"There are many audiences for this volume, but, read in tandem with Headman's *Dictionary of the Ponca People* (2019), it speaks most powerfully to the children, grandchildren, and great-grandchildren of the Ponca people. Here are the embers left to rekindle Ponca culture and language!"

—BETH R. RITTER, *Great Plains Quarterly*

"An important work for the Great Plains region and for the growing literature of Indigenous-produced histories."

—PHOEBE LABAT, *South Dakota History*

"This book is a jewel because it presents an insider's view drawn from the insights of Ponca elders with whom the author talked during many years while simultaneously bringing outside scholarly assessments into the mix. Specialists on the American Indian, whether anthropologists, archaeologists, sociologists, political scientists, or historians, as well as the general reader, will gain insights from the work."

—BLUE CLARK, professor of American Indian Studies at Oklahoma City University

"A welcome model of how to do collaborative ethnography from within a culture and how to synthesize and evaluate information from multiple sources.... This volume, in an accessible way, leads the reader toward an understanding of how to see the Ponca as the Ponca see themselves."

—REGNA DARNELL, Distinguished University Professor of Anthropology and First Nations Studies at the University of Western Ontario

WALKS ON THE GROUND

Walks on the Ground

A Tribal History of the Ponca Nation

LOUIS V. HEADMAN
Foreword by SEAN O'NEILL

University of Nebraska Press

LINCOLN

The University of Nebraska Press is part of a land-grant institution with campuses and programs on the past, present, and future homelands of the Pawnee, Ponca, Otoe-Missouria, Omaha, Dakota, Lakota, Kaw, Cheyenne, and Arapaho Peoples, as well as those of the relocated Ho-Chunk, Sac and Fox, and Iowa Peoples.

♾

First Nebraska paperback printing: 2024

Library of Congress Cataloging-in-Publication Data
Names: Headman, Louis, author. | O'Neill, Sean, 1969– author.
Title: Walks on the ground: a tribal history of the Ponca nation / Louis V. Headman; foreword by Sean O'Neill.
Description: Lincoln: University of Nebraska Press, [2020]. | Includes bibliographical references and index.
Identifiers: LCCN 2019020043
ISBN 9781496212801 (cloth)
ISBN 9781496241016 (paperback)
ISBN 9781496219350 (pdf)
ISBN 9781496219336 (epub)
ISBN 9781496219343 (mobi)
Subjects: LCSH: Ponca Indians—History. | BISAC: SOCIAL SCIENCE / Ethnic Studies / Native American Studies | HISTORY / Native American
Classification: LCC E99.P7 H43 2020 | DDC 976.6004/9752539—dc23
LC record available at https://lccn.loc.gov/2019020043

Set in MeropePonca by Mikala R. Kolander.

Contents

Illustrations

Foreword

SEAN O'NEILL

With this work, tribal elder Louis Headman offers up an intimate portrait of his own people—namely, the Ponca Tribe of Oklahoma and their brethren in Nebraska, the Northern Ponca—who have, to this day, mostly been portrayed by outsiders. Headman, for his part, speaks with great authority on this subject, as a distinguished elder in the Ponca Tribe of Oklahoma and as a direct descendant of Chief Standing Bear, in addition being one of the last remaining speakers of the language.

Right from the start, one begins to see how far off anthropologists and historians have been up until this point—how little outsiders have been able to see the intimate details of Ponca history as the Ponca people understand it, from the perspective of close family relations, in terms of the intimate lessons learned in the home and throughout the course of life, among close associates, speaking purely in the Ponca language. And in this way, the book belongs to a small handful of works aimed at describing indigenous ways of life first and foremost from an internal perspective—with an eye to passing these traditions on to the next generation.

To take one example, the Ponca have all too often been seen as one of the quintessential tribes of the plains, alongside their close relatives among other Siouan-speaking peoples—such as the Lakota, Dakota, Omaha, Osage, Kaw, and Quapaw. Taken together, these groups are among the most heavily romanticized (and mythologized) peoples of the Americas, both North and South, with such films as *Dances with Wolves* giving a one-sided snapshot of the past, including their encounters with the heartless colonial forces of the day. The horse, the tipi, and the buffalo are some of the popular images here, along with iconic ceremonies, such as the Sun Dance or even the Ghost Dance. Yet it does not take much reflection to see that these are merely recent artifacts—products of the colonial encounter—providing little sense of the deeper history before contact with Europeans. For much of the world, however, this is the image that continues to circulate, even among scholars, when it comes to the indigenous peoples of the Americas. The flipside of the intense romanticism is, of course, the harsher reality of the oppression these people faced at the hands of colonial forces, up to the present day at the hands of the U.S. government, for example, as seen today with the struggles that continue to unfold at Standing Rock, among the tribes on the northern plains. This book, in particular, begins to address these many misconceptions, borne of recent historical misunderstanding, even going so far as to provide an antidote, as a direct response to these misleading images.

Countering these popular misconceptions, Headman does not place the origin of his people on the plains, where the present-day Ponca Tribes of Oklahoma and Nebraska now have their headquarters, as but an artifact of recent history, in the aftermath of European contact and colonialism. Rather, according to the ancestors themselves, the original home of the Ponca people was toward the east, somewhere near what is now known as the Smoky Mountains of Tennessee, where their ancestors begin their long journey toward the Great Plains only in recent memory. Of course, colonial forces, at the hands of the U.S. government, brought the Ponca to the plains—another fact that is often obscured from view in sanitized historical accounts, even throughout much of the history of anthropology, where colonialism itself was obscured from view, with more sanitized views of the past.

The portrait given here does much to remedy these inaccuracies in the historical record, along with the many misconceptions that continue to circulate in popular consciousness. Between the covers of this book, Headman provides a detailed history of his own tribe, down to the minute details of everyday language and life—not only in terms of recent historical times, since the era of European contact, but going back many generations before that. Here one will find a vivid portrait of the early history of the tribe, as remembered in oral narratives and songs, long before the historical record begins to set in, with recent accounts; a history of the Ponca Trail of Tears, the tragic and devastating forced relocation to Oklahoma in the late nineteenth century; a description of the hard times the Ponca encountered in Indian Territory, before it was opened to outsiders; the lineage of Ponca chiefs;

a description of family structure and marriage patterns, along with the associated clan and personal names; an ethnographic account of popular games and art forms; and the rites surrounding birth and death, including within the Native American Church. Few ethnographies give this level of detail from an insider perspective. In a significant sense, the reader of this book has the privilege of witnessing the expert testimony of a person who can directly attest to an era of history that would otherwise have been lost, much as we see in the posthumous work of Zora Neale Hurston (2018), in her work with the memories of the last survivor of the Middle Passage.

Born in the 1930s, Headman grew up in the last generation that was raised speaking the Ponca language fluently in the home—among parents who retained a living memory of the Ponca Trail of Tears of the 1880s, when much of the tribe was forced to relocate to Oklahoma, then known as "Indian Country." Thus, his childhood was filled with the immeasurably rich tradition of songs and stories passed down by his ancestors from time immemorial, far beyond the reach of historical records. Here, in this work, Headman gives a composite portrait of stories from his childhood, including the many echoes he heard from his friends, neighbors, and elders through the course of his own life. And along the way, Headman continued his education, earning a degree in seminary school, with additional training in psychology, linguistics, and anthropology at the college level. Thus, in addition to being a distinguished elder, steeped in his own cultural traditions, he has also earned a position as a distinguished scholar in many areas of advanced knowledge, culminating in a series of books, including this history as well as a dictionary and grammar of his own language. Few people have accomplished this much in a lifetime, even among professional linguists, anthropologists, and historians, working strictly within the academy. Yet Headman was also a preacher most of his life and raised a family of his own along the way.

Much of what Headman has to say in this book was originally passed down to him in the oral tradition, as stories and songs going back many generations, into time immemorial. For countless generations, these stories were passed down strictly by word of mouth, starting early in life with the lullabies of the cradle to songs and ceremonial speeches one encountered throughout the course of life. That is, until relatively recent times, the tribe had no formal writing system, something that only began with the work of James Owen Dorsey (1899) in late nineteenth century and continued with the sophisticated system of writing advanced herein by Louis Headman. Yet massive bodies of learning were passed down by word of mouth, starting with the nursery rhymes of childhood. Some of these histories were passed down as songs, with names and places embedded in the lyrics, as seen throughout this book. Others were transmitted as oral narratives, in storytelling mode, which Headman had the foresight to collect in his youth, when many of the elders still knew the original language of the tales, which they passed on in great detail, as Headman acknowledges throughout the book, with the names given in abbreviated form. His sources were in this sense impeccable and numerous, allowing for cross-references seen through the book. As is so often the case, Headman gives more than one source for his observations on Ponca history.

Like many prominent scholars in the fields of anthropology, history, and religious studies, Headman conducted his work first and foremost in the Ponca tongue. Here he follows in the footsteps of many of the scholars and priests who painstakingly translated religious literature, while retaining a deep respect for the local literary traditions where they worked. Likewise, Headman continues in the tradition of many anthropologists and historians who listened to indigenous experts, carefully transcribing their knowledge of local storytelling traditions, songs, and spiritual practices. Going back to the source has always been important in these areas of scholarship, and one needs to know the local language to truly hear (and understand) people in their own words and on their own terms, as they are comfortable expressing themselves—their most intimate thoughts and feelings. In this way, Headman stays close to the source throughout his many years of research, giving countless examples from his own language, to illustrate the key concepts throughout this book. For this reason, Headman intersperses his speech—here given primarily in English—with a great many words from the Ponca tongue.

For Headman, these humble word forms serve as one of the primary sources of information throughout this book, as he dwells on their meanings—and etymologies—to reveal deep historical legacies, passed down through the generations, in the form of personal names, geographical sites, ethnographic practices, spiritual practices, and song lyrics. Many of these words distill history lessons of their own, as the reader encounters the original names for people, plants, animals, ceremonies, and places — indeed everything in the Ponca world, including the often-intangible spiritual realm. In this way, through the window of these words, one begins to get a sense of how the ancient Ponca people saw this world, before the time of European contact. In this sense, the linguistic anthropologist Edward Sapir used to say that language is heuristic; you can learn a lot by dwelling on the meanings of ordinary words, listening to the delicate wisdom imparted by the ancestors, as passed on through these powerful verbal symbols, which almost float in the air.

Given the intense focus on language, the book resonates with many of the classics in early anthropology, which were taken down and translated from Native languages — only to appear secondarily in English. As Edward Sapir (1985, 162) used to say, culture is built on a symbolic edifice and, to understand something, even as simple as a poem, requires a great deal of insight into the meanings of words, as they resonate with the whole life of a community. In this sense, Headman offers a detailed and layered account of how the Ponca traditionally saw the world, through the lens of their ancestral tongue, encompassing everything in the universe of everyday experience.

Most ethnographies, in contrast to this work, have been penned by outsiders, either as anthropologists or historians who derived their understanding, secondhand, by working closely with the local peoples they came to portray from a considerable distance. Here we must count even such classics as *Black Elk Speaks* (Neihardt 2008) in this genre of ethnographies compiled by technical experts outside the community, working only with secondhand knowledge — even where the primary source was a distinguished elder. Ultimately, we know Black Elk only through his translators, through Black Elk's son (Ben) and Neihardt — who, in the end, we must trust, in the absence of a single word from Black Elk himself. Yet with *Walks on the Ground*, which you now hold in your hands, every word was penned by Louis Headman, deliberated and carefully revised over the course of many years, in both Ponca and English, the two main languages he invokes herein. And yet Headman relies on more than a handful of experts in compiling this narrative, so the voices we hear in this study are many. His authority is thus shared, making it all the more profound. Along the way, I have vetted many of his insights, as both a linguist and anthropologist myself.

Thus, throughout this work one hears the echoes of the many voices within the Ponca community, addressing one of the central concerns on ethnographic writing, which is the distributed nature of culture, going beyond the individual and even the generation, reaching people over the great span of time. Thus, in every chapter, Headman carefully weighs his sources, which he often identifies by the initials given in the preface. In a curious historical twist, Sapir (1985, 569–77) once addressed precisely this concern in an essay he penned about the Ponca and Omaha; slightly before Sapir's day, the early linguist and ethnographer James Owen Dorsey took the time to document the discrepancy within the Omaha and Ponca communities, finding an elder, named "Two Crows," who adamantly disagreed with the rest of the community, in a way that was worth noting, for historical reasons. Culture is not uniform, as anthropologists and literary theorists have come to observe (see Bakhtin 1981). On this model, anthropologists now strive to write "polyphonic" ethnographies, capturing a sense of the great wealth and diversity of perspective within the community (Clifford 1988).

Going beyond even the Americas, this book provides a rare portrait of indigenous culture and history from an internal point of view— not just from the perspective of one authority, but from many sources within the community. Conveying a sense of this internal frame of reference was, of course, one of the original goals of Boasian anthropology, with its collaborative methodology. Thus, this book belongs to a small handful of works in the history of the indigenous peoples of the Americas. Boas himself collaborated for many years with George Hunt, eventually coauthoring a number of works (Boas and Hunt 1905). But Headman goes beyond just a handful of sources in compiling this composite portrait.

At the same time, there is a growing body of literature on indigenous ethnography, which is ultimately where this book probably belongs— however unique and therefore distinct from other works within this genre. Lucy Thompson, for example, was one of the first Native American authors (1991) to write an ethnography in direct response to the work of anthropologists, revealing the inner workings of her own culture, among the Yurok of northwestern California—from the perspective of both a fluent speaker and a distinguished elder and as gifted writer in the colonial tongue, English.

Even in the realm of indigenous ethnography, Headman's work makes striking contributions of its own. To begin, Headman often goes beyond his own authority as an elder, channeling the views of many of his own elders, who in turn stood on the shoulders of the giants who came before them. As Clifford Geertz (2017) has said, ethnography is "thick description," based on layer upon layer of interpretation. If the voices and authorities are many, the one strives for a polyphonic ethnography, capturing a sense of the great wealth and diversity of perspective within the community, as Headman has done with such virtuosity here.

Though deeply historical in its main thrust, this book also provides many prescient lessons for future generations. Rather than simply offering an esoteric lesson in the remote past, Headman speaks directly to the reader about the present, with poignant lessons for those who are willing to listen, Native and non-Native alike. We all have so much to learn from this man. But the perspective is not merely his own; he offers here a composite portrait. In writing this work, Headman was not only setting the history books straight, he also had an eye to the future. Historians generally have a mission, a compelling vision to share, in ways that challenge our present-day understanding, with an eye to a future in which some of these past injustices may be undone, a movement James Clifford vividly presents in his book *Returns* (2013)—as something that is now sweeping the planet, among indigenous peoples everywhere, the foremost victims of colonialism. Thus, Headman's work takes one large step in the direction of restoring the damage that has been done by carving out a place for the Ponca language and culture on the world stage—leading the way, by extension, for other indigenous peoples the world over. And in an exciting way, the ethnography given here is truly polyphonic, capturing a sense of the great wealth and diversity of perspective within the community.

Headman started this work over sixty years ago now, in his youth, as someone with a heartfelt conviction that the stories of his elders would matter again someday, even during a time when they were being forcefully undermined by the powers at play in politics and education. Thus, over the past sixty years, he has been able to take the time to finish a work he started many decades ago, as a teenager determined to document and preserve the traditions of his ancestors. For decades, he listened to the stories told by the elders of his youth, many of whom knew the Ponca language and culture from birth, taking extensive notes on the vocabulary of the Ponca language, often written on whatever materials he had at hand—from ordinary paper notes, at one point, to extensive computer files, as time progressed. These notes eventually furnished the material for the book manuscript he recently completed, with assistance from me, Dr. Sean O'Neill, along with long-term support from his nephew Randy Ross and the Cherokee playwright Mary Kathryn Nagle.

Over the past six years—during which time I served as his friend and assistant in these efforts—Louis Headman devoted countless hours of his own time to synthesizing and organizing all of these materials, in addition to conducting follow-up research on some of the central questions he has been pursuing all of his life—such as delineating the many memories that still exist when it comes to the Trail of Tears the Ponca endured in the late nineteenth century. Then, a considerable fraction of his time was spent verifying the materials he had collected in the past, such as conversations, stories, and handwritten notes he compiled after the fact, which he took the time to carefully review before publishing. Publishing this work in an academic setting, at the University of Nebraska Press, was another matter that took a great deal of attention to detail, in terms of the formatting of the special fonts and the structure of the citations. For me, this was a great pleasure, offering my services, as a pro bono effort (without compensation), to such a rewarding end, with the collective good in mind.

We hope that this book, along with the *Dictionary of the Ponca People* (2019), will lay the foundations for preserving the culture and traditions of the Ponca Tribe. Someday soon, future generations will discover Louis Headman's many amazing lifeworks.

References

Bakhtin, Mikhail. 1981. *The Dialogic Imagination: Four Essays.* Edited by Michael Holquist. Translated by Caryl Emerson and Michael Holquist. Austin: University of Texas Press.

Boas, Franz, and George Hunt. 1905. *Kwakiutl Texts.* Publications of the Jesup North Pacific Expedition, vol. 3. Leiden, Netherlands.

Clifford, James. 1988. *The Predicament of Culture: Twentieth Century Ethnography, Literature, and Art.* Cambridge: Harvard University Press.

———. 2013. *Returns: Becoming Indigenous in the Twenty-First Century.* Cambridge: Harvard University Press.

Geertz, Clifford. 2017. *Interpretation of Cultures,* with a foreword by Robert Darnton. New York: Basic Books. (Original work published in 1973.)

Hurston, Zora Neale. 2018. *Barracoon: The Story of the Last "Black Cargo."* Edited by Deborah G. Plant, with a foreword by Alice Walker. New York: Amistad.

Neihardt, John G. 2008. *Black Elk Speaks: Being the Life Story of a Holy Man of the Oglala Sioux.* Annotated by Raymond DeMaille, with illustrations by Standing Bear. Albany: State University of New York Press. (Originally published in 1932.)

Sapir, Edward. 1985. "Why Cultural Anthropology Needs the Psychiatrist." In *The Selected Writings of Edward Sapir,* edited by David Mandelbaum, 569–77. Berkeley: University of California Press.

Thompson, Lucy. 1991. *To the American Indian: Reminiscences of a Yurok Woman.* Berkeley CA: Heyday Press. (Originally published in 1916.)

Preface

Writings of the history and culture of the Ponca Tribe of Native Americans were done in the past by non-Indian or non-Ponca people. There are multiple reasons this work is being presented. First, no Southern Ponca have written an extensive work on the history and culture of the people. Second, most historians and anthropologists have attempted to group or canonize the Ponca as part of another tribe. Even though they are linguistically related, the elders said that the Ponca have always considered themselves a distinct, separate people. And as such, they felt there was an overlapping of or duplication of their tribal cultural practices with others based on the work done by others at the beginning of the twentieth century. The elders also noted that their testimonies given during that time were never published in the ethnography of the Ponca people. Third, whether the Ponca are of the "Eastern Woodland" or "High Plains" variety, this monograph views only part of the anthropological data on Ponca origins. And fourth, this writing stands on its own merits where the elders of the tribe offered their knowledge of history and culture.

In the beginning the writings were never intended to be a book. I have no formal training in the writing arts. This work should be viewed as a record of my personal study of the Ponca people. This study began in my teen years. Most of the material was written down over a period of many years. It may be seventy or more years. The intention was that perhaps someone in the tribe or family, in the future, could use these materials to formulate a book on the Ponca people. While writing stories from the Ponca language, it became clear that the culture and history of the tribe could not be fully understood because this aspect of learning required the historian to know the language. The culture and practices are imbedded in the language. Under this premise, non-Indian historians and anthropologists (Indian and non-Indian alike) were handicapped and could only record something by observation, hearsay, and opinion. Writing has always been an interesting feature of the ongoing dominant society. It is seen in varied books of knowledge, magazines, newspapers, cartoons, poetry, drama, and so forth. Untrained and untaught, I mimicked these various writers. There never was a problem or a burden to write about the Ponca people.

Although remarks are made in connection with the Northern Ponca people and other tribes, this is primarily recorded data and testimony of the Southern Ponca. No effort was made to trace changes of the Ponca culture or the tribe's connection with previous or other tribal cultural affiliations. The obvious changes in the tribe are seen in the educational processes, the influences and effects of the federal government, and the dominant societal structure and ongoing culture. The gradual progression of the Ponca people into the modern world has been described by some as being "fifty years" behind all of America.

The layout of the book begins with the historic notation of the Ponca people having their origins in the east. The last of the true Ponca speakers and storytellers entered Indian Territory in 1877. Most of them lived up to the 1940s. One of the significant practices common to the Ponca people was that they told of their history often. There is much involved in Ponca oral history. As a learning historian, you were required to listen to elders tell stories and to engage yourself in all practices of the culture. According to tradition, it was always the eldest son who received instruction on tribal history and cultural practices. The younger siblings heard the stories and cultural practices, but they were essentially directed to the oldest son.

Near Niobrara, Nebraska, probably in the eighteenth century, the Ponca had a love-hate relationship with a number of tribes in the north for about a hundred or so years. It was recorded in the nineteenth century by non-Ponca historians that the Ponca were not well liked by other tribes. In our heritage, the history of Ponca individuals is told in our *Heđúškà* songs. This Ponca fraternal organization passed on history to young members through singing and storytelling. I primarily learned about the songs by singing with known ceremonial singers, such as Harry Buffalohead; Ed Littlecook; Oliver Littlecook; Eli Warrior; Dr. Sherman Warrior, son of Sylvester Warrior, known singer of Ponca songs; Roland No Ear; "Pee-wee" Clark; and others. These singing sessions were done at the homes of these men.

The book also includes writings of children's stories. These stories are included in the learning episodes of Ponca children. Stories were told to children at bedtime. Our homes were not large and were somewhat akin to the old tribal dwellings that housed the entire family. Through acculturation, the idea of separate bedrooms seems to have become the ideal, but for family stories, one room was sufficient. Grandma Headman's surname was Big Soldier. Her keen mind remembered many children's stories. Some stories are similar to Aesop's Fables. I believe they are purely coincidental. Sometimes the story had no logical conclusion. Children had to determine the meaning of the story.

There were no formal interviews. Most elders simply love to tell stories of the tribe. Once they begin to speak, if you are present, you listen intently to all details. Menfolk typically tell stories after the noon meal following a Native American Church (NAC) meeting. Later, when tape recorders were available, stories were recorded. Some individuals were glad to have their voices recorded. My father, Kenneth Headman, who seldom spoke the English language, shared the majority of this writing on history and culture. During the winter nights, after he put a large log into the fireplace, he would begin his storytelling. The other elders in the tribe confirmed his insights. They also knew and contributed other stories in the history of the Ponca people.

This work also recognizes the contribution made by Ponca servicemen who served during the First and Second World War, the Korean Conflict, Vietnam War, Desert Storm, and the ongoing conflict in the Middle East. Minor accounts told by veterans do not tell the whole story; however, they strongly indicate the conditions of a war at the front lines. The tribe honored most of those who served during wartime by giving them a song in the order of the Ponca *Heđúškà*.

After Public Law No. 93-638, the Indian Self-Determination and Education Assistance Act, was passed, a younger generation of Ponca men assumed leadership for the Southern Ponca. It was then that the idea of political governance became apparent. This effect has not yet reached its potential use for the people. The interpretation of the enactment of the law was primarily left to the younger Ponca men who initiated tribal programs and projects. Education was the key to success for all Indians. Education committees were established and promoted incentives for the students.

Acknowledgments

Writing a book was not my intention in the beginning. I wanted to know about my people and their history. I have asked questions since I was a child. I am demure to say or tell what was told to me in confidence. The information given to me was given in faith that I would not alter or embellish any part of it. If anything, I probably left out much of what was conveyed to me during the times I listened to the elders speak. The elders of the tribe were straightforward in relating their stories, history, and culture. The elders quoted herein were the first generation of Ponca born in Indian Territory (Oklahoma). Their parents were the Ponca who were forcibly removed from their homelands in the North Country. Most of them learned the English language at the Ponca Boarding School, which was abolished in the early part of the twentieth century. Although many Ponca tell stories in this work, the major contributors are listed below:

Kenneth Headman (KH), 1891–1984, was my father and was born in Indian Territory. His Ponca name was *Mącú Žįgà* (Little Bear). He was the primary informant on Ponca history and culture. Although a quiet man, he spoke to and responded to all persons wanting information on Ponca tribal history and culture throughout his life. He was a member of the Ponca *Đíxidą̀* clan, the Ponca *Heđúškà waną́xe* fraternal organization, and the Ponca Native American Church, and he served in the First World War. He was the son of *Gak'úwixè*, a clan chief of the Ponca, and grandson of *T'ądé Ámądį̀* (Walks on the Ground). He was called upon many times in probate hearings on heirship matters pertaining to land ownership. His knowledge of tribal family members and family structure gave credence to court determination of heirship in many cases. When the modern "powwow" cultural practices were initiated, he withdrew from dancing and singing at such events.

Norman "Willie" Cry (Cries for War) (NC), 1892–1978, was born in Indian Territory. His Ponca name was *Nążítiđè* (Sudden Rain). He was a member of the *Hísadà* clan and a leader of the Ponca Native American Church who conducted meetings at various places on the Ponca reservation and provided native medicines for healing. He was also called on to use his medicines at individual homes. During the early years of oil exploration in Oklahoma, E. W. Marland approached him to drill for oil on his land. Although he was cautioned by the then elders of the tribe to resist the offer, he did sign a lease. His oil field was the start of what ultimately became the Continental Oil Company. He was a generous man who many times paid for the meals of people in restaurants. He was the grandson of *Nagé Áxa* (Cries for War), a chief of the Ponca. J. O. Dorsey in his *Omaha and Ponka Letters* mentioned Cries for War. He too did not participate in the modern powwow movement.

James Poore (JP), 1890–1979, was born in Indian Territory. He was of Ponca/Lakota descent and was given the names *Maxp'iázi* (Yellow Cloud) and *Ạbédo Wašt'è* (Good Day). As a leader in the Native American Church, he conducted many meetings at his "home place." In his position as a church leader, he often recounted tribal codes and beliefs when needed. He was knowledgeable of Ponca culture and history. He was the son of *Šáge Xdàha* (Poor Horse). A conscientious man, he was one of few Ponca who farmed his own land. Although he did not participate in the modern powwow world, he enjoyed camping out at the annual Ponca powwow at the White Eagle community.

Albert Makes Cry (AMC), 1893–1981, was born in Indian Territory. He was a member of the *Ðíxidà* clan. His Ponca name was *Íbe Žąkà* (Scissortail), and he was the son of *Wáđi Xagè* (Makes Cry), who was a great singer and warrior in the old days in the North Country. "Uncle Albert" as he was known on the Ponca reservation was a great Christian man who was also a public speaker and composer of traditional Ponca Christian hymns. He was a veteran of World War I. During the Second World War, he took charge of the local church when no ministers were available. He was a man of integrity and stood out among tribesmen as one who was known as a Bible teacher, singer, historian, and man of prayer.

Adam LeClair (AL), 1903–82, was born in Indian Territory. As a non-clan member, he was named *Ádamà*, the Ponca version of the name *Adam*. He was considered a "tribal or cultural enthusiast" and had good knowledge of Ponca legends and history. He was one of the last Ponca doctors who practiced the art of "hacking and bleeding" as well as vein cutting. He built a large enclosed arbor at his home where many tribal activities such as hand games and feasts were held. He was a man who recalled many comical and serious incidents that occurred on and near the Ponca reservation. He was a singer of *Heđúškà* songs and a singer for all tribal events.

Ronald D. Hopper (RDH), 1941–93, was the youngest of the men providing information on the Ponca Tribe. He contributed current and historic policies of the federal government concerning the Ponca Tribe. He is credited for much of the chapter that deals with political governance. He spent most of his young life studying Indian law. Thus, his information on tribal laws was invaluable. As a paralegal for the Ponca Tribe in the 1980s, he provided guidelines for the first high-stakes gambling operation in the United States—save the Seminole Nation of the State of Florida, which does not have a treaty agreement with the United States—on the Ponca reservation. At the time of his demise, he was formulating the procedures for establishing legal community ordinances and precedents in laws to be regulated on the Ponca reservation.

Virginia Big Soldier Headman (VBSH), 1854–1957, was my grandmother and was born in the North Country along the Missouri and Niobrara Rivers. She was a member of the *Wašábe* clan of the Ponca Tribe. Her Ponca name was *Mídagđį* (Pleasant Sun). She was the daughter of Chief Big Soldier (*Wanáše T'ągà*), a clan chief of the Ponca. She was a survivor of the forced removal of the Ponca from their homelands in 1877. She did not speak English. When speaking of the teachings and culture of the Ponca people, she more often than not spoke of them in a matter-of-fact way. In the 1950s she gave an informal testimony to the Indian Claims Commission of the tribe's forced removal from their homelands. She quietly lived her life in the traditional Ponca lifestyle until her demise in 1957.

Katherine Cry (Cries for War) Headman (KCH), 1895–1986, was my mother and was born in Indian Territory. She was a member of the *Hísadà* clan of the Ponca Tribe. Her Ponca name was *Íye Skà* (Interpreter). She was the granddaughter of *Nagé Áxa* (Cries for War), a chief of the Ponca. J. O. Dorsey in his *Omaha and Ponka Letters* mentioned

Cries for War. In her unassuming demeanor she shared her knowledge of Ponca culture and history. Her parents and other relatives taught her the art of sewing and making traditional moccasins and Native clothing. As an excellent bead worker, she was well informed of Ponca tribal designs for ceremonial clothing and ornaments. She was knowledgeable of Ponca names of flora and fauna and of where to find various edible roots, nuts, and wild fruits.

Nancy (Big Snake) Maker (NM), 1903–89, was born in Indian Territory. She was the granddaughter of *Wés'a T'ǫgà* (Chief Big Snake), who testified in the trial of Chief Standing Bear. She said her grandfather often accompanied Standing Bear in his efforts to bring justice to the Ponca people. She was a member of the *Wašábe* clan of the Ponca Tribe. She was an active member of the Native American Church. In addition to her stories, she corroborated historical accounts given by other elders. She was a homemaker for all her life and quietly raised her children in the Ponca lifestyle.

To give thanks to each individual from among the Ponca people would be an incalculable task. The unmentioned names and faces of our people that I am indebted to are embedded in this production of the history and culture of the Ponca people. I thank Ponca Tribal Chairman Earl Howe III and the Business Council for their insight regarding the importance of completing this historical documentation of the Ponca people. The office space provided by the council was a peaceful and quiet workplace at the Dana Knight Building. To them I give my humble thanks and appreciation.

Individuals I wish to acknowledge for their kindness and friendship to me in the completion of this work are Randy Ross, tribal planner and grant writer; Ms. Mary Katherine Nagle, attorney at law; and Dr. Sean O'Neill, professor and linguistic anthropologist at the University of Oklahoma. They were instrumental in acquiring the Tribal Heritage Grant for the editing, updating, and completion of the manuscript.

This material was produced with assistance from the Historic Preservation Fund, administered by the National Park Service, Department of the Interior. Any opinions, findings, conclusions, or recommendations expressed in this material are those of the author(s) and do not necessarily reflect the views of the Department of the Interior.

Introduction

It has been hypothesized that American Indians were travelers who entered the North American continent by way of the Bering land bridge that existed tens of thousands of years ago. Others say that the spread of early civilizations to South America may have occurred by way of a reed boat from Egypt. There is also a theory that our ancestors came here by traveling from island to island on a seaworthy craft crossing the Pacific Ocean from the Orient. While popular theories seem to suit most people, most American Indians have very little to say about their origins. When such theories have been exhausted, it will probably still be of little importance to the average Indian. Future technologies will probably piece together the history of mankind more accurately. With the exception of a few elders who told stories of their beginnings, most stories are centered on experiences on this continent.

One of the modern historical statements made about the Ponca prescribes that they arrived in the north central plains by way of the Middle Mississippian culture. In light of research, this conclusion could be reached because of the many artifacts associated with that culture. The migration patterns explained by the tribe too give credence to that theory. Also, other tribes that are said to have emerged from the same culture usually have similar languages and customs. The customary beliefs and social forms of the Ponca tend to complement those of other plains tribes that came into the plains from the east and southeast. In the simplest terms, we know this connection exists from the development and use of material culture: the construction of the bastioned palisade fort, the earthen lodge, the bow and arrow, pottery, and so forth. However, some marked differences do appear. Material culture may be the same, but languages may differ. The Ponca adapting to the plains may have adopted a lifestyle significant to any people who had moved there.

Consequently, it is concluded that we are descendants of an ancient people who established propitious patterns of living by which they survived the onslaught of famine, disease, and many other unfavorable conditions. Evidence shows that sociocultural changes occurred over a long span of time. It would be presumptuous to assume that these early inhabitants were innovative and inventive. Their interests surely must have been survival rather than experiment. The development of their social life, the discovery of medicine and food came through a myriad of favorable and adverse circumstances.

Historical perspectives are mostly conceived by the written page in Western civilization. The basis for conclusive evidence is that what happened was written down by someone. Unfortunately for the Ponca, only small pieces of historical material were recorded. Historians and military records attempted to account for people. The census records of village populations were often inaccurate leaving outsiders totally unaware that the Ponca were separate from other similar-speaking people. These were honest mistakes but had far-reaching consequences in placing the Ponca people as part of another tribe. As a result, to place the Ponca into some reasonable historical perspective, the only records at hand were the living elders of the tribe. Therefore, in this work, we will focus on the elders as they recount their history and ways of life from their memories as well as from other resources that verify the Ponca story.

Phonetic Key

The following phonetic key provides information about the pronunciation of Ponca words appearing in this monograph. To assist the astute reader who would successfully pronounce the words correctly, the diacritic use of the acute and grave accents as well as the ogonek (or forward hook) are explained. The letters of the Ponca alphabet are as follows:

Vowels

Unnasalized Vowels

A/a as in the *a* in "father"

E/e as in the *a* in "ate"

I/i as in the *e* in "me"

ʃ/ʃ as in *i* in "tip"

O/o as in the *o* in "go"

U/u as in the *u* in "flu"

ə (schwa) as in the initial *a* in "America"

Nasalized vowels

Nasalized vowels are indicated by the diacritic ogonek (˛) and appear as follows:

Ą/ą as in the *a* of "father," but pronounced with air passing through both the mouth and nose

Ę/ę as in the *a* of "ate," but pronounced with air passing through both the mouth and nose

Į/į as in the *e* of "me," but pronounced with air passing through both the mouth and nose

ʃ as in the *i* of "tip," but pronounced with air passing through both the mouth and nose

Q/ǫ as in the *o* of "go," but pronounced with air passing through both the mouth and nose

Ų/ų as in the *u* of "flu," but pronounced with air passing through both the mouth and nose

Consonants

B/b as in the *b* in "book"

Č/č as in the *ch* in "church"

D/d as in the *d* in "dog"

Đ/đ as in the *th* in "them" (an approximation — in the Ponca sound, air also passes over the sides of the tongue)

G/g as in the *g* in "go"

H/h as in the *h* in "hat"

J/j as in the *j* in "judge"

K/k as in the *k* in "kin"

M/m as in the *m* in "milk"

N/n as in the *n* in "no"

P/p as in the *p* in "put"

S/s as in the *s* in "see"

Š/š as in the *sh* in "show"

T/t as in the *t* in "tall"

W/w as in the *w* in "walk"

X/x as in the *ch* of the German name "Bach"

Y/y as in the *y* in "yes"

Z/z as in the *z* in "zest"

Ž/ž as in the *s* in "leisure"

The Ponca language does not include the letters *c, f, l, q, r,* or *v.*

Phonetic Descriptions

Detailed phonetic descriptions based on the International Phonetic Alphabet (IPA) can be found below for each letter.

Vowels (both nasalized and unnasalized)

i   high, front, close, unrounded [i]

ʃ   high, front, open, unrounded [ɪ]

e   mid, front, close, unrounded [e]

ə   mid, central, close, unrounded [ə]

u   high, back, close, rounded [u]

o   mid, back, close, rounded [o]

a   low, back, open, unrounded [ɑ]

Consonants

STOPS

p   bilabial, unaspirated, voiceless [p]

b   bilabial, unaspirated, voiced [b]

t   alveolar, unaspirated, voiceless [t]

d   alveolar, unaspirated, voiced [d]

k   velar, unaspirated, voiceless [k]

g   velar, unaspirated, voiced [g]

ʼ   glottal, unaspirated, voiceless [ʔ]

NASALS

m   bilabial, voiced [m]

n   alveolar, voiced [n]

FRICATIVES

đ   interdental, flat, voiced [ð]

s   alveolar, grooved, voiceless [s]

š   alveo-palatal, grooved, voiceless [ʃ]

z   alveolar, grooved, voiced [z]

ž   alveo-palatal, grooved, voiced [ʒ]

x   velar, flat, voiceless [x]

h   glottal, flat, voiceless [h]

AFFRICATES

č   alveo-palatal, voiceless [tʃ]

Accents and Apostrophes

An acute accent over a vowel indicates primary stress, while a grave accent over a vowel indicates secondary stress.

´   primary stress
`   secondary stress

The acute and grave accents are not always used on the first or last syllable. They may be used on any syllable for correct pronunciation.

The apostrophe (') is used to indicate two distinct articulations in Ponca. Following a p, t, k, or sometimes x, the apostrophe indicates that the preceding letter should be pronounced with an ejective or glottalized release. Physically, these sounds are produced by releasing a short puff of air that has been built up in the mouth by briefly closing off the vocal cords. Examples are below:

P'/p' as in the Ponca word *P'áxe* ("I made")
T'/t' as in the Ponca word *T'á'* ("dehydrated meat")
K'/k' as in the Ponca word *K'ą́de'* ("plums")

The second use of the apostrophe, following all other letters, indicates a glottal stop, a related articulation in which the vocal cords are closed briefly. A glottal stop is used in the English expression "uh-oh," but in Ponca, glottal stops are phonemes, meaning-bearing letters, as shown in the examples below:

Nú' ("man")
Wá'đate ("table")

The orthography is intended to be unambiguous, with each word pronounced as written.

WALKS ON THE GROUND

1
Beginnings

The elders began by saying that the Ponca were a single, distinct cultural and politically separate group of people. This saying may have transpired because somebody recorded that the Ponca were part of a larger group of people. For all practical purposes, especially in light of past studies, the Ponca (*P'ą'k'a*) people have been identified as one of several tribes that speak a similar language. This includes the Kansa (*Káze*), Omaha (*Umáhą*), Osage (*Wažáže*), and Quapaw (*Ugáxpè*). History in the oral tradition of the Ponca tells us that they came from the east. The elders said, "*Mi'édąbet'ąđišą et'át'ą ągáti*" (We came from where the sun rises). Some of the landmarks they made on their westward migration included the Niagara Falls (*Ní'uxp'áđe*), Smoky Mountains (*P'ahéušúde*), Ohio Valley (*Ohá'i*), Kahokian Mounds (*P'ahé'žíde*), and Mississippi River (*Nišúde t'ągà*). These locations were not simply landmarks but established village sites where they lived for long periods. Relative to descriptions given by elders of the Ponca, it is appropriate to identify these tribes with the great cultures of southeastern North America. In retrospect, tribal tales, religious structure, construction of crafts, identity of landmarks, and other cultural elements would indicate a common ancestral beginning (KH, NC, AMC, JP).

Other tribes with a similar language that have also been classified as other Southern Siouan, include the Iowa, Otoe, and Missourian. James Howard (1995, 6) said that the Mandan and the Southern Siouan carried forms of the great southeastern culture into the plains. He drew this conclusion because these tribes evidenced the many elements of their Middle Mississippian heritage. The most obvious element exhibited by the Ponca was the building of a palisade fort. This type of fortification was a common practice during the earlier cultural period. The last fort was built in the 1700s and used by the Ponca people who lived along the Niobrara and Missouri Rivers. This historic fort is located in Knox County, Nebraska. The term for a fort is *Nązá*. KH and NC said there were other forts built along rivers, but their locations are unknown. There are stories of the tribe defending its territory from the fort in Knox County. In addition to living in permanent villages, the Ponca were also separated by bands.

Louis Knight, grandson of Chief Black Hair Horse, said each band had at least two village sites that they occupied. According to tribal custom, they moved every two years. This, he said, was to allow the ground to replenish itself with natural plant growth. During the Land Claim testimonials of 1912 and 1914, when the Omaha Tribe attempted to claim the entire state of Nebraska, the Ponca testified that they had lived at twenty-eight different village sites. These sites are found along the Missouri, Niobrara, Elkhorn, and lower Platte Rivers in Nebraska. Others were located along the White, Keyapaha, and Missouri Rivers in South Dakota. Other landmarks included the Black Hills Wind Cave, the twin buttes south of Winner, South Dakota, and a meteorite near the Keyapaha River. Many of these village sites later were confirmed by archeological digs (Wood 1965). More recently, studies have disputed these sites as being Ponca, but material culture indicates they are Ponca in origin.

The following is an oral testimony given in 1976 by KH. Because of his keen insight on Ponca genealogy, he had been called into many probate hearings on land ownership in Oklahoma. He also served as interpreter for his mother, Virginia Big Soldier Headman, concerning the Ponca land claim case in the 1950s. He was called upon by many of his contemporaries for information on tribal culture and history. He refused personal recognition for his knowledge. His interest in Ponca cultural and historical data had made him one of the few Ponca who knew about the lands and stories that surrounded the Ponca people.

We don't really know where we came from. We just tell what our parents told us. Long time ago the Ponca lived back east along the ocean . . . Níʼtʼǫgà. We don't know where it was. Our folks always tell us that we came westward—Mí idétʼadišą [where the sun sets]. As they traveled, they heard a loud sound. I guess they curious about it, and some of the young men said they wanted to go over there to see what it was. So the leaders said it was okay to do that. When the young men returned they said it was "falling water." That's where we get that name for it—

Ni'úxp'áde. They traveled on farther west and came through Ohio. That word *Ohá'ì* means "coming through." I guess they liked that place cause there was good water there. And there was good hunting there. They must have stayed there for a long time because they remember it. But they kept coming west and come to a big river—*Nišúde t'ǫgà* [the Mississippi River]. There wasn't any kind of bridge to cross over it. But our ancestors understood those things, so they got across it somehow. They came to a place what is now called Missouri. That's where the Missouri River flows into the Mississippi. There is a big hill there, and they know about it already. It is called *P'ahé'žíde* [red hill]. As long as we have heard about it, it has always been called that. It is at St. Louis, Missouri. That is why they call St. Louis *P'ahé'žíde* now. They traveled on farther until they came to the Missouri River. I guess they camped along this river as they went northward. They say the Osage, Kaw, and Quapaw stopped somewhere along this river and the Ponca and Omaha went up the river. The Omaha stayed with the Ponca for quite a while afterward, but they separated and went downstream someplace. The Ponca kept traveling around until they settled at a place near what is now called Ponca, Nebraska. They like that place cause there was good water and plenty of game. The Ponca call it *Míxe bdǫzè* [small grave] because many Ponca children died there while they were living there. So the Ponca stayed there. After they lived there for a while, some of those men who like to travel said, "*Mǫžá baxú ǫgádet'è*" [Let us go "mark" this land]. They used to hunt all over that place. They also lived along the Elkhorn River—*Waté'* [no meaning]. They hunted all the way to the Black Hills in South Dakota. I guess they lived there long time. The Ponca have a name for all those places up there. They [the white people] call the state of Nebraska after a Ponca word—*Níbdá'ska*. It means "flat water." The Missouri River is called *Ní šúde* . . . it means "water that smokes." There are places all along the Niobrara and Missouri River that have names. There is a place called *Į́'e áidǫdì* . . . it means "where he landed on the rock." They say a medicine man flew across the river as a bird and turned back to a man just before he stepped on a rock and left his footprints on that rock. There is another place up there where the old people used to mark their height. It is called *Į́'e k'ip'áxudǫdì*. This means "where they marked their height." Many persons came by this place and put a mark on a wall of rock to show how tall they were. There is a place where the Iowas (Iowa Tribe) tried to plant a garden on Ponca territory. It is called *Máxudè wa'áidądì*. It means "where the Iowas dug the ground." The Ponca ran those Iowas out. A place along the Missouri River is called *Uhé átą* . . . "bridge." Way up north, the Ponca say there is place where the river is narrow and easy to cross over. It is called *Ní šúde ágažadèdądì*. It means "standing over the Missouri River." They call the Black Hills *P'ahé sabè*. A place that is closer to the city of Niobrara, where there are two creeks [that] run into the Missouri River, one river is call *Xádagdè'* . . . that means "going back." That other one is called *Xáda'dè užíga* . . . "small, going back." They say when the big river floods, these little creeks flow back the other way. A creek west of Niobrara is called Ponca Creek today. Our people called it *Ní'udít'ę wačíška* . . . it means "die in the water creek." Way out west of there, there are two buttes where the Ponca used to have sports. That place is just south of Winner, South Dakota, where those two buttes stand. At those buttes they used to shoot their arrows from one butte to the other. They called that place *Mą́ dédé dądì* . . . "where they shoot the arrows." The Poncas used to live in that place for a long time. They used to shoot arrows from one butte to the other to see who could shoot the farthest. The Sioux Indians used to come south to that place where they fought with the Ponca. Another place close by, toward the south, near the Keyapaha River there was a meteorite. The Ponca used to see who could lift it and throw it. They named that place *Į́e dihądądì*. That means "where they lifted the rock." There are other places long ways from there that the Ponca went to. They called Pike's Peak *P'ahé'žé'egą̀*. It is a word that's kind of bad language in English. The Ponca used to travel all over. They hunted in those mountains in Colorado. They met some people over there one time. They called them *Niášigà nušiáha*. It means "short people." They don't know who they were. They just called them short people. The old people used to visit other tribes around there. Then the government [U.S. government] moved them to Oklahoma.

There is a story of the aforementioned fort that tells of the Comanche people who came and occupied the fort when the Ponca had moved to another area. According to KH and AMC, that occupancy was short-lived when, after the Ponca had returned, there was a short battle. It was not unusual for the tribe to encounter other people in their territory. One of their oldest villages is near present-day Ponca, Nebraska. The Iowa Tribe came and began to cultivate the farming area there when that group of Ponca had gone to live in another area. Upon returning, the Ponca found the Iowa digging up the ground to plant crops. The Iowa, of course, were asked to leave the area. This camp became known as *Máxudè wa'áidạdì*, or "where the Iowas dug up the ground." Stories such as these are based on places where the Ponca traveled or hunted or where unusual happenings occurred where they lived. They also give evidence of locations of various village sites and landmarks. AMC, one of the finest men among the Ponca people, gave the following account of Ponca origins and travels:

> What I heard was that we came from somewhere east to this place. They [the Ponca] were on the water and finally got on the land . . . but there was a wall of rock there [cliff] . . . so they looked for an entrance to get on the land. A few men then looked for a way to get through. They found a split in the rock . . . "big enough for a man and a bundle to get through," they said. After they got on land there, they lived there for many years and then begin to move north and westward. The place that they first came to was Ohio [state]. They called it that because they saw that somebody or some people had been there before. They saw articles [artifacts, remains of dwellings, etc.] there and said, *"Oháikè"* [It has been traveled through before]. They went all over that place . . . *P'ahé'židè* [near St. Louis, Missouri] . . . also to the pipestone quarries in Minnesota where they got pipestone. They finally came to the Missouri River. They called it *Ní šúdè*. If you happen to be up there in the morning, it looks like smoke. That's why it's called *Ní šúdè* . . . "water that smokes." Those people gave names to several places up there [Nebraska and South Dakota]. They named those places by what it was known for. They called one village *Hubḑą́* because that village people ate just fish. They called one village *Wa'í'xúde* . . . it means "Gray Blanket." That third village was called *K'úhewadè* . . . "scary place." But all those places up there had names. Our people stayed there for long time and finally moved to Oklahoma because the government ordered them to move.

According to tradition and oral historical accounts, the Ponca people established land boundaries by landmarks significant to them. The process is called *Mążá baxù*, or "land drawing." When this process was established, that is, seeing that no other people occupied these lands, the territory then became theirs to live in. Migrating tribes who came into occupied territories usually proceeded through without interruption. Usually, it has been said, the leaders of such tribes carried a white deerskin aloft to let the resident tribe know that their passage was peaceful. The boundaries of any tribe, when recognized by those passing through, were usually respected. According to the elders, the known Ponca lands in the modern setting can be drawn beginning with present-day Omaha, Nebraska, aligned to Ponca. Nebraska to the confluence of the Missouri and Niobrara Rivers, to the Missouri and White Rivers in South Dakota to the southern part of the Black Hills, viz., Wind Cave, and from the Wind Cave very close to a straight line south to the Platte River and then in a straight line to where it flows into the Missouri encompass the Ponca territory. These lands were occupied by the Ponca people. James Howard (1970) in "Known Village Sites of the Ponca" indicated that testimonials given during the Omaha land claim showed that the Ponca people had occupied the above land description. These testimonies were given by Ponca Indians who remembered the names of the sites. Names given here are names known by their physical appearance; some unusual happenings that occurred at the time of the occupancy, such as the great meteor shower of 1834; and other incidences that affected the tribe. As in the earlier mentioned land claim case, the elders confirmed the names for these villages as follows:

P'ahé šnabè	dirty hill, village at the fork of the Niobrara and Keyapaha Rivers.
[Village name unknown]	village at the mouth of the Platte (located southwest where the Platte flows into the Missouri)
T'í wádì	St. Helena village
Uhé átą	bridge
Omádì	to walk a way of life
Máxudè waáedądì	where the Iowas dug the ground
Ní' xué'	roaring water

Mí gašúdè	moon when it was dusty
T'enúga sábe waáedądì	where Black Buffalo Bull dug the ground, village near O'Neil, Nebraska
Žą́ wídądą̀	few sticks of wood
Mikáe uxp'ádè tedądì	village location during the great meteor shower of 1834, village at the mouth of Burgess Creek
Xdabé t'í'à'	dead (*t'í'à'* = rotten) tree village
T'ądé waáedądì	farming ground village
Ną́zà	fence and earthworks, the Ponca Fort site, occupied 1700s to early 1800s
Hubdą́	fish smell village, occupied at the time of forced removal
Xádagdè	going back, Ponca Creek (may have been called *Ní'udít'ę̀ wačíška*)
Xádagdè užíga	little going back, Bazile Creek
Žábè t'í	Beaver village
Ní púki	Norfolk, village near Wayne, Nebraska
Gaxdíbiwadè	where it was appropriate to whip someone, Big Bend village
Míxè bdązè	small grave, very early occupation
Waí xúdè	gray blanket village, occupied at the time of forced removal
K'úhèwadè	scary place village, occupied at the time of forced removal
Į́'e dihą́dądì	where they lifted the rock-meteorite

Note: Date of occupation for some of these sites has not been clearly confirmed because they are said to be very old.

A representative of one of the schools of archeology presented a lecture on some of the village sites in Nebraska and South Dakota a few years ago. He attributed some of those sites to other tribes of Indians. His theory was based on small amounts of material culture and on burial methods. Consequently, he vaguely stated, some of these village sites could have been occupied previously by those tribes identified with what archeologists term central plains tradition. The elders said these are the kind of records made by white men who never consulted with the true inhabitants of the land (KH, NC, AL). Joseph Jablow (1974) wrote a most fascinating ethnohistory of the Ponca Tribe in reference to their claim to lands in Nebraska and South Dakota. I must admit that I (being a layman in such matters) am amazed that some of the written material confirmed stories told to me by the elders, for example, the "acquisition of the horse." In Ponca history, in the oral tradition, some horses were acquired from the Comanche, and acquisition of horses is part of the story of Little Bear, a Ðíxidą Ponca warrior. This story predates the historical record of the French trader Juan Munier, who had filed a petition to establish trade rights with the Ponca for "a period of ten years" in 1793. Additionally, a disclaimer that said "the Poncas are nothing but Mahas (Omahas) who have left the tribe" was filed by Jacques Clamorgan in 1794. This evidently was done to prevent Munier from trading with the Ponca because he was benefiting from trade with the Omaha as well. Clamorgan's statement is probably the basis of Fletcher and La Flesche's claims that the Ponca were part of the Omaha Tribe.[1] In the race to establish name and capital gain, the European traders sought to create inroads to every Indian nation by offering gifts and trinkets to their recipients. The Ponca would have nothing to do with these activities. Where were the Ponca before these contacts? They were where they always were. Some Ponca took advantage of some European trade goods while they could. They were aware of the trading going on among the Omaha and could go there without detection and trade without notice. The history of exploration by Europeans too had its downfalls. A. P. Nasatir (2002) wrote that Frenchmen "of all kinds" had "penetrated the whole Trans-Mississippi West country and in a general way had made known the country contained in the watershed of the Mississippi-Missouri rivers" lacked accuracy and precision. Nasatir inferred that exploration "had not reached a point much beyond the Platte River" and "except for that stretch of river above the Platte and below the White or Cheyenne River" (2002, 56). No white explorer knew anything about the Ponca: "Thus did the light of history fail to shine, as yet, upon the Ponca, for they were in an area far above the Platte and well below the White River, to say nothing of the

Cheyenne River" (Jablow 1974, 69). This would suggest that the territory mentioned earlier had never been explored by anyone or had not been recorded by anyone who might have been able to confirm the existence of the Ponca people before 1785. It should be pointed out that reference is made to this historical documentation only as a subjective evaluation necessary for this section. As stated earlier, the Ponca lived and carried out their lives in the aforementioned area.

Following European contact, they mysteriously became a small tribe recorded as having a population ranging from two hundred to sixteen hundred (Jablow 1974, 335–38) at different periods from about 1780 to mid-1800. The census was taken over fifty times and presumably by over thirty-five different sources. In seventy years, their population fluctuated so much one wonders how they survived. Were these figures recorded for only one or two villages? It is reasonable to suggest that this could be one of the problems surrounding the wide differences in counting heads. However, some other questions surround the smallness of the tribe. These questions, to date, have not been answered by other known resources. They are centered on approximately twenty-eight (or more) known Ponca villages in the above description. The contradiction between the size of the Ponca Tribe reported by elders and the size that was recorded necessitates inquiry. To quantify supportive material for this supposition, this writer had to rely solely on oral history of the elders. For instance, from the two-room shack where I was born and lived to the old White Eagle train station is approximately one mile. Grandmother (VBSH), who was born about 1854, said the camp circle (*Húdugà*) at a Ponca sun dance held in the 1700s was that far across. This circle with a diameter of one mile across would have been composed of several thousand people. The *Húdugà* was four circles deep! This was told to her by her grandparents. If the Ponca Tribe was larger than what has been recorded, what happened to them? Many Pawnee people suffered annihilation by blankets infested with smallpox given to them by federal officials. The Ponca have some stories of the tribe suffering from smallpox. They called it *Dí'xe*.

Culturally, the Ponca stayed in one village for no more than two years and then would move back to their former village. That being the case, the number of villages the Ponca occupied could have been at least fourteen. Was their disappearance caused by the same source that diminished the Pawnee (that is, smallpox)? If so, the outbreak would have had to have happened before the Pawnee ordeal and been undisclosed throughout history. Someone was unable to hide information concerning the Pawnee. Ponca lands were ceded to the Teton Sioux. Why didn't the Teton occupy this land after the last three Ponca villages had been vacated? The Sioux was a large tribe. Why is it they could never annihilate the Ponca people? The Ponca fought them from time immemorial. Historical records tell of the "speeded-up attacks" of the Sioux on the Ponca after they (the Sioux) learned that the land was theirs. If that was the case, why did Standing Bear and his small band want to go back to such deplorable conditions after being taken to Indian Territory? The Sioux were a threat to the government, and the government was opening this territory for settlers. The government had to appease the Sioux?

The home of the Ponca people was desired, not by the Sioux or any other tribe. It was a desirable place to live. The federals had to get them out. What has to be admitted is that a federal ring of land grabbers was at work at this time. These are the culprits who twisted the truth. They lied, cheated, and corroborated with other federal officials for capital gain. Recorded letters, trade agreements, and other federal documents in state and national archives are stacked high to prove the Ponca were a small tribe and roved about; were only a part of the larger Omaha Tribe; were begging for food; were hiding behind white farmers; and were attacked unmercifully by the Sioux, who destroyed their crops and killed dozens of Ponca at a time. Some even reported and recorded that the Ponca were in alliance with the Sioux or the Pawnee at different times because they were the much larger tribes. They reported that this was done to protect themselves against the Sioux or Pawnee. Such rubbish and ridiculousness was presented to the U.S. Claims Commission in an attempt to centralize the Ponca in their last and final stronghold at Niobrara. Such is the description of the Ponca before their removal to Indian Territory. They unfortunately had no written language to counter such claims. These statements, according to the elders, were derogatory, slanted, and without grounds (KH, NC, AL). This should have caused historians to investigate why this action was taken during the Indian removal era. Inasmuch as the archives, anywhere, should be researched, the Indians were never consulted. But why was there so much ado about documenting the conditions of those "poor, desperate, starving Ponca"? The idea of the complete genocide of Native peoples was still in the thinking of many Europeans. Not too long before, a U.S. president had sought to annihilate a tribe of Indians. In the case of the Ponca, records were made and letters were written because they needed a reason to remove them. The act of any forced removal of Indian tribes to Indian Territory or to any other area in the country was simply done to acquire the land. Additionally, it was recorded later that the governor of Nebraska too stated he wanted no Indians in his territory.

2

Niobrara

The last and final stronghold the Ponca people possessed was a favored site in the north central part of the state of Nebraska. They called the area *Níúbdadà*, or "broad water." (Some historians said the Ponca called it "rushing water"; however, the word description is from the French *Eau-qui-cour*.) The Ponca term for rushing water is *Ní xué*, which was not the name of the river. The French were apparently referring to the river when it flooded. I was told that in the old days, it could be a violent river when it flooded. But the area was a desirable place to live. Its geographical location has beautiful physical characteristics. At first appearance to the newcomer, one's instincts are awakened to its aesthetic values. Even the journals of Lewis and Clark, in reference to the Ponca Fort site, said it was built on a "butifull plain." If you go there during the springtime, summer, or fall, you will see green native grasses covering the hillside with bright green trees along all the rivers and creeks that seem to last for all seasons. The confluence of the Missouri and Niobrara Rivers provided good fishing (and still does). The beautiful, smaller Ponca and Bazile Creeks, along with the Verdigre River, also provided an abundance of food fish. The high hills and valleys provided excellent cover for wildlife. Hunting was good. The plains south and west of Niobrara were known for great herds of bison, which the Ponca bison hunters delighted in. It was a "land of plenty," and the inhabitants were well taken care of. The low, rich productive lands adjacent to the rivers, the high hill, the valleys, and the timber speak of a quiet peaceful place. Even though the Ponca established villages in many other locations as mentioned above, this was the last area of land they considered as theirs before the removal.

Other village sites are along the Missouri River, the Niobrara and Elkhorn Rivers in Nebraska, and the Keyapaha and White Rivers in South Dakota. The Ponca always made their villages near rivers and creeks. A well-known village was located north of the Missouri River along Chouteau Creek. Of interest to the Ponca was the Black Hills (*P'ahé sabè*). A village site is located at the foot of the Wind Cave. (Many stories are derived from Ponca knowledge of the cave. In the stories, a character called *P'ahé wadáhunì*, "The Hill Swallower," emerges especially for children.) The Ponca established villages at different locations, at different periods, over a large territory. Since they had lived in as many as twenty-eight different villages at one period in their history, this territory then is where they made their homes and lived in peace among themselves. Intruders were dealt with quickly and taken to the borders of their territory. These people were a resourceful people who defended their territory like most civilizations. The strategic geographic features of the northern Nebraska hills and rivers were chosen to be their final defense against surrounding tribes and the onslaught of the Europeans. Here, for nearly two hundred years, they defended themselves against natural disasters, drought, disease, and other people.

A much talked about hill in Knox County, Nebraska, was that fortification they built and used in the seventeenth and eighteenth centuries. Other such forts were built by other bands of Ponca according to some of the Ponca elders. Peter LeClair said one such fort was located near present day Ponca, Nebraska. The unique feature of the forts is that they were built at locations where they could withstand the enemy. The fort (*Náza*) in Knox County was built as a means of protecting women and children. Inside the fort were four large mound dwellings (*Máit'ì*). Any intruder, in time of war, able to ascend that hill would have had to be an unusually agile person. The earthwork surrounding the fort (which lies only a few feet from the hill's edge) was maintained by Ponca bowmen. Behind the earthwork was the palisade fort. The description of the Ponca Fort site is as follows:

> The Ponca Fort site may be characterized as the remains of a fortified earth-lodge village. It is located in sec. 29, T.33N., R. 7 W., Knox County, Nebraska.... The fort was well situated from a defensive point of view, being located on a prominence, one of the bluffs of the Missouri, some 50 or 60 feet above the floor of the valley of Ponca Creek.... The fort covers an area of 3 acres, and measures 380 feet east and west and 320 feet north and south. On at least one side of the fortification, protuber-

ances or bastions were built from which the village inhabitants could rake attacking forces with a murderous crossfire. (Howard 1995, 11)

In times of warfare, the Ponca were thorough in letting the enemy know that they would not tolerate any attacks. The manner in which they dealt with intruders would be considered barbaric in modern times (assuming our modern civilization doesn't do those kinds of things). The Ponca never took scalps; they took the whole head. The University of Nebraska, for decades, held Ponca remains for study. It was recorded that seventy-five remains were dug up at the Ponca Fort site and other Ponca burial grounds in that area. There were twenty skulls among these remains. They had been buried in a common grave. A Ponca elder said that those skulls could not be Ponca. He said it would be unsympathetic, in modern times, to tell whom they probably belonged to. I climbed up to the top of the hill from the north side and found it to be quite a workout. It makes one wonder how it would have been if someone was throwing rocks and shooting arrows at the people trying to ascend that hill. That fort was strategically built. No small mind could have thought it out.

The high rolling hills too served the people well. Harry Buffalohead, a Ponca singer, now deceased, told the story about a neighboring tribesman who attempted to prove his prowess and bravery. The story goes that he would come from the east and south. Sitting on his horse, he would holler at the man and blow his whistle indicating he was ready to fight barehanded. The Ponca man did not hesitate to pursue him and to decapitate the enemy. The Ponca knew their territory. An enemy might have been able to escape once in a while, but more often than not, it was folly to come onto their land. From the beginning of the time when the Ponca occupied lands north of the Platte River in Nebraska and in the southern parts of South Dakota, they often encountered people passing over their territory.

For as many years as can be recalled, the tribe has recorded incidents affecting the people through singing. When things of interest happened to an individual or to the whole tribe, song makers were present to sing about it. In many instances, when travelers came onto their lands, they either welcomed them or defended their territory. If these encounters were significant enough, they were recorded in song. These stories are found in the songs of the Ponca *Heđúškà* fraternal organization (see "The Ponca Drum" in chapter 12). The songs indicate who the Ponca had conflicts with. Some of these people were the *Ihátawì* (Yankton), Teton, Oglala (*Ogđádà*), Omaha (*Umáhą*), Pawnee (*P'áđì*), Comanche (*P'ádak'à*), and Iowa (*Má xudé*). And in modern times, although no songs are remembered or have been made of these encounters, the Ponca aided Lewis and Clark and the Mormons, in addition to various federal officials, geographers, topographers, and private entrepreneurs.

But all was not defense and warfare. On the lowlands just north of the fort site, approximately two thousand feet from the Missouri, they built their permanent earthen lodges (or mound dwellings), which were occupied most of the time. Situated just a few hundred yards west of the confluence of the Niobrara and Missouri was the *K'úhe wađè* (scary) village. About five miles westward, the *Hubđą́* (fish smell) village was built. This location is near the Ponca Creek northerly from the hills where the Ponca fort site is located. From the Missouri up the Niobrara as it curves westward was the *Waį́ xúdè* (gray robe) village. (These were the last three villages the Ponca built before the removal.) The lowlands were fertile, especially close to the rivers. This was a good place to plant crops. The elders said the Ponca cultivated up to forty acres of land. Growing foodstuff was not significant to the Ponca because most tribes living along the Missouri had a similar economic base. A similar village site is located approximately thirty miles up from where the Niobrara enters the Missouri. Here the Ponca built an earthen lodge and tipi village. The village was occupied before 1860 by a band of Ponca known by U.S. Cavalry and Army doctors who wrote about them and drew maps of their location.

Economic Pattern in the North

Economic patterns of various tribes of Native peoples varied slightly and were primarily contingent on game population, natural vegetation, and a fertile land base. Tribes accustomed to a horticulture economy sought fertile ground where natural fruit and vegetable plants grew. Usually these grew along rivers and streams. The climate was also a factor. Nebraska is said to have light precipitation, but it has cold winters and hot summers. Average temperatures range from below freezing to the upper seventies for winter and summer. The plains of Nebraska have some rivers and streams with timber. Natural vegetation of the plains originally included tall prairie grass; in the much more arid regions of the west, drought-resistant grasses grew. Elm, hackberry, box elder, cottonwood, oak, and ash trees grew along the major rivers. At least three varieties of willows grew along streams. The wood from the willow trees was used for religious purposes. Normally, ash was used for making bows, but Osage orange was favored because of its potent resiliency. Water played an important role in the lives of the Ponca as it was used for many purposes, which included some irrigation and watering of transplanted trees. J. H. Howard (1995) said that most upper central plains tribes had practiced the art of transplanting trees. This, he said, was self-evident by observing trees located sometimes far away from streams and rivers. A clump of trees in the plains for the anthropologist or archeologist could reveal, for example, old campsites. The current state of Nebraska still has a "sand hill" region in the west. These "dunes" are covered with short grass, and according to our elders, they were uninhabitable.

Horticulture and Agriculture

From the earliest time when the Ponca migrated into the north central plains, their first impression of the land was its rich and productive soil. They found the land rich with "all kinds of fruits," according to KH. He said the land was *Wašé* (plenteous) — it had everything. The land was good for growing plants and for transplanting. He himself was known for the "seeding" of "Indian perfume," or *P'éžep'à*. He said this type of seeding and the seeding of other kinds of plants were commonly done. Sometimes a whole plant was dug out and replanted where it would most likely grow and produce fruit. Those kinds of seeds that required good soil for maximum growth, like corn, squash, pumpkins, and so forth, were usually planted on lowlands or near streams and river bottoms. Good examples of this are the last three Ponca camps where they planted and reaped good produce. At the time of occupancy, the Ponca families communally cultivated many acres of land. Some individual families cultivated about ten acres. Corn or *Wahábà* being a food staple was prepared in different styles. The following are

Ponca names for types of corn, other plants and vegetables, and their extended use as food:

TYPES OF CORN

Watą́zì	corn (grain)
Wahábà	corn on the cob
Wahábà ukédì	blue corn (now called decorative corn)
Wahábà bízeđè	dried or dehydrated corn
Watą́zi skíđè	sweet corn

PREPARED CORN DISHES

Wabíšnudè	hominy (This is the process by which hominy is made. The corn is cleaned with ashes to remove the hull.)
Wabđúgà	hominy (usually cooked with meat)
Watą́zi skíđè	cooked sweet corn with meat
Bibđúbđúgà	corn ball dumpling (This is made from ground corn.)
Wašą́gè	corn pudding (made from ground corn)
Wahába žéąhè	parched corn
Watą́zì wažégđą̀	corn bread
Wanáxe	grain corn parched on griddle (pounded and mixed with dried meat)

OTHER VEGETABLES, GRAINS, ROOTS, NUTS, AND SO FORTH

Watą́	pumpkin
Mąžą́xè	wild onion
Watą́ múxà	squash
Hįbđíge	wild sweet peas
Watą́ hášugà	thick-skinned squash
Hįbđíge	beans
T'ą́deáha nú'	wild potato
T'ą́deáhà hįbđíge	ground beans
Núgđè	wild turnip

Síwanidè	wild rice
Nú	potato
Žá	land squatters (greens)
Núskidè	sweet potato
Waxdá	milkweed sprout
Wažídè	tomato
T'édawì	water lily (chinquapin)
Mikáe xdí	morel
T'ágè	nut
T'áge t'ągà	black walnut
T'áge žįgà	pecan
Nąsi'	hickory nuts
Ą́žįgà	hazelnuts
Búdè	acorns
Waxt'á	fruit
Bat'é	raspberry
Agdą́gamągè	strawberry
Ną́p'a	chokecherry
K'ą́de'	plum
Unknown	crabapple
Unknown	Juneberry
Unknown	sand cherry
Ną́šąmà	blackhaw
Wažídè	buffaloberry
T'asp'ą̀	persimmon
T'užígà	pawpaw
Unknown	elderberry
Unknown	ground cherry
Šé'hįškubè	peach
Házì	grapes

Sugar (*Žąní*) was made from wild honey, box elder, maple, and hickory. People with a sweet tooth liked honey and nuts mixed together. Beverages, usually tea (*Xádè mąk'ą̀*), were made from wild mint, wild verbena, and wild anise. Salt (*Niskídè*) was dug out of the ground in chunks. Salt, at the time the Ponca lived along the Niobrara, was taken from an area near current Lincoln, Nebraska. This work was done by the women of the tribe. Meats were processed from the following large and small mammals:

T'é	bison
Žábè	beaver
P'ášt'ągà	moose
Mik'á	raccoon
T'axt'ì	deer
Sísnejèwagidè	muskrat
T'ačúge	antelope
Mąsčíge	cottontail
Ápą	elk
Mąsčí skà	jackrabbit
Mąčú	bear (any)
Wasábe	black bear
Mąsčíge sísnedè	snowshoe rabbit
Haxúde	sheep
Haxúde hé't'ągà	bighorn sheep
Sígà	squirrel

MEATS FROM FISH AND FOWL

Húhú	fish (generic term for any fish)
Huhú ít'ągà	largemouth bass
Hup'ásisnedè	sturgeon and gar
T'úzè	catfish
Hu žíde	buffalo carp
Hubđáska	carp, drum
Hubđáska žígà	sun perch, crappie, and so forth
G'é	turtle
G'ét'ągà	snapping turtle
G'éhábedà	sand turtle

G'égdézè	terrapin
G'ét'at'áxì	snapping turtle
Wažįga	bird
Míxat'ǫgà	geese
Míxà	ducks
Úšįwadè	quail
Đítit'ǫgà	turtledove
Zizík'à	turkey
Šú	prairie chicken (now, pheasant and Chinese ringneck)

Women and children always gathered fruits, nuts, and other edible plants and caught smaller game, especially waterfowl, rabbits, and turtles. Women seldom went fishing but participated in the food preparation for all catches and kills. KCH said dehydrating chokecherries was a process that went something like this: Large baskets were filled and brought to a rocky ledge, on a hillside, where they crushed the berries with smooth stones. The crushed berries were then made into patties and laid out in the sun to dry. Periodically, the patties were turned over so that they would dry evenly. The patties, when completed, were sacked and stored. Peaches and other fruits were cut in half and were dehydrated in the same fashion. The Ponca very seldom seasoned foods. Ponca foods, by our standard food preparation today, would have to be classified as very bland. However, in addition to salt, other seasoning types included anise, cedar, and ashes. Meats and vegetables were commonly cooked together. Squash and venison cooked together with anise, for example, was a favored dish at certain times of the year, according KH and AL. They indicated the small purple seeds from cedar trees were also used to season some soups. The ashes from the fireplace were used to season hominy dishes.

The Ponca Bison Hunter

Whereas the economy of the people who live in the tropical rain forests in South America, where the land is heavily timbered with large quantities of broadleaf evergreen trees and a very large number of species of both animal and plant life, the Ponca who lived in the plains established an economic base that included horticulture, some agriculture, and hunting. Following the dispersion of the Middle Mississippian culture, the Ponca, according to Howard (1995), made many adjustments in the north central plains. By the time the Ponca made first white contact, they had become bison hunters. Adaptation to the plains, apparently a slow process, brought a new economic system that would alter the planting economy of the former cultural period. They continued, however, to plant vegetables, which were now largely supplemented with bison. The American bison is a gregarious animal with a large head and hump over the forequarters. This short-horned animal is a descendent of the giant bison (*Bison antiquus*) that is said to have been about three times as large in prehistoric times. During Ponca occupancy of the northern plains, the smaller version roamed the plains in large herds. The behavior pattern of the animals was known by the hunters and tracing their whereabouts was easily done. Finding the herd seemed unimportant when speaking with the elders. Retaining herd size and sufficient female population for procreation and for ecological purposes was never given consideration by the hunters. Because there was so many bison and the tribe took only what they would use, there apparently was no need to take preservation into consideration.

Ponca bison hunters and the hunt were described by VBSH in the early 1950s during the Ponca Land Claim investigation. At that time her eyesight was failing. She said on occasion that sometimes she could "see" the Ponca shooting bison as she looked toward the woods on her homestead in Oklahoma. The following is translated from the Ponca language:

The bison hunt (*T'e' wakíde*) occurred two times a year. The first one was during the new year (in springtime). When they killed bison, they killed only what they would use for meat, for making tipis, huts, tools, robes and other clothes. When they prepared for hunting and killing the animals, they used to pray first. When they got ready, they fixed all their hunting equipment. They got their best horses for this kind of hunt, got the best trackers and the hunters ready. When the time came to leave, the men who were in front were the ones who would find the bison. Sometimes it took several days before they came where the bison were feeding. When the herd was found, they made camp in a circle. Before they went to kill them, those who would shoot the bison made plans among themselves. Some would speak to others about how they would help each other during the slaughter. They took precautions by encouraging one another so they wouldn't make mistakes during the kill. The tribe depended upon them for the meat, so they had to do it right the first time. Everyone was happy at this time because they were going to have much to eat. Those men who were in charge usually knew how to get to the bison they wanted to kill. On the first day of the hunt, they always looked at the herd and saw which direction they should come close to them. Sometimes they would ride into the herd to separate the cows from the bulls. They did that so they could get those cows for the meat and skins. Their meat was tender and the skins were soft. They also killed one or two calves too. Some people liked to eat the meat from the young bison because of some sickness they believed it to cure. The skin from the bull bison was tough, so was the meat, but they could use the meat and skin too. Young bulls were good, and their skins were good too. When they went in to shoot the bison, some men had to ride up close to the running animal to get a good shot. If they had guns, it was easier to do it, but bow and arrow was harder. If there was cliff nearby or a dry creek bed, they ran those bison in that direction hoping that one might stumble and fall. After they killed the bison, we followed our parents who began butchering the animals. When they finished, the people prayed. Then we went home and passed the meat around to everyone who didn't go on the hunting trip.

Some historians, who have described the Ponca bison hunt, have suggested that the Ponca had "buffalo police" to keep overzealous hunters from spooking the herd. The elders said that they had never heard of such men. The term for helping or aiding is *Uk'ík'ą* or, depending on context, *Ákinąžì* in the Ponca language. The words are described in full in chapter 13. These terms had been ingrained into the minds of young men. They always had this teaching. This suggests that the hunters depended on each other for a successful hunt and kill. There was no time for individual self-praise and glory. This time was for procuring the tribes' foodstuff for that period of need.

Other stories about traditions in the bison hunt say that families always tried to get to the kill made by a family member. However, this was not always done. Following a kill, the first person to come to the kill was entitled to take a choice cut of meat for the first meal. KH, AMC, and AL said the *T'ǫ́hè* (a section of the large intestine) was usually the first cut made. Butchering was a tedious job that included dehydrating the meat, packaging, and separating some parts of the bison bone for tools. The scapula, for one, was used to make spreaders for the roach headdress and garden hoes. The lower leg bone above the fetlock to the knee was used as a flesher. Other bones were used for arrow straighteners, spoons, ladles, and so forth. The horns were principally used in tribal medicines. Varied sizes of spoons (*T'éhê*) were also made from the horns. Sinew was used for thread, heavier string, and rope (KH, NC, JP, AMC). Other large mammals contributing to the economy included pronghorn antelope, deer, elk, and moose. The elk horn had many uses as tools, especially for digging and scraping. KH said that a flint blade was attached to the end of an elk horn that was cut at the first fork of the antler. Later when metal tools were introduced into the upper plains, metal blades replaced flint. Deer and antelope skins (already mentioned) had many uses, especially for clothing. Smaller animals were eaten, and some hides were used for various purposes. For example, the otter hide was used as a bag, namely, for medicine. Caps and other ceremonial dancing paraphernalia were also made from this hide. The elders said only those men who practiced the art of medicine wore the skin of the otter around the back of the neck with the two ends hanging down parallel to each other in the front. The skin was cut about four to five inches wide. Some Ponca differ on their descriptions of the uses of wolf and coyote hides. Peter LeClair stated that the Ponca never used the hides in hunting experiences. But KH, AMC, AL, and others said the hides were used for hunting and ceremonial purposes.

Known Creek and Stream Tributaries to Major Rivers

From the earliest times of civilization, every nation and its people have traveled, marking trails in their memories. Topographic patterns of the landscape on the plains and, even more striking, valleys and mountains reminded the traveler of his direction of travel and location. It has been said too that game led him in varied directions, but his innovative mind kept him aware of his steps, which passed distinctive indicators of his whereabouts.

The elders used to say the Ponca people had leanings toward discovery of new places. The stories of travels into the North Country as well as to the south were marked by the significance of the land. From the East Coast to the great Southwest, the Ponca lived near and named various landmarks. Already mentioned are names of places where the Ponca traveled as they moved westward from the east. Once settled in what is now Nebraska, they named many of the tributaries along the Missouri, Niobrara, and Elk Horn Rivers. The tributaries to these rivers seem to cover the extent of Ponca territory. According to the elders, although they established permanent villages, the Ponca never stayed in one place to fish and hunt. This was done to prevent exhausting the land resources and to preserve wildlife.

Two major tributaries entered the Missouri River (*Nišúde*). The first was the Niobrara River (*Níúbdàdà*). (Part of the Niobrara was called *Mázitą̀*, "where there are many cedars.") The other was the Elkhorn River (*Wat'é*), which flowed into the Platte River (*Níbdá'ska*, "flat river"). This major tributary flowed into the Missouri River. Hunters and travelers named streams or landmarks along these tributaries according to an incident that may have occurred there or an obvious natural characteristic of the land.

The Ponca people hunted near and fished in these streams and creeks. Some buttes along the Niobrara were called *P'ahéšnábe*, "dirty hills." When I was a young man of about fourteen years, Peter LeClair told me and KH that near his home was a place called "Where a stone was lifted," "Roaring water," and "Where Buffalo Bull" was killed, among other names. The Southern Ponca elders of the 1960s and 1970s knew some of the streams and creeks but had no knowledge of their location. They could recall stories from their parents and grandparents of traveling and hunting expeditions naming some of the streams, creeks, and other topographical landmarks.

The following is one historical story of how the Ponca people acquired the use of the smoke from cedar as a healing balm. Interestingly, the geographic location of the experience may have occurred near a place called *Mázi nádįgè dàìdą́*, "where the cedars were burned." The story was told by KH as follows (my translation):

The Ponca people were going through a period of sickness. No one knows what the sickness was. They had suffered many symptoms of sickness. Medicines given to them by the doctors would not help them. It was a time for those who practiced the art of healing to find the source of help that would be given by the Great Mystery. In those days, medicines were considered sacred or "*Waxúbe*." Special preparations were made before they left the village. They would search the land in their own way, as it was the custom of the people to be led by the spirit of God.

It seemed hopeless after many attempts were made by men and women to find a medicine to help. According to the elders, it was at this time a Ponca man of the Hísadà Clan came upon a scene that drew his attention. It was a time of a drought in the land. He had been traveling for days. They say he never ate any food during this time. He only drank a little water.

The scene unfolding before him was a pillar of dust in the distance. He observed an object moving on the dry earth causing the dust to rise into the windless sky. Coming closer, crawling up a knoll, he was able to see the cause of the disturbance. An eagle was flapping a wing. He noticed the eagle was dragging the other wing. In doing so, it spun in a circle causing dust to rise. One wing was broken.

He concluded that the eagle was destined to die from starvation or would be killed by a predator. He continued his search for the next days. As he traveled, each morning and evening he would think of the fate of the eagle. After he had traveled many days from his village in a wandering fashion, the scene of the eagle haunted him. It must have been days since he was at the sight where he had watched the eagle. Thinking perhaps Wakąda was offering him something; he returned to see if the eagle was still there or if it died of starvation or had been killed.

When he arrived at the site, he was surprised to see the eagle was alive and still attempting to lift its wing. The broken wing was now being lifted and flapping clumsily but was indeed very close to matching the good wing. The bird was hopping and flapping until, the fourth day of his return to watch, it went to a tree that stayed green all year long. The elders said it was a large cedar tree, or *Mázi hi* as the Ponca call that tree.

They say the bird began to climb the tree using its beak and talons to pull itself up until it reached the pinnacle of the tall evergreen. Up to that day, the drought was still in effect. But from the northwest, the man noticed clouds forming and approaching quickly. The wind began to cause the tree to sway. He noticed the eagle had its wings spread wide facing the wind. Suddenly as a huge gust of wind came, the eagle jumped into the wind with its wings spread. Catching the strong wind, the eagle began to rise into the air. As it rose to the heights of the clouds, the man said, "It has gone back to where eagles dwell."

The man had watched and saw a natural phenomena of a bird healing itself and left the site to pursue his quest for the medicine that *Wak'ada* would show to him. But as he was leaving, he thought perhaps there is something at that tree where the eagle showed me it could fly again. Returning to the tree, he found at the base of the tree one of the tail feathers of the eagle lying upon a small branch of cedar.

At that time, the Ponca never knew nor used the feathers of the eagle for any purpose. But the man decided he would take the two items back to the village. Being respectful to nature and its offering, he went to a nearby stream and cleansed himself with ritual washing.

When he arrived at the village, he told his household what he experienced and showed them the two items he brought home. An elder in his family told him, he had burned cedar before because it had a pleasing smell. He said this one may be sacred, or *Waxúbe*, and different because it is telling you a mystery. The man thought of it for days. Then, on the fourth day, he concluded that *Wak'ada* had showed to him that if the eagle had given up by sitting still the wing would have never healed. It had to move about and use its natural want to fly again.

This man of medicine went among the people from that day and burned cedar on ashes in each dwelling. He fanned members of the families with the eagle feather saying their sickness will leave them if they would get up and move about. He told them to keep using the healing herbs given to them by others. It is said that to this day, the Ponca people still burn cedar in their homes and feel that *Wak'ada* is with them.

Based on what the elders say, there is a historic relationship with many geographic locations in the North Country where the tribe once

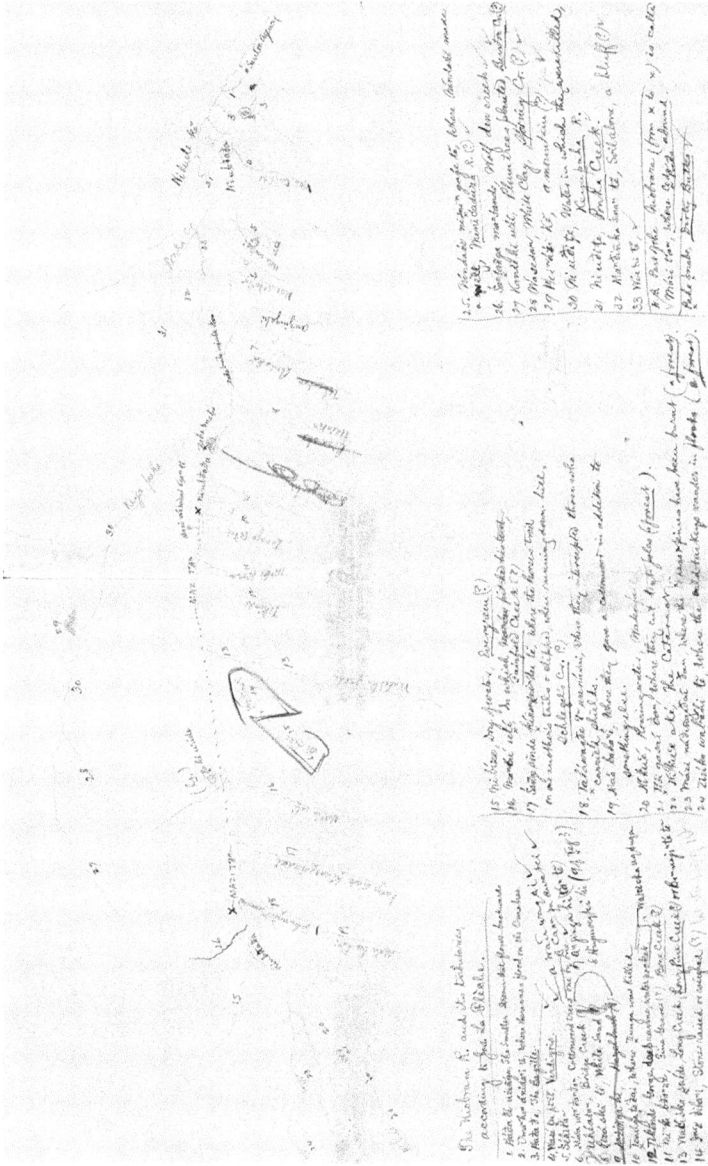

MAP 1. Tributaries to the Niobrara River. National Museum of Natural History National Anthropological Archives, Siouan-Catawban series, James Owen Dorsey papers (NAA MS 4800).

lived. Other personal family stories were often told during the winter months of incidents occurring around the known landmarks and streams in the North Country. Mentioned elsewhere, KH and NC said they never told these types of stories during the summer. No reason was given for this practice.

In the nineteenth century, Mr. Joseph LeFleche, a Frenchman who married a Ponca woman, according J. O. Dorsey, contributed much to the names given to small streams, creeks, and small landmarks in the Ponca territory. Map 1 (forwarded to Headman from the National Museum of Natural History National Anthropological Archives by Charmain Baker during her study in research of the National Archives) shows the extent of his knowledge of what the Ponca people knew of their territory. Although maps 1 and 2 are readable by any Ponca-speaking person, the following names of the streams are written according to the current writing system of the Ponca language:

Xáđađè užį́ga	small going back, a smaller tributary entering the Missouri River
Umą́hą ánidąì	where there was a flood on the Omahas (This is not a creek, according to Alfred L. Riggs in correspondence to J. O. Dorsey.)
Xáđađè	going back, Bazille Creek flows into the Missouri River
Wasét'u p'eží	bad blue clay, a stream that flows into the Niobrara called the Verdigris
Šéhitą̀	the crab apple tree
Má'à' wídąđą̀	few cottonwood trees
Uhé átą	the bridge
P'izá ská	white sand (Another stream entering the Platte River was also referred to as *P'izá ská*.)
Á'žį̀gà hì tą̀	the hazel bush or tree
T'é núga t'ę́đaì	where Buffalo Bull was killed
T'íxį̀đè	a gorge or deep ravine, a water pocket
Míxe bđą̀ze	narrow grave (According to KH, a village near Ponca, Nebraska, also bears that name.)

Wačíška snedé	long creek
Į́e đihą́i	where they lifted the rock (A temporary village site where men lifted and threw a meteorite. Peter LeClair, who lived a short distance from this location, said the meteorite was said to be over four hundred pounds.)
Ní'bizè	thirsty, dry of water
Mąčú út'i	where a bear lives (On the north side of the stream as it enters the Niobrara was a hill called *P'ahé u'úde,* "hill with a hole in it.")
Šą́ge sį́de k'inąsnidè	where a horse stripped away the hair off its tail
T'aháwagđè į' ma wánąsaì	those who carried shields were stopped
Má'á' bahą́i	cottonwood tree hill
Ní' xué'	roaring water (probably referred to a small waterfall)
T'íši gasáit'a	where they cut tipi poles
Ní'xué' aké	the cataract
Mázi nádįget'à	where the cedars were burned
Zizíka wabáhi đą	where turkeys wander in flocks
Nídažì ní'sní gáxe	where *Nídažì* made a well
Šą́tągà mąšą́de	wolf den
K'ą́de hi uží	where plum trees are planted
Wasésą	White Clay
Xé'į ázi kè	a mountain
Ní'uđít'ę	where someone was killed or drowned in the water
Ní'uđít'ę	Ponca Creek
Mąđį́ka šnà	soil alone, a bluff? (*Mąđį́ka* refers to the soil or dirt. *Snà* refers to something that is flat or even.)
Wé'e' ái tè	where they dug the earth with a hoe

Communication was also made between J. O. Dorsey and a Mr. Alfred L. Riggs concerning the maps. Before March 16, 1882, Riggs wrote to Dorsey stating that he had interviewed Standing Bear about the names of the streams and creeks. Since this was the first time these men identified these small tributaries, it is reasonable that there was more than one source to determine the names. In his letter he wrote:

Santee Agency, Neb
Mar. 16, 1882
Rev. J. Owen Dorsey

Dear Friend,

I have at last seen Standing Bear and have gone over those names on the map with him. Or rather he gave me the names and I compared them with the map list. And here are his corrections

2 *Umáhą ánidą̀i* is at the main forks of the Bazil Creek and not either one of the branches.

4 & 5 as the map

A *Wau waxđi* (Winohica ton cicaktipi.)

B *Šaą́ p'a úwačí* (Dakota pa wacipi.)

No. 6—Same as map

Next—*Ą́žįga hí*—What the map has as No 9.

C *Hiyuwihci hi*—(*Ceca wanjidan*)

D *Mąá íđitį̀ Maya wankantuya wakpa*

7 & 8 Inter change = *P'izá skà* first then *Uhéátą*

E—*Né' t'ągà wačíška Mdetanka wakpa* (large water holes at the mouth.)

F—*P'anaho t'è te Hihankaga ta*

12 is *Wačíška Uxđúga*

13 & 14 The same as in map

15 is a Dry Run

16 Same as map

17—Same as map

18—Same name as 12 *Wačíška Uxđúga* or *uhđuga* [which is it?]

19 Does not know the name or stream

20 The main falls is near the mouth—Does not know the second falls. He speaks of it as mini hunin-bent = water Can the Ponca word mean that? *Ní' baxą́ đą̀*

23, 24—does not know

25, 26, 27, 28, 29 All right

G.—*P'ahé ú'úde* Split hole in the mountain is also a stream

30 Is not known to him What is the proper name for Ponka Creek—*Ní údi t'è*

32—Unknown

33—Right

34 (Which I put in): between Ponka Creek and Niobrara is *K'úhe waɗè-Okokipi*— So called from the thick wood about the crossing.

Mázitą and *P'ahé šnábe* are right.

On the list of Buffalo Chip that Standing Bear you see, has added a few names to the list—which either I failed to take or he did not give me with the map yesterday.

A.L.R.

In their effort to secure names for the streams and creeks, Buffalo Chip gave them yet another list titled "Tributaries of the Niobrara and other landmarks." I have copied the list as it was written. There are some Lakota words or names that I have left as is.

ON THE SOUTHERN SIDE

1. *Wasétu p'eǯì*	bad green clay, Verdigris
2. *Mázi nihága ugɗé*	pines or cedars set up in the (ground) by a spring
3. *Gahí k'ipáhi*	where they elected their chiefs (?)
4. *Mížįgà šánudà ík'inaì te*	where the dogs contended for the body of a girl
Máugde & Schitan & Wauwagdi & San pa waci	come in here wrong place
5. *Ą́žįgà hì t'ą̀ te*	where the hazel bushes abound
6. *P'izá užì te*	where it is filled with sand
7. *Šaą́ p'á áwačì te*	where they danced over the head of a Dakota
8. *Má'ạ̀ wí ɗą́ ɗą*	where cottonwood trees grow, one by one
Ą́žįgà hì	comes in here
9. *Hįwexčì uɗą́i te*	where *Hįwexčì* was arrested

Mąá iḋitì te	the bend in the river where it passes close to the foot of a cliff
10. *P'izá skà*	white sand
11. *T'ašnąge uží*	where ash trees are planted [*Pinkpinza wakpi, Mąḋixudè, Uhéatą̀ & Gubéhi & (Né' t'ągà = Neḋuḋasin)*]
12. *P'ánuhù tę́ te*	where *P'ánuhù* died
13. *T'enúga tę́ḋaì*	where *T'enúga* was killed
14. *Wačíška nąbá uxḋúxa te*	two creeks flowing through ravines
15. *P'á nązi̧ t'ę́ te* (or *Ban nžin te*)	long pine, *Wačíška snede*
16. *Wačí-waḋúpi te, Mą̀čú utì; Dak.-Kanta wakpadan*	many bears, animals, not a man
17. *Sį́de k'iną snide*	See *Ş̌́áge sį́de k'iną sníde*, on map (the same name)
18. *K'ą́de uží*	where plums are planted (on north side of Niobrara)
19. *Ní' xué*	cataract that makes the sound "X-x-x-!"
20. *Zizíka wabáhi te*	as on the map. Not a stream

ON THE NORTHERN SIDE

1. *Wa-ú-ga mąšą́de upé te*	
2. *Į́'e ík'itį̀ te*	
3. *P'ahé ú'úde te*	the hill that has a hole in it. Also not a stream.
4. *Mą́čú waḋį́hisà úti te*	where Savage Grizzly bear pitched his tent
5. *Mázi wábahà égą te*	the pine that serves as a landmark
6. *Mázità̧ uhą́ge te*	the end of that part of the Niobrara called "*Mazi tan*," where pines and cedars abound
7. *P'ahé waį́' egà̧*	the hill like a pack
8. *Wasésą ái te*	where they dug for white clay
9. *Į̧gḋą́ žą́ ḋixí aḋaì te*	
10. *Xéki áži te*, see *héin áži*	on map
11. *P'ahé šnábe užáta te*	see map

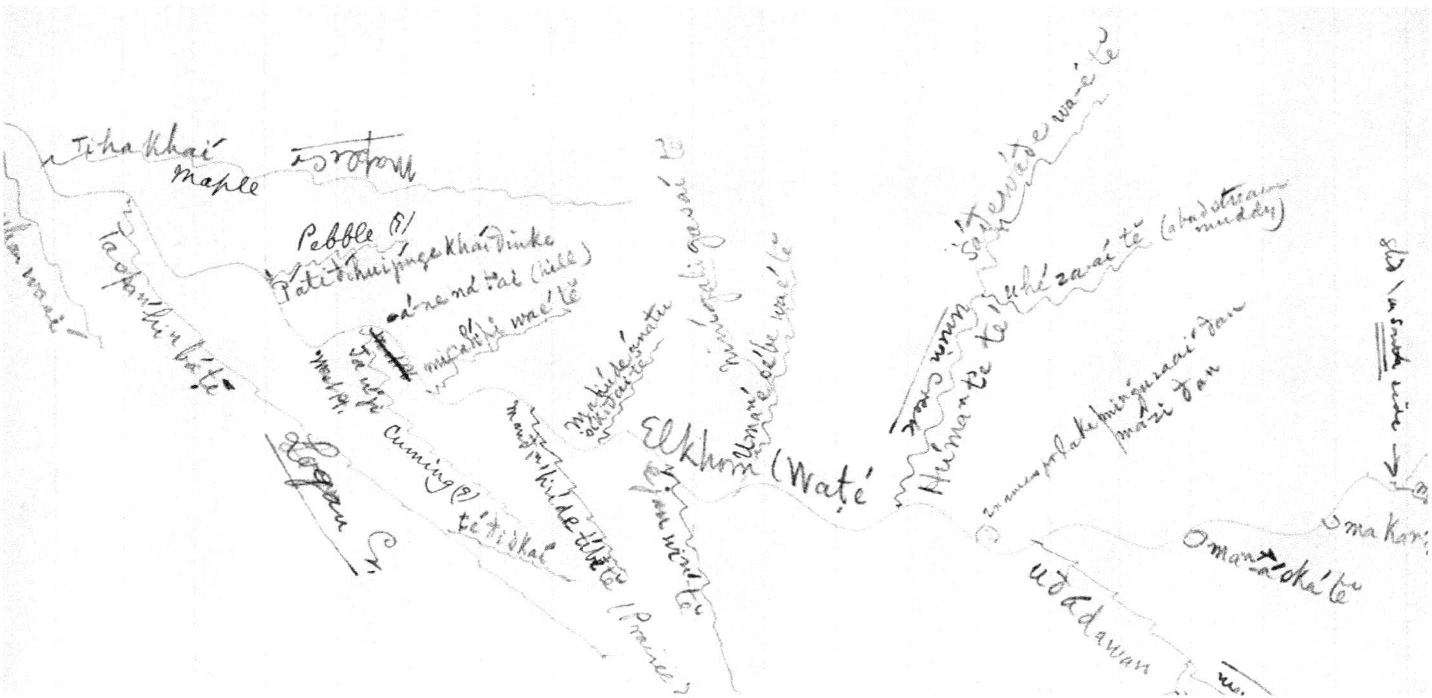

MAP 2. Tributaries to the Elkhorn River. National Museum of Natural History National Anthropological Archives, Siouan-Catawban series, James Owen Dorsey papers (NAA MS 4800).

Map 2 shows the names written in Ponca. As cartography was not as sophisticated as it is today, a rough drawing of a map shows the names of creeks and places of interest.

After reviewing several modern maps of the streams entering the Elkhorn, plus English notations made on the map, it appears that the map is upside down. Beginning at the east side of the map, the names of the streams are listed as shown on the archival material below:

NORTH SIDE OF THE ELKHORN

Hąmą́digdą̀ wáxdì te	where Hąmą́digdą̀ whipped (or killed) them
	Head of Bazille
Gdedą́	hawk
Hidédįgè te	where there are trees and water doesn't flow out
Mázi te	cedars
Mąk'ą́ ninída ái te	where they dug for Mąk'ą́ ninída
Mąá skà	white cliffs, a landmark
Udádawą̀	appears to be Udádadą̀, "to get accustomed to"
Má ugdè tè	
Míxa ázaì dą̀	a lake where ducks made loud squawking, a second name is Mázi dą̀
Hu'mą t'ę́ té	where Hu'mą died
Šadéwadè wa'é té	where Šadéwadè planted crops
Uhézaaì té	a bad muddy stream
Umą́'esébe wa'é té	where Umą́'esébe planted crops
Nínígahì gasái tè	where they cut tobacco
É'žą wí tè	one elm tree
Máxudè ą́natù ák'idą̀ì tè	where they disputed with the Iowas for a place (where they traditionally planted crops)
Mą́díxudè t'íbe tè	where prairie dogs live
Mikáxp'e wa'é tè	where Mikáxp'è planted crops

Ánenà taì	a hill
Žá úd̨àžì	bad brush and grass
P'atídihù ižíge x'aí d̨ikè	
T'asp'áhi bate	cluster of persimmons
T'é d̨iškaì	
T'íha x'aí	
Um̨áh̨a waái	where the Omaha had planted

In 1965 Dr. W. Raymond Wood, archeologist, cited the Ponca hunting camps and villages in his monograph called "Redbird Focus, the Problem of Ponca Prehistory." The interest here was to determine that some of the cultural material uncovered in the Redbird focus could be of Ponca origin. He writes:

Eleven camp sites on the Niobrara and Elkhorn rivers are identified as components of the focus (Redbird Focus). Five of them, on small tributaries some distance from the Niobrara, are forty to ninety miles west of the mouth of that river. Six of them, on the banks of the middle reaches of the Elkhorn, are about fifty miles south of the mouth of the Niobrara. Pottery, end scrapers, knives and other chipped stone tools, and other cultural detritus are rare to abundant at these sites, but none of them yield any hint of earth lodges. Perhaps they are temporary stations occupied while the people were on bison-hunting expeditions. The quantity of material at some of them suggests they were used over a long period of time, or on successive occasions. (Wood 1965, 114–15)

Since my interest here is identifying cites by name and tribal stories about lands the Ponca once inhabited, I, as a layman, can only read materials that suggest and substantiate a locale where the Ponca people once lived. Considering that archeology places the Ponca historically or prehistorically in that area and a map also suggests Ponca habitation, it is believed that it was part of their territory. Even in modern times the elders could recall, by name, places where families planted crops along some of the tributaries of the Elkhorn. There are many stories that can be cited of events that occurred there.

The story told here may have happened around a place called *Hidéd̨igè te*, "no bottom." The term suggests "where there are trees and water doesn't flow out." This is located near the Elkhorn River. KH told a story of a bison crazed from eating some grasses. He called the bison "*T'ę́núga dádį*." The following story was originally told in the Ponca language and is my translation:

This is a story of a man who slew a crazed bison. It was an animal that had a reputation of chasing travelers in a place called *Hidédįgè*. They say it even killed a man. You should remember that there are other places called *Hidédįgè*. It is a place where there are trees and where water has no outlet. Because of that crazed bison, people avoided going near that place. So no one traveled that area. Some hunters tried to kill it but were unsuccessful.

It was in the middle of summer when Little Bear told his family that he would go and kill the bison. His family knew he would try anything that is a challenge, so they never discouraged him to go. As our custom is, he took with him only those things he would need to do what he intended to do. They said he carried the bow and a quiver of arrows and his knife. But he also took soft buckskin with him. In those days they didn't ride horses. In his journey, he would have to stop and eat his parched corn and dried meat. Sometimes he would kill some small game. When he arrived at the general area of the place called *Hidédįgè*, he made camp. It must have been a drought season because the ground had great wide crevices on the ground. It was here that one man escaped being gored to death by that bison.

It was told the man lay in one of those big cracks in the ground that was just big enough for a man. The bison couldn't reach him because its head and horns were too wide to reach into that crevice. The bison was determined to get to the man but could only reach him with its tongue. They say it began to lick his back and with each stroke of its tongue, it would tear the man's skin. They say that man was a friend of Little Bear. It was then that he decided to kill the animal.

Where the trees grew in a group and thinned out, there was a pond. Water in the pond was only waist deep. You could see the tracks of animals that had come to drink because of the muddy edge of the pond. Little Bear took note of all the surroundings. The day after he got there, he looked for the bison. It wasn't long before he spotted the bison feeding in the distance. He didn't do anything at that time, but he watched it for two or three days to see when it came to drink. He also found out how deep the pond was. Then on the fourth day, he went out to lure the bison to him.

This is how he got the bison. He went toward the place where it had been feeding. From that distance, he began to wave that buckskin he brought with him. When he got its attention, it started to come in his direction. It did not charge at that time, but came at a slow canter. Little Bear also moved back toward the pond that was about a quarter of a mile away. The closer he came back to the pond the faster the bison came at him. Now at a full charge the bison bull was right behind him as he reached the pond. He jumped as far as he could into the pond with the bison behind him. The say that bison bull was very big and heavy. The pond being muddy at the water's edge, it sunk down into the deep mud and could hardly move. Little Bear got out of the pond and stood on the edge telling it to come get him. As the bison moved, struggling toward the edge, Little Bear came forward and threw the buckskin over its head hooking the skin on the bison's horns. It shook its head violently trying to free itself of the buckskin but could not. Little Bear, in the meantime, got behind the bison and cut the tendons just above and behind the hooves of its hind legs. Upon doing this, the bison had no power to stand and fell on its haunches. The bison bull could not move at all. He walked in front of the bison and said, "I said I would kill you, and now you will die for what you have been doing." With that he jumped on its back and reached to the lower side and plunged his knife into the animal. Little Bear's acts of bravery with his devil-may-care attitude are remembered by clansmen to this day.

In modern times we, as tribal members, are not knowledgeable of the many significant places where our ancestors visited or lived. We only have stories such as this one told by elders of the tribe when they lived in the North Country in ancient times.

Other stories mention battle sites where individual Ponca fought other tribesmen in man-to-man fights to the death. The map does not show the names of battle sites. But there are two particular places where individual Ponca warriors defended their villages. These incidents are sung about in the songs of the *Heđúška* organization. Although they sing about battles in many places, they sing about individual fights that took place only in these two places. One is called *Mǫá zì*, or "yellow cliffs." The other is called *P'aƌágè*, or "bluffs." The following song is based on a story of two young men who had hard feelings toward each other:

Ąnak'ina' škǫ'na?	Do you want to fight me?
Ąnak'ina' škǫ'na?	Do you want to fight me?
Sįde gƌéška mà, ƌikúde gą́	Spotted tail, come quickly
Žúwǫgƌè ígà	to engage in this confrontation
Ną́wip'a mǫ̀ži	I have no fear for this exchange
Mǫá zí' udánagè t'a šá de kè	You want to fight in the yellow cliffs
Sǫ́ǫ žįgà, t'aháwagƌè gƌízagà	Young Sioux, get your shield

In the latter days of his life, Logan DeLodge, a well-known singer of Ponca songs, shared a story of an Omaha Indian who taunted a Ponca man with contempt because of the affection his lady friend had for a Ponca warrior. As the story goes, the man came to the Ponca village. Sitting on his horse, he hollered, blew his whistle, and called the man's name asking him to come out to fight. The Ponca man would not go out to fight. After this happened several times, other Ponca men urged him to go and fight. When the man finally agreed to fight this man, he prepared to go in the traditional ways of the people. He called on the "Great Mystery" to give him guidance and to be victorious in this fight.

The day came when the man blew his whistle in his usual way and the Ponca warrior went to meet him for battle at the place called *P'aƌágè*. When he arrived at the place of battle, the Omaha man was not there. He returned to the village. Three times the man came, but each time the Omaha would not be at the place of battle. The Ponca warrior had figured out where the man had gone by following his tracks. The fourth time he came, he intercepted the Omaha on his secret passage and slew the man. Showing he was victorious in the man-to-man battle, he came back to the village carrying the head of the enemy on a pole. A song was made about this incident, but the Ponca warrior's name is not mentioned. The song is still sung today. As in most Ponca songs, the following words in the song only relate part of the whole story:

P'aƌáge ket'à, ugƌá'a t'i ƌǫbà	Someone is hollering from *P'aƌágè*

P'adáge ket'à, ugdá'a t'i dabà	Someone is hollering from *P'adágè*
Nisúde gdíhutè íya be	He blows his whistle, he speaks
P'adáge ket'à, ugdá'a t'i dabà	Someone is hollering from *P'adágè*
P'adáge ket'à, ugdá'a t'i dabà	Someone is hollering from *P'adágè*
Nisúde gdíhutè íya be	He blows his whistle, he speaks
P'adáge ket'à, ugdá'a t'i dabà	Someone is hollering from *P'adágè*

The elders who confirmed this story said the incident occurred when part of the tribe was living somewhere along the Elkhorn. The elders of the Southern Ponca said the area of the Elkhorn was called *Wát'è*. The word is an old term meaning "plenty." They said the area had a lot of wildlife, edible plants, a lot of wild fruits, and so forth. (The modern term *Wášè*, which means "plenty" and relates to foodstuff, seems to have derived from the ancient term *Wát'è*.) In their memories, they spoke in terms of how much wildlife and plants existed in that part of their territory. The economic conditions in their lifestyle or culture were of primary importance. It is no wonder then, they marked that land with names and names of incidents that occurred.

3

Trade Agreements, Indian Treaties, and Indian Removal

The Ponca who were satisfied with their land and homes were to see many whites come across their territory. A petition requesting exclusive trade with the Ponca was made by Juan Munier to Governor Carondelet on September 16, 1793 (Jablow 1974). This was the first official contact with white traders. This contact was followed by other companies that also made trade agreements with the Ponca on the Missouri, Niobrara, Elkhorn, and Platte Rivers and in other areas. This was the beginning of exploration by Europeans into the interior territory of the Ponca people and also the start of taking virgin lands through their shrewd entrepreneurship and government backing.

Treaty agreements with the Ponca apparently existed before 1817, but a treaty of peace and friendship was made in this year with the United States. The treaty agreement was made to equally forgive both parties for "every injury or act of hostility that may have been committed." "Perpetual" peace and friendship would exist between them. The Ponca would acknowledge themselves to be under the protection of the United States. Unfortunately, the United States and private businessmen did not take into consideration Indian laws. Violation of the unwritten laws sometimes placed the white people in jeopardy with the tribe. For instance, the white people would "squat" on Indian lands. Boundaries were respected by other tribes as indicated previously. The Ponca sometimes encountered people squatting in their territory. If such circumstances were reported to federal officials, the government was slow to respond. The process of "settling" the country using this tactic of squatting was apparently sanctioned by the government because nothing was done to prevent further occurrences.

On the other hand, if the Ponca violated their end of the treaty agreement, they were quickly made to comply with the agreement. They, on one occasion, were said to have committed "deprivations" on "private citizens of the United States" and were made to pay back losses suffered by the white citizen. When the trafficking of whites became serious and squatting became uncontrolled, the government sought a new treaty agreement. The treaty of 1825 made no mention of land assignments to the federal government but dealt primarily with possible crimes and means of punishment for offenders. Subsequent treaties were quite lengthy and entailed the ceding of lands to the government. In the treaty of 1858, for example, they ceded all their claims to land in Nebraska. This repeated process resulted in their removal to Indian Territory. A precursor made by federal officials is found in "The Annual Report of the Commissioner of Indian Affairs" (1855). He reported that it is "understood that the Ponca are anxious to make some treaty arrangements" regarding the ceding of their lands to the government. The Ponca, who had survived drought, famine, warfare, and the demise of fellow tribesmen from time immemorial, were now ready to move away?

In 1868 a treaty agreement with several bands of Sioux was made by the government, which absorbed the Ponca Reservation or lands they (the government) had centralized around Niobrara. The treaty agreement with the Sioux was done without consultation with the Ponca. The war status the Ponca had with the Sioux began to be renewed. Now the federal government was backing them to raid the Ponca at will. Being longtime enemies of the Ponca, the Sioux always respected the tribal boundaries. The larger Ponca Tribe, which in past times could withstand any attack from any direction, was now reduced to a small number of people by government trade blankets infested with smallpox (Dí'xe). The years of sickness and death decimated the Ponca to a very small group of people. It was at this time that the Ponca repeatedly asked the government to protect them from their enemies, as provided by the 1858 treaty. The guarantee of protection was never given to them. Historians called the ceding of Ponca land to the Sioux a "federal blunder." The twisted historical accounting of the Ponca is a classic example of what lengths the Europeans would go to, to acquire the land.

The Indian Removal Act was enacted when Congress decided that it was time to quit lollygagging and get those Indians somewhere. (This act affected many tribes.) To understand the relationship that various tribes have with the U.S. government, one must begin with the initial entry of the white Europeans into this country. The first treaties ever made were made not only with the British, but also with the Dutch, French, and Spanish (RDH). Reasons for treaties varied from tribe to tribe but essentially ranged from keeping peace and preventing war to gaining tribes as allies. These early treaties considered Indian tribes as nations within themselves. When the United States became the controlling government of this country, the Indian tribes remade numerous treaties with them.

Following the treaty period, the government created a system that placed Indian tribes in a certain geographic area in the country. Of the five types of reservations, the Ponca were affected by two. The first was called a *treaty reservation*. This was done when they ceded their lands to the government in 1825, 1858, and 1865. The remaining lands, by federal input, created a *treaty reservation* in the amount of approximately 125,000 acres of land. The second (present reservation) was an *executive order reservation* that placed the Ponca in Indian Territory (RDH). This was done by government appropriation of $30,000, and an order from the chief executive to remove the Ponca from Nebraska. The first intention of the government was to remove them to the Kaw River in Kansas. Then a subsequent bill that appropriated more money to move them to Indian Territory was passed. In the fall of 1876, the tribe received information from a missionary that the government agents were planning to move them to some other place. Following a tribal council meeting during which there was great concern about the possibility of being removed from their homes, an Indian agent came to the Ponca. The agent stated that somebody in Washington said they had to be moved to Indian Territory. He told them the land was much better and they didn't have to work as hard. The Ponca had been good farmers in addition to being bison hunters. The response from the tribal council said the tribe did not want to go, that they wanted to stay there in their homelands because they had known this land for ages and that they wished to live and die there. Additionally, they rejected the agent's offer (bribe) to give them a piece of land of equal value and money in Indian Territory. The council repeated again that they did not want to sell their lands because they had already acquired implements through trade and were making a good living there (KH, NC, AMC). The Indian agent continued to bargain and asked them to just go down there to see the land. If they didn't like it, they could come back to live forever. The agent speaking convincingly caused about eight chiefs to go to Indian Territory with him and his men to inspect the land. After seeing the land, the chiefs said they didn't like the land and wished to return to their homes around Niobrara. When they made this decision, remembering the agent's promise to take them back to "live forever," the Indian agent began to tell them they could not return. He said that they would have to stay and select their land because they would not be allowed to go back. He further told them if they didn't stay as they (the agents) had planned, they would be left to starve to death because he would not give them any provisions. KH said:

> Edí wádį atí tedądì, wanáše áma, égidąitè: "Đewadì danáži škánaži tedí, gá' déwadì đat'é t'amašè', ewégaìte."

> When they brought them here, the soldiers told them: "If you do not stay here," they said to them, "you will die here."

The elders stated that the Indian agents had been planning to bring the chiefs to Indian Territory and keep them there and then go back to Niobrara and convince the tribe that the chiefs were satisfied with the new land and were waiting for the tribe to join them there. Unfortunately, that was not the case. The chiefs were left there to die. The chiefs set out on foot, without provisions, back to their homes along the Niobrara and Missouri Rivers. Over five hundred miles they walked in sub-zero weather. As they passed through what is now Kansas and Nebraska, they ate dried-out corn from some farmer's field. They spoke of their hunger, the cold, and the sickness when they reached the Otoe Reservation in southern Nebraska. Their feet were bleeding because they had worn out their footwear. They reported that when the Otoe had seen them in their condition, they showed compassion to them and gave them provisions and horses. A few days later the chiefs arrived at the Omaha Reservation, where they rested. Eight of the chiefs returned to their homes. At this time Chief Standing Bear (Mąčú Nążį), one of the chiefs, made his first complaint to the president from Sioux City. From there he telegraphed a letter to the president through an English-speaking Omaha Indian. The message essentially told the president of the chiefs' ordeal in Indian Territory and about the Indian agents abandoning them there. This was the beginning of other contacts that would be made to the president or other government officials. These events were only a prelude to moving the entire tribe to Indian Territory.

On April 12, 1877, an order was issued to remove the Ponca to Indian Territory. Accounts of the removal relate to how notification was given to the tribe, when there was none given; how well the government agents treated them, when they did not; and how the agents placated the Ponca to move, when no dialogue about the move was ever had. It seems historical accounts also avoided remarks that would be offensive to readers and researchers. In 1981 one elder of the tribe made a statement to a group of young boys as to what they thought about the trip when the Ponca were brought to Oklahoma. "Do you think the children were just sitting in the back of a wagon eating oranges and apples as they rode down here?" Some of the boys thought that could be possible. The elder using "bad white man words" said, "#@!+ no! They walked every damned step of the way . . . hungry and sick." The elder had heard the dreadful story of the removal many times over from his parents, relatives, and other tribal members who made the trip. Not to mention those other unspeakable experiences they suffered during the removal that were never reported. The degrading of the people was such that those offenders should have been executed. The white people would have been prosecuted by their own laws had their offenses been committed on their own people. In the effort to hide these kinds of incidents, some historians spoke of it in lighter tones. In the process of bringing truth and giving credence to some history and the field of anthropology, some came closer in describing the forced removal and showed a more realistic picture. In one aspect of his description of the removal, James Howard (1995, 33) wrote,

> On April 28, 1877, Howard [E. A. Howard of Hillsdale, Michigan, who was appointed agent for the removal] arrived at Columbus, Nebr., where he expected to meet Agent Lawrence with the assembled tribesmen. He found Lawrence with only 170 Ponca, the remainder having resisted removal, stating that they would rather die in defense of their homes than abandon their country and live in the "hot country" to the south.

There were many who wanted to remain but were forced to leave their homes and belongings. The elders said there were many accounts of families who tried to go back to their homes on that infamous day. Remembrance of harsh treatments and even murder were part of the epilogue to leaving Niobrara. Those Ponca who told the truth of the forced removal by gunpoint were never recorded. Among the first to be removed was the family of Virginia Big Soldier Headman, who gave the following account:

> One morning the soldiers came and pointed their guns at us and told us to get out of our houses and leave. We were not allowed time to gather our clothes or any personal belongings. Without food or anything but the clothes we had on, we were forced out of our homes. The men were not allowed to get their horses. They herded us toward the river like animals. . . . The next thing that is vivid in my mind is the Ponca standing on the banks of the Niobrara River — weeping. We didn't weep for fear or defeat but of regret and sorrow for the disrespect shown to the tribe. They wept for the acts of dishonoring them who many times defended their lands; for showing disrespect for them who showed compassion to hungry whites crossing their lands in search of a place to live; for the disrespect shown to them who shared the use of the waterway for business purposes, especially furs and other goods; and, for those who created distrust and who conspired for self-advancement and gain. That is why we wept. The other thing I remember is the long walk, the hot temperature, the rain and people dying . . . many people. I remember the soldiers offering us some sort of herb to eat. We refuse to eat it because we were certain that they were trying to kill us.

What an amazingly different picture to that of E. C. Kemble, U.S. inspector, who reported how he had allowed the Ponca to load as many of their personal belongings as possible on their wagons and horses. Records indicate that on April 30, 1877, Kemble asked agent Howard to inform the Ponca to move. Those who had not yet been notified of the move were still in their respective villages. They were to be moved without force (as ordered by Washington), yet there were twenty-five armed U.S. troops under Major Walker accompanying Howard. The United States instigated one of the most atrocious and unjust acts committed on a tribe of Indians. This group of tribesmen departed May 16, 1877.

The story of *T'esą́wį̀* (White Buffalo Girl), one of the first children to die on the trip to Indian Territory, was told (KH, NC). Barely thirty miles from the Niobrara, the little girl died. She was the daughter of *Hexágà Sabè* (Black Elk) and *Mí Gdedą́wį̀* (Moon Hawk). At the burial of the child, her father asked the townspeople of what is now Neligh, Nebraska, to take care of her grave. He said, "I ask this of you because I may never come this way again." The people of Neligh agreed to do this and to this day have brought flowers to that little grave site. There were some white people along the way, I'm sure, who had compassion for these Native Americans. Recently, when traveling through Nebraska, I went to the town of Neligh, where I met a gentleman who seemed to have great understanding of the Ponca removal. He indicated that historical records tell that White Buffalo Girl had originally been buried a mile or so north of the township. He said some of the townsmen felt it proper to have her buried in their cemetery. As a result, the remains were moved to the current location. His interest and concern for the care of the grave site of White Buffalo Girl has gone beyond the maintenance and care of the grave. In 1997 there was a growing interest in the surrounding communities, including Neligh, to erect a statue to commemorate this touching episode of the death of a little Ponca girl. A theatrical play was also written about the incident.

On a lighter side, some Ponca hid out among some white settlers who aided them. They were protected for a brief period and are accounted for as those who did not make the trip to Indian Territory. There is a story of one young woman who fell in love with a white farmer who loved her so dearly that he took and hid her with his parents. They eventually married and had several children. The Ponca remember her to be an "uppity" woman. There were many who did not make the trip to Indian Territory and successfully remained in the area. Others took refuge among the Sioux.

Now, after their forced removal to Indian Territory, they came to a strange land that they had never seen before. It was after a period of extreme hardship. The death of over 157 tribal members was still fresh in their memories. The mourning and grief that enveloped the people seemed as though it would never go away. Their original condition of perplexity seemed to have forced them to accept their dilemma. But something familiar and recognizable came back to their memories: the earth. As it is perceived by most Native Americans, the elders said the earth was truly God-given and was to be respected. The moon, sun, stars, and all the elements of the heavens portrayed to them the existence of *Wak'ą́da*, the "Great Mystery."

Now here was their new home. Here they would live. Here they would raise their children. Here they would hunt and build their lodges. The plains topography was familiar. The rolling hills and places of small rocky bluffs were reminiscent of their former places of residence. The blushing colors of *T'ą́gaxdą̀* along streams and rivers brought fond memories to these inhabitants in a new land. The wind-swept plains of the new territory too did not go by unnoticed. The familiarity of fresh smells of the coming seasons, the still unsettled lands showing promise of game, the rich untouched soil all spelled peace and contentment.

As in former times, the men of the tribe explored the entirety of the area they would now call home. The limited space of land in Kay and Noble Counties set aside for them became immediately known to them. The *Ní'skà*, or "Arkansas River," was familiar to them, since they have followed its flow into the south in ancient times. They saw for the first time the river *Ni'ží'dè*, or "Salt Fork River," a tributary to the Arkansas River. They saw the Chikaskia River, a tributary to the Salt Fork River. The Chikaskia is a mispronunciation of the word *Žegá'skà*, which means "white buttocks and thighs." The Bois D'Arc Creek is called *Níp'à*, "bitter water." It was a new beginning for the tribe.

4

Chief Standing Bear

The trial of Chief Standing Bear started with the removal conditions described in the previous chapter and with the death of his son. It was after the move to Kay and Noble Counties that Chief Standing Bear's leadership role became clear. According to KH, men who spoke out for the tribe centered on a man by the name of *Ubískà*. It seems that this man had some influence among the tribesmen and encouraged them to remain strong throughout this ordeal. There is no trace of his family affiliation, but his name was spoken of by the elders as one who led in keeping the people together. Some of the tribesmen, although beaten, hungry, sick, and weak, still had the intent of fighting and returning to the North Country. The Ponca Tribal Council had been discontinued and was not recognized by the federal government.[1] This was done to disable the tribe. It became necessary at that time for men to "rise up" and speak for and to the tribe. With due respect to Chief White Eagle, the tribe was without leadership because he was left without proper powers to govern his people. Regrettably, but truly, the tribe had no leader to govern the people. AMC, KH, AL, NC, and JP said, without his recognized tribal position, White Eagle was unable to speak to his people. At this time men had to rise to the occasion and lead. It should be understood that White Eagle eventually regained his status as a recognized highly esteemed chief of the Ponca once they were settled in Indian Territory.

Standing Bear's return to Dakota Territory has been recorded and documented. Consequently, the account of this historical event is provided here as known by our tribal elders. When Chief Standing Bear's son died, he proceeded to make plans to return to Niobrara. He did not notify anyone, that is, the other Ponca leaders, of his intentions to take leave. It was after he had gathered provisions to take the trip with his friends and relatives that word got out of him taking his son to be buried at the Niobrara. Some of the elders of the tribe objected to his actions saying that he would be brought back or even killed by the soldiers. He told them that his intention was not to stay at the Niobrara but simply to bury his son. But some believed that he, like many of them, wanted to go back. KH said, "It seems like everybody wanted to go back up north." They thought perhaps if he could go back and convince the government that their northern homeland was more suitable for them, they too could return. It is obvious that Standing Bear did not plan to go to the Omaha Reservation, get arrested, go to court, and sue the government. He had no knowledge of the U.S. justice system, much less what a writ of habeas corpus was. However, he did have a previous experience with the judicial system. In the month of March 1879, with the government officials unaware of his leave, he and his wife and twenty-nine other Ponca set out for their old homeland. Standing Bear chose those families that were close to him to accompany him and his family back to the Niobrara. Additionally, an interesting selection of tribesmen were in the group. KH pointed out those men to be members of different clans. These names are also recorded in the court proceedings of Standing Bear. Each clan was represented by at least one adult male member. They were as follows:

Mąčú Nąžį́	Standing Bear of the *Wažáže* clan
T'éžé Bat'é	Buffalo Chip of the *Wašábe* clan
Mąčú Dádi	Crazy Bear of the *Níkap'ašną̀* clan
Šáge Hįzí	Yellow Haired Horse of the *Wažáže* clan
Nagé Áxa	Cries for War of the *Hísadà* clan
Wádixè K'áˀì	Long Runner of the *Néˀt'à* clan
Míxa Žįgà	Little Duck of the *Đíxidą̀* clan
T'é Sigđè	Buffalo Track of the *Núxe* clan

Was this "clan thing" a coincidence, or did Standing Bear, Buffalo Chip, and others plan to stay in the north or where they might be led? There is nothing said about it in our history. Among those returning to the north was a man by the name of *Wačígaxè Žįgà*, or "Little Dance" of the *Mąk'ą́* clan, who was not mentioned. When word reached the federal officials, they were ordered to intercept Standing Bear and his small band and, if at all possible, detain him at the nearest fort. Before the Ponca went on to the Niobrara, they stopped at the Omaha Reservation, where they stayed with friends who tried to convince them to stay there. The Omaha Indians were fearful that the government might move them to Indian Territory and were apprehensive of the Ponca's visit. The so-called Omaha Citizens Committee was more sympathetic than the traditionalist. The citizens band of the Omaha wished to abandon their tribal customs and live like the white man while the traditionalist favored the old ways of hunting and horticulture (KH, NC, AMC). The Ponca, before their removal, had set a pace in farming at the Niobrara and were known for their farming skills in better days. These skills were substantiated during Standing Bear's trial (Tibbles 1972, 74) after his incarceration. It was no surprise that those who favored the modern technique would be supportive of Standing Bear. The necessary and logical direction to take was to adhere to a set of standards prescribed by the federal government. Hence, the citizens band satisfied the federal mandate. As stated above, the ordeal of the Ponca removal records one of the most vicious atrocities committed upon a people. The government's use of its powers and sanctions through its several offices and officers was out of control. Washington had to contend with lower government agents appointed to negotiate and establish a just relationship with Indian tribes. Government treaties were broken by crooked "Indian agents" who sought personal gain by taking advantage of opportunities to capitalize on tribal lands (RDH).

Chief Standing Bear had some knowledge of treaty agreements. As previously stated, Indian tribes had a mutual understanding of boundaries. With this knowledge, Chief Standing Bear protested the action taken by the government. He knew (as did many others) that it was against government policy to remove a tribe without its consent. He was aware that the Ponca council never signed or knowingly placed their thumbprint on papers giving up their lands.

Xįháskà ma, ebé ukíabažì. Įdádą gáxaìke, ebé štiwą úwagidabažì. Níkagahì ma . . . íš'áge ákaštì. . . wabáxu wébahà bažì aí'. Nąbá ábit'a bažì. (VBSH)

The white people did not speak to anyone. What they did, they never told anyone here about it. The chiefs . . . including my husband [who was also clan chief] . . . they never showed any [legal] papers to them, he said. They never put their thumbprint on it [the papers]. (VBSH)

With this knowledge, Chief Standing Bear was prepared to argue his cause should he be arrested. On the Omaha Reservation, the Ponca began to work alongside their hosts. They had just begun to sow wheat on plots given to them by the Omaha when they were arrested and brought to Fort Omaha by Brigadier General George Crook, commander of the Department of the Platte. Reasoning for the arrest was based on the assumption that "Indians were not persons" and did not have the same civil liberties and freedom as members of the dominant white society. Indian status was like "wards" of the government, and as such, they were not permitted to travel at will (RDH). Under this premise, General Crook was ordered to arrest Chief Standing Bear and his fellow tribesmen.

The thirty people arrested included relatives of many Ponca living today. This dreadful experience remains clear, even in the minds of modern-day Ponca. The tribal elders, namely, KH, AMC, and NC, said the Ponca were taken into a stockade, much more like a corral. Their first consensus was that they would probably be returned to Indian Territory. The federal officials had already concluded that the logical procedure was simply to take them there. But as circumstances and unforeseen conditions often interrupt what would be the most normal thing to do, something happened. The Ponca had been detained in the stockade for some time when the townspeople heard of it. Out of curiosity or pity, they came to see these Indians held in the corral. KH said,

> They said there was some preacher who come to see them. I guess he tried to talk to them but didn't say too much. He went back to his people and told them about what he saw. He didn't like what he saw, so he wrote letters to many people he thought would help out.

It was essentially the clergy who had first seen the conditions in which the Ponca were being held. They protested. The clergy of various Christian denominations voiced their objections to this detestable treatment of the Ponca. Among those who had seen the Ponca was Thomas H. Tibbles. He, being a newspaperman (who later was labeled as a fighter for Indian causes), wanted to know why these people were being kept under guard. He noted that they were without food, proper clothing, and other necessities. The people coming around to see them alerted the Ponca that there might be a chance of being released. Anticipating what would transpire or what this would develop into was impossible. KH said Standing Bear used a Ponca-speaking white man by the name of Hamilton to speak to Tibbles. When he was asked why they were locked up and under guard, Standing Bear said that he did not know. But he stated that before the white man came, in past times, if he wanted to go hunting or visiting he could go where he wished to go. He said,

> If I wished to go where the sun sets, I can go; if I wished to go in the direction where the sun rises, I can; if I wish to travel where it is hot, I am free to do that; and if I want to go where it is cold, I go.

KH said, "These words, as far as I know, were never recorded." He said the chief was saying, "I had my own freedom to travel before the white man came here." It was evident that Tibbles had a good story to tell, but more than that, he also would take this idea of an "uncivilized" Indian and make it a social issue. Because, in Chief Standing Bear, he saw a person being judged and labeled as something less than human, but he knew through the interview that this was a very intelligent individual he was dealing with. Tibbles's interview with *T'ĕžĕ Bat'è* (Buffalo Chip) also centered on why they were being held prisoner. If they had committed a crime, what was the crime? KH, NC, and AMC said the Ponca would ask questions like, Why can't we live like white people? Why can't we travel anywhere we wish like the white people? Do the same laws apply to everybody? Are white people imprisoned for traveling? As an assistant editor of the *Omaha Daily Herald*, Tibbles had the tool to spread the word about the Ponca. Up to now, no Indian tribe or person had the right to sue or protest under the U.S. court system. Enlisting the aid of John L. Webster and A. J. Poppleton, attorneys at law, Tibbles was able to convince them to draw up a petition for Standing Bear to appear in court. Normally, a writ of habeas corpus could be acquired only by people who were white citizens. However, Webster and Poppleton filed for the writ in the U.S. Circuit Court for the District of Nebraska. It said something like, The Ponca, namely, those mentioned above, were illegally kept as prisoners, were deprived of their natural liberty, and had not committed any crimes (RDH). Simultaneously, the aforesaid clergy drew up petitions objecting to the treatment of the Ponca. These were also mailed to the president of the United States (Tibbles 1972).

The case involved many people, including private citizens, soldiers, the commissioner of Indian Affairs, and the secretary of the interior, in addition to legal procedures involving letters (telegraphed and written), testimonials, and court arguments. The prime issue was whether an Indian was a person or not. According to RDH, Indians (Native Americans) were considered to be animals and had limited or no rights at all. Some questions directed toward Chief Standing Bear by the government's representative centered on whether he was a "chief" of the Ponca Tribe. These questions were asked to prove that he was not "like other citizens" and still retained the traditional lifestyle of the Indian people. On one hand, if he admitted to being a chief of the tribe, he would be representing a different political entity and would be opposed to the U.S. government. If he said he was not a chief, he would be lying as the Indian people still regarded him as a Ponca chief. His arguments centered around the idea that he simply wanted to live as he always lived. He farmed land, hunted on occasion, and protected his territory since there was no law (as we know it today). The Ponca, according to Howard (1995), were not only horticulturists but were also advanced in agriculture.

> The climate of this Ponca "heartland" is of the general continental type. Summers are long and warm, and well suited to the raising of crops. The spring is usually cool, with considerable rainy weather, and the autumns are long and pleasant, with only occasionally rainy spells. Indeed, the Ponca preferred the fall of the year to both spring and summer. The mean rainfall is 24.1 inches. About 77 percent of this occurs during the principal part of the growing season, from April to September, a very fortunate circumstance for the agricultural Ponca.

I was raised on foodstuff produced by my father in Kay County on the Ponca Reservation. Seeds were taken from the best growth and kept for planting the next year. It was not unusual for Ponca families to keep seeds each year to plant large vegetable gardens. It was unheard of that families never planted. In a pretrial interview, T'éžé Bat'è (Tibbles 1972, 21), one of Standing Bear's followers, made the following statement:

Eight days ago I was at work on my farm which the Omahas gave me. I had sowed some spring wheat, and wished to sow some more. I was living peaceably with all men. I have never committed any crime. I was arrested and brought back as a prisoner. Does your law do that?

In response to questions put to him by Mr. Lambertson, U.S. district attorney, Chief Standing Bear made the following statement (Tibbles 1972, 81) concerning his way of life and his intention when they had come to Indian Territory:

I saw the land, and land was not good to my eye; some places it looked good, but you kick up the soil a little, and you found lots of stones. It was not fit to farm. When we got down there we heard we were going to get clothing, and get money, and everything that we wanted, but I have not seen it yet. When I was told to go down there, I thought, perhaps, the land was good, and I could make a living, but when I got down there it was entirely different from the land in my own home. I couldn't plow, I couldn't sow any wheat, and we all got sick, and couldn't do anything.

On May 1, 1879, the trial began, and it lasted two days. Because the bison had been killed off and deer and other large animals were becoming scarce, the Indian people had to accustom their lifestyle to that of the white man, that is, by using modern implements originally acquired by trade. The Ponca, however, were already accustomed to doing horticulture and some agriculture. The Omaha Citizens Committee could have supported Standing Bear in his court case, although it was never considered or mentioned. The elders claimed Standing Bear used every possible means to show the prosecuting attorney and the judge that he would live like a white man once he was released from his imprisonment. It seemed that the court wanted to hear that he and his people had abandoned their former lifestyle and now were taking up the white man's way of life. It was assumed that this was the "civilized" way of living. In the course of the trial, Chief Standing Bear (Tibbles 1972, 80) was questioned as to what the Ponca were doing to become like white men. He said:

The white men are great workers, some of them are and some are not . . . it is about the same with Indians . . . some want to work, and some don't . . . I want to work, and become like a white man, and I have tried my best.

The point made here is not to say that he fabricated a story to get the favor of the court, but he made these kinds of statements more than once to agree that "Yes, I do work for my living, and always have." Besides, this is what the court wanted to hear. The issue for the government, through Lambertson, was to prove that Chief Standing Bear had not abandoned his Indian ways and was still, indeed, a chief of the tribe. Inasmuch as that he could have claimed a nonchief status with the court, he was still regarded as a chief by the Ponca to the day he died (KH, NC, AMC).

During an earlier interview, he had answered a question about his religious beliefs. The Ponca people from time immemorial have always worshipped one God. The belief in a monotheistic God among the Ponca is as old as the legends that relate to their relationship with the one supreme God. Peter LeClair once made a statement that religious practices of the Ponca included a "commandment" that they should have one God. Their belief in the spirit of God is also embedded in their religion. It is questionable whether Chief Standing Bear had abandoned all his tribal beliefs in pursuit of the Christian faith. The Ponca came to the knowledge of the Son of God in the early 1800s. The following statement of his religious beliefs was made by Chief Standing Bear. It is apparent by his own words that he embraced the principles of the Christian faith, which were similar to tribal codes and ethics. These words were not difficult for him to make because of his aforesaid religious background:

There is one God, and He made both Indians and white men. We were all made out of the dust of the earth. I once thought differently. I believed there were happy hunting grounds, where there were plenty of game, and plenty to eat, no sickness, no death, and no pain. The best of the Indians would go to these happy hunting grounds. I thought that those who were bad would never live anymore; that when they died that was the end of them. But I have learned that these things are not so, and that God wishes us to love Him and obey His commandments, follow the narrow road, work for Him on earth, and we shall have happiness after we die. I am told His Son died for us, died that we might live. I want to try to do something for Him, to be like Him, follow in His footsteps as nearly as I can. I think there is but one God. I need help to do right, and I pray to Him that he will help me for His Son's sake. I do not wish to do anything wrong. I wish to follow the narrow road of happiness. God never does anything wrong. He knows what is best for me. No man can understand God, or know why He deals with us as He does. Sometimes what we think is the worst is the best for us. When I was arrested by the soldiers and brought down here, I thought for a little while that God had forsaken me, but now I see that, perhaps, it is the best thing for me and my people. If they would only hearken to His word, they would find that all is for their good. He sees me all the time. He watches over me, and knows all I do. He knows my thoughts. He knows when I think wicked thoughts. He knows it all. If He did not watch over me, and take care of me, I should die. I want Him to watch over me and take care of me, and I believe He always will. He helps me. I can do nothing without His help. I love His truth. I hate lies. I wish to follow the truth always. God has control of the whole earth and everything is in His power. He sees over all things at once, every man, woman and child, and knows their thoughts and actions, and everything they do. He watches over me wherever I go. He sees me here today. He has been with me through all my wanderings, and has taken care of me. He has seen how I have been taken away from my land. Through all this He has been close to me. When I have felt that I had no friends, I remembered that He was my Father. His people have been good to me, but the people of the devil are trying to send me to Hell. They have tried to make me believe that God tells them what to do, as though God would put a man where he would be destroyed, and they have destroyed many already, but they cannot deceive me. God put me here, and intends for me to live on the land they are trying to cheat me out of. I pray to God every day for Him to help me to regain my rights, if I am worthy of it. For His Son's sake I have asked it. He made the whites, and me and although we are of a different color, I think men's hearts are all alike. If I were to go back to my land today, the first thing I would do would be to fall down on my knees and thank God for it. I think in the future, as I grow in years, I will try to love Him more and more every day, do that which is right and be afraid to do that which is wrong (Tibbles 1972, 62–63).

Arguments for and against the major issue between Webster, Lambertson, and Poppleton lasted approximately fifteen hours (Tibbles 1972, 92). Following the attorney's conclusions, the court allowed Standing Bear to speak. The famous words that standout prominently to this day are quoted below and are known by most Ponca speakers today:

Nąbé agút'aì tè, xįhá tè, ʃáwakígąbažì, đažą̀ ak'ížahètedì aniet'amikè. Đíʃtì đakížahètedì đaniet'anikè. Wamí xt'atè úgaxètè ʃáwakígąt'aitè. Niášigàbđí há. Wakądà enąwiteną̀ wądą wáxaì há'.

My hand is not the color of yours, but if I pierce it, I shall feel pain. If you pierce your hand, you also feel pain. The blood that will flow from mine will be of the same color as yours. I am a man. The same God made us both.

Judge Elmer S. Dundy, U.S. district judge for Nebraska, filed his opinion on May 12, 1879, concluding that an Indian was a person within the meaning of the law under the Constitution of the United States. A discussion on English and American writ of habeas corpus law also had its impact on the case. The English law apparently stated that the law applied only to those who wrote the law and who were non-Indian. Judge Dundy stated that if this was the case, it was at a disadvantage when compared with our own. In review of the habeas corpus statutes, he said that a "party" or "any person" who applied for the writ included all mankind. And in regard to people such as Chief Standing Bear, he stated, "I must hold, then, that Indians are 'persons.'" Following the decision handed down by Judge Dundy; Chief Standing Bear thanked those people who had aided him. This had a far-reaching effect on the white community.

The Nebraska State Historical Society Museum has in its collection a headdress currently on display. It was evidently considered an object of high honor by the Ponca people. This hairpiece or wig was worn only at important council meetings by the tribal leader. This ornament was given to Poppleton by Chief Standing Bear as a token of his appreciation. Caroline L. Poppleton, widow of Andrew J. Poppleton, loaned the headdress to the museum on January 26, 1915. In the accession records on the headdress to the museum, an accompanying statement said in part of Chief Standing Bear:

Out of the poverty of his worldly possessions, he gave such visible token of his appreciation as he could, while out of the wealth of his human soul, and out of the fullness of his manly heart, he uttered sentiments, and expressed purposes which distinguish him as chief among ten thousand. . . . The keepsake given by the Chief to the great attorney, is a rare gift, being esteemed the most sacred, as it is the most venerable object in the possession of the tribe. It resembles a wig and was worn by the head chief at their most weighty councils.

Chief Standing Bear and his people were ultimately allotted lands back on the old homelands along the Niobrara River. However, there was much to say about the status of the land. It appears that an agreement was made between Chief Standing Bear and the Sioux, namely, the Oglala. They were able to reclaim part of the land. On the legal side, there are reports that relate to Webster and Poppleton aiding Chief Standing Bear to sue the Sioux, stating that the Ponca had more right to occupy those lands than the defendants. They had named Red Cloud as the head of the Sioux Nation. This case resulted in favor, again, for the Ponca.

This first Indian civil rights case involving the Ponca had far-reaching effect on federal Indian policy at that time. Many changes occurred on Indian reservations nationwide. Standing Bear subsequently made a number of trips east with Thomas Tibbles and Suzette LeFleche making speeches to churches and other civic groups. His prominence as a civil rights leader now stands significant among all Indian tribes and people of the world. It can be said that without the help of those Christian ministers, Tibbles, Webster, Poppleton, Judge Dundy, and others, this could not have happened. Standing Bear and his fellow tribesmen very well could have been returned to Indian Territory with nothing said.

5
Indian Territory

While Standing Bear and others were seeking their freedom in Nebraska, what happened to the Ponca who remained in Oklahoma (Indian Territory)? The initial acculturation process restricted them to a small reservation with the grantor of the land being the federal government. The bill to move them to a place along the Kaw River in Kansas fell short of its original intent. They then were taken to an area near Baxter Springs, Kansas, where they stayed for about one year. The Ponca protested that the location was not suitable for farming and raising a family. For one thing, according to the elders, they figured the ground was hollow because some had seen caves in that part of the country. They said many who could not acclimatize to the weather conditions contracted malarial fever and other maladies, causing much misery and death. En route to Indian Territory in that first year an estimated 157 Ponca had died. On July 21, 1878, when they departed for the new location in Kay County, the hot and humid weather remained a problem for the people. From Baxter Springs to the new reservation is 190 miles. It took eight days' travel in temperatures above a hundred degrees to get to the new reservation. The Ponca people were accustomed to mild summer temperatures and cold winters. Additionally, they knew nothing of malaria or remedies for such sicknesses. However, there were no deaths during this trip.

Before the second move, they had examined this location (a place where the eight chiefs had originally come). A high protrusion of land in Noble County enabled the tribal leaders and a federal official to select the land. From that high point, *Į'e basnádè*, or "high rock" as it is called, they were able to see clearly approximately six miles north and seven miles south. The east boundary of the reservation would be the *Ní'skà*, or Arkansas, River and the west boundary, the Chikaskia, or *Žegá'skà*, River. The north boundary, as told by the elders, is aligned east and west with the Big Spring, *Nihága t'ągá*, on South Avenue in current Ponca City, Oklahoma. The south boundary is the old Condit Road in Noble County. Here they accepted approximately 101,894 acres of land.

When they arrived at their new location, they camped on the land, near the Big Spring, at the northeast corner of the reservation, but the Indian agent urged them to scatter out onto the reservation land to avoid contact with others because of prevailing sickness. KH and AMC said the elders stated that they would not move because their tribal social system was such that they customarily stayed and supported one another in difficult times. However, some families did move. By 1879 the government had begun talks with the Southern Ponca chiefs to determine the leadership of the tribe. The reorganization of the tribal political structure, not clearly defined, was handed down from the War Department (now the Interior Department). Political changes began to go into effect in which all half-breed Ponca took full responsibility. Joseph LeRoy, a Frenchman who married a Ponca woman, had already assumed leadership while working with other Indian agents in Nebraska. The Ponca claim that he was the man who "sold the Ponca." They say in the Ponca language, "Jú' sí' dįgè aká, éi wiʃádįwį." In English, "Joe No Foot, he sold us." The original plats of the Oklahoma Ponca lands show the Mike Roy (formerly, LeRoy) allotment on the north jurisdictional line. Across the road on non-Indian land, his father, Joe LeRoy, had two 160-acre plots of prime agricultural land.

The Ponca were affected by the Indian Allotment or Dawes Act of 1887. The full-blood Ponca were aware that those *Wáxe hebè*, or "part-white people," got the best or prime agriculture lands. It was clear that the government was not concerned about the situation nor had any interest in making it easy for the Ponca. If the Ponca were to survive, they would have to do it on their own (KH, NC, AL). The government assumed that a man and his family could survive off at least 160 acres of land. The Ponca began to move onto their allotted lands, but not all tribal members received that amount of land. According to Louis Knight (now deceased), who was a tribal member and retired Bureau of Indian Affairs (BIA) land management officer, some Ponca received only 80 acres of land. The Ponca who had shared in, participated in, or commonly used land were now forced into an individual-type existence.

The approximate date when the true Ponca assumed the leadership role for the tribe is unclear. It could be reasoned that they suffered from mass cataclysmic trauma caused by the removal. They were broken in spirit by bad treatment, sickness, and death and now had little to survive on. The time required to adjust to the new way of life was disheartening for all Ponca. For two years, the tribe existed without aid, causing many leaders to capitulate to lesser leaders. The former governing body of the tribe was ignored by the government, and the aid came slowly. During that time, only a select few were spoken to as a part of the federal government's scheme to break down the tribal system (KH). The government finally allocated some funds in partial repayment (they said) for lands taken from them previously. With this, not quite understanding the concept of American capitalism, the Ponca attempted to build an economy while retaining their former lifestyle. But problems continued to mount.

They Killed Big Snake

Following the Standing Bear trial, the status of Indian citizenship in this country was still unknown to the Ponca people as well as to some bureaucrats. The idea of citizenship was never understood nor made clear in former times either. From the time the Ponca first came into contact with the Europeans and made treaty agreements, they had been obligated to consult with them about their travels. Before white contact, they had traveled and respected other tribes who lived and hunted on the land. They even shared major hunting areas. For the Indian people, this continent was simply a land where they lived and raised their families (KH).

Since there was no formal knowledge of their citizenship status in the interior United States or of other negotiations made by the world powers of the time, the Ponca lived according to their own political governance and cultural standards. They were unaware that parts of the country were being sold, as in the Louisiana Purchase, or that Europeans were claiming parts of the country. They heard about wars going on "between white men" (KH). The powers at hand had assumed that God had given this land to them, and they proceeded without regard for its inhabitants. When the question of what to do with the Indians came up, some reasoned as Andrew Jackson did. He thought that the Indians should be annihilated, starting with the Creek Indians. President Abraham Lincoln also held the same position. On the day he signed the Emancipation Proclamation, it was rumored that he also signed a document approving the execution of forty Sioux Indians at Mankato, Minnesota.

Indian people, like other nations, had problems, but they knew how to deal with them. When the Europeans came to this continent, real big problems came with them. They came with all kinds of new ideologies, philosophies, religions, and governments. Those who espoused these new ways would eventually affect the inhabitants of this country. These were the conditions that Chief Standing Bear faced in the court in Nebraska. The winning of the case did not immediately affect the nations of Indians throughout the country. Nor did it affect every Ponca Indian. The rights of Indian people, although determined by an American court, were not forwarded to Indians on reservations. Such were the circumstances on reservations that news traveled. Chief Big Snake, a brother of Chief Standing Bear and Standing Elk, had heard and knew the law. It is unclear whether Big Snake was a biological brother of Standing Bear because Big Snake was a member of the *Wašábe* clan whereas Standing Bear was a member of the *Wažážè* clan. Big Snake was a typical Ponca Indian, perhaps a little taller than some of his tribesmen. He had fine facial features—a strong chin, piercing eyes, prominent cheekbones like his brother Standing Bear, a gentle smile—and a kind disposition toward his people. He loved his family, his many relatives and friends, and his tribe. He had a commanding stance, which is typical of great leaders. He was a man of integrity who respected his fellow man. He was not a man who tolerated lies, cheating, and stealing. He easily saw through deception and dishonesty. He typified the Ponca, who were honest in all their dealings (KH).

As early as 1877, before the removal, Big Snake and Standing Bear had been incarcerated at Fort Randall for protesting the actions of the federals. The reason for the arrest and incarceration at Fort Randall was because they had protested that E. C. Kemble had withheld rations from the Ponca to get them to move to Indian Territory (Lake 1981). KH said the government had accustomed the Ponca to receiving certain provisions as a trade agreement for passing through their lands and using the Missouri River. The agreement with the tribe resulted in the building of a dock near one of the village sites. He said:

I guess they made some kind of agreement with those government people. They wanted to use that Missouri River up there. From way back they talked to those white people. They promised those old Indians they going to give them things — food, cloth, cooking pots — like that. So those people allowed them white people . . . government . . . to come through.

Withholding provisions and additionally giving repeating rifles to the Sioux was intolerable. The conditions were such that the Ponca were in need of assistance as per their treaty agreement with the government. The government, however, did not respond positively, and that's why Big Snake and Standing Bear protested. This was significant in that it gives one insight into the mental and emotional condition of the Ponca people. The brothers did not act as two rabble-rousers separate from the tribe, but as the voice of the majority who resisted the removal. Big Snake was always the fighter, making things happen that ultimately would have to be dealt with by those who made laws and policy governing the Indian people. According to KH, he seemed to be a man feared by federal officials. At the time the Ponca were semi-settled in Indian Territory; on one or two occasions Big Snake had taken leave to visit with friends among the Cheyenne and Pawnee. His absence and travels from the Ponca reservation, according to KH, were to show the federal officials that the decision handed down by Judge Dundy, in the Standing Bear trial, entitled him to travel as any citizen. Accordingly, he traveled to the Cheyenne and Pawnee Reservations. The news of the trial and the decision made by Judge Dundy was heard of by tribal members. This meant that tribal members could go as they pleased.

A Senate document in the National Archives gives an interesting account of an investigation conducted by the Interior Department titled "The Killing of a Ponca Chief by Soldiers" (S. Ex. Doc 46-14 [1881]). The account began with apologies that the original documents about the killing were lost. But other "copies" had been forwarded to the proper people conducting the investigation. The document targeted Big Snake as an "unruly member of the tribe," along with Antoine Roy, a "half-breed" Ponca. Big Snake was accused of causing unrest among the Pawnee and Nez Perce Indians. The Interior Department report said some young Nez Perce were looking up to Big Snake as a leader to take them back north. It reported that Big Snake's influence on the Pawnee was as such that "there is to be a revolt by the Pawnee, which will have its influence upon the Ponca." Regarding the occasion that Big Snake went to visit the Cheyenne, the report accounted for thirty-five people by name — including the Chief, Standing Buffalo, Little Picker, Big Snake, Cheyenne wife and child, No Heart, Packs the Horse, Little Shooter, Buffalohead, Yellow Bird, Thick Bull, Little Water, Little Soldier, Harry King, Child Chief, Fore Stop, Cheyenne, White Spirit, Bears Ear, Blue Back, Not Afraid, No Ear, Pretty Hawk, Louie Primeaux, Stands Black, Little Walker, Prison Hunter, Walking Sky, Little Voice, Antoine Roy, McDonald, White Buffalo Bull, Pawnee Chief, Makes Noise — and about twenty-five others. The report was made by William Whiteman, the Indian agent at Ponca Agency, who was ultimately responsible for the death of Big Snake. The correspondence between government officials, that is, Indian agents, U.S. Army soldiers, and those in the high offices in Washington DC, put themselves into good stead with all federal officials. It seems that whatever Mr. Whiteman requested was in concurrence with what other federal officials believed, whether it was true or not. Relating to his brother's case, Big Snake evidently mentioned the decision handed down by Judge Dundy that Indians could travel at will. In direct response to Big Snake, General Sheridan wrote to Washington DC. The following came from General W. T. Sherman:

> Headquarters, US Army,
> Washington, D. C.
> May 22, 1879
>
> To: Gen. P. H. Sheridan, Commanding Division, Chicago, Illinois
>
> The honorable Secretary of the Interior request that the Poncas arrested and held at Fort Reno in Indian Territory, as reported in your dispatch May 18th, be sent to the agency of the Poncas. You may order this to be done. The release under the *Writ of Habeas Corpus* of the Ponca in Nebraska does not apply to any other than that specific case.
>
> W. T. Sherman, General

This telegram, then, was basically in response to Big Snake's statement that he was free to travel at will because his brother Standing Bear had won his case for Indian people. To summarize the correspondence, it was simply one man, William H. Whiteman, who ultimately killed Big Snake. To do this, he had to conjure up some sort of story to justify his own hatred for Indian people and Big Snake.

U.S. Indian Service
Ponca Agency, Oct 20, 1879

Sir:

I have the honor to state that since the return of Big Snake from consignment at Ft. Reno about the 4th day of August, 1879, he has conducted himself in an extreme sullen and morose manner, and plainly shows that the consignment did him no good, and that he is harboring a grudge against me, which I have no doubt he will endeavor to satisfy whenever he can get a good opportunity. He has never spoken to me since his return; he very rarely comes about the agency when I am at home, but in my absence frequently comes to the agency and in a very offensive manner orders the employees to go and do work for him, or orders them to do their work in a different manner from the one I had instructed them in. He had several times sent very insulting messages to me, at one time ordering me to put up a large frame house for him right away, and another time, sent a message ordering me to put up hay for him over by his house; he has repeatedly said that he intended to kill me, and has gone as far as to set the time within which he will kill me. Since his return from Ft. Reno, where he was arrested and confined for inciting the Indians to run away from the agency for the purpose of visiting other tribes, he has upon two occasions left the agency without permission and made visits to the Pawnee Indians, at each time bringing back a considerable number of ponies with him, which were given to him by the Pawnees.

The liberty which Big Snake takes in spite of all I can do to restrain him has a very demoralizing effect upon the other Indians; they see him go off and return with ponies and they are immediately fired with a desire to do likewise. At this time a number of Indians and among them several employees are absent without permission upon a visit to the Pawnee Indians, and may go further. "Big Snake" is the most brutal Indian in appearance and manners I have ever seen; the Indians are all afraid of him, and he is a terror to the employees. I am informed by Mr. Chapman, who obtained his information from Yellow and Henrs Keutte, that Big Snake has been talking and consorting with the most dangerous elements among the Nez Perce, inciting them to rebel against the authority of the government and make their way north; they say that Big Snake told some of the Nez Perce young men that he intends to kill me, and these young men are looking to him to lead them in an outbreak. It is my own opinion that Big Snake is preparing to make a break as soon as he receives his annuity and goods; whether he will attempt to carry out his threat of killing me, I am not prepared to say, but I do not think he should be given the opportunity; it is very disagreeable for me to always be on my guard against him; I am not of the disposition to be influenced by morbid fears of danger which does not exist. I believe it that Big Snake has it in him to carry out his threat. I am constantly on my guard against his violence; and should kill him at the first demonstration he makes; but this is an alternative which I very much dread, and one which I should not be left to take.

I therefore, most respectfully and earnestly request that the commanding officer of U.S. Troops at Fort Reno or Arkansas City be directed to send a detail of soldiers to this agency to arrest Big Snake and convey him to Fort Reno and confine him for the remainder of his natural life.

William H. Whiteman, U.S. Indian Agent

(to)

E. A. Hyatt, Commissioner of Indian Affairs

Washington, D.C.

The description of Big Snake and the accusation that he disobeyed government authority by this man is in complete contrast to the true story of the Ponca people. The wars between Indian and white people were coming to an end. It makes one wonder if this man wanted to make a name for himself. The accusation of Big Snake's influencing and leading the young men of the Nez Perce tribe was said to be a ludicrous lie. KH made the following comment on the Nez Perce:

Those old Indians (Ponca) used to have meetings at our place [ref. Land description, tract number 0423-B3, Sarah NH Big Soldier, Sec 23, 25N, 02E on N/2 Lot 6] right where our old homestead is. During that time there wasn't any house there. There were four big cottonwood trees on the southeast corner of the homestead. They used to sit there and talk. They also went over there south of Dana Knight's house too . . . where there are some cottonwood trees. One time they was sitting there talking . . . in those days they had menfolk who were "lookouts" . . . they always watching for somebody to come. If somebody come . . . they come and tell those old men. My father was there at that time when those *P'é gazadè* came there. He said one "lookout" came back from that hill toward that river west of there. He said, "There's some men coming on horseback." *Šáge ágđì aí', áitè*. They come not too close to those chiefs . . . they holding up a white piece of buckskin . . . *Há ská*. That means they come in peace. They sent one man out to meet them. When he came back . . . he said, "They are Nez Perce . . . Chief Joseph is with them and he wants to talk with us." In those days . . . they always have interpreter . . . somebody can talk Ponca or some other language. They came over there where those chiefs was sitting. Chief Joseph said he wanted the Poncas to join in with him. He said he was going to get the Pawnees and some other tribes too . . . to start back north. He told them it would be easy to wipe those whites out if they joined in . . . together. They heard him out. But they told him they were satisfied where they were . . . lots of Poncas died coming down . . . now they had to stay here. They don't want to to leave them here. So he left them and went his way.

Joseph was in charge, not Big Snake. The Ponca who had been known by their neighbors to be hostile could also be friendly and reasonable. They made friends with many different tribesmen. J. H. Howard said of Virginia Big Soldier Headman, "She was able to describe the tribal hunts along the Elkhorn and Keya Paha Rivers and she vividly recalled a visit paid to a Pawnee earth-lodge village on the Platte when she was very small" (Howard 1995, viii). Visiting friends of another tribe was a common practice with the Ponca.

The account of the killing of Big Snake as reported by the Indian agent went as follows:

U.S. Indian Service,
Ponca agency, Oct 31st, 1879

Sir:

I have the honor to state that Lt. Mason, of the 4th US Cavalry, arrived here last night in command of 13 men for the purpose of arresting Big Snake and conveying him to Ft. Reno, Indian Territory. I had an interview with Lt. Mason immediately after his arrival, and advised him to postpone making the arrest until today, as I had sent out word to all the Indians who have freighted the supplies for the agent that I would pay them off today and I believe that the notice sent out would bring Big Snake to the office, at which time I thought he could be arrested without difficulty or causing much commotion among the Indians. Big Snake came to the office today between 1 and 2. 2 o'clock as I expected. Lt. Mason went into the office with 2 or 3 of his men, and, through the interpreter, informed Big Snake that he was ordered by the Big Chief to arrest him and take him to the commanding officer at Ft. Reno. At first Big Snake took the matter very quietly; he wanted to know what he had done . . . doth he arrested. The Lt. informed him that the officer at Ft. Reno would inform him of that when he got down there. Big Snake professed so much ignorance so much on this subject that I undertook to inform him, but was continually interrupted by him, and I finally ceased to talk to him. Big Snake then demanded an interpreter be sent with him. I replied then that he was in custody of the soldiers, and that I had no further control over him period. He then demanded then of the officers that he take with him an interpreter for his benefit, and also one of his wives. Lt. Mason then told him that he had no orders to take anyone but himself, and that he must come along without further parleying. Big Snake refused to go. The Officer, in my opinion, acted very considerately. I had told him several times that I desired that the arrest be made without harming Big Snake, if it was possible to do so; and upon Big Snakes refusal to go, the officer talked to him and reasoned with him for some time, advising him to go along quietly, and not put him to the necessity of using violence or putting irons upon him. Two chiefs who were present also talked with him and advised him to go along quietly. Big Snake replied to them that he would rather die than go with the soldiers.

I said to Big Snake that he had not very often taken my advice, that he had sometimes refused to take advice from me and by so doing, had got himself into trouble; that he would do well to take my advice now; that the soldiers had orders to take him, and they would be sure to do so, even if it should be necessary to hurt him in doing it. The officer then, seeing that Big Snake did not intend to go along, save he was forced to do so, ordered the corporal "Dobbins" to bring in 6 men to assist him; they took hold of Big Snake and told him to go with them; he hung back and would not stir. The officer then ordered his men to handcuff him. At this time Big Snake began to make use of all the wonderful strength with which he possessed. He threw the soldiers from him like chaff. A soldier struck him over the head with the butt of his gun, a blow that would have brought an ox to the ground, but still Big Snake kept his feet and would not be taken. The soldiers say that at this time Big Snake drew a knife, and the corporal, seeing the knife and believing that he would kill the Lt., who was struggling with him, shot him dead. I did not see Big Snake have any weapon, but several of the soldiers were between him and myself, he may have had it and I did not see it. Mr. Frisbie, the agency carpenter, said he noticed Big Snake reaching into his blanket or shirt as if searching for something and that he did not see him draw any weapon.

The Indians, after the killing of Big Snake, became very much excited. They are now, this the morning of the 1st of Nov., more quiet, and holding a council among themselves over the matter. I do not think any trouble will grow out of it. I have requested Lt. Mason to remain here with his men for the present, which he has agreed to do. Big Snake was a very bad, insolent, and dangerous Indian. I regret that he should be killed in this manner, but am of the opinion that the tribe will be more tractable, now that he is dead.

Willliam H. Whiteman, US Agent
(to)

E. A. Hyatt, Commissioner of Indian Affairs, Washington, D.C.

According to KH the above is not what happened. Chief Headman of the Đíxidạ̀ clan, who was a clan chief under the old order of chiefs, was charged with the responsibility of providing security for the Ponca camp in Nebraska. His duty now, under the federal government, was to provide leadership for the newly organized tribal police. He was present when Big Snake was killed. His account of the incident was told to KH over and over. KH had lived with this all his life. He told the following:

> The tribal police heard that they were going to arrest Big Snake. That day ... they sent for him to come to the agency. When he got there ... there was several soldiers on horseback. One of the Indian police was also there ... but my father was just getting there in a wagon. When he got off, there was lots of hollering. They were standing outside the agency building. All at once they started struggling with Big Snake. Big Snake bumped two soldiers' heads together and knocked them down. My father tried to get to them when he heard the Indian police say to Big Snake, "*Gákè, mạhì wít'àkè đizágà! T'é' diđètamà! Wí t'é' žúgđàgà!*" (Here is my knife [on my belt]! Get it! They're going to kill you! Let one of them die with you!) He knew that Big Snake had no knife. The Indian police struggling with them ... while those soldiers kept trying to turn his body toward the building ... I guess he didn't hear him. When that Indian police was knocked to the ground ... the rest of those soldiers got hold of Big Snake and turned him toward the office building. From that office building ... on the second floor ... that Indian agent had a rifle. He was real close to them, about ... maybe fifteen ... twenty feet away. From the window ... he shot Big Snake in the chest. Word went out that day ... they said, "They killed Big Snake."

As was the custom of the Ponca people, they mourned the death of one of their great chiefs. Big Snake was a man who did what any man would do to cause the government to live up to its agreement that Indians were people and citizens of the United States, that they were entitled to travel, conduct business, or simply visit friends if they wanted to do so. His death was caused by one man, Whiteman, who had a personal dislike for Big Snake, who evidently disagreed with the government and got many to agree with him. Whiteman was the dangerous man.

6

The Selection of Ponca Chiefs

The time-honored tradition of selecting chiefs for the tribe occurred for the last time in 1903. The principal chief at the time was White Eagle (*Xiđá Skà*) of the *Đixidą̀* clan. According to KH, although White Eagle was in charge, he called for Standing Bear (*Mąčú Nąžį̀*) of the *Wažážè* clan to come from Nebraska to preside over the selection process because of his respect for him and his knowledge of the ancient tradition. The meeting was held on the No Ear allotment in Kay County (KH). All chiefs selected are lifetime positions. According to tribal tradition, all seats in the council are filled by the oldest son. This is done when a member is deceased. This process is determined by the clan chiefs. Those present in the clan chief council meeting were *Gakúwįxè* (also known as Headman) of the *Đixidą̀* clan, *T'áxtì Skà* (White Deer) of the *Níkapášną̀* clan, *Waną́šè Žį́gà* (Little Soldier) of the *Mąk'ą́* clan, *P'édègahì* (Fireshaker) of the *Hísadà* clan, and *Óhođà* (No Ear) of the *Wažážè* clan. Two other clan chiefs did not show up for the meeting. Names were not mentioned but were from the *Wašábe* and *Núxe* clans. The *Néšta* clan was nonexistent at that time (KH, NC, AMC, JP). This meeting occurred following the inception of the "business committee" instituted by the federal government. Some apparently felt it was unnecessary. KH said that his father, *Gakúwįxè*, who sat in the clan chief council before the selection session, related that there was a problem with selecting the principle chieftain position. White Eagle had three sons. They were Horse Chief, George, and Frank. The second oldest, George, was active in political matters concerning the tribe. He was a good speaker and was very visible in tribal gatherings. White Eagle had requested that the council approve George as his successor. The council, however, said it could not be done. They agreed that George was the man they would listen to in tribal matters, but because of the age-old custom of honoring the eldest son, it was not allowed. In the end, it was agreed that Horse Chief would be the succeeding chief.

Although Horse Chief was a kind man, it was said by the elders that he did not participate in matters pertinent to the tribe.

The bicameral political system had eight positions for the eight Ponca clans. By 1902 the *Nèšta* clan had become extinct except for two elderly women in the tribe who were members of the clan. The selection of chiefs for the remaining seven clans then was followed by the selection of the lesser chiefs. These chiefs represented their clan according to size; that is, if a clan had more members, it had more chiefs. The selection process of the chiefs took three factors into consideration. The first was that the eldest sons of the chiefs were to be recognized and would assume chieftain responsibilities from that time on. Many of the men who had been selected as chiefs previously remained in their seats. The second was that certain seats in the council had been vacated because of death. The eldest son of the deceased, of course, would fill that seat. Third, the oldest sons not yet adults were to be recognized as future chiefs of the tribe. These little boys were "shown" to the chief's council. In Ponca they say, "*Žígàama wábahà wáđi ahí nái, áki níkàgàhiámà đàbè wakiđè nái*" (They bring the little ones to be seen, and they let the chiefs see them). KH said it was at this time that the fathers of the boys were given an opportunity to honor the old chiefs of the tribe. His gift to Chief Standing Bear was a black stallion with white hair from the knees to the fetlocks. The chief said to KH, "*Đaʃáđadext'i, ítą, áwaket'à bđá k'i šáge ágđi bđé t'amikè. Gađáđiše t'anikè!*" (Since you have shown compassion on me, I will ride upon this horse. [*Made tribal sign language.*] You will come to here.) KH said the sign was for "long life." KH lived to the age of ninety-three years. The boys were then seated outside for the duration of the meeting. The chiefs who were selected in 1902 and those who already had a seat in the council are listed below. The list was supplied to me by KH.

Bear's Ear	*Mąčú Nit'á*
Little Walker	*Mąđí Žįgà*
Biggoose	*Míxa T'ągà*
Makes Cry	*Wáđixagè*
Big Snake, Sam	*Wés'à' T'ągà*
McDonald, Page	*Péjè*

Blue Back	Ną́k'à T'ú
Mixed Cloud	Gamą́xp'ì
Buffalohead, Robert	Hésatigdè
Morgan	K'ą́zè Hą́gà
Cerre, Lemuel	Wašką́mą́dì
Pollak	T'é Núgà
Crazy Bear	Mą̌čú Daďì
Raises the Other	Gak'á
Cries for War	Nagé Ą́xa
Red Leaf, Lesley	Taníšì
Fire Shaker	P'édè Gahì
Rough Face	Įdé Xágà
Gives Water	Wažį́ga Umà
Running over the Water	Ní' Ánągè
Hairy Bear	Mą̌čú Hįxtè
Thick Nail	Šágè Šugà
Hinman	Níkagahì Skà
Warrior	Nudą́ Mą̌dì
Horse Chief	Šą́gè Níkagahì
Washington, Robert	Áhį Skà
King, Harry	P'úďugahì
Yellow Berry	Waxtá Zì

Other older chiefs who kept their seats in the council were as follows:

White Eagle	Xiďá Skà
Standing Bear	Mą̌čú Nąžì
Big Elk	Ą́pą T'ągà
Standing Buffalo	T'é T'ągá Nąžì
Big Soldier	Wanąše T'ągà
Standing Elk	Ą́pą Nąžì
Headman	Gakúwįxè
Walking Sky	Wagíą Skà
Little Dance	Wačígaxè Žįgà

White Deer	*T'áxtì Skà*
Little Man Stands Up	*Wagₐé Žįgà*
White Tail	*Sįde Skà*
Little Soldier	*Wanₐše Žįgà*
Yellow Bull	*T'é núgà Zí'*
No Ear	*Óhoₐà*

KH said Robert Buffalohead, whose father was deceased when he was a child, automatically filled that seat. He was the youngest of the chiefs selected, at the age of twenty-seven years. The selection of the Ponca chiefs was done to retain their internal governing body. The government officials were aware of the meeting but made no move to interrupt the process. In fact, the government issued certificates confirming the men as recognized chiefs of the Ponca Tribe of Oklahoma. With the exception of Standing Bear, the Ponca chiefs mentioned here were those residing in Oklahoma and do not include the chiefs of the Northern Ponca.

7

The Ponca Reservation in Oklahoma

The Salt Fork River cuts through the reservation and enters the Arkansas River and, thus, resembled the Niobrara River entering the Missouri in Nebraska. Above the confluence of the Arkansas and Salt Fork Rivers, a site was chosen for the government agency. Several frame buildings were erected to provide offices and houses for the non-Indian employees. Originally, the location was called Ponca Agency. Its location was adjacent to lands that were designated to Chief White Eagle and other unallotted lands. Two other significant structures were built around the agency. The Ponca Boarding School was built south of the agency. The agency was renamed when the government workers moved away in the 1920s. It is currently known as the White Eagle Community.

Two acres of land were also set aside for the Methodist Church. Some early missionary changed the number from 2 to 20 by adding a zero. For years it was assumed the church "owned" that land. The title of the property was held by the church women's division of the denomination. In the late 1960s they turned the property back to the local congregation. This included the church building, a gymnasium, parsonage, and two acres of land. Its location was near the agency.

The rivers in Kay County were important to the people. They called the Arkansas River *Nı́'skà*, or "clear sparkling water"; the Salt Fork *Nı́'žı́dè*, or "red water," because when flooded it became a muddy reddish color; and the Chikaskia, *Žegá'skà*, or "white buttocks and thighs." Those allotted lands in the area were given to the *Wáxe hebè*, or "part-white" Ponca. The Chikaskia River was so named because *Wáxe hebè* teased themselves about their white skin. These rivers were used for various purposes, such as drinking water, bathing, bathing horses, breaking horses, fishing, and playing. Even though this was to be the new Ponca Indian territory, as they understood it, they still reminisced of the lands in the North Country. Here in their new lands, according to KH, AMC, JP, and AL, game was plenteous and wild fruit grew abundantly. Pronghorn antelope were often seen grazing along the Chikaskia River as well as in current Noble County. Some bison were still present in the area. Rabbits (cottontails and swamp rabbits), squirrels, raccoons, and prairie dogs were often part of a meal for the Ponca family. A variety of wild berries grew along the rivers. Wild turnips, onions, water lilies, and a variety of other edible plants were bounteous. Pecans, walnuts, and acorns were also plentiful. The Arkansas River being "crystal clear," the elders recounted a time when they could "see to the bottom of the river." The river contained a variety of fish, and many Ponca were good fishermen. Trees and bushes along the river provided excellent cover for game.

Mandates were issued through the federal government's "long arm" to reach and teach the Indian people. In the case of the Ponca, it seemed that the help transpired because of the terrible ordeal they had experienced. The acquiring of lumber, for instance, for house building was a priority. KH said the men in most families were knowledgeable and skilled in house building. The Ponca who were familiar with farming had no difficulty in growing their first crops. Unfortunately, some families were unable to do as well. Those who were more productive were the half-breed Ponca who received the better agriculture lands on the west half of the reservation. The full-blood Ponca received the less productive lands. There were creeks, gullies, and so forth running through their lands. Where there had always been social equality and fairness among the people, now the tribe became divided by favoritism and biases (KH, NC, AL, JP). Additionally, the elders stated that in the years to come, the 101 Ranch in cooperation with the government Indian agent apparently targeted the full-blood tribal members as those who would lose their lands.

The First Years in Kay County

KH, NC, AL, and AMC said that a hut village had been erected when the Ponca first came to what is now Kay County. The village was located at the northeast corner of the reservation. They also said the reservation boundary should have been located on South Avenue of present Ponca City, Oklahoma. But the boundary was set along what is now Highway 60. There was no city, oil refinery, or highway present at that time. The Ponca lived there several months but gradually moved southward along the Arkansas River, possibly influenced by fishing and hunting. Additionally, many white people were moving into the area north of the reservation.

The use of this new land and two rivers was beneficial to the tribe. The Arkansas was pure enough to drink. Fishing in the Arkansas River was accomplished in several ways. According to the elders, during summer and winter the hook and line was used. Strong cord and hooks replaced formerly used sinew or rawhide strings and fish bone hooks. Baits consisted of small insects, especially grasshoppers and worms, and entrails of fowls. Gigging fish was done in shallow water and practiced throughout the year. Noodling was done only in the summer. Ponca men tried to find holes or cavities on the banks of the river where large flathead and blue catfish rested. One or more of the fishermen would block one side of the hole while another poked around the other end. This caused the fish to exit from one end where the other men grabbed or hooked the fish by the gills. AL said they used a gunnysack to cover the exit. Other types of fishing were done in natural ponds at certain times of the winter when fish came close to the water's edge. Martin Blueback Sr. said they chipped away the ice to find fish along the bank. Also during winter, the ice was cut, and corn was dropped into the water. Fish coming to feed on the bait were either gigged or hooked with bailing wire.

In addition to fish, a variety of turtles were also eaten. According to NM, turtles were caught and cooked during the summer, and girls looked for turtle eggs. KCH said that trees and other plants yielding nuts and fruits grew along the rivers. Wild fruits grew on a variety of trees and bushes, such as plums, fall plums, black haws, pawpaws, grapes, blackberries, strawberries, and persimmons. Morel was found in most wooded areas during the early spring. Greens, water lilies, milkweed, and other edible plants were gathered from spring to fall time. Deer and pronghorn antelope were hunted periodically through-out the year. Deer inhabited timbered areas along the Arkansas, Salt Fork, and Chikaskia Rivers. Techniques for hunting larger game were not much different than those of the modern bow hunter save those with compound bows. Some men were able to procure some small guns through trade. Men also trapped beaver for the pelt and food.

Waterfowl, such as ducks and Canadian geese, were hunted at certain times of the year, as were doves and quail.

Farming and Leasing

From a very early period of the Ponca occupancy of lands in Indian Territory, they continued to correspond with their northern brothers from the Omaha Reservation concerning their successes and failures of crops. One *Gahígì* wrote to Chief White Eagle: "I wish to know all about the kinds of food which you have planted in the land in which you dwell" (Dorsey 1890, 490). Others told how well they were doing. A person by the name of *Nąmą́mąnà* also wrote to Chief White Eagle, stating, "I sowed fifteen acres of wheat" (Dorsey 1890, 491). *Dúba Mądì*, an Omaha, wrote to McDonald, "What we planted is very good. All the vegetables which we planted are abundant. I hope you do well in the land [in] which you dwell, whatever kind of land it may be I hope that you may have a great abundance of the vegetables which you plant" (Dorsey 1890, 492).

Except for a few large farms, the Ponca farms were usually small. The communal farming concept was the predominant farming technique for the Ponca from ages past. This went through some modifications under the Allotment Act. KH said those families that did no more than growing a vegetable garden usually aided the families who planted larger crops, namely, wheat and corn. At the time when the Ponca arrived in Indian Territory, they planted wheat. Corn was planted for personal use, while wheat was for selling. KH said the major crop by 1900 was corn, and this was sold as well. But as the government agents would have it, wheat again became the major production.

The procurement of farm implements in Indian Territory was, in a manner of speaking, repayment for lands taken from them. They received the implements within the first five years after arriving in Indian Territory. Although some of the elders say that some federal contributions were made to the tribe, others said they had to make more bargains on their own. Starting a new farming lifestyle led to a new philosophy for the people. Namely, what had to be done by the individual had to become more important than the supply of goods provided.

The indigenous person then had to design his lifestyle within the predominant influences at hand. The Ponca became subjected to government policy as well as the offers made to them by private citizens. The offering of livestock, implements, and other supplies as a reimbursement for lands taken from them was not immediately termed as a payback but more often was interpreted as "what the government is doing for you" (KH, NC, AL, JP). These kinds of statements directed toward the people seemed to be a diversionary device to acquire the new lands from the Ponca. It also caused the tribe to assume a passive role toward acculturation. Concerning the early Ponca adjustment period, NM quoted a Ponca saying,

Itígą́deákà égidą̀ì: "Wadít'ą̀tè itédaìgà. Gą́' Wáxeàmà, mažą́dą́ unàt'amà. Điséƒ dažą́ wanáte t'abiƒ."

The government people said: "You don't have to work. Just lease your land to the white people and let them do the work. They said you can lie on your side and eat."

The absurdity of this federal mandate was known among the Ponca, and they spoke of it when they spoke of the times the Ponca had successfully farmed their lands in Nebraska. This statement was one of the government agent's solicitation phrases to remove the Ponca from Nebraska. The leasing and buying of lands from the tribe was a new concept, and the payback for the land's use may have seemed reasonable to some. Those white landowners who did no physical labor in the south, where black workers and sharecroppers did all the work, appeared to be doing quite well for themselves. If this was a pattern that would benefit them too, then why shouldn't they lease their lands? The concept of slavery and sharecropping was unknown to most Native Americans. But misinformation spread about by the government agents caused the Ponca, who were adjusting and accepting the new lifestyle, to succumb to a lifestyle of survival at its lowest level. The adjustment period for the tribe in Oklahoma entailed many problems in their economic and political worlds (KH, NC, JP).

Since the Ponca people had been engaged in horticulture and some agriculture before European contact, it seemed logical for some federal authorities to assume that they should continue to practice farming. Since Indian Territory was open to white settlers, and most were farmers, it seemed reasonable to assume that the territorial populace would soon be growing foodstuff. The option to raise cattle would have been closed since the amount of land was restricted to a small acreage, and the Native people had no knowledge of business enterprise. The concepts of expansion and growth, supply and demand, were unheard of. The influx of white settlers brought one family into the absolute center of the Ponca Indian Reservation. How this was accomplished hasn't been revealed by the government, but this family did come into Indian country and establish one of the largest ranches in the world. Since the Ponca had a little over 101,000 acres of land, this family saw that if they could manipulate the system the way wanted it, they could own the entire reservation. Hence, they named their ranch after the acres of land owned by the Ponca. This was the first contact with the Whites. The Ponca were to learn of trickery and sham land deals after all smiles had faded (KH, NC, JP, AL).

Income received from lands was contingent on the kind of land leased and the amount of acreage. The Miller brothers of the 101 Ranch started leasing Ponca allotments in the 1920s. These were mostly pasture lands. The 101 Ranch had a company store, where many Ponca purchased foodstuff. Because they had no formal education, many lost their lands. Louis Knight (deceased), retired BIA employee and tribal member said,

> They had quite a store there . . . the Indians would buy flour, baking powder, potatoes . . . and would run up their bill, so they'd have to sell their lands to them in order to make their payment to them. This was back in the 1920s now; that's a long time ago . . .

It worked something like this. KH said,

> They had everything you want. You could go there anytime and eat in the cafeteria . . . and sign your name on a sheet of paper. If you need groceries . . . sign a paper . . . and you got what you needed. They put you to work . . . helping with cattle, horses, plowing, butchering, gardening . . . this was to work off what you spent. It was a good time . . . fun time . . . everybody had plenty. Some folks camped out near that place just to be close by. Some of us got to act in movies as cowboys, so we dressed-up like bandits and rode our horses pretending like we

were going to rob a train. Some danced for crowds of people that came to see Indians. They made our people put plenty feathers on our dancing costumes. They said the White people that were coming . . . wanted to see Indians with plenty of feathers. Some of our people lost their lands by getting things [credit from the store] from them.

On the leasing of Ponca lands, it was assumed that the fair market value of leased lands was the responsibility of the Indian bureau and was to be determined by them. Alice Eagle was asked when the white farmers began to lease Ponca lands. She could not recall the year but did indicate that the 101 Ranch leased a considerable amount of Indian lands. She said,

My sister's land was leased. She had 160 acres and got paid for it. I don't know what kind of dealings they had with the government and leasers.

Concerning the government giving the Ponca farm implements and the amount of money received for leased lands Knight said,

Following the Allotment Act, the Poncas received 120 to 160 acres of land dependent upon the value of the land. They also received some horses and plows . . . They, the 101 Ranch, leased mostly pasturelands and very few agriculture lands. They were primarily interested in raising cattle and horses. Those were the "horse and buggy" days, you know. And sometimes they leased their lands for a buggy and pair of horses. There was no set price per acre. It was not until the 1950s when they started appraising Indian lands. Otherwise, the farmer would go out and make a bid to the Indian and say, "I'll give you so many dollars" or "I'll give you a team of horses or a new buggy if you'll let me lease your allotment." Sometimes a lessor would offer them chickens, beef, or hog to help them live.

The elders suggested that a commissary that housed supplies be located on the reservation. The commissary was part of the federal input in repayment to the tribe. Although the initial farm implements were provided by the government, many families purchased additional equipment. Most families had their own horse-drawn walking plows, harrows, and listers. The government, however, did provide a mowing and thrashing machine. Knight said that the conservation office initiated the land appraisements. This was done according to the fair market price or value of the land. He said that other responsibilities of the Indian Soil Conservation office since 1947 included checking pasture conditions, checking Indian farms, determining needs for terraces, aiding Indian farmers to raise better crops, and others.

The Ponca participated and were successful in the raising of wheat and corn to sell until other factors began to interfere with the new agriculturists. As in most civilizations, adaptation to something new always has its drawbacks. *Competition*, for the Ponca, was a new word added to their vocabulary and philosophy. The influx of white settlers from September 16, 1893 — the great "land rush" — caused a large portion of Kay County to be inhabited by many of the approximately 100,000 non-Indians who "rushed" into Indian Territory. The city of Ponca City, then called Cross, was founded in 1899. Adjacent to the Ponca Reservation, the non-Indian farmers were soon to learn of the BIA policy of Indian allotment leases. The early representative of the BIA was called an Indian agent. This individual was solely responsible for handling Indian leases. He approved all leases and other business transactions. Although private citizens were able to approach an Indian family offering money and materials in exchange for the use of their land, the Indian agent gave final approval. Was this practice protecting the Indian family? Not likely. The main purpose for the Indian agent was to get his share of the deal (KH, NC, AL). By that statement, KH, NC, and AL implied that the Indian agent was getting money for himself.

Later years, Knight said, the white farmer offered a "bonus" to Indian families above the lease agreement that was usually a competitive venture on the part of several farmers. The farmer making the best offer usually got the lease. Their bonuses were usually money, blankets, or even livestock and were dependent on the kind and amount of the land leased. The lease monies were paid into the office at the Ponca Agency by the farmers and were redistributed to the landowners through government checks. He said this may have been why white people have always thought "Indians get government money." NM said she heard that the tribal members were supposed to have received money from the government. She said,

Those white people in town always say to us, "You Indians are rich, you get two hundred dollars a month." I don't know where they heard that, but I never got any kind of money from anyone. I did hear, though, through my father (Big Snake), that the government was supposed to pay us that much for our lands they took from us.

Knight said that the general public had a "misconception [about receiving money] due to the dividends received from our tribal lands."

Communal Farming—Ponca Style

Even though the government encouraged the leasing of lands, the traditional Ponca economic structure continued. Corn was continually cultivated and remained a food staple for decades into the twentieth century, as were other wild fruits and vegetables (KH). In the transition period, there was a combined system of both white and Ponca ways. Although children were learning the English language and doing school chores, parents were continuing a lifestyle similar to their fathers of the old days, that is, dehydrating various foodstuffs and hunting small game. KCH, NM, Alice Eagle, and others mentioned the dehydrating of fruits, vegetables, and meats even though white-oriented farming was done. Alice Eagle said,

> They used to say, "We're putting this away for when the blowing snow comes." My grandmother used to put up a small tipi and make smoke in it. She use to cut up rabbits and hang them in there to smoke and dry them. To dry meat, you slice it with the grain and make it very thin. Then we put salt on them and hang them out. When they get kind of dry we pound them with a rock and kind of make them flat . . . maybe to get the juice out . . . then we hang them out again. We keep turning them over and over until the meat gets dark . . . and it becomes hard. It gets soft again, though, when you cook it. When you're drying the meat, you have to watch for the thicker parts because it can spoil. I guess that's another reason why they used to pound on them. They made a scaffold of wood really high to hang the meat on . . . to dry. We also dried apples, wild grapes . . . and of course, corn.

The keeping of foods for future use is reminiscent of the earlier Ponca who buried foods in caches in their earth lodges. KCH described the process of dehydrating corn for making hominy. This is called *Wabíšnudè* in the Ponca language. The term is made in reference to breaking away the bran from the corn grain. She said in the Ponca language (my translation):

> We use the "plain" corn [*Wahába ukédį* is called "plain" corn in the Ponca language and is now referred to as "decorative corn"] to make hominy. Grandmother (Virginia Big Soldier Headman) and I used to get the dried-out corn on the cob and peel the kernels off. We cooked the kernels with the ashes from oak or elm wood. The ashes made the skin of the corn come off. It is cooked for just the right length of time because the taste of the ashes can get into the corn. It has to be watched closely. When the hull comes off, it is ready to be used. We used to cook some of it, but we dried the rest of it to save for some other time.

Families' dehydrating foods such as those described was a vital part of the tribe's survival in the early years into the mid-1900s. To show the extent of the use of the "old ways" in modern times, Sylvia LeClair Iron told how she currently dries meat:

> First, I go to the grocery store and select a choice roast . . . very lean. Your knife has to be sharp to slice the meat. I hold the meat in the palm of my hand and slice the meat very thin . . . with the grain. I cut the meat in the middle first and then slice it. A four pound roast usually is about eight inches wide and about ten to twelve inches long. The hard part is cutting it without making holes in it because it has to be thin. I use coat hangers to dry them out. I put wax paper on the hanger to keep the meat from sticking on the hanger. I hang them in my dining room window to dry out for about four good days. I turn them over periodically to aide the drying. The meat will change to a dark color by the time it is thoroughly dried out. It can keep for a long time. I have some stored now that I've had for about a year and a half now. It is just as good as it was when I first made it. I keep it in Tupperware and use it for stews and a favorite Ponca dish called *T'ágát'ube'*. This is pound meat.

The economy of the tribe included traditional methods of preserving foods and small farming. This was supplemented with very few employment opportunities. KH said working for wages was available only to "white folks." And the farmer who wanted hire had little to pay with and wanted long working hours from the employee. Lacking in education and trade skills, the people could not meet the requirements of the dominant society. So they relied on their age-old survival skills. There is that period when, in the history of the Ponca, they were enthusiastic about their accomplishments in farming. That the Ponca farmed before and after the turn of the twentieth century is hardly known by the younger generation of Ponca and non-Ponca. Commenting on this, at her home, NM said,

> My father used to farm this land here. Lot of people don't know it or believe it . . . but lots of those old Poncas used to farm their lands when they first came down here.

Testimonials given by elders of the tribe concerning their family farms were numerous. The following statement on a larger extended family–farming endeavor was given by Molly Cerre:

> When they were ready to plant their wheat, some families came in to help out. They all camped out around my father's place. My mother and some of the women made aprons to put the seed wheat in. They would line up across the field side by side and walk across the field sowing the wheat . . . throwing it as they went. They did the same with corn . . . each person took a row and planted their corn. There weren't any weeds in the field because they kept it clean. When harvest time came, they would all help out again. They didn't have cars or trucks in those days, but they had lots of horses and wagons. They would load up the grain and carry it to the mill at Marland [then Bliss, Oklahoma] or to the other place . . . Those people who had allotments planted gardens too . . . every year. My father didn't buy hogs or didn't get any from the government. The way he got his was when the white settlers came asking for fence posts. They [the whites] really wanted fence posts to fence in their properties and would trade hogs for them. So my father and his relatives cut lots of trees to make fence posts to trade for hogs. They also traded fence posts for cows.

On the growth of wild fruits in Kay and Noble Counties, agreeing with KCH, she said that there was an abundance of wild fruits that grew along the Arkansas River:

There was lot of wild berries across the river [Arkansas], but most of ours grew on our side. Blackberries and strawberries grew along the river. We picked *Ną́šamą̀* [black haw], persimmons, and wild grapes. We had lots of nuts . . . pecans, walnuts, hickory, and so on. As far as food goes, we had enough.

The practice of putting away these types of foods in storage was done by digging cellars or underground caches. The cellars served families twofold. They were used for storages for foodstuff and protection from bad weather, especially from heavy windstorms.

Alice Eagle said that her parents did farming in cooperation with members of their extended family. She spoke of planting wheat, drying corn, and canning wild fruits.

My dad farmed wheat. I helped shock corn. Nelson [Roughface] and John [Gayton] and myself used to work all day. We also shocked wheat. Our close families used to help each other. Those were the good old days. We used to go out and pick plums for canning, and we picked wild grapes to make grape jelly . . . and we canned potatoes. We used to haul our wheat to Marland. . . . We sold it there. We also put up wheat and put up hay.

It is apparent that there was a good use made of the land for food production. The planting of gardens by young Ponca at the Ponca School too encouraged many families to plant vegetable gardens. Many families began to can foods at this time even though drying foods for the winter was done. The technique for drying corn was a yearly endeavor by all tribal members. AMC said his family

cooked it . . . corn on the cob. My folks always used big lard buckets to cook it. It gets really hot. They boil it, but not to the boiling point. When it's done, they take off the kernels and then lay them out to dry. It takes up to four days to dry it good. It can be eaten then. We dry a whole lot of it. We go down in the field and get armloads at a time . . . it's some work. We shocked the corn too. . . . It had to be cut just right and tied into bundles. After that we picked them up to use later on.

The procedures for drying corn are much the same for all families with small differences. The elders stated that once the corn was thoroughly dehydrated, members of the extended family took some home. The dividing of the corn was customarily done at this time. According to the elders, some families kept some corn for feed. KH gave the following testimonial on the use of government equipment and the cooperative efforts of the extended family:

> On our twenty acre plot of my father's . . . he planted wheat. After he planted . . . during harvest time, a mowing machine belonging to the government was brought around. You have to use your own horses to pull it. The neighbors . . . them that live close by . . . some who live farther away come to help out. The menfolks get behind the machine and rake up enough for making bales. Those bales were tied by two other men, and it took time. Then two men stacked them. A thrashing machine was brought around when they were through using them somewhere else. Before the machine was used, the shocks were picked up . . . put on a hayrack. They pull the machine alongside the hayrack . . . two men threw bundles into the machine . . . one of them threw the bundles while the other cut the cord when it went into the machine. A wagon on the other side caught the grain coming out of the machine. We hauled it way to Arkansas City to sell it. This was about 1900. I was a little boy then. Later years, we took it to that other place. Those old people sure like to work hard. Later on, we had our own farm implements . . . all horse drawn.

As the Ponca ventured into a new cultural era, they seemed to adjust well in the farming enterprise, but the first quarter of the twentieth century brought on other economic and cultural conflicts.

It was understood that the original federal conservation program for all of America was to conserve all lands. Federal programs such as the Tennessee Valley Authority (TVA), the Works Progress Administration (WPA), and the Civilian Conservation Corps of 1933 provided employment for the Ponca for the first time in their history. It is interesting to note that while the dominant society was in a "Great Depression," the Ponca's economic condition skyrocketed. For the first time in their history, they could go to work for money. The work entailed construction of ponds on tribal lands, roadways, terraces, and so forth. The method used to haul dirt was by pick, shovel, and wheelbarrow. They built ponds for the prevention of soil erosion and access roads to their lands. From the late 1920s to the 1930s, the men of the tribe were able to procure employment and pay in the amount of one dollar a day (KH). A certain cultural aspect of the Ponca served as a deterrent toward their socialization and acculturation. The noncompetitive philosophy of the tribe encompassed practically every part of their lives. In opposition to competition was the sharing concept in which the tribe shared all that they had. No one possessed a large stock of material things to the extent of denying another the same. They retained this part of their culture and heritage despite the urging of the government officials to get into the mainstream thinking of American capitalism. In moderate progression, some had left others behind holding onto the age-old philosophy of sharing. Remnants of this practice are still evident in some cultural practices today.

This section about the Ponca in Indian Territory demonstrates that they entered a period of self- and tribal adjustment. The issuance of mandates and various federal laws regarding the tribe's removal to Indian Territory have had far-reaching consequences that exist to this day. In the early days, the use of the Arkansas, Salt Fork, and Chikaskia Rivers gave temporary means of support, and the lands yielded sufficient natural foodstuff in addition to something like communal farming.

8

Ethnography

The Ponca, being horticulturists, bison hunters, and somewhat agricultural, were a self-reliant people who used all they procured from the natural world. The elders said that anything they could find for tools, for eating, for clothing, for decorations, for shelter, and so forth, they "picked it up." The manufacture of artificial material was unknown. Obviously, hides, furs, bird claws, brush, wood, dirt, and stone, for instance, provided many uses. The Ponca also used clay, sand, crustaceans or seashells, fish bones, and bones of the bison, elk, deer, and other large animals for construction of tools and decorations. Any usable item in its natural state was fair game to the people.

Dwellings

There were several types of dwellings and shelters common to the Ponca. The elders said the common lean-to was hardly ever used by them. As with all Ponca dwellings, permanent or temporary, the entrance was always on the east side facing the sunrise. Temporary dwellings included the *T'iúdip'ù*. This was a small domed structure made of slender poles, about eight to ten feet in length, that were placed in the ground. The poles were set in a circle about three feet apart. These then were bent toward the center of the circle and tied together. The structure was then covered with hides. This type of shelter was used by hunters and travelers. KH, AMC, NC, and JP said in the "old days" these were also used by families that were in mourning. In that earlier period, the family gave away everything at the death of a family member and moved outside the camp circle and lived in this type of dwelling.

A larger structure similar to the above was called *T'iúdip'ù snedè*. The structure had the appearance of a Quonset hut. The construction was same as the *T'iúdip'ù* but was wider, taller, and elongated. This type of structure was used for meetings, rituals, ceremonies, and various other purposes. Such a structure was used up to recent years. The last long huts built and used were at the residences of the late Ed Primeaux Packhorse and JP. They were used for having hand games and feeding attendees at Native American Church functions during the winter months. These dwellings could be used to sleep in as well. In place of hides, canvas and tarpaulin are used in modern times.

The arbor, or *Sadégde*, is a structure for shading. Almost every family dwelling had an arbor built nearby. The elders stated that a typical arbor was made by using eight poles to serve as a support for "rafters." The rafters or poles lain across were covered with straw, and smaller poles were laid on the straw to hold it down. This then was covered with fresh willow branches with leaves. This provided adequate shade during the summer months (KH, AMC, NC, JP). Like their earlier cultural affiliates who built their villages along the Mississippi River and its tributaries, the Ponca built permanent dwellings called *Mąít'i* (or earthen lodges) near rivers. KH, reminiscing, said about 1914 he was taken to an area west of Niobrara, Nebraska, near the Missouri River by his uncle Jack Peniska (this land is currently underwater). Here he was shown the remains of an earthen lodge village that appeared at that time to be nothing but piles of dirt and rotten logs. They were not placed in a circular fashion, as they appeared to be scattered. The earthen lodge had a heavy wooden frame of cottonwood. Four large upright center poles were placed in the center of the construction to serve as the foundation to hold other large poles meeting concentrically at the top with the larger ends supported by shorter posts on the outer circle of the dwelling. This large circular dwelling was described by Peter LeClair (Howard 1995, 56):

> There were four main posts in the center. They were as much as a foot thick. They had crotches in the top, and other poles were laid in these crotches. Then poles were leaned on these center poles all the way around. There was also a series of outer posts but there was no set number for these. The poles that were laid on the center poles also rested on these outside posts. When the framework had been built brush and kind of red prairie grass were piled on. No wicker work was used in these houses. When this stuff had been piled on the whole thing was covered with dirt.

The elders stated that at the outer wall (about eight feet tall), the floor was at least eighteen inches higher than it was toward the center of the structure. This gave the structure a sunken living room effect. The purpose of this was twofold. The first was to elevate the sleeping quarters from ground level. The sleeping quarters were sectioned off for the family members. The dwelling was large enough to house the entire family of paternal grandparents, sons and their wives and children, and unmarried daughters. Additionally, personal belongings were placed on this level. The second was related to the fireplace, which was located between the four center poles. This was the cooking and eating area, and a smoke hole was directly above. At a point west of the fireplace, a trench was dug out, extending to the outer wall of the floor. The trench (about ten inches square) was then covered. This allowed fresh air in through an opening from the outer west wall, where a flat rock (damper) was used to regulate the amount of air entering the dwelling.

The *T'iúkedį*, or "tipi," was lived in during the summer months. It was also used for ceremonial purposes and when the tribe went on bison hunts. It was easily constructed and could be readily taken down. The tipi could be packed and carried on a travois (*Wahé'ą*) when the tribe was on the move. According to KH, the conical-shaped structure could be constructed with as many as twenty-seven poles. AL said eight bison hides were used depending on the size and its purpose. KH said three poles served as a foundation; they were tied and then raised like a tripod. The three poles are set and called by the direction where they stand. He said one pole is placed at *Mí'édąbè t'adišą*, "the direction of the rising of the sun"; the next pole is at *It'áxeat'à*, "the northwest direction"; and the third pole is at *Íšnugà t'adišą*, "the southwest direction." Each additional pole was added, beginning at the right of the entrance and proceeding counterclockwise to the southwest pole. Then the remaining poles were added from the left of the entrance and proceeding clockwise to complete the frame. The bison hides, *T'é'hà* or *T'í'hà* (house hide), were then placed over the frame to complete the structure. At the smoke hole, or *T'íhukà*, a hide served as a vent where the tips of two long poles were fitted into slots to regulate ventilation by turning these "flaps" in relationship to the wind. Other parts that held the tipi together were called poles (*T'íšì'*), wooden fasteners (*T'íubažą̀*), and stakes (*T'íúgadą̀*). Appropriate decorations or artistry were added to show family or clan insignias. Medallions made of porcupine quills and horse hairs were placed on the back side of the tipi. AL said some families used polished deer hooves, which were hung in a "bunch" to make noises or sounds. No explanation was given as to why this was done. Tipis are used today for religious (Native American Church) and camping purposes.

Tanning Skins and Clothing

Buckskin or deerskin and elk skin were used to make clothing. The tanning process included taking the animal's brain matter and rubbing it into the skin to loosen the hair and to aide in the softening process. A stretched skin on the ground enabled the worker to remove fat on the inside as well as the hair on the outside. A scraping tool called *Wébaù'* was used to remove the hair. Martin Blueback Sr. conveyed to me that his father, Ernest Blueback, remembered seeing the softening process being done by using a smooth blunt pole. This, of course, was done after one had completed the process of using the brain matter to remove the hair. The pole, about four inches in diameter, was used by making a succession of taps or blows on the skin, which was staked out on the ground. Blueback said the skin was also drawn to and fro tightly over the blunt part of the pole when it was stood erect. This also helped the skin soften. Skins that were kept natural white color normally were used for ceremonial purposes. To get the desired color, the finished tanned skin was stretched on an upright rack. The rack stood at an angle and a corncob fire was built next to it to allow the smoke to blow upon it (KCH, KH). This created the smoke that colored the skin. The shading of varied colors included white, yellow, light brown (tan), and dark brown. Some have suggested that the skins were sometimes dyed black for moccasins. The primary use of tanned deerskins was for clothing.

Men's basic clothing consisted of a shirt, leggings, a breechcloth, and moccasins. A belt of a sort was used to hold up the breechcloth and leggings. During the winter months, in addition to the above, buckskin shirts, fur caps, and bison robes were also worn. In the event long walks had to be made, for example, for winter hunting, wraparound buckskin strips were used around the lower legs to protect the traveler from the snow or otherwise cold weather. Summer clothing consisted of breechcloth, sometimes leggings, moccasins, and vests made of buckskin, although some younger men and boys went bare chested. Women's clothing consisted of a buckskin wraparound skirt about ankle length, a blouse, and moccasins. During the winter, the women added high-topped elk skin moccasins and leggings that came up to the knees. Like the menfolk, they also wore bison robes. Children's clothing was made like that of adults (KCH, KH, AMC, NC, NM). For ceremonial purposes, KCH said, special clothing was adorned with varied ornamentation. Throughout her life, she made beaded designs for Ponca clothing and other ceremonial paraphernalia. She gave the following description (my translation):

Decorations consisted of individual designs made of porcupine quills. The quills are usually flattened, softened, and colored with natural dyes. Shirts, leggings, belts, and moccasins have integrated geometric designs. On men's shirts, a design of the width of two to three inch strip of quill-work is done on the outer sleeves from the shoulder to the wrist. The design is also placed on the front of the shirt. Each design starts from the shoulder and extends to the length of the front of the shirt. The length of the shirt usually reaches to the upper thighs. To embellish the design, the old folks used to add locks of horsehair along the outer side of the design, spacing them about two to three inches apart. Otherwise, buckskin fringes are added to the design. The design is placed on the outer leggings but is about a half inch wide. The slightly modified design extends to the length of the leggings. The quillwork is dressed up with buckskin fringes, which are about ten to twelve inches in length. In the place of fringes, sometimes men's leggings had a flap where the quillwork is done. The flap is flushed at the top and widened to about four inches at the bottom. The edges of the flap also have the same quillwork design. The moccasins are also designed the same. Men's moccasins usually have two narrow strip designs on the instep as well as around the bottom edges near the soles. The fringes are sewn in graduated lengths from the toe to mid-instep, with the shorter fringes at the toe. These are along the outer edge of the narrow strip of designs on the instep. Men's ceremonial moccasins have several strands of fringes on the heel—the longer fringes on the bottom [about six inches long] recessing to about two inches at the top of the moccasin. Both men and women moccasins can be completely designed with quillwork for ceremonial purposes. Men's breechcloth normally has floral or trail designs. The ceremonial dress style also includes an otter skin bandolier. For such occasions as in the *Ská ágɖì,* or "One Who Sits upon the White," women wear especially designed ceremonial clothing. The two-piece skirt and blouse are befringed and decorated with quillwork designs. Their moccasins usually have floral designs on the instep with coordinated designs on their knee-high leggings. They wear long quilled pendants called *Nąžíha ík'at'ą* that are also coordinated with the designs on their knee-high leggings. These are tied to their braids, which are worn on the back. It is the custom of women to wear their braids in the back as opposite of men who wear their braids hanging in the front. Small pouches, scabbard, and knife are attached or looped through the belt. These items too are embellished with quillwork fringes and/or horsehair.

Members of the *Heɖúškà* fraternal organization also wore their earned dance paraphernalia at appropriate times (KH, AMC, NC, AL).

Early Dance and Encampment Sites in Oklahoma

When the Ponca first came to Oklahoma, their only social life consisted of visiting friends and relatives. Reminiscing of the North Country dominated most conversations. The Ponca, who were yet to be affected by the Dawes Act of 1887, still camped as a tribe in the traditional way along the Arkansas River. Even when they were eventually told that they had individual allotments, they continued to live in the camp. Living singly and away from tribesmen and relatives was unheard of. The forced acculturation could not keep the people apart. As late as the 1930s they continued to go back to camping at those campsites. The use of lands along the Arkansas River for ceremonial and living purposes was known by all elders. The land descriptions from previous research are credited to Dr. James H. Howard, who also researched the Ponca use of the Arkansas River bed in connection with water rights litigation. To understand the riverine-oriented lifestyle of the Ponca people, KH, AMC, AL, and JP, identified the following dance and encampment sites:

Dance and Encampment Sites

At the Buffalohead allotment, NE 1/4 of Section 3, T 25N, R 2 E, Kay County, Oklahoma, the Ponca held dances and ceremonials. KH said the first Ponca Native American Church had its beginnings here. Ruben Taylor, a Cheyenne Indian and friend of Robert Buffalohead, allotee, introduced the religion to the Ponca.

At the Little Dance allotment, SE 1/4 of Section 3, T 25N, R 2 E, Kay County, Oklahoma, Heđúškà and scalp dances as well as other tribal meetings were held, according to KH and NC.

At the Standing Buffalo allotment, NE 1/4 of Section 3, T 25N, R 2 E, Kay County, Oklahoma, traditional dances and tribal meetings were held, according to KH, NC, AMC, and JP. Chief Standing Buffalo held the office of T'iáđį (House Keeper) of the Heđúškà, and at his demise, he was buried on this site. A large roundhouse was built on the Roughface allotment located in the NE 1/4 of Section 23, T 25N, R 2 E.

The roundhouse was precisely on the dividing line with the Big Soldier allotment. This campsite was the last large camping place for tribal activities. KH said land surrounding the roundhouse was used for various purposes that included summer and winter dances, meetings for tribal leaders, dances for both male and female organizations, and numerous other activities. He added that it was here that members of the infamous Capone gang from Chicago camped and gambled with the Ponca. During this time, many visitors from the Comanche and Cheyenne tribes came to stay and acquaint themselves with the Ponca. They praised the Ponca for their hospitality and their good fortune for having such an ideal location for camping, hunting, and fishing.

The Raise the Other allotment, NE 1/4 of Section 26, T 25N, R 2 E, Kay County, Oklahoma, was the location of the Ponca Ghost Dance encampment, according to KH. Although the dance was held at other locations, the significance here is that the absence of other activities indicated the dance was considered a highly sacred one. The dance, which is nonexistent today among the Ponca, was last held on this allotment.

The Sits on the Hill allotment, SE 1/4 of section 26, T 25N, R 2 E, is located on the west bank of the Arkansas, directly east of the present-day White Eagle Community. Dora White Deer Buffalohead said the

Ponca held their "Big hand game," or *į'ų́tį t'ągà*, here and it was also a large encampment. This hand game included the Ghost Dance. Mrs. Buffalohead's father, *T'áxt'i Ská* (White Deer), was the leader of the Ghost Dance. At this location, according to KH and AL, the infamous Dalton gang often crossed the Arkansas River. Some Ponca families that befriended them were paid by the gang to provide meals for them.

An unalloted acreage (an island of approximately 160 acres), Section 15, T 25N, R 2 E, was also used by the Ponca for summer and winter encampment dances. KCH and NC said this island was favored by children because of the many activities there. They played, swam, and looked for turtles and turtle eggs in the surrounding waters and sandbars.

KH said that another unalloted island (no description), approximately one-half-mile long, adjacent to the 160-acre island, was also used for encampment and dances. This island is currently being washed away by water released periodically from the Kaw Dam upstream. Both islands are accessible from Kay County, Oklahoma. James Howard (1995) said the encampment and dance sites were necessarily located along the Arkansas River because it related to the Ponca's former riverine lifestyle. KH, AMC, NC, and AL said when the Ponca first came to Kay County, they accepted the area primarily because of the rivers that surrounded and crossed the reservation. Their orientation to water usage, then, necessitated that they camp near the rivers. They camped and benefited from the rivers from 1879 to approximately 1930, although tribal ceremonies and dances continued to 1936 (KH).

The use of the Arkansas was ended following the discovery of oil in Kay County. The first oil well on the Ponca Reservation was drilled on the Willie Cries for War (Norman Cry [NC], tribal elder) allotment. The E. W. Marland Oil Company secured the lease through the Miller brothers of the 101 Ranch. The Continental Oil Company in Ponca City, which took over the Marland Oil Company in 1922, began using the Arkansas River to dump their waste products from their refinery. Ponca City, too, used the river for its raw sewage. The *Nį́skà*, "clear, sparkling water," was now polluted and unfit for use. While many continued their ceremonials and dances along the Salt Fork and Chikaskia Rivers, they too eventually became polluted.

Ritual and Ceremonial Dances and Songs

The Ponca, up to this period, had retained many of their tribal customs. The elders described the principal ceremonial and ritual dances in addition to social dances associated with the Ponca. These included the *Nidą́bewačì*, "Sun Dance"; *Heđúškà*, now called the "War Dance"; *Wáwaą̀*, "Pipe Dance"; *Ská ágđį*, "One Who Sits upon the White"; *Xđexđé*, "Tattoo Ritual"; *Waną́'xe wačígaxè*, "Ghost Dance"; *Nudą́ wačígaxè*, "Women's Victory Dance" or "Scalp Dance"; and *Šą́t'ągà wačígaxè*, "Wolf Dance." In connection with each dance and ceremony, songs too were retained by singers. Since each facet of tribal customs required the singing and recounting of past events, songs were essential. Songs of the Ponca are held in high regard by tribesmen and are taught to each ensuing generation. In addition to songs for the abovementioned ceremony and ritual dances, the Ponca also had names for other types of songs. For instance, KH said that songs for the ritual of bringing in the Sun Dance Pole through the encampment were called *Ígadizè waą́*. These types of songs were, however, not limited to the Sun Dance. The songs, called *Wéwači waą́* were also used as an introduction to various rituals and ceremonials. They were similar to the *Ígadizè waą́* and were also used in connection with other rituals and formal gatherings. The toe-to-heel dance step of the Ponca *Heđúškà* had several other dance styles, and each type of song and dance had names. A *Heđúškà* dance called the *Waną́šè wačígaxè*, or "Soldier Dance," is a new name for an old dance that had its own drumbeat and dance style. The *Heđúškà Ną̀stáp'i wačígaxè*, "Tiptoe Dance," and *Sésasà wačígaxè*, "Trot Dance," also had a different drumbeat and dance style. The songs of the Ponca *Heđúškà* number in the hundreds, and each dance style of each song tells the same story with a different drumbeat and tune. As mentioned earlier, Sylvester Warrior stated that the songs of "Scalp Dance" told the same story as the *Heđúškà* songs. This is Ponca oral history.

Dances

The Ponca in Oklahoma successfully continued their social, economic, and religious practices despite federal laws prohibiting certain religious practices. Socially, they enjoyed activities that collectively involved the entire tribe. The aforementioned *Heđúškà* dances, for instance, were intertwined with religious observance. The dance has been called the "War Dance" but does not have much to do with going to or coming from war. This activity would ultimately become a social function. In Oklahoma, there were four Ponca *Hedúškà* organizations. According to elders, the number of organizations had no significance. KH named the four groups as they were known in the earlier part of the twentieth century. *Hedúškà wanáxe*, or "Ghost *Hedúškà*," were said to be men held in high regard by tribesmen. The Ghost *Hedúškà* danced on the Standing Buffalo allotment mentioned above. *Hedúškà wasísíge*, or "Energetic *Hedúškà*," danced on the John Bull allotment; *Hedúškà wahádigè*, or "Orphan *Hedúškà*," comprised older men and danced on the White Tail allotment; and *Hedúškà gdádi*, or "Crazy *Hedúškà*," was so named because they danced anywhere and with any group. They were not connected to the "Contraries," or *Gdádi*, who were a separate society of men.

Sylvester Warrior said there were men selected to "keep the house," or *T'iádi*, of the *Hedúškà*. This means that the *Heduškà* dances were held at the homes of the individual designated as *T'iádi*. As a fraternal organization, the meetings of the men included doing good deeds, feasting, dancing, and giving away material goods to individuals in need. Originally, the giveaway was done at the changing of the seasons, but it evolved into a sporadic function continuing up to 1936 (AL).

In the early 1900s in Oklahoma, there were four societies of "scalp dancers." According AMC, the proper name for the Scalp Dance was *Nudá wačígaxè*, or "Warrior Dance," but it could also be called "Victory Dance" because the celebration connoted victory for the Ponca warriors returning from battle. In the old days, when the warriors were returning from battle, the singers and women ran to the center of the village and began to sing and dance. Whether they were victorious or not they danced as if to say, "We were victorious." It was good psychology. The people were encouraged and future hope for peace and contentment was felt by everyone.

AMC said this dance function also became purely social. As in the Ponca *Hedúškà*, the Ponca Scalp Dance societies also were appropriately named. *Nudá waú'*, or "Warrior Women," danced on the Standing Buffalo allotment. KH and AL said this group was considered the "elite group" of scalp dancers. This was said primarily because the dancers comprised chief's wives, daughters, granddaughters, and nieces. Mothers and grandmothers of chiefs also were members. *P'ádát'ą*, or "Drinks Bitter," danced on the Crazy Bear allotment along the Bois D'Arc Creek. According to AMC, AL, and KCH, they were so named because they featured coffee as a special drink that was served to members and visitors. Although coffee may have been plenteous, it was a rare and new drink to the Ponca at that time. *P'á díge*, or "Has No Bitter," danced on the John Bull allotment and were so named because their organization was founded following the *P'á dát'ą* group and did not serve coffee as a special drink. The elders said that the original term for coffee was *P'á* because the drink was bitter. The current term for coffee is *Mąką sábe*, "black medicine." *Mązeskà ną́p'į*, or "Wears Money," was the last of the Scalp Dance societies to be organized and danced near the 101 Ranch. These dance groups were purely social and provided a social meal for members and visitors.

Some dances and dance ceremonies of the tribe were held in high regard. These rituals and ceremonies are no longer performed, but the purpose and place of these customs were shared by KH, KCH, and AMC. The intent here is not to give a method of how it should be done, but to provide the reader a general description of the custom in the early 1900s. The following rituals are described in their simplest form for historical purposes as given by the elders.

Wáwąą (Pipe Dance)

The meaning of the term is vague. It has been suggested that the closest interpretation is related to singing. The term *Wąą́* means "to sing." *Wá* is an instrumental prefix meaning "to initiate action upon a person or thing." If this is correct, then the term *Wáwąą* could mean "to sing upon." However, the term still remains vague. Some probable causes include the stigma attached to the discussion of sacred rites, ceremonialism, relics, and dances. To speak of such things was forbidden by the people except for those to whom it was relegated. It was believed that to speak of religious matters as an unqualified person would bring sickness or even death to those who violated this unwritten law. Not unlike the Hebrew religion, in which their religious leaders too forbade all to say the name of their God, the Ponca people also avoided practicing religious rites without proper religious leaders. The Ponca, however, could and did call on the name of their God.

The absence of the dance in the present Ponca culture, the absence of singers who knew the sequence of songs for the dance, and some uncertainty as to who had sufficient knowledge to initiate the ceremony are other reasons why this ritual has lost significance in the Ponca culture. But the ritual and its various and well-defined procedures are still known. In modern times, it is possible that this ancient dance and ceremonial rite can be reintroduced. For our purposes, the loss of the word meaning to this once beautiful ritual will not prevent discussion of its purpose and scope.

The Purpose of the Wáwaą̀

The ritual Wáwaą̀ honored a child of a prominent family in the community. These types of families usually exemplified fairness and showed compassion toward all tribal members. Individuals were chosen on this basis rather than on the basis of the family's wealth. The child would be taught every moral and ethical teaching of the Ponca people. The act of inculcating these ideologies and religious values would require intensive parental guidance. Additionally, grandparents and other family members too would contribute to the upbringing of this child. Central in the teaching were several Ponca philosophical concepts, but more so was the idea of compassion, Wadáedè, and becoming "poor" for the sake of others, Wáxp'adį k'igáxe. The latter connotes humbling one's self in acts of love for fellow tribesmen. In the lapse of time, the "honored" one would learn to love and give with complete concern for their people. These people, as adults, usually sought out ways and means to be of help to anyone in need. They served as exemplary members of the tribe (KCH, NM, AMC).

The "Taking Tobacco" Ritual

This ritual was initiated by a respected man in the community. Had we lived during his time and seem him walking across the camp in the 1800s or early 1900s, we would have known that he was taking tobacco to some family for a ritual purpose. The first act in taking tobacco to a family is to make it known to the family by an intermediary. This would allow the family time to think about it and decide whether they would accept it or refuse the tobacco. Assuming they were agreeable to accept the tobacco for the *Wáwą̀* rite, the family would evaluate their belongings and potential for giving away gifts at the time of the ceremony. They would, of course, have others to assist at that time. Foremost was their willingness and commitment to have their child assume this great responsible way of life.

As the man proceeded across the Ponca camp, we might see him stop to smoke and pray. He would do this four times before he arrived at the dwelling of the family to whom he would present the tobacco. Upon arrival, the family would invite him to share a meal. The head of the family then would inform him whether they would accept the honor. If they accepted the honor, they then would proceed to set the time when it would be most appropriate to carry out the rite (KH).

The Giving Away of Gifts

Depending on the material wealth of the family, the rite required the giving away of many things of value, which included horses, robes, clothing, and other Indian valuables. After European contact and influence, the gifts included blankets and money. This act of giving away personal items was a shared responsibility of family members of the honored one. These helpers, *Wagáxdą̀*, were an important part of the ceremony because they were showing the tribe their support of the purpose of the ritual and of the honored one (KH, KCH, NM, AMC, NC, AL). In this light, it was also felt that other tribal members too would see and know of the acts of love and compassion. (Discussed elsewhere, the Ponca terminology used for gift giving has four different meanings.)

But why was gift giving important to the Ponca people? It would seem other channels of recognition and requirement would be more appropriate; however, during the height of their cultural development, the essential survival techniques show that sharing one's wealth enabled the tribe to remain intact during hard times. When they faced drought and famine, it was imperative that all members of the tribe cooperated. KCH said the internalizing of moral principles became an intrinsic part of their lifestyle. This then required a model that the tribe could distinguish as one conforming to those standards. The elders concluded that the *Wáwą̀* song and dance ritual came into existence to exercise this sacrificial way of living and the practice of giving.

The Ceremony and Dance

When the time and place for the ceremony was determined and the people were notified, they commenced the prescribed form of rites. The person in charge began with a speech followed by prayers. Usually, the speech thanked the people for coming and explained the parents' feelings and love for their child. He spoke of the parents' desire for their child to grow old in wisdom—understanding, trusting, and believing in their people—and to live a life without sickness and hardship. The speech might have included many hopes for the honored one (KH, KCH, AMC, JP, NM). When the speech was concluded, prayers of supplication and intervention were offered to the Maker for the people and the honored one. This speech and prayer was made where the people were seated. During the time when the Ponca people built large earthen lodges (*Mɑ́ít'i*), this ritual might have taken place there (KH). After their removal to Indian Territory in the late 1800s, the people built large-frame roundhouses to accommodate such activities.

Dora Buffalohead (now deceased), who went through the rite as a child, once told me that the leader of the ceremony then went to a dwelling (*Mɑ́ít'i* or *T'iúkeɖi̜*) to get the honored one. This rite was known as *Hɑ́gaɖizè*. She said here the honored one, his or her parents, *Wagáxɖɑ̀*, the leader, dancers, and singers were assembled to proceed to the place where the people were seated. The child, if a toddler, was carried by the leader. Older children were put on a robe or blanket and carried by four men or women. In front of the procession were the two *Wáwaɑ̀* dancers followed by the singers and helpers. Behind them followed the leader of the ceremony and the honored one, his or her parents, and close relatives. As they proceeded toward the place where the ritual would be consummated, the songs of the *Wáwaɑ̀* were sung.

KH and AMC said that in the ritual, the two dancers were trained to perform this special dance. These men had to be physically fit, about the same height and weight. They wore no special paraphernalia for the occasion. Their dress consisted of the roach, *T'ahį́' wagɖɑ̀*; breechcloth, *Žeáɖigɖɑ̀*; moccasins, *Hįbé'ukéɖi̜*; and deer hooves wrapped around their lower legs as noisemakers. (In later years, sleigh bells were used.) In their left hands, the dancers carried staffs. One staff, or *Niníbažɑ̀*, resembled a pipe stem of about four feet in length and had seven white eagle tail feathers of the bald eagle attached to it. The other staff had ten dark or black golden eagle tail feathers attached to it. In their right hands, the dancers carried gourds, *P'éxè*.

As the procession moved, the two dancers led the group, dancing intricate choreographic steps. The procession stopped four times before reaching the dance and ritual area. At each stop the leader would cry out in a loud voice that the one coming was honored to live his or her life in this sacrificial way. Upon arrival the honored one was sat at the inner west side of the circle. Here, he or she sat for the duration of the ceremony. Following the proper seating of the procession, the leader again presented the child to the congregated group. At this point, the leader spoke to the people or designated a speaker to explicate the purpose of the ritual. Again, he expounded on the meaning of living a moral and ethical life. He might have spoken on the virtues of fairness and justice. He might have suggested that the honored one would have to be an arbitrator in family disputes, that they should always honor the wisdom of his or her advice. So went his speech to the Ponca. Prayers of thanksgiving and petitions to the Creator would have been made after the speech (KH).

Upon completion of the speech and prayers, the singers began singing for the *Wáwaǫ̀* dancers. The two dancers performed the ritual dance directly in front of the honored one. Not unlike some South Seas Islanders who express stories with their hands, the Ponca *Wáwaǫ̀* dancers depicted the many pitfalls of life through dance steps, which included birth, successes, failures, victories, losses, times of happiness, times of sadness, sickness, death, and so forth. The simultaneous movement of the dancers appeared as if only one dancer was dancing. Intermittently, the speaker made further comments on the values of giving and sharing, refraining from selfish behavior, admonishing one another, defending individual rights, and so on.

In the finale of the dance, the cadence sped up with each dancer standing in one place stamping one foot in time with the drumbeat. At a given point, the dancers would make one circular movement with body bent low and come to an abrupt upright stop with the beat of the drum. Once the dancers had completed their part in the ritual, which lasted quite a long time, they seated themselves among the people (KH, AMC).

During the ritual dance, the people remained quiet because of the message being "sent" to them through the dance steps. The leader of the ritual, following the dance, walked through the crowd with a staff called the *Wábažǫ*. The act of walking with the staff through the crowd was called *Wábažǫ*. In this ritual, the leader would use the staff to "push" the people as he went among them. This act was to mimic differences and separation of the people caused by certain conditions in life. This, in turn, would be corrected by the acts of giving and sharing. While the honored one observed, the people too were reminded of their duties and responsibilities to their fellow tribesmen (KCH). The elders stated that at the place where the ritual was performed, the dance and speeches were presented only to the adult community.

The Eagle Plume

The feathers of the golden and bald eagles were held in high esteem by the Ponca people. In practically all Ponca rituals, certain feathers of these magnificent birds were used. The eagle plume was particularly used in the *Wáwąǫ*. The eagle plume in the *Wáwąǫ* ritual was used to signify that the individual who wore it was a member of this unique number in the tribe. At tribal gatherings for various purposes and dance, these individuals usually wore their eagle plume on the left side of their head.

When the leader completed his "round" with the *Wábažǫ*, he returned to the honored one's side and spoke of the plume, *Hįxpé'*, and its significance to the one who would wear it. After his speech, he tied the plume on his or her hair saying that to wear it was a great honor. It would now be the honored one's responsibility among others to exemplify those values that had been taught from ages past. His private advisement to the honored one would have included statements such as "listen to your parents and grandparents"; "listen attentively to the elders when they speak"; "be good to people"; "say good things about people"; and so forth (KH, KCH, AMC, AL).

The elders said it was appropriate, after the plume had been placed on the honored one, for the singers to render a song for the family to arise and join together in dance to show their approval and give honor to the honored one. This dance and song was shared by all those who assisted and gave of their belongings for the purpose of the event. (Family songs were songs made by a song maker who observed or heard of the deeds of a family member. It may have been acts of kindness or an act of bravery in defense of the village.) This dance was led by the honored one, if he or she were old enough to dance, and the parents.

The Giveaway

The giveaway ritual was handled by the helpers, *Wagáxdą*. Gifts were taken to each person who was present. Since children were not allowed to be there, only adult tribal members were present at this rite. There could not be disturbance of any kind during the course of the ceremony. This would suggest that perhaps many people had to remain home. Be that as it may, the gifts were distributed first to the needy or those with less material wealth and then to others. The ceremonial occasion ended with a prayer for all members of the tribe. It is believed that this ritual was one that served the people well. The quality of principles established over a long period was due, in part, to the *Wáwą* ceremony. Even though the meaning of the word is vague, we have explored its potential use for establishing ethical and moral values for men and women to live by. The tobacco-taking rite is only one way of conveying intent and acceptance. It worked well with the *Wáwą*. The use of tobacco in other rituals connotes its entitlement to reverence and respect. Gift giving suggests the sharing principle as well as an expression of love, especially in this rite. The dance, a lively and beautiful expression, shows life's many pitfalls and victories. Not being ashamed to be that person the people wanted as the example, the honored one wore the eagle plume identifying him or herself in all social gatherings.

Xdexdé (Tattoo Ritual)

The "tattoo ritual" as it is commonly called also gave impetus to the value system of the Ponca people. This ritual prepared a young woman for a lifelong service to the tribe as a helper of people in need.

The ritual consisted of tattooing a solid circle, about one inch in diameter, on the center of a young girl's forehead. The tattoo was referred to as *P'ebát'ù* by the Ponca. Sometimes a more elaborate tattoo, a star, for example, was placed on the girl's upper back or the top of the left hand. In this rite, like the *Wáwą*, the teaching is giving one's material wealth away as well as receiving gifts from others at appropriate times. The rite was less elaborately done and was attended by fewer people. The rite was done at the immediate family home. Usually a tipi was erected for this purpose. Extended members of the family unit were also present (KH, KCH, AMC, AL, JP).

The Purpose of the Ritual

The elders said it was expected that the young girl would be set aside from others to exemplify a high moral and ethical standard for her people. She was to perform her regular household duties like others, but additional responsibilities entailed a benevolent attitude toward all people. Her duties included dancing when it required the giving away of personal belongings; having respect for all people; feeding the poor and needy; showing concern for the aged by actual deed; and if she possessed some knowledge of curing certain ailments, using her skills without bias for all people. Most commonly, if a person was having great difficulties in life, it was appropriate to approach this special person and ask for help. She then would help or find help for the person.

These represent only a few examples of the many duties and responsibilities that the girl had to perform in the course of her life. A reciprocal relationship was established with the people in that they gave to her at giveaways in private and public settings (KH, KCH, AMC).

The Taking of Tobacco and the Initiator

The taking of tobacco to the family was also used in the *Xdexdé* rite, but the responsibility rested on the person who initiated the rite. If this person was not the father, grandfather, or any other family member who served as initiator, that individual assumed the total responsibility of the ritual. His duty was to give much to the family, which, in turn, would be given to others. He himself had to evaluate his wealth and determine whether he was able to give many material things. Once determined, he could not accept assistance from others, that is, relatives and friends. He then would bear the "cost." Two things had to happen at this point. The primary act was made by the initiator and the second by the recipient, who would be designated to carry out a lifelong duty to her people. Assuming it was a person outside the ranks of her immediate family, the "initiator" was the person who would honor the young woman by taking tobacco to her family. KH related the following example of a man who honored two step-daughters:

> That old man was a good man ... quiet, stay-at-home man. He never say any bad thing toward people. Always good. He marry this woman ... has two daughters, and they are nice girls ... everybody like them. They kind of show kind ways toward the Ponca people when they young ... never fight ... never talk bad. So he had this done. He wants them to live like that ... do good to people ... say good things ... help out where people need help. He pay for everything ... give away lots things to people because he want them to know. Everybody thought a lot of [respected] that man.

This man was a person of distinction, a person of discriminating character with exceptional judgment of people and families. His name was *Wáxt'a Zì* (Yellow Berry). An eminently considered gentleman, he was a man who set the example for living (KH).

The Young Lady

This young girl had to be held in high esteem by her peers—and parents. The Ponca refer to this as *Áxt'idè*. At a young age, especially from toddler age, she might have impressed her family, close family friends, and other relatives as special. As an adolescent, she was already liked by everyone in the community. This, in addition to being from a prominently "good" family, would have been a preconditioned status for selection to be honored in the *Xdexdé* ritual (KH, KCH).

The Ritual

In the late 1800s and early 1900s, a tipi was usually set up for this purpose. The person who was skilled in tattooing was summoned by the person in charge. This person was given many gifts for his services. Women who previously had this honor came to support and encourage the young lady. The one who initiated the rite also brought with him a speaker to reiterate the purpose of the *Xdexdé*.

He spoke of the parents' hopes for the young lady and the support of the family members. At the beginning of the ritual, appropriate songs were sung. This ceremony was not an elaborate public affair like the *Wáwaǫ* but was rather private in nature. Those people present usually stood on the east side of the tipi facing east and danced in one place during the singing. Other onlookers might have heard the speeches and prayers and remained respectful during this time (KH, KCH, AMC, AL, JP).

The Ritual Dance

The elders stated that this dance style only required a slight bending of the knees to the beat of the drum. The singing and drumming was done by one or two people. The initial song that was sung was called a *Wéwači waą́*. This type of song was rendered before any ceremony or ritual was to be performed (AL and Harry Buffalohead). The ritual songs related to the gift of the *Xdexdé* by the Creator and the gift of the flesh by the Creator. The songs referred to the flesh being one with the acts of compassion and giving. The female relatives, including the mother and grandmother, as well as close friends of the family, participated in this ritual dance. There was no particular dress or paraphernalia required to dance. This dance was a preliminary act before the actual tattooing would take place in the tipi (KCH).

The Tattoo Ritual

Following the speeches, prayers, song, and dance, the girl was taken into the tipi by her parents. When the girl was seated at a suitable place and was comfortable, the person who would place the tattoo upon the girl would first offer prayers and then encourage the girl to be proud of this honorable state of being. During the actual act of tattooing, he would sing songs of the Creator's goodness to the people. Again, he would sing songs relating to the skin, which would, in turn, serve as a reminder to the people of the goodness and fairness that should be present in our existence (KCH). Once the tattoo was completed (sometimes the tattooing was carried on for a great length of time), a meal was prepared for the girl in her honor. It was a shared meal with all present, including others who might be nearby. Following the meal, gifts were taken to those people in attendance, as well as to others in the community. The requirement of living a clean, ethical, and moral life then was the responsibility of the girl and her family.

These rituals that set young people apart as "role models" required high moral character and ethical living. Again, they were taught to honor and to show respect for the Sacred Pipe and other ritual and ceremonial activities of the tribe. The Sacred Pipe was the main thrust of Ponca religious practices and beliefs. Inasmuch as this honor was bestowed on certain girls, the Ponca people held all young girls of the tribe in high esteem, and they were regarded as capable leaders in their gender (KH, KCH, AMC).

Ská ágdį (One Who Sits upon the White) Ceremonial Dance

The term *Ská ágdį* means "one who sits upon the white." This term in modern times is known as the "White Horse Rider" song and women's dance. The English title "White Horse Rider" is a misnomer. Originally, the term was used in the story of an enemy warrior riding a white horse in battle. He was referred to as the one "riding upon a white horse" who took the lives of the elderly and children. However, the elders stated that the term literally referred to "one who sits upon the white." This apparently was in conjunction with honors bestowed on a female individual who would be caused to sit upon the robe made from the skin of a white bison or bear. The elders also stated that the ceremonial dance and giveaway honored the wife or wives of a chief and could also be done for a daughter, granddaughter, or niece of the chief. The dance and giveaway were ceremonies in themselves and could be done separately from other activities, as in the *Wáwaà* and *Xdexdé*.

In modern times, *Ská ágdį* has been done in conjunction with other tribal dances. About the turn of the twentieth century, in Oklahoma, at least two tribal celebrations were held. These particular tribal celebrations were held for several years. One was held in the late summer and the second in midwinter. At these dances the ceremony was performed (KH, KCH, AMC, JP). An announcement would be made that this ceremony would be taking place. The Ponca would tell each other, "They are going to have *Ská ágdį* at the dance today." This was an indication that gifts would be given by those participating in or sponsoring it.

The Purpose of the Ská ágdį

The primary function was to redistribute material goods that a chief had accumulated over time. The act of gift giving was important to the tribe, as mentioned. In this ritual dance, the tribal leaders (chiefs) had the opportunity to give back to the people. A solid economic base and wealth of the tribe was shared equally by its members. This, of course, could not be done if the sharing principle was not present. Hoarding, stockpiling, squirreling, and so forth was not within the economic structure of the Ponca people. The practice of stockpiling was not forbidden but would have drawn extreme criticism. This type of practice, essentially, would have put a family at odds with the tribe, and the family probably could have been shunned or spurned. The purpose of the ceremony was to honor one female member of the chief's family and then give the chief a chance to give back to the people (KH).

The Ceremonial Dance

The elders stated that those who danced at in this ceremony were the wives, daughters, granddaughters, and nieces of the chief who would be giving away. The accumulation of material goods by the chief himself, in addition to those that would be given by the women dancers, would be a considerably large number of gifts to be distributed to tribal members. The basic rule "give to those with less material wealth" would be the standard for giving. For the purpose of teaching the values of giving, the women of this family, from the youngest to the eldest were obligated to dance. This was done, in part, because they were of the chief's family and extended family members. Their buckskin dresses were elaborately fringed and beaded with intricate designs (before European influence, the Ponca had used porcupine quills). Worn with the traditional buckskin dress was a belt that included a beaded knife scabbard and beaded pouches for personal items. Their moccasins were also completely beaded following European contact. They also wore knee-length fringed leggings, laced bone bead necklaces, chokers, beaded or quilled pendants attached to their hair, and other jewelry, such as quilled medallions and rosettes (KCH). If any of these women were eligible to wear an eagle plume, these became part of the ceremonial dress for the *Ská ágⱥį*.

Usually, at the beginning of the dance, the first song gave the women time to arise to dance. At the second chorus of the song, the women, led by the wife of the chief, began dancing. The dance style was the type of short steps keeping in time to the slow tempo of the drum.

The cadence of the drum changed at certain intervals of the singing. In particular, at the drumroll, the women stopped dancing until the drumbeat resumed the slow tempo. The closing of each *Ská ágdį* song is indicated by three strong beats. A series of songs are usually sung for the occasion. The finale songs and drumbeat are faster, and dancers add style and variety to the dance at this point. These songs connoted victory and accomplishment, and the dance expression became spirited. Ponca singers and drummers say these songs are composed of vocables but speak their own language of life, love, happiness, sickness, and even death. These songs talk about overcoming life's problems, and the finale songs show joy and victory.

Following the dance, during which a series of *Ská ágdį* songs were sung, the giveaway commenced. The speech would include the accomplishments of and hopes for the honored one who sat upon the white. Some known incident and difficulty she might have gone through would be mentioned, drawing attention to her patience and willingness to see it resolved. If she accomplished some significant thing, this too would be spoken of. The speech might have also included the hardships and adversities of the chief and his family and their final victory over the vicissitudes of life. Following the giveaway, prayers of thanksgiving were offered for the lives of the chief and his family. When the prayers were completed, this ended the ceremonial dance and giveaway.

9

The Ponca Giveaway

The practice of giving away material goods can be described as an act of redistribution of goods. Giving away material goods to another person has been practiced by the Ponca for as long as anyone can remember. The principles of giving away are still part of the Ponca culture. An elder said, "It begins in the home." Children are taught to give by observance and by practice. When a person or a family visits for the first time, the host and hostess usually present a gift to them when they leave. People who have not visited for some time are also given a gift when they come calling. There is no need to reciprocate, but it is commonly done. In receiving a gift that was badly needed by the recipient, they would exclaim *"Wéšną́ ą́đađè!"* (You have caused a wonderful thing to happen to me) (KH). As stated above, the purpose and concept of sharing originate in the family-based Ponca social structure, that is, the caring for and sharing with family members their basic physical needs.

Other forms of giving away were accomplished at certain ceremonial dances. The giving of personal property to another could be classified as a sharing philosophy, which is exemplified when a person shares material wealth in a ceremony. In the actual giveaway, gifts could be given to anyone, but they were usually given on the basis of personal thoughts and feelings toward others. (There was no romantic gesture in these acts of giving.) The recipients of the gifts were usually people who were not relatives. Friends could give to each other informally anywhere, but sometimes they were included at the giveaway. Usually people of high status in the tribe, especially leaders of social standing beginning with chiefs, war leaders, women held in high esteem because of their benevolence, and so forth, gave away on different occasions. The accumulation of gifts by these individuals was ultimately redistributed to the needy or to people who were less fortunate.[1] This included the elderly, widows, orphaned children, the infirmed, and others. In the 1800s and in times past, material wealth or goods could have comprised foodstuff, cooking and eating utensils, clothing, pipes, furs, hides used for shelter, weapons, and animals, namely, dogs and horses. Items of adornment could also be classified as personal property and could be given away (KH, NC, AMC).

As stated above, it was thought that to accumulate material goods was a sign of selfishness; however, if the individuals or families were traditionally recognized as people who gave away to the less fortunate, then the accumulation of goods was acceptable (KH).

The procedure for giving away began at some point in the general dance activity. Usually when a family wished to give away, they told the person who served as the spokesperson for the dance occasion or another person who would speak on their behalf. Usually the speech preceding the actual giveaway embodied some favorable attributes of the family or individual. The spokesperson normally noted the family's status in the community, the family's sentiments, and the purpose of the giveaway.

Following the monologue, he proceeded to call the names of individual recipients who came forward to accept the gift and shake the hand of the donor. The recipient of the gift was, and is, not allowed to make any public statement of thanks. Also, in some ceremonial acts of giving, an individual may honor another person in the act itself. For example, in the *Heđúškà*, an individual dancer may be honored by family members and friends. As he dances to the special song (usually individual or family songs), they come by him placing robes on him or any item they wish to give away. In modern times, Pendleton blankets and shawls are usually put on the honoree. He is expected to give these items away after he dances. For example, as mentioned, in the *Ská ágđį*, or "One Who Sits upon the White," ceremony, the individual (usually a female member of the family) is considered "honored" by having her give away the accumulated goods received by her father, grandfather, uncle, or other family member who is chief (KH).

Clothing and Other Items That Might Be Given Away

As stated elsewhere, the Ponca people used natural materials to make all clothing and other personal material items. The materials used to make clothing included deerskin or buckskin (*T'ahá'*), elk skin (*Ą'pą* hà), and bison skin (*T'ȩ' hà*). Skins were sewn together with sinew. The following are examples of some clothing items (KH, KCH):

Há unáži	buckskin shirt
Ųtá, há utá, há utátá	leggings
Hįbé ukédį	moccasins
Žeádigdą̀	breechcloth
Hįbé ábaè	moccasins (beaded)
Ųnáži t'ągá	coat
Nušnáha wadage	otter skin cap
Nąbé udíšį	gloves
Waį xúdè	robe
Wadágè	hat/cap (any)
Mášą p'agdą̀	feathered headdress
Há'waté	buckskin dress
Hįbé ukédį ádist'à	moccasin leg wraps
Íp'idagè	belt
Waíkáhazì	broadcloth
Waígdabè sábe	black shawl
T'éhį žíde	woven strap
Gasné žíde	red braid wraps

Broadcloth, sometimes referred to as trade cloth or coat lining, was of European origin.

Ceremonial paraphernalia and other items were constructed with hides, furs, hair, feathers, shells, claws from both the black and grizzly bears, horns of bison and big horn sheep, wood, stone, and copper, including the following:

Níkidè wanáp'į	shell gorget
Nąžíha mą́ša ábaxà	feather lock
Úwį gazą́de	beaded gorget
Nusí' áxdadè	bandolier
Niní úžihà	tobacco pouch
Niní'	tobacco
Nidą́bewačì nisúde	Sun Dance whistle

Hįxp'é	eagle plume
Heđúška nisúde	*Heđúška* whistle
Nisúdè	whistle
Axíbè	bracelet
Nąžíha ík'ąt'ą̀	hair beads
Nąbéúđixđà	ring
Wanáp'į	necklace
Úwį	earrings
Hįská	beads
Mášą hągà	center tail feather (eagle)
Káxè migđà	crow belt
K'áxe migđà̀ síde	tail to crow belt
Mą́ge wahí	breastplate
Ímągđè	staff
Wábažą̀	short staff
Niníbažą̀	pipe staff (stem)
P'éxe	gourd
Níkidè	shell amulet
Wégasap'ì	whip
T'aháwagđè	shield
Nudą́ wétį	war club
Wabáxte	pouch (any)
Wabáxte	bag
Mąčú šágè wanáp'i	bear claw necklace
T'aí wágđà̀	roach
Mą́'	arrowhead
Mą́de hí'	arrow shaft
Mądę́'	bow
Mą́dę hí'	spear
Mą́hi	knife
Mí'iđáp'è nisúde	flute
Mą́zep'è žįgà	hatchet
Wasé žíde	red ocher

Wasé t'ù	blue ocher
Wasé zí	yellow ocher
Nąxdé	charcoal
Ųgásnè	braid something within
P'ę́'	adz
Niníba	peace pipe

Some of the above terms carried over into modern clothing items with slight modifications. The following clothing articles are some examples (KCH):

Nídeudíšį	pants
Ųną́žį	shirt
Ųną́žį t'ągà	coat
Ųną́žį čéška	jacket
Ųną́žį zizigè	sweater
Nídeudíšį čéška	shorts (sport)
Mąze Ųną́žį	metal breastplate
Nídeudíšį mą́te	shorts (under)
Hįbé	shoe (any)
Hįbé uwákihą̀	overshoes
Hįbé sidéde mąšì	woman's high heels
Hįbé zízíge	galoshes
Hįbé t'ągà	work shoe
T'éska basí hįbé	cowboy boots
Hįbégawįxè	socks
Hįbé sidéde bdáskà	woman's flats
Waté	dress
Waté xé'a	short dress
Waté mątè	slip
Nídeudíšį mątè	panty
Đíʃdadisądè	vest
Díʃmątè	bra
Waté snedè	gown

Hįbégawįxe	stockings
Ųnáži xáxadè	thin shirt / blouse
Ųnáži puki	thick shirt / coat
Wadáge	hat
Sáhį wadáge	straw hat
Wadáge bút'a	cap
Wá'batè	ribbon

Since there is a constant change in cultural values, the processes and procedures for giveaways have deviated from former times, when giveaways were more elaborately and ceremoniously done. For instance, other items that may be given away at modern Indian dances today include money. Candy and toys are given to children. The drummers are given cigarettes. And when someone calls for their family song to giveaway, the money they gather as they dance is normally given to the drummers. Long gone are the days when fine riding horses and teams of horses were given away. The family also gives a Pendleton blanket to the person who started their family song. Pendleton blankets are favored by the recipient, but lots of Mexican sarapes are also given away. Some Pendleton blankets, called "Chief Joseph" types, are more elaborately designed, are larger, and cost more. The recipients of both types of Pendleton are usually men. Rarely, someone might give away his red and blue "broadcloth" blanket.

The Ponca now participate in the pan-Indian gourd dance. They also have adopted some giveaway customs. Bonnie Kent McElroy (now deceased) said one of the ways a giveaway can be accomplished is to take a person, who is either dancing, singing, or simply standing on the sidelines looking on, to a vacant spot in the arena. And then take a second person, who is the recipient, to stand beside him dancing. You are "honoring" the first person. You then place money before the second person. Other dancers or spectators may come by and also place money before him. They too will dance with the honoree and recipient. When the song ends, the "honored one" picks up the money and hands it to the second person who pockets the dough. He has an option. He may keep the money or give it to someone else.

Before, during, and after World War II, the economic status of the tribe was as such that giveaways at dances were meager. It was not unusual for people to give to one another twenty-five and fifty cent pieces in giveaways at the hand game. Sometimes it was a serious gift, but more often than not, it was done in a fun or joking way. There is the story of one Omaha Indian, visiting from the north, who danced to give away some cookies for the next hand game. He couldn't pronounce the word *cookie* very well. But he told the speaker he was giving "koo-kies" for the next dance. It sounded as though he was saying the Ponca word for pig— *K'úkusì.* So the announcer, who really did know he meant to say cookie, told the audience in the Ponca language, "He said he's going to give a pig for the next hand game." The man tried in vain to correct him. Everyone present had a good laugh on the northern brother. They could hardly afford a meal in those days, much less a pig.

Property

To understand the tribal concept of property, it is necessary to refer back to the time when the Ponca lived in Niobrara, Nebraska. According to KH, the ownership of local lands, that is, lands on which the tribe was currently residing, was a vague concept. Howard (1995, 96) quoted Peter LeClair as saying that land ownership rested with the tribe, but this ownership seemed dependent on where the tribe was located at a particular time. This conclusion was reached based on the time the tribe had taken in Mormons, who, in desperation, came seeking help from the Ponca people. Apparently, the territory at the time was sparsely populated by white folks, and the tribe had signed a treaty with the federal government saying it would not accept other people, particularly a religious order, on its land. Yet the Mormons came to the Ponca people asking for land to live on until they could find a suitable place to live. Harry Buffalohead said his great grandfather had told him that the Mormons offered the Ponca a small cannon and gunpowder. He said the tribe quickly accepted the cannon because the government was supplying repeating rifles to its longtime enemies, the Sioux. He said the only defense the Ponca had was their single-shot black powder rifles. The land yielded such good crops that the enterprising Mormons dug out a canal near the Niobrara River and built a mill to process their wheat and corn. According to tribal custom, when the tribal clan (the original "owners") and family members returned, the Mormons moved on. The land on which the Mormons resided is currently marked by a monument on the west bank of the Niobrara River near present-day Niobrara, Nebraska.

In modern times, on lands where their annual powwow is held, the Southern Ponca families have camping sites that are understood to belong to them because they have always camped there. This is reminiscent of the earlier practices when the tribe recognized lands used for agricultural purposes. KH said that all land claimed for living on, that is, for dwellings and raising crops, was owned by the tribe. Hunting territory, he said, was shared by several tribes. That kind of land was large, covering thousands of square miles. Some things owned by the tribe, clan, and individuals were incorporeal in nature. Names and songs represent some of the more intangible items. Names, for instance, are affiliated with clans. The patrilineal kinship system demands that names come from the father's clan. Under certain provisions a non–clan member or even a non–tribal member might receive a name from a given clan. This was done under special circumstances, particularly when an orphaned child whose paternal parent was not Ponca was adopted. It was not uncommon about the turn of the twentieth century to select a name from the child's father's tribal background. JP, who had two Sioux names, had a Ponca mother and a Sioux father. His names were *Mąxp'íázi* (Yellow Cloud) and *Ąbédo Wašt'é* (Good Day). He also gave his children Sioux names, according to tradition.

If the father was non-Indian, since the 1800s, the maternal parent, grandparents, and relatives called the child by his or her white name or a corruption of the same. Howard (1995, 97) wrote that the Ponca had a custom of "trading names with other tribes such as the Omaha and Dakota." According to the elders, as far as the Ponca were concerned, the name was owned by those tribes. Perhaps out of coincidence some names were the same as Ponca.

Songs, especially individual songs (mentioned elsewhere), were and are considered personal property. These songs, in the days when the Ponca lived in the North Country, were earned by the individual for his extraordinary feats of bravery or his exceptional talent and benevolence. Each of the Ponca clans also has songs that cannot be used by any other clan or person. Songs of the Ponca *Heɖúškà* also belong to the *Heɖúškà* organizations (see chapter 13).

Rites and Ceremonies Not Owned

According to KH, rites and ceremonies were not "owned" by any one person. There were, however, certain individuals in the tribe who knew the procedures of practice and application of such rites and ceremonies. Although they could not formally give away the ritual or ceremonial, their knowledge could be passed on or given to another person who showed interest. The tribe relied on these people to carryout these ceremonies according to custom. The Ponca Sun Dance leader in 1912 was a man by the name of *Mąčú Pʼá Xúde* (Gray Headed Bear). KH said this man was given the responsibility to lead and organize the Sun Dance ceremony according to tribal custom. He had been instructed by an elder of an earlier period. At the demise of *Mąčú Pʼá Xúde*, the dance coincidentally was discontinued when the government placed a law prohibiting the Ponca to practice this ancient religious ceremony. Although the Sun Dance leader had left no instructions formally to any person to continue the procedure and practice, there were many who knew the procedure and understood its significance. But out of respect for him, they chose not to continue the practice. There seems to have developed a concept of intertribal co-ownership of the Sun Dance, but each tribe of Indians believes that the dance has its origins among themselves. Some rites and ceremonies were kept by one person or a group. These were formally passed on to another through special ceremonies that amounted to a small gesture of sharing a meal and exchanging gifts. Alanson Skinner (1920, 307) said that members of the Ponca Medicine Lodge might pass on their knowledge, by purchase, to their eldest son or nearest relative. This seems to suggest that knowledge alone was not "passed on" but would have included all paraphernalia used in those rites and ceremonies. KH said this was a common practice in his lifetime.

If this can be termed as corporate property, it would be tribally owned or clan owned in nature. Whatever was considered *Waxúbe*, or "sacred," whether owned by the clan, tribe, or an individual, could not be given away without some proper tribal custom. Some items falling under this heading included pipes, long and short staffs, medicine bundles, certain shell amulets, ceremonial robes, shirts, leggings, and moccasins. The material culture considered sacred to the owner could include some of the other items mentioned elsewhere (KH, KCH, NM, NC, AMC, AL, JP).

On occasion, a person might have ulterior motives for giving an item to a certain person in the tribe. Under these rare circumstances, some of the items considered sacred could not be given away except to other individuals who understood their significance. Should someone acquire such an item through a malapropos gesture, its signification ultimately would be lost. Therefore, in the context of giveaways, one must understand the concept of ownership. In the past it was said that individual recipients were warned not to accept gifts that might hold special meaning for the owner. In one case, whatever purpose the donor might have had in mind in the act of giving in the first place was foreseen by an elder or wiser observer who cautioned the recipient. The misuse of the types of medicines being given away, in this particular case, would bring havoc to the recipient. The person doing the giving evidently did not like the recipient for some reason. KH said the Ponca have a saying: "*Niášigà mąk'ą́ íbahą̀ mà, éi ídihidè ną́i. Niášigà íbahą̀ži mà, ínąk'à k'idè wadái . . . it'ę štì ną́i*" (In medicines, only those who understand it can handle it. If it should fall into the hands of someone who does not know its values, he can get hurt . . . even die).

10

The Old Ponca *Heǧúškà*

The *Heǧúškà* is the name of a fraternal organization of good men within the Ponca Tribe. From ancient times, the organization existed to teach the male population how to live. Men were taught from childhood to entreat and greet one another with proper social amenities, to extend aid to members of the organization and other tribal members, to speak and show compassion to tribal families in need, to recognize the economic needs of the tribe, to learn the skills of tracking and the hunt, to show respect for the religion of the Ponca people and participate in appropriate rites and ceremonies, and to defend the community with their lives, if necessary (KH, NC, AMC, AL). The dress of the *Heǧúškà* member was significant in that it represented accomplishments and deeds of bravery. Hunters, gatherers, planters, warriors, singers, and men with medicinal knowledge could be recognized for their contributions to the tribal economy and security (KH). The *Heǧúškà* of the Ponca people were organized by groups and by special skills and abilities.

Tribal historians stated that the earlier *Heǧúškà*, in Nebraska, had specific duties in the tribe. Before the Ponca removal to Indian Territory, remnants of these organizations still existed. Numbering from four or more organizations, they were called *P'áǧánìk'ì*, *Tokáǧà*, *T'é nặp'àžì*, *T'é gáxè*, *Wašná t'ặgà*, and so forth. KH and AMC said members of the *Ðíxiǧặ* and *Níkap'àšnặ* clans composed a group called *P'áǧánìk'ì* and were considered "shock troops" by the tribe. These men were required to be ready at all times to protect the community. This meant that they had to have access to weapons. Some even carried weapons with them at all times. And when they went to war, they painted their faces black with charcoal to symbolize death. The *Tokáǧà* was composed of the young men of the tribe who were proven and tested in defending the camp. The *T'é nặp'àžì* was called, as the name implies, "Not Afraid to Die." KH and AMC said this group stayed at the place of battle to the end, whether it was for victory or defeat. At dances, they stood together and danced in one place. The *T'é gáxè* was known for waiting for the enemy to come close to them before they fought—hence the name "Pretend to be Dead." The *Wašná t'ągà*, or "Big Belly group," were retired elderly men. They were known for coming to dances and showing their bravery and "toughness" to the younger men by reaching into a hot kettle of soup with their bare hands to retrieve a piece of choice dog meat. These men practiced the *Heđúška* values and were very able to defend the camp.

According to KH, the first teachings received in the *Heđúškà* organization were threefold: *Wanąp'ažigà* (overcoming fearfulness), *Wažįska k'iđagà* (making your mind clear), and *Mążáke ígip'ahągà* (being knowledgeable about your environment). Overcoming fear was probably the most challenging to members. Children, for example, can be fearful of many things. The process of instilling concepts of bravery and courage could be exciting and rewarding to each participant.

Experiences of older members, for instance, were recounted at gatherings and at home. The young men hearing these stories, although uncertain at times, were willing to meet the challenge. "Making your mind clear" meant the development of their knowledge of their immediate surroundings through peripheral vision. Learning from the elders, focusing their eyes on objects straight ahead, and concentrating on the surrounding area accomplished this. I have heard in modern times that "Indians don't look you in the eye." It is possible that this practice may still be in use. Being knowledgeable of the environment did not simply mean knowing the surroundings in the home, although that was important, but more knowing the topography of the country and wilderness. Additionally, the men had to have a willingness to explore and a clear understanding of ethical values. The following organizational values were taught to me by KH. In 1981 he reiterated them, especially how social cohesiveness developed in the membership of the organization (my translation):

Ákinąžį—This means "to depend on one another," that is, to be dependable and be willing to give aid to any member of the group when the need arose. A member had to commit his life to the welfare of all members of the *Heđúškà* group of which he was a member. If one had a particular problem, he should have been able to go to any member of his *Heḋúškà* group and ask for help and receive it. Every member had to be dependable, reliable, trustworthy, and responsible. There was no place for selfish motives in the Ponca *Heḋúškà* societies.

Ųkík'ą—The word is closely related to *Ákinąžį* and means "to help one another." The group of men who were members of a *Heḋúškà* organization was expected to help each other in every situation. When hunting season was coming, he made preparation for participation in it and helped others to prepare as well. In times of warfare, he calmly stood his ground protecting Ponca land. A good *Heḋúškà* member partook of each opportunity to give assistance to fellow warriors in every crucial incident.

Íye ákinąigà—The meaning of the word is "listen to one another" or "communicate with each other." The sayings or truisms of the Ponca all point to communication when dealing with all human situations. Therefore, appropriate communication is essential to helping and asking for help. Children admonished or reprimanded by parents for some unwanted behavior also received instruction from the *Heḋúškà* organization of which they would become a member. *Šįgažįgà ámà úwagikiáigà*, or "Speak to your children," is an ancient statement given by the elders to young parents. The many sayings of the Ponca suggest communication is the answer. It breaks down barriers if differences of feelings occur. As a member of the *Heḋúškà*, a man's communication had to be clear and concise. Assuming he followed the teachings of the organization, his words were wise and all who came into contact with him admired his teachings.

Ḋáékidaìgà—This means to "have compassion for one another." To develop a high moral character, he was instructed early on in his membership. He was told to have compassion and give to the poor and needy, and to give comfort and counsel to the bereaved. He was taught to be honest in his dealings with other men, to be truthful in his words, and to be faithful and enduring in his station in life. He always conducted himself in an ethical manner in the presence of others. He danced and gave away, not to be seen of men, but because it was instilled within him to give. He was not boastful of his deeds of bravery, because others knew him for what he was. He could be selected from his organization to serve food as *Úhąšigḋè* when a tribal feast was held. The term means and suggests "cook's helper as one who serves food." This was one of the duties of all *Heḍúškà* organizations. He was a good man in every way.

K'iwáhǫigà — This word means "to be grateful toward one another." A single word expressing thankfulness in the Ponca language is absent as in the English "thanks." Being grateful or thankful to another usually entails statements such as "you have done me a great favor," "this good thing would not have happened without you," and so forth. Mentioned elsewhere, the term *Wéšnaǫdaḍè* means "you have given me something I really need." Simply stating *Wíbḍahǫ̀*, or "I thank you," would be incomplete. Usually a statement preceded this final remark. This could be followed later by some act of reciprocation. Some members of the tribe in modern times have been said to be "stingy." These types of people have been ignored at tribal gatherings.

K'iwíkaigà — "Be truthful to yourselves" or "be prudent" is a statement that can be characterized as one of the cardinal virtues of organization members. But all was not serious talk among members. The Ponca like to tease one another. Sometimes they would make up a story to get a laugh, but all in fun. An exaggerated tale can be noticeably fabricated. For example, a man once told a true story of how he traveled north (in Ponca, *Qsni átà* "where it is cold") many days and encountered a very different kind of people. He told of their way of life and how he stayed with them for a while. At the point of completing his story, a man known for telling "stories" spoke up immediately. He said, "I, too, went on a trip. But I went way up north [in Ponca, *Qsni átaxtì*, "where it is *really* cold"] where I, too, met people. But those people I met, they didn't have any arms. And they didn't have any mouths. Anyway, they called me to eat with them." Someone asked him, "If they didn't have any arms and mouths, how could they eat?" He answered, "Oh, they just smell the food and get full." Everyone laughed, but they knew it was for the purpose of breaking the monotony that sometimes enters such gathering. Because of prudent living, social cohesiveness is solidified.

K'igḍiéžubaìgà — "Dignify yourselves" or "walking circumspectly" is a word that truly characterizes an individual who is known for fair play. His behavior also gives evidence of his status in the camp. He is cautious with his words. His attire also becomes him. His dress is appropriate for the occasion so that his appearance is identified with that status.

K'iwášḳąìgà—The word means "practice your own prowess" or "tend to your own powers of strength." The word also implies personal fortitude and physical strength. Implicit meanings suggest having the ability to evaluate and determine a solution for one's individual personal dilemma or problem. The term can be applied to the collective organization or to an individual.

The teachings of the *Heдúškà*, not unlike the Ponca *Wáwąą* and *Xдexдé*, had high ethical and moral standards, and those behavioral expectations of the *Heдúškà* became the normal criterion for all its members. Although all members were required to live by the teachings, only those who were desirous of and dedicated to those ethical codes for living found fulfillment. The organizational requirements for membership were sometimes fulfilled only in part as it was not unusual for some to ignore some of the rules (KH, NC, AMC). For most, however, the responsibilities and duties became a part of their daily living.

The Induction

A young Ponca boy could become a member of the *Heдúškà* when he reached the age of six or seven years (KH, NC, AMC). His *Heдúškà* group was required to teach him the aforementioned standards. It was a time to hear old stories of victories, defeat, and a time to learn that a man does not always win. Even though they were boys, they were instructed to be men in every human situation. From this comes the saying, *"Nú k'isíдaigà"* (Remember that you are a man). Practically every male in the Ponca Tribe in the first half of the twentieth century received this teaching from his father, his mother, and other family members.

The inductees were initially called to a meeting of the *Heдúškà* at an appointed place. They had a dinner followed by *Heдúškà* dancing. This was where the boys were brought in to be inducted into the group. In the initial meetings, the boys were instructed in the philosophy of the *Heдúškà* and Ponca way of life. AMC said as members they would learn about high moral and ethical standards. Their etiquette and behavioral standards would cause them to have better interpersonal relationships with other tribal members. There seemed to be a promulgation of these standards among their fellow tribesmen for future generations. They were encouraged to practice these values. Having been taught to be conscious of the needs of the tribe and the members of their own group of *Hedúškà*, they had to give special attention to proper etiquette at tribal gatherings. Whether it was a religious or a social function, they practiced acts of kindness to the elderly and participated in giveaways.

At the initiation, the boys were given a black eagle feather called *Mášą sábè*, which was taken from a young eagle. They were allowed to dance at their own organizational dances. With the black eagle feather tied to the hair at the crown of their head, they wore only their breechcloth and moccasins when they danced. During the winter, they wore their buckskin leggings and shirt. This feather was a lifelong ornament of the *Hedúškà* that would be worn with other earned ornamental paraphernalia (*Wékìą̀*). Other teachings given to children, according to KH, included hunting, facing the enemy, entreating strangers properly, feeding the poor, giving away to the needy, comforting the bereaved, and showing kindness to the aged, plus a sundry list of other ethical and moral teachings. In addition to the teaching they received from their *Hedúškà* group, the parents, grandparents, and other relatives of the boys also had a large part in training these young men for their responsibilities to the tribe. As they matured into manhood, when appropriate, the organization allowed them to participate in all dances and ceremonies pertaining to the tribe. Further, they were expected to participate in the protection of the camp.

The *Hedúškà* Giveaway

Among the Ponca, the act of giving away encompasses practically every formal activity. When an individual is honored, the honor is also given to his family. The family members then must reciprocate and help the one honored by giving away some things of value to others. The type of gifts in earlier times included horses, robes, or other items considered valuable. Every family obligated themselves to give when their son was inducted into the *Hedúškà* organization. This was done when the boys were first brought into the circle wearing the black eagle feather (*Mą́šą sábè*), breechcloth, and moccasins. At this first dance, the parents gave away. This finalized their induction into the *Heđúškà* organization.

The Organizational Structure of the Ponca *Heđúškà*

From time immemorial the Ponca people had the *Heđúškà* organization. When speaking to the elders of the tribe in 1965 at White Eagle, Oklahoma, they confirmed that the organization was present in the days of their grandparents and beyond. One elder thought that it could have begun in an early cultural period, such as during the Adena and Hopewell cultures. They said that the *Heđúškà* was a major source of the tribal way of teaching. They further said it was an organization that supplied the means by which the tribe provided itself security. Sylvester Warrior was a well-known singer and interpreter of Ponca *Heđúškà* songs. Being raised by grandparents whose roots were in Nebraska, he had a rich background in Ponca history and culture and was war leader of the Ponca *Heđúškà*. He gave the following description in 1968:

It was an organization of men composed of the male members of the tribe who were the warriors, leaders, and sons and grandsons of chiefs, men who were known for their ability to talk, and were good men. The structure is as follows:

Nudą́hągà—War leader . . . He chose his committee that could be from four to eight people. He was responsible for the organization. He saw to it that all the members did their duties. He gave material things to the organization and saw to it that the dances and feasts were completed accordingly . . . also helped the committee to carry out their duties.

Whip man—He was responsible to see that each man started to dance appropriately. He danced in a semicircle. When he returned, anyone who had not risen to dance, he would "whip" them to make them dance. This was done especially to young boys who were either ashamed or bashful to get up and dance.

Tail dancers—These men danced the "tail" of the song. This is the finale of the songs . . . the short ending of the songs.

Head singer—He saw to it that all the singers were there. He started the singing. After the first four songs were sung, he would turn it over to the rest of the singers. He also helped the organization by offering donations to the committee when the war leader songs were sung. These are commonly called giveaway songs today.

Water boys—The water boy's position is important. This is connected to the fact that water is life and is sacred to the tribe and this organization. He makes sure that the singers and dancers have water when it is needed.

Cook—This person is a man. He can have his own staff, but his duty is to the *Heđúškà* first, and he too must dance and give away when it is appropriate.

The *Heđúškà* organization may have more people on the committee if they want it. Among the Ponca *Heđúškà*, there is no "drum keeper." The singer usually keeps his drum in a safe place at his home. There is, however, a "keeper of the house," or *T'í'wáđì*. He is the keeper of the house of the *Heđúškà*.

The giveaway in the *Heđúškà*—Once the organization is completed, the leader places each man in the semicircle. Each man is given a seat in the circle, and he keeps that seat from then on. He cannot change his seat because he has "paid" for his seat in the War Dance circle. This applies to all members. The whip man is placed on the north side of the semicircle with one of the tail dancers. The other tail dancers sit on the opposite side.

Each of the members of the *Heđúškà* must pay for his position. Your first duty is to the organization. When you give away, it must be to the organization. However, there will be opportunity to give to others at an appropriate time. If, for instance, a whip man who had already paid for his position enters the semicircle, he must "pay" by dancing to a giveaway song or the leader's songs. If he had not paid previously, and this was the first time he enters the circle, he must give away without a song to let the people know why he is giving away. This is showing your gratitude and appreciation to the organization for being selected to be a member. You are allowed to give to your friends, but this can be done at another time when the time is appropriate. You have no obligation to members in the initial giveaway, but you can give to any one of them or all of them at some other dance.

The committee songs—There are four committee songs that require the war leader, whip man, tail dancers, and other committee members to dance and give away. At the end of the dance, you sing these committee songs. This can be done about one hour before you intend to quit dancing. The songs are sung in the following way: Two committee songs first, then the whip man, and then the cook. The head singer can get up and dance at any of these songs.

When a person has a lot to give away, he gives to persons of importance first. The person who receives the gift shakes hands with the person who gave the gift. The order of giveaway: No one in particular gets first gift. First time dance member comes into the semicircle . . . gives away to the organization and then he can give to others. There is no song in this giveaway.

The leader in the Ponca *Heđúškà* is in the organization for life. I attempted to leave my position or resign from the organization but was told that I could not do this. A leader of this nature cannot resign from the organization. This was confirmed by the elders of the tribe. Other committee members can resign. If they fail to come to a meeting one or two times, they are out automatically. It is up to the organization whether to follow this policy. In modern times, a job can take a person away for the weekend or when the dance is being held.

There is no limit to age. They start at the age of six or seven years, and this is restricted to men only. Children of a younger age should not be allowed in the circle. Women can dance only where they were sitting. They could stand up and dance in one place. Due to changes in modern times, they are allowed to get up and dance in the arena to give away. But at a regular *Heđúškà* dance, they are not allowed to dance except outside the arena.

In regard to the drum, it was highly respected. It was thought that through the drum, the people benefited from it and got a good feeling from it. In the old days, a man even spoke to the drum because it was respected. The songs are very old. They have words in them. They pertain to the enemy much of the time. They tell of battle experiences. These songs also acknowledge the present of the horse and buffalo. Stories tell of challenges of the enemy. In the *Heđúškà*, there is a song for the whistle and the crow belt. This was honorable, and he who wore it had to be a brave man, a proven man in battle. The Creator is mentioned often in these songs . . . asking the Creator to give him strength to overcome the enemy. There are songs that have no words in them.

[The elders said those songs that have no words in them in modern times were lost to the past. They say that all Ponca songs originally had some words of a story of some accomplishment or deed.] They were songs that were dreamed of or man had a vision in which these songs came to him by animals such as the wolf and coyote. Man who fasted four days to get the tune and words. They came to the Ponca in that manner. There are very few new songs sung today. Some songs were composed in regard to the servicemen who went to the first, second, and Korean War. Our songs are divided into four versions: *Hedúškà* or War Dance that includes the fast War Dance, the Trot Dance (*Sésàsà wačígaxè*), and a dance that is called Tiptoe Dance (*Nąstápʼi wačígaxè*). Also included is the so-called Soldier Dance that is essentially another form of the *Hedúškà* or War Dance. The organization dances are usually done on the weekends. They usually dance in the afternoon and at night. The Ponca people used to dance for four days. Some apparently used to dance at night and some danced in the daytime.

The tail dancers carry the coup stick. The war leader sits at the center of the semicircle. The committee members sit on each side of the leader. If, for instance, you had eight members, you would have four on each side. The war leader gives each man his seat. He keeps that seat from then on. This is done before the dance begins. Before you get ready to place your members of the *Hedúškà* organization, you may have the whip man to meet each one and to point out their seats. The war leader should stay in his position. This is because we don't want to have him walking around the dance ground. He is the headman, and his officers are there to help him. The places of seating would have to be prearranged between the war leader and the whip man. This is one of his duties.

The Dance Paraphernalia of the *Hedúškà*

A young man was allowed to wear, at the onset of his involvement with the group, the items mentioned above. However, numerous items were added to his dancing paraphernalia in the course of his life. KH gave the following as a partial list of those items (my translation):

Tʼaí wàgdą̀—This is a roach. The roach is placed on the head and tied to the hair at the crown of the head. This headpiece was worn by those members who had participated in a raid on an enemy camp or in conflict with an enemy. As a young man of about twelve or thirteen years, they might be allowed to accompany the men to hold horses, gather firewood, keep the fire going in the winter, find and bring water to the men, and other menial tasks that would contribute to the welfare of the group. This entitled the young men to wear the roach.

Mą́šą hągà—This is the center tail feather of the golden eagle and fits on the roach in an upright position. This item was added when the young man accompanied the men for the second time.

Káxè migdą̀—The crow belt—This item was an earned piece. To wear it, a *Hedúška* member had to enter into actual combat with an enemy tribe. The crow belt was composed of four different bird feathers. They were all meat eaters. These predators included the eagle, hawk, owl, and crow. Although the crow is known for eating carrion, it is also known for killing other small animals. The feathers were used to identify with the taking of life. When a warrior took a life, he added an eagle "spike" (a long wing feather) to the top of the crow belt. At the tip of the feather, he tied strands of the hair of his enemy. At another time, a second eagle "spike" completed the composition of the crow belt. Only two spikes were placed on the crow belt. If the individual had been wounded in the battle, he would be allowed to add a tail to the crow belt.

Šą́t'ągà hà—This is the skin of the wolf. The head section was worn over the right shoulder while the rest of the skin draped down the back of the man. This was also worn when hunting. Some elders have suggested that the ornament was worn during certain types of ceremonial dances.

K'áxe hà—The skin and feathers of a crow—This was an identifying item, sometimes a predator and sometimes not, of the *Hedúška* that was worn on the back of the left shoulder.

Nusí áxdadè—Bandolier—This item was worn across the chest over the left shoulder. The bottom hung on the right side where a bag was attached. The bag, depending on a given situation, could contain food or medicines. The bag was different from the tobacco pouch, which it resembled.

Niúk'igdás'į̀—This is a mirror. This item was used to signal others from long distances. The first type of mirror used was made out of shale. The shale was put inside of a wooden frame. Sometimes they decorated them according to their own clan designs.

KH, KCH, AMC, NC, and AL named other identifying paraphernalia worn for ceremonial purposes, including a decorated feather placed on a headband pointing downward in front of the face. This item seems to be the original black eagle feather, or *Mą́šą sábè*, given at the initial entrance into the organization. Other identifying ornaments included otter skin caps (*Nušną́hà wadágè*) and deer hoof noisemakers (*T'áxtì šáge' nąšádù*) tied below the knees. The men also wore armbands, wrist cuffs, hair pipe beads for breastplates, decorated breechcloths and moccasins, necklaces made of bear claws, and paints. They used red and yellow ochre, in addition to white and blue clay. Depending on the time of the year, they wore leggings, shirt, and vest. The Ponca *Hedúška* took pride in their organization and what it stood for.

The *Hedúškà* Dance

Originally, only the men danced in the circle. Women were allowed to dance outside the circle in one place. The circle was the area or arena where the *Hedúškà* dance and rituals were carried out. The dance was simple. By alternating each foot in a toe to heal movement with the beat of the drum and song, the Ponca dancer can mimic a hunting experience, a movement in battle, or any significant experience that might have affected his life. Variation of body and foot movement adds to style. According KH, AL, and NC, this dance was done at the changing of the four seasons. Some have suggested that the *Hedúškà* dance is a "war dance" and that such movement depicts a warrior's approach to his foe. Many Indians and non-Indians tell this. Perhaps this is done to dramatize the "warrior image" of the American Indians. Even though the dance may show "movement in battle," it has been said that it has nothing to do with going to or returning from war. Some elders suggested the steps and movement in the dance depict a man hunting for game. Others have said it could depict a person seeking medicines. Unfortunately, according to some of our contemporaries, it would seem that all Indians did was fight each other in combat.

In 1970 I was in attendance at the Gallup Indian Ceremonial in Gallup, New Mexico, where the San Carlos Apaches performed a "war dance." This performance was presented from a proper historical perspective because, when their ancestors fought the American soldiers (*Máhi t'ągà*), they undoubtedly prepared themselves physically and mentally for the encounter. To achieve their objective before the fight, they would dance with pistol and rifle in hand, shouting and shooting their guns.

This was what the Apaches felt and pursued in their war against the United States. That war dance was done in conjunction with intent to fight. The Ponca *Hedúškà* dance, again, did not precede or follow a war. The *Hedúškà* first should always be perceived as a society of honorable men who did good deeds, including facing an enemy in warfare.

The Origin of the Ponca *Hedúškà* as Seen through Dance and Song

The meaning of the term *Hedúškà* is unclear and cannot be clearly interpreted for loss of appropriate word meaning. The inception of the fraternal organization may have begun before the dispersion of the Middle Mississippian culture. Those tribes claiming the *Hedúškà* probably emerged from the same cultural group as the Ponca. This could account for the use of the term *Hedúškà* among other tribes, or their use of the term may simply be a corruption of the Ponca term. The difficulty in identifying the term itself does not indicate in any way that it is a derivative of other Ponca words. Words of the Ponca people are known with exception of the suffix *-dúška*, or "curved." The late Joe Rush, a noted singer of *Hedúška* songs, used this term. He said this story about a vision seen by two Ponca boys while hunting was given to him by a Ponca elder in the early 1900s. He told the story in 1975.

One time there was a group of Ponca hunters who were long ways from home. Two of them got lost from the rest of the hunters and couldn't find their way home. As they tried to find their way back, they came to a hill and climbed to the top. That's when they heard a sound that sounded like thunder or maybe a drum. On top of that hill, they looked down the other side and saw a buffalo dancing. It was stomping its hooves on the ground, and it sounded like a drum. At the tip of its horns were eagle feathers. A tail feather and a plume were on each horn. The buffalo also shook its head as it did this ceremony. That's where that word *Hedúškà* comes from. The horns of the buffalo are curved—*đúška*. That word means curved and the horns are curved, so the word means "curved horn" ... *Hé'* means horn. The eagle feathers tied on the ends of the horns got the boys' attention. The buffalo that was dancing gave this dance to the Poncas, so they called it *Heđúškà*. That buffalo said these words to them: "*Wak'áđa* sends you these words. Use this dance when you are happy or when you are sick and I will come to you with blessings." So this is how the *Heđúškà* came to the Poncas.

This story may be a part of the total story of how the fraternal group was initiated. Others have suggested the *Heđúškà* came by quixotic experiences. KH, AMC, NC, and AL said they heard that animals, such as the deer, antelope, buffalo, and elk, all contributed to the song and dance of the *Heđúškà*. The Ponca people, who were close to the natural things of the earth, found many of their beliefs in their environment as the Creator revealed them. This can be accounted for by their prayerful and spiritual life. Even though the words of the prayers have been lost in the past, the songs and the dance have been a part of the culture of the Ponca people. The elders have agreed that the term *Heđúškà* has always been the name of the Ponca fraternal organization.

The Ponca belief that the *Heđúškà* is of Ponca origin is based on the evidence of songs that relate to the Creator giving the organization to them. In an interview in 1970, Sylvester Warrior said, "This is our belief. The Creator gave us songs to go with the dance." The purpose of this section is not to claim its origin as Ponca but rather to show how the *Heđúškà* was a vital part of the total philosophy and psychology of the tribe. For example, it coincides with the philosophy of the *Wáwaą* (Pipe Dance), *Xđexđè* (Tattoo Ritual), *Ská ágđį* (One Who Sits upon the White Ceremony), and other rites and dances of the tribe. The second consensus is that the songs (of which there are hundreds) have stories of *Heđúškà* experiences that are also told in the Ponca women's *Nuđą wačígaxè* (Women's Warrior or Victory Dance), *Šąt'ągà wačígaxè* (Wolf Dance), and other forms of the Ponca *Heđúškà* dance called the *Wanąšè wačígaxè* (Soldier Dance), *Sésàsà wačígaxè* (Trot Dance), and the *Nąstáp'į wačígaxè* (Tiptoe Dance).

The techniques for preserving the history of these events over millenia might have been crude markings on sticks, poles, or even rawhide. The latter was used by Chief Standing Buffalo, as a young man, who drew a picture of a battle between the Ponca and Sioux. But the ability to keep such records would have been limited because of the wear and aging of the material and the loss of meaning of symbols. The retaining of historical events then required a medium that could not be lost. So they sang about it. The vocables in any Ponca tune are set and do not change. When words are added to the tune, the song includes some aspect of our history. The next step would be to have a new tune because the old one would become tiresome, repetitive, and boring. Songs and tunes were composed by song makers (*Waą́ gáxe*) to record historical events in the abovementioned men and women's dances. The original songs are known as *Heđúška* songs, and as such, they belong to individual members of the organization. Since the drum makes the rhythm for the *Heđúška*, the tempo should be understood. The tempo can range from a slow to a very fast beat depending on the occasion for which the men are dancing. The drumbeat for the *Heđúškà* is one steady beat. Drumrolls are also used in some of the songs.

The songs for the women's *Nuđą́ wačígaxè*, or "Victory Dance," have at least three completely different drumbeats. At the beginning, the drumbeat and song are usually very slow. After the initial songs are sung, they are followed with a roll of the drum, and the tempo for the next songs is faster and allows the women more variety in their danc- ing style. A lively one-beat tempo for some songs is sung intermittently. These songs for this particular women's dance tell the same histori- cal event as told in the men's *Heđúškà* dance and song. The complexi- ties of the vocables with words that are sung give impetus to historical retention. The tempo of the *Nuđą́ wačígaxè* drum, which is completely different from the *Heđúškà*, adds to the historical record. I would suggest to the reader that this is oral history. Non-Native historians have often said oral history was done by storytelling. This is usually depicted with artwork showing an elderly Indian sitting by a camp- fire with a group children listening to his story. That may have been done, but with the Ponca, oral history happened as described above.

The Legend of *Waą́* (Song)

It may have started out with rhythmic and repetitive chanting such as one hears from the birds and water flowing in a brook, or even from the roar of the waterfalls. It was a discovery that aided in their memories and retention of events (KH). As time passed, they entered words intermittently in their chanting. It may have been somebody who accomplished or performed a deed that benefited the people. These words would remain in the tune. Heroic deeds too were recorded. The following is an excerpt of the story of Song told by the elders (my translation):

> There was a being called *Waǫ́* (Song) in a legend told by the elders. This spiritual entity desired to dwell on this continent. It looked for places among different peoples. In those days there were many groups of people living from the big water in the east to the big water in the west. In the legend, it ultimately found the Ponca people. They were the kind of people it wanted to live among. They expressed compassion for each other. Their generosity and fairness to one another were the traits it wanted. They were a people who were attempting to find a medium to preserve their history and heritage. So Song came to live among the Ponca.

Different members of the tribe have told the legend. This short version gives the reader insight into a sometimes long story.

How the Ponca May Have Acquired the *Heḍúšk̀à* Dance

The following is an account of five hundred years' involvement in one episode in the lives of the Ponca people. According to a "winter count" in the 1800s, the Ponca in modern times recalled receiving the *Heḍúšk̀à* dance and ceremony from the Lakota. KH gave the following oral historical account:

> A group of Poncas went hunting . . . *Abaye aḍáitè* . . . they traveled several days . . . *Ą́ba ánǫžǫ̀* . . . away from the Ponca village . . . they can't find game. They're using their own provisions up. After they traveled . . . for several weeks, they ended up near a creek . . . about dried up . . . little water there. They got real hungry . . . got tired . . . no food. Some got sick . . . too weak . . . can't go any farther. So they stay there. They think maybe somebody will come by. So they stay there. After some time . . . *Ą́ba ánǫžǫ̀* . . . several days some of those men died from sickness . . . maybe starve to death . . . someone came there. One man was

watching them. This man said to another, "There's somebody watching us." After a while another man stood with him. They're looking at the Poncas. Finally, one of them come down to see. He use sign language . . . ask them who they are and what happened here . . . so they talk . . . *Wagáxaìtè*. They told him they were looking for game and ran out of food. That man left after that. He bring food . . . try to help those who are sick. They stayed with them until they feel better and could get up. They took those Poncas with them north. They say they traveled many days. When they came to their village, they stay there. They don't know where they are . . . but it was far north of where they came from. Their leaders told them about some kind of sickness and finding game. They said, "We got a way when we can't get well from no food . . . we have a dance that heals. We want you to learn about it . . . maybe your people can use it one of these days." So they learn about that war dance way . . . some songs too. After they're strong enough to go back, those people gave them provisions . . . *Umą̀ì waìtè* . . . a drum and songs to take with them. Those people took those Poncas back to the place where they first met. At that place . . . they paid respects to those who died there . . . then they went back after they thank those Sioux people for their help. So the Poncas got that dance from those people. They said they should do this dance when the New Year comes . . . that's when the grass grows to your ankles. It's then when they dance. Some call it "the dance when the grass grows in the New Year." *Pą́càamà* . . . they added new songs . . . *Heɖúškà waą́* . . . put words in them songs . . . tell about Ponca warriors . . . their deeds. They like that dance . . . enjoy dancing. For many years they carried it on . . . maybe over 250 years. We don't know what that word means . . . *Heɖúškà*. There's some old folks who said it was a way of living way back . . . when the Poncas lived along the ocean back east. Whatever it means . . . they called that dance that name, but that word has to do with how you live. Then one day after that the Poncas . . . *Ši'abaye aɖáitè* . . . went hunting and traveling, they came to a place where they saw some men lying on the ground . . . they look like they're dead. Somebody went to look close . . . come back . . . say they're not dead. These men . . . they're hungry . . . sick. So the Poncas fed them . . . took pity on them . . . encouraged them. You might say, it happened just like what happened to the Poncas 250 years before then. They took those men with them back to Ponca village where they told that story . . . how the Poncas ran into that same thing. They listened, but they don't know anything about that *Hedúškà* way . . . *Íbahạbažiíte*. They said, "Maybe our people had that one time . . . but we don't know about it." So these people learn some songs like our people did . . . many years before. They invited those people to come back after that every New Year . . . springtime. For the next 250 years they keep that . . . tradition. But later years the Poncas and the Sioux never got along . . . fight . . . like that. But those old-time Poncas always tell this story . . . how they got that *dance*. So they keep making songs and dance.

Many times oral tradition dictates to us language we do not wish to hear because of our pride and presumption that what we have has always belonged to us. Not too long ago it was said that the Japanese had to swallow their pride when it was revealed that their production of radios, televisions, and other technological devices was only a variation of American technology. Although we are not far removed from our northern brothers, we sometimes think that we are a product of our own and refuse to accept alternative thoughts concerning our material and cultural way of life. We are impelled to accept pan-Indian values as part of our heritage. Because cultures change, the Ponca *Hedúškà* has evolved into something different than was understood by our ancestors (KH).

11

New *Heⱦúŝkà* Dance Paraphernalia

The original Ponca *Heⱦúŝkà* dancer wore the already mentioned crow belt, roach, center tail feather of the eagle, and buckskin vest. About 1900, the dancer discontinued wearing the crow belt and, consequently, was referred to as the "straight dancer." Again, in modern times, to wear the crow belt was considered a great honor because its symbolism was derived from the act of participating in warfare. At the time the center tail feather was added to the young Ponca boy's roach, he actually participated in the war experience. He normally accompanied the war party only to see to it that the horses were watered and fed accordingly. He might also have been required to take food from the enemy (Dorsey 1891, 376). Other ornaments for the upper body included a choker (*Wanⱥp'į̀*) made of hair pipe bone beads. Some were trade beads that were usually made in the "netted-style" with horse's hair. A flat circular seashell (*Níkidè*) of about one and a half inches in diameter was placed on the choker center. A hair pipe beaded breastplate (*Mⱥ́gè wahí wanⱥp'į̀*) and bandolier, usually made of hair pipe beads strung together with dried mescal beans (*Wasé žídè*), were part of the upper body ornaments. An otter skin cap was worn during the winter months. According to KH, AMC, and AL, certain Ponca *Heⱦúŝkà* organizations wore the coyote or wolf skin over the right shoulder and the skin and feathers of a crow over the left shoulder. The wolf and coyote skin was used also in the bison hunt. Some hunters, it was said, wanted to get as close to the game as possible. This was during the time when the Ponca did not have horses for the hunt. A stole-like ornament made of otter skin was worn around the neck and hung down the front reaching to the waist level of the dancer. This item in modern times is attached at the back of the neck with the one end hanging down the back. The otter tail, like the skins of the wolf and coyote, as well as the feathers of the eagle, hawk, owl, and crow symbolized meat-eating predators with which the Ponca warrior identified himself. When I was fifteen, my father (KH) and my mother visited Peter LeClair near Wewela, South Dakota, on his homestead. During the visit I remember vividly the description that LeClair gave of his buffalo (bison) headdress. From the crown of the headdress, he tied the feathers of what he call "meat eaters." This included the feathers of the eagle, hawk, owl, and crow.

The otter, an aquatic mammal that feeds primarily on fish, was also thought to possess some medicinal powers. As a decorative item, the otter tail is still used by the Ponca *Heⱡúškà* dancer. Howard (1995, 64) wrote,

> Tied at the dancer's neck, so as to fall down his back and stream out behind him when he dances is a long otter skin dance tail, ornamented with beaded disks and eagle feathers. The thongs used to tie this ornament about the neck are concealed by the dancer's neckerchief. The Ponca claim to have introduced this otter skin tail into the Oklahoma area, and OYB (Obie Yellow Bull) said that formerly the otter skin was twisted and sewn round, like a rope. Those tails used at present, however, are flat.

Originally, the disks were made of quills while some were made of the formerly mentioned seashells (*Níkidè*). In addition to buckskin leggings (*Ųtą́ or Há utą́*), the *Heⱡúškà* dancer wore his breechcloth (*Žeⱡdigⱡą́*), belt (*Íp'iⱡagè*), and moccasins (*Hįbé ukéⱡį*). The dancer carried a whistle (*Nisúdè*), which was sounded at the beginning of each song and dance. In former times, the Ponca war dancer also carried his war club *(Wétì)*. In modern times, a dancer usually carries a coup stick. (The elders said the Ponca never counted coup. Therefore, they did not carry a coup stick.) One elder said the so-called coup stick may have been a faux object symbolizing the whip carried by the whip man. It was not known by the elders why the modern dancer wore sleigh bells other than to provide noise to keep in time with the drumming and singing (AL). In times past, AL said, many dancers wore deer hooves as noisemakers. Additionally, dancers carried cedar in their hands along with a fan (*Idé áganì*) of eagle feathers. KH said the Ponca received the cedar and eagle tail fan as a gift from the Creator through nature. From that day, he said, the Ponca people have honored and venerated the eagle feather and have used the cedar that heals the spirit and helps the people to reach their goals in life. It has taken on a special place in our lives, he said, and we are taught that God (*Wak'ⱥda*) will hear our prayers, see our hardships, correct the imbalance, and bring us peace.

In connection with the ceremonial dress and dance, the performance was done, in part, for the promulgation and perpetuation of religious and other socialization processes of the tribe. The song and dance, including the acts of certain rituals and ceremonies, had the additional feature of socialization toward better intratribal and personal adjustment. Consequently, the end product from this tribal activity is retention of history, social cohesiveness, and culture. From a personal perspective, the individual received an education in his tribal culture, a proper behavioral attitude toward life, respect for all people, and development of his status in the social structure of the tribe. The songs and ceremonies of the Ponca served many purposes to aid the young, as well as the aged, to understand the actions and attitudes of others. Certain types of dance activity provided opportunity for the individual Ponca to express their gratitude and benevolence to other people. This was, of course, accomplished through the giveaway songs that are sung at various gatherings.

Changes in Ceremonial Adornment

At the time when European trade goods became commonplace with the Indian people, beads began to replace quills. In modern times, or after European contact, trade cloth or broadcloth replaced much of the formerly used deer and elk skins, especially for men's leggings and women's wraparound skirts. Cotton cloth shirts and blouses too became part of everyday and dance dress. Ribbons sewn on men's shirts in place of fringes also became common. Women's skirts also had ribbons sewn around the garment's hem. In the latter parts of the 1800s and early 1900s, elaborate ribbon designs begin to appear on women's wraparound skirts. The six- to eight-inch wide designs usually were placed on the length of the front and along the hem of the garment. Women's costumes now included beaded purses and cloth with ribbon-work shawls. Strings of glass and metal beads were worn in the earlier part of the 1900s. Now modern hair styles included the eagle plume and beaded hair ties, which are worn in the front rather than the back. Hair pipe beads strung perpendicularly are also worn on the front and back.

Changes in the Ponca *Hedúškà* dance paraphernalia took on the look with feathers. This dance costume (which it was—a costume) was instigated and encouraged during the era of the 101 Ranch by its owners because customers from the East wanted to "see Indians with feathers"—with lots and lots of feathers. So the former crow belt became a large feathered bustle. Not one but two bustles. The smaller one placed above the larger one on the upper back of the dancer. A feathered headdress or roach was also worn. A uniform color scheme of feathers was created by the dancer to his individual likes. The original single "tail," which was earned by a warrior who was wounded in the legs, was now replaced on the new fancy dance costume with two tails. The tail was symbolic of being wounded. The "fancy" dance costume also consisted of either sleigh bells or goat bells worn around the lower legs just below the knees. Some of the fancy dancers today have returned to the deer hoof noisemakers, in addition to a beaded belt, a necklace, a headband, a metal or beaded armband, cuffs or gauntlets, and a suspender-like ornament hanging from the shoulders. They also wear ankle bands made of some long-haired animal skin and fur, such as that of the Angora goat.

The use of the enlarged eagle bustle in modern powwows also has its origins in the crow belt. This excessively large bustle, now very popular, has become significant as an ornament of the so-called traditional dancer. Usually the dancer will wear the bustle with the roach, hair pipe breastplate with glass and metal beads interlaced, metal armbands, wide belt, breechcloth, buckskin leggings, goat bells or deer hoof noisemakers, and moccasins. He may or may not wear leggings. A variety of other paraphernalia is attached to the bustle, to the tail, to the belt, or around the neck, arms, and head. Some dancers attach one or two feathers extending from the roach outward or a decorated stick extending from the roach with a feather or two dangling at the end of the stick. Others have used feathers fanned out in front of the roach, giving the appearance of a pioneer woman bonnet. Same type of fanned-out feathers is sometimes attached to the shoulders. A circular beaded ornament that may be multic olored or may have at least four colors in its four sections is sometimes attached to the belt or below the belt. Other strips of decorations also hang from the belt. The modern traditional dancer has ornaments that are significant to his likes and tastes. It also appears that much of the costume is pan-Indian. One young man who has been photographed often indicated through friendship with dancers of other tribes that he has received gifts of several pieces of dance equipment. Some of the elders said that this was an age-old practice of the *Heðúškà* organization. But under the old order of the *Heðúškà*, the ornaments were passed on from veteran members to the younger men who had earned the right to wear them.

According to the elders, the original items worn by members of the Ponca *Heðúškà* were made very plain and simple. Some tribal craftsmen, in modern times, have attempted to keep their work simple; however, those requesting certain items desire more than the common decorations used by dancers. The simplistic approach to making ornaments was part of Ponca living. This was in line with the Ponca's former philosophy that espoused inconspicuousness as a virtue. To exhibit one's self publicly would be to elevate one's image to a status above others. This kind of behavior was thought to be showy and arrogant. But alas, times have changed. As years pass, changes continue in the dance paraphernalia.

Dance Contests

In this century, acculturation processes affected practically every aspect of Indian life. The loss of religion and ceremonialism in the social realm, as well as food gathering and hunting in the economic sphere, have resulted in adaptation to the dominant thought of the Western philosophy of competition. This could only be achieved if one was mentally, physically, and emotionally prepared to enter the domain of the non-Indian. Even with this ideology, many still displayed their tribal heritage through dance and song. Thus came the opening for competition in the dance arena. Consequently, questions like, "Who is the best dancer?" or "Who dresses the best?" had to be answered through contests. The Ponca, who are known for their retention of *Heðúškà* songs and dance, have claimed the title as the home of "Where Champion Meets Champion." This slogan is used in connection with the annual Ponca powwow. This claim was made in 1926, when Augustus McDonald won the first fancy dance contest held at the Haskell Institute at Lawrence, Kansas (now Haskell Indian Nations University). Since that time, many dancers from various Indian tribes have won the title of world's champion. Some dancers of the Ponca Tribe who have been outstanding and have won this title and trophy include Henry Snake, Andrew Snake, Dennis Roughface, Wilbur Waters, Rudolph "Rudy" New Moon, Vance Buffalohead, Clyde Warrior, James "Pee Wee" Clark, Edward Calls Him, and R. G. Harris. Other champions from surrounding tribes include Nick Webster, Elmer Brown, Johnny Moore, George Watch Taker, Charles Chibitty, Ted Moore, Robert Murray, and Larry Daylight. Contests for children's fancy dance also became a part of the main event in dance competition. Costumes for the fancy dance are known today as "feather costumes." Men as well as boys must be in perfect physical condition to maintain the speed and rhythm provided by song and drum. The simple toe to heel dance in the *Heđúškà* dance is done with variation of step and movement to the beat of the drum. Since rhythm, speed, and style are essential in professional dance, the contestant must also know the song and beat of the drum in order to stop on time. Keeping abreast with new "trick songs" is essential if one expects to win contests.

A straight dance contest is also included in the powwow dance competition. The dress style of the original *Heđúškà* described above is found in this dance contest. Although there is a slight variation of the dance dress, it still is identified by tribal members as the straight dance costume. This form of *Heđúškà* dance is slow, allowing dancers to show dignity and eloquence in their steps. This dance is a difficult contest to judge because each dancer shows their personal steps. But the dance contest continues to be one of the favorites of the audience because of its historical importance to the tribe. In recent years, young boys of about seven or eight years of age have competed in the dance competition in the straight dance category. These boys are competing in straight dance in part because their parents wish to return to the old dance dress style of the early 1900s.

In recent years, a new look in dance paraphernalia has taken the powwow world. The above described "traditional dancer" now is popular in contest circles. These elaborate costumes add to the dancer's appearance of fierceness. The songs and drumbeats are usually slow, unlike in the fancy dance competition, and require the dancer to add his own steps and body movements. Once called the "sneak-up" dance, this dance mimics the warrior's approach to his foe. Colorful and lively, the traditional dancer now has a big part in the powwow dance competition.

The Powwow Princess

Like all of modern America, Indian communities too have to select their princesses to represent their tribes at special gatherings for one year. During the first years of selecting a princess for the Ponca dance gathering, a young woman was chosen by the prominence of her family and personal beauty. Christine Calls Him, my sister, was the first to be selected in 1936. In modern times, the criteria by which young women are chosen include their interest in tribal culture, education, beauty, and congeniality. Throughout the year, they are expected to represent the tribe at intertribal gatherings and dances. Unlike non-Indian pageant winners, the Indian princess and family are required to give much of their time and money. These young women must have parents who are willing to support them during the year so that they can attend and participate in all tribal dances. If the princess is invited to be "head woman dancer" at a dance, for example, the young lady is expected to give away gifts to some of the people in the audience. This usually does not present a problem for the parents or grandparents, as they feel a sense of being honored by these types of invitations and relatives and friends usually help. On occasion, the princess too could be a recipient of gifts from others, such as male head dancers or head singers.

12

The Ponca Singers

The Ponca singer must have ability and talent to sing and recall songs. The elders have stated that individuals who are tone-deaf should not sing. A natural singer is one who possesses the ability both to sing and to recall songs. There are no books and page numbers nor titles in Ponca singing. A Ponca singer must also have coordinated rhythm because he must keep time of his singing with the beating of the drum with his fellow singers. Singing and drumming takes the special talent to sing fixed vocables that are set and are never changed. A singer cannot make slurs or stops when there are none, and he must maintain a constant blending of voice with his fellow singers. The unique harmony of voices is recognized by inflection, resonance, and modulation. Unlike a choral arrangement in which singers maintain tempo for soprano, alto, tenor, and bass, the Ponca singer must keep tempo in unison with drumbeat and song. Songs then are performed with enthusiasm and feeling. The musical element of crescendo suggests that the singing is good and dancing becomes a great joy; they complement each other.

The inspiration that caused men to sing and make songs is an integral part of the creative mind of the Ponca people. Some Ponca singers in the 1890s made cylinder recordings. Only vaguely recalled, these men carried the tradition of learning and singing into the twentieth century. From the American Folklife Center at the Library of Congress in Washington DC in the 1960s, Sylvester Warrior acquired copies of a few songs recorded before the turn of the century. Although there were other singers present, the principal Ponca singers associated with these early recordings were Frank Eagle, Old Man MacDonald, Chief White Eagle, and Francis LeFlesche Sr., who was largely responsible for having the recordings done. This was the first glimpse of Ponca singers retaining songs.

The elders remembered singers of the early to mid-1900s, such as

Oscar Makes Cry, Big Kansas, Pete Washington, Albert Makes Cry Sr., Robert Little Dance, Leonard Smith, Charley Waters, Tim Little Voice, Francis Eagle, Hugh Eagle, McKinley Eagle, Franklin No Ear, Josiah Thicknail Sr., Adam LeClair, Logan DeLodge, Turner "Snake" Elk, and William Kemble. An Otoe Indian by the name of Morgan Faw Faw used to sing with the Ponca in the early part of the century (KH, AMC, NC, AL, JP). Mid-twentieth-century singers joined the older men and carried on the tradition. Some of those singers were Sylvester Warrior, Louis Yellowhorse, Lamont Brown, Russell Rush, Joe Rush, Harry Buffalohead, Bob Collins, and Albert Waters. In the latter half of the century, many singers emerged who were related to the previous generation of singers. Now all deceased, they were John Kemble, Ellsworth Kemble, Eli Warrior, Roland No Ear, Max No Ear, and Edwin Little Cook. Those in the later generation who are still actively singing are Oliver Little Cook, Henry Collins, Douglas Eagle, and Wilkie Eagle. In every generation, new singers arise, but only those who take time to learn the songs and their stories are successful. Those who are of mixed Ponca blood also sing. Some of these, in modern times, were Edwin Hinman, Maynard Hinman, James "Pee Wee" Clark, and Wilford Clark. Still leading songs of this group are Kinsel Lieb and Jimmy Kemble. These men are well-known singers who know every Ponca song. They, like other Ponca singers, are capable of composing songs for veterans, prominent families, and other significant individuals and occasions.

The Songs

Music has always been a vital part of the Ponca culture. In its unique application, the Ponca people have used music in preserving their history, documenting events, honoring leaders, recalling acts of bravery and accomplishments, or simply, dancing. The depth of its usage is not fully known to us, yet we can understand its emotional qualities that reach even to the youngest of our tribal members. That "something" that attracts and holds us spellbound when we hear our songs perhaps comes from man's innermost being. In it are pride, humility, self-esteem, respect, reverence, dignity, and sundry other religious and social characteristics significant to the Ponca people. Whether for religious purposes and prayers or for the joy of dance and expression, the Ponca people sing their songs. Our music's origins are from times unknown to us. We only know that we have always sung. It must have been in prehistoric times that it began. Harry Buffalohead told me the following legend of Song (my translation):

> In the legend of Song (*Waą́*), it is said that Song was a person. He had sought out a place to dwell throughout this continent and could not find rest. Traveling from people to people, he tried to find a path that led into their camp but was unable to find it. Then one day, he found the people who were doing what he was seeking. He saw that these people were worshiping the Creator through their music. This was how he found the path that led to the Ponca. You might say that path was a path that led to the heart of man. From the heart came every emotion—joy and happiness to anger and hatred. But here, the Poncas were seeking a way to live that they might have peace of mind. So it was that Song said, "Here are the people that I am seeking. Here, I will stay. Here, I will make my home."

The legend of Song perhaps is the basis of Ponca songs. Through inspiration, the Ponca people perceived the natural world that gave them their songs. Sounds of thunder, wind, and rain; sounds from rushing waters; from large and small animals; from birds and insects; even sounds from man himself gave them chants. These sounds, in turn, were followed by words of wisdom, prayers, accomplishments, words that describe good deeds, words that praised man, and words about animals and their contributory existence to mankind. These were all recorded in the songs. The songs also told of specific places and individual incidents. At times, only two or three words are present in the singing, but stories told by parents and grandparents give the chants and words meaning. In modern times, many of the stories have been lost, except for a few that have been retained. This is how history is retold through singing.

The Ponca Drum

The drum was made of bison hide in the early days. The hide was cleaned of hair and stubble and stretched over a hollow log. The Ponca called it *Néxegak'ù*. The act of beating the drum is *Gak'úgè*. In modern times, the drum is called *K'úge*. For the Ponca, the drum is the center of the dance arena. Its prominence is important to the people because with it singers relate that which is historical and religious. The drum resonates in all directions and equally touches those who hear it and become part of it in the dance experience. Harry Buffalohead said that when people "get up and dance around the drum, all their sicknesses leave them." As the dancers proceed clockwise around the arena, they feel an affinity to the drum. The drum is, therefore, in the center.

According to Edwin Little Cook, there are probably more than four different beats (tempos) for songs and dances. For the *Heđúškà* dance, the cadence is one even beat. The tempo can be slow to fast. Three strong beats indicate the chorus of the song. Toward the end of the song, one strong beat is given to indicate the end of the song. The slow *Heđúškà* song always has the chorus sung. In the Ponca *Heđúškà* organization, only the "tail dancers" are allowed to dance the finale, as indicated earlier. The *Nąstápʼi* and *Sésàsà* dance styles are variations of the *Heđúškà*. As mentioned, songs for these dances tell the same stories told in the regular *Heđúškà* dance songs. The drumbeat is about the speed of a trotting man. Unlike the regular slow *Heđúškà* songs, in which the two or more vocables or words are held within drumbeats, the rhythm of the vocables and words of the *Nąstápʼi* and *Sésàsà* are at a different counterpoint with the beat of the drum so that they play against each other. Ray Cantwell, a non-Indian musician, listened to the drumbeat and song to determine the above musical description. Additionally, the chorus is not sung at the end of these songs.

Another variant of the *Heđúškà* dance is the *Wanąšè wačígaxè*, or "Soldier Dance." The dance style is movement from the right to the left in a side-step motion. As the dancers proceed around, the left leg is lifted with a slight snap with each step. All dancers are in accord in a single line encircling the drum. Each dancer is in step with the lead dancer. The drum tempo is one strong beat followed by a soft beat. Songs for this dance too tell of the same story in the *Heđúškà* dance.

The Women's Dance, *Nudá wačígaxè*, has a faster dance step than the Soldier Dance, although the dance style is similar. Dependent on the song, there may be some variation in the dance step. The drumbeat in these songs may include a drumroll at the beginning of the dance. It is followed by a very slow tempo. Other songs have a drumbeat somewhat like the Soldier Dance but more pronounced; that is, they have one strong beat followed by a soft beat. Another woman's dance called the *Šąt'ągà wačígaxè* (Wolf Dance) has a much faster beat. These songs also relate to the stories told in the *Heđúškà*. Women participating in this dance usually begin by taking short single steps in time with the drumbeat. At the chorus of the song, the women stop and dance in one place. Then they resume the single step.

The *Ská ágđį* (One Who Sits upon the White Dance) for women has nothing to do with the *Heđúškà*. The drumbeat is a single slow cadence. The dance step is a slow walk in time with the drumbeat. Songs have no words but connote matters pertaining to life, such as times of calmness or contentment in life, sickness, death, and ultimately, victorious accomplishments. The beginning songs require a drumroll followed by a very slow beat of the drum. In the finale songs of this ceremonial dance, victory is evidenced by the fast single beat of the drum. The dance is lively, and the dancers add their own style (KH, AMC, AL, NC, JP).

Requests for Ponca Singers

From earliest times, Ponca singers were requested to come and sing at other tribal celebrations and dances. In the due course of time, when the tribe was established on its reservation in Indian Territory, its members were invited to come and visit other neighboring tribes. Usually the tribes having a close affinity to the Northern Plains traditions were located in the north, west, and southwest parts of Indian Territory.

Very common to the Ponca was friendship with the Osage Tribe. Along with the Kaw and Quapaw Tribes, they spoke the same language with minor differences in the dialects. The Osage, who, in early twentieth century, acquired wealth from oil resources, often called on the Ponca singers to come and sing at their annual dances. In 1997 at his home in Bethany, Oklahoma, Albert Makes Cry Jr. told me of a typical experience of his family singing at Gray Horse, Oklahoma. Still fluent in the Ponca language, he related the following (my translation):

> At the Gray Horse annual Osage dance, the Ponca singers were the drummers and singers in the early 1900s. Approximate start-up of these dances coincided with the established wealth of that tribe. The Ponca singers were invited from the beginning to provide the songs for

the dance occasion. From earliest times, those singers involved with theses dances included Pete Washington, Grandpa Oscar Makes Cry, Papa Albert Makes Cry Sr., Charley Waters, and Bob Little Dance. One man of their tribe called "Old Man Osage" sang with the Poncas. They sang at all these camps and made some songs for some Osages. Ponca dancers who went over there were Dennis Roughface, Henry Snake, Gus McDonald, Frank C. War, Frank Buffalo, and Charles LeClair. Sometimes the elderly men of the Ponca Tribe joined in the dances. They were George Eagle, Robert Washington, Old Man Crazy Bear, Ed Smith, and Charles Pappan. At times other Ponca dancers came. They were Franklin No Ear, Alfred No Ear, Perry Crazy Bear, Andrew Snake, Norman Kemble, Albert Cole, Willie C. War (he was just a boy), and Fred Roy . . . and Julia Roy who married Edgar Maker, an Osage, was always present at the dances.

An Osage friend, Mrs. Watson, from Gray Horse, referred to Grandpa Oscar Makes Cry as grandfather and had established a relationship with the Ponca through this friendship. Also a Mrs. Pryor was also a friend of the Ponca. Patricia Butler, of the Watson family, considered Papa Albert Makes Cry Sr. as an uncle. Grandpa Oscar made a song for Josephine Pryor. Our family did not live off the Osages while they were there. But they used to bring us food or what they called rations. The Osages did not have the war dances until the 1920s. Their costumes were new and were very well made. They practiced their old Indian ways and showed their generosity to everybody. It goes back to that old saying that an Indian, if he has anything, he's going to give you part of what he has.

Other Ponca singers who sang at various tribal events and pow-wows throughout the state are mentioned above. Many stories can be told of how the Ponca singers established their reputation as great singers around the country.

Knowledgeable Non-Ponca Men Who Sing Ponca Songs

In recent years, Ponca songs have been of interest to many singers among many tribes. Among Indian people, it is not unusual for any individual to want to learn something from another tribe of people. Morgan Faw Faw of the Otoe Tribe and "Mutt" Pratt, a Pawnee tribal member who had sung with the Ponca, were well-known singers of Ponca songs. A Kiowa Indian by the name of Jim Anquoe and his son Jack Anquoe were considered excellent singers and were informed on the history of the songs. Melvin Pacquin, a Zuni Indian, learned and leads Ponca songs at various Indian powwows in the Great Southwest. Even one of the strongest traditionalist tribes in the United States, the Navaho, or *Diné*, now sing Ponca songs at their powwow events. A group of Ponca singers led by Johnson Taylor Jr. in Ignacio, Colorado, called themselves the "Yellow Jackets." They are of the Southern Ute tribe. In Baltimore, Maryland, a group of white hobbyist singers led by Dr. Jon Orens sings Ponca songs at their annual and special dances.

Ponca singing groups have been invited to sing at celebrations such as the Red Earth intertribal event in Oklahoma City. Usually there are many singing groups present at these types of events. According Oliver Little Cook, among the Indian tribes, singing groups are referred to as "drum groups" or "drums." Groups have names such as Fort Oakland Ramblers, Yellow Hammer, Southern Boys, Southern Thunder, Yellow Spotted Horse, and Ponca Singers. These particular groups are all Ponca drums. Although Ponca in origin, these groups sometimes include men from neighboring tribes. Each group of singers is composed of men who have sung together for a period.

13

Ponca *Heđúškà* Songs

In this chapter, the discussion of Ponca *Heđúškà* songs is limited to only a few songs. The number of songs composed by Ponca song makers would fill pages with accounts of leadership, heroism, valor, hunting expeditions, acts of compassion, deeds of mercy, and prayers to *Wak'áda* for guidance. Included also are atrocities committed on the enemy in retaliation. These songs may have been one of the reasons why the Ponca were called *P'a máse*, or "head cutters."

After members of the *Heđúškà* had been notified of and had prepared for an upcoming dance ceremony, they met at the designated *Heđúškà* Keeper of the House (*T'iáđį*) for their group (KH, AL, AMC, NC). Each Ponca *Heđúškà* organization had an agenda to follow as it began a dance. This essentially consisted of singing special songs intermittently with rituals. The first four songs were sung at the beginning of the dance. No one dances to these songs. However, they each had a purpose in the organization. The following is an interpretation of a typical Ponca *Heđúškà* dance procedure and the songs used:

BEGINNING SONGS

a. The Calling Song
b. Song for Bringing in the *Heđúškà* Pipe
c. Song for the Receiving of the *Heđúškà*
d. Pipe Lighting Song

a. The Calling Song was used to call all members of the *Heđúškà* into the circle. Once the dance rituals began, latecomers were told to stay back until the war leader (*Nudá hągà*), at a given time, allowed them to take their seat. The Calling Song is as follows:

| Leader starts song: | Ya ha e ya ha e ho we yo he đè đè |
| Singers second song: | Ya ha e ya ha e ho we yo he đè đè |

Ya a ha ya e ya ha ya eho we yo he ɖè ɖè

Ya a ha ya e ya he yo he yo he ya eho we
yo he ɖè ɖè

Ya a ha ya e ya ha ya eho we yo he ɖè ɖoì

Chorus of song: *Heɖúškà Wak'ą́da dą́babè* yo e ho we yo
he ɖè ɖè

Ya a ha ya e ya ha e ho we yo he ɖè ɖoì

The term *Haskáɖą̀* (the flag) in the twentieth century replaced the nineteenth-century *Wak'ą́da* (AL, AMC). This was probably owing to the allegiance the Ponca felt they owed to the United States. Many Ponca served in the foreign wars. Each song phrase also begins with the leader starting a particular song. The rest of the singers join in as they "second," or repeat, the same phrase of the song that continues into the chorus and the remainder of the song.

Interpretation: Most of the song is composed of vocables that suggest getting the attention of the members.

Heɖúškà Wak'ą́da dą́babè. "The mystery power (God) is looking upon the *Heɖúškà*."

b. The Song for Bringing in the *Heɖúškà* Pipe was sung after the war leader had spoken and had given the purpose of the meeting and dance. At this time, every person within the dance circle and others who might be visiting outside the circle were required to arise from their sitting position. The song is as follows:

Leader starts song: *Ųhé šubɖé mą́ši ną̄žį́ga*

Singers second song: *Ųhé šubɖé mą́ši ną̄žį́ga*

    Mąbɖíáɖìhè ąɖą́baigà, mą́ši ną̄žį́ga

    Ųhé šubɖé mą́ši ną̄žį́ga

Chorus of song: *Žįɖé mąbɖíáɖìhè ąɖą́baigà, mą́ši ną̄žį́ga*

    Ųhé šubɖé mą́ši ną̄žį́ga

Interpretation: *Ųhé šubɖé mą́ši ną̄žį́ga.*

    "Arise where I come walking."

Mạbdíádìhè ạdą́baigà, mą́ši nąžį́ga.

"Arise, and behold where I walk."

Ụhé šubdé mą́ši nąžį́ga yo he dè doì.

"Arise where I come walking" (plus vocables).

Žį́dé, mabdíádìhè adą́baigà, mą́ši nąžį́ga.

"Elder brother, arise and behold the place where I walk."

c. The Song for the Receiving of the *Hedúškà* was usually sung after the pipe had been brought in. Following the prayer, the third song was sung.

Leader starts song:	*Hedúškà te dédù waí'bè* yo he dé dè
Singers second song:	*Hedúškà te dédù waí'bè* yo he dé dè
	Hedúškà te dédù waí'bè
	Te dédù waí'bè yo he dè yǫ he ya ha
	Hedúškà te dédù gáxabè yǫ he dé doì
Chorus of song:	*Hedúškà te dédù waí'bè*

The interpretation shows only the words or statements in the song. The pipe bearer set the pipe and other paraphernalia in front of the war leader. After the people sat down, the leader arose to speak to the members of the *Hedúškà* organization and offered a prayer or designated someone to pray.

Te dédù waí'bè yo he dé yǫ he ya ha

Hedúškà te dédù gáxabè yǫ he dé doì

Interpretation:	*Hedúškà te dédù waí'bè.*
	"The *Hedúškà* was given to us here."
	Te dédù waí'bè.
	"It was given to us here" (plus vocables).
	Hedúškà te dédù gáxabè yǫ he dé doì.
	"The *Hedúškà* was made here" (plus vocables).

d. The *Hedúškà* pipe-lighting ritual was done after the foregoing song had ended. The pipe bearer removed the pipe from the encasement and handed it to the war leader. The length of the stem was three to four feet; therefore, it had to be lit by the pipe bearer. The pipe bearer started a fire by using flint, cottonwood tree pulp, and a striking stone. Once the pulp caught fire, small branches were set aflame. According to KH, NC, and AL, if the dance was held at night, a branch was taken from the main fire to the east of the dance area. The pipe bowl was filled with tobacco and kinnikinnick. The leader then began to draw on the stem while the pipe bearer placed the flaming stick to the tobacco. Once the tobacco was lit, the leader stood, stepped forward with it, and raised the mouthpiece to the four winds, giving thanks to the Creator. Then the pipe bearer took the pipe to each member, proceeding counterclockwise, and they each smoked the pipe (KH, NC, AL). He then took the pipe to the center, where the singers also smoked the pipe. It was then returned to the war leader. The Pipe Lighting Song was then sung as follows:

Leader starts song:	*Nudą́ hągà įwįdabè, Nudą́ hągà įwįdabè*
Singers second song:	*Nudą́ hągà įwįdabè, Nudą́ hągà įwįdabè,*
	įwįdabè, Ahaú, įwįdabè yo he đé đé đoì
	Nudą́ hągà įwįdabè yo he đé đoì
Chorus of song:	*Nudą́ hągà, niní đetè íđašudetè įwįdabè*
	Ahaú, įwįdabè yo he đé đé đoì
	Nudą́ hągà įwįdabè yo he đé đoì
Interpretation:	*Nudą́ hągà, įwįdabè.*
	"The war leader has told me."
	Ahaú, įwįdabè.
	"Accordingly, I have been told."
	Nudą́ hągà, niní đetè íđašudetè įwįdabè.
	"When the war leader blew the smoke, he told me."

One of the war leader's many responsibilities was to inform the members of the meaning of the use of the *Heđúškà* pipe, that is, its sacredness to the organization, its symbolic representation of prayers rising to *Wak'ą́da*, the respect it deserved, and its use in the circle.

The procedure from this point began with the songs of the *Heđúškà*.

Some of the first songs are those pertaining to the *Heɗúškà*. These songs have words relating to the organization. Some of the songs with words say in effect: "God gave us the *Heɗúškà*," "Arise (and dance) *Heɗúškà*," "He gave to us the crow belt," and so forth. Usually old songs that have no connection to anyone follow these. The purpose of this process was said to be to give respect to those men and women whose lives are lost in memory, to afford them a time for remembrance. Harry Buffalohead said these songs, in some cases, were common songs and were used to "warm up" for the more active songs. He said, "*Waą́ úxt'ažìtè, éi p'ahą́gà ą́' nąi̧*" (They sing the uninteresting songs first). He said the songs could be divided up between "uninteresting songs" and "very interesting songs" and "from slow to fast song." A "head singer," he said, "needs to control these songs. Some singers don't know any better and will start a good lively song in the wrong place, or a slow song in the wrong place." He added, "The beat of the drum and song should keep pace as the dance moves on. Each set of songs usually moves up to a livelier pace, and the better songs are sung for each level." He said, "There is a time in there, when they'll call for committee member's songs or other individual songs."

AL said if the head singer wants to do it, he could lead out in either the *Sésàsà* or *Nąstáp'i̧* songs. These are the "Trot" and "Tiptoe" songs. When the singers sing these songs, they sing a whole set of them. He said, "*Waą́tè, bɗúgà é'kigą́ ą́' nąi̧*" (The songs are of the same type). Like the regular *Heɗúškà* songs, when these songs are sung, they are sung in sets. He said a set of songs used to be composed of eight songs sung consecutively. Some say four are a set. Some wordless songs are usually sung early at the start and are sung intermittently throughout the dance.

Songs for the officers of *Heɗúškà* organization
   a. Song for the *Nudą́ hągà* (war leader)
   b. Song for the Whip Men
   c. Song for the Tail Dancers
   d. Song for the Cook
   e. Songs for other committee members

The officers of the *Heɗúškà* organization (committee members) had songs they were required to arise and dance to. These songs were not necessarily sung as a part of any dance but were sung when the time was appropriate. During those times, these leaders were required to give away material goods. The following are songs for leaders of the *Hedúškà* organization:

a. The Song for the War Leader, or *Nudą́ hągà*, was to recognize and show respect and honor to him for his leadership and dauntless courage. The song is as follows:

Leader starts song:	E ya ha i he i he đe he ya ya he yo
Singers second song:	E ya ha i he i he đe he ya ya he yo
	E ya ho wi he i he đe đe *Nudą́ hągà*
	Nąžį́ge yo he đe đe
	E ya ha wi ha i ha i ha he *Nąžį́ge* yo
	he đe đoì
Chorus of song:	E ya ho wi he i he đe đe *Nudą́ hągà Nąžį́ge*
	E ya ha wi ha i ha i ha he *Nąžį́ge* yo he
	đe đoì
Interpretation:	Most of the tune is composed of vocables.
	Nudą́ hągà Nąžį́ge.
	"Arise! War leader."

b. The Song for the Whip Men was to recognize and show respect to the men whose duty it was to keep order in the dance circle. According to Sylvester Warrior, the whip men were responsible for seeing to it that the younger men participated in the dance.

Leader starts song:	Ya e he ya ya e he ya ya ho we yo he đe đe
Singers second song:	Ya e he ya ya e he ya ya ho we yo he đe đe
	Ya e he ya ya e he ya ya e he ya ya e he ya
	Waną́še ke nąžį́ge yo he đe đoì
Chorus of song:	Ya e he ya ya e he ya ya e he ya ya e he ya
	Waną́še ke nąžį́ge yo he đe đoì
Interpretation:	Vocables. *Waną́še ke nąžį́ge.*
	"Arise! Whip men."

c. There is no current information on the Song for the Tail Dancer. Tail dancers, according to tribal elders, are those Ponca warriors who stayed at the battle site when the fight was over. This was to ensure that there would be no further fighting or to see to it that the enemy was not making a second attempt to attack. They stayed in the area as the main body of Ponca warriors started for home. They then left the battle site to return home. In every *Heðúškà* song, the chorus is sung after every dancer has returned to his seat. Only those who have been designated as tail dancers danced to this part of the song. In modern times, there are several groups of men from the Osage Tribe who have been designated as tail dancers. At the annual *Heðúškà* dance at White Eagle, for instance, several men from their respective tribal *Heðúškà* organizations serve as representative tail dancers for their group.

d. The Song for the Cook was normally sung before the meal was to be shared. According to AL, there were two cook songs. One was used to bring the dance to a halt and share the meal. The second one was used to honor the cook. This gave him opportunity to give away material goods. The first song is as follows:

Leader starts song:	*T'iát'à í ðabè,* ðe he ðo ho
Singers second song:	*T'iát'à í ðabè,* ðe he ðo ho
	T'iát'à í ðabè, ðe he ðo ho *úhà ní'dè* ho
	T'iát'à í ðabè yo he ðe ðoì
Chorus of song:	*T'iát'à í ðabè,* ðe he ðo ho *úhà ní'dè* ho
	T'iát'à í ðabè yo he ðe ðoì
Interpretation:	*T'iát'à í ðabè, ðe.*
	"Start to come into the house, now"
	(plus vocables).
	T'iát'à í ðabè, ðe he ðo ho úhà ní'dè.
	"Start to come into the house, now.
	The cooking is done" (plus vocables).

e. Songs for other committee members were sang at appropriate times in the course of the dance in keeping with the rules of the organization. Currently, some of these songs are sung at tribal dances in honor of individuals who serve in some capacity for the dance.

Song for Women Singers

This song was especially made for the women singers according to Sylvester Warrior. He said they were a part of the Ponca *Heḍúška* organization but sat outside the semicircle of the dance area. They, in the Ponca language, were called *Úḍazè*. The term refers to a person who would chime in on the ongoing singing. This was done on the chorus of the song, and the women singers would gradually increase the volume toward the ending of the song. In the "old days," according to AL, the women would not stop simultaneously with the drumbeat but would hold the final vocable or word trailing off to silence. However, there were particular songs when they were not allowed to do this. There were many songs when this could not be done. This song made for the women singers gave them opportunity to dance and give away in modern times.

Leader starts song:	Ya e ha ya he ya ha we yo he ḍe yo he ya e ya
Singers second song:	Ya e ha ya he ya ha we yo he ḍe yo he ya e ya
	Ya e ha ya ya he ḍe ha we yo he ye ḍe yo he ya e ya
	Ya a ho we yo hi ye ya he yo
	He ya he ha e ha ya ho we yo he ḍe yo he ya a yo
	Ya e ha ya ya a ho we yo he ḍe ḍǫì
Chorus of song:	*Heḍúškà tè ḍe wit'ą́ge nąžį́ga waḍą́babè* yo he ye ḍe yo he ya e ya
	Ya a ho we yo hi ye ya he yo
	He ya he ya e ha ya ho we yo he ḍe yo he ya a yo
	Ya e ha ya ya a ho we yo he ḍe ḍą̀
Interpretation:	Vocables *Heḍúškà tè ḍe wit'ą́gè nąžį́ga waḍą́babè.*
	"The *Heḍúškà*, this [way of life], elder sister arise and behold the way."

Individual Songs

These songs originally were sung during the course of the dance. While the Ponca lived in the North Country, according to KH, they danced simply to the singing of songs. And those songs were the "earned" songs of members of the *Heđúškà* as well as other songs about tribal incidents or significant individuals. They were the songs that the organization danced by. Over the years, some of the songs were "put back in the drum" because the original owner of the song was deceased. Some families too want the songs "put back in the drum." This means they wish their family song to be sung anytime, at any *Heđúškà* dance. An individual song in modern times is usually requested by the individual who wishes to give away material goods. The composition of songs is based on events occurring within the tribe during the year.

VBSH told the story of how her husband, *Gakúwįxè* (Chief Headman), was in a small conflict with the Sioux that ended in the death of several Ponca men.[1] She related how he and ten other Ponca men were on a hunting expedition when they were accosted by a Sioux war party. Under no circumstances does one run from danger, she said. The Ponca took cover behind a small knoll and begin firing back at the enemy. The following is my translation from the Ponca language:

> There were many *Šaą́*. The Ponca kept firing on them, as they would come. When they got up close, the Ponca shot some of them and the rest would turn back. They kept coming and killed one or two Ponca each time. But they [the Ponca] also killed some of them. In the end only five of them were left. Walking Sky, Cries for Ribs, Running after Arrow, and Old Man were the ones left. One other man was there, but I can't remember his name. He was wounded very bad but lived. The rest were killed. Running after Arrow, who was a small man, got shot. Old Man was shooting and killing the enemy when he was shot in the upper leg. The bullet hit one of the main blood vessels [artery?], and he became unconscious. One of them tied a strap around his leg to keep it from bleeding. Cries for Ribs also got shot in the neck. Walking Sky was the only one left. He told them to leave and get home if they could. Cries for Ribs was a big man . . . he was tall. Old Man awoke when they spoke to him. They told him what they intended to do. He told them it was good and wished them success in getting home. Cries for Ribs

packed the small man on his back. He was holding the blood from running out of his neck with his fingers. Running after Arrow, who was being carried, put his thumb into the hole on Cries for Ribs's neck to keep it from bleeding. The enemy chased them on horseback. But the man, who carried the small man, was a fast runner. He was known for that among the Ponca. The enemy could not catch him.

When the enemy came back, Old Man and Walking Sky began to shoot at them again. They pulled back, but the *Šáǫ́* were determined to kill them. Again, he began to pass out from the loss of blood. In that space of time, he saw and heard Walking Sky say, "If they come again, I will defend until I die." He said Walking Sky stood up and tied a rawhide thong around his waist and attached it to his knife. He stuck the knife into the ground. He then hollered as men holler in battle facing the enemy and firing at them. The second time Old Man began to wake up, he heard men crying. Someone was singing in the distance. Then he heard horses passing by. It was the enemy taking their dead. The last man stopped and was looking at the Ponca men lying dead. As he came by, Old Man opened his eyes and stared at the man. He said the man got really scared and made his horse run from the scene. The next thing he remembered was when he became conscious back at his home. He and the rest of the men, even those who died, were honored at the *Hedúškà* meeting. He and Walking Sky, who survived the onslaught, were praised by Cries for Ribs and Running after Arrow for their bravery and courage. The *Hedúškà* gave him an eagle feather to wear on the left side of his hair because he was wounded on the left side.

Gak'úwįxè was honored with a song that is still being sung today at many Indian dances throughout Indian country because it was "in the drum" from the beginning. "Old man" among the Ponca is a title of respect. The term was also used to refer to the husband. The song is as follows:

Leader starts song:	*Ųk'íteámà ꝺǫ́ nagé šaíbedǫ̀*
Singers second song:	*Ųk'íteámà ꝺǫ́ nagé šaíbedǫ̀*
	Ųk'íteámà ꝺǫ́ nagé šaíbedǫ̀
	Gak'úwixè nǫ̀žį́ tidábè yo he ꝺe ꝺoì

| Chorus of song: | *Ųk'íteámà ɖá̧ nagé šaíbeɖą̀* |
| | *Gak'úwixè nąžį́ tidábè yo he ɖeɖoì* |

Interpretation:	*Ųk'íteámà ɖá̧ nagé šaíbeɖą̀.*
	"Because the enemy is coming to fight."
	Gak'úwixè nąžį́ tidábè yo he ɖeɖoì.
	"*Gak'úwixè* [Turning Clouds] arose
	immediately [to face the enemy]."

The first reference is made to the enemy as they kept charging them. In the second reference, even though he is wounded in the legs, he gets up to face the enemy.

Songs can be earned by anyone who shows courage to defend the camp. Child Chief was just a young boy when he accomplished a notable deed. In 1971 I visited with Adam and Bessie LeClair, who related the story of how Child Chief earned his song. Mrs. LeClair was the granddaughter of the chief. The story is as follows:

The Poncas went off hunting somewhere. Just a few people were left at the village. The grandfather of grandpa Child Chief was blind. He was sitting inside a tipi alone when he had a vision. In his mind he saw two men coming in the direction of the Ponca village. He didn't know what their intention was, but he said that *Wak'ą́da* had given them to him. He got upset by this. He stood up and went to the entrance of the tipi and called out for anyone to come. A man came to him to see what he wanted . . . because everybody knew he was blind. He said, "Bring my grandson here." So the man went off to look for him. Grandpa Child Chief was just a boy then . . . maybe about twelve years old. When he got to his place, his grandfather begin by telling him that *Wak'ą́da* had given to him two men . . . and that they were walking over there. He repeated this to the young man because he sensed that he didn't understand what he meant. Finally he said that these men walking over there may be trying to do something to the Poncas. The boy asked him what he wanted him to do. He said to take his young friend with him and intercept the men coming and if they could . . . kill them.

Grandpa Child Chief and his friend went out to meet the enemy. Although they might be a little afraid, they went. Hiding behind some bushes, they looked in the direction they were told and saw the men coming. They waited until they were able to shoot them. But those men saw them too. They began to come closer toward where the boys were. Even though they knew someone was up ahead, they didn't know that the boys were expecting them and were surprised when grandfather Child Chief stood up and shot one of them. When the man fell, the other tried to hide behind a bush. Grandpa shot into the bush and heard the man groan and fall. They waited for a while and then went to see what happened to them. They found both of them dead. When the other boy seen it, he picked up a clod of dirt and hit them with it. He claimed the victory along with Grandpa Child Chief. Some of the elders of the tribe who were able to get around went out to see. One old man made a song right there. He put Grandpa's name in that song. It's a song that is sung everywhere today. He and the other boy were honored at the next *Hedúška* dance.

This song, too, is in the drum. The song immediately makes reference to the two men walking over there. It is one of the few songs that have an unusual start. A drumroll at the beginning of the song precedes the regular drumbeat as the words of the song are sung. The chorus is sung with the regular drumbeat, but it stops abruptly at the end without the singing of the vocables. The second time the song is sung, it follows the same procedure as in the first, but the chorus is sung with vocables. As the song continues for the third time, the song is sung from the beginning to the end as regular a *Hedúška* song. The song is as follows:

Leader starts song:	*Ṇabá dédomè, deáma dédomè*
Singers second song:	*Ṇabá dédomè, deáma dédomè*
	Ṇabá dédomè, deáma dédọmè
	Ṇabá dédomè, deáma dédọmè yo he ye de doì
Chorus of song:	*Žįgá Gahígi, ažáwa tí ídomè*
	Ṇabá dédomè, deáma dédomè
	Ṇabá dédomè
Interpretation:	*Ṇabá dédomè, deámà dédomè.*

"Two are walking over there,
they are walking over there."
Žįgá Gahígi, ažáwa tí įdomè.
"Child Chief, they have come here to take
'pleasure and enjoyment'" (plus vocables).

The above songs are given as examples of the individual songs (now referred to as "family songs").

The verb *ažáwà*, "to take pleasure or enjoyment upon," in the old days meant someone coming to take advantage of any situation whereby they enjoyed it. In this song, it is used to describe an attack on another group of people or the stealing of horses, material goods, and food.

Some individuals have been honored with more that one song. One such man was *Mącú Žįgà* (Little Bear), an outstanding warrior of the Ponca. According to Sylvester Warrior, this man had six or seven songs because of the large volume of stories that the Ponca have about him. These songs were made to honor him for his bravery and great deeds. He was a member of the *Ðíxidą̀* clan (see "The Story of Little Bear" below). The following two songs are examples of songs attributed to him:

Leader starts song:	*Šé ahíámà ąwą́ne áma, Šé ahíámà ąwą́ne áma*
Singers second song:	*Šé ahíámà ąwą́ne áma*
	Šé ahíámà ąwą́ne áma yo he ɖe yo he ya e yo
	Šé ahíámà ąwą́ne áma yo he ɖe yoì
Chorus:	*Úk'itèàmà awą́nè hííbè*
	Šé ahíámà égą awą́na
	Ðúdà íígà yo he ɖe yò
Interpretation:	*Šé ahíámà ąwą́ne áma.*
	"Those men, over there, are searching for me" (plus vocables).
	Úk'itèàmà awą́ne hííbè.
	"The enemy [tribes] came searching for me."
	Šé ahíámà égą awą́na.

"You, over there, search for me in that manner."

Đúdà íígà.

"All of you, come here!"

This song was probably made subsequent to Little Bear's deeds in gaining the chieftainship. The story that follows includes additional and unexpected details that are part of the history of the Ponca people.

The Story of Little Bear

As indicated elsewhere, the songs of the Ponca embrace various acts of bravery and compassion, deeds of kindness, participation in hunting and war experiences, and a sundry list of common occurrences. In addition to this system of recording history, the Ponca also told stories by word of mouth to each succeeding generation. This section deals with the stories of Little Bear. Many songs about his prowess and bravery have been made. KH, AMC, NC, JP, and AL concurred on the following story of Little Bear, chief of the Ponca. This story also relates the original chieftainship of the Ponca and the way it came to the *Đíxidą* clan.

The original clan holding the highest position in the chief's council was the *Mąk'ą́*, or "Medicine Clan." The name that stands out among these clansmen is White Tail, or *Sįde Skà*. He presided over all council meetings, or *Gahìè*. The Ponca had eight clans and thus eight clan chiefs. The position of principal chief is said to have been given by the Creator (*Wáxe*) to a man before the clans were formed. His clan would ultimately become the Medicine Clan. From that time on, the eldest son would inherit that position. Other chiefs, in the beginning, were selected by the virtue of "goodness" in them. Wisdom, ability, and leadership were considered in the selection process. Their positions would also be inherited by their sons (KH, NC, JP).

All matters concerning the welfare of the tribe were handled in the chief's council. This provided a fair management of all tribal affairs. In the story to follow, there seems to be a suggestion that the main chief may have had absolute authority in decision making; that is, he could veto any plan made by the council. According to the elders, for the most part, the council generally had to agree before any act could be passed. And according to the tradition, the transfer of the main chieftainship could not be done. The unusual circumstances related in the following story by KH about the accomplishments of Little Bear show how the Đíxidạ̀ clan acquired the position of the principal chieftainship:

> Long time ago there was a chief who had no sons when this happened. He was the main chief. They say he had two daughters . . . He thinks a lot of them [loves them] . . . proud of them. The Poncas liked them too because they always show respect to people. They help out . . . aid their people any way they can. So, White Tail, he lived like that. At the time this happened . . . it was harvest time for picking fresh corn. Women folks usually pick the corn with young boys and girls. In those days no one was required to gather food for the chief . . . so the daughters went out to the fields one day to bring corn to their father. Even though they didn't come back soon, nobody said anything because people visit and help each other out. Before the sun went down that day . . . someone found the chief's daughters. Somebody killed them and took their scalps. The whole camp felt real sad about what happened . . . so they came to the chief and mourned over these girls. It was a big tragedy . . . everybody cried over it. The family in those days used to stay home for four days. People bring them things. They bring food, clothing, horses, or anything to help that family. After those four days were over . . . he called all the chiefs together. White Tail . . . he's the one who called that meeting. Some of those chiefs didn't feel good about this thing. I guess they wanted to go on the warpath against those who did this. They knew it was a different tribe. They left a trail . . . marks on the ground.
>
> So the council came together to hear what White Tail had to say. In that council, he said it was a hard time for him. They say he wanted to do what is right . . . but it wasn't that way. He wants to take revenge because he's going through lots of sorrow. Sad . . . and hurting. So he wants something done to avenge his daughters' deaths. He asked the council to think about what he was going to ask them. He said first, that he had no sons to take his place, and that his daughters were now dead. He said that if any one Ponca man would do what he was about to ask . . . he could sit in his position in the council . . . he wants to give

up his seat for all times. He wants to relinquish his position . . . to that man and to that clan. The chiefs didn't like that but didn't say so . . . they want him to finish what he's saying. He said it like this: "*P'áca níkašigè, ebédištiwà, húdugadądì dúbàhà áši adáíkì, ukít'è níka nążíha ądì agdík'ì, ugdí abdítè edì gdì é'kąbdà. Áwàketà adáitešti údą. Šígažįgà wì, mižįga wì, nú'wì, waúžįgà wì . . . gaégà . . . t'éwadaìkì, nążíha wédizaì k'í, šągèšti dúba wadí agdíkì, éi níkašigà dįkè Níkagahì užú ugdí'te adí' t'atè*"* (If any man of the Ponca people will go out of camp and bring back the hair of a person of the enemy, I desire for him to sit in my position as principal chief. Wherever he goes is good. He may kill one child, one young woman, one man, one old woman, or the like, and bring back four good horses, that man will have the principal chief seat). He meant that whoever goes and does what he asks . . . that person would be the principal chief.

When he finished talking, those old chiefs talk to each other. They said that this couldn't be done because of the rule . . . only the oldest son or close relative . . . a brother or nephew could take that seat when there wasn't any son to inherit that seat. That main seat belongs to that *Mąką́* clan. They can't change that. They said that would violate the rule that was made by the Creator . . . *Wáxe*. They said that they always lived in peace . . . never started wars . . . conflict of any kind . . . never took revenge. They don't believe in killing children or anybody without reason. They said if they ask anybody to do this, they wouldn't do it. Those chiefs asked White Tail not to do this. But he was angry and kept saying it had to be done.

Because he wants this done . . . they told those who tell things to get the word out . . . that anyone who is willing to do these things to come to the council. They didn't want to do this, but I guess they had to agree . . . because he's the main chief. So word went out to the camp. There were lots of Ponca at that time . . . maybe ten to twelve thousand. When word went out, those other tribes heard about it. Some said they would be ready if anyone tried to come to their camp and do this. After word went out, the chiefs sat in council every day waiting for an answer. Those people who tell messages . . . they came back every day . . . and no one wants to do these deeds. Then, one day, somebody told them that there was one such person who could do what White Tail requested. So the man went to tell the council . . . tell them that there was a man in the camp who could do what they wanted done. They said, send him to us . . . we want to talk to him. When they brought him to the council, they said . . . "The man is standing outside. His name is Little Bear of the Ðíxidą clan." Little Bear is known by our people as Mąčú Žįgà. He was a brave man. When he was growing up, they say he always tried to do what anyone else wouldn't do. At times he hunted alone . . . fought the enemy by himself. He wasn't afraid of anything. He was what they call Wašką t'ągà . . . very strong . . . Wašúšè . . . not afraid to die. He likes to stay by himself. Some people are kind of afraid of him, but they respect him.

The council said, "Let him come in." When Little Bear come into that council, he kneeled down on one knee. He lifted both hands, toward the chiefs, and draw them down. This means "thank you," but you usually do that with one hand . . . right hand. The Poncas call this Wadístubè. The way he did this was showing his boldness but was almost disrespectful to the council. Those who know Little Bear personally know that this was the kind of man he was. He was Wašúšè. He can meet any challenge. His deeds of bravery were known by many Poncas.

White Tail talk to him . . . told him everything and what he wanted done. If he could do this, he will become the main chief of the tribe. Little Bear said, "Okay . . . I can do that." He went out of the council to his own camp. It is the custom of Ponca families to share . . . so they made a feast for this man. When everybody come there, somebody explained what White Tail wanted done. They said that Little Bear was going to do this thing. At that feast . . . some person who prays for things was there. He pray for Little Bear, so he can accomplish these deeds . . . have good judgment . . . guidance . . . that whatever had to be done would be done quick . . . fast . . . so he could come home. When the feast was over and everybody left, his folks fixed his food. He's going on the warpath so he's going to take only those foods that men carry at times like that . . . pounded dry meat and corn. They only take a little bit when they travel. No water . . . they know where water is. They understand . . . for each trip . . . four of them . . . he will get the same kind of provisions . . . Umąi.

Before he left, he thought about where all the neighboring tribes was located. The Ihátąwì were always enemies . . . also the Pádì. Even the P'ádak'à who roamed up and down . . . along the great mountains to the southwest could have done this. The *Isą́ą́tˀi* were friendly and gentle people. He's going to pass by the Arikara and *Mawádani* too. So with his provisions . . . he set out on his first trip. He carried a knife . . . that's all . . . no bow and arrow. He's going to kill those people with that knife.

On his first trip, he went up to Sioux country. He walked long ways . . . came to a camp. That night . . . he waited until night . . . to get those horses . . . good horses. He got four of the best ones and tied them up away from that camp. He knows that . . . that man who owns them is going to come looking for them when the sun comes up. Before the sun came up, he waited close to that man's camp. Sure enough, that man came out to check on his horses. He watched him . . . looking around . . . looking at tracks. That man started in the direction where Little Bear laid waiting on him. It wasn't quite sunup, but you can see. That man didn't know he was laying there . . . he passed by. Little Bear came up behind him and cut his throat. To do this kind of thing . . . they say a man has to do what he was told. He can't think about anything else. He took his scalp and horses . . . returned to Ponca land. His folks was happy to see him . . . but he had to leave again . . . right away . . . so he got his food and left.

On his second trip, it was late in the day when he found that next camp. He rested that night . . . I guess he traveled several days and was tired. But before sunup, he looked around to see a place where women folks pick their wood. He found a place like that . . . and a place to hide. They say he found a tree that had big roots sticking out above the ground. So he laid there all day. Lots of women came around that place . . . and they leave. Just before sundown . . . an old lady came by. All the other women had already left. While she was picking up wood . . . he killed the old lady and hid her body under that tree. By nightfall he spotted some horses . . . good horses. They was hobbled. They must have thought that old lady was visiting somebody because nobody came to look for her. Little Bear took four of the best horses he could find . . . and that old lady's scalp back to Ponca land. By this time . . . other tribes were getting suspicious of these killings. They know that Little Bear is trying to gain the chieftain position.

On the third trip, he come to a place where the Sioux tribes are having a meeting . . . and dance too. He can speak many languages.

He heard about this meeting . . . and wants to come there . . . on this trip. So he went over there . . . dressed up like Sioux Indian. Walked into their camp. He started talking to some Sioux and went with him to the dance grounds. He sat down with all those Sioux men folks . . . some of them big warriors. He listened to their leaders talk for long time . . . and even danced with them. After a while, one of the leaders stood . . . said, "There's a person among us who is not Sioux. We will dance to this song . . . and if that person is here he will overstep in the song." This special song was one that stops at a certain place in the song. A person had to know that song . . . to stop on time. They didn't know that Little Bear understood their language. So when they danced . . . he danced with them. When the song stopped, he stopped on time. This was done several times . . . but they can't spot him. They danced until quitting time.

When everybody went to his or her own camp . . . Little Bear pretended he was going to his camp too. Since it was dark by now . . . stayed close to one camp talking to a man. After a while it got real quiet . . . he heard a boy crying . . . so he left and went toward where that boy was crying. He stood outside that tipi where that little boy was crying . . . and heard a woman say, "If you don't stop crying, I'm going to send you outside. Little Bear's out there and he'll get you." As I mentioned before . . . all those tribes heard about the Ponca and what Little Bear was doing. That woman didn't know . . . while she's trying to scare her boy . . . that Little Bear was standing just outside their doorway. When the boy kept crying . . . the woman pushed him out the door . . . and said, "Here! Little Bear! Get this boy!" She shut the doorway . . . and at that same time, Little Bear grabbed him . . . put his hand over his mouth and ran from the camp carrying the child away. The mother . . . thought that the boy was scared and was standing still outside the doorway. By the time she checked on him . . . Little Bear already been running . . . many miles away from there. Again, he got four good horses and the scalp of that dead boy. This was probably hard to do . . . but he had to do that. He can't feel sorry . . . sympathize . . . he has to do this and take it home to the chief.

Even though that third trip was hard to do . . . this fourth one was even harder. He had to kill a young girl . . . maybe . . . fourteen or fifteen years old. This was dangerous for him . . . people . . . they watch their young girls close. Give them things to do . . . chores . . . so they always know where they are and what they do. Everybody knows. Now . . . since it was two young Ponca girls who died . . . they know . . . whoever is going to take scalps will be looking for young girls. So at this time . . . young girls are being watched . . . protected by their folks . . . tribe. On this trip, it was hard for Little Bear to find a camp. But he finally found one . . . this one . . . *P'ádak'à* . . . a Comanche camp. They was camped out along a river. They say he looked for a place where girls got water for their folks. He was watching from far off . . . nobody knows he's there. The next day he got in that water early in the morning . . . came down stream . . . under water. He came to that place where they got water. There was a bank overhanging along that river . . . close by. He stayed in the water there all day. In the evening he could hear the women folks . . . girls . . . laughing and talking getting water and leaving. Just before sundown he heard two girls coming to get water. They were joking with each other . . . saying, "Little Bear is down there." They would come to the river edge . . . run back. One of the girls said, "I'm not afraid" and come closer. The other girl become scared . . . maybe she think something wrong up there . . . but she went back toward camp . . . maybe to get someone to come with her. The other girl . . . she's going to get water . . . reached down to get the water. Little Bear grab her wrist and pull her in the river . . . drowned her . . . *mížįgà dįkè níú t'édaìtè*. He took her scalp . . . and swim away. It was late but he had to get the horses. That camp was in turmoil . . . looking for that girl . . . girl never did come home. But Little Bear . . . he's a brave one . . . he goes back into that camp sometime during the night and stole four good horses and headed for home.

By this time he's tired. He's been going for several weeks without resting. When he comes home . . . all the Ponca seen him coming. Those women folks that dance that Victory Dance . . . they run out to the center of the camp. The singers start singing. Everybody's happy . . . cause he accomplish his deed. So for this victory, the women danced . . . holding their enemies' scalps in their hand . . . they laugh . . . danced. After that celebration . . . Little Bear rested. The council was called . . . people came to hear the announcement. White Tail's going to give up his position as principal chief of the Ponca. When they heard that, they were satisfied. But Little Bear didn't accept it. He said it was good that he was honored like that. He said that the honor was a high honor . . . it deserved to be given to somebody who could lead. He told the council and people, "You know me . . . I live by myself . . . hunt alone . . . travel and sometimes face the enemy alone. I cannot take this." He said he did not have a wife and that he had no sons to carry it on. He asked the council to allow him to give it to his oldest brother . . . *Wégasàpʼį* . . . Whip. His second oldest brother was *Tʼaíkʼawahò* (also known as Walks on the Ground) . . . who was also a chief. Of those three, Little Bear was the youngest. Whip was respected . . . clan chief. This position was a good thing for him . . . he took charge from that day on. This is how the *Đíxidà* clan became the holder of the principal chieftain position in the Ponca tribe.

Little Bear was a great man . . . never married . . . had no sons. He lived like that all his life . . . always dare to do something . . . bravery. He knows who he is . . . never pretend to be anybody . . . just himself. He was a Ponca warrior . . . hunter to the end of his life.

The story of Little Bear was written as it was told. The story is authentic and has no embellishments to glamorize the account. The act of this one man at the direction of the principal chief, White Tail, eventually brought retaliation upon the Ponca. A small portion of the story of *Mącú Žįgà* (Little Bear) was written by Fletcher and La Flesche (1992, 49, 50) as a vengeful act requested by "Zhinga gahige (Little Chief), of the Washa'be band." The elders said the account was not true because Little Chief was not the principal chief. Fletcher and La Flesche also referred to Little Bear as "*Wasábe Žįgà*," which means "little black bear." According to the elders, that was incorrect. His name in the Ponca language literally means "Little Grizzly Bear." The elders believed that either the inaccuracies were deliberate or the story was not known. It is assumed that Fletcher and La Flesche did not know the story.

The next phase of the oral historical account of the Ponca shows their bravery rather than tragedy and loss of life. KH told the following story about an act of retaliation by the Comanche:

They say when you disrupt . . . confuse people . . . they going to do something. Those Comanche were upset over the death of that young woman. The Sioux . . . always fight with the Ponca . . . took Little Bear's acts . . . just like they always do. So they didn't do nothing. It was at this time . . . that Little Bear took some of his relatives to visit the Omaha . . . and the rest of the menfolk went on a hunting trip . . . *Ábaè adáítè*. In those days . . . some family went along. They take children . . . womenfolk . . . but some old people stay home. Some crippled people stay too . . . along with some women and children.

So those Comanche want to take revenge on the Ponca. They must have watched that Ponca camp. They know . . . that they were going on a hunting trip. The Ponca had many camps at that time. So the Ponca went on their hunting trip. The Comanche came . . . those left behind didn't know what was going to happen. The old folks say . . . "*P'ádak'àmà ahí*" . . . (the Comanches came). "*Šą́gè ágdì*" . . . (They rode horses) . . . carried spears . . . tied rawhide loop on the end. They used it to kill people . . . maybe animals too. They hook it around your neck and jerk it. Sometimes . . . they say . . . they can pull your head off. They was killing old folks children . . . women. They rode back and forth through the camp. Some of those old Ponca ran . . . but didn't get far. But there was one woman who got away.

That woman was . . . *Wašábè Waú* . . . member of the *Wašábè* clan. She escape . . . run toward where the Poncas went. This woman known for her strong voice . . . people know her. She began calling for them to come back. She run long ways . . . long distance. Finally, somebody heard her. The first person to hear her call . . . a man by the name of *Wahátągà*. He started back right away. When he got to where she was . . . she told him what was going on. She said, "There's a man who's riding a white horse . . . *Ská ágdì* . . . he's the worst killer." *Wahátągà* rode as fast as he could to get back to camp.

At that time . . . those Comanche never used bow . . . arrow. That man *Wahátągà* was a big man. He began to shoot at them as he ride in. He crippled some of them . . . killed some. The rest of the Ponca got back . . . began to shoot those Comanche. Right in the middle of the fight . . . *Wahátągà* saw that man on the white horse. That man painted himself all red . . . I guess that's their ways. He went for him. The man saw him coming . . . so he turned his horse . . . he's going to fight him. He was hollering when he come toward *Wahátągà*. But *Wahátągà* . . . got off his horse and threw his knife . . . bow . . . arrows to the ground. He's showing he wants to fight him bare-handed. That Comanche warrior . . . saw that . . . got off his horse . . . put down his weapons. With all that was going on ... hollering ... shooting ... riding ... that Comanche didn't pay too much attention to the size of *Wahátǫgà*. He's a big man ... about six feet eight ... ten inches tall ... all muscle. But it's too late ... he already got off his horse. *Wahátǫgà* killed that man ... with his bare hands. He got hold of him and crushed him to death. That ended the fight. Some of those Comanche were trying to get away. That spear and loop was no match ... for the bow and arrows.

Some time later, they came back. The new leader rode up ... white buckskin in his hand. That means "We come in peace" back in those days. They say he spoke in the Ponca language, *"P'ádàk'à ǫ̀dì. K'ík'ínatè šą́ agáxaì. Niášigà wì agúnè ǫgáti. Niášigàdìkè, Mǫ̀cú žįgà dadàì. Éi agúnè agátì"* (We are Comanche. We have quit fighting. We have come to look for a man. The man is called Little Bear. He is the one we are looking for). They told the Comanche that Little Bear was not there ... that the loss of lives of those people ... was caused by another. They told them the story about what happened ... the death of Chief White Tail's daughters ... and what he requested. The Comanche were sad ... over the death ... and their own warriors' too. When they heard the whole story, they left.

The Comanche ... they didn't want these bad feelings to go on ... continue. They like that bow and arrow. Maybe ... they think that if they can trade something for the bow and arrow ... and make peace with our people. Some months later they sent people ... delegation ... back to the Ponca. They said they wanted the bow and arrow. In exchange ... trade ... they're going to give the Ponca some good horses. Comanche know how to ride ... good riders ... and they are going to teach those Ponca how to ride. The Ponca said it was okay ... so they gave them the bow and arrow ... teach them what kind of wood to use to make it ... how to use it. Ever since then ... the Ponca and Comanche never fought each other. They live in peace with each other ... good to one another ... all the way to this day.

When speaking with some urban Indians in Wichita, Kansas, in 1973, Marlin Otipoby, a Comanche Indian, remembered the trade of horses for the bow and arrow. He also reiterated the story of how the bow was used for a staff in the Native American Church.

The story of how the *Đíxidǫ̀* clan acquired the principal chieftainship as related above has been told to each generation of the Ponca people, especially the Đíxidą and Mąk'ą clans. The process by which Little Bear acquired the principal chieftain seat—by the killing others and bringing back to White Tail scalps and horses—has also been a point of debate among tribesmen. Some tribal members insisted that Little Bear committed the acts and only subsequently offered the spoils to White Tail. Misinformation accounts for most of the confusion in the stories of Little Bear and the battle between the Ponca and the Comanche.

Seemingly of little importance to some historians, the story is significant to the Ponca people and must be included as part of the historical account of the tribe. The Ponca have had a good ongoing relationship with the Comanche people into the twenty-first century. Howard said the Ponca term for the Comanche was Padouka, but the Ponca have always refered to the Comanche as P'ádak'à.

Fletcher and La Flesche (1992, 79–80) recorded what they called a traditional story of how the Ponca met and fought the Comanche while on a hunt. They said these were first horses the Ponca had ever seen. They said that after peace had been established between the two tribes, the Ponca gave the bow and arrows to the Comanche and received horses from them. They also wrote that the Ponca stole more horses from them and drove them out of their village. According to KH, NC, AL, and AMC, the Ponca had horses before this encounter with the Comanche. Since the Comanche were known for their ability as expert horsemen, they said, it was this that the Ponca wanted to learn. Also, the Comanche had owned large herds of Appaloosa, or Nídeskà, horses. This type of horse was desired by most Indian tribes. For more information on the bow and arrows, see chapter 20.

Some of Little Bear's songs are titled as Wašúšè songs. The term has been interpreted as "bravery"; however, it connotes more of a devil-may-care attitude. Little Bear was that and more. In his second song, the tempo is faster. The words are as follows:

Leader starts song:	Nudą́ hągà wašúšè udínè ahíbabè yo he ye đe đǫ
Singers second song:	Nudą́ hągà wašúšè udínè ahíbabè yo he ye đe đǫ
	Nudą́ hągà wašúšè udínè ahíbè dą
	Udínè ahíbedą̀

	Nudą́ hągà wašúšè udínè ahíbabè yo he ye de dǫ
Chorus of song:	*Mą̃čú žìgà, nudą́ hągà wašúšè udínè ahíbedą̀*
	Udínè ahíbedą̀
	Nudą́ hągà wašúšè udínè ahíbabè yo he ye de dǫ
Interpretation:	*Nudą́ hągà wašúšè udínè ahíbabè.*
	"A fearless war leader has come looking
	for you" (plus vocables).
	Udínè ahíbabè dǫ.
	"He has come looking for you."
	Mą̃čú žìgà, nudą́ hągà wašúšè udínè ahíbedą̀.
	"Little Bear, a fearless war leader has come
	looking for you."

Songs are sometimes made about individuals who play a significant role in international conflicts involving the United States. For example, during the First World War, the kaiser of Germany was said to have run for his life after his closest friends had left him. A Ponca Indian who had served on the front lines in that war told our people of the incident. In addition to singing about the Ponca soldier in a *Hedúškà* song, they also composed at least three songs for the kaiser in the *Hedúškà* Soldier Dance. One of the songs says, "*Kaísašt'ì, dikágeámà digábadą̀ dadhe*" (Kaiser, all your friends are gone and you are fleeing). The connotation in the Ponca language is that he was fleeing from death. Apparently, the Ponca were so astounded by the disgusting behavior of the kaiser, a high official, that they composed several songs relating to this incident. The first of the four songs is the *Hedúškà*, or War Dance, song (Joe Rush recorded and made a remark that it related to the kaiser):

Leader starts song:	*Ųkít'è dé ešédą̀*
Singers second song:	*Ųkít'è dé ešédą̀*
	Ųkít'è dé ešédą̀
	Ųkít'è dé ešédą̀
	Ųkít'è dá wína wašúšè dǫ he ye de dǫì

Chorus of song:	*Kaízaštì, ukít'è đé ešédà*
	Ųkít'è đé ešédà
	Ųkít'è đá wína wašúšè đǫ he ye đe đǫ

Interpretation:	*Ųkít'è đé ešédà.*
	"This enemy, you said."
	Ųkít'è đá wína wašúšè.
	"This enemy, he said, I alone have a devil-may-care attitude" (plus vocables).

The term "*Ųkít'è*" originally meant "enemy." In modern terms, it means a person of a different tribe or nation.

The following are the three *Hedúškà Wanąšè wačígaxè*, or "Soldier Dance," songs made for the kaiser of Germany (the songs are not necessarily sung in this order):

Leader starts song:	Ya ha he ya he yǫ e yǫ he đe đe
Singers second song:	Ya ha he ya he yǫ e yǫ he đe đe
	He a ya ha e ya he yǫ he yǫ e yǫ he đe đe
	He a ya ha e ya he yǫ e yǫ he đe e đe
	He e đe yǫ he e đǫì

Chorus of song:	*Kaísašt'ì, đikágeámà đigábadà đaáhe* he yǫ
	he đe đe
	He a ya ha e ya he yo e yo he đe e đe
	He e đe yǫ he e đǫ

Interpretation:	*Kaísašt'ì, đikágeámà đigábadà đaáhe.*
	(Vocables) "Kaiser, all your friends are gone and you are running for your life"
	(plus vocables).

The next song tells of the emotional condition of the kaiser when he found himself abandoned by his friends:

Leader starts song:	He a ya e ha e a ya e ha
Singers second song:	He a ya e ha e a ya e ha
	He a ya a ha ya he a ya e ya ya ha ya e ya ha yoì

Chorus of song:	*Kaízaštì ną xágèha*
	Ị́tą xágèha ya
	E a ya he ya ya ha e ya ha yǫ

Interpretation:	*Kaízaštì ną xágèha.*
	(Vocables) "The kaiser is weeping now."
	Ị́tą xágèha.
	"He is weeping now" (plus vocables).

The third song is as follows:

Leader starts song:	Ya ya he ya he ya he yo oh ya eh
Singers second song:	Ya ya he ya he ya he yo oh ya eh
	Ya e ya he yo oh ya e ha ya e ha
	Ya e ya he yo oh ya e ha ya ha e ya ha yoì

| Chorus of song: | *Kaízaštì kagéá nú niážìtą̀* ehe ya e ha ya e ha |
| | Ya e ya he yo oh ya e ha ya ha e ya ha yoì |

Interpretation:	*Kaízaštì kagéá nú niážìtą̀.*
	(Vocables) "Kaizer, friend, you are not a man"
	(plus vocables).

Three particular Ponca men who served in the First World War also earned songs. According to Sylvester Warrior, an old Ponca *Heđúškà* tune was used to honor those men who had fought in a battle. This *Heđúškà* song is of the Soldier Dance variety and names Richard Hinman, George Calls Him Sr., and Alfred Buffalo. Their Ponca names are *Ník'agahì Skà*, *Íbahabè*, and *Wés'a T'ągà*, respectively. These men were the only Ponca to fight on the front lines in Europe. The song is as follows:

Leader starts song:	He ya i ha ya ho he ye đe yo
Singers second song:	He ya i ha ya ho he ye đe yo
	He ya i ya a ha o đo ho we yo he đe đoì

| Chorus of song: | *Ník'agahì skà e šuhíʃdè đǫ* hi ye yo hi ye đe o |
| | E ya e ya o ha o yo ho we yo he đe đoì |

Ní ą́mąt'à hiʃdè šugdíʃdè yo hi ye yo hi ye đe o
E ya e ya o ha o yo ho we yo he đe đoì

Interpretation: *Ník'agahì Skà e šuhíʃdè.*
(Vocables) "White chief, he went there
[to the front lines]."
Ní ą́mat'à hiʃdè šugdíʃdè.
"He went beyond the water. He has
returned."

The names *Ník'agahì Skà* (White Chief), *Íbahabè* (He Who Knows),
and *Wés'a T'ą̀gà* (Big Snake) are inserted in the song each consecu-
tive time it is sung.

Their names were also entered in songs of the women's Scalp Dance.
These men also have their own individual songs. The use of an old tune
was unusual to the Ponca people because song makers were always
present. It may have been that such song makers were not present
during the First World War. This conflict is especially significant for
the Ponca because some of the Ponca people were not yet considered
citizens of the United States, and these men (and many others) joined
the armed forces because they were simply interested in the welfare
of their kinsmen during the war. Other Ponca who joined the armed
forces during the First World War were honored with songs of valor
and recognition. There are a variety of songs in the *Heđúškà* organization designating honor to individuals who did not go to war but were
good men who accomplished something for the tribe.

One of many such songs tells of the scarcity of bison. Albert Makes
Cry Jr. (*Wétį Wasà*) told the story of a man who was responsible for
finding game. The story is as follows (my translation):

This man was called upon to aid the tribe. As the story goes, after his
initial fast, he summoned the Ponca hunters to the edge of the hill
country where he said game would come. It had been a dry summer
and the winter looked bleak without their usual food source. There
were no clouds in the sky, but he said for them to watch the sky, warning that when the bison came he would give the signal. No one was to
proceed without his signal. As they stood watching the sky, suddenly

a dark cloud arose from the west growing as it came. When the cloud was yet in the distance, it began to drop toward the ground beyond the hills. As suddenly as the cloud dropped, there came the sound of hoof beats and over the hills came the first bison. A young hunter, anxious to make his kill, caused his horse to jump forward, galloped as fast as his horse would go toward the bison. The bison then began to rise like a cloud back into the sky. The man who had warned them again told them to wait for his signal. The second time he hollered, the hunt was on. The signal he gave was something like: "*Hiyá· íyá·.*" When that signal was followed this time, the Ponca men entered into the act of killing the bison.

The major point of the story is the signal. All other factors point to this, so the song maker chose terms and words that point to the signal given. The song is as follows:

Leader starts song:	Hi ya· iya· *t'é wí tidą́bidè*
Singers second song:	Hi ya· iya· *t'é wí tidą́bidè*
	Hi ya· iya· *šą́gè wí tidą́bidè*
	Šą́gè tidą́bidè he ya
	Hedúškà dą́babè yo he dè dǫì
Chorus of song:	Hi ya· iya· *šą́gè wí tidą́bidè*
	Šą́gè tidą́bidè he ya
	Hedúškà dą́babè yo he dè dòє
Interpretation:	*T'é wí tidą́bidè.*
	"Here comes a bison."
	Šą́gè tidą́bidè.
	"Here comes a horse [and rider]."
	Hedúškà dą́babè.
	"*Hedúškà*, behold the exhibition"
	(plus vocables).

The Story of the *Mą̨tó*

Bear (*Mą̨čú*), as a child, was captured by the Ponca in the old days when they fought with the Sioux. The Sioux word for bear is *Mą̨tó*.

The Ponca word, which is similar, is *Mąčú*. The word that is part of his name or follows his name is the suffix -*štimà*, which means "he or him too." The following story was told by Sylvester Warrior:

As Bear grew up around the Ponca, one day someone told him that he wasn't Ponca and that he was a Sioux Indian. From that day on, he would go back to his own tribe, but he would come back. Finally, they discovered him missing, but they guessed that he had gone back to the Sioux people.

A day came when the Sioux attacked the Ponca, and in that fight, they saw him. At other times when the Sioux came to fight, they would notice that he would be among them. So the Poncas singled him out and recaptured him. When they brought him back to the Ponca camp, he begged them to allow him to live. He said that if he was allowed to live and go back to his people, they were going to give him his father's seat on the chief's council. But the Ponca warriors thought it was comical that he should beg like that. They laughed at him and didn't spare his life. To betray the trust of the people who nurtured you and taught you how to live had severe consequences in the old days.

The song for *Mątó* is as follows:

Leader starts song:	*Áníkà bɖiá ešédą̀ Áníkà bɖiá ešédą̀*
Singers second song:	*Áníkà bɖiá ešédą̀ Áníkà bɖiá ešédą̀*
	Hátaɖò ešédą̀ Áníkà bɖiá ešé bé yo he ye
	Ɖe ye ɖoì
Chorus of song:	*Mąčú štimà įkágè ą̀daɖè ešédą̀*
	Hátaɖò ešédą̀ Áníkà bɖiá ešé bé yo he ye
	Ɖe ye ɖoì
Interpretation:	*Áníkà bɖiá ešédą̀.*
	"You said, 'I am a human being.'"
	Hátaɖò ešédą̀.
	"You said, 'Hátaɖò'" (plus vocables).
	Mąčú štima ikágè ą̀dáɖe ešédą̀.
	"Even the Bear, you said you were my friend" (plus vocables).

The term *Hátadò* is unkown to both the Ponca and the Sioux Indians.
A *Wé'wačì waą̀* song based on the same story:

Leader starts song:	Ya he e he ye ya he e he ye
Singers second song:	Ya he e he e dè e ahé a he e dè e dè a
	Ya e ya he a he dè a he yo he doì
	Mą̀čú štimà níkàgáhì udágdadą̀
	Kagé íxà dàdà e áì
	Ya he ya e ya he dè a he da he doì
Chorus of song:	*Mą̀čú štimà níkàgáhì udágdadą̀*
	Kagé íxà dàdà e áì
	Ya he ya e ya he dè a he da he doì
Interpretation:	*Mą̀čú štimà níkàgáhì udágdadą̀.*
	(Vocables) "Bear, he told about how he would become chief."
	Kagé íxà dàdà e áì.
	"Friend, there is laughter everywhere [about what you just said]."

The Story of *Šedówagagižè*, a Sioux War Leader

The incidents that occurred in this story are cited in these songs. This following story was told by KH:

One afternoon when it got late, everybody was sitting around . . . one "lookout" . . . I guess he see somebody on the hill moving around. They say he don't run and tell people right away because he's trying to see how many they are. After while . . . he tells one person and they tell another person. Those Poncas back then can do things we don't know about . . . but they told those men folks at one of the other villages about those men at the top of that hill might be getting ready to steal horses . . . or come to fight. They get ready and they all come up to that dried-out pond where those enemy was hiding. *Šedówagagižè*'s men run from the area with the exception of three others who were shot and killed. They say those men was trying to hide among the cattails in a dried pond, some of them run . . . but they got shot. After those Ponca had surrounded *Šedówagagižè*, who was left behind, one Ponca man said, "*Šką́ą́ži nąží'igà. Wí' t'ę́'ádèt'amikè*" (Be still. Let me take care of this). *Šedówagagižè* was crawling on his knees among the cattails. He hold his hands up to show he had no weapon. The Ponca man with a knife in his hand rode upon him and, with a single blow, cut his head off. They say the head of that man rolled on the dry pond bed and rested with its eyes open and looking up. The Ponca jumped off his horse, went to the head, and said, "*Į́dádą uɖáneà? Gáke uwáne*" (What are you looking for? This is what I'm looking for). And he took his head. One of the songs tell about *Šedówagagižè*'s crying (weeping) by saying, "Stand there and weep. You brought this upon yourself." I guess they was waiting for the sun to go down . . . so they was trying to steal Ponca horses.

Leader starts song:	*Šéɖu xagé nąžíga yo, Šéɖu xagé nąžíga yo*
Singers second song:	*Šéɖu xagé nąžíga yo, Šéɖu xagé nąžíga yo*
	Šéɖu xagé nąžíga yo, xagé nąžíga yo
	Šéɖu xagé nąžíga yo he e ɖe ye doì
	Xagé nąžíga yo Šedówagagižè, ɖíʃwaɖáki'à
	Xagé nąžíga, Šéɖu xagé nąžíga yo he e ɖe ye doì
Chorus of song:	*Xagé nąžíga yo Šedówagagižè, ɖíʃwaɖákià*
	Xagé nąžíga, Šéɖu xagé nąžíga yo he e ɖe ye doì
Interpretation:	*Šéɖu xagé nąžíga.*
	"Stand there and weep."
	Xagé nąžíga yo Šedówagagižè, ɖíʃwaɖákià.
	"Stand weeping, *Šedówagagižè*, you brought it upon yourself."

Again words when sung are pronounced differently. The term *nąžíga* (stand) when sung is *nąžíge*.

The Scalp Dance song speaks of the same story but says, "Look at you, little Sioux, you wanted to capture horses." The song then proceeds to deride *Šedówagagižè* by saying, "Little Sioux, you wanted to drink water." This was probably in reference to the dry pond bed. The song continues as it says, "You have left behind your *Šedówagagižè*," scorning those who had fled.

NUDÁ WAČÍ'GAXÈ SONG (SCALP DANCE SONG)

Leader starts song: *Eí didábagà, Eí didábagà*

Singers second song: *Eí didábagà, Eí didábagà*

                        Šaá žįgà, šágetà nágdè danądà

                        Eí didába he ya he yo

1st Chorus of song: Hi yé, hi yé e de he de e ha

                        Šaá žįgà, nidát'a gądą

                        Šaá žįgà, nidátą gądą

                        Ya ya o he ya he yo

2nd Chorus of song: Hi yé, hi yé e de he de e ha

                        Šedówagagižè dagíądà dà

                        Šedówagagižè dagíądà dà

                        Ya ya a he ya he yo

Interpretation: *Eí didábagà, Eí didábagà.*

                        "Look at you, look at you."

                        Šaá žįgà, šágetà nágdè danądà.

                        "Little Sioux, you used to steal horses."

                        Eí didába.

                        "Look at you (now)" (plus vocables).

                        Šaá žįgà nidát'ą gádà.

                        "The Little Sioux wanted to drink water."

                        Šedówagagižè dagíąda dà.

                        "You have left your *Šedówagagižè*."

WÉ'WAČÌ WAÀ SONG (PRE-RITUAL SONG)

Leader starts song: He ya a e ya e ya he de

Singers second song: He ya a e ya e ya he de

                        He ya a e ya he ye

                        Ye he dǫ he ya a he a he de a he de a he ya

                        he dǫì

Chorus of song: *Šedówagagižè dagdáxubà edà̀*

> *Wak'ą́da ma iwídikà ye*
>
> Ye he do he yǫ a he a he de a he de a he ya he dò

Interpretation: *Šedówagagižè dagdáxubà edą̀.*

(Vocables) "*Šedówagagižè* is the one you thought to be '*xubé*.'"

Xubé connotes having "sacred powers."

Wak'ą́da ma iwídikà ye.

"I asked God to aid me" (plus vocables).

Note: The line "*Wak'ą́da ma iwídikà ye*" seems to suggest the word *but* is part of the statement, in which case the statement would be "But I asked God to aid me." This is also a woman's way of speaking; -*ye* is a feminine suffix. Although the incident surrounding *Šedówagagižè* was carried out by men, the song ridicules the enemy from a woman's point of view. Could it be that a woman composed the song? Also, as it is with Ponca singers, women sing the endings of songs, and it may be that the song changed over time and the -*ye* was added. Additionally, the slow beat for *Šedówagagižè* is one of several songs sung in connection with the beginning of a ritual dance. In this case, it appears that this song was one used with the women's Scalp Dance.

Trot Dance (*Sésàsà wačígaxè*) Songs

The Trot Dance, or *Sésàsà wačígaxè*, is a style of dance classified as *Hedúškà*. There is a similar dance called the *Nąstáp'ì wačígaxè*, but it has songs without words. The *Sésàsà wačígaxè* tells the same stories as in the regular *Hedúškà*, or War Dance, songs.

	SÉSÀSÀ SONG
Leader starts song:	*Ą́ba déte wíną ądíhe dó'*
Singers second song:	*Ą́ba déte wíną ądíhe dó'*
	Ą́ba déte wíną ądíhe dó'
	Ą́ba déte wíną ądíhe dó'
Chorus of song:	*Uk'ít'emašè wíną ądíhe dó'*
	Ą́ba déte wíną ądíhe dó'

Ą́ba déte wíną ądíhe ðǫ́'

Interpretation: Ą́ba déte wíną ądíhe ðǫ́'.

"This day, I am the one."

Ukítèmašè wíną ądíhe ðǫ́'.

"You [pl.], enemy, I am the one."

SÉSÀSÀ SONG

Leader starts song:	Tiðą́ðíšè šedétabè ðǫ
Singers second song:	Tiðą́ðíšè šedétabè ðǫ
	Tiðą́ðíšè šedétabè ðǫ
	Tiðą́ðíšè šedétabè ðǫ kagéhà
	Tiðą́ðíšè šedétabè ðǫ
	Tiðą́ðíšè šedétabè ðǫ

Chorus of song:	Éi Šúkabì hà, Šahíʃðà Tiðą́ðíšè
	Tiðą́ðíšè šedétabè ðǫ
	Tiðą́ðíšè šedétabè ðǫ kagéhà
	Tiðą́ðíšè šedétabè ðǫ
	Tiðą́ðíšè šedétabè ðǫ

Interpretation:	Tiðą́ðíšè šedétabè ðǫ
	"He is charging! Look over there!"
	Éi Šúkabì hà, Šahíʃðà Tiðą́ðíšè
	"They, Thick Clouds, the Cheyenne
	are charging."

A man is calling out to Šúkabì (Thick Clouds), a Ponca warrior that "they, the Cheyenne, are charging [on to fight]."

SÉSÀSÀ SONG

Leader starts song:	Ukítè wašúšè įðíga tíbedà
Singers second song:	Ukítè wašúšè įðíga tíbedà
	Uwéhedątè įðígabedà
	Ukítè wašúšè įðíga tíbedà
	Uwéhedątè įðígabedà

Uwágašątè įdígabedą

Uwéhedątè įdígabedą yǫ he ye đe ye đoì

Chorus of song:

Ukítè wašúšè įdígabà

Ábakà đihenò

Wak'ąda éskaną mą́šì đaną́žįtè

Uwágašątè įdígabedą

Uwéhedątè įdígabe yǫ he ye đe ye đoì

Interpretation:

Ukítè wašúšè įdígabà tíbedą̀.

"A brave enemy with a devil-may-care attitude came here to say to me."

Uwéhedątè, įdígabedą̀.

"He said about me, that I should come out to fight."

Uwágašątè įdígabedą̀.

"He said about me, that I should 'travel'" (plus vocables).

Ábakà đihenò.

"He continually provoked me."

Wak'ąda éskąną mą́šì đaną́žįte.

"God [Creator], I desire that you stand above [by] me."

The term *Uwéhedątè* normally means "to get involved" with any given situation.

The connotation here suggests a hand-to-hand combative activity. The term *įdígabedą̀* literally means "He said about me," and *Uwágašątè* means "to travel" or to go and take "spoils" from the enemy. In this case, the enemy is asking him to come out to try to do the same to him. The main story, according to Harry Buffalohead, was that the enemy kept taunting this Ponca man to fight for some personal reason. He said this individual who came into the Ponca village was a brave person. He said the Ponca man did not want to fight but was provoked to the point that he prayed to *Wak'ąda* to aid him as he went out to fight the enemy. He, of course, was victorious in the fight with this brave enemy.

Leader starts song: *Đidígè dà šadádišè (adá) sabe dà*

Singers second song: *Đidígè dà šadádišè (adá) sabe dà*

                         Đidígè dà šadádišè (adá) sabe dà

                         Đidígè dà šadádišè (adá) sabe dà

                         Đidígè dà šadádišè (adá) sabe dà

                         šadádišè (adá) sabe dà

                         Ápa Žigà đidígè dà šadádišè (adá) sabe dà

                         Ánit'adíhè (adá) sabe adíhèdà

                         Đidígè dà šadádišè (adá) sabe dà

Chorus of song: *Šadádišè (adá) sabe dà*

                         Ápa Žigà đidígè dà šadádišè (adá) sabe dà

                         Ánit'adíhè (adá) sabe adíhèdà

                         Đidígè dà šadádišè (adá) sabe dà

Interpretation: *Đidígè dà šadádišè (adá) sabe dà.*

                         "Since you have been gone (since your death)
with sudden distress, I have had deep sorrow."

                         Šadádišè (adá) sabe dà.

                         "With sudden distress, I have had deep
sorrow."

                         Ápa Žigà đidígè dà šadádišè (adá) sabe dà.

                         "Little Elk, since you have been gone
(since your death), I have had deep sorrow."

                         Ánit'adíhè (adá) sabe adíhèdà.

                         "I am alive, and I live with deep sorrow."

The term *adá* is not sung, although it is part of the word, and *dà* is used in the place of *dà*. It is in this that the elders said that the Ponca were "stingy with their words." The term *šadádišè* when spoken is *gadádišè*. The word connotes "to come to this condition." The song speaks of a man by the name of *Ápa Žigà*, or "Little Elk." According to the elders, this man was a man well liked by the people. They indicated that he was one of the Ponca chiefs. It may have been that he was also a great counselor or doctor. He was honored by this song in memorial to him.

Leader starts song:	E ha ya hi ya e he đe he đe he
Singers second song:	E ha ya hi ya e he đe he đe he, đe
	Ya ya e ha i ha yo ho we yo he đe đoì
	E ya he ya he e đe he
	Ya he ya he a i ho yo ho, ho o wi he đe
	A he đe ya he ya a yo o
	Ya he ya he a i ho yo ho we yo he ye đoì
	Ąpą Žįgà íyà đeđè, kagé wađíšušè, ešé, wídakè đé
	Đikágè ámà udínąą̀ ya e ya he a i ho yo ho
	we yo he đe đoì.
Chorus of song:	*Ąpą Žįgà íyà đeđè, kagé wađíšušè, ešé, wídakè đé*
	Đikágè ámà úđínąą̀ ya e ya he a i ho yo ho
	we yo he đe đoì.
Interpretation:	*Ąpą Žįgà íyà đeđè, kagé wađíšušè, ešé.*
	"Little Elk, you have spoken [sent words
	forth]. 'My friend, you are fearless beyond
	bravery,' you said. You told the truth."
	Đikágè ámà udínąą̀.
	"Your friends, they have heard about you."

This slow beat song is about the same man mentioned in *Sésàsà* song.

Ending Songs

These types of songs called for the conclusion of the *Heđúškà* dance. In modern times, only one is identified as a "quitting song." It is, however, identified as one of the songs used to draw the dance to a close.

Leader starts song:	*Heđóška nąžíge* yo he đe đe
Singers second song:	*Heđóška nąžíge* yo he đe đe
	Heđóška nąžíge yo he đe đe
	Heđóška nąžíge yo he đe đe
	Heđóška nąžíge dą́babè yo he đe đe
	Heđóška nąžíge dą́babè yo he đe đe

Chorus of song:	*Šenóžįgà uhétè wegáxàbè* yo he de de
	Wak'áda gaxábè nąžíge yo he de de
	Hedóška nąžíge dábabè yo he de de
Interpretation:	*Hedóška nąžíge.*
	"*Hedóška*, arise!" (plus vocables).
	Hedóška nąžíge dábabè.
	"*Hedóška*, arise! Behold [these men]."
	Šenóžįgà uhéte wegáxabè.
	Young men, the path has been set [made] for you.

The words in some songs are pronounced differently when spoken. *Hedóška* is *Hedúškà* when speaking, *wadábagè* is *wadábagà*, and *nąžíge* is *nąžígà*. Aside from the order of the *Hedúškà* dance procedure, many songs of the *Hedúškà* are now sung at powwows and are used indiscriminately without regard for their ownership or for descendants who might want to claim (as some have) their ancestors' song by taking it "out of the drum." The act of taking a song out of the drum requires the giving away of gifts to the singers and the people.

"Ponca songs are great to dance by," said one dancer from a nearby tribe. The drumbeat and songs have an enticing rhythm that causes even the bystander to keep rhythm with his heel. Ever since the Ponca tribal singers made two records, the songs have gone to all powwow enthusiasts throughout the country. Those singers Sylvester Warrior, Lamont Brown, Harry Buffalohead, Joe Rush, Russell Rush, Louis Yellowhorse, and Jim Waters (all deceased) paid a great tribute to the Ponca people as well as to Indian people throughout the United States. These two volumes have inspired many singers who now sing at different powwows and Indian gatherings. The songs recorded in the 1960s include songs that are now commonly sung at all powwows.

Old Individual (Family) Songs of the Ponca

The songs in this section were chosen randomly. These songs are very old, and some have been used by each successive generation. They, of course, were attributed to individuals in the nineteenth century but may have had origins in an earlier period. As indicated elsewhere, these songs were made for individuals who had accomplished some worthy deed. In many of the songs, the stories relate a special relationship with the Creator. Others mention acts of bravery, a strong philosophical statement of life, the *Heđúškà* way of life, and other accolades that marked distinction upon certain individuals.

The following songs were written as they came to mind and were attributed to the men whose names appear in the title:

WHITE EAGLE'S SONG

Leader starts song:	*Heđóška mąđí kiđà be* yo he đe ho
Singers second song:	*Heđóška mąđí kiđà be* yo he đe ho
	Mąžą́ đéđu mąđí kiđà be yo he đe yo he ya i ho
	Heđóška mąđí kiđà be yo he đe đoi
Chorus of song:	*Xiđáskástì* đe ho
	Heđóška mąđí kiđà be yo he đe ho
	Mąžą́ đéđu mąđí kiđà be yo he đe yo he ya i ho
	Heđóška mąđí kiđà be yo he đe đą́
Interpretation:	*Heđóška mąđí kiđà be.*
	"The *Heđóška* let him walk this way of life."
	Mąžą́ đéđu mąđí kiđà be.
	"On this earth, it [the *Heđóška*] let him [taught him to] walk this way of life."
	Xiđáskástì đe.
	"Here, White Eagle too [walked this way of life]."

The term *mąđí* literally means "to walk"; however, in this situation it is used in reference to the *Heđúškà* way of life. The connotation we also receive from this song is that the *Heđúškà* taught this way of life, and White Eagle received the teaching as a young boy.

STANDING BUFFALO'S SONG

Leader starts song:	Yə e he yə e ha
Singers second song:	Yə e he e yə e ha
	Yə e he e yə e ha

Yə e he ə ya ho we yo he ɖe ɖoi

Chorus of song: *Šaą̀mà šáibe, Ašáwagè*
                   Šáibe ya ho we yo he ye ɖe ɖą́

Interpretation: *Šaą̀mà šáibe, Ašáwagè.*
                   (Vocables) "The Sioux are coming,
                   Ašáwagè."

Spotted Horse, or *Ašáwagè*, is of Pawnee origin. Ponca singers say the name was given to him to honor him. His Ponca name is *T'é t'ą̀ga Ną̀ží* and is sometimes pronounced as *T'atą́ga Ną̀ží*. Both words mean "Standing Buffalo."

ROUGHFACE'S SONG

Leader starts song: *Šą́ge ną́ge kiɖè dą́bagà*
Singers second song: *Šą́ge ną́ge kiɖè dą́bagà*
                         Šą́ge ną́ge kiɖè dą́bagà
                         Ðikáge Wak'ą́da íɖa be yo he ye ɖe doì

Chorus of song: *Į̀dé Xágà*
                         Šą́ge ną́ge kiɖè dą́bagà
                         Ðikáge Wak'ą́da íɖa be yo he ye ɖe doì

Interpretation: *Šą́ge ną́ge kiɖè dą́bagà.*
                         "Behold this man. He caused his horse to run."
                         Ðikáge Wak'ą́da íɖa.
                         "Your friend has seen the things of Mystery [God]" (plus vocables).
                         Į̀dé Xágà.
                         "Roughface."

THICKNAIL'S SONG

Leader starts song: *Šéɖì gáxabè Wak'ą́da gáxabè*
Singers second song: *Šéɖì gáxabè Wak'ą́da gáxabè*
                         Šéɖì gáxabè Wakądà gáxabè mą́ši mą̀dí be yo he
                         ye ɖe ye ɖoì

Chorus of song:	Šáge šugà Wak'ạ́da gáxabè
	Šágè šugà Wak'ạ́da gáxabè mạ́ši mạ́í be yo
	he ye ɖe ye ɖoì

Interpretation:	Šéɖi gáxabè Wak'ạ́da gáxabè.
	"That person done the things of
	Mystery [God]."
	Mạ́ši mạ́í be.
	"He walks above."
	Šáge šugà Wak'ạ́da gáxabè.
	"Thicknail has done the things of
	Mystery [God]."

RUNNING OVER WATER'S SONG

Leader starts song:	Šéɖì ik'áge ɖigé ɖạ̀
Singers second song:	Šéɖì ik'áge ɖigé ɖạ̀
	Šéɖì ik'ágè ɖigá be yo he ye ɖe ye ɖò
	Šéɖì ik'áge ɖigé ɖạ̀
	Šéɖì ik'áge ɖigé ɖạ̀
	Šéɖì ik'ágè ɖigá be yo he ye ɖe ye ɖò

Chorus of song:	Íš'gadabè, Šéɖì ik'áge ɖigé ɖạ̀
	Šéɖì ik'áge ɖigé ɖạ̀
	Šéɖì ik'áge ɖigé ɖạ̀
	Šéɖì ik'ágè ɖigá be yo he ye ɖe ye ɖò

The name Running over Water in the Ponca language is Ni'ánạgè. Many of the tribesmen had two names. In this song he is called Íš'gadabè.

Interpretation:	Šéɖì ik'áge ɖigé ɖạ̀.
	"That person has no friend" (plus vocables).
	Íš'gadabè, Šéɖì ik'áge ɖigé ɖạ̀.
	"Íš'gadabè, that person has no friend."

BIG ELK'S SONG

| Leader starts song: | Kagé nít'atè ábe yo he ye ɖe ɖe |

Singers second song:	*Kagé nít'atè ábe* yo he ye ᵈe ᵈe
	Kagé nít'atè ábe yo he ye ᵈe ᵈe
	Kagé nít'atè ábe yo he ye ᵈe ᵈoì
Chorus of song:	*Ą́pą t'ą̧gá, nít'atè ábe* yo he ye ᵈe ᵈe
	Wak'ą́da áka gáxa be he ᵈe ᵈe
	Nít'àte ábe yo he ye ᵈe ᵈą̀
Interpretation:	*Kagé nít'atè ábe.*
	"Friend, this is life, it is said."
	Ą́pą t'ą̧gá, nít'atè ábe.
	"Big Elk, this is life, it is said."
	Wak'ą́da áka gáxà be.
	"The Great Mystery or Power [or God] has done this."
	Nít'atè.
	"This is life."

YELLOW PICKER'S SONG

Leader starts song:	*Šéᵈò ayámà uᵈínà be* yo he ᵈe ᵈe
Singers second song:	*Šéᵈò ayámà uᵈínà be* yo he ye ᵈe ᵈe
	Šéᵈò ayámà uᵈínà be
	Šéᵈò ayámà uᵈínà be yo he ᵈe ᵈe
	Šéᵈò ayámà uᵈínà be yo he ᵈe ᵈoì
Chorus of song:	*Wawénąhì, Šéᵈò ayámà uᵈínà be*
	Šéᵈò ayámà uᵈínà be yo he ᵈe ᵈe
	Šéᵈò ayámà uᵈínà be yo he ᵈe ᵈą̀
Interpretation:	*Šéᵈò ayámà uᵈínà be.*
	"Those who are coming are seeking you" (plus vocables).
	Wawénąhì, Šéᵈò ayámà uᵈínà be.
	"You Who Approve, those who are coming are seeking you." (Yellow Picker is *Wabáhi Zí'.*

He was also known by the above name, *Wawénąhì*, in the song).

JOHN DELODGE'S SONG

Leader starts song: *Đúdà hí'íbe yo he đe o ho*

Singers second song: *Đúdà hí'íbe yo he đe đoì*

Niášigà đéđù í'ibe yo he đe o ho

Đúdà hí'íbe yo he đe o ho

Đúdà hí'íbe yo he đe o ho

Đúdà hí'íbe yo he đe o ho

Đúdà hí'íbe yo he đe đoì

Chorus of song: *Hexága wakíđè ha*

Đéđù í'íbe yo he đe o ho

Đúdà hí'íbe yo he đe o ho

Đúdà hí'íbe yo he đe o ho

Đúdà hí'íbe yo he đe đoì

Interpretation: *Đúdà hí'íbe.*

"[You who are there,] here, come to this place" (plus vocables).

Niášigà đéđù í'ibe.

"People from here are coming to this place."

Hexága wakíđè ha.

"Shoots the Elk!"

Đéđù í'íbe.

"Here, they are coming to this place."

GIVES WATER'S SONG

Leader starts song: *Đikágè šaíbè*

Singers second song: *Đikágè šaíbè*

Đikágè šaíbè

Đikágè šaíbè

Đikágè P'ąkà be yo he ye đe ye đoì

Chorus of song:	*Wažį́ga umą̀*
	Đikágè šaíbè
	Đikágè šaíbè
	Đikágè P'ą̀kà be yo he ye đe ye đoì
Interpretation:	*Đikágè šaíbè.*
	"Your friend is coming."
	Đikágè P'ą̀kà.
	"Your friend, the Ponca, is coming."
	Wažį́ga umą̀.
	"The Đwelling Place of Fowls of The Air."
	Đikágè šaíbè.
	"Your friend is coming."

RUNNING OVER WATER'S SECOND SONG

Leader starts song:	*Đét'à kođà šewádįbe*
Singers second song:	*Đét'à kođà šewádįbe*
	Đét'à kođà šewádįbe Uhéwakiđažì šewádįbe
	Đét'à kođà šewádįbe yo he ye đe ye đoì
Chorus of song:	*Đét'à kođà šewádįbe Uhéwakiđažì šewádįbe*
	Đét'à kođà šewádįbe yo he ye đe ye đą̀
Interpretation:	*Đét'à kođà šewádįbe.*
	"Friend, there, he had the enemy confused."
	Uhéwakiđažì šewádįbe.
	"He Would Not Let Them Pass By" had the enemy confused"

Note: It was not unusual for men in the "old days," according to the elders, to have more than one name. In this song, we see that Running over Water is called by a different name — *Uhéwakiđažì*, "He Would Not Let Them Pass By."

BLACK BUFFALO BULL'S SONG

Leader starts song:	*Šą́ge wít'à ešé đą̀*
Singers second song:	*Šą́ge wít'à ešé đą̀*

Šáge wít'à ešé đà

Šáge wít'à ešé be yo he ye đe ye đoì

Chorus of song: *T'é Núgà Hì Sábè*

Šáge wít'à ešé đà

Šáge wít'à ešé đà

Šáge wít'à ešé be yo he ye đe ye đoì

Interpretation: *Šáge wít'à ešé đà.*

"Those are my horses, you had said."

T'é Núgà Hì Sábè.

"Black Buffalo Bull."

LITTLE FLYER'S SONG

Leader starts song: Ya e hi ya ya hi ya ho we yo he ye đe ye đe

Singers second song: Ya e hi ya ya hi ya ho we yo he ye đe ye đe

Ya e hi ya ya hi ya ho we yo he ye đe ye đe

Ya e hi ya ya hi ya ho we yo he ye đe ye đe

Ya e hi ya ya hi ya ho we yo he ye đe ye đoì

Chorus of song: *Giá Žįgà, đe đanážįtè đidábe gáđa be* yo he ye đe

ye đe

Ya e hi ya ya hi ya ho we yo he ye đe ye đe

a e hi ya ya hi ya ho we yo he ye đe ye đà

Interpretation: *Giá Žįgà, đe đanážįtè đidábe gáđa be.*

"Little Flyer, you, where you are standing,

they wish to behold you" (plus vocables).

MIKE ROY'S SONG

Leader starts song: Ya e ha đa yo e ha đa ho e ha đa ho we yo he

ye đe ye đe

Singers second song: Ya e ha đa yo e ha đa ho e ha ya hi he ye đe

ye ho yo

Ya e ha đa yo e ya e ho e ha đa ho we yo he

ye đe ye đe

Ya e ha ɖa yo e ho e ha ɖo ho we yo he ɖe ye ɖoì

Chorus of song: Mąnąkugè ha, ɖa, ižáže ɖít'à udínąą be ɖe ye
ho yo
Kágè ha, ɖa, úɖą škáxè ga aɖísiɖà be yo he ye ɖe
ye ho yo
Ya e he ɖa e ya e ha ɖa ho we yo he ye ɖe ye ɖò

Interpretation: Mąnąkugè ha, ɖa, ižážè ɖít'à udínąą be.
"Stomps The Ground, you, they [the people]
have heard of your name" (plus vocables).
Kágè ha, ɖa, úɖą škáxè ga aɖísiɖà be.
"Friend, you, because of the good deeds
you performed we remember you"
(plus vocables).

BLUEBACK'S SONG

Leader starts song: Wašúše uɖíginàbe
Singers second song: Wašúše uɖíginàbe
Wašúše uɖíginàbe
Wašúše uɖíginàbe
Nągetidè, uɖíginàbe yo he ɖe ɖoì

Chorus of song: Wašúše uɖíginàbe
Wašúše uɖíginàbe
Nągetidè, uɖíginàbe yo he ye ɖe ye ɖò

Interpretation: Wašúše uɖíginàbe.
"Those who are brave [with a devil-may-
care attitude], they are looking for you."
Nągetidè, uɖíginàbe.
"He Who Runs By, they are looking for you"
(plus vocables).

MACDONALD'S SONG

Leader starts song: Ya e ha ɖa ho wi yo
Singers second song: Ya e ha ɖa ho wi ɖe

Ya e ha ɖa ho wi yo
Ya e ha ɖa ho wi ɖe
Ya e ha ɖa ho wi ɖe
Ya e ha ɖa ho wi ɖe
Ya e ha ɖa ho wi ɖe ya a ho we yo he ye ɖe
ye ɖoì

Chorus of song: *T'é núgà níkàgahì wašúšè, Heɖóška wašúše*
Ya e ha ɖa ho wi ɖe
Ya e ha ɖa ho wi ɖe
Ya e ha ɖa ho wi ɖe ya a ho we yo he ye ɖe
ye ɖoì

Interpretation: *T'é núgà níkàgahì wašúše, Heɖóška wašúše.*
"Buffalo Chief, you are brave [having a
devil-may-care attitude], a *Heɖúškà* who is
brave [having a devil-may-care attitude]"
(plus vocables).

The term *Wašúšè* has been translated liberally by other interpreters;
however, after consultation with the elders, it seemed that the phrase
"devil may care" was better than "brave."

GEORGE PRIMEAUX'S SONG

Leader starts song: *Ɖigé hút'à nàžĩ̀dè*
Singers second song: *Ɖigé hút'à nàžĩ̀dè*
Ɖigé hút'à nàžĩ̀dè
Ɖigé hút'à nàžĩ̀dè
Ɖigé hút'à nàžĩ̀dè
Ɖigé hút'à nàžĩ̀dè yo he ye ɖe ye ɖoì

Chorus of song: *Ɖét'à koɖá, Mãhi skàštì, hút'à nàžĩ̀dè*
Ɖigé hút'à nàžĩ̀dè
Ɖigé hút'à nàžĩ̀dè
Ɖigé hút'à nàžĩ̀dè yo he ye ɖe ye ɖà

Interpretation: *Ɖigé hút'à nàžĩ̀dè.*

"There was no 'war cry' given as he stood."

Đét'à kođá, Mą́hi skàstì, hút'ą̀ nąžį́đè.

"My friend who stands yonder, White Knife too, he gave a 'war cry' as he stood."

NO EAR'S SONG

Leader starts song:	*Į̀dádą udáne'à? Į̀dádą udáne'à?*
Singers second song:	*Į̀dádą udáne'à? Į̀dádą udáne'à?*
	Į̀dádą udáne'à?
	Žį́đe, đégà uwánè yo he ye đe ye đoì
Chorus of song:	*Óhođà Šaą̀ wanąxe į̀dádą udáne'à?*
	Žį́đe, đégą uwánè yo he ye đe ye đà
Interpretation:	*Į̀dádą udáne'à? Į̀dádą udáne'à?*
	"What are you looking for? What are you looking for?"
	Žį́đe, đégą uwánè.
	"Friend, this is what I am looking for."
	Óhođà Šaą̀ wanąxe į̀dádą udáne'à?
	"*Óhođà*, Sioux ghost, what are you looking for" (addressing the slain enemy).
	Žį́đe, đégą uwánè.
	"Friend, this is what I am looking for" (plus vocables).

Note: The supporting story for this particular song indicated that the eyes of the enemy were still open after his decapitation. Hence the question, "What are you looking for?" The phrase "this is what I am looking for" suggests the taking of a scalp.

WHIP'S SONG

Leader starts song:	*Awát'ané'à?, awát'ané'à?*
Singers second song:	*Awát'ané'à?, awát'ané'à?*
	Awát'ané'à?, awát'ané'à?
	Awát'ané'à?, awát'ané'à?

<table>
<tr><td></td><td>Wégasap'ı̨, awát'ané'à? yo he ye de ye dǫ</td></tr>
<tr><td>Chorus of song:</td><td>Awát'ané'à?, awát'ané'à?</td></tr>
<tr><td></td><td>Awát'ané'à?, awát'ané'à?</td></tr>
<tr><td></td><td>Wégasap'ı̨, awát'ané'à? yo he ye de ye dǫì</td></tr>
<tr><td>Interpretation:</td><td>Awát'ané'à?, awát'ané'à?</td></tr>
<tr><td></td><td>"Which direction are you taking?</td></tr>
<tr><td></td><td>Which direction are you taking?"</td></tr>
<tr><td></td><td>Wégasap'ı̨, awát'ané'à?</td></tr>
<tr><td></td><td>"Whip, which direction are you taking?"</td></tr>
</table>

Note: This is a call upon the principal chief to make a decision on an important matter concerning the tribe.

WHITE ELK'S SONG

<table>
<tr><td>Leader starts song:</td><td>Éi Wak'ą́da Í'bahąbidè</td></tr>
<tr><td>Singers second song:</td><td>Éi Wak'ą́da Í'bahąbidè</td></tr>
<tr><td></td><td>Šédì Wak'ą́da Í'bahąbidè</td></tr>
<tr><td></td><td>Šédì Wak'ą́da Í'bahąbidè</td></tr>
<tr><td></td><td>Šédì Wak'ą́da Í'bahąbidè yo he ye de ye dǫì</td></tr>
<tr><td>Chorus of song:</td><td>Hé xágà skà Wak'ą́da Í'bahąbidè</td></tr>
<tr><td></td><td>Šédì Wak'ą́da Í'bahąbidè</td></tr>
<tr><td></td><td>Šédì Wak'ą́da Í'bahąbidè yo he ye de ye dǫì</td></tr>
<tr><td>Interpretation:</td><td>Éi Wak'ą́da Í'bahąbidè.</td></tr>
<tr><td></td><td>"He knows the way of the Mystery [God]."</td></tr>
<tr><td></td><td>Šédì Wak'ą́da Í'bahąbidè.</td></tr>
<tr><td></td><td>"That one knows the way of the Mystery [God]."</td></tr>
<tr><td></td><td>Hé Xágà Skà Wak'ą́da Í'bahąbidè.</td></tr>
<tr><td></td><td>"White Elk knows the way of the Mystery [God]."</td></tr>
</table>

Note: *Hé Xágà Skà* is interpreted literally as "Rough White Horn." *Hé Xágà* is another Ponca name for Elk.

Old Man Bear

During the winter of 1996, I had a visit with my brother-in-law in Bethany, Oklahoma. Albert Makes Cry Jr. was one of the only surviving Ponca speakers who still remembered some of the stories related in the *Heđúškà* songs. Before speaking with him, I had heard some of the Ponca singers tell of a great Ponca warrior that no one knew anything about. His name was *Mą̨čú Išáge*, "Old Man Bear." I asked Albert about it, and he said, "He was a great warrior alright, but not the kind you might think of." Smiling, he said, "*Mą̨čú Išáge* was a dog." He related the following story:

> This is a story of how a dog earned a song. *Šą̨nudà wí wáą wí' gígaxaì tè.* They said that this dog was a close friend to his owner who used to go with him wherever he went. Everybody in the camp knew this dog. When they went hunting, they say his dog would go with him. His name was *Mą̨čú Išáge* . . . Old Man Bear. They say he even went on the buffalo hunt with the menfolk. *Gaxą̨ adá kí' wiúhe adé ną̨ite.*
>
> In this story, a day came when an alarm was made by the tribal lookouts . . . *Úwadą̨bè.* They said, "There are some men coming this way." In those days, the lookouts could tell how far away a person or a group was from the village and who they were. That was their job, you might say. In the Ponca camp, there were also some men who were always ready to defend the tribe. These men were from the *Đíxidą̨* and *Níkapášną̨* clans. They were the first to meet the enemy. This was part of the Ponca strategy to go into warfare.
>
> As the warriors began to leave the village, *Mą̨čú Išáge* started to follow them because his owner was a member of the group. But his owner talked to him and told him he could not go. He said, "We may fight over there and you might get kicked and get hurt. You have to stay." But *Mą̨čú Išáge* wouldn't stay back. His owner pretended to hit him with a little stick and *Mą̨čú Išáge* ran back toward the village.
>
> But as the men approached the enemy, they suddenly noticed that the enemy was in turmoil. When they came close, they saw *Mą̨čú Išáge* jumping at the enemy's legs and biting them. Their horses were bucking and turning round and round. The Ponca battled the enemy, and when it was over, they looked for *Mą̨čú Išáge.* But they could not find him. So they returned to the village victorious but without *Mą̨čú Išáge.*

About four days later, a man came to the owner's dwelling and said, "There is a dog lying in the bushes. It looks like your dog." He immediately went to see with other men. Sure enough, it was *Mącú Išáge*. He was hurt, but he was alive. The man who doctors people and animals came. Also present was a song maker . . . *Waą́ gáxe*. This is the song he made for *Mącú Išáge*, a heroic and brave dog.

Leader starts song:	*Áwate t'éxiadą̀, ną́wap'adè ąkidedą̀*
Singers second song:	*Áwate t'éxiadą̀, ną́wap'adè ąkidedą̀*
	Áwate t'exíadą̀ Sáą žįgà ną́wap'adè ąkidedą̀
	Áwate t'éxiadą̀, šéwabdì bde yo he ye de ye do
	Mącú isága áwate t'exíadą̀ Sáą žįgà ną́wap'adè ąkidedą̀
	Áwate t'éxiadą̀, šéwabdì bde yo he ye de ye do
Chorus of song:	*Mącú isága áwate t'exíadą̀ Sáą žįgà ną́wap'adè ąkidedą̀*
	Áwate t'éxiadą̀, šéwabdì bde yo he ye de ye do
Interpretation:	*Áwate t'éxiadą̀, ną́wap'adè ąkidedą̀*
	"Where is it difficult, that you would think I should fear?"

Veteran's Songs

A number of veteran songs were composed in the twentieth century. These songs are sung at special times during a tribal dance today. The following are written in no special order.

SONG FOR VIETNAM VETERANS

Leader starts song:	Ya e hi ya yo oh e yo he ye de ye de
Singers second song:	Ya e hi ya yo oh e yo he ye de ye de
	Ya e hi ya ya e hi ya ya he yo oh
	Ya e hi ya yo oh e yo he ye de ye de
	Ya e hi ya yo oh e yo he ye de ye dǫì
Chorus of song:	Ya e hi ya ya e hi ya ya he yo oh
	Ya e hi ya yo oh e yo he ye de ye de

Ya e hi ya yo oh e yo he ye đe ye đǫì

Final chorus of song: *Háskà đéđò t'éxì áđe* yo he ye đe ye đe

Šenúžįgà uđánagè

Háskà đéđą̀ ađí agđí đéđò đą́bàbe yo he ye
đe ye đe

Ya e hi ya yo oh e yo he ye đe ye đǫì

Interpretation: *Háskà đéđò t'éxì áđe.*

"This flag is a difficult way"
(plus vocables).[2]

Šenúžįgà unágè àhì.

"The young men fought for and through it."

Háskà đéđą̀ ađí agđí đéđò. Đą́bàbe.

"This flag, they brought it back. Behold it."

The next song was sung at the Gives Water dance arbor when Kennis Headman returned from the Vietnam War. He had received medals of valor including the Bronze Star.

THE VIETNAM SONG

Leader starts song: He ye ya e hi ye hi yo *wađą́bagè* yo he ye
đe ye đe

Singers second song: He ye ya e hi ye hi yo *wađą́bagè* yo he ye
đe ye đe

*Heđúškà mà wađą́bagà. Nuđą́ hiámà
wađą́bage* hi ye yo he ye đe ye đe

He ye ya e hi ye hi yo *wađą́bagè* yo he ye
đe ye đǫì

Chorus of song: *Heđúškà mà wađą́bagà. Nuđą́ hiámà wađą́bage*
hi ye yo he ye đe ye đe

He ye ya e hi ye hi yo *wađą́bagè* yo he ye
đe ye đǫì

Interpretation: *Wađą́bagè.*

"Behold these men" (plus vocables).

Heđúškà mà waḍ́bagà. Nuḍ́ hiámà
waḍ́bagè.

"Behold the Heđúškà. Behold these who
have gone on the warpath."

Note: The term Heđúškà connotes the teachings of the fraternal organization. The song refers to these principles.

VETERAN SONG

Leader starts song:	Wiáhidè ahíbè, waḍ́be yo he đe đe
Singers second song:	Wiáhidè ahíbè, waḍ́be yo he đe đe
	Wiáhidè ahíbè, waḍ́be yo he đe đe
	Wiáhidè ahíbè, waḍ́be yo he đe đe
Chorus of song:	Šenúžįgà, wiáhidè ahíbe ma̧' đidą́be yo he đe đe
	Wiáhidè ahíbè, waḍ́be yo he đe đe
	Wiáhidè ahíbè, waḍ́be yo he đe đa
Interpretation:	Wiáhidè ahíbè. Waḍ́bè.
	"They have gone to a far distance [to war].
	Behold these men" (plus vocables).
	Šenúžįgà, wiáhidè ahíbe ma̧' đidą́be.
	"The young men have gone to a far distance.
	They have 'pulled the bow'" (plus vocables).

VETERAN SONG

Leader starts song:	Šenúžįgà nudą́ đéđǫbè
Singers second song:	Šenúžįgà nudą́ đéđǫbè
	Šenúžįgà nudą́ đéđǫbè
	Šenúžįgà zaní đéđomè yo he e đe e đoì
Chorus of song:	Mažą́ đéđù ákìnǫ̀žì đéđomè
	Nudą́ đéđòbè yo he e đe e đoì
Interpretation:	Šenúžįgà nudą́ đéđǫmè.
	"The young men are going to war"
	(plus vocables).

Mažą dédù ákìnążì dédomè.

"This land here, they are depending upon and protecting each other, they are going."

VETERAN SONG

Leader starts song:	Adúhagà téxìtè
Singers second song:	Adúhagà téxìtè
	Adúhagà téxìtè
	Adúhagà téxìtè
	Hedóška tè yo he e de e doì
Chorus of song:	Nudáhągà Adúhagà téxìtè
	Adúhagà téxìtè
	Hedóška tè yo he e de e doì
Interpretation:	Adúhagà téxìtè.

"Go first in this difficult way."

Hedóška tè.

"The Hedúškà way of life" (plus vocables).

Nudáhągà Adúhagà téxìtè.

"War leader! Go first in this difficult way." (The word Udúhagà means "to follow." Adúhagà means "go first." This is consistent with in all songs that call for the war leader to initiate or to do something.)

VETERAN SONG

Leader starts song:	He ya e ya ha e ya ya ha e ha e ho we yo he de de
Singers second song:	He ya e ya ha e ya ya ha e ha e ho we yo he de de
	He a ya ha e ha ya ha e ha e ho we yo he de de
	E ya he ya he ya he ya ya e ha yo ho we yo he de doì

Chorus of song:	*Šénužį̀gà nudą́ ɖaitè eí̀ wadą́babè yo he ɖe ɖe*
	Ų̀hé téxì ho, Káge, Wak'ą́da gáxabè yo he ɖe ɖà

Interpretation:	*Šénužį̀gà nudą́ ɖaitè eí̀ wadą́babè.*
	"Young men who are going to the warpath, behold these them."
	Ų̀hé téxì ho! Káge, Wak'ą́da gáxabè.
	"The way is difficult! Friend, God made it that way."

VETERAN SONG

Leader starts song:	Ye e he ya, ya e ho we yo he ɖe ɖe
Singers second song:	Ye e he ya, ya e ho we yo he ɖe ɖe
	Ye e he ya, ya e ho we yo he ɖe ɖe
	Ye e he ya, ya e ho we yo he ɖe ɖe
	Ye e he ya, ya e ho we yo he ɖe ɖoì

Chorus of song:	*Šénužį̀gà, ukít'è à mà xagáíyedè, wadą́bagè yo ɖe ɖe*
	Ye e he ya, ya e ho we yo he ɖe ɖe
	Ye e he ya, ya e ho we yo he ɖe ɖà

Interpretation:	*Šénužį̀gà, ukít'è à mà xagáíyedè, wadą́bagà.*
	"Young men, the enemy weeps. Behold these men."

VETERAN SONG

Leader starts song:	*Šuhí'ʃdè wadą́babe yo he ɖe ɖe*
Singers second song:	*Šuhí'ʃdè wadą́babe yo he ɖe ɖe*
	Kagéá há P'ą́kà mà nudą́ híámà
	Uk'ít'è amà uhéwaɖaì
	Kagéá šuhí'ʃdè wadą́babe yo he ɖe ɖoì

Chorus of song:	*Wadą́babe yo he ɖe ɖe*
	Kagéá há P'ą́kà mà nudą́ híámà
	Uk'ít'è amà uhéwaɖaì

Kagéá šuhíʃdè wadábabe yo he de dóɛ

Interpretation: *Šuhíʃdè. Wadábabe.*
"They went there [to war]. Behold these men"
(plus vocables).[3]
Kagéá há P'ákà mà nudá híámà.
"My friend, these Ponca have gone on the
warpath."
Uk'ít'è amà uhéwadaì.
"There, they met the enemy."
Kagéá šuhíʃdè. Wadábabe.
"My friend, they went there [to war].
Behold these men" (plus vocables).

VETERAN SONG

Leader starts song: *Nudá šaíbedà, nudá šaíbedà*
Singers second song: *Nudá šaíbedà, nudá šaíbedà*

                  Nudá šaíbedà, nudá šaíbedà

                  *Nudá šaíbedà, šénužįgà nąžįtidabe yo he ye
de ye doì*

Chorus of song: *Ukíteámà Nudá šaíbedàdà*
                  Žįgá dít'à nudá dé dedò
                  Nudá hágà nąžįtidabe yo he ye de ye dó

Interpretation: *Nudá šaíbedà, Nudá šaíbedà.*
"They come warring, they come warring."
Nudá šaíbedà, šénužįgà nąžįtidabe.
"They come warring, young men! Arise!"
Ukíteámà Nudá šaíbedà.
"The enemy comes warring."
Žįgá dít'à nudá dé dédò.
"Your young men are going to war."
Nudá hágà nąžįtida be.
"War leader! Arise!"

VETERAN SONG

Leader starts song: *Šénužįgà wadábedédàbe yo he ye đe ye đe*

Singers second song: *Šénužįgà wadábedédàbe yo he ye đe ye đe*

P'ákà šénužįgà ma nudá đáiſdè

wadábedédàbe yo he ye đe ye đe

Uhétè Wak'áda wedé p'ahágat'é yo he ye đe ye đǫì

Chorus of song: *P'ákà šénužįgà ma nudá đáiſdè*

Wadábedédàbe yo he ye đe ye đe

Uhétè Wak'áda wedé p'ahágat'é yo he ye đe ye đò

Interpretation: *Šénužįgà wadábedédàbe.*

"Behold these young men as they leave" (plus vocables).

P'ákà šénužįgà ma nudá đáiſdè.

"The young Ponca men are going to war."

Wadábedédàbe.

"Behold these men, as they leave" (plus vocables).

Uhétè Wak'áda wedé p'ahágat'é.

"Mystery [God] go before them in the pathway" (plus vocables).

VETERAN SONG

Leader starts song: *Hedóška nąžįgè yo he ye đe ye đe*

Singers second song: *Hedóška nąžįgè yo he ye đe ye đe*

Hedóška nąžįgè yo he ye đe ye đe

Hedóška nąžįgè yo he ye đe ye đe

Hedóška nąžįgè dábabè yo he ye đe ye đe

Hedóška nąžįgè dábabè yo he ye đe ye đǫì

Chorus of song: *Šénužįgà, uhétè wegáxabè yo he ye đe ye đe*

Wak'áda gaxábè nąžįgè yo he ye đe ye đe

Hedóška nažigè dábabè yo he ye đe ye đò

Interpretation:	*Heđóška nąžį́gè.*
	"*Heđóška* arise!" (plus vocables).
	Heđóška nąžį́gè. Dą́babè.
	"*Heđóška* arise! Behold these men"
	(plus vocables).
	Šénužįgà, uhétè wegáxabè.
	"Young men, the path has been made."
	Wak'ą́da gaxábè. Nažį́gà.
	"The Mystery [God] has made this path.
	Arise!"

VETERAN SONG

Leader starts song:	Hi ya ya ha i ya he e he ya e ho we yo he đe đe
Singers second song:	Hi ya ya ha i ya he e he ya e ho we yo he đe đe
	He ya ya ya i ya ha ya a e ho we yo he đe đe
	Ya i ha ya e ho hi ya ya e ha ya ho we yo he
	đe đǫ̀ì
Chorus of song:	*Šénužįgà nudą́ đaítè eí wadą́babè* yo he ye
	đe ye đe
	Nú' tè t'éxì ho kagéá Wak'ą́da gáxabè yo he
	ye đeye
	đòi
Interpretation:	*Šénužįgà nudą́ đaítè eí wadą́babè.*
	"Behold these young men as they go to war"
	(plus vocables).
	Nú' tè t'éxì ho kagéá Wak'ą́da gáxabè.
	"Being a man is difficult. Friend, the Mystery
	[God] has made it that way" (plus vocables).

There were veterans' songs made especially for the Ponca *Heđúškà* organizations. These songs, according to the elders of the tribe, were made for all *Heđúškà* members regardless of their organizational affiliation. There are numerous songs of this type. In modern times, as in the past, certain songs were composed by song makers who designated certain individuals as recipients. Particularly those who participated in the First and Second World War were honored by the gift of some of these songs. In recent years some Ponca men received their songs for serving in the Korean, Vietnam, and Persian Gulf (Desert Storm) Wars.

A HEÐÚŠKÀ SONG

Leader starts song:	*Wak'ą́da wagít'ąbagà, Wak'ą́da wagít'ąbagà*
Singers second song:	*Wak'ą́da wagít'ąbagà, Wak'ą́da wagít'ąbagà*
	Wak'ą́da wagít'ąbagà, Wak'ą́da wagít'ąbagà
	Wak'ą́da wagít'ąbabe yo he e ᵈe e ᵈoì
Chorus of song:	*Heᵈóška tè t'éxiʃdè, p'áxeʃdè, ą́kihidà*
	Wak'ą́da wagít'ąbagà
	Wak'ą́da wagít'ąbabe yo he e ᵈe e ᵈą̀
Interpretation:	*Wak'ą́da wagít'ąbagà.*
	"God watch over us."
	(Repeat five times then vocables.)
	Heᵈóška tè t'éxiʃdè, p'áxeʃdè, ą́kihidà.
	"The *Heᵈúškà* is a difficult way. I am living it. Watch over me."

A HEDÚŠKÀ SONG

Leader starts song:	*Heᵈóška tè waíbedą́, ké, ną̨žį́gà* yo he e ᵈe e ho
Singers second song:	*Heᵈóška tè waíbedą́, ké, ną̨žį́gà* yo he e ᵈe e ho
	Heᵈóška tè waíbedą́, ké, ną̨žį́gà yo he e ᵈe ᵈ'e
	Heᵈóška tè waíbedą́, ké, ną̨žį́gà yo he e ᵈe ᵈoì
Chorus of song:	*Heᵈóška mà Wak'ą́da akà waíbedą̀, ké, ną̨žį́gà* yo he e ᵈe e ᵈe
	Heᵈóška tè waíbedą́, ké, ną̨žį́gà yo he e ᵈe e da
Interpretation:	*Heᵈúškà tè waíbedą̀, ké, ną̨žį́gà.*
	"The *Heᵈúškà* has been given to us" (plus vocables).
	Heᵈúškà mà Wak'ą́da akà waíbedą̀, ké, ną̨žį́gà.

"God has been given the *Hedúškà* to us"
(plus vocables).

Note: AL said the *Hedúškà* "way of life" was a gift from God. In the phrase, *Hedúškà mà Wak'ǫ́da akà waíbedà*, a connotation is made that the Ponca already had the *Hedúškà* concept but the "way of life" that one should live was a gift from God.

Quitting Song

In one of his recordings, Sylvester Warrior mentioned the *Hedúškà* organization had what is commonly call the "Quitting Song," which he said should be titled the "finale song," which connotes the final event in a series.

Leader starts song:	Hi ye ye *danǫ́žite de, ǫ́nǫžitè dè*
Singers second song:	Hi ye ye *danǫ́žite de, ǫ́nǫžitè dè*
	Hi ye dé *anǫ́žite de, Kodá da anǫ́žite dè*
	Ịdádi gáxedà nǫží dé dé
	Wak'ǫ́da gáxedà nǫ́ži dé yo he dé dǫ
Chorus of song:	*Hedúškà té dédu gáxabè dé, ǫ́nǫžitè dè*
	Ịdádi gáxedà nǫží dé dé
	Wak'ǫ́da gáxedà nǫ́ži dé yo he dé dǫ
Interpretation:	*Hi ye dé anǫ́žite de, Kodá da anǫ́žite dè.*
	(Vocables) "Here I arise, friend, we arise here!"
	Ịdádi gáxedà nǫží dé dé.
	"Father composed this, therefore, arise here!"
	Wak'ǫ́da gáxedà nǫ́ži dé yo he dé dǫ.
	"God [or Great Mystery] composed this, therefore, arise here!"
	Hedúškà té dédu gáxabè dé, ǫ́nǫžitè dè.
	"The *Hedúškà* was made here, so I stand or arise."
	Ịdádi gáxedà nǫží dé dé.

"Father composed this, therefore,
arise here!"

Wak'ą́da gáxedą ną́ži đé yo he đé đą.

"God [or Great Mystery] composed this,
therefore, arise here!"

Some names that are associated with making songs in the first half of
the twentieth century in Oklahoma are Oscar Makes Cry, Pete Washington, Charley Waters, Sylvester Warrior, Lamont Brown, Albert Waters,
and Harry Buffalohead. In very recent years, Joe Hairyback (deceased),
James "Pee Wee" Clark (deceased), Henry Collins (deceased), and
Jimmy Kemble have made songs. Songs from the nineteenth century
and back are still being sung. Composers for such songs are unknown.

14
Family Structure and Kinship System

Previous to the removal to Indian Territory, a typical household consisted of grandparents, mother, father, sons, and daughters. If the sons were married, their wives and children also lived in the same dwelling. Living with parents was a practice that covered a period when the Ponca lived in earthen lodges, or *Mąít'i*, that extended well into the twentieth century (KH). The first thing that impresses me about the family structure, especially the kinship system of the Ponca, is that it showed great warmth. Members of the family always expressed consideration for each other as well as for other members of the tribe. Comparatively speaking, this kind of warmth in the English system extends only to immediate members of the family unit and encompasses only mother, father, daughter, son, and sometimes grandmother and grandfather. The indifference begins in the use of the term *cousin* when referring to one's parent's sibling's offspring. This concept can go into infinity as in first, second, third cousins, and so forth. Where that closest feeling of warmth to family members ceases to exist in the English system, the Ponca system continues to reach the extended family and tribe.

Although the tribe has assimilated in the dominant society, the kinship system is still being used. In the past, many attempts were made by our people and others to find English words suitable to use in the place of Ponca terminology.

At first, it seemed appropriate to use terms that appear to be equivalent to the Ponca language. But as one proceeds into the system, breakdowns of terms occur, and English words do not apply. According to the elders, the breakdown is based on the researcher's failure to understand that Ponca words connoted nuances unfamiliar to them. In their evaluation of the Ponca system, it seems that the habitation of the dwelling (any large dwelling) and clan system played an important role in the structuring of the kinship system. Designated sections of the dwelling were described as places for living, cooking, eating, sleeping, and storage.

Some Ponca and English terms have the same meanings, namely, words for the one who has fathered a child and the one who gives birth. The Ponca terms are the same as English for mother (Įnahà) and father (Įdádi). The meaning of the term for grandmother, Wiką̀, is unknown. The term for grandfather, Witígą, suggests "the house I am of." Ponca terms also take on a different meaning when applied to other family members. For example, in addressing one's siblings, the proper term describes whether they are younger or older, before or after by birth. These kinds of terms are most descriptive and appropriate when applied to other family members. Accordingly, ego being male, his younger brother is called Wisą́ga because he was "born after" him and his older brother is called Wižį́de because he was "born before" him. This rule applies to his sisters as well. His younger sister is called Wihé while his older sister is called Witą́gè. The words, of course, are more meaningful and give impetus for closeness to the one being addressed or vice versa. The terms, additionally, are applicable when addressing ego's father's brothers and his mother's sister's sons and daughters (first cousins in the English) (KH, KCH, AMC, JP, NC).

The relationship of ego, ego being male, to his mother's brother's daughter is Wižįge, or "son." She in turn is called Įnahà žįgà (little mother) or Įnahà (mother) by ego. Age is not a factor because the "little mother" may be younger or older than ego. There is a connotation in the system that some socio-behavioral pattern developed through the generations. One of the most common practices among children is that they play together. This included a visiting relative's children and other children. Close relatives, such as these, played games with each other. Girl relatives could play with boys until they were about eleven or twelve years old. The word for "play" is T'í gáxè (to make a house). Playacting among all children is also common. Boys and girls sometimes mimicked their parent's roles in the family. Ponca boys pretended to go on hunting expeditions. They also practiced with bows and arrows, as though they would fight with enemy tribes. Girls mimicked the role of mother in the dwelling by playacting gathering sticks for firewood, cooking, mending clothing, and

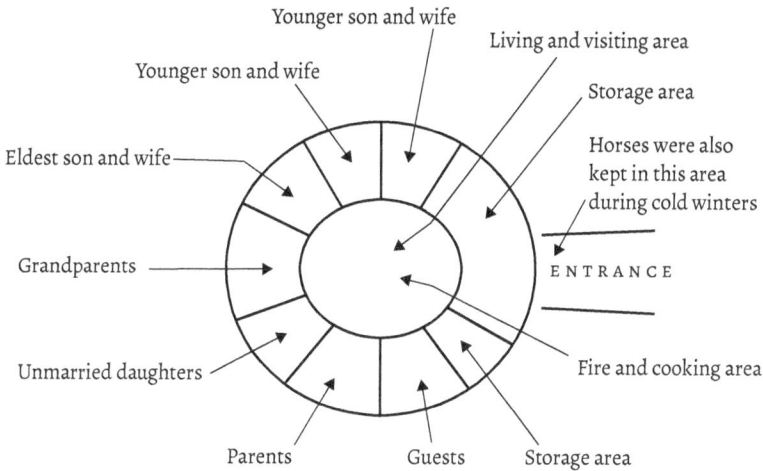

Younger son and wife
Younger son and wife
Living and visiting area
Storage area
Eldest son and wife
Horses were also kept in this area during cold winters
Grandparents
ENTRANCE
Unmarried daughters
Fire and cooking area
Parents   Guests   Storage area

DIAGRAM 1. Floor plan of *Mąít'i*. Created by the author.

so forth. It stands to reason that this relationship would make little girl cousins (especially first cousins) *Įnahà žįgà*, or "little mothers."

The diagram of the earthen lodge shows how the living arrangements might have been in earlier years. The dwelling (*Mąít'i*) was as large as 120 feet in diameter. The living space was large enough to house these families together. According to KH and KCH, when a son's family become large enough that they needed more room, they built a new dwelling with the help of family members. These, then, were the conditions or the environment in which children were reared. From the quarters of the dwelling, their clan affiliation, and children's play came other terms that normally applied to adults, such as mother, father, uncle, aunt, son, daughter, brother-in-law, "little mother," "little uncle," and so forth. Whether their relatives were of close or of distant bloodlines, the family continued to address them according to the social mores. Visiting friends too were given a special place to sleep in the dwelling. The Ponca family sometimes adopted these tribal and nontribal members as relatives. The kinship terms were applied to them as if they were blood relatives (KH, KCH, NC, AMC).

In 1987 I met with Stanford Whitestar, Dr. Sherman Warrior, and Edwin Littlecook concerning the kinship system. After we had identified and categorized terms for every possible relationship, we decided the phrase "closest English equivalent" for the translations was inadequate. It seems that each identifying characteristic of the terms used is elusive and not easily interpretable, although some credible definitions were discussed and suggested by other researchers. For our purposes, we are obliged to do the same. The Ponca kinship system has many features, unlike the English type. In the following, the prefix Wi- suggests the relationship as "my" as in Witígą, "my grandfather." Because some words were spoken differently by male and female, the principle terms below are listed separately or for both when they are the same.

Ponca Word	English Word	Said By
Witígą	Grandfather	Both
Wiką́	Grandmother	Both
Įdádì	Father	Both
Įnahà	Mother	Both
Wižį́ɖe	Older brother	Male
Witínu	Older brother	Female
Wisą́ga	Younger brother	Both
Witą́ge	Older sister	Male
Wižą́ɖe	Older sister	Female
Wihé	Younger sister	Both
Wižį́ge	Son	Both
Wižą́ge	Daughter	Both
Winégi	Uncle	Both
Witími	Aunt	Both
Witą́ška	Nephew	Male
Witúška	Nephew	Female
Witížą	Niece	Male
Witúžągè (also wihé)	Niece	Female
Witúšpa	Grandchild	Both

Witáhą	Brother-in-law	Male
Wiši'e	Brother-in-law	Female
Wihą́ga	Sister-in-law	Male
Wišíką	Sister-in-law	Female
Míwadixè	Daughter-in-law	Both
Witáhą	Son-in-law	Both
Wigáxdą	Wife	Male
Wiégdągè	Husband	Female
Witígą	Father-in-law (Grandfather)	Both
Wiką́	Mother-in-law (Grandmother)	Both

The following terms are listed as a possessive pronoun with the use of the prefix *Wi-*, for example, *Witígą*, or "my grandfather." The term for daughter-in-law is *Míwadixè*. The instrumental prefix *Mí-* is feminine and is in the possessive case. The prefix *Į́-*, "his, her, or its," is used to modify the noun as in "his father, his mother," for example, *Itígą*, "his grandfather." The term *Wádixè* means "to be married" when referring to women. The term used for men is *Mígdą*, which is also in the possessive case but is used with the male form *Gdą́*, "to be married."

The following statements show the Ponca word for every possible relationship (m = male / f = female):

Son is called *Wižíge*.

Son's wife is called *Míwadixè*.

Daughter is called *Wižą́ge*.

Daughter's husband is called *Witą́de*.

Son's son and daughter are called *Witúšpà*.

Daughter's son and daughter are called *Witúšpà*.

Brother's wife is called *Wihą́ga* (m) *Wišíką* (f).

Brother's son is called *Wižíge* (m) *Witúškà* (f).

Brother's son's wife is called *Míwadixè*.

Brother's daughter is called *Wižą́ge*.

Brother's daughter's husband is called *Witáde*.

Sister's husband is called *Witáhạ* (m) *Wišíʼe* (f).

Sister's son is called *Witą́škà* (m) *Wižíge* (f).

Sister's son's wife is called *Míwadixè*.

Sister's daughter is called *Witížạ* (m) *Wižą́ge* (f).

Sister's daughter's husband is called *Witą́de*.

Father's elder brother is called *Ịdádi*.

Father's younger brother is called *Ịdádižịgà*.

Father's sister is called *Witími*.

Father's brother's wife is called *Ínahà*.

Father's sister's husband is called *Winégi*.

Father's brother's son is called *Wižídẹ/Wisą́ga* (m) *Witínu/Wisą́ga* (f).

Father's brother's daughter is called *Witą́ge/Wihé* (m) *Wižą́dẹ/wihé* (f).

Father's brother's son's wife is called *Wihą́gạ* (m) *Wišíkạ* (f).

Father's brother's daughter's husband is called *Witáhą́* (m) *Wišíʼe* (f).

Father's brother's son's son is called *Wižíge*.

Father's brother's son's daughter is called *Wižą́ge*.

Father's brother's son's son's wife is called *Míwadixè*.

Father's brother's daughter's daughter's husband is called *Witą́dè*.

Father's brother's daughter's son is called *Witą́škà* (m) *Wižíge* (f).

Father's brother's daughter's daughter is called *Witížą́* (m) *Wižą́ge* (f).

Father's sister's son is called *Witą́škà* (m) *Wižíge* (f).

Father's sister's daughter is called *Witížą́* (m) *Witúžạgè* (f).

Father's sister's son's wife is called *Míwadixè*.

Father's sister's daughter's husband is called *Witą́de*.

Father's sister's son's son is called *Witą́škà* (m) *Wižíge* (f).

Father's sister's son's daughter is called *Witížạ* (m) *Witúžạgè* (f).

Father's sister's son's son's wife is called *Míwadixè*.

Father's sister's daughter's daughter's husband is called *Witą́de*.

Father's sister's daughter's son is called *Witą́škà* (m) *Wižíge* (f).

Father's sister's daughter's daughter is called *Witížạ* (m) *Witúžạgè* (f).

Mother's brother is called *Winégì*.

Mother's brother's wife is called *Witímì*.

Mother's brother's son is called *Winégižįgà*.

Mother's brother's daughter is called *Wiháźįgà*.

Mother's brother's son's son is called *Winégižįgà*.

Mother's brother's son's daughter is called *Wiháźįgà*.

Mother's brother's daughter's son is called *Wižíɖe/Wisága* (m) *Witínù/Wisága* (f).

Mother's brother's daughter's daughter is called *Witágè/Wihé* (m) *Wižáɖe/wihé* (f).

Mother's brother's son's wife is called *Witímì*.

Mother's brother's son's son's wife is called *Witímì*.

Mother's brother's daughter's husband is called *Įdádi*.

Mother's brother's daughter's daughter's husband is called *Witáhạ*.

Mother's sister is called *Wihá*.

Mother's sister's husband is called *Įdádižįgà*.

Mother's sister's son is called *Wižíɖe/Wisága* (m) *Witínù/Wisága* (f).

Mother's sister's daughter is called *Wižáge/Wihé* (m) *Wižáɖe/wihé* (f).

Mother's sister's son's son is called *Wižíge*.

Mother's sister's son's daughter is called *Wižáge*.

Mother's sister's daughter's son is called *Witáška* (m) *Wit'úška* (f).

Mother's sister's daughter's daughter is called *Witížạ* (m) *Wižáge* (f).

Mother's sister's son's wife is called *Wihága* (m) *Wišíkạ* (f).

Mother's sister's son's son's wife is called *Míwaɖixè*.

Mother's sister's daughter's husband is called *Witáhạ*.

Mother's sister's daughter's daughter's husband is called *Witáɖè*.

Use of Žįgá (Little)

The Ponca kinship system has "little fathers," "little mothers," and "little uncles." Unlike the English system, these terms of endearment give one a sense of direction and understanding of his or her status in the family circle.

The rule for using the term *žįgá*, or "little," is based on the age of (male) ego's relative. The term *Winégì*, or "uncle," is normally used for ego's mother's brother. Ego also refers to his uncle's male children as *Winégì* or *Winégì žįgá*. This terminology is derived from the virtue of being ego's mother's male siblings (older or younger). The Ponca term *Winégì* is applied to all male members of the lineage of ego's mother's brother's male offspring whether they are his sons, grandsons, great-grandsons, et cetera. Even though it would be appropriate to call them *Winégì*, or "uncle," in modern times, it loses significance when applied to ego's *Winégì žįgá*. For our purposes, this means "little uncle." If ego's "little uncle" is older than he is, the term *žįgá* is dropped. If he is younger, the term, of course, is *Winégì žįgá*. This latter rule on age applies to *Įdádi* (father), *Įnahà* (mother), and *Winégì* (uncle), especially ego's mother's brother and his male offspring. In the case of *Įdádi*, who is ego's father, the term is also used for his father's brother. If ego's father's brother is younger, he is referred to as *Įdádi žįgá*, or "little father." If he is older, the term *žįgá* is dropped. He then is called *Įdádi* as his natural father. This is done out of respect for his age. Ego's father's brother's wife is always called *Įnahà žįgá* with no regard to age. Ego's mother's sister likewise is called *Įnahà žįgá* if she is younger. If she is older than his mother, the term *žįgá* is dropped. The term *Įnahà žįgá* is likewise applied to ego's mother's brother's daughter. When she becomes married, her children become ego's brothers and sisters. All of ego's mother's brother's male offspring are called *Winégì žįgà* and their sisters are *Įnahà žįgá*. The rule at this point is set. It cannot be changed. The rule for ego's mother's sister's husband is that he is always called *Įdádi žįgá* or nothing at all. He is just there. Perhaps out of respect he is called *Įdádi žįgá*.

As a rule, the Ponca family was considered "very close," that is, they held each member of the family in high regard. The closeness of the family and extended family included friends who were considered an essential part of their family unit. Consequently, these adopted "relatives" fit into the scheme of the family structure. Howard (1995) in his work on the Ponca Tribe quoted Dorsey (1890, 291) that the "relationships between parents and children of the same sex were very close." As described in the folktale "The Bear Girl," her mother combed her hair although she was grown. This was customary. The relationship between mother and daughter as I saw in my own family was always very close. William Whitman (1939, 187) described a relationship between father and son as "quite restrained." Mutual respect and honor have always existed in the relationship between father and son.

Even though each person was shown respect, the development of a teasing relationship became acceptable for certain relatives. For example, a teasing or joking relationship existed between uncle and nephew, aunt and niece, brother and sister-in-law, and sister and brother-in-law. Sometimes the teasing or joking became extreme until one or the other declined to continue. KCH said on one occasion that she and her sister were fetching water when their uncles rode up on horseback. The uncles began to taunt them with joking statements. They were speaking Ponca, of course. One said, "What are they?" "Are they some kind of bugs—look at that one—it's long and tall and looks just like a Teátatà [praying mantis]." KCH's sister responded, looking at one of them and without a blink of an eye, "I know what kind of bug that is— it's an Įǥé babútà [dung beetle]!" Without another word, the uncles rode off. One of the uncles was short, fat, and very dark skinned! Who said Indians didn't have a sense of humor?

An extreme mutual respect existed between father-in-law and daughter-in-law, as well as between mother-in-law and son-in-law. Communication between these relationships was indeed limited and on occasions could borderline something comical. Many stories tell how the father-in-law sought to ask his daughter-in-law some question— when she was in the same room. He would proceed to ask his son to ask his daughter-in-law. The son then would repeat the question to the daughter-in-law—the same question that she had already heard—and she would respond to her husband, who in turn relayed the answer to his father. One occasion, in modern times, a son simply said, "Why don't you just ask her yourself? She's sitting right there."

The husband and wife relationship in earlier times was sometimes a stringent one in which the husband was the absolute head of the home. But they had deep affection for one another. The husband assumed a protective role over his wife and children. Being the strongest in the household required that he be able to hunt with success and provide his family with the necessary sustenance for survival. Wives, not unlike women of the early twentieth century, took care of the home and children. Other members of the family shared certain responsibilities as well. KH and NC said that uncles in the "old days would teach their nephews about girls and sexual things." Aunts too told their nieces what to expect in their relationships with boys and men. Grandparents served as mentors to the young, especially their grandchildren. Brothers and sisters, that is, those who could be thus called, were not permitted to play together beyond the age of about eleven or twelve years. At that time they had to assume a relationship of deep respect that would last for the remainder of their lives. They spoke to each other only when necessary, and statements were curt and to the point. This has been relaxed, however, and today there is an open and frank relationship between brothers and sisters. They can tease and speak to each other without fear of offending one another.

The eldest son was always given the best of everything. He inherited the right to the father's seat in the council if his father was a chief of any rank. Normally, he did not inherit medicines or medicine bundles from his father. But it could be done. Usually medicines were considered a gift from nature, and individuals with medicines were said to have a special understanding of that gift. In the story of *Čígadišížè*, medicines could be stolen and not considered a gift. The eldest son, however, did have advantages not provided to his younger siblings. In the past this may have been acceptable, but it is no longer practiced in modern times. Some children began to resent this practice in the mid-twentieth century, and as a result, the custom has been abandoned. Some families have tried to follow this practice but with little success. One reason is that one or more of the other siblings have caught the spirit of competition in the dominant society. Even though that is the case, some families have insisted on giving the eldest son or daughter the favored treatment whether they were successful or not. Few families still attempt to hold on to this ancient custom.

15
Marriage and Property

Marriages among the Ponca were prearranged during the time they lived in what is now Nebraska and South Dakota. When a family had a son who became of age to marry, they picked the girl to whom he would marry (KH, AMC, AL, VBSH). However, other family members and friends sometimes participated in making personal suggestions concerning the prospective couple's compatibility. The elders said some families were circumspect and wanted their children to marry into certain families. KH, AMC, and AL said that some boys and girls were known to have "liked each other," and this was known by most people, including their families. It was not unusual for families to recognize these special relationships and allow marriages to take place between the couple.

When conditions were in order, the parents of the girl were usually spoken to by some person who had a close relationship with both families. If the family of the girl agreed to the marriage, the mutual friend conveyed this to the boy's family. The marriage rite was then carried out by the parents of the young man.

Girls married at approximately sixteen to eighteen years of age. Dorsey (1884, 259) said that in former times "men waited until they were twenty-five or thirty, and the women till they were twenty years of age." Others have suggested girls were fourteen to sixteen years of age when they married. We assume that the established system of pre-arranged marriages did work as there were few divorcements among the Ponca at that time. Influences from the social mores, it is said, kept couples together. Young couples were given emotional support as well as gifts and other resources by both parents. As they joined together in marriage, they were promised help from the female parents to raise their children.

The act of gift giving among the Ponca people was and is practiced in all social activities.[1] After proper intentions were conveyed to each parent and agreements were made complete, the act of marriage was initiated. The procedure for uniting a couple in marriage was given by KH as follows:

> The parents of the young man . . . they go to visit the girl's parents and offered gifts to them. The gifts were usually horses, blankets . . . other things of value. The girl then has to go with the boy's parents back to their home. After they lived together for a few days . . . the parents sent their son and new daughter-in-law to her parents with more gifts. That's the end . . . this makes the marriage complete. Sometimes . . . if everything is alright . . . the parents of the girl give their son-in-law something to take back to his parents.

Well wishes for the newlyweds were made by family and friends as they began their marriage. The young couple usually stayed with the boy's parents as mentioned. This still is, somewhat, the trend among the Ponca. But more often couples in modern times like to get their own apartments or home. Additionally, we are seeing more and more church weddings with all the trimmings.

Property

The right to possess, use, and dispose of something is a good concept of Ponca ownership. The use of land and its natural resources was recognized by neighboring tribes. This included game, trees, streams, and topographical areas, such as mountains and plains. Some locations were considered sacred to the people and were respected by all people. Among the Ponca, individual places near the village site were also considered sacred and were avoided by tribal members. The elders said the land, in some cases, was held communally for hunting. During those times, the identification of the land held by the Ponca and some tribes was known by natural boundaries. These boundaries were known by other tribes, and certain procedures were required to cross the territory. Without the proper entrance into the land, a tribe could take the trespass as an aggressive act.

The right to possess and use certain lands was indeed respected and the unwritten law obeyed. Originally, personal property was marked by the owner. These properties included clothing, weapons, horses, robes, tipis, and other dwellings. Sometimes, certain kinds of property belonged to a clan. These were religious in nature, namely, clan pipes and medicines. Incorporeal property is intrinsically part of an individual, clan, or tribe. This type of property would then include clan names, clan ceremonials, tribal songs, songs of individuals or families, dances, and games (KH, AMC, AL, NC). Ownership of tribal songs, for instance, has come to be a great social issue with the Ponca people. These songs, new and old, have been composed for individuals for their personal acts of kindness or accomplishments that were significant to each individual. There is a problem with the tribal ownership. For some tribes, songs to dance by are simply songs to dance by. Not so with the Ponca. The songs are respected because they are personal and can only be shared by the individual who allows the song to be sung.

In the earlier part of the twentieth century, this type of property, namely, Hedúška songs, was given away by tribal singers. Songs were given away by Ponca singers to the Osage Indians. In return for the songs, the individual singers received much money and material gifts from the oil-wealthy Osage. Differences of opinion arose as to the ethics of this practice, but most agreed that once it was done it could not be taken back. It has been disclosed for some time now that certain families of that tribe possess "old Ponca songs" on old-time cylinder recordings. Again, because of the money they had, they could buy the latest advances in recording technology and record our songs. But those Ponca who have been privileged to hear the old recordings stated that the songs were very common songs sung by our people. The Osage now claim the songs as their own because "the songs were given to them by the Ponca." Modern singers have no problem with this. They say, "Just remember, their origin is Ponca." Unfortunately, they have replaced the old Ponca words with Osage words. In some cases, other tribes have done the same (AL, AMC, and Harry Buffalohead).

Community property included land, animals (bison, elk, deer, etc.), plants, water, fire, and air. Food, for instance, was considered community property because it was derived from the land, that is, an animal or plant. Foodstuff grown in the fields was equally divided among tribal members. The meats, scapula, sinew, and so forth of bison brought home by hunters was shared. The biblical concept that espouses "If a man not work, he should not eat" would have destroyed a tribe, for the infirmed, lamed, or those traveling at the time would have been left out. Acts of benevolent sharing would have altered the social and religious structure. Consequently, if game was plentiful, all ate. The elders said gathered fruits and vegetables were shared by all. And the butchering of a new kill of bison allowed for the first comer; that is, the one who would butcher could take what he desired. The second person took the second-best piece and so forth, but everyone got a fair share. In those days, violating certain customs could result in unwanted consequences. VBSH used to tell the following story of how some Ponca families left the main body of the tribe following an episode of being left out in the distribution of sinew (my translation):

> After the bison hunt, the men divided the meat and sinew. Everyone was happy after they received their share. But a few families did not receive their share of sinew. They protested in their quiet way, but there were no leaders to speak for them. They became withdrawn from the rest of the people, and one day they packed their belongings and left the tribe forever. No one knows where they went, but those who watched them go said that they went north. Some believed that they probably ended up very far north in the cold country. They refer to them as *Pá̜ca dúba taká̜ uxí̜ʼe ayáḍaì* (the Ponca who went away complaining about sinew).

The disposition of property was restricted to personal property. This was done at any gathering that included giveaways. As mentioned elsewhere, there are four types of giveaways. The first is called *Wagáḍè*, "to give away something." This can be done anytime. The second is *Waḍʃḍè*, "to cause someone to have," or the act of giving in public dances, especially *Ská ágḍį*, "One Who Sits upon the White." The standard procedure in giving is to "look around you and see if anyone present is in need and give to that one." The third is *Ḍįgéḍè*, "to give away everything." This was done in earlier times when death occurred in a family. They gave away all their property, including the dwelling. KH, AMC, AL, and NC said that in Oklahoma, the family gave away only those items used by the deceased, such as bedroom furniture, rifles, knives, awls, and so forth. This is called *Waḍísi*. (The deceased's clothing and bedding were burned at the time of their death.) This giveaway was done several months following the passing of the relative.

The family set the time when they would sponsor a feast in memoriam of the deceased. The gathering of material goods, such as blankets, shawls, cloth material, and so forth, from family members and friends set the stage for this occasion. During these times, the gifts were given to individuals who were the approximate age of the deceased and to others who were help to the family (KH, KCH, AMC).

The modern church today ritualizes the "giving away" of the bride. This rite has its historical roots in many cultures worldwide. In a certain way, the Ponca considered the wife as property of the husband. KH and AL said in an ancient custom, the husband was permitted to give away his wife. The act of giving away one's wife is unknown to most Ponca. As an adolescent, I once heard Uncle Simon Henderson, Osage Indian and rancher, say in a man's conversation during the afternoon following a peyote meeting: "The Ponca have all us tribes beat in giveaways, they have a wife giveaway song. When you get up to dance, you can give away your wife." The menfolk laughed and asked my father if it was so. He nodded yes, it was true. Later he explained this in the following:

> In the early part of this century . . . the last of the Ponca wife givers . . . gave away his wife. At the old roundhouse, they was having a dance and a man gave away his wife. His mother-in-law got real mad and gave her daughter a knife to stab her husband. She said that they was making fun of them. The old lady told her . . . if you don't do it . . . I'm going to stab you! That girl walked behind that man . . . he was sitting next to a window at that roundhouse . . . she reached around him and stabbed him in the shoulder. That man bled to death.

According to the federal law, he said, the elder woman was charged with duress and was sentenced to life imprisonment. She died in the Leavenworth Federal Penitentiary. The practice of giving away one's wife no longer exists.

Today's concept of ownership is basically the same as in the ongoing world. The "what's mine is mine and what's yours is yours" philosophy is predominant in most cultures. The Ponca, as well as other tribes, have only one property item that belongs to the U.S. government — land. Since the Ponca are a federally recognized tribe of Indians, they are like wards of the government. This means that our lands are not ours to manipulate; that is, we cannot run a business on it or sell it without the due approval of the federal government, namely, the Interior Department's Bureau of Indian Affairs. Certain governmental procedures must be met in order to sell or lease our lands. Even though Indians have use and right to possess the land (which are nontaxable) without due approval from the BIA, they cannot do much with the land. For example, if a tribe or any Indian wishes to open a business on tribal trust or individual trust lands, they must acquire a "third-party agreement," which usually includes the tribe, the company doing business, and the BIA, which approves or disapproves the transaction (RDH). Indians who live off reservation comply with all tax laws as would any American citizen. Since all reservation Indians are U.S. citizens, they must also pay appropriate taxes. The only taxes they do not pay are lands they possess, which are considered federal trust lands. The government cannot tax itself.

FIG. 1. *Moonlight*. Oklahoma Historical Society, 19687.IN.PON.5.2. Chester R. Cowen Collection. Photographs. Box 6. Indians-Ponca-camps. Copyrighted 1907 by George B. Cornish, Arkansas City KS. Printed by the Albertype Co., Brooklyn NY.

FIG. 2. Ponca Indians on horseback lined up double file. Oklahoma Historical Society, 6482.8. E. M. Fry, Mrs. Collection. Photographs. Box 1. Events-Wild West Shows-101 Ranch. *Celebration 101 Ranch before Statehood.*

FIG. 3. Ponca Indians on horseback. Oklahoma Historical Society, 6482.10. E. M. Fry, Mrs. Collection. Photographs. Box 1. Events-Wild West Shows-101 Ranch. *Celebration 101 Ranch before Statehood.* Photo by J. Drake, Ponca City, Oklahoma Territory.

FIG. 4. *Ponca Police Court.* Oklahoma Historical Society, 19383.99.1. Frederick S. Barde Collection. Photographs. Box 2. Indians-Ponca-law. 1890–1916.

FIG. 5. Sun Dance, 1900. Oklahoma Historical Society, 3447.B. Frederick S. Barde Collection. Photographs. Box 2. Indians-Ponca-Sun Dance-1900.

FIG. 6. Sun Dance. Oklahoma Historical Society, 19383.101.15. Frederick S. Barde Collection. Photographs. Box 2. Indians-Ponca-Sun Dance, 1890–1916.

FIG. 7. Sun Dance. Oklahoma Historical Society, 19383.101.11. Frederick S. Barde Collection. Photographs. Box 2. Indians-Ponca-Sun Dance, 1890–1916.

FIG. 8. Chief Crazy Bear of White Eagle, Oklahoma. Oklahoma Historical Society, 5288. John L. Coffey Collection. Photographs. Box 1. Indians-Ponca-Chief Crazy Bear of White Eagle OK. Printed c. 1918–22.

FIG. 9. Weak Bone, Ponca Chief. Oklahoma Historical Society, 16204. John L. Coffey Collection. Photographs. Box 1. Indians-Ponca-Weak Bone, Ponca chief. Photo by Solomon Trompetter, c. 1926–39.

FIG. 10. *Council and Dance Ponca Indians Okla. Terr.* Oklahoma Historical Society, 20315.14.4. Kent Ruth Collection. Photographs. Box 1. Indians-Ponca. Photo by Christopher Stotz, El Reno, Oklahoma Territory.

FIG. 11. *#113 Indian Agent with the Chiefs of the Ponca Nation.* Oklahoma Historical Society, 20687. Oklahoma Historical Society Photograph Collection. Photographs. Indians. Indians-Ponca. Photo printed by S. J. Morrow, Yankton, D.T., c. 1881. 1860s–2006.

FIG. 12. Stands Yellow. Oklahoma Historical Society, 15650. Ruth Mohler Collection. Photographs. Box 1. Ponca Indians-Stands Yellow. Photo by Croft of Arkansas KS.

FIG. 13. Antoine Ray at a Sun Dance. Oklahoma Historical Society, 15676. Ruth Mohler Collection. Photographs. Box 1. Indians-Ponca-Dance-Antoine Ray at a Sun Dance.

FIG. 14. Max Black Hair
Horse. Oklahoma Historical
Society, 15687. Ruth Mohler
Collection. Photographs.
Box 1. Indians-Ponca-Max
Black Hair Horse.

FIG. 15. Earnestine Blueback
and Betty Joe Buffalohead.
Oklahoma Historical
Society, 20912.20.65.
Tartoue Negative Collection.
Photographs. Box 1. *l. to r.*: 1.
Earnestine Blueback, age 5. 2.
Betty Joe Buffalohead, age 5.
Poncas. White Eagle OK 1947.

FIG. 16. Irontail, a Ponca. Oklahoma Historical Society, 20588.12.B.20. Thomas-Foreman Home Collection. Photographs. Box 1. Indians: Irontail, a Ponca. Photo by Vincent Dillon, Fairfax OK.

FIG. 17. Sun Dancers, including Plain Chief, Robert Raise the Other, and Oscar Makes Cry (Little Cottonwood). Oklahoma Historical Society, 5014. Thomas N. Athey Collection. Photographs. Box 1. Indians-Ponca-dance-Sun-Dancers. *l. to r.*: 1–11. Unidentified, 12. Plain Chief, 13. Robert Raise the Other, 14. Oscar Makes Cry (Little Cottonwood), 15–16. Unidentified.

FIG. 18. Indians dressed ready for dance. Oklahoma Historical Society, 16558. Virgil Robbins Collection. Photographs. Box 2. Indians-Ponca-dance-Indians dressed ready for dance. Postcard.

FIG. 19. Chief Good Boy. Oklahoma Historical Society, 16293. Virgil Robbins Collection. Photographs. Box 2. Indians-Ponca-persons-groups-Chief Good Boy. Postcard. Photo by Vince Dillon, Fairfax OK.

FIG. 20. Logan Cerre. Oklahoma Historical Society, 3628.2. W. P. Campbell Collection. Photographs. Box 1. Indians-Ponca-Logan Cerre, 1918. Photo by Love, Pawhuska OK, 1899–1928.

16
Clans of the Ponca

The elders' interpretation of the word *clan* is a group of people who are related through their fathers. Their mothers are of a different clan. The elders believed through lineage a clan has a common ancestry. Being exogamous, the Ponca are allowed to marry outside their clan. Therefore, children of any clan cannot marry within their own clan. In tribal organization and political governance, the clans were connected according to the elders.

There was a rush of searching for information on the clanship system of the Ponca people in the early 1970s, when it was again apparent that the elders of the tribe would not be with us much longer. During the interviews, there was a general agreement about the origins of the Ponca clans and their position in the summer encampments. As mentioned elsewhere, the Ponca camped in four circles. The Lower Brule once called the Ponca *Oyáte dúbà*, or "four camps," referring to the four circles. Other Sioux people referred to Ponca as *Oyáte yamni*, or "three villages," probably in reference to the last three Ponca villages before removal to Indian Territory. KH, NC, JP, AMC, and AL said that the Ponca people had divisions within the tribe called *Tą́wągdą̀*, or "clans," and that they camped according to their place in the circle or circles. The modern term means town or city.

Although there was no apparent evidence that the clans were affiliated with the directions, the division of the clan encampment coincided with the eight directions. The Ponca people had eight clans, which were patrilineal. KH supplied the names for the directions in the following diagram:

Beginning with east and moving counterclockwise, the English translation of the Ponca terms for the directions are as follows:

East: *Mí édąbet'à*   where the sun rises
Northeast: *Ítat'à*   that which is touchable

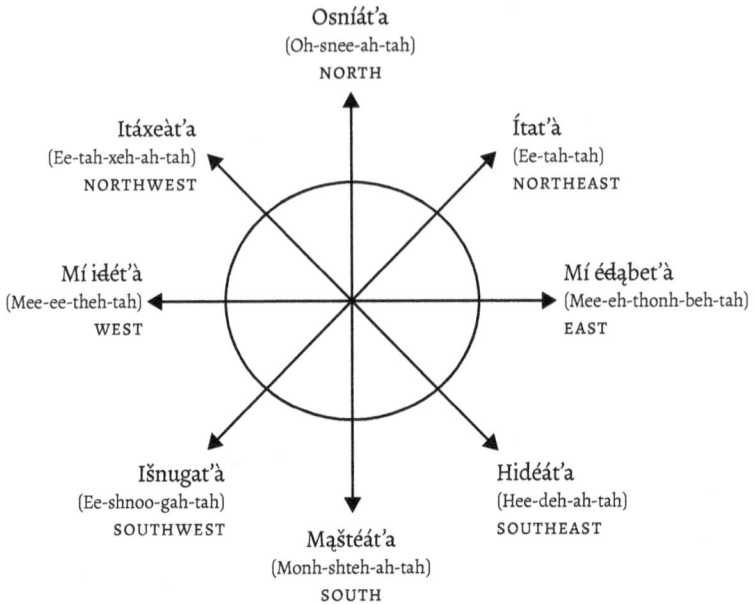

Osníát'a
(Oh-snee-ah-tah)
NORTH

Itáxeàt'a
(Ee-tah-xeh-ah-tah)
NORTHWEST

Ítat'à
(Ee-tah-tah)
NORTHEAST

Mí iɗét'à
(Mee-ee-theh-tah)
WEST

Mí éɗạbet'à
(Mee-eh-thonh-beh-tah)
EAST

Išnugat'à
(Ee-shnoo-gah-tah)
SOUTHWEST

Hidéát'a
(Hee-deh-ah-tah)
SOUTHEAST

Mạštéát'a
(Monh-shteh-ah-tah)
SOUTH

DIAGRAM 2. Cardinal directions. Created by the author.

North: *Osníát'a*	where it is cold
Northwest: *Itáxeàt'a*	at the top or ending
West: *Mí iɗét'a*	where the sun goes down
Southwest: *Išnugat'à*	meaning lost
South: *Mạštéát'a*	where the sun shines
Southeast: *Hidéát'a*	at the bottom or beginning

Prehistory of the Ponca People

There were no songs made of the prehistoric period of the Ponca. The only source of information comes from elders who probably sat around the campfires relating stories about their travels and landmarks they had seen. Stories of great accomplishments of individuals in hunting and in meeting other people were inculcated in the minds of young men and women. Children's stories too, of animals, ran parallel with real life experiences of the people. The oldest story of Ponca origins begins with the phrase *P'ahágadìxt'ì*, meaning "in the very beginning." The elders agreed that "in the very beginning" the Ponca were traveling and came to a place where the land narrowed and there was water on both sides of the land they traveled on. (The term *Ugášą* means "travel" but can mean "discovering to find." This means taking from the enemy, if necessary, to acquire varied provisions for the tribe.) This is the context for the legend of how the Ponca came to this continent.

The Ponca people have always traveled, and their knowledge of the directions and the position of the stars became essential. It has been said that the establishment of names for the directions coincided with the stars. A short description of the stars and their importance to the Ponca people is given by AMC:

> The old time Poncas paid a lot of attention to the stars, and had names for many of the constellations. The Ponca *Húdugà* or camping circle was based upon the circles of stars in the sky. The Milky Way we call *Wak̨áožągè*, or the holy path. Its movement was used for reckoning time. The North Star is called *Mikáʼe šk̨ážì*, or the star that doesn't move. It was used by hunters and travelers to find their way. The old time Poncas watched the moon too. In its last quarter the moon was called *Mí tʼè* or dead moon. We look for signs of storm at that time. (Howard 1995, 75)

The Ponca clans, as explained by the elders, are fixed in the following positions in the ceremonial camp circle.[1] Originally, the Ponca circle was entered from the east, and like the directions mentioned above, the clan positions were located by proceeding counterclockwise. In modern times, however, the procedure is to the left of the center or clockwise. This change is probably due to influences from southern plains tribes. Fortunately, the position of the clans in the circle remain intact. The illustration shows the camp represented by four circles.

The Ponca have three or more legends concerning the origin of the clans. They have been agreed upon by the elders. The first was shared with me in 1980 by AMC, who was eighty-six years old at that time (my translation):

> The Poncas were on water, and as they came to a sand bar they could see land. When they got on shore, there was a high cliff there. It stretched out as far as they could see to either side of them. They tried to climb the cliff but could not get on top. They searched for a way up the cliff

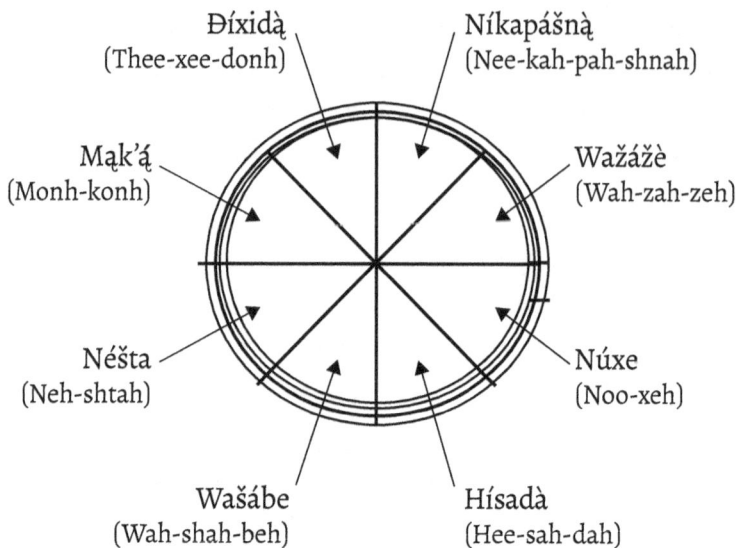

DIAGRAM 3. Position of clans in the Ponca circle. Created by the author.

but could not find the way. Finally, one day a man came back to the camp and said, "I have found a way but it is a crevice in the rock cliff, and it is big enough for only one man and a small bundle to climb and go through it." He further stated, "Up there is land and there are all kinds of game: bison, antelope, deer, elk, moose, rabbits, squirrels, and birds of every kind. Also there is a man there who has invited us up there to live. He said there is a way that is right and good way to take [kill] these animals, and that we must follow his ways." As was the custom of their time, men carried large bundles perhaps twice as large as themselves. Some tried to fit into the crevice but found that they could not. They then laid their belongings on the ground and began to pack them into small bundles. Some were anxious to get up there to see, and perhaps see the animals they could kill for food. But they were admonished by the leaders and told to proceed slowly because they did not know the land. After they were settled on land and had camped, they began to explore only to be told to stay near the camp. In those days, there was no order to their camp. They camped where the grass grew and in any fashioned they wished. After some time had past, the man who was there called the leaders of the people and began to instruct them how they would go about in taking the animals for food. Since this was the first time they would go hunting, they were told to follow the instructions given to them. The killing of animals would occur under conditions that permitted leaving those animals about to give birth and those that were too young to take. Some animals should be killed at various times in the year. There were parts of animals too that they were to consider as forbidden to eat, such as heads, tails, skins, tongues, blood, and so forth. There were reasons for such things then. Today we do not know why. They killed some animals because they were hungry and immediately ate them. The end result was that these people became sick and carried a malady throughout their lives. The disobedience to the *man* there was the main reason. It happened in the following way: The *man* there had told them to wait for particular time to kill these animals. As they prepared to go for the hunt, the men divided up by relationships. Their groups included grandfathers (if they were able), fathers, sons, nephews, etc. Some had close friends who joined. Although they were not aware of it, they were forming the beginnings of the Ponca clans.

So when that time came, the men went forward to the hunt. But the majority of the men did not only kill the designated animals but killed others as well. After the kill, they laid out the animals for the rest of the people to see because they were proud of their accomplishments. They had killed practically every known animal there. They also built a huge fire, and some took the charcoals to make separate fires. But the *man* there was disappointed in them and told them to leave the animals where they lay. But the people were hungry and ate them. The *man* there said, "Since you violated the instructions I gave to you, those of you who ate the meat parts which are forbidden to eat will never eat it again. The generations of children to come will also be forbidden to eat those meat parts. Some of you who took the skin of the animals will not be allowed to touch them again." The ones who first took the charcoals were forbidden to touch or cook upon charcoal nor could they use it for paints. The clans were named by these acts. The *man* there told them that they now must abide and live according to these rules. They called this man *Wáxè*. This means Maker or Creator in the Ponca language. He was also called *Wak'ądạ* and *Níkawasà* depending upon the kind of ceremonial or ritual the Ponca were performing.

The second legend is by KH. He agreed with the above, but the deliberation on the sacred pipe is predominant. The following is given in his own words:

The Poncas were coming ... walking ... traveling on land. There was water everywhere, but they were on dry ground. They could see land up ahead ... maybe mountains and trees. They kept coming until they arrived to the main land. The leader at that time was *Mikáe Skà* ... White Star. He was the chief. After they settled ... camped and take notice of the land ... they say that White Star used to go out toward east and pray. In those days then ... people depended upon each other ... especially those who could pray. They helped one another like that. Sometimes others would go out to pray too. They did that in the early morning ... about sunup. One day the people saw a wall cloud that come down to the ground. They heard a voice talking ... come from that cloud ... telling them about the land. He told them that in this land there was plenty of game ... animals of all kinds. He said that there was plenty of good things in that land ... good water, plants, berries, and all kinds of nuts to eat. He said that they have to take care of it in a good way.

They say he stretched his hand out through that cloud ... and he gave them the sacred pipe (calumet). He told them to take it and use it. The person White Star accepted it since he was the leader. They say he was told how to use that pipe. There were all kinds of prayers for different things ... for finding food, getting rid of sickness, keeping peace among the people, finding answers to different kinds of problems that the people might run into, and other things. From that time on ... he told White Star ... that this pipe would passed on to each generation in his family. He's supposed to teach the one who's going to take care of it ... everything about how to use that pipe ... what it means and how to pray for the people.

Probably the most important thing that was said by Almighty is a saying that was handed down from the beginning. The saying is this: "*Gákè Nińba kè, tą́wągdą̀ idágiškaxètaì.*" This means, "With this Pipe you will make yourselves a people." That word, *Tą́wągdą̀*, has different meanings. It can mean city or clan too. In these words ... it means that as long as we got the pipe and we are using it in the right way, we will always be a tribe of people ... and will be taken care of by Almighty. There was warning given too. He said that if we didn't handle it right, we would be scattered everywhere and wouldn't be a tribe anymore . . . that when that day came, we would not even know our own relatives. He said there would be no respect shown to one another if we failed to take care of that sacred pipe. So, that's how the Poncas got the sacred pipe from Him. The Poncas called him *Wáxè*, which means Creator or Maker.[2] Today they change that name to mean those white people. In our meetings [peyote meetings], we call Him Almighty. But sometimes we say Creator. In those days there was no such thing as a clan, but they were going to do that [i.e., the clans would be formed]. After some time after they first spoke to Him . . . those Poncas went against the rules and killed lots of animals. They say they were not supposed to kill certain kinds of animals. They weren't supposed to kill young buffalos and other animals with their young. Certain times of the year there are animals that shouldn't be killed . . . but they did that. By family members, the Creator divided the tribe up. There were eight groups that went hunting . . . that represented the families so they became known by clan and were forbidden to eat certain animals or parts of animals. Some clans could not eat . . . touch the skin of deer, elk, antelope, and moose. Some clans could not touch the tail of the buffalo or eat its tongue. There are rules for each clan in the Ponca tribe. To this day, if clan members eat these (forbidden) foods they become sick or break out in a rash.

When we were children, an elder would relate some historic element of the tribe. The third legend was told following an inquiry about Ponca origins made by one of the missionaries who came to the Ponca people in the 1940s. Helen Washington Little Dance, a staunch Christian woman, told the following story:

The old people tell us that the Ponca people were traveling between two bodies of water. They saw a big land in the distance and wanted to get there. They said they lived along the way by hunting and fishing. They finally came to that big land. There they camped and hunted for game. They said that land had lots of good things to eat . . . plants, berries, and different kinds of nuts and roots. They say every morning a man used to go out east of the camp and talk to *Wak'áda* . . . that's the way we say God, the Creator. The real Ponca name for God is *Wáxe*, "the one who made us." One day as he was talking to God, the clouds came close to the ground. From that cloud . . . or mist, he heard God say to him, "This land is yours to live in. You must respect it, and it will take care of you. Don't kill animals when you don't need the food." They say God gave him all the instruction on how to live there. With that He gave the Ponca the Sacred Pipe to worship with and pray to Him. We don't know anything about those words given to that man. But he used to take that pipe out once a year and talk to God. They say he had prayers for everything that the Ponca people needed. When God gave that pipe to him, he said, "*Gáke niníba ke t'ąwągdą idágiškax-et'aì*" (With this pipe, you will make yourself a tribe). I guess you could say, ". . . a city, a community, a town, or a special people." So, to this day we still have that pipe and they take it out once a year and pray to God for our needs.

The legends told above represent what the elders remembered in modern times.

Our people give credence to them with deep respect because of the age-old adage that the elders speak with no intention of deceiving hearers. They stated that the Ponca clans had, at one time, been divided into two parts. Each clan had one major group with a subgroup. For example, one part of the *Đíxidą* clan was called *Đíxidąxt'ì* while the other was called *Đíxidà xúdè*. No reason was recalled by elder clan members why the clans were thus called. In another story, part of the *Wažážè* clan was called *Wažážèxt'ì* while the other was called *Wažážè xúdè*. Concerning the *Wažáže* clan, Obie Yellow Bull said:

The hereditary chief of the clan, who was conducting the rite, had finished tattooing half of the members when an eagle flew out of the sky and, in spite of a fusillade of arrows, entered the lodge and blinded the chief by scratching his eyes out. The ceremony was thereupon discontinued. The members of the clan who had been tattooed before this event thenceforth called themselves *Wažážèxtì* (real or complete *Wažážè*) while those who had not been tattooed called themselves *Wažážèxúde* (Gray *Wažážè*). (Howard 1995, 90)

Legends such as the one above and other characteristics of the clans suggest a division of the clans. It should be mentioned that divisions in the clans by no means suggest any form of social strata (as we understand social strata today) or half tribe. As mentioned earlier, the social structure of the tribe had its foundation in the exogamous patrilineal clanship system. Each clan of the tribe had certain features and traits, such as names, hereditary chiefs, responsibilities, and taboos. The existence of the clan system also enabled the Ponca to identify people according to names that were significant to a particular clan. This also provided a means by which the tribe could make a selection of tribal chiefs. The clan and kinship system helped identify people for marriage purposes. The clans were easily identified, and their responsibilities could be carried out without interference from others. This would have been seen when the Ponca numbered in the thousands. A populace of this size would have necessitated a camping structure of a sort to maintain order. The four circles indicate dwellings that housed all Ponca families. The lines running across the encampment show the divisions of the tribe by clan. As indicated above, the clan members lived in a set section of the *Húdugà* (the camp circle) at all times and never changed their place in the circle. A specific place in the circle is a reasonable system for keeping track of each clan and member of the tribe (KH, NC, AMC). The circular-shaped community in the diagram shown above seems to contradict drawn maps of the 1800s that show a mixture of both earthen lodges and tipis. Again, adaptation to the plains brought about significant changes.

Since children followed their father's lineage, children of both sexes remained in the clan division. And since the Ponca system is patrilineal, those born of other than Ponca descendancy cannot be clan members. They are referred to as *Ukít'e hébe* (part other tribe), *Wáxè hébe*, or *Xįháska hébe* (part white).

In 1874 an Indian agent with the help of other federal officials took a census of the Ponca and found 139 half-breed Ponca. This group was larger than any other band of the tribe. This was not a clan. *Wáxè hébe*, or "part white," was a word designating a non-clan tribal member. There were eight bands under eight chiefs. The largest full-blood band was under Big Soldier and numbered ninety-seven. That census was sent to the commissioner of Indian Affairs, Washington DC, in 1874.

When girls became marrying age (sixteen to eighteen years of age), they went to live with their husbands' families. Their children, of course, were members of their father's clan. Females of a given clan who married in another clan were usually identified by their clan and name. This provided instant knowledge of who the young women were. One could not marry within his or her own clan because the bloodlines were too close. It stands to reason that close relatives could be members of another clan. But a stricken suitor would be immediately set straight when he heard a girl's clan name and personal name and then knew who her father was. Marriage patterns, however, never presented a problem for the people (KH, NC, AMC).

From a Ponca perspective, the clans and clan taboos are listed below. In some cases, the meanings of the clan name have been lost and only attributes of the clans and clan taboos remain. Proceeding counterclockwise from the entrance in the ceremonial camp circle, the elders, namely, KH, AMC, NC, JP, KCH, and NM, described the clans.

Wašábe

a. Meaning: Dark bison. The description is one of a bison standing darkly against either the rising or setting sun.

b. Responsibility: They planned with other clansmen for the tribal bison hunts. They set time and appointed men to certain duties in the bison hunt. They painted about half of the arrow shaft red as a clan-identifying mark. Arrows belonging to individual hunters were also identified using additional color or ties. This clan was spoken about as having medicines concerning thunder and thunderstorms. They were knowledgeable about keeping material valuables dry in times of heavy rain.

c. Taboos: They do not eat bison tongues or bison calves, and they do not touch the head of bison.

Néšta (extinct)

a. Meaning: Where there are places of water (lakes).

b. Responsibility: Unknown.

c. Taboos: Same as those for Wašábe and Núxe clans.

Wažážè

a. Meaning: Snake.

b. Responsibility: Guarding the entrance to the camp. They were known for being good hunters and could track an animal for days and find it.

This clan was known to be warlike and would join in any conflict. They were beneficial to the tribe in defending the camp. Chief Standing Bear was said to have been a member of this clan. Being clan chief in his time, he spoke openly to all tribal members as well as other tribes and chieftains.

c. Taboos: They do not touch snakes, and they do not enter dwellings except through the entrance for fear that they will make a way for snakes to enter. They do not touch charcoal or verdigris.

Níkapášnạ

a. Meaning: Person with bald head (in reference to male members "roach" hairstyle).

b. Responsibility: They led tribal members in deer hunts. What are now termed "shock troops," they were always ready to protect the camp and were members of the *P'adánekì* war society with the *Đíxidạ* clan. They were known to have remedies for curing headaches or other ailments of the human head.

c. Taboos: They do not touch the skin of deer or other members of the deer family.

Đíxidạ

a. Meaning: Derived from a type of hawk. They were referred to as *Ịgdạ́sisnedè* (puma) or *Ịgdạ́sisnedè Wét'ì* (dwelling place of the puma). This was in reference to their wrapping pipes with the skin of puma. They wore a "roach" hairstyle with a braided tail. They were referred to as *Síde ágdè*, or "those who wear a single braid or locks of hair as a tail." The hair was long from the crown, although the sides were shaven. The hair was made into a single French braid to the neck and then completed with a regular braid.

b. Responsibility: They officiated the installation of chiefs. They were one of two clans who were considered "shock troops" and went out to meet the enemy first. They were members of the *P'adánekì* war society. Arrow shafts were painted black where the feathers are tied. Sinew was dyed red, which is symbolic of the taboo "does not touch blood," or *Wamí ítaži*. The unfortunate loss of the daughters of Chief White Tail of the *Mąk'ą* clan resulted in his relinquishment the principal chieftain position by his own cognition. The *Ðíxidą* clan became the holder of the principal chieftainship in the tribe following certain tasks and accomplishments by Little Bear, a *Ðíxidą*, which were dictated by White Tail. The last of the principal chiefs of the Ponca was *Šą́ge Níkagahì* (Horse Chief).

c. Taboos: They do not drink or touch the blood of bison. They do not touch rodents. They do not use or touch *Wasé'tù*, "blue paint."

Mąk'ą

a. Meaning: Medicine

b. Responsibility: They had charge of the Ponca Sacred Pipe. From the beginning they were responsible for the proper care and use of the pipe as the Creator gave direction. No other clan or outsider was allowed to touch or handle the pipe. In the event that the Ponca moved, the Sacred Pipe went first; hence, the *Mąk'ą* clan was always in the lead position. From this clan came the principal chieftain. The earliest chieftain remembered was White Star, who was said to have accepted the Sacred Pipe from the Creator. They were also one of two clans who were in charge of the bison hunt. They were known to have knowledge of plants and herbs. The *Mąk'ą* painted their dwellings (tipi) with yellow and black stripes.

c. Taboos: Unknown.

Note: According to Fletcher and La Flesche (1992) "it was a man of the Monkon [*Mąk'ą*] subgens who in the race was the first to reach the Pole" (i.e., the Omaha Sacred Pole).

Núxe

a. Meaning: Ice. This clan is also referred to as the red- and yellow-haired bison.

b. Responsibility: They had part in the bison hunt. They were known to have knowledge of the attributes of water and ice.

c. Taboo: They do not touch the head of bison or the hide of bison calves. They do not eat bison tongues.

Hísadà

a. Meaning: Stretched-out legs, that is, a bird running with out-stretched legs.

b. Responsibility: They were in charge of the rainmaking ceremony. According to legend and clan historians, when a member of this clan dies, rain follows. Arrow shafts were painted red where the feathers were tied. They defended the entrance of the camp. The *Hísadà* clan always lived at the entrance of the *Húdugà* (camp circle). They were called *T'í uhǫge*, which means "the dwelling at end of the camp." The dwelling was located on the south side of the entrance into the camp. The term *Wasábe* (black bear) was a name attributed to some clan members because of the taboo that "they do not eat the flesh of the black bear." This reference was made of them at an earlier period. They were "related" or were a sister clan to the *Wašábe* clan. Legend of this division has been lost. Members of the clan were known to be "quick to anger." This clan was also responsible for the use of cedar in tribal ceremonies. The male members of the clan were taught early in their lives how to identify the kind of cedar to be used.

c. Taboo: They do not eat deer or the flesh of the black bear.

Other Views of Ponca Clans

Because of the time lapse between the era when the elders of the tribe could recall clan names and meanings, their position in the camp circle, and the duties of the clans and the present, the following description is given to show what some historians have concluded. This description should not be absorbed as absolute truth. Lists were made by various writers, and according to Howard, these lists are all questionable. Keep in mind that at different times in the history of our people, those who recorded information did not always speak to people who may have been able to give good information. Additionally, KH quoted an old Ponca adage that says the Ponca people were "stingy with their words" (*P'ǫk'a ámà íyè gíwaštabažì*).

Dorsey (1891, 331–32) gave a number of names and taboos that elders have said are inaccurate. This was unacceptable to the elders because Dorsey said that each clan had subdivisions or component parts. I believe that some parts of the descriptions given may be accurate; however, the gentes have been confused with other tribes who speak a similar language as the Ponca. This was also concluded by the elders. Because of their close contact with other members of the Đégihà-speaking people, they knew the differences as compared to the Ponca clan system (KH, NC, AMC, JP, AL).

Dorsey accounts for eight clans. In the *Tsízu* (*Č'ížu*) half tribe, he listed the following:

Gens 1 *Hísada*, Thunder people

Gens 2 *Wasábe-hitàzi* [*Wasábe ítažì*], Touch not the Skin of a Black bear

Gens 3 *Díxida* [*Đíxidà̩*], Wildcat, Wears tails or Locks of Hair

    Had two subgentes:

        (1). a. *Mágde-itàzi* [*Na̩xđé ítažì*], Touches no Charcoal

           b. *Wasétu-itàzi* [*Wasétù ítažì*], Touches no Verdigris

        (2). a. *Wamí-itàzi* [*Wamí ítažì*], Touches no Blood

Gens 4 *Níkapàsna* [*Níkapášnà*], Bald Human Head Elk people

    Had three subgentes:

        (1). a. *Te-síde-itàzi* [*T'é si̩dè ítažì*], Touches no Buffalo Tails

        (2). a. *Te-déze-datàzi* [*T'é đé'zè đatážì*], Eats no Buffalo Tongues

        (3). a. *Táxte-Ki-apa-datàzi* [*Táxtì kí á̩pa̩ đatážì*], Eats no Deer or Elk

In the *Wažážè* half tribe, he further listed:

Gens 5 *Maká* [*Ma̩k'á̩*], Medicine, a buffalo gens, also called *Te-síde-itàzi* [*T'é si̩dè ítažì*], Touch no Buffalo Tails

    Had two subgentes:

        (1). a. *Pákaxtì* [*Pá̩caxtì*], Real Ponkas, Keepers of a Sacred Pipe

        (2). a. *Páka-xúde* [*P'á̩ca xúdè*], Gray Ponkas

Gens 6 Wasábe [Wašábe], Dark Buffalo

    Had two subgentes:

        (1) a. *Te-síde* [*T'é side*], Buffalo Tail

           b. *Te-déze-datàzi* [*T'é đé'zè đatážì*], Eat no Buffalo Tongues

           c. *Te-zíga-datàzi* [*T'é ži̩gà đatážì*], Eat no very young Buffalo Calves

        (2) a. *Te-pá-itàzi* [*T'é p'á ítažì*], Touch no Buffalo Heads

In the second *Wažáže* half tribe, which he called Water Phratry, he listed the following:

Gens 7 *Wazáze*, Osage

Had two subgentes:

(1) a. *Wazáze sàbe* [*Wažáže sábè*], Dark Osage, Keepers of a Sacred Pipe

b. *Wasétu-itàzi* [*Wasé t'ù ítažì*], Does not Touch Verdigris, or *Nágde-itàzi* [*Nax̣dé ítažì*], Does not Touch Charcoal

(2) a. *Wazáze-xude* [*Wažáže xúdè*], Gray Osage, or *Wesá-wetàzì* [*Wésa ítazì*], Does not Touch Snakes

(3) a. *Necta* [*Néštà*], an Owl subgens, is now extinct.

The subgentes of the *Núxe* clan were uncertain; however, three taboo names are listed:

Gens 8 *Núxe* [*Núxe*] Reddish-yellow Buffalo miscalled *Núxe*, ice

(1) *Te-pá-itàzi* [*T'é p'á ítažì*], Does not Touch a Buffalo Head

(2) *Te-zíga-itàzi* [*T'é žįgà ítažì*], Does not Touch the Yellow Hide of a Buffalo Calf

(3) *Te-déze-datàzi* [*T'é dé'zè datážì*], Does not Eat Buffalo Tongues

According to the elders, the confusion of Dorsey's work begins with the Ponca circle and clans being divided in two half tribes—the "*Tsízu* and *Wazáze*." KH and AL said the concepts of division and name, in part, may be significant to the Osage Tribe. KH, NC, AL made the following observations of the work:

1. The term *Tsízu* (*Č'ížu*) is of Osage Indian origin. The Ponca have no specific division as described, although they do have a *Wažáže* clan.

2. The two half tribes were unknown among the Ponca. KH said Dorsey may have been confused by the "old-time" ways when the tribe recognized certain clans as "sister clans." As mentioned earlier, the *Wašábe* and *Hísadà* were considered relatives (KCH).

3. The subgentes mentioned are taboos of the respective clans they fall under.

4. A "Water Phratry" is mentioned probably owing to confusion about the relationship between the two above clans. There were cer-

tain beliefs about them concerning water, namely, rain, thunder, and thunderstorms.

5. The *Mąk'ą* clan was indeed the original keeper of the Ponca Sacred Pipe.

6. The elders said they never heard of the terms *Poncaxti* or *Ponca xudè*.

7. The *Néštà* (not a subgentes) was one of the eight clans of the Ponca. It is now extinct.

Fletcher and La Flesche (1992, 41–42) also give a questionable account of the Ponca clans. They account for seven clans. This work was also criticized by tribal elders as being incorrect. Fletcher and La Flesche's work was written following long discussions with tribal leaders. The elders were disappointed with the finished product because the authors had been able to speak and understand Ponca. The following is an excerpt from Fletcher and La Flesche:

> There are seven gentes in Ponca tribe, namely: *Waçábe, Thixida, Nikapashna, Poncaxti, Washabe, Wazhazhe, Núxe*. These camped in the order indicated in the diagram . . . beginning on the southern side of the eastern entrance of the tribal circle, to which the Ponca give the name *huthuga* . . .
>
> 1. *Waçábe*, Black Bear. Subgentes: (a) *Waçábe*, (b) *Hiçada* (stretched, referring to the stretch of the legs in running); *tabu*, birds. 2. THIXIDA. Meaning lost. Subgentes: (a) *Thixida*; *tabu*, blood. (b) *Ingthoncincnedeweti* (*ingthoncincnede*, puma; *weti*, [*Wét'ỉ*] to dwell in); *tabu*, blue or green paint. 3. NIKAPASHNA. A mans skull. Subgentes: (a) *Tahaton itazhi* (*ta*, deer; *ha*, skin; *ton*, possess; *itazhi*, do not touch); *tabu*, deer. (b) *Tecinde itazhi*, (*te*, buffalo; *cinde*, tail; *itazhi*, do not touch); *tabu*, buffalo tail. 4. PONCAXTI Real or original Ponca. Subgentes: (a) *Poncaxti*; (b) *Monkon* (mystery or medicine); one *tabu*, buffalo head. 5. WASHABE. A dark object, as seen against the horizon; *tabu*, skin of buffalo calf. 6. WAZHAZHE. (Wazáze) An old term. Subgentes: (a) *Wazhazhe* (real *Wazhazhe*); name said to refer to the snake after shedding old skin and again in full power. (b) *Wazhazhexude* (gray *Wazhazhe*) refers to the grayish appearance of the snakes cast off skin; one *tabu*, snakes. 7. NUXE. Ice; *tabu*, male buffalo.

After reviewing the above, the elders again stated that there was no *Poncaxti* clan. They suggested that the authors had confused the Ponca system with the Osage Tribe's clan system. The elders observed the following regarding the above excerpt:

1. *Wasábe* (Black Bear) was incorrectly listed as a clan with the *Hísadà* as one of two subgentes. Again, according to the elders, the *Hísadà* clan was sometimes called "black bear," or *Wasábe*.

2. Fletcher and La Flesche stated that the meaning of the term *Đíxidà* was lost. They further stated that the *Đíxidà* was a subgentes of itself.

3. Most of this is acceptable as written; however, there is more on the taboo -*ítažì*, or "does not touch."

4. There never was a *Poncaxti* clan. There is a *Mąk'ą́* clan. The meaning of this word is no mystery; it means medicine.

5. This item seems acceptable as written.

6. Most of this is acceptable as written; however, Obie Yellow Bull's legend gives a different origin of the terms *Wažážèxtì* and *Wažážè xúdè*.

7. The *Núxe* clan seems to be ignored, or perhaps the authors could not get information on this clan. The taboos listed in Dorsey's work are acceptably recorded.

Taboos Associated and Unassociated with Clans

When it is lightning,
> do not stand by the window.
> do not lie on your back if it is lightning when you go to sleep at night.
> cover your mirrors.
> do not smoke.
> do not build a fire.
> do not stand under a tree.
> do not run.
> do not walk close together.

If you are a *Hísadà* clan member,
> do not throw water out of the dwelling because it causes rain.

do not hang your feathers outside the dwelling because it causes rain.

do not eat deer, antelope, or elk meat because it will cause your skin to break out.

When you are a child,

learn not to walk in front of a person who has medicine.

do not walk in front of an elder.

do not make unnecessary noise around elders.

sit quietly when an adult is speaking.

If you are a member of the Đíxidą clan,

eat meat that is well done.

do not eat rodents.

do not touch or drink blood.

Other practices that sound like taboos include the following:

When you are walking, let the women and girls walk behind.

Get home before sundown.

Tell a tree you must use it to build or build a fire before cutting it down.

Excuse yourself if you accidentally move a large rock or stone in a pathway.

Excuse yourself if you accidentally cut the root of a plant that is used for medicine.

Do not look into the eyes of another person when speaking with them.

Do not stare at another, even from a distance.

Light a smoke if a spirit follows you at night.

Scare a spirit away by farting.

If a spirit comes at night to your dwelling, place a knife where you eat.

Do not leave your eating utensils unwashed. Spirits will come to wash them.

Do not leave food at the table where you eat.

Burn cedar in the dwelling if spirits come around too often.

When a relative dies, take food to the burial site only once.

Parents, give to your oldest child anything he or she wishes for.

Parents, speak to your children. Do not beat them.

Be good to old people.

When somebody visits your dwelling for the first time, give them a gift.

Do not imitate a crippled person's walk.

Walk quietly in the dwelling where medicines are kept. They are sacred.

One final statement in connection with the clans of the Ponca is about the governmental structure. The Ponca government was a highly organized and structured system, contrary to what Howard (1995) suggested—that the Ponca system was "of the very weak type which has sometimes been termed tribal." The elders of the tribe described what could be termed a bicameral governmental system. This is associated in part with the clan system and its divisions. They said that without the clan system, the government could not work or would not exist for that matter. Originally, the Ponca council consisted of one principal chief, eight clan chiefs, and as many chiefs of the third rank depending on the size of the clan.

It is understandable why these earlier works could have been confused with other tribes. The tribes of the Ðégihà Siouan linguistic family have the same roots in origins and share a language analogous to the other. After a long period, over which the tribes separated, changes occurred that affected concepts of cultural patterns and practices. The Ponca, who are "stingy" with their words, made certain that much of our cultural heritage went by unrecorded and lost to the past. Those responsible for attempting to preserve our heritage can be credited, insofar as their insight permitted, for what was written.

17

Ponca Names

Names probably exist for several reasons for all peoples of the earth. Some of the probable causes for using two or three names came from the need to accommodate the vast population and to avoid duplication of identity. Webster's dictionary suggests that *name* is a "word or phrase that constitutes a distinctive designation of a person." When we distinguish a thing, we perceive a difference in two or more things. Names then served to distinguish individuals one from another. Name giving usually takes place at the birth of the child for most Americans. Books are published in modern times to aid expectant parents in choosing a name. In the case of the historic Ponca, more often than not, phrases were used to distinguish newborn tribal members. However, one-word names were not uncommon among the people. Some names have as many as seven English words.

The Ponca family usually named their children at birth. The hopes that a father had for his son or daughter gave impetus to the naming of the children. Grandparents, of course, were the name givers. They suggested names and were usually honored with being allowing to name the children. All Ponca male children kept their name until they were able to exercise some talent or became known for something when they were old enough to join the adult men in their hunts and other activities. At this time they were given a second name. Personal attributes lent to the naming of children. A child who seemed not afraid of anything, was fast on his feet, was a quick person, was strong, was intelligent, was a good speaker, and so forth could be named according to those traits and characteristics. The Ponca took inspiration from a wide variety of sources in naming newborn children and the giving them their second names, including animals, earth, sun, moon, clouds, rain, hail, thunder, lightning, and so forth. The eight clans of the tribe had names significant to them. Names were used only by those clans and were not allowed to cross clan lines.[1] This allowed the tribe to identify one's clan and relationship to tribal members. For example, if a person had a name with *bear* in it, he would likely be a member of the Đíxidą̀ clan. If a person had a name that had anything to do with the weather, especially rain, he would be a member of the Hísadà clan. If a person had a name relating to reptiles, he would be a member of the Wažážè clan. Names relating to certain animals, the weather, reptiles, and so forth would identify a person's clan and family. A person's name was usually connected in some way to the clan taboos (see chapter 16). Some clans forbade members from eating or touching certain animals or parts of animals. Consequently, some personal names of clan members were derived through their clan affiliation and taboos. These names belonged to the clan. However, in some instances, names were given to non–clan members. These people could use the name for their lifetimes, but the names reverted back to the clan at their death. This practice is unknown in modern times. The giving of a clan name required the person receiving the name to be an upstanding person in the tribe or neighboring tribe. The giving of the name constituted the "adopting" of that person into the clan and tribe.

In acquiring a name, a young man might become known for his interests in animals. According to KH, it was thought that animals were agents that provided insight and understanding of certain types of sickness and medicines that effected cures. Bears, for instance, have always been revered by the Ponca. They held these magnificent animals in awe, considered them sacred, and believed them to possess some medicine that benefited the tribe. Other attributes of the bear that were revered were its physical qualities. The strength, intelligence, and appearance of the grizzly bear, for example, were respected by the people. Other traits and distinguishing qualities of the bear too did not go unnoticed. Their diet, which consisted of meat, vegetables, nuts, and fruits, and their man-like appearance when standing caused them to rise in status. Thus, the bear was venerated and held in high esteem. But these animals were still simply animals to the Ponca people. If the family, then, observed that a young man had an interest in the bear, he would then be named accordingly. Others chose names from different animals as some clans and families were known to hold them in high regard. Additionally, as stated above, some names fell under the violation their ancestors had committed in the beginning when the clans were formulated.

Naming Ritual

Parents, grandparents, relatives, and friends were all involved in this ritual of giving of the second name. Between the ages of six and twelve, a child began to identify himself and became significant. At this time one of the members of the family, usually the father, noticed, and would speak of it to his wife and other members of his family. Normally, names thought to be appropriate for the youngster were selected by the family. Usually, an elder of the family would name the child. However, if so desired by the elder of the family, another person could be called upon to come and do the honor of naming the child. Also if there was no elder in the family to assume this duty, then a respected elder of the tribe could be called upon to carry out the wishes of the family. A typical process to initiate this naming-giving ritual is as follows (KH, KCH, NC, JP, and AMC):

> After the decision of the parents to name their child and the names which were considered, they would tell the elder of the family. If the name the parents suggested seemed appropriate, or if he felt another name would be more fitting, he would tell them. A discussion would follow and the name would be selected.
>
> A day would be set for the name-giving ritual. The parents would then plan a meal to be served to other relatives and friends to be invited to the occasion. On the day of the name-giving ritual, the elder would rise to speak. He would tell of the child's interests, and his family background. He could also speak of a person in the child's clan who had accomplished something significant in the camp. His speech ended by saying, "From this day on he shall be called [name]." Following the meal and name giving, gifts would be presented to the one who gave the name.

Not all name-giving rites followed this procedure. Also, the one giving the name could be honored at another time. Some received names in unusual places and under different circumstances. (In modern times, some people request names according to their profession.)

As a member of the *Hísadà* clan (on my mother's side), my great-grandfather Cries for War (*Nagé Áxa*) lived during the time when the Ponca still had periodic conflicts with their ancient enemy, the Sioux people, as well as the Pawnee. His early childhood name was *Nažįtidè*, which means "Sudden Rain." He was about eleven or twelve years old when he received his name—Cries for War. The following is a translation of his story (Dorsey 1890, 372–73) about how he received his adult name:

> At the very first, when I was small, they spoke of going on the warpath. And when I said, Father, I wish to go to those people, he said No! Do not say that again to anyone. When I was young, my child, I used to travel, but I used to know difficulties. Because you are young, I fear you would cry if you got into trouble. Nevertheless, said I, persons of any size at all who decide for themselves invariably travel; therefore, I do that. Well, you shall go thither. When they attack one another, you shall go among them. Even if they kill you while you take hold of a man, it would be good, said my father. So I went to the persons who had assembled. Behold, they were all grown. (It is customary among Indians for the wounded ones to become great men by means of their suffering.) Ho! It is right. It is his son, but he has come. They shook hands with me. They departed, traveling throughout the month. At length the moon was dead, and it was very dark. Ho! bring ye hither the boys of different sizes who have come. Let them abandon their old names. Bring his son hither, said they. They meant me, and they called my father's name. The messengers took me thither. You shall go thither, said they. *Šúde gaxè* (Smoke-maker), *Nágetidè* (He starts to run), *Mixá ska* (White Swan), and the others made me sit in the center. Oho! said they, you shall abandon your name. Behold, his friend shall have a name, for there is a great abundance of them. When we were coming hither on the warpath, this one, his friend, cried for it; therefore, he shall have *Nudá áxà* (He Cried For The War-Path) [now Cries for War] for his new name. And *Šúde gáxè* lifted his voice to tell the deities. He is indeed speaking of abandoning his name, Há-o-o-o-oh! He is indeed speaking of having the name *Nudá áxà*, há-o-o-o-oh! Ye big headlands, I tell you and send it to you that you may indeed hear it, há-o-o-o-oh! Ye clumps of buffalo-grass, I tell you and send it to you that you may hear it, há-o-o-o-oh! Ye big trees, I tell you

and send it to you that you may indeed hear it, há-o-o-o-oh! Ye birds of all kinds that walk and move on the ground, I tell you and send it to you that you may indeed hear it, há-o-o-o-oh! Ye small animals of different sizes, I tell you and send it to you that you may hear it, há-o-o-o-oh! Thus have I sent to tell you, ye animals. Right in the ranks of the foe will he kill a swift man, and come back after holding him, há-o-o-o-oh! He also told the old name. He speaks indeed of throwing away the name *Nažįtiđè* (Starts to Rain), and he has promised to have the name *Nudą́ áxà* há-o-o-o-oh! Said he.

Circumstance then, sometimes determined the receiving of a new name. The words shouted out to things in nature and mankind was truly the Ponca way of telling all things on earth that this was to be the person they would interact with.

Sources of Names

In the process of name giving, the most logical contributor of names had to be animals. But other sources were also important to the Ponca. The following names are composed of a man's interaction with animals and his fellow man.[2] The descriptions of animals and of birds from which many names come are examples of known names.

T'é	Buffalo (bison)
T'é Hą́ga	Buffalo Leader
T'e Núga Žįgá	Little Buffalo Bull
T'e Núga	Buffalo Bull
T'e P'á Žįgà	Head of Little Buffalo
T'e Núga Dáđì	Crazed Buffalo
T'e Sigđè	Buffalo Track
T'é T'ągà Nąžį̀	Standing Buffalo
T'e Žį́ga	Little Buffalo
T'e Wáđihį̀	Scares out the Buffalo
T'e Žį́ga Sabè	Little Black Buffalo Bull
T'e Núga P'à	Head of Buffalo Bull
T'e Núga Ská	White Buffalo Bull
T'e Núga Sàbe	Black Buffalo Bull

T'e Žíga Skà	Little White Buffalo Bull
T'e Núga Hį Sabè	Black-Haired Buffalo Bull
T'e Núga Nąžį Žįgá Ská	Little White Standing Buffalo Bull
Šą̀ T'ǫgà	Wolf
Šąt'ǫgà Skà	White Wolf
Šąt'ǫgà	Big Wolf
Šą́ge	Horse
Ašáwagè	Appaloosa (Pawnee name)
Šą́ge Nąsè	Horse Hunter
Šą́ge Hį Sábè	Black-Haired Horse
Šą́ge Sábe	Black Horse
Šą́ge Hį T'ú	Dappled Horse
Šą́ge Xdahà	Poor Horse
Šą́ge Hį Zí	Yellow Horse
Šą́ge Níde Skà	Appaloosa
Míkasì	Coyote
Mą̀čú	Bear (grizzly)
Mą̀čú Dádį	Crazy Bear
Mą̀čú Sábè	Black Bear
Mą̀čú Dúba	Four Bears
Mą̀čú Skà	White Bear
Mą̀čú Hįxtè	Hairy Bear
Mą̀čú T'ǫgà	Big Bear
Mą̀čú Máze	Iron Bear
Mą̀čú Waží P'iážì	Angry Bear
Mą̀čú Nąbà	Two Bears
Mą̀čú Wíáxčì	Lone Bear
Mą̀čú Nąžį̀	Standing Bear
Mą̀čú Zí	Yellow Bear
Mą̀čú Nitá	Bears Ear
Mą̀čú Žįgà	Little Bear
Šą́nudà	Dog
Įštá Dubà	Four Eyes

Šą́nudà Skà	White Dog
Wasábe	Black Bear
Wasábe Žį̀gà	Little Black Bear
Wasábe Xⱡahà	Skinny Bear
Mą̃ščį̃ge	Rabbit
Mą̃ščį̃skà Mą̃ⱡį̀	Walking Rabbit
Táxtì	Deer
T'atą́ga Mą̃ⱡį̀	Large Walking Deer
T'áxtì Skà	White Deer
T'atą́ga Ną̃žį̀	Large Deer Standing
Sį́de Skà	White Tail (deer)
T'áxtì Sį́de Sábè	Black Tailed Deer
Miká	Raccoon
Miká Žį̀gà	Little Coon
Ą́pą	Elk
Ą́pą Ną̃žį	Standing Elk
Hexága Mą̃ⱡį	Walking Elk
Ą́pą Žį̀gà	Little Elk
Hexága Sabè	Black Elk or Black Rough Horn
Ą́pą T'ą̃gà	Big Elk
Hexága Skà	White Elk or White Rough Horn
Hexága	Rough Elk Horn
Hexága Wakíde	Shoots the Elk
Xúgà	Badger
Xúga Žį̀gà	Little Badger
T'ačúge	Antelope
T'ačúge Ną̃gè	Running Antelope
Žábe	Beaver
Žábe Skà	White Beaver
Žábe Žį̀gà	Little Beaver
Čą̃bé Skà	White Beaver
Xiⱡá	Eagle
Xiⱡá Skà	White Eagle

Xiđá Gáxe	Makes Himself an Eagle
Xiđá Xùde	Grey Eagle
Xiđá Gią́	Flying Eagle
Xiđádawį (fem.)	Eagle
Xiđá Hą̀gà	Eagle Leader
Xiđá Žíde	Red Eagle
Xiđá Žį̀gà	Little Eagle
Xiđá Sabe	Black Eagle
Xiđá Mą́šigđè (fem.)	Rising Eagle
Gđedą́	Hawk
Gđedą́ Sabè	Black Hawk
Gđedą́ Xùde	Grey Hawk
Gđedą́ Žíde	Red Hawk
Gđedą́ Ną́pabì	Afraid of the Hawk
Gđedą́ Ginà	Hawk Calls His Name
Gđedą́ Skà	White Hawk
Gđedą́ Hą̀gà	Hawk Leader
Gđedą́wį Tégà (fem.)	New Hawk
Gđedą́wį (fem.)	Hawk
Gđedą́ Žį̀gà	Little Hawk
Gđedą́wį Téxi (fem.)	Difficult Hawk
Wažį́ga P'à	The Flicker
Wažį́ga Zì	Yellow Bird
Wažį́ga P'à	Bird Head
Wabáhi Zì	Yellow Picker
Wažíga	Bird (any)
Pánahò	The Owl
Míxa Skà	The Swan
Héga	The Buzzard
Míxa T'ą̀gà	Big Goose
Į́be Žąkà	The Scizzor Tail
Šúína	Prairie Chicken Coming
Káxe Ną̀bà	Two Crows

Šútimá	Prairie Chicken Came
Káxe Žįgà	Little Crow
Wažį́ga	The Bird
Káxe Sàbè	Black Crow
Wažį́ga P'à	Birds Head
Mą́ge Zì	Yellow Breasted
Wažį́ga Skà	White Bird
Míxa Žįgà	Little Duck
Wažį́ T'ù	The Blue Bird
Há Baxđúde	Sheds His Skin
Kigđíbutà	Curls Himself
Há Gđéže	Stripped Skin
Ǫkípatą̀	Wraps around Himself
Ít'ągà	Large Mouth
Wés'à	The Snake

The Weather

There is a correlation among the names of the months, seasons, and weather conditions of the year. And mainly, in this section, we see a further relationship that existed between the births of children and the weather. Further, to understand the name-giving process, it was necessary to note the position of the moon, the growth of plants, types of ceremonies, clan responsibilities, and weather. There were many types of weather conditions known to the Ponca people when they lived in the North Country as well as in Indian Territory. From the beginning they were familiar with the weather and its varied elements. The migration from the East Coast had led them through all sorts of weather conditions. They saw and experienced the weather at Niagra Falls (*Ní'uxp'áđe*), the Smoky Mountains (*P'ahéušúde*), the Ohio Valley (*Ohá'ì*), and near present-day St. Louis, Missouri and the Kohokian mounds (*Pahé žídè*). From the frozen northland to the wind-swept plains, they adjusted to the natural conditions of earth's elements. There were lands that were dry (*Mąbízè*), such as the Badlands of South Dakota (*Pahé šúšúdè*), as well as wetlands (*Níštáštà*). There were incidences in the tribe's history when they traveled to areas that were said to be arid or wet. This was to and from the great southwest (*Íšnugatà*) to the great lakes area (*Néštà*), particularly where there are many lakes (KH, AMC, NC, JP). Their knowledge of these conditions would ultimately influence the process of name giving; that is, some names would be derived from the current weather conditions when the child was born.

Weather patterns put the people at a disadvantage. The Ponca relied essentially on a cloud on the horizon and its density to determine just what was going to happen in the weather. Some rainmakers and rain stoppers evidently knew some secrets of the weather and appropriately named all the elements and conditions of the weather and climate. For our purposes, the varied elements and conditions of the weather and climate are listed below in addition to the Ponca terms for the months of the year and the seasons (KH, AMC, NC):

English term	Ponca term	Interpretation
April	*Mé p'ahą́ga*	Springtime begins
May	*Ną́žį́štą*	Always rains
June	*Mą̀šté p'ahą́ga*	Sunny days begin
July	*Nugé oską́skà*	Midsummer
August	*Waⱦápipižè*	Prepare corn for drying
September	*Ą́pą hút'ą*	Elk bellows
October	*T'ą́dè mą̀šą́de uží*	Store food in caches
November	*Ǫsní uhą́ge*	The edge of winter
December	*Máⱦè ǫską́ska*	Midwinter
January	1. *Má spą̀*	Thawing snow
	2. *T'áxtì má ną́ga*	Deer paw the snow
February	1. *Mí uⱦúną́žį̀ waⱦáži*	Undependable moon
	2. *Wažį̀gàmà waékè mí*	The birds scratch for food
March	1. *Míxa agⱦái kedí*	When the ducks go home
	2. *Į̀št'áukią̀dà*	Sore eyes caused by snow glare

Approximately in the month of April, the Ponca New Year begins. It was said that the "first growth" (of grass) was observed at this time of the year in the north central plains. Some months were given dual names that primarily related to animal behavior.

The seasons of the year coincide with the number four. According to the elders, the number four is similar to the number seven in the Christian faith. As the number seven was considered a perfect number, the number four in the Ponca cultural pattern was also considered a perfect number.

English term	Ponca term	Interpretation
Spring (springtime)	Mé	Spring
Summer (summertime)	Nugé	Summer
Fall (falltime)	T'ą́gaxd̨ą	Fall
Winter (wintertime)	Mád̨e	Snowing

The following terms for conditions of the weather or forms of these terms were used to name children and all family members:

Ponca term	Ponca interpretation	Closest English interpretation
Ániwì	Drop of rain	Raindrop
Dá	Frozen	Frozen
Mądá	Frozen ground	Frozen ground
Đią́bà	Cause to light up as day	Lightning
Đigígd̨izè	Lightning spreading across the sky	Electrical storm
G'éd̨à	Clear or clearing sky following cloudiness	Clearing skies
Gamą́tigd̨è	Sudden heavy rain	Sudden heavy rain
Įgd̨ą́ hútą	Thunder Gods cry	Thunder

K'ímąhà	On the sheltered side	On the sheltered side
Má	Snow	Snow
Mádè gašúde	Blowing snow	Blizzard
Mąšt'è	Warm/hot sunny day	Sunny
Mągášudè	Blowing dust from the ground	Dusty
Mási	Snow seeds	Hail
Mási žįgá	Small snow seeds	Sleet
Mąskáskábe	Sticky dirt	Mud/muddy
Mąxdíxdíbe	Mud that clings to you	Mud/muddy
Mąxp'í	Cloud	Cloud
Mąxp'í sá	Bright clouds	Bright clouds
Nákadè	Hot	Hot
Nąžį́	Rain	Rain
Nąžį́ gáxe	Rainmaker	Rainmaker
Nąžį́ ubíxà	Rain sprinkle	Sprinkling
Núxe	Ice	Ice
Ogásnì	Cool	Cool
Osní	Cold	Cold
P'úidì	Hot and humid	Sultry
Štíde	Warm	Warm
Šúdemąhà	Fog	Fog
Šúkabì	Thick clouds	Thick clouds
T'adą́he	Whirlwind	Whirlwind
T'adé	Wind	Wind
T'adésagí t'ągá	Big hard wind	Tornado/cyclone
T'ušnìgè	Rainbow	Rainbow
Ugánądà	Turns cloudy	Turns cloudy
Waú mąxpì	Woman cloud	Woman clouds

Xékì	Fog hanging over the valley	Fog
Xuéginà	Storm comes roaring	Coming storm
Žą́ą́dašnà	Ice on the wood and ground	Ice storm (black ice)
Žídą̀	Dew	Dew
Zigígdì	Sleet while sun is shining	Sleet

Some names seem to suggest that the Ponca people had knowledge of how to make rain. But did they make rain? According to Peter LeClair (Howard 1995, 75), it was so. He suggested that the *Hísadà* clan were rainmakers and used burning weeds to cause rain. He described the rainmaking ceremony of this clan as follows:

> The *Hísadà* clan are noted as rainmakers. . . . They make rains by rolling up bunches of redgrass, like is used in building earth lodges, and making a fire and burning some. Then some more is dampened, and this is put on top. This forms a gas and it explodes. This brings rain. It never fails. All of this is done with prayers.

Those of us who were born in the twentieth century never knew nor heard of this; however, from the stories told at informal family gatherings, it is apparent that these kinds of occurrences were many. Oral history, tribal ceremonies, and other practices give evidence that it did happen. The practice of name giving, in particular, seems to validate these kinds of stories. Names used by various clans and families pertaining to the weather were derived from some ancient custom regarding tribal medicines. These types of names connoted a segment of a philosophy relative to their religious practice. My great-grandfather (on my father's side), *T'áíkawahò*, who was also known as *T'áde Ámądì*, or "Walks on the Ground," was a known and learned man in tribal medicines. A member of the *Đíxidą̀* clan, he was said to be *Įgdą́ ídaedè* and *Manądiwadè ídaedè*. The former suggests that he "understood the things of the clouds, thunder, lightning, rain, and water." The latter meant that he used techniques given to him by some phenomenally little people. In one episode of his life, he learned the nature and the behavior of animals. His subsequent learning experience dealt with the animals' relational behavior to the weather. In this, the components of some processes of the weather patterns brought about additional knowledge. He named his children by occurrences of various weather patterns, probably to remind him of the signs that dictated his summation of the weather conditions (KH). His children were named as follows:

Gakúwįxè	Clouds Moving in Different Directions
Ganážį Ubíxą	Caused to Rain Upon
Įgdą́ Sábe	Black Cloud / Dark Thunder
Niágiwadè (fem.)	One Who Gets Water
Nudą́ Mądį̀	Warrior (Approaching Rolling Wind Clouds)
T'idétigdè	Makes Noise (Thunder in the Distance)

The names he gave to his children seem to be out of the ordinary, but his gift of medicine and knowledge of the weather through some natural phenomena justified the giving of the names. According to KH, the names are centered around the properties of an approaching storm, but *T'áíkawahò*'s knowledge of additional signs foretold the coming of the seasons, set expectations for the coming winter (e.g., the growth or lack of growth of certain plants could tell of a long hard winter), and indicated the disruption of normal migrating habits of birds (i.e., migrating too early or too late). Thunderheads spiraling in the distance told him of the nature of an approaching storm, and lightning striking in a straight or angled line told the direction the storm was headed. And he knew many more natural processes.

In modern times, some jokingly have said they could make it rain or stop raining. A Comanche Indian said all one needed to do to make it rain was to spank a turtle. When we were children, if it had not rained for some time and sudden clouds came up and it began to sprinkle, we were encouraged to go out into the light rain and play *Dábi*. We stretched our arms out as far as we could and spun round and round. We got dizzy, but they said it would make it rain harder. Again, when it continued to rain too long, we were encouraged to go outside and draw the figure of a turtle on the ground going east. Sometimes the rain stopped immediately and sometimes it didn't. Were the Ponca rainmakers? We who have lived in the twentieth century do not know. But we believe that their insight of the coming storm was certainly understood through centuries of experience on the planet Earth because they live here.

The great men and women of the Ponca Tribe's *Hísadà* clan used the elements for many names. The number of their stories is multiplied by each family and includes throwing water on another person causes rain, hanging out feathers causes rain, the dying of a clan member causes rain, and so forth. However, regardless of clan affiliation, the elements became part of the name of the Ponca people. The following examples are given to show the extent of the usage (most of the names below are from the *Hísadà* clan):

Ániwį (f.)	Rain Drop
Nąžígaxè	Rainmaker
Áxewà	Frost Upon
Nąžíxùde	Gray Rain
Điába	Lightning
Nąžítidè	Sudden Rain
Điába Žįgà	Little Lightning
Niágiwadè (fem.)	One Who Gets Water
G'édawį (fem.)	Clear Weather
Ní Ákibanà	Goes Toward the Water
Gamátigdè	Sudden Downpour
Ní Ánągè	Running over Water
Gamáxp'ì	Becomes Cloudy
Ní Wá'ì	Gives Water
G'édadadį	Jubilant on a Clear Day
Šúkabì	Heavy Clouds
Mási Mądì	Hail Walking
Xuéginà	Comes Back Roaring
Mási Žįgà	Little Hail
T'adé Ása	Fast Hard Wind
Mąšt'éwį (fem.)	Sunny Day

T'adé Údą	Good Wind
T'ádewį (fem.)	Wind
Mąxp'í Sábe	Black Cloud
T'íúbixà	Sprinkle upon the Dwelling
Mąxp'í Sá Mądì	White Clouds Everywhere
Mąxp'í Ámądį	Walks on the Cloud

The Ponca people, like many other tribes, hold the earth sacred, so they used the natural setting of the earth. To name their children, they used the *Tą́de* (Ground), *Pahé* (Hill), *Mąžą́* (Land), *Wadíška* (Creek), and *Mą́ ną́šudè* (Dust from the Ground) to formulate the following names:

LAND

Mąžą́ Átą	Over the Land
Pahé Óđišà	Around the Hill
Mąžą́ Íbahà	Knows the Country
Pahét'ap'į	Top of the Hill
Mąžą́ugášą̀ (fem.)	Travels the Country
T'ą́de Ámądì	Walks on the Ground
Mą́ Nąšúde	Dust from the Ground
P'ahé Žįgà	Little Hill
P'ahé T'ągà	Big Hill (Mountain)
P'ahé	Hill
P'ahé Ágđį	Sits on the Hill
Wačíškà	Creek
T'ą́de Nąkúge	Stomps on the Ground

Male names were also derived from weaponry objects such as a *T'aháwagđè* (warrior's shield), a *Mą́* (arrow), a *Wégasap'ì* (whip), a *Wétį* (war club), a *Mą́hì* (knife), and the *Heđúškà Niníbà* (pipe or calumet).

Mą́ Ákibanà	Running after Arrow
Niníba	Pipe
Mą́ Í'dadì	Crazy Arrow
T'aháwagđe Skà	White Shield
Mąčú T'aháwagđè	Bear Shield

Wégasàp'ì	Whip
Mą́hį Đįgè	No Knife
Mą́hį Skà	White Knife
Wétį Wasà	He Cut Their War Club

Although the practice is not limited solely to female members of the *Đíxidą̀*, *Hísadà* and *Níkapášną̀* clans, these clans name their female offspring according to the moon (month) in which they were born. Also, it was common to name these babies according to the condition of the moon. The Ponca have names for each quarter of the moon. Sometimes names related to the quarter or to the waxing and waning of the moon.

Mí Gašą̀dį̀	Pouring Moon
Mí T'ą́i	Full Moon
Mí Gđedą́wį̀	Moon Hawk Woman
Mí T'ą̀i Đįgè	No Full Moon
Mí Gđidą̀į̀	The Return of New Moon
Mí Tenà	Only the Moon
Mí Hìdabì	Waning Moon
Mí Wahúsa	Scolding Moon
Mí Husą̀	Bright Moon
Mí Wása	White Moon
Mí Hùsą̀są̀	Sparkling Moon
Mí Íjabè	Narrow Moon
T'ą̀i Ginà	Moon with Halo Coming Back
T'ą́iđì	Moon with Halo
Mí P'ahą́ga	First Moon (Quarter)

Only three female names could be found relating to the sun.

Mí Đágđì	Good Sun[3]
Mí Wáxubè	Sacred Sun
Mí Skà	White Sun

Personal Attributes in Names

The Ponca used personal descriptive attributes in the giving of nick-names. One name relating to a personal attribute for female children in the *Níkapášną̀* clan is *Mą̀šiát'a Xɖíťu Mą̀ɖį̀*, which means "Walks in Meanness above Others." This type of child's name usually remained with a girl until she was given another name. Other names that were prominently known at the turn of the twentieth century were *Xiɖádawì Waú Žį̀gà*, which means "Old Lady Female Eagle"; *Hį́ziwì*, or "One Yellow Hair"; and *Mísį̀wì*, the meaning of which is unknown. Men too had nicknames such as *Újà̀*, "Good" (*Újà̀* is a corruption of *Úɖà̀*); *Wahába*, "Corn"; *Mą̀ɖį́ Čáki*, "One Who Walks Awkwardly"; *Nąhégažì*, "One Who Does Not Run Fast a Little"; *Mágažį̀gà*, "Little Skunk"; and *Žį̀gáp'ežì*, "Bad Boy." Nicknames for women included *Waú Wiáxčì*, "One Woman"; *Bɖékažį̀gà*, "Nickle"; and so forth. Sometimes these kinds of names stayed with them throughout their lives.

Use of the Feminine *Wį̀*

The feminine gender *Wį̀* in names was used with clans, weather, and so forth.

Ániwį̀	Rains Upon
Néštawį̀	*Néstà* Clan Woman
Časkáwį̀	(Sioux name)
Mašt'éwį̀	Sunny Day Woman
Gɖedą́wį̀	Hawk Woman
Núxewį̀	*Núxe* Clan Woman
Hísadàwì	*Hísadà* Clan Woman
Ɖíxidą̀wì	*Ɖíxidą̀* Clan Woman
Pą́cawì	Ponca Woman
Mą́nąt'ęwì	Kills the Arrow Woman
Mąką́wį̀	*Mąk'ą́* Clan Woman
Wašábewì	*Wašábe* Clan Woman
Wažážewį̀	*Wažážè* Clan Woman
Níkapášnąwì	*Níkapášną̀* Clan Woman

Clan Names

In the distant past, as mentioned previously, names were attributed to clan members probably by some natural process. The names in each clan were given to each subsequent generation and each generation added more names (see chapter 16). The names for male and female members of the tribe were given at birth, and at puberty, young men received their second name. Some received the same name of a relative in their clan. If a young man was not named after an ancestor, he perhaps would be named for a predictable personal attribute seen in his behavior. But the name had to match given attributes of his individual clan (KH, KCH, AMC, NC).

After conducting interviews with the elders, lists of clan names were made. *Tract Books Indian Schedules*, volume 22 (December 7, 1894) was also helpful. This document shows the distribution of land or acreage to individual Ponca Indians according to the Dawes Act of 1887. The allotment description in this document shows the relationship of each family member, namely, husband, wife, sons, and daughters. It appears that there was not an acceptable written alphabet to accommodate Ponca sounds. Further, since there were no Ponca individuals schooled in the English language to aid translation, the names in the tract book were spelled according to what the recording agent heard. Also, it was evident that some individuals had the same name, and the agent used a different spelling of the name for each individual, probably in order to distinguish one from the other.

Although these lists do not include all clan names of both Ponca men and women, the following are names of Ponca women derived from various clans:

HÍSADÀ CLAN

Ániwì	Rains Upon
Mą́nąt'ęwį̀	Kills the Arrow
T'adéze	Buffalo Tongue
Mí Đágđį̀	Good Sun
G'édawį̀	Clear Day
Mí Wahùsa	Scolding the Moon
Há Wáđizè	Takes the Hide

Mí Wasà	Cut Moon
Há Wátè	Buckskin Dress
Nązéízè	Meaning Unknown
Hísadàwį	*Hísadà* Clan Woman
Šabekéwadè	Darkened Them
Hínąxpèwį	(Meaning unknown)
Winážįgà	Little Sister
Húčą	Sounds of Birds
Žáį Wadè	Carry Wood
Íye Skà	Interpreter

ÐÍXIDÀ CLAN

Bdékažigà	Nickle
Mí Gdedáwį̀	Moon Hawk Woman
T'áidì	Moon with Halo
Mí Hídabì	Waning Moon
Ðíxidąwį	*Ðíxidà* Clan Woman
Mí Hùsąsą̀	Sparkling Moon
Enábabì	The Only One
Mí Wahùsa	Scolding the Moon
Gdedáwį	Hawk Woman
Míhusà	Bright Moon
Íbaàmà	Unknown
Nązéįzè	(Meaning unknown)
Ínidabì	The One Healed By
Ní Agíwadè	Let Us Get Water
Mí Ábadį̀	Day Moon
Waú Wiáxči	One Woman
Mí T'ąì	Full Moon
Wétįwì	Club Woman
Mí Gášądì̀	Pouring Moon
Xidá Mą́šigdè	Rising Eagle
Mí Gdìt'ąì	When Moon Comes with Halo

MĄK'Ą́ CLAN

Gdedą́wį T'égà	New Hawk
Mí P'ahą́ga	First Moon
Mą̊žą́ Ugášą	Travels the Land
P'ą́casà	Light Ponca
Mí Akądà	Moon Goddess
T'áí Mądì	Walking
Mí Hídabì	Waning Moon
Umą́ágdè	Gets Provisions
Mí Ną́p'abì	Fears the Moon

WAŠÁBE CLAN

Ááwį	(Meaning unknown)
P'ą́cawì	Ponca Woman
Gdedą́wį T'égà	New Hawk
T'é Mížįgà	Buffalo Girl
Mąšt'éwì	Sunny Day
T'é Míwaù	Buffalo Woman
Mí Gdedąwì	Moon Hawk
T'é Są́wį	White Buffalo Girl
Mí Đágdį	Good Sun
T'é Wáu	Buffalo Woman
Mí Wáxubè	Sacred Sun
Míbdiwì	(Meaning unknown)
Zí Mądì	Walks Yellow (Buffalo)

NÚXE CLAN

Éšnà T'ąì	She Alone Is Made Clear
Núxewì	Ice
Giwáčìbè	Comes from the Battle
T'é Waú	Buffalo Woman
Mímitè	Dying Moon
Wétanà	(Meaning unknown)
Misą́ Mądį̀	Walks in Shimmering Moon Light

WAŽÁŽÈ CLAN

Mí T'ą́igè	The Moons with Halos
Míteną̀	The Moon
Míakądà	Moon Goddess
Užą́gèdąbè	Sees the Pathway
Míbdįwì	(Meaning unknown)
Waką́wì	Gambler
Míhągà	First Moon

NÍKAPÁŠNĄ̀ CLAN

Gdedą́št'ewì	One Hawk
Mí Gdedą́wì	Moon Hawk
Mą́zè Wažì	Puts Metal upon Them
T'ą́iginá	New Coming Moon
Mašiáta Xdít'ù Mądí	Walks in Meanness above Others

NÉŠTA CLAN

No names were remembered by the elders for this now-extinct clan. At the turn of the century, ca. 1900, there were two sisters who bore the English name Kemble (KH, NC, AMC). The elders said the area of Minnesota and the Great Lakes was called *Nésta* by the Ponca people. The term connotes "lakes," or "at the lakes." The only additional information on this clan was found in Dorsey's work on Ponca clans. A name in the feminine gender of the term would be *Néštawì*.

Male Names

WAŠÁBE CLAN

P'ahé Udíšą	Bison around the Hill
Niníba	Pipe
Šúkabì	Bunch of Clouds
Giną́žągè	Makes a Pathway
T'e Ágahà Mądì	Bison Walks Above
Hé Xudè	Grey Horn

T'ežįgà	Little Buffalo (bison)
Hį Zí Žįgà	Little Yellow Hair
Waną́še T'ągà	Big Soldier
K'išt'áwàgu	(Meaning unknown)
Wažį́dadì	Angry Thoughts
Žą́ Xùdè	Grey Wood
Mą́ Xága	Jagged Arrow Head
Wažíágahigì	Anger Chief
Ágahà Mądì	Walks Upon
Wésà T'ągà	Big Snake
Ní Ákibanà	Runs for the Water
Mą́ge Zí	Yellow Breast
Ną́kà Édąbè	Back of Bison Comes into View
Pá Mą́gdè Nąžį̀	Bison Holds Head up Standing
Ábagdè Nąžį̀	Bison Standing Reserved
Gaxáta Nąžį̀	Bison Standing Apart from the Herd

WAŽÁŽÈ CLAN

Ábe Žíde	Red Leaf
P'ádįgahì	Pawnee Chief
Đéze Sábe	Black Tongue
Síde Gdáką	Tail Across
Há Baxdúde	Sheds His Skin
Šáge Šugà	Thick Nail
Há Gdežé	Striped Hide
Taníši	Unknown
Héga	Buzzard
T'e P'á Žįgà	A Small Bison Head
Hú Žįga	Little Voice
Ukípatà	Wraps around Self
Įdé Sábe	Black Face
Úkinądì	Can't See It
Įdé Xagà	Rough Face

Ųxúđa	No Ear
Kigđíbutà	Makes Itself into Ball
Wašką́hì	Strong
Mąčú Bđą̀	Bear Smell
Waką́hągà	Gambling Chief
Mąčú Ną̌žì	Standing Bear
Wádašibè	Makes Them Open
Mą́ge Sábe	Black Chest
Wadáhut'à	Makes Holler
Mą́xeàt'a Mąđí	Walking Sky
Wádidaxè	Makes Rattling Sounds
Nąą́be	He Heard It
Wažįga Zì	Yellow Bird
Pahé Žįgà	Little Hill
Xidáhągà	Eagle Chief
Xidá Žįgà	Little Eagle
Šą́ge Zí	Yellow Horse
Ápą Nąžį̀	Standing Elk
Nąxíde Đįgè	No Ear

NÍKAPÁŠNĄ̀ CLAN

Čumą́dì	Spits Walking
Ną́getidè	Runs Suddenly
Gdedą́ Ną́pabì	Hawk Fears Him
Ną́kat'ù	Blue Back
Gdedą́ Sabè	Black Hawk
Ną́djbažì	Makes No Error
Gdedą́ Ská	White Hawk
Nąxdé Sábe	Black Coal
Gdedą́ Xudè	Grey Hawk
Niškúšku	(Meaning unknown)
Gdedą́ginà	Hawk Returns
T'awážįgà	Little Deer

Húḓugà Sapì	Straps the Camp Circle
T'áxt'i Ská	White Deer
Mąčú Daḓį̀	Crazy Bear
Wažį́t'u	Blue Bird
Waséką	Fast

ĐÍXIDĄ̀ CLAN

Áhįdubà	Wings
Nudą́ Mąḓį̀	Warrior
Čąbéskà	White Beaver
Nudą́ Đį̀gè	Has No War
Đúdaḓįgè	(Meaning unknown)
Pahé T'ągà	Big Hill
Gahíží̧gà	Little Chief
Šą́nugahì	Wolf Chief
Gakúwį̀xè	Turning Round
Šą́ge Níkagahì	Horse Chief
Ganą́ži Ubíxą̀	To Sprinkle Upon
Šéki	Rattle Snake
Hé Žáta	Forked Horn
Šimąšadè	Kneels on One Knee
Hé Xága Ská	White Elk
Šką́tigḓè	Moves Quickly
Íye Mąḓį̀	Goes around Talking
Šúde Gaxè	Smoke Maker
Į́be Žąkà	Scissor Tail
Šúde Waḓè	Cause to Smoke
Į̀gḓą́ Sabè	Black Cloud
T'aháwagḓè Skà	White Shield
Káxe Nąbá	Two Crows
T'aíkawahò	(Meaning unknown)
Kixíḓabaží	Not Afraid to Try
T'ą́de Ámąḓį̀	Walks on the Ground

Máá Žįgà	Little Cotton Wood Tree
T'é Núga Nąbà	Two Buffalo Bulls
Mą́šą	Feather
T'idé Tigdè	Makes Noise
Mąšt'ínugà	The Bull
Úgadè	Gives Away
Mąčú Dúbà	Four Bear
Uhé Gaxè	Makes a Way
Mąčú Nąbà	Two Bears
Wábadizè	Man Who Scares Them
Mąčú Žįgà	Little Bear
Wadá Đįgè	Has Nothing
Mąčú Skà	White Bear
Wádixagè	Makes Cry
Mąčú Waną́xe	Bear Spirit
Wažį́ Skà	Clear Mind
Mą́'kapà	Quick Arrow
Wažį́ga Umą̀	Where Birds Gather
Miká Žįgà	Little Raccoon
Wat'ę́ Žįgà	Kills Little
Míxa Žįgà	Little Duck
Wé'e' Žįgà	Little Hoe
Nąbá Watą̀	Treads on Two
Wégasapì	Whip
Nąhídabì	Grows Old
Wéti Wasà	Cuts Their War Club
Ní Wá'i	Gives Water
Xéga Đixé	(Meaning unknown)
Níkà Waką́da	God Man
Xidá Skà	White Eagle

MĄK'Ą́ CLAN

Gahígidabè	Made Him Chief

Nugá	Bull
Gaká	(Meaning unknown; That One?)
Sįde Skà	White Tail
Gdedą́ Sabé	Black Hawk
T'é Hągà	Buffalo Leader
Hą́gažįgà	Little Leader
Hé Xága	Elk or Rough Horn
Nihą́ga Žįgà	Little Spring
Úhąbè	Cook
Nádè Wáxa	Heart above Others
Žįgá Nudą̀	Little Warrior
Íniàbe	Healed By
Wačígaxè Žįgà	Little Dance
Mą́ Ákibanà	Running after Arrow
Wagíą	Sing for Us
Mikáe Ská	White Star
Mą́ną́šudè	Dust from the Ground
Wáxa Nąžį̀	Standing Beyond Others
Xidá Gaxè	Makes Himself into an Eagle
T'í Úkiàbažì	Does Not Speak to His Household

NÚXE CLAN

Bą́ Nąžį̀	Stands Black
Núxe Žįgà	Little Ice
T'é Sí Žįgá	Little Buffalo Feet
Šábetą Nąžį̀	Stands Black
Nąhégažì	Runs Swiftly
Sįde Dúbà	Four Tails
Núxe	Ice

HÍSADÀ CLAN

Áhį Skà	White Wing
Nąžį́tidè	Sudden Rain

Áxewà	Covered with Frost
Ní Ánągè	Running over Water
Điába	Lightning
Niába Žįgà	Little Moonlight
Điába Žįgà	Little Lightning
Nudą́ ą́xa	Cries for War
Điti Áxa	Cries for Ribs
P'ádįgahì	Pawnee Chief
Gédadadì	Clearing Weather
Šúkabì	Puffy Clouds
Gamą́tigdè	Sudden Downpour
Tabdúga	(Meaning unknown)
Hąmą́di Žįgà	Walks Little at Night
Tanúka	Meat
Hé Xága Nąžį̀	Standing Elk
T'é Níxa	Buffalo Belly
Hésatigdè	(Meaning unknown)
T'é Núgà P'à	Buffalo Head
Į̀št'á Pedé	Fire Eyes
Ug'ádežą́	Aside from Others
Mási Mądì	Hails Everywhere
Ukíabè	Spoken To
Mási Žįgà	Little Hail
Wahába	Corn
Mądį́ Čakì	Walks Carelessly
Wažį́ga	Bird
Mąxpí Są́ Mądį́	White Clouds About
Wasábe	Black Bear
Nąžį́ Gaxè	Rain Maker
Wasábe Xdahà	Poor Bear
Nąžį́ Mądì̀	Rains Everywhere
Xaéginà	Comes Back
Nąžį́ Xúde	Grey Rain

Žúga Uđíšp'è	Cuts the Flesh
Úhą̀ Žįgà	Little Cook
T'iúbixą̀	Chimney Swift
Kiážiwađè	Cause Them Not to Come Home

Names from Census Roll

Several censuses were taken in the nineteenth century.[4] The one acquired here is primarily composed of male names interspersed with a few female names. The purpose of the census is unclear, but as stated previously, over thirty-five different censuses were taken by over fifty different people. The following census was taken by U.S. Special Agent I. Shaw Gregory on July 6, 1860, at the Ponca camp. The date on the document is a strong indication that the Ponca were probably still living in the three camps near the confluence of the Niobrara and Missouri Rivers. The names here include some known Ponca individuals, particularly chiefs of the tribe; however, some of the names are unfamiliar. Because the writing of the Ponca names was not clear, the current Ponca alphabet is used to make the names readable. It was either written by someone of French descent or someone who wrote what they thought the Ponca word sounded like. Where the translations were also incomplete or inaccurate, I have taken the liberty to make some corrections. These are noted in parenthesis. Again, I am obliged to acknowledge the assistance from the elders. Without their knowledge and willingness to help, these interpretations and corrections could not be made. Although some pages seem to be missing, the names are listed as they were taken from material available to me, that is, the census roll.

	BAND OF
Ešną́ Níkagahì	Lone Chief
Wašką́mą̀đì	Strong Walker
Gđáwabì	Man That Loves
Waí Waú	The French Woman
Į́'e Skà	The White Stone
Hexága Wakíde	Man Shoots Elk
Náxđį̀	The Blaze

Mixá Skà	The [White] Swan
Tą́de Nąkúge	Man Rings the Ground [Man Stomps on the Ground]
Wábazè	Man That Scares
Wažį́ga	Little Bird [Bird]
Wés'a Žįgà	The Little Snake
T'é Núgà Įštà	[Bison] Bulls Eye
Đítì Áxà	Cries for Ribs
Gđedá Wažį̀	The [Angry] Hawk
Máa Žįgà	Little Cotton Wood [Tree]

BAND OF

Wégasapì	The Whip
Šą́t'ągà	The Wolf
Mą̌čú Wádihì	Man Scares the Bear [Man That Scares Up the Bear]
Nudą́ Hągà	The Main Chief [War Leader]
Šą́nugahì	Chieftain [Wolf Chief]
Mą̌čú Wiáxčì	Lone Bear
Xégà Đixè	Man Breaks Wood
P'á Gažá	Man Shakes His Head
Wášpažì	Man That Moves Always [Man That Misbehaves]
Hįbé Piážì	Bad Moccasin
Nišúdè Žá	Missouri River Wood
Šą́ge	The Horse
Wadá Đįgè	One Who Has Nothing
Pážì	Man Carries Hay
Nąą́bà	Man Walks All Night
Wažį́skà	White Brain [Clear Mind]
Waígđabà	Man Spreads His Robe [Spreads the Robe]
Niágiwađè	Man [Woman] That Gets Water
Mą̌čú Sabè	Little Bear [Black Grizzly Bear]
Mąštį́ge	The Rabbit

Wahútǫdì	The Gun
Šúde Gaxè	The Smoke [Smoke Maker]
T'é T'ǫgà	The Bull [Big Buffalo]
Uhé Gaxè	Path Maker
Miká Žįgà	Little Coon
Hįbé Mazè	Iron Shoes
Niníba Išáge	The Old Pipe
Gdedąwi	The Little Hawk [Hawk]
Éšnǫ Nąžį̀	The Lone Man [The Only Man Standing]

BAND OF

Gíštawágo	Hard Walker
Gahígi	The Chief
Qkíabè	The Man That Talk
T'é Wádihì	The Man That Raise the Buffalo [One That Scares Up Bison]
Šuína	Prairie Chicken Coming
Akíčidà	The Soldier
Tidíba Wažį́ga	The Sawyer
T'é Dítį	The Rib [Bison Rib]
Há Xduà	The Hollow Skin
Edą́ Nǫ́ge	The Man That Runs Close
Žįgá Pežì	Bad Boy
Wažį́ Wáxa	The Bad Man [Anger above Others]
T'at'ą́ga P'á žįgà	Small Bulls Head
Nąbé K'iúì	Wounded Hand
Mąčú Hį Šabè	Bear with Long Hair [Dark-Haired Bear]
T'é Núga P'à	Big Bull Head [Buffalo Bull Head]
Wakądagì	Devil [Prehistoric Animal]
Baxága	The Bull Sheds His Hair
Axúde [*Hé Xúdè*]	The Grey Horn
Nušiáha	The Small Man [Short]
Žábe Skà	White Beaver

Tanúkà Nąžį̀	Standing Buffalo [*T'át'ą̀gà Nąžį̀*]
P'ádį Gahígi	Pawnee Chief
Wé'e' It'ą́điàdì	Old Hoe
Edítą	One That's [from] There
Mą̀čú Nąžį̀	Standing Bear
Néxe Gakù	The Drum
Mą̀čú Đatè	Bear Eater
Wađáge	The Hat
T'adą́he	Whirlwind
Ųhą́ge Žą́i	Man Sleeps at the End
T'í Ugíą	Man Flies in His Lodge
Mą̀čú Dúba	Four Bears
Wašáđu Sábè	Negro
Wabáhì Žį̀gà	Little Eater [Little Picker]
Mą̀čú Ké Nąpà	Bear That Goes Out [Fears the Bear]
Mą́zemà̀ Nápį̀	Ball in the Neck [Cartridge Necklace]
Wáđixè KáSì	Man Runs Far [Long Chaser]
Hexágà	The Elk
Wažáže	The Osage
Aabè Židè	Red Leaf
T'í kè Tiúpà	Man Comes from the Lodge
Į̀dáđą Đį̀gè	Poor Man
Čú Ké Skà	Man Spits White
Mą̀žą́ UgáSą	One Travels the Earth
P'á Đišágè	Curly Hair [Head]
Šą́gè Hį́ T'ú	Grey Horse [Dappled Horse]
ÁnąhàSì	Last Man [*Ená háSi?* The Last One]
Hébadì Žą́i	Man Sleeps This Side
T'ahį́ T'ą̀gà	Big Mane
Waą́	Singing Man [Sing]
WagđíSkà	The Bug

Mąčú Skà	White Bear
Nudą́ Žį̀gà	Small Warrior [Small War Party]

BAND OF

Ágahà Mąđì	One That Walks over the Other
Wažíga P'à	Birds Head
Máxèát'a Nąží	Standing Cloud [Stands Above]
Mázè Unáž̨į	Iron Shirt
Mąčú Síde Đį̀gè	Bear with No Tail
Į̀dé Mą́šađì	Dirty Face
Šą́ge Sábe	Black Horse
Míkasì Xđahà	Poor Wolf [Skinny Coyote]
Hexága Sabè	Black Elk
Áązè	One That Don't Run [Resting]
Mą́ga Žį̀gà	The Skunk [Little Skunk]
T'ahį̀ Šábe	Black Cow [Black-Haired Buffalo]
T'esą́ Waštà	White Cow
Nąbá Mąđì	Double Walker
Ní Ánè	Man Climbs upon Water
Mą́ge Zí	Yellow Breast
Gđínidą̀	Man Sits Down
Šahíɾđà	The Cheyenne
Žį̀gá Wašúše	Little Soldier
T'ežé Baté	Cow Dung [Buffalo Chip]
T'é Žį̀gà	Small Calf [Little Buffalo]
Zį́	Man Carries the Yellow [Yellow]
Į̀dé Sábe	Black Face
Pádį̀ Pizá	Pawnee Sand
Mázitą̀	The Cedar
Mąšt'į́gè	The Rabbit
Wábašibà	Lost Man [Lets Them Out]
Mąšt'éwì (fem.)	Sunny Day

Sí Ðįgè	One Leg [No Foot]
Šánąžíá	Man That Stands
Wašúše Žįgà	Little Brave
Mąxp'í Ámądį̀	Walking Cloud [Walks on the Clouds]
Waką́ Ną̀žį̀	Man Head of All [Standing Gambler?]
T'ągádihà	The Big Man [A Large Area]
Pétą Áxa	Man Cries for a Crane
Xiðá Gaxè	Eagle Maker
Mą́ Ákibanà	Running after Arrow
T'é Hągà	Buffalo Chief
Mąžą́ Íbahà̀	Knows the Country
Į̀štá Pedè	Fire Eyes
Pahé Mąšì	Big Hills [High Hills]
Wahá Tągà	Big Kettle
Į́'e Nąp'ì	Wears Stones
Wašką́ Žįgà	Man Not Strong
Ðéba Xą́	Broken Jaw
Nugá	The Stud [Bull]
P'á Šį́	No Tail [Flat Nose]
Sį́de Ská	White Tail
Wagíą	Thunder [Sings for Us]
Mąžą́ Háde	Humpback [On the Land]
Hé Ðíšižè	Crooked Horn [Cracked Horn]
Wažį́ Šidà	Bad Temper
Į̀št'á Mą́ze	Iron Eyes
Káxe Sábè	Black Crow
Mą́šą Skà	White Feather
Mąną́átà̀	The Scratcher
Išáge P'ežì	Bad Old Man
Mąčú Ðigúže	Crooked Bear
Mą́hì Ðįgè	No Knife

Gahígi Wašúše	Brave Chief
Íwetĩ Žĩgà	The Hammer [Little War Club]
Mąčú Wažĩ Piážì	Bad Bear [Angry Bear]
Wadíšnažì	Not Seen
Sádetą	White Spot
Ságe Nągip'àbažì	Man Not Afraid of His Horses
Xúga Žĩgà	Little Badger
Nągètidè	Fast Runner
Čú Mądì	Spitter
Xúga Nąpĩ	Badger Necklace
Žĩgá Asà	Head Small Man
Hánukadì	No Leggings [Naked]
Ĩdé Hĩ Škubè	Big Beard
Má Žĩgà	Little Arrow
Mí Gdedáwì (fem.)	Moon Hawk
Manáutà	Ground Scratcher

BAND OF

Oska Đužià	Rush in the Battle
Núxe Žĩgà	Little Ice
Đaégà	The Poor Man
Wasábe	Black Bear

The following names come from a census roll taken on December 26, 1862. It also divides the tribe into eleven bands. It is presented to show the nature of names in that period. Some names are the same as in the previous census, and some new names are included. Also, there are some names missing in this roll. The names are only a part of the full document.[5] This sample of names from the document includes only some of the names of the heads of households.

Again, there are only a few female names on the list.

Wégasap'ì	Whip
Mąčú Wadihĩ	One Raises the Bear
Mášą	Feather
Šąt'ągà	Big Wolf [Wolf]

Nudą Mądì	The Warrior [On the War Path]
Nudą Hágà	Headman [War Leader]
Šúde Gaxè	Smoke [Smoke Maker]
Uhé Gáxè	Road Maker
T'atąga	Big Bull [Large Bison]
Mąčú Nit'á	Bears Ear
Mąčú Wiáxčì	Lone Bear [One Bear]
Hįbé Piážì	Bad Moccasin
Wasábe T'ągà	Big Black Bear
Ną Ába	Travels until Daylight
Didé Tigđè	Makes Noise
Wadá Đįgè	Has Nothing
Nišúde Žą́	Missouri Timber
Šą́ge	Horse
Wáspažì	One Who Does Not Behave
Wahút'ądį	Gun
Niníba Išáge	Old Pipe
Miká Žįgà	Little Raccoon
Hįbé Mą́ze	Iron Shoes
Gđedą́ Ké	The Hawk
Íyè Mąđį̀	Great Talker
Đehétawì	Good Girl
Mąčú Žįgà	Little Bear
Wagđé Žįgà	Little Man Stands Up
T'é Są́wį	White Buffalo Girl
Íbahąbè	One Knows Something
Waį̀ Gabđà	Open Robe
Míxa Nidè	Goose Rump
Kíšt'awágù	Hard Walker
Šúkabì	Heavy Clouds
Agášità	Soldier
Wasábè Žįgà	Little Black Bear
Šúínà	Prairie Chicken Coming

Nagé Áxa	Cries for War
T'é Núgà P'à	Bull Head
Nabé Úbɖà [Nąbé K'íu]	Wounded Hand
T'e Ɖíṭį	Buffalo Ribs
Pédè Gahì	Fire Shaker
Žábè Skà	White Beaver
Ukíabè	One Talks to the Other
Gahígi	Chief
Áškà Nągè	Close Runner
Žá Snà	Hairy Man [Cut Self on Bushes]
Ápà Nąžį̀	Standing Elk
Wahá Xɖúà	Hollow Hide
T'atągà P'á Žįgà	Small Calf Head
Máhi Gahì	Crazy Knife
Wakádagì	The Devil [Prehistoric Animal]
Dúbà Wažįga	The Lawyer [Some Birds]
Íkuhabè	The Thief [Afraid Of]
Žįgà P'ežì	Bad Boy
Hé Xudè	Grey Horn
Wažįga	Bird
T'e Wáɖihį̀	One Starts the Buffalo
Ɖíti Áxa	Open Ribs [Cries for Ribs]
T'atąga Nąžį̀	Standing Buffalo
Wažįga Zì	Yellow Bird
Nąábi	Listener
T'é Wáu	Buffalo Woman
T'í Ugíą	Flies in the Lodge
Wé'e'ɖahà	The Hoe
Wahá P'agɖè	The Hat [Leather Head Cover]
Wáxe Sabè	The Negro
Wabáhi Žíga	Little Picker
Mącú Ɖaté	Bear Eater
Wašúše	The Brave

Nąbé Gasè	Cuts the Hand
Wažáže	Osage
Šáge Skà	White Nail
Į́'è P'è	Rock Hammer
Waą́dehè	Singer
Mą̌čú Skà	White Bear
Adúhagà	One Walks Behind [One Goes Ahead]
Wagđíškà	The Bug
Hexágà	The Elk
Nušíáha Ginà	Short Man [Short Stature Coming?]
Tawáđì	Sniper [Snipe]
Gahígì T'égà	New Chief

Following the above two censuses, another head count was made of all male members of the three camps occupied by the Ponca near the Niobrara and Missouri Rivers. The document is dated November 19, 1874, and was submitted to the Honorable Ed P. Smith, commissioner of Indian Affairs, Washington DC. It was evidently written by a U.S. Indian agent whose name is not legible but appears to be P. Birkett. As in the other documents, the census taker divided the tribe by bands. This is probably correct as they accounted for nine bands, one of them being a half-breed band. Since the Ponca had eight clans, the chiefs whose names are listed as band leaders were probably clan chiefs. The names on the list were basically the same with few exceptions.

Names for Non-Clan Members

The census roll taken at Ponca Agency, Dakota Territory, on November 19, 1874, showed that there were 139 people who possessed some degree of Ponca blood. These people were considered members of the tribe and held all benefits and rights as tribal members. In effect, they were Ponca, but the Ponca clanship system is patrimonial, and as such, children follow the clan of their fathers. The naming process was broken down at this point and adjustments had to be made. Some names were borrowed from a parent's clan. Other names were made up to fit the individual and seem to be no different from clan names. Few male names have survived. They are listed below:

Ešną́ Níkagahì (Lone Chief)	Mitchell Cerre
Ą́pą T'ągá (Big Elk)	Robert Primeaux
T'é Nugá Níkagahì (Buffalo Chief)	McDonald
Mą́hi Ská (White Knife)	Peter Primeaux
Uhé Wakiḍažì (Won't Let Them Pass By)	Louis Primeaux
Wanáxè Mą́í (Ghost Walking)	
Mikáè Uxpádè (Falling Stars)	
Mą́šą̀ P'agḍą̀ (Feathered Headdress)	
Wábisą̀dè (Press Them Down)	Louis Roy
Maną́kugè (Stomps the Ground)	
T'é Núgà Níkagahì (Buffalo Bull Chief)	

Corruption of English Names

One of the most common practices was to call non–clan members by their given French or English name. Since non-English-speaking Ponca had difficulty pronouncing the non-Ponca names, a corruption of the name developed. Some of these names are listed below with the Ponca corruption by which these people were known.

Ponca corruption	English name	Ponca corruption	English name
MALE			
Ádamà	Adam	*Ḍamútè*	Lamont
Boína	Paul	*Mišéna*	Mitchell
Ḍǫ́dè	George	*Pétą̀*	Pete or Peter
Ḍamí	Lemuel	*Pí'ke*	Pinck
Jímì	Jim	*Salíse*	Silas
Jú	Joe	*Šánì*	Charles
Luwí	Louis	*Tómà*	Tom or Thomas
Lóginà	Logan	*Jánà*	John
FEMALE			
Alísè	Alice	*Losána*	Rosanna
Ḍisí	Lucy	*Magaḍíte, Magḍítè*	Margaret

Đizá	Elizabeth	*Madíšą*	Martha
Edénì	Ellen	*Madí*	[Martha?]
Émédè	Emily	*Médè*	Mary
Supína	Sophia	*Jiniwí*	Jenny
Luwísa	Louise	*Suzáni*	Suzanna
Žudí	Julia, Judith, or Julie		

Some Ponca words (some meanings unknown) were used as names for these non-clan members. Some examples for males are *Bimą́*, *Bazína*, *Bdazú*, *Hádamà*, *Náxdį̀* (Burning), *Į́'è Skà* (White Rock), *Pidišį́*, *Paská* (White Head; also Bald Eagle), and *Sásuwè*. Female examples are *Madíána* (Mary Ann?), *Madídéčè* (?), *Madižąwį̀* (?), *Bdiží* (Brazia?), and so forth.

Non-Indian Titles

Non-Indian people, including federal government workers, had contact with the Ponca people beginning in the late 1700s. For that reason, they were given names. Some rules for Ponca name giving may have been used; however, these non-Indians were just given names that seemed appropriate. The Ponca gave names of honor and respect to the president of the United States and to other high-ranking officials and representatives of the U.S. government. Although the Ponca had no diplomatic relationship with England, the queen of England was given a name despite having no relationship with the tribe. Also included are individuals with a position of significance in the community or government who had direct contact with the Ponca.

Ponca name/word	English name	Ponca meaning
Itígądè	President of the United States	Grandfather
Žagdáša Waú	Queen of England	
Itígądè Žįgà	Indian commissioner	Little Grandfather
Idádidài	Indian agent	Adopted Father

Mążą́ Uná	Farmer/rancher	Land Borrower
Uɖíwį T'í Áɖį	Storekeeper	Has a House Where You Buy
Wabáxu Į́	Mailman	The One Who Carries Paper
Wagáze Wáɖį	Teacher	One That Has School
Waką́da Wáɖahà Níášigà	Minister	Person Who Prays to God
Waną́še (Orig. *Wéną̀šè*)	Soldier/police	One That Takes Away
Waúwe (*Waú íyè*)	Attorney	Woman Talk
Wazéɖe	Doctor	One That Doctors
Wazéɖe Waú	Nurse	Woman That Doctors
Wanáštą	Gypsy	Beggar

Other non-Indian individuals with whom the Ponca came into contact before and after the twentieth century were ranchers, farmers, storekeepers, and neighbors. They became known by their personal characteristics or profession. The following is a listing supplied to me by KH:

Į́hį' Židè	Mr. Souligny	Red Beard
Į́hį Sabè (more recent)	Mr. Alfred Matthews	Black Beard
Į́hį Sabè (original)	Mr. VanSellous	Black Beard
Jú Sí Ðįgè	Mr. Joe LeRoy	Joe No Foot
Mą̀šíáta Mąɖį̀	George Miller	Walks above Others
Mą́ze Įštá Úgɖà̀	Mr. ?	Eye Glasses
Mą́ze Kamà̀	Mr. Bell	Bell
Ną̀žíha Židè	Mr. Nick Fitch	Red Hair
P'á Bɖáska	Mr. Wycoff	Flat Nose
Šą́gè Gɖežè	Zack Miller	Spotted Horse
Ųgípì	Mr. ? (Father)	Full
Ųgípi Žįgà	Mr. ? (Son)	Filled up a Little
Úɖįwi T'ì Àɖį̀	John Hron	One Who Has Store

Wahút'ądį	Joe Miller	Gun
Wáxe Gdądį	Mr. Cummings	Crazy White Man

In modern times there seem to be no additional names given to non-Ponca people. Those responsible for naming those people listed above were Ponca people who spoke only the Ponca language (KH, KCH, AMC, NC, JP, AL). These names were given out of necessity, designating individuals whom they sometimes interacted with on a daily basis.

Names of Tribes and Nationalities

The Ponca people had met and interacted with various tribes and foreigners in the North Country as well as those whom they met following their residency in Indian Territory. Some of the tribes and foreigners, of course, were known by the Ponca during the pre-removal era. (The generic term for non-Ponca people is *Ukítè*, which means "enemy" or "one you would fight with"). The following list was provided by KH, KCH, NC, AMC, JP, and AL:

English term	Ponca term	English term	Ponca term
Arapaho	*Mąxp'íátą̀*	Kickapoo	*Hígabù*
Ponca	*P'ą́'k'a*	Bannock	*Bánikì*
Kiowa	*K'áiwà*	Pottawattomie	*Wahídaxą̀*
Blackfeet	*Sihá sabè*	Mandan	*Mawádanì*
Quapaw	*Ugáxpè*	Caddo	*P'aúdè*
Missouri	*Ní utátsì*	Sac and Fox	*Zágè*
Cherokee	*Šedekì·*	Nez Perce	*P'é gazą́dè*
Santee	*Isą́ą́tì*	Cheyenne	*Šahíʃdà*
Oglala	*Ubdádà*	Seminole	*Žíbè nąsádù*
Commanche	*P'ádakà*	Ojibway	*Waxtáwį̀*
Sioux	*Šą́ (All Sioux)*	Creek	*Wačíškà*
Rosebud Sioux	*Šą́xt'i (Real Sioux)*	Pine Ridge Sioux	*Sičáxu*
Omaha	*Umą́hą*	Tonkawa	*Níkà datè*

Crow	*Káxè; Húpatì*	Osage	*Wažáže*
Wichita	*Wišíta*	Hunkpapa	*Húkpapà*
Otoe	*Waɖúdadà*	Winnebago	*Hú t'ǫgà*
Iowa	*Máxudè*	Pawnee	*P'áɖì*
Yankton	*Ihą́tąwì*	Kaw	*K'ą́zè*
Southwest Indians	*Niášigà Nušíáha*	Lower Brule	*Kúda wičáša*

English term	Ponca term	Meaning
Caucasoid	*Xįhá ská*	White skin; also white people
Japanese	*Įštá músnadè*	Slanted eyes
Chinese	*Áskù snedè*	Long single braid
Mexican	*Špaúnì*	Corruption of the word *Spanish*
British	*Niášigà mǫsà*	"Uppity" person
Negroid	*Xįhá sábè*	Black skin; also black people
French	*Xįhá ská ukéɖì*	"Ordinary" white person
Russian	*Waɖáge púki*	Big fluffy hat
German	*Íyè Ɖašáɖu*	Speaks with gutteral sounds
Spanish	*Špaúnì*	Corruption of the word *Spanish*

The term for Caucasian people originally was *Xįhá ská*, but as they began to populate the land and build houses and other buildings, the Ponca began calling them *Wáxè*. The term literally interpreted means "One who made us." As previously mentioned, the original use of the term *Wáxè* meant God the Creator. The elders speculated that early on, the tribe attributed the name to the white people because of their incessant need to build buildings and fences. When used in that sense, the term means "those who build."

This section has given a fair number of names attributable to each Ponca clan. I have further given the sources for names of individuals with whom the early Ponca people interacted. Additionally, included are some names of our ancestors that are no longer used. It will be up to future generations to determine whether they will use these ancient names.

Many names of our Ponca ancestors are still being passed on to each generation. Members of specific clans have no difficulty in naming their children. However, non-clan members reach out to close relatives to find appropriate names for their children. Unless a new and acceptable system is initiated, these names will be lost to the past.

18

Toys, Games, and Sports

Making toys, playing a variety of games, and participating in sports were part of the Ponca world in early times. As in most cultures, the adult members of the family made or created games and toys for their children. Although they were originally made by the parents, the activities were taken over by the older children, who taught their younger brothers and sisters. Some games for children and adults developed into a tribal function, that is, games or activities that first involved only children ultimately involved the tribe. These games and activities provided an opportunity for tribal members to participate and exercise their individual abilities. Games for children, however, were simple and were normally played when relatives came to visit. The toys, games, and sports remembered by KH, AMC, KCH, and NC are discussed in this section.

Some of the toys included a spinning disk called *Đidą́gigì*. The ends of a leather thong about three feet long were inserted into a wooden disk with two holes. The wooden disk was slid to the approximate center of the thongs and twirled. The child then could pull outward on the thongs and cause the disk to spin. A pulling and releasing motion caused the disk to spin continuously and make a buzzing sound. Indoor activities included children making shadow pictures on the wall with their hands. This was done by most children, but older children and adults sometimes participated.

Small children played a game called *Tahádazìzì*. Four or five children facing each other would pinch the top of each other's hand until all hands were linked together by their pinches. They then would lift their hands up and down saying "*Tah-HAH-thah-ZEE-ZEE!*" The first one to let go got tickled. This game kept children busy while parents visited. It also helped children to interact with others, especially visiting relatives.

Mą́ ą́dadedè, or "arrow throwing," was a favorite outdoor activity for boys. A flat piece of wood about twelve to eighteen inches long was carved in the shape of an arrow. A notch was cut about one-third of the length of the arrow shaft close to the point. A twelve-inch leather thong with a knot on one end was tied to a stick about two or three feet long. The thong was inserted in the notch of the arrow, and the knot served to hold the arrow as the child threw it. A good thrower could throw the arrow about two hundred yards. This was a good activity for friendly competition.

Mǫdį́ka ą́dadedè was played by boys of about nine to thirteen years of age at the swimming hole. They used a limber stick about twenty inches long. They put a ball of mud at the tip of stick and slung it at each other. There was no teams or scores kept. The boys avoided being hit by ducking underwater. This game was often played when one of the swimmers wanted to quit and go home. He was usually splattered with mud and had to get back into the water and stay longer. We, as boys, called this "making sure on him," that is, making sure he stayed longer and didn't go home.

Gasnúgidè means "sliding on ice and snow." Young people played on the icy surface of riverbeds during the winter. Running and sliding to see who could slide the farthest was one of the common games. Besides running and sliding, a game like ice hockey was played. The game was similar to the Ponca shinny game but was played on ice.

Kikíbanà, or "racing on foot," was not restricted to children. Foot racing was held yearly during the spring when the annual shinny game was being played. This sport was also held at many other tribal gatherings. Older youth and young adults also raced. Footraces predominantly happened in the springtime. KH said one of the rituals before the Ponca Sun Dance was a race called *Žą́ ákibanà*, or "race for the pole." In this race, a young Ponca man could exercise his religious stamina and physical prowess. He would dance for the next four days without food or drink.

Mą́íbagì was played by teenage boys and young adults. The name of the game connotes sliding a spear on the ground. The spear, about six feet long, was slid on the ground toward a rolling hoop. A distance of about thirty yards away, another player would roll a twelve-inch hoop made of willow across the target area. The object was to slide the spear through the hoop. This increased the Ponca men's skills at hunting and spear fishing. Again, this game was played during tribal gatherings. It was an opportunity for men, women, and children to participate in physical activity.

Mą́ dédé, or "arrow shooting," was a noncompetitive way to try out new bows and arrows. In Tripp County, South Dakota, where two buttes stand side by side, Ponca men used to shoot arrows from one butte to the other. In 1949 my father and mother took me to visit Peter LeClair at his home near Wewela, South Dakota. They took me to those two buttes. I was sure that those Poncas back in the old days must have been giants. They told me that those Ponca men shot arrows from one butte to the other. The buttes are approximately a quarter of a mile apart.

Įe dihą means "lift the rock." This "rock" was a meteorite found in Tripp County. The location of the meteorite became a landmark and a place of encampment for the old-time Ponca. The weight of the meteorite was unknown. KH said, as a sport, certain strong men of the tribe would try lifting the meteorite and tossing it.

Ką́sì, or "plum seeds," were used to play a fun game. The seeds of the plum were cut and polished to serve as dice for the game. In modern times dice are made of bone and have many shapes and designs. Some are cross-like designs (usually representative of the four directions), and others are triangular, star, and starburst shapes. High-scoring pieces were animal shaped and were usually bear, fish, horse heads, and the like. This dice game was played as a gambling game by adults. Gambling is a cultural complexity that fit into many aspects of tribal traditions. Alvina Waters Primeaux (now deceased), who owned a set of the game, gave the following description of the game in 1982:

> The dice are flat and made of bone and are colored dark on one side. The other side is left in its natural bone color. This set I have is made of beef-rib bones. The two main dice are shaped like horse's heads. The other buttons have eight sides. They are about three-fourths of an inch in size. There are nine pieces total. The highest score you can get is twelve, and that's what wins the game. The dice are placed in a wooden bowl to play the game. The way you score is each person has a turn and hits the wooden bowl on a pillow or something soft, and the dice bounce up to show what kind of score you make. The scores are kept with chips. When you score, you get a chip for each point that

shows. Here's how you get points: Two horses' heads count twelve points when the rest fall on the dark side or vice versa; one horse's head alone in its own color counts ten points; if all are one color, it is eight points; odd color buttons count five points; one horse's head and one button is two points; and two buttons count two points. Any other combinations do not score points . . . like you can't score one, three, four, seven, nine in one hit. If you have a score of eleven already, you can score twelve with any of the other scores . . . like when you hit, you might come up with all dice in one color, which is eight points, but it will count only one point because you already have eleven points . . . and twelve points wins the game. If you don't call your game, you may lose your turn.

This game was played from ancient times up to the 1930s as a gambling game. When the first card games were introduced to the Ponca for gambling purposes, the "Indian Dice" game became a family social game. It is still played in modern times.

Wabášnadè was and is a game played by girls and women of all ages. KCH and NC said this was a noncompetitive sport played like the men's shinny game. Their description of the game is as follows: Two corncobs are tied about four inches apart with a leather thong or cord. Each player carries a stick of about two and a half feet in length. The tip of the stick is usually cut at the fork to provide a natural bent of about one and a half inches used to hook the thong between the corncobs. The playing field is about fifty to sixty yards long and about twenty-five yards wide. The goalposts stand about four feet high and six feet apart. The object of the game and scoring is to pass the corncobs between the posts for a point. At the beginning of the game, sides are chosen without discrimination, that is, players are not chosen to play on a certain team or side. The selection process, as in the shinny game, is done by piling up all the players' sticks in the center of the playing field. The leader then grasps two sticks with both hands at random and tosses them in opposite directions. This is done until all sticks are separated. The players then look for their sticks on either side. The side their sticks are thrown to is the goal they will defend. Once teams are chosen, the corncobs are placed in the center of the playing field and two people closest to the center commence the game facing each other on opposite sides of the cobs. They count to four simultaneously lifting their stick to touch, and on four, they begin to try to hook the thong and throw it in the direction of their goal. Other players too try to stop the cobs and send them toward their goal. There is lots of laughing and running. Sometimes it seems that every player is trying to get to the cobs, but once a player hooks the cobs, she can run with them or throw them. The game in modern times includes boys and men. So goes the game called *Wabášnadè*.

The Ponca Shinny Game

Tabégasè, or "shinny game," is a man's game played every spring as the big tribal sports activity. Four games are played every seven days at the beginning of the New Year. Springtime is the New Year, and the first of April is the approximate time the New Year begins, so the early Ponca begin to play in April on Sunday afternoons. In ancient times, the Ponca began to play when the grass began to grow. The clan charged with keeping and leading the game was the *Níkapášnà* clan. According to the elders, when the Ponca Tribe was eventually settled in Indian Territory, the Blueback family had charge of the game, beginning sometime in the early 1900s. Martin Blueback Sr., who was in charge of the game at the time of this interview in 1980, gave the following information:

This game is played the first part of the year. The old people say: We have come through the fall and winter . . . the days that cramped our bodies by the temperature . . . which kept us cold and kept us in tense feelings. Now we are given another year. The Great Spirit is renewing everything and putting new clothing on all its creation . . . so let's all stretch ourselves and stretch our legs and exercise our hearing, our sights, and move the way the Great Spirit wants us to be. So, the Ponca Indian shinny game was played. The man who was responsible for the game prepares for himself and his followers in a prayer and offering of food to the Almighty. He asked for guidance and for the fortitude of all the young men and the aged who take part in this great game of shinny. He further asked the almighty for all grievances to be set aside, and to help them forget for a day . . . all offenses that had been committed against each other, and for good fellowship and to conduct themselves in a sportsmanlike way to their fellow man.

The game was played in Nebraska for as long as anyone can remember and was played each year after the Ponca had arrived in Oklahoma. The time of the year it was played was obviously important to the people. Blueback said they determined the time to play as follows:

When the grass gets thick or just below the ankle . . . the leader calls the day when it is to be played.

To begin the game, sides were chosen as described in the women's *Wabášnadè* game; players were chosen by random selection. Blueback said this was done once for each day the game was played.

They throw all the shinny clubs in a pile and the leader . . . kneeling down . . . throws the shinny clubs right and left . . . at random, and then they choose their goal . . . the opposite side from where your club was thrown. The goals used to be about one mile apart in the old days, but now they are closer . . . The leader then takes each side to the center of the field, and they line upon each side toward their goalposts. Then the leader tosses the ball on the ground between the goalposts. Sometimes six or seven goals are made in a game . . . The game is played like hockey . . . the white man's game.

Shinny is a rough game, and younger boys play on the edge of the playing field, waiting for a stray ball to come their way. Blueback said the roughness in the game served several purposes:

If you got hit on the shins or any part of your body, it was considered a great honor because you could enjoy another year without sickness and enjoy good health. The game is pretty rough once you are caught in the thick of it. Its the closest thing to a hand-to-hand battle so those who are timid and feint of heart stay away from the main body of players and hit the ball when it is accidentally knocked to him . . . Sometimes you see things that are pretty rough, but grievances are brought to the front when two enemies bump into each other accidentally or intentionally. If a fistfight develops, everybody tries to keep it from happening.

He said the equipment used for the game included: the shinny club; three sizes of balls that were used at different intervals during the game; and special clothing.

Shinny clubs are made by bending a second growth of ash wood in a curve at one end . . . like a hook or cane. It was tied with a wire, or in the olden times, with stripped bark . . . sometimes the club is tied in the winter months and left curved until spring, then they do not have to cook it over a fire . . . then it has retained a natural curve. Those old fellows used a thicker club and those younger fellows who are fast use a thinner one. The length of the club is from the hand to the ground. The old time warriors stripped of their clothing except their breech-cloth, as if preparing for a battle. Moccasins and whistles were also put on as well as a black band on their heads to keep the sweat out of their eyes. There are three sizes of balls. The first one is big . . . about ten inches in diameter . . . they usually kick that one. We throw in the medium size one about halfway in the game. The little ball is used toward the end of the game . . . it's a fast one. Usually the first one is kicked around, and when we put in the next size, they try to kick it, but they'll miss it, so they have to use their sticks.

Blueback said the ball has a yellow cross design that represents the four winds. It is placed at the center of the playing field. The leader draws a similar design on the ground where the ball is placed so that the cross on the ball touches the cross on the ground. There was no mention of why this was done, although Blueback said that in earlier times there was some ceremonialism that preceded the game. Today the leader usually informs the players that they should observe fair play, obey the rules, and have a good time. He then will offer a prayer to commence the game. In the old days, there was much ado about how to protect oneself from injury. In modern times, if one gets hit, one gets hit.

According to KH and NC the clothing style has changed over the years from the old style of wearing breechcloth and moccasins. Presently, the players wear gym shoes (which are part of America's everyday attire), jeans, T-shirts, and caps. Occasionally, older players wear an "Indian" shirt. Blueback said some of the rules included no fighting, no batting the ball, and no running with the ball. A player, however, is allowed to stop the ball with his hand, feet, or body. In the old days, Blueback said, many activities occurred at the time the shinny game was going on: side betting; other gambling games, such as *Ką́sì* (already mentioned); rope-pulling contests; horse racing during intermission of the shinny game; and footraces. He said spectators, especially women, wanted to touch the ball that was knocked out of the playing field. They believed they too would receive a blessing from it, and then they would throw it in the direction of their husband's or boyfriend's goal. A spirit of frivolity was the overall atmosphere of this tribal sports activity. Although the other activities have been done away with in modern times, the shinny game is continually played each year.

Competitive Sports and Teams

In the early 1900s in Oklahoma, the young men of the tribe participated in competitive sports. In those days a team could play against any other team willing to play. The Ponca formed a baseball team called the Ponca Indian Cyclones and challenged local teams in the northern Oklahoma area. However, they also played other teams, such as the Kansas City Monarchs. Some of the team members were Pete Mitchell, Ed Smith, Charley McDonald, Francis Roy, Phillip Others, Frank Roy, and others. A later team called the Ponca Indians was organized, and team players were Ernest Blueback, Walter Blueback, Kenneth Headman (KH), Charley Makes Noise, Ralph Pack Horse Sr., Obie Yellow Bull, and others.

When the tribe organized its first football team, they played against Ponca City, Northern Oklahoma Junior College, Pawnee, Newkirk, Perry, and a college in Oklahoma City. Jim Fireshaker coached the Ponca team. Team members were Jim Poor Horse, Kenneth Headman, Charley Makes Noise, Ed Roy, Maky Kemble, Frank Waters, Earnest Blueback, Cyril Others, Jeffrey Knows the Country, Jim Waters, Walter Blueback, Logan Cerre, and Archy Little Walker. One incident occurred in a game against the Northern Oklahoma Junior College. KH, NC, AMC, JP, AL, and others recalled that the Ponca team was scoring high in the game when the opposing team and their cheering section became upset and came out into the field with apparent intent on attacking the Indian team. A big red-bearded man by the name of Souligny drew his pistol, fired it into the air, and said, "Leave these

Indians alone! They're winning fair and square. If any man tries anything, he'll have to come through me first." With that, the crowd disbursed. The Ponca team never wanted to go back there again.

In the early years, the Ponca owned many horses, and thus, they were accustomed to riding horseback and were good horsemen. Some became amateur rodeo cowboys and excelled in calf roping. Francis Pappan was the only Ponca to succeed as a professional cowboy. As a saddle bronco rider, he rode in the National Finals Rodeo in Madison Square Garden in New York City. Blaine Buffalohead played college basketball in the 1950s. George Arrow and Steve Buffalohead boxed professionally in the 1950s. Recently, Clendon "Sim" Warrior also boxed professionally and worked in the George Foreman boxing camp as his sparing partner.

Among golfers, a popular sport among the Ponca, Ben Waters and LeRoy Warrior Sr. (both now deceased) qualified for professional status in the 1960s. Ty Headman qualified for the 1988 world Olympics for the butterfly stroke in swimming. The best outdoorsman was Phillip LeClair. Skilled as trapper of fine animal furs, he was once featured in the *Oklahoma Fur, Fishing and Game Magazine* (1966) on trapping beaver. These are but a few of those who are known by tribesmen. Others who reside away from Ponca City and Oklahoma have, too, excelled in athletics of whom we are only acquainted with names.

As we enter the new millennium, the past hundred years has held many fascinating and challenging moments for the Ponca. In the sports world, the Ponca now involve their children in all aspects of competitive sports, especially basketball, baseball, and football. Beginning with T ball and flag football, children can learn and participate in sports throughout their youth. Boxing clubs too allow for children to learn the art of pugilism. The Ponca Tribe has periodically formed a boxing club at the White Eagle community. These boxing organizations gave those young boys insight and purpose for their individual developing lifestyles.

19
Arts and Crafts

The ethnographic section describes some Ponca crafts that are still being made today. The constructions of crafts from one cultural period to another were somewhat different. The changes in craft construction occurred because of the movement of the tribe in former times, that is, from a southeastern culture to a plains-oriented culture. Other influences came with modern materials and new methods for making crafts. The use of materials varied. But certain things do not change, like stones, skins, hides, bones, shells, clays, feathers, bear claws, quills, and so forth. However, it seems that the use of these items and the like were influenced by taboos, religious practices, and things that applied to an individual clan. Exchange of gifts with other tribes too caused some changes. For example, they traded Ponca bows and arrows for Comanche horses, Ponca craft materials for Mandan rice, and trade goods from early traders and white settlers. Once white contact was made with the Ponca, they traded furs and skins for glass and metal beads. Other popular items purchased through traders and other traveling entrepreneurs included trade cloth or broadcloth; beads of many sizes and colors; mirrors of all sizes and shapes; pots, pans, dishes, knives, forks, and spoons; strings, cords, and ropes; and many other goods that the Ponca used to create arts and crafts.

Old pictures of the nineteenth century show evidence of the use of some of these materials. Some pictures of early Ponca leaders (about 1858) show them wearing the traditional two-piece buckskin shirt, breechcloth, and leggings. Quillwork shows that the Ponca made geometric and floral designs on many of their crafts and ornaments. Their fringed leggings also showed the use of porcupine quills and modern beads. The breechcloth was bordered with a single straight line of quillwork while the center designs were floral oriented. Something like vines reached outward. There were usually eight points at the end of the "vines" on each breechcloth. Although the points appear to be geometric, they are "floral" (see chapter 8). Early pictures also show the Ponca men wearing turbans and otter skin caps. A variation of the otter skin cap was made of fox skin. It had a flat vertical wing-like piece attached to it extending outward from the side of the cap. It had a quilled designed. One picture, dated ca. 1868 in Washington DC, shows one Ponca wearing an eagle-feathered headdress. Whether this item is a true Ponca headpiece is not clear. But the elders said they had always seen old men wear them. They could not verify that the headdress in Washington was of Ponca origin because that type of headdress was worn by other plains Indians. Styles of hard-soled moccasins shown in old pictures are made the same today. Tobacco pouches and medicine bags too are highly decorated with quill and beads. Presidential gifts of metal pendants are worn by the chiefs. Earrings, bear claw neck pieces, and bandoliers too are shown as part of the dress style. Hatchets and calumets are held by these men. Howard told me he suspected these were props and were given to all Indians to hold when they had their pictures taken.

Pottery and other earthenware were no longer made by the early part of the nineteenth century because of the introduction of metal pots and pans. J. H. Howard conveyed to me that some potsherds excavated in Nebraska were of the grit-tempered type rather than the shell-tempered type that was common among the north-central plains tribes. Identified with the Woodland period, the grit-tempered potsherd of the Ponca was like the Otoe and Osage variety, which also had its origin in the east. Howard described the pottery as having a wide mouth, rounded bottom, and sharply keeled shoulder with wide trail designs. KH, NC, JP, and AL said these were trail designs believed to be of Ponca origin and said other potsherds excavated at the Ponca Fort site were of Arikara Indian origin, suggesting that the Ponca took a few Arikara women for wives.

Wood carving by the Ponca is an art that dates back to previous cultural periods. This is known to us because some relics have been kept in families for generations. For example, the carved handles of some items used in the peyote religion show many carved geometric and trail designs. Some of these designs are found on calumets and drumsticks. Carved figurines on Ponca flutes (over the air passage) include elaborate figures of animals, birds, and the simple saddle type (KH, NC, JP, AL).

The art of quillwork was done in the Ponca's old homelands in Nebraska. This art is no longer done primarily because of the absence of the porcupine. VBSH said the quills were bitten or chewed on to make them flexible. They were then placed in a bowl of water containing natural dyes for a period to make a permanent color. Once it was dyed to the desired color and dried, the quill was then sewn or wrapped onto the skins of animals for robes and other surfaces being decorated. Wrapping quills on tubular surfaces such as handles and calumet shafts was common. Quillwork no longer exists among the Ponca. Quills have been replaced with modern beads, and beadwork is done on practically every clothing item as well as other decorative ornaments. The predominant use of quills in the North was for flat rather than rounded or tubular surfaces. Since the beginning of the Oklahoma period, beadwork has been done on every kind of material, including handles of feathered fans and gourds. The type of stitch used varied according to the material to be beaded. Stitches commonly used are the so-called lazy stitch, loom beadwork, a kind of a netted stitch, and spot stitching. Lazy stitch work is done on moccasins, tobacco pouches, purses, and so forth.

Looms are used to make belts, headbands, or any decorative pieces such as watchbands. Netted stitching was done in the former Dakota Territory period and in the early Oklahoma period (KH, KCH). Common use of this technique was for making a necklace called Úwì gazⱥdè. The beads were interwoven with horsehair. In modern times, the stitch is used for gourd and fan handles, as well as for other tubular surfaces. Spot stitching is done on gauntlets, medallions, or any of the many items used on dancing costumes. Among others, KCH used to use spot stitching on special items, such as hairpieces, belt buckles, and rosettes for parts of women's necklaces or pendants as well as for dance costumes. She made moccasins for all ages and used the lazy stitch technique to make traditional patterns of Ponca designs. Some Ponca beadworkers who still do quantity and quality beadwork do peyote gourds and fans with the netted stitch as well as other techniques.

Dancing paraphernalia and ornaments (now crafts) originally had some religious meaning pertaining to the tribe. Designs and draw-ings were said to come by dreams or thoughts as the craftsmen and women constructed the craft. KH, who had made crafts for many years, said that a design comes to you as you construct the craft. A veteran of World War II once told him to think of him when he was soldiering during that time. He said:

> That was okay . . . the way he said that but in our [Indian] ways, we don't do that. That's the way the white people do. I guess they got their ways too. When we make things . . . there's a way . . . it comes from somewhere. *Wak'ą́da akà eì waí' ną̀* . . . the Creator, he gives it. It comes from him.

This man of a different tribe wanted a beaded handle for his eagle fan. Even though telling KH of his wartime experience during World War II was not in accord with Ponca cultural practices, KH took those thoughts in mind and created the religious object. He said he never thinks about or draws a design before making it. In some instances, he said a person might be inspired by something. Walter Blueback said he dreamed of what he was drawing:

> I wanted to draw something, but I didn't know what to draw. All night I dreamt all night long. I dreamt I went there and drew something. I went over next morning and drew what I had dreamt . . . (Whitman 1939).

Not unlike the English, who waited on the muse or inspiration for poetry and writing, Ponca craftsmen found inspiration through nature. Some craftsmen still seek spiritual guidance when creating new crafts. Some time ago, I spoke with Bill Collins (now deceased) who had done oil paintings of Ponca history. He said his inspiration came from stories he had heard from childhood. There are many such stories of Indian artists and craftsmen. It seems then, in all Ponca arts and crafts, that the initiated piece comes directly from within the individual rather through some mechanical means.

Today's crafts require that special attention be paid to the materials used for the work to be done. There are many ornaments for ceremonial clothing. Modern beads, precut wood, leather, metal, plastics, and so forth now used for crafts have replaced formerly used quills; clays; natural dyes from roots and flowers; red, yellow, blue, and black ochre; woods; bark; straw; seeds; flint; obsidian; copper; and animal parts such as horns, antlers, bones, entrails, skins, furs, hair, and hooves. Gone is the need for battle shields, bows and arrows, and stone hatchets that were constructed with sinew and wood, as is the need for bone fishing hooks and equipment, bison scapula gardening tools, tanning tools, and so forth.

Indian Art

The modern concept of Indian art is founded on ancient Indian pictographs and petroglyphs. It is a two-dimensional art technique that is widely used by many Indian artists throughout the United States and Canada. A few Ponca artists have been trained in schools of art, but most are self-taught, like many artists who just simply have natural talent. (Oils, acrylics, and water-based paints are also used by Indian artists.) Not unlike their ancestors, who drew pictographs on buckskins or buffalo hides, the modern Indian artist draws simple pictures depicting ideas. The old pictographs on skins called "winter counts" are now lost to the past. Only one known item was preserved in Washington DC. The piece was done by Standing Buffalo, or *T'é T'ǫgá Nǫží*, who was also called *T'a T'ǫgá Nǫží*. The art piece was said to depict a war between the Ponca and the Sioux. However, the Standing Buffalo family (descendants) said it was an accounting of a battle with the Pawnee. The two-dimensional art piece shows both Ponca and their enemy with firearms and bows and arrows. It was painted approximately in the 1850s. The configuration shows the top and bottom figures to be of equal size and appears to be flat. No distance or roundness indicates depth. The pictorial representation in its simplest form was due to certain restrictions in religious and philosophical practices. The development of this type of art seems to be the extent of Ponca Indian art. There seemed to be more freedom of growth in the graphic arts as seen in other crafts.

The application of the paints in Indian art requires a careful preparation of the mixture of water and paint. Chief Terry Saul (now deceased), Choctaw Indian and former professor of art at Bacone College, Muskogee, Oklahoma, said the onetime application of the paints must be spread evenly on the surface. He said that the texture of the paints seemed to be contingent on room temperature and the amount of water included. High humidity, for instance, might allow for a smoother application of the paint, but it might also cause problems such as watermarks. Watermarks on the applied paints constitute a poor production and must be discarded.

The initial step in Indian art is selecting the art paper. Ideal media include standard watercolor paper of different grades, matte boards of various colors, or any surface that will hold the paint. Although the technique varies according to the artist, the process may have some similarities described herein. An outline of the desired painting is pencil-drawn on newsprint or similar paper. The back of the paper is blackened with a darkening solution or graphite tracing paper, and the sketch is traced onto the master painting surface. Each color of paint to be used it mixed separately. The paints are applied separately and must be dry to eliminate unwanted mixture of the colors as well as watermarks. Watercolors dry rapidly. In the early stages of the painting process, usually a fine line of color is used to outline the painting, although in some cases this is done as a subsequent phase toward the completion of the painting. The outlining is often composed of one or more hues to give the painting a transfigured effect. Lighter shades proceed into darker shades toward modification of the main color scheme. Some Indian art pieces are not outlined at all. Shading of the painting, as an additional effect, is done as part of the painting process. Varied hues of one color give the effect desired. The softening of the colors too from bolder colors to lighter shades gives the painting a quality that causes the subject matter to emanate.

Perspective and depth in Indian art is minimal, and large empty spaces surround the subject or subjects. Representations of ground level and clouds are sometimes done with only an outline of various tints of one color. Natural vegetation is drawn with some detail but in the simplest form; painted vegetation does not appear to be an exact replica. A suggestion of life as well as of death seems significant in most pictorial representations. Some Indian art may stress details of clouds, horizons, vegetation, and ground levels with some roundness, although certain graphic lines are used in combination with the same. The main subject matter or focal point is usually centered, but not necessarily in the middle of the painting. Being a rather tricky kind of art, one may perceive the layout as empty yet full. The focal point may very well be items drawn within the total scheme or may be a single item surrounded by others.

Ponca artists, like many artists, usually express some deeper emotion about legends, experiences, and relics. Figures of man, animal life, earth, and the universe are perceived as one part of the other, that is, they are fused together as the same. Additionally, philosophical interpretations consider each part of the painting not as separate segments of a larger part, but rather as a whole. Ponca tradition and heritage, which was surrounded and influenced by all creation, seems to be the central theme, with emphasis on man and nature.

Among those Ponca artists who have captured the philosophical ideologies of the tribe in Indian art were Franklin Fireshaker, Mars Biggoose, Paldine Roy, Ponca Warrior, and Burgess Roy (all now deceased). Other Ponca artists include Gordon Warrior, Brent Greenwood, Ty Headman, and Perry Arkeketa. To identify Indian art, as opposed to early European techniques, it is essential to note the slight differences in painting application and style. Indian art is not simply painting Indian life with any medium, such as oils or acrylics, but rather using specific techniques as describe herein. Some Ponca artists have used oils and acrylics to depict Indian life. The late William Collins Jr., mentioned above, was a well-known Ponca artist whose oil paintings have been widely circulated in the country.

Today there are many promising young Ponca artists who explore other subject matter and art techniques. But they still concentrate on early Native American folklore and crafts depicting neo-Indianism.

20

The Ponca Native American Church

Probably the only religious ceremony held in common by many Indian tribes is the Native American Church. Historically, this religion has existed among the Ponca since 1903. The "peyote meeting," as it is called, was held in Oklahoma in the late 1800s among other tribes. Some researchers believe this to be the first pan-Indian religion, a movement that began in Kay County in northern Oklahoma. According to KH, JP, NC, AMC, and AL, the Ponca learned of this religion at the turn of the twentieth century, and the adherents of the religion have always been minimal. JP, NC, and AL were leaders in the Native American Church who conducted peyote meetings throughout their lives. In the earlier part of the century, the religion had only a handful of followers, but gained momentum in the 1920s through the 1940s. Following the Second World War, membership seemed to dwindle because of deaths, but it rose during the 1960s and early 1970s probably due to the civil rights movement and tribal cultural awakening. Modern Ponca exponents always tell you that there has been no change in the religious practice and that the church came into existence by a mandated decree issued by tribal leadership. However, for our purposes, we intend to examine the church's origins, testimonials of its origins, and other influences of pan-Indianism that gave the religion impetus for growth among the Ponca as well as other pan-Indian features that seem to solidify tribal and intertribal components in the religion.

The Native American Church cult has many features that resemble the Christian church in modern times. The order of worship, for instance, has procedures that include prayers, songs, speeches, and announcements. Upon entering the place of worship, there is a sense of quietude, reverence, and sacredness. Tipis are usually used for the meeting; however, the Osage have or had special buildings built for the same purpose. The theological structure is such that many tribes can find commonality in the worship experience. The worship experience itself has a procedure that many tribes can identify. Most tribal religious ceremonies or rituals usually have a feature that addresses the needs of others.

The religious differences of tribes were the result of their geographic location. This affected their particular beliefs in the old days. For instance, the tribes located in the arid Southwest compared to the northern plains had quite different perspectives on religious practices. The basis for their rites and ceremonials were specific in character and description for their particular tribe. The Native American Church rituals encompassed some aspect of the religion of every tribe. Also the phrase "Indian ways," which is commonly used by various tribes, provided the means for many who wished to build fellowship with other tribes. Adopting another's religion was not an acceptable practice in most tribes, but the "Indian way" provided the essential standard or avenue for acceptance. Even though rites and ceremonials of tribes were different, the basis of this religion, that is, the worship of one god, and certain other elements furnished the ingredients that people could easily accept. In 1964 I asked the tribesmen about the origin of the religion. They stated that they always "kind of believed like that" but made little comment on origins.

The cacti peyote (*Lophophora williamsi*) was used as a medicine in the country of Mexico long before American Indians learned of it. The peyote has a central place in Native American Church meetings. Unlike the use of other herbs in healing, the peyote is a cure-all for both physiological and psychological ailments. At the inception of the religion among the Ponca, many wanted to know its history. According to KH, AMC, NC, and JP, Joe Marcus, a Tonkawa Indian and staunch believer in the religion, told the following story of the origin of peyote as a medicine:

> There was a woman who belonged to some tribe of Indians in Mexico . . . those people told this story to our people. This woman's husband died, and she was grieving over it. They say she couldn't get over it and went away with her little girl. She just walked anywhere and didn't know where she was going. They say she was hungry along with her girl. They were hungry when . . . they realized they were in a

mountain. So they lay down to sleep on the ground. She been walking around for many days and nights. When she went to sleep . . . this woman had a dream, and there was a person who spoke to her. That person said, "I see you are tired and hungry because you have been grieving over your husband's death. Where you are sleeping, you are using a medicine for your headrest. You must get up and pray to the Creator and eat that medicine. It will cause you to get well. And take another one to your people. It will help your people when they are having a hard time." So this woman took the medicine to her people and told them all about what happened to her.

Although several tribes of Indians in Mexico have used peyote and are using it, the Tonkawa, whose original home is Mexico, are credited by many peyotists in America with bringing the religion and medicine to them (KH, NC, AMC, JP, AL). KH also told the following story that has been shared by several men of different tribes:

A Tonkawa man befriended a man of another tribe. On one occasion . . . he took opportunity to visit this religious ceremony. He ask his friend what it was that he had heard during the night. His friend said it was a drum . . . gourd shaking . . . singing. His friend told him that they had medicine and they ate it during the night. He said if a man was sick and needed help . . . *Wéwahái naítè* . . . they prayed for him right there . . . eat that medicine and get well. He said that persons who were sick always went there to get help. He said shaking that gourd . . . beating that drum and singing was their ways. They talk to the Creator that way. He said . . . through it they all would be encouraged . . . get help in life. That Tonkawa man wanted to know more about it . . . *Upáitè* . . . so he attended one meeting. At the first meeting, he liked it . . . the way they conduct it. He wanted to take it back to his people. So they gave it to him . . . that ritual and medicine . . . and he took it to back to his people. They teach him how to conduct a meeting, sing, beat drum and all that. They say the Tonkawa people had this religion when they came into New Mexico and Arizona.

They say they were friends to those Apaches and gave that religion to them. Many years later . . . when some of those Apaches were captured and brought to Oklahoma, the Comanche learned it from them.

The origin of the peyote cult is attributed to a woman, according to most exponents of the religion. The popular belief is that the Tonkawa Indians of Mexico introduced the cult to the Indians of North America. The Ponca eventually learned of the religion in Oklahoma. The Ponca refer to the membership of their church as *Mąką́ ɖatéámà*, or "those who eat medicine." The peyote is called *Mąką́ɖą̀*, or "the medicine."

According to adherents and the elders, the Ponca became aware of the religion in 1903, when a member of the tribe brought it back to the Ponca Reservation in Oklahoma. The first Ponca advocate of the religion was probably Robert Buffalohead, a member of the *Hísadà* clan. He was known by the tribe as a "tough man." He was a fellow who enjoyed fighting and brawling. He befriended a Cheyenne by the name of Reuben Taylor and often exchanged visits at their respective reservations for periods that lasted for months. During these visits, they usually "partied" together. Taylor was also known "as one tough guy" among his people. As the story goes, Buffalohead had not seen Taylor for over a year. In that space of time, Taylor evidently had joined in with his tribesmen in the NAC. It was after his induction to the cult that he got "straightened out" and brought Buffalohead into a group of peyotist among the Cheyenne. Buffalohead did not return to the Ponca Reservation for over a year. When he returned, he was said to be a "new man" who had a different perspective on life (KH, NC, AMC, AL, JP).

The Ponca did not accept the religion immediately. Their own religion centering on the *Niníba waxúbè* (Sacred Pipe) should have prevented the entrance of any new religion. But several factors affected the Ponca people during this time. KH referred to the years between 1890 and 1910 as "bad years" for the Ponca. Numerous entrepreneurs, including those peddling whisky, came to the borders of the Ponca Reservation. Many men using alcohol lost self-esteem and pride. He said,

> This peyote way was a good way . . . because our people became bad people. They even kill each other during that time. So this way was good for our people. These people . . . one time killed a man and laid him on the railroad track to make it look like the train run over him. Another time some woman was killed. The man you named one time . . . *Uškádèžìą̀* (Rushes into the Battle) . . . was killed during a drinking party.

They didn't have the peyote church yet. At that time . . . they did have some but some men didn't like it . . . so they formed a delegation to send them to Quanah Parker.

Many Ponca had suppressed their ancient religious practices in favor of the oncoming new ways. Still the elders of the tribe continued to caution their fellow tribesmen about accepting the new ways and the new peyote religion. AMC said his father, Oscar Makes Cry, said, "*Úškąkè ądíwagazuítè. Sabáži adíp'íbažitai*" (This situation is something we should investigate and scrutinize. We might make a mistake). Additionally, he said that the Ponca should be slow in accepting it, if some did indeed accept it. This meant that acceptance should be based on close scrutiny of the way that was being taught and the sincerity of those advocating it. Interestingly enough, those who investigated it became the first Ponca members. However, they were ridiculed for practicing the new religion. Many times, the elders stated, other Ponca men would stand outside the tipi-meeting place and try to intimidate them and laugh loudly. Some men, who had previously known Buffalohead as a man who liked to fight, would come to the meeting place and challenge him to come out of the tipi and fight. But Buffalohead seems to have handled it without incident. The harassment went on without anyone getting hurt, but the men scorned the new religionists to no end. The members were now convinced that the cult did teach a "good way" and that the old Ponca philosophy of doing good to your fellow men was identifiable in the religion. The Cheyenne "fireplace" was the first to come to the Ponca. (The term *fireplace* simply means ritual.) The first members were Robert Buffalohead, who had the first fireplace; Phillip Others; Jess Waters; Charley Pappan; Ed Roy; and "Old Man" Little Walker (KH, NC, AMC).

Although the Cheyenne fireplace was satisfactory to those first Ponca who accepted the religion, other Ponca were not satisfied. Their dissatisfaction arose because of the person who brought the peyote religion to the Ponca. They felt that it should have been a reputable person of the tribe. The story of the Comanche fireplace is rather lengthy, but for our purposes, it gives deeper historical insight into the bond created by our ancestral fathers of both the Ponca and Comanche tribes. KH gave the following account:

This is what was told to me by several people who knows about this. After the Ponca came to Oklahoma in 1877 . . . there was many problems the people faced. They say lots of people died when they moved here. I guess . . . at first . . . they lived over there near Baxter Springs, Kansas . . . right next to the Quapaws. They finally moved over here where we live now. After they got here . . . they let those white people come in. When they did that . . . they brought all kinds of bad things with them. So . . . many Poncas picked that up and did like the white man did. In those days . . . everything was hard . . . food was hard to get. But our people know how to grow things, so they did that. It looked like everything was going all right until those white people came here. Many people . . . many menfolks took up drinking whisky. They lived in a bad way. Many families were afraid of them. Sometimes a woman and children have to hide in the fields at night because they were afraid of them menfolks. They carried guns and shoot around . . . so women and old folks . . . afraid of them. They live like that for a long time . . . maybe from . . . about 1890 to 1910 or 12. During that time, there was a man by the name of Robert Buffalohead . . . his Indian name was *Hésatigdè*. He was also known as *Ukíábè* . . . a man who was one of them that like to drink. He was a heavy drinker . . . likes to fight. He fight anybody . . . not afraid of anybody. I heard he had a friend among them Cheyennes whose name was Reuben Taylor. I guess they like to drink together. Sometimes they stay at each other's homes on the Cheyenne and Ponca Reservations. It was one of these times . . . *Hésatigdè* went to Cheyenne country that this experience happened. He didn't go there for a long time . . . when he come there . . . he found that his friend quit drinking. It was told to me that Reuben Taylor quit drinking because he took up the peyote way. I guess he prayed to God too . . . changed his whole life. They say he took his friend Robert Buffalohead to meetings while he was there visiting. He learned about the peyote way and learned to pray to God too. They say he stayed there for long time. After he got back to Ponca . . . he told his folks about it . . . they don't know what to think about this . . . they know he always drinks and fights. You might say they were puzzled over this. So he put on meeting at his place . . . invited people to come there . . . pray. I guess his friend, too, bring some Cheyennes to help out. At first some of the older Ponca men don't like it. They said we have our own ways. We don't like this. We don't know nothing about it. I guess some of them came out of there. Even those Poncas who used to drink and fight with *Hésatigдè* didn't like it. They come by at nights when they were having peyote meetings and make fun of them. They even mock them . . . when they pray and sing songs. Sometimes they said to him . . . Come and fight . . . you're supposed to be tough. But he would tell his group of followers, *Íyàìžigà* . . . "Don't say anything." So this is how the Poncas got the first peyote fireplace. They had meetings there on the Buffalohead allotment for long time. Those Ponca men who took it up were Old Man Little Walker, Jess Pappan, Charley Pappan, Ed Smith, Jess Waters, and a few others. Later on, he [*Hésatigдè*] gave that Cheyenne fireplace to several of them. Charley Pappan was a good man . . . kindhearted, helpful . . . treats everybody good. He carried on that way all his life and passed it on to his son-in-law Willie Cry [Norman Cry]. It was done in a good way. When you give a fireplace to someone, it has to be done according to a certain way. I guess he followed that way, and Willie Cry got the right to run meetings. By this time, there was lot of Poncas following the peyote religion, but there was some who didn't like the way it came to the Poncas. They know *Hésatigдè* . . . and think that maybe it should be done according to those people who know where it came from . . . origin. It so happened that Ol' Man Ed [Ed Packhorse] was acquainted with Quanah Parker, Comanche Indian . . . he use that peyote too. So Ol' Man Ed got his bunch together and went to see him.

Now, right here, I'm going to tell you part of a story I told you about once before . . . because it has something to do with this peyote way. You know about Little Bear [*Mąčú Žįgà*]. It was after all those things he did that caused the Comanches to come and attack the Poncas. It was during one of the Ponca's buffalo hunts when this happened. *Mąčú Žįgà* didn't go on that hunt because he was invited to visit with the Omaha. They say he encourage his whole clan . . . *Đíxidą̀* clan . . . to go with him on that visit. Well, it happened that the Comanches were looking for him because of all that dirty work [murder for revenge] he did for White Tail . . . *Níkagahì užú* . . . "the main chief of the Ponca." It happened like this. The Ponca were traveling some distance from home when the Comanches came. Only old folks and some women and children were left behind. They begin to kill anyone in sight. There was one Ponca woman there who ran from the fort . . . that's where some of the

Ponca lived then. They used to have a place where they put up a high wall made of logs . . . around four big *Mąít'i* [earthen lodges] . . . was inside that fort. I guess they live like that in those days. This woman . . . she run in the direction the hunters went. She stopped on top of hills and holler for them. They say she had a powerful . . . strong voice. Finally, somebody heard her. That man . . . they call him *Wahátągà* . . . he was the first one to come back. She told him that the Ponca were being attacked by some tribe. He asked her a question about who was the worst one . . . warrior . . . attacking the Ponca. She said, "*Ukítè aká ská ágdì. Ą́kì, bdúgà wasé žídè ą́kikida aké*" (The one that rides a white horse. And he's the one who paints himself all red). *Wahátągà* rode off . . . going as fast as his horse would take him. When he got back to camp . . . that camp was below that fort . . . close to the Missouri River . . . he saw what was going on. He began to look for that man who rode on a white horse. When he saw him . . . he went toward him . . . and that man saw him coming so he rode in his direction. He wants to fight him and that man knows it too . . . he come toward *Wahátągà*. When he got there, *Wahátągà* threw down his bow and arrows and walked toward him barehanded. That enemy warrior got off his horse too . . . came toward him with a knife. Those Comanches used to use a long spear with a loop on one end. If they can ride close by you they can loop and pull your head off. But this man wants to fight . . . hand to hand . . . you might say. He don't know *Wahátągà*. This Ponca warrior was a big man. They say he was . . . maybe seven feet tall. By the time this enemy warrior find out, it was too late for him. *Wahátągà* grabbed him and crushed him with his arms. After that they say he used his bow and arrows on the other enemies. By this time . . . rest of those Ponca warriors got there, they were all shooting arrows at these enemies. They began to ride away . . . but did not stay away. After a little while, they come back holding a white buckskin up . . . *Há ská* . . . that's a sign of coming in peace. When they rode up . . . one of them . . . a man who spoke for them. He made this statement in Ponca, "*Pádakà ądì. Niášigawì agúdixìdè ągátì. Mącú žįgà dadaí. É' ągúnè ągátì*" (We are *Pádakà*. We have come here looking for a man. They call him Little Bear. He's the one we came here looking for). "*Šá ągáxaì. Ądíkinà ągádabàžì. Ągágdetaìtehá*" (We quit. We do not want to fight you. We are going home). I guess they asked where Little Bear was . . . but nobody tell them where he is . . . so they rode away. The Ponca camp was sad . . . they were in big sorrow over those people who died during that time. They say these *Pádakà* came back after several weeks and made agreement that they would not fight again. They like that bow and arrow . . . want to know how to use it. So they stay with the Poncas for several days . . . maybe weeks . . . learning how to make the bow and arrows. They gave the Ponca some real good horses for that. After this all happen . . . they always got along with each other.

In this story, that bow and arrow is important. You must not forget that. When Ol' Man Ed [Ed Packhorse] went to see Quanah Parker, he went with Louis McDonald, Old Man Crazy Bear, and Mike Roy. When they got there, Quanah Parker fed them and gave them a place to sleep. After they settled down, they said, he came to them and asked them, "Okay, now you tell me what it is you want, maybe I can help you." So Ol' Man Ed told him about the Cheyenne fireplace and how it came to the Poncas. He asked that maybe he could do something to make it right. They believed that Quanah Parker was a powerful medicine man. He told them that he can't do anything about that other fireplace because it was already done. But he said this, "It's good that you came to see me . . . you did the right thing, because I'm going to tell you a story that is connected to this peyote way." He told them that story I just told you about Little Bear. At the end of his story, he talk this way, "We used this bow and arrow now for many years . . . long time. When we Comanches came to know about this peyote way, we used this bow like a staff. We hold it in our left hand with one end on the ground when we sing. It is symbolic . . . it is a source of our existence. We can get food with it. It protects us. That point to the ground and upward means that earth provides for us through prayers and our singing to Almighty. It is important. When you use these [peyote paraphernalia] you must think like that." I guess he talk like that long time about the peyote *Wékià* . . . staff, gourd, feathers, cedar, sage, drum, and drumstick. He put on meeting for them there in Comanche country and prayed for them. Then he said to them, "Now, I'm going to give these to you . . . *Wékià* . . . and I'm going to give back to you the bow and arrow. It was once used to kill animals and even humans but now it is our staff to live by. If you use it in a good way, Almighty will take pity . . . provide for you . . . help you in your time of need." That morning when he talk to them, he talked about that *Mąk'ą* . . . peyote. He said, "This is a good medicine. Remember when you use it . . . I'll be there too . . . praying for you." Some of these boys . . . kind of misunderstand that. They thought he said, I'll be in it. That's not right. It is just like someone praying with you when you pray. In the Indian way, you pray all the time. When you eat, work, quit working, hunt, come home, visit, and so on. That's what he meant . . . like maybe, I'll be praying with you. He gave them instructions to go back to Ponca and put up four meetings. He said at the end of that fourth meeting, they would know who will run the meetings from there on. He told them how to run those meetings. But they didn't do that . . . they wanted Ol' Man Ed to run them. Quanah Parker said to them privately, "He's not the man. But if you want it that way . . . you can go ahead." So that's the way it was done. Ol' Man Ed run those meetings until he went up north. He didn't come back for a long time . . . maybe for twenty to twenty-five years. But that Comanche fireplace is still here.

Those Ponca who wanted satisfaction in receiving the peyote religion could be content. Ed Packhorse conducted meetings until his death in 1975.[1] He was born in 1879. The Cheyenne and Comanche fireplaces are now considered Ponca. They take pride in their leadership in the church's functions.

The Ponca Fireplace

The term *fireplace* up to now has been used indiscriminately. In simplest terms, as previously stated, fireplace refers to the ritual of the NAC. The Ponca refer to it as *Unéde*. Usually, the statement or term *Mąką́daté ną́gidè akà* refers to the person who is authorized to conduct a meeting and the way he conducts it. The ritual has been set and is done in a certain order so that one ritual is not the same as another. The following is a short description by KH and NC of the procedure in running a meeting according to the original Cheyenne way:

In the meeting . . . sometimes a medicine man can do this doctoring . . . because they did it like that in those days. When a person was doctored . . . afterward everybody prayed for him. They use tobacco or smoked. When they finished . . . the fireman gathered the stubs and put them at that fireplace. The leader then gives four peyote to each person there. They sing until midnight. He makes smoke and drink water. This water is smoked or fanned . . . *Ášudè*. Sometimes they fan everyone. After this the leader goes out and prays. He prays in four directions. When he comes in, he is fanned and sits down. After this anyone can smoke and pray. Sometimes a person is fanned. This smoke is sacred. When someone uses it, everyone respects it. They sing again . . . but anyone can smoke and pray at this time. At morning . . . the leader sings four songs . . . morning songs. The water is brought in by the wife of the leader. She is fanned, and she kneels and prays for everybody. After that the leader sings four quitting songs. The woman goes out and brings in food . . . *Ní* [water] . . . *Wanáxè* [grain corn cooked on griddle], *T'a gatúbè* [pounded dry meat], and sometimes wild honey and nuts. After eating . . . they go out . . . it is finished. This is a Cheyenne meeting . . . fireplace.

The Native American Church is probably the only source of religious practice among the Ponca that still uses the stars to tell time. In his writings Howard (1995, 74) wrote,

> Adam LeClair told me that the Peyote fire chief still keeps track of the time during a ceremony by noting the position of the stars. He keeps the road chief or leader informed, and this official regulates the ceremony accordingly.

Both KH and NC explained a longer version of the Cheyenne peyote ritual to me. The following outline shows the ritual procedure in its simplest form in accordance with the Cheyenne variety Ponca style:

- A talk is given by the leader.
- The person who called the meeting is given time to talk and give information and the reason for the meeting. The information is for the benefit of everyone attending, and the specific purpose is explained in detail.
- The leader then passes tobacco to all participants.
- The "fireman" gets a stick from the fireplace for lighting the tobacco for those who would smoke and pray. Sometimes a special tobacco lighting stick is made. The wood is about two to two and a half inches

in diameter, and is decorated with carved-in designs for the purpose of the meeting. The stick is passed around clockwise to everyone.

- Everyone prays at this time as directed by the leader.
- Following the prayers, everyone present uses the sage, which is given to them by the leader. The leader then prays and burns cedar.
- The leader proceeds to fan (*Ášudè*) the peyote staff (*Ímǫgdè*), feathers (*Mǫ́šǫ*), drum (*K'úge*), and other paraphernalia.
- The leader sings four starting songs.
- Each participant will then sing four songs. Depending on the number of participants who will sing, they normally will go one round (that is, beginning at the left of the leader and proceeding clockwise, each man is allowed to sing four songs of his choice).
- At midnight, the staff, gourd, feathers, drum, and so forth are called back to the leader's seat. At this time he will smoke tobacco and pray.
- The fireman brings water and prays. He then makes tobacco (lights it) and brings the water and smoke to the leader, who smokes and prays.
- He uses the water and then goes out of the meeting place.
- When the leader goes out, the cedar man sings four songs. The leader's exit is primarily done to offer special prayers to *Wak'ǫ́da*. He prays toward the four sacred winds.

According to KH, the prayers offered are similar to those of other Ponca rituals, particularly those that deal with the giving of thanks, sickness, and hardship. The prayers usually include giving of thanks to the Creator for the earth. Depending on the time of year, the prayer includes thanks for the natural things of earth. For instance, in the springtime, thanks is given for the new growth of plants, birds of every kind that make their sounds protecting their nests, small burrowing animals that bring forth new life, large animals bringing new life and food, and the life cycle of mankind. The prayers are composed of beautiful words in the Ponca language. Following the prayers of thanksgiving, supplication is made for the sick and needy. Diagram 4 shows the points where the leader stands and prays.

- Participants quit singing when the leader reenters the tipi.
- The leader is fanned when he comes in.

The 3rd prayer is given
at this point facing
northward. He blows
the whistle here.

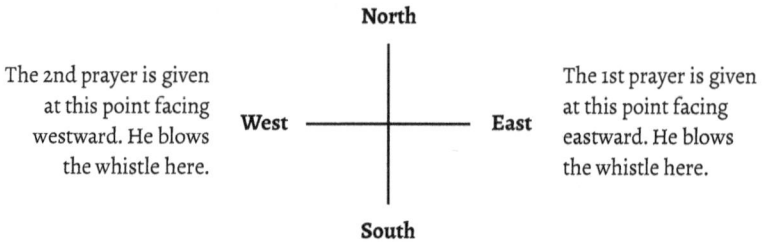

North

The 2nd prayer is given
at this point facing
westward. He blows
the whistle here.

West —————————— **East**

The 1st prayer is given
at this point facing
eastward. He blows
the whistle here.

South

The 4th prayer is given
at this point facing
southward. He blows
the whistle here.

DIAGRAM 4. Position of Native American Church prayer leader.
Created by the author.

- The leader and participants sing one round.
- The person who puts on the meeting smokes and prays. He then passes it to the leader.
- The leader then prays and fans the person who put the meeting on.
- At daylight the leader sings morning songs.
- The leader's wife brings in the water and is fanned.
- The leader's wife makes smoke and prays. When she is finished, the fireman takes it to the leader. The leader will then pray.
- The water is passed around for all participants to drink. She then will bring in parched corn, fruit, and pound meat (in that order).
- Four quitting songs are sung at this time.
- The leader may ask anyone to pray.
- The drum is untied. The staff, feathers, gourd, cedar, sage, and drum are passed around to the participants. They can "use" these items by touching them.[2]
- The food is then passed around.
- Anyone, at this time, who desires to speak may speak. This concludes the meeting.

The Cheyenne fireplace seems to be the same as the Comanche fireplace with slight variation in the ritual. For instance, Grandpa Ed Packhorse ran meetings according to the Comanche ritual. He used eight songs at the beginning of the meeting, at midnight, in the morning, and at the end. He gave a fireplace to individual Ponca who were authorized to conduct meetings; they were people who possessed leadership qualities and respect from their tribesmen. For example, one of the early followers and leaders of the NAC was Norman "Willie" Cry (Cries for War), oilman. At the time of his demise in 1975, it was stated that he was the only living NAC leader who had been properly inducted into the leadership role. He received his fireplace from Charley Pappan, who was elderly and could no longer carry on his responsibilities as an NAC leader. He held a meeting and called the elders of the church to announce that his son-in-law Norman "Willie" Cry would now assume the responsibility of conducting meetings. NC said it was a solemn and dramatic act that morning when "Old Man" Pappan stood from the sacred seat and called him to be seated there. After accepting that position of leadership, Willie Cry carried on his duties according to the Native American Church tradition. He was helpful and benevolent toward his people. He always held meetings for people who were sick.

According to KH, NC, and JP, those Ponca who were authorized to conduct meetings and from whom the authorization came included the following (no dates for when the men received the authorization were given):

Reuben Taylor to Robert Buffalohead (or *Ukíábè*) to Mark Buffalohead (*T'é Wáđihį̀*)

Quanah Parker to Ed Primeaux Packhorse (*T'iúbixą́*) to Napoleon "Bird" Buffalohead (*Wažį́ga*)

Cheyenne to Charley Primeaux (*Mą́zè Nąpį̀*) to Lamont Primeaux (*Lamútè*) to Adam LeClair (*Ádamà*)

Robert Buffalohead to Old Man Blueback (*Ną́kà T'ú*) to Walter Blueback (*Wažį́ T'ù*)

Cheyenne to Old Man Pollak (*T'é Núga*)

Comanche Billy to Lem Cerre to Logan Cerre (*Lóginà*)

Cheyenne to Lem Cerre to Albert Primeaux

White Face Bull (Cheyenne) to Robert Washington (*Wažį́ Ágahigì*) to James Poor Horse (*Mąxp'íazì*)

Cheyenne to Tom Primeaux (*Támà*)

Cheyenne to Jess Waters to George Smith

Cheyenne to Charley Pappan (*Mázè Nąpį̀*) to Norman Cry (*Nąžį́tidè*)

Quanah Parker to Ed Primeaux Packhorse (*T'iúbixą́*) to Lester Biggoose

There have been numerous leaders since the above were commissioned to conduct meetings. In each generation since its inception, the NAC has continued to pass that authority on to those men willing to accept the responsibility. Not unlike the Christian minister, the NAC leader is expected to pay attention to clean living and self-discipline, show compassion to all people, and lead a prayerful life. In the Ponca language, these practices are called *Wáspè mądí*, *Kigdíežubà*, *Wadáedè*, and *Wahą́ìšigdè mądí*, respectively. This is only a part of the total responsibility of the leader. For instance, in the first years, the NAC leaders paid for all expenses for the peyote rites and feast. Whether the idea of paying for all expenses was mandated by the original religionist or whether it was suggested by those from whom the Ponca received it is unknown. Most meetings today, however, are paid for by the one requesting it. The current Ponca NAC leaders are Oliver Little Cook and Dwight Buffalohead. Parrish Williams, Roland No Ear, and Rayburn LeClair, who served recently, are deceased.

In the earlier days, when the church was in its beginnings, the Ponca peyotists were known as men of prayer. They had an identifying mark that was only worn during the peyote meeting. In his discussion on "Ponca Dress and Adornment," Howard (1995, 68) wrote,

> According to Ed Primeaux . . . it was the custom of Ponca peyotists, in the period 1902–30, to wear a downy eagle plume, dyed red, attached to the *ásku*, as well as a silver button with two pendant buckskin strings, ornamented with silver and ending in two beaded tassels. This same headdress was sometimes worn, in connection with the roach headdress, by straight dancers.

Members of the church used to wear moccasins when they entered the tipi. Recently, members also wore specially sewn narrow bed sheets resembling a cummerbund with the ends tucked in at the sides with the excess hanging down. Jewelry consisting of pins, brooches, earrings, and so forth was usually made to resemble the *T'úzè* (water bird). Jewelry was made of either nickle or beadwork. Oklahoma Indian metalsmiths and beadworkers were primarily responsible for creating these ornaments. Favored feathers for members at one time included both bald and golden eagle tail feathers. These feathers served as a fan with beaded handles and buckskin fringes. Other feathers used were "water bird" or water turkey (*Anhinga anhinga*) tail feathers and scizzortail. In recent years, some members added one or two carefully trimmed and decorated macaw tail feathers to the water bird feathers. This fan was the loose-hanging feathers type. Another identifying characteristic of the Ponca Native American Church is the tipi. Some members felt that the tipi was the last identifying mark of Indian religion (KH, NC, AMC, JP, AL).

Membership in the Church

The following is a list of deceased members (from about 1940 to the 1980s, during my lifetime) who advocated and participated in the Native American Church meetings and functions:

Kenneth Headman	Norman "Willie" Cry	James Poor Horse
Logan Cerre	Ed Primeaux Packhorse	Louis McDonald
Robert Little Dance	Nepoleon Buffalohead	Pete Buffalohead
Amos Little Cook	Joe Rush	Amos Warrior
Fritz Warrior	Sylvester Warrior	Adam LeClair
Josiah Thicknail	Tom Primeaux	Walter Blueback
David Buffalohead	Roy Buffalohead	Jim Waters
Lincoln Buffalohead	Harry Buffalohead	Franklin Smith
Mark Buffalohead	Pershing Roughface	Jimmy Clark
Louis Yellow Horse	McKinley Eagle	Ed Roy
Tom Roy	Parish Williams	Lamont Warrior

David Eagle	Simon Eagle	Franklin White Tail
Charles "Šáni" LeClair	Hugh LeClair	Tim Little Voice
Logan DeLodge	Kenneth Burt	George Smith
David Jones	Lamont Cerre	Lamont Primeaux
Gary Blueback	George New Moon	Leon Biggoose
Arthur Buffalohead	William Overland	Zack Smith Sr.
Bill C. War	Henry Jones	Jimmy Clark
Albert Waters	Lamont Brown	

Examples of Ponca Native American Church Songs

The Ponca have prided themselves as good singers of any type of tribal ceremonial songs. The drum (made from a kettle and buckskin cover) and gourd (rattle) are the two instruments used when singing "peyote songs." Sometimes an eagle bone whistle is used, but only when the ritual calls for its use. Like other Ponca church songs, the meanings include praise, appeal, thanksgiving, and prayers. The following are two examples of Ponca Native American Church songs:

Jísasà Wanídè hó	Jesus Savior
Đahą́ údą nì he ya na he ne no wai	You are good to praise
Waɖáeɖè áta ni hó heya na ne ho	You have great compassion
Đahą́ údą nì heya na ne ho	You are good to praise
Đahą́ údą nì heya na ne ho	You are good to praise
Jísasà Wanídè hó	Jesus Savior
Đahą́ údą nì he ya na he ne no wai	You are good to praise

The cactus peyote is referred to as *Mąk'ą́* and is venerated in the following song.

Waką́da, mąką́ɖaną̀ aɖí ɖaną́žį ́ áɖą̀	God, because you stand with the medicine
Wíbɖahą̀ hiya na ne ho	I praise and give thanks to you.
Waką́da wíbɖahą̀ hiya na he ne no wai	I praise and give thanks to you.

Waką́da, mąką́daną̀ aⱡí ⱡaną́žį̀ ádą̀	God, because you stand with the medicine
Wíbⱡahą̀ hiya na ne ho	I praise and give thanks to you.
Waką́da, mąką́daną̀ aⱡí ⱡaną́žį̀ ádą̀	God, because you stand with the medicine
Wíbⱡahą̀ hiya na he ne ne	I praise and give thanks to you.
Waką́da, mąką́daną̀ aⱡí ⱡaną́žį̀ ádą̀	God, because you stand with the medicine
Wíbⱡahą̀ hiya na ne ho	I praise and give thanks to you.
Waką́da, wíbⱡahą̀ hiya na he ne no wai	I praise and give thanks to you.

Again, the Ponca like to sing, and song makers still make a personal religious expression through their singing. There have been many songs made by singers since the inception of the Native American Church.

Presently, many claim membership in the Native American Church, but few practice it. The fireplaces are now Ponca, and thus, members still take pride in the leadership and their churches' functions.

21

The Christian Church in the Ponca Community

The logical sequence of good missionary work had to begin with learning the language of a non-English-speaking people. Reverend James O. Dorsey, a linguist, evidently learned and spoke Ponca fluently. The Ponca people called him Đásì. He was one of the first missionaries to come to the Ponca in late nineteenth century. "After being ordained deacon, 18 April, 1871 he was sent as a missionary of the Protestant Episcopal Church to the Ponca Indians in Dakota where he remained for 2 years" (Wilson and Fiske 1887, 207). He lived near and among the people. Although a missionary, he is mostly spoken of by modern-day historians as a linguist and ethnographer. However, as a missionary, he is remembered by the Ponca as using various methods in teaching. Dorsey, according to the elders, used stories from old literature to convey certain moral and ethical Christian teachings. In this particular case, he used tales from Aesop's Fables (KH, AMC, NC, AL). These tales were told to children along with tribal Hígà. He probably used the fables because the Ponca Hígà were stories about animals that also taught morals and ethics. Some of us learned them from grandmother VBSH, who never spoke nor understood English.

The morphology of Dorsey's work on the Đégihà language is exceptional. A note made in his *Omaha and Ponka Letters* indicates that some Ponca men, at that time, learned to use his alphabet to write letters. So began the introduction of Christianity among the Ponca Indians.

Because of the direct relationship of one Edward Howe to the Ponca people, the following account of the church is elaborated on. According to Eugene Howe, in the early 1920s, Reverend Edward Howe, Eugene's grandfather, was assigned to the church near the Ponca Agency near Niobrara, Nebraska.[1] His records show he was "catechist" for the church. He was one of five brothers born to George Howe Sr., who was known by the Ponca as Nǫbésnà (Scarred Hand). They had one sister by the name of Hannah. Rev. Howe was married to a half-breed

Ponca woman by the name of Emily who bore him several children. Of those who came to Oklahoma in the early 1900s were Oliver and Elmer Howe, who married two sisters, Mattie and Agnes Headman. His other children were Marvin (Buzzy), Loretta, Myrtle, Elsie, Pam, and Viola.

According to Rev. Howe's diary, he recorded church data each Sunday that included attendance, offerings taken, baptisms, deaths, and so forth. On one occasion, because of the cold winter, he became stricken with sickness. In his diary he wrote that he requested help from the church members to cut wood for the heating stove in the church, but no one responded. On another occasion, he wrote to the Diocese of Nebraska requesting assistance for repairs on the church building and some damage on the road to the church. The following letter from the Rt. Rev. Ernest V. Shayler shows his response to that request:

July 11th 1928
The Diocese of Nebraska, Omaha

My Dear Mr. Howe:

I have your letter and regret that I have no funds whatever with which to meet its appeals. The Diocesan Council in January did not put a single dollar at my disposal for additional work in the diocese this year, or for emergencies.

Since my visit to Niobrara last Sunday, and seeing the splendid gathering of your people there, I have been thinking that they ought to do something toward the support of your work. I discovered in my conference with them that practically all of them own land and could help if they would. We do not appreciate the things that cost us nothing as much as those for which we have to work for or pay for, and giving to the support of the Church and to others is an important part of the Christian duty. It is not right that you should do all the work and the giving of your time and they do nothing . . .

With kind regards, I am
Yours sincerely,
Earnest V. Shayler, Signed, Bishop

There were other times when members of the church did supply wood for the church. Times were difficult in those days as he recorded the offering on one Sunday as being only seven cents. On another particular Sunday, he wrote down that Ma-sha-de-lin, the wife of Little Duck, had died. She had been baptized by the Rev. James O. Dorsey at the time he had come to the Ponca people in about 1871. It was recorded that she was the oldest living Ponca tribal member (age 115) in Niobrara on April 13, 1925. The funeral service was held at the St. John's Chapel near the old Ponca Agency, Niobrara, Nebraska. Rev. Howe served as catechist in charge for the funeral service.

Other missionary endeavors in the nineteenth century ushered in new religious practices espousing a theology not unlike that which the Ponca already possessed. The only other religious leaders who came into the Ponca territory in Nebraska were the Mormons mentioned earlier. According to the elders, their main interest in the area evidently was to find shelter. Since they were seeking refuge, they showed their weakness and never had any Ponca converts. However, most exponents of the Christian faith during that period in the history of America considered anyone not adhering to its teachings as per its set of standards as heathen, sinner, or both. John Wesley, the founder of Methodism and advocate of Christian perfection, came to the East Coast of America trying to convert Indians. His conclusion was that they were hopelessly lost and were not worth the time.

Acculturation and a new era of civilization brought about disregard for the main thrust of the Ponca religion, which was the Sacred Pipe. But there were many who retained their belief in their own religion and continued to follow their ancient practices of praying to *Wak'ada* according to the old Ponca customs.

During this period when the Ponca showed interest in other religious faiths, the tribe was in a state of mass confusion over their lands and possible removal to Indian Territory. Christianity apparently provided a peace of mind to those who followed the early missionary's teachings. This in effect aided the people seeking new ways to live when they moved to Indian Territory and into the twentieth century.

The Church in Indian Territory

Because the Methodist missionary had traveled with the Ponca to Indian Territory, the tribe set aside two acres of land for the construction of a church building. The tribe built a Methodist Episcopal Church at the

Ponca Agency (now White Eagle Community). Other religious advocates of various denominations made their impact on the Ponca Reservation in Kay and Noble Counties in Oklahoma, but those Protestant denominations establishing churches were of the Methodist, Nazarene, and Baptist faiths. Today, some Ponca have joined the Roman Catholic and Pentecostal Churches. Few have membership in other faiths or cults.

The Ponca (Protestant) churches on the reservation have features of worship that are similar in many ways. This is primarily due to the tribal cultural pattern. From ages past the people were taught to show compassion and understanding to their fellow man. Prayers and praying were always a part of their daily lives. Giving encouragement and moral support to people in need was and is commonplace among tribesmen and women.[2]

The Ponca churches function similarly to any Christian church throughout the world. Their Sunday morning order of worship consists of singing service; special songs; choir numbers for special occasions; special prayers for people, projects, and so forth; the sharing of tithes and offerings; and preaching. Messages from the pulpit inform, challenge, and inspire as in most churches. Since these churches are also connected to their various denominational ministries, they are assessed financial responsibilities. These monies are directed toward denominational mission projects, evangelism, hospitals, education institutions, and so forth. Although inadequate, these churches also pay salaries to their pastors and pay for all utilities of the church and parsonages. Every year the churches select their appropriate delegation for their particular denominational annual meetings.

The Methodists

The Southern Ponca were Christianized primarily under the missionary work of the Methodist Church. In the early years in Indian Territory, the church fathers established a congregation. Its constituency was mostly women and children. In later years a gymnasium was constructed, and most tribesmen assisted in the construction of this building.

Preachers and Evangelists

Some of the missionaries who came among the Ponca were Mr. White, Mr. Maggner, Mr. Baker, and Mr. Clinginsmith. In the early years of mission work on the reservation, an evangelist by the name of Mr. I. G. Martin came to hold a tent revival among the Ponca in 1903. An interesting turn of events occurred at this meeting. As recalled by KH, KCH, and AMC, Mr. Martin claimed to be a Nazarene. The Church of the Nazarene was not yet known by that name. While he was preaching, Mr. White became upset, slammed his Bible down on the pulpit, and walked out. To this day, no one knows why he became angry, but they remembered the incident. We, of course, are aware today that the Church of the Nazarene was organized by discontented Methodist preachers. In modern times, some church historians say the split came because of the "slave issue" in the 1800s while others say it was the contemporary thought in Christian theology.

The many Indian ministers who pastored the Ponca church included Revs. White Parker, Lynn Paughtey, Lee Motah, Robert Pinezaddleby, Tony Hill, Melvin Boyiddle, Kenneth Edmonds, Gibson Davis, Levi Biggoose, Thomas Roughface Sr., George Miller, Abraham Jackson, and others. The church's first called Ponca Indian minister in modern times was Thomas Roughface Sr. Serving as pastor of several churches for years, he was made the general superintendent of the Oklahoma Indian Missionary Conference. Other Ponca ministers coming from the Ponca Methodist Church were Levi Biggoose, George Callshim Jr., Stanford White Star, and Edwin Hinman.

About the turn of the twentieth century, a Ponca man by the name of James Williams attended a school on the East Coast and became the first Ponca ordained as a minister. According to the elders, his ordination fell under the Presbyterian Church. It is unclear whether he served as minister under that denomination. He was educated at Haskell Institute at Lawrence, Kansas, Hampton Institute at Hampton, Virginia, and Dartmouth College at Hanover, New Hampshire. Williams returned to the reservation and was known as an excellent orator at public gatherings.

Although the majority of the Ponca people claim membership in the church, there are those names of church members that stand out predominantly. Since about 1940, these former members who are now members of the church triumphant include Aline Roy, Ellen Roy Cerre, Molly Roy Cerre, Mary Horse Chief Kemble, Cora Burt Cry, Nellie King Blueback, Christian Blueback Others, Dorothy Blueback

Buffalohead, Louis and Mattie McDonald, William and Helen Over-land, William and Hattie C. War, Francis and Alice Eagle, McKinley and Lucina Eagle, Stella McDonald Yellow Horse, George and Alice Smith, Mitchell Roy, Cornelius and Cordelia Hardman, Alice Grant Primeaux, Lamont and Lucille Feathers, Lillie Biggoose White Tail, Leona Biggoose Roughface, Vernon and Theodorsia Roberson, Stan-ford and Faye White Star, George Callshim Jr., Levi and Francine Eagle Biggoose, and Thomas and Patricia Roughface Sr.

Like other churches, the modern Ponca Methodist Church is com-posed of the children and grandchildren of those former members. In recent years a new church building was constructed under the auspices of the St. Paul's United Methodist Church in Ponca City. A beautiful sanctuary, chapel, and education classrooms are a part of the building. The old mission gymnasium still stands.

The Oklahoma Indian Missionary Conference of the United Meth-odist Church normally conducts its annual meetings at one of its three district centers located at Preston, Antlers, or Anadarko, Oklahoma. In the early years, only a few people from the Ponca church attended these meetings, but one man always attended the Methodist Annual Conference. According to Bishop Angie Smith (now deceased), Louis McDonald (also deceased) was the only representative present from the Ponca Indian Methodist Church attending these conference meetings.

According to Bishop Smith, at the Hog Creek District Center at Anadarko, Grandpa McDonald always got up and came to the front of the congregated church representatives and sang a traditional Ponca Indian church hymn. Afterward he would report to the conference. As the Ponca Methodist Church grew and became more involved in the conference, many members began to attend these annual meetings.

The youth programs in the three Ponca churches were very active for years. Each sent young boys and girls to summer camp. The Indian Methodists originally sent their children to Turner Falls. Then the denomination established a camp at Lake Texhoma, near Kingston, Oklahoma. The Methodist Indian Conference boys and girls from the Arapaho, Cheyenne, Comanche, Euchee, Kiowa, Pawnee, Ponca, and Five Civilized Tribes attended this senior high camp. There they played, studied the word, sang, and generally fellowshipped with one another. This week of fun for kids helped raise fine Christian men and women.

The Methodist Church (now United Methodist) has a long-standing relationship with the Ponca Tribe of Oklahoma. And they are very enthusiastic about their church functions.

The Nazarenes

The first Nazarene ever to come to the Ponca Tribe of Oklahoma was a man by the name of Mr. I. G. Martin, who at the time, was working with the Methodists as an evangelist. About 1903, at a camp meeting, he preached to the Ponca people. Even the chief of the tribe attended and was converted. In about 1937, according to AMC, a man by the name of Brother Smith came to the Ponca Reservation from Blackwell, Oklahoma, to hold services. The story goes that as he walked down the road, he asked different Ponca men and women where he could go to hold these services. Someone directed him to David and Suzette Buffalohead's home, saying, "Go over there to that house, they will let you conduct services there." So it was there the Nazarene Church got its start. In 1939 the Church of the Nazarene organized a mission church on the reservation under the supervision of the Reverend Mr. Luther Cantwell. Its first pastor was Rev. Amos Komah, a Comanche Indian from Cache, Oklahoma. Some of the pastors assigned to the Ponca church were Revs. Bass, King, Barney, Partane, Curtis Shook, Carroll Wilbanks, Richard Martinez, Nino Buffalohead, Bradford Golding, Edward Satilla, Lula Morton, James Browning, Samuel Mackety, Julian Gunn, Lloyd Hughs, Charles Young, and me. The first Ponca ministers entering the ministry from the church were Albert Makes Cry Sr., Nino Buffalohead, Tony Cerre, and me. The membership of the church has never been more than sixty people. Attendance, however, has exceeded a hundred in different years. During the war years (World War II), the church had no pastor. AMC and his family assumed responsibility for the church and continued church services. AMC became recognized by tribesmen as one of the best public speakers and composer and singer of Indian hymns. His son, Albert Makes Cry Jr., attended the Southern Nazarene University (then Bethany Peniel) at Bethany, Oklahoma, and ultimately became the choir director of a large Nazarene Church in Oklahoma City.

The first frame church building was constructed with money received from what the Nazarene Church called "Alabaster Offerings" (AMC). The menfolk of the church were primarily responsible for the labor. In the 1960s a new church building was constructed with the church's own money and labor. With the help of the Rev. Samuel Mackety, a Pottawattomie Indian, and Mr. Pontiac, a Saginaw Chippewa Indian, both from Mount Pleasant, Michigan, the church was built assisted by church members Millard, Ben, and Paschal Cerre. The building is small and seats about 125 people. Some members of the past who are now members of the church triumphant include Helen Washington Little Dance (who donated land for the construction of the first church), Albert and Beatrice Pappan Makes Cry, Prudence Primeaux Rush, Suzette DeLodge Buffalohead, Mitchell and Dora Fire Shaker Cerre, Gary and Martha Fire Shaker Blueback, Emily Fire Shaker Page, Marcella C. War Waters, Dora Eagle, Eugene Eagle, Edna Little Dance Primeaux, Ben and Edna Cerre Waters, Pete and Ada Grant LeClair, Perry and Nora C. Bear, Genevieve Washington Pollak, Bernadine C. Bear Roy, Evangeline Little Dance Wedell, Nino Buffalohead, Ben Cerre, Pascal Cerre, Vinola Cerre Rosborough, Julie Cerre No Ear, Ernie Blueback, Adolfus Warrior, LeRoy Warrior, Anthony "Tony" Warrior Sr., Suzanna Makes Cry White Eagle, Marion Cerre, Elizabeth Blueback Goodman, and others.

In modern times, those leading the church include Hazel Makes Cry Headman, Clairene C. Bear Arkeketa, Millard Cerre, Virginia Buffalohead, Louise Roy, Dolores Waters Decorah, LaVonne Headman Steeprock, Caroline Steeprock, Christiana Kemble Simpson, Paula Buffalohead Mendoza, Nathaniel and Edith Rose Primeaux Johnson, Bruce and Christie Johnson, Tamara White Eagle Bear, Cynthia White Eagle, Galvis White Eagle, Rolf and Virgie Sue Headman Clements, and others.

The Church of the Nazarene District Assembly for the Indian churches was held annually in different locations. In the early years, the Ponca Nazarenes, who owned an old gray school bus in the 1940s, would take as many people as possible to their annual meetings. These annual meetings were held in either El Paso, Texas, or Albuquerque, New Mexico. The elders said that attending this annual meeting was planned well ahead and was worth waiting for. For the Ponca church, every member saved enough money for food and gasoline for the bus. Church members got to see new places and meet other Christians.

Following the inception of the North American Indian District, Church of the Nazarene, the Indian churches had their annual meetings in Albuquerque, New Mexico. Some of the tribes attending the meeting were of the Arapaho, Cheyenne, Cocopah, Comanche, Laguna Pueblo, Maricopa, Mojave, Navaho, Tohono O'odham, Pima, Ponca, and other Pueblos.

Each tribe had its opportunity to sing in their language. AMC led and sang Ponca hymns with other Ponca delegates. They put harmony into their translated hymns. This was enjoyed by all tribes attending the annual meeting. Apparently impressing the Southwest Indians, they were referred to as the "Singing Birds of the Plains." As these meetings became more centralized, AMC always took at least three carloads of church members to the meetings.

The Nazarene youth always had their summer camp at Navaho, New Mexico. In the beautiful mountain setting, these children learned of God through songs and the Bible with boys and girls from the Arapaho, Cheyenne, Cocopah, Comanche, Laguna Pueblo, Maricopa, Mojave, Navaho, Tohono O'odham, Pima, Ponca, and other tribes. At camp they played games and fished in the lakes.

The Ponca church is now in the Northwest Oklahoma District, Church of the Nazarene. Although many members of the church and other tribal members did not want their relationship severed from their fellow Indian Christians in the Southwest, the future of the church is promising as young men and women come freely to join hands in this fellowship.

The Baptists

The first Baptist work among the Ponca started in 1923. Mrs. George English, of the Chilocco Indian School, established a center of a sort at Ponca City that continued for one year under the supervision of Rev. M. B. Hurt. A building was erected for worship purposes in about 1927. Money was donated by the Osage Baptist Church. It was during those years when the oil-wealthy Osage had shown benevolence by helping other struggling churches, including the Ponca's. The Southern Baptist Church began its formal mission work among the Ponca in 1926 and was organized in 1927 by Rev. C. C. Bowles. In 1928 Rev. A.

W. Hancock became the pastor of the Ponca church. Assisting in that work was also a woman by the name of Miss Mary Sharp.

Revs. Thomas Wamego, John Stoneroad, Bruce Conrad, Jasper Saunkey, Jonas Dyson, Allen Corbet, Eddie Lindsey, and Ted Freeman were some of the pastors assigned to the Ponca church. The church has also had interim retired pastors from other churches. In the early beginnings of the church, some of its first members included Mary LeClair Gayton, Eva LeClair Primeaux, Maggie LaDue, Grace Little Warrior, Mattie Headman Howe, Lula Headman Thicknail, Nellie Headman Jones, Agnes Headman Howe, Beulah Running over Water Roy, Lizzie Makes Cloud Roy, Baptiste and Lizzie DeLodge, Leland and Bessie Pappan Sr., Irene LeClair Warrior, Henry Snake, Eugene Howe, Isaac Headman, Duane Buffalohead, Carmel Howe Roy, Alice Howe Fisher, and others. One of the most fascinating functions of the church was the water baptism that took place once a year down at the river. Everyone wanted to get baptized, and each person had a different story to tell concerning they're baptism. The congregation met faithfully in a one-room frame building until the 1960s, when a new sanctuary was built. The construction of a fellowship hall and classrooms by its members has added much-needed space for activities. In modern times, the church leadership consists of the following Douglas and Lillian Pappan Eagle, Thomasine Grass Blueback, Dewey and Dolores Stands Black Crain, Molly Pappan Eagle, Michael and Susan Crain Cornell, Tully Red Corn, Susan Williams Freeman, Dorthea Walkingsky Blueback, Kay Walkingsky, and others. The Ponca Indian Southern Baptist Church, being an autonomous body, normally sent their reports to the local (Kay County) Baptist Association and to the Oklahoma State Baptist Conventions annually.

Other Churches

The Roman Catholic Kateri Circle, recently organized under the auspices of St. Mary's Church in Ponca City, has well-organized meetings and is drawing more Ponca people. Their meetings and fellowship occur once a month. They are bringing into the church the rich Ponca traditions of song and scriptural readings in the Ponca native language. The leaders of the group are Betty Pensoneau Primeaux, Vanessa Knight

Good Eagle, Ted and Ruth Knight Felix, Phyllis Rush, Darlene Pensoneau Harjo, and others.

The Ponca Full Gospel Church, a recent church organized by local tribal members, has services every Sunday. This church organization is the most recent of the Ponca churches. A man from the Pawnee, Oklahoma, area probably initiated it. His name was Sam Young. Mr. Young was a leader of this independent church movement, that is, people who followed this belief. The Ponca men who knew him said he was a godly man who spoke the truth of how a man should live. He had held prayer meetings among the Pawnee people as well as in other parts of the state. He and Mr. Thurman Buffalohead (now deceased), a member of the Ponca Tribe, led the beginning of the Ponca church. Its membership is composed of Mr. Buffalohead's family and other relatives and close friends.

The Singing Church

Since the Ponca people have always had special interest in singing, each church has their favorite singers who add to the worship experience on Sunday mornings. Some of these talented soloists from many years ago were Albert Makes Cry Jr., Robert Others, Mitchell Cerre, Maynard Hinman, Thomas Primeaux, and Alice (Howe) Fisher. They sang in most of the Ponca churches until their demise. Jesse Fisher, son of Alice Howe Fisher, is a talented singer and businessman. He is one of the great-grandsons of Edward Howe, who was a priest at the Niobrara, Nebraska, Episcopal Church. Barbara Wilson and Tony Cerre sing on special occasions in various churches.

The Nazarenes were the first to compose and sing Ponca Indian hymns. This was probably due to the leadership of Rev. Amos Komah, who sang traditional Comanche Indian church hymns. The first members also translated many English hymns into the Ponca language. The early church members were inspired to compose unique Ponca Christian tunes by the ancient prayer songs of the people. AMC said they held special prayers to find the words and tunes for the Ponca traditional hymns. These particular tunes were not used but were inspirational, in that they gave impetus to creating new and meaningful Christian songs. The original tunes were prayer songs, uttered in the private setting, to the Creator. Cross-culturally, the words in the songs related clearly the Christian message to many non-English-speaking Ponca.

In the order of worship, songs were sung thematically, that is, appropriate songs fit the message, scripture, or occasion. Some songs were made for various worship experiences, such as regular worship services, revivals, and special prayer meetings for the sick, funerals, and birthdays. The songs can be categorized as praise hymns, thanksgiving hymns, funeral hymns, and hymns for the altar call, or call to Christian discipleship. These songs, normally, were and are sung through two times.

From the early 1940s on, Ponca men and women who were members of the Ponca churches, including the Native American Church, were actively involved with the religious and spiritual needs of their people. Some composers (all deceased) of traditional hymns included Albert and Beatrice Makes Cry, Robert and Helen Little Dance, Prudence Primeaux, Suzette Buffalohead, Tom Primeaux, James Clark Sr., Harry Buffalohead, Napoleon Buffalohead, Lamont Brown, Francis Eagle, McKinley Eagle, Cornelius Hardman, William C. War, Logan Cerre, George Smith, Mitchell Roy, and William Overland. According to AMC, the tunes came from songs of the ancient past. He stated they were prayer songs to *Wak'ą́da* called "Captive Songs" (*Nágdè waą̀*). He said these kinds of songs were sung in times of extreme hardship or some perplexing situation.

The following is an example of a praise hymn composed by Robert Little Dance:

THE SON OF GOD IS WORTHY OF PRAISE

Wak'ą́da Ižį́ge đahą́wadenì	The Son of God is worthy of praise
Wíbđahą̀ mąbđį́	In my walk of life I praise you
Wak'ą́da Ižį́ge Waníđe	Son of God, Healer (Savior)
Đahą́wadenì wíbđahą́ mąbđį́	Worthy of praise, in my walk of life I praise you
Wak'ą́da Ižį́ge đahą́wadenì	The Son of God is worthy of praise
Wíbđahą̀ mąbđí, ą̀đáginą̀atè	In my walk of life I praise you, hear me (my God)
Į́đáđą ą̀đágiškaxekè	What you have done for me

Wadáedadè daháwadenì	You are compassionate and worthy of praise
Wak'ada Ižíge daháwadenì	The Son of God is worthy of praise
Wíbdahà mabdí, adáginaatè	In my walk of life I praise you, hear me (my God)
Idádą adágiškaxekè	What you have done for me
Wadáedadè daháwadenì	You are compassionate and worthy of praise
Wak'ada Ižíge daháwadenì	The Son of God is worthy of praise
Wíbdahà mabdí, adáginaatè	In my walk of life I praise you, hear me (my God)

The Ponca Nazarene Church always had a mini choir. Each generation in the church has at one time or another sung in the choir. For example, in 1947 the choir was composed of Genevieve and Drew Little Warrior, Edna and Alison Waters, Perry and Nora Crazy Bear, Rachel Makes Cry, Etheline and Evangeline Little Dance, Lucille Little Voice, Melvin Buffalohead, Eugene Eagle, and Albert Makes Cry Jr. The current members are Louis and Hazel Headman, Clairene Arkeketa, Virginia Buffalohead, Christi Simpson, LaVonne Steeprock, Paula Mendoza, Edith Rose Johnson, Jennifer Feathers, and Bruce Johnson. The following is a translation of the hymn "The Savior for Me."

THE SAVIOR FOR ME

Adúha mašiáta táwadágištąbé	From heaven above He made a great provision for us
Jísas wanide datíte	Jesus came to be Savior
Níta wadágidè téxikè udáha	He gives us life through his agony
Jísas niádagidè datí	Jesus you came to heal my spirit.
Idádą bdúgà ázegidè dédaì	He has sent forth His calmness
Jísas udížedà dagdí	Jesus in tiredness (earthly) you have sat
Uwíką digéxtì	Without (earthly) help.
Idádì ákà edí	(But) the Father is there (to help).
Jísas niádagidè datí	Jesus you came to heal my spirit.

Chorus

Jísas waníde átanì	Jesus is the great Savior
Wadáedadè wídakè	Your compassion is Truth.
Náxè díta ǫdáhąì	We praise the Spirit you gave
Wíke ǫdígaxaì	We have made you the Truth.
Waníde dí ǫdádinidąi	We cling to you Savior

For over a hundred years, the Christian church has been actively involved in the lives of the Ponca people. There has been some resistance to the church by some tribal members. This is understandable because of the high moral and ethical values taught by parents and tribal elders in past times. It has been said by some tribal members that the Christian church is not teaching anything different from what we have been taught. However, as we enter the twenty-first century, these teachings have all but disappeared leaving the church a great responsibility. It will be up to the younger generations to pick up the torch of moral values and ethics. We are seeing the younger group grow as they offer special prayers for people celebrating birthdays, graduations, marriages, and other tribal events that take place. They also request prayers for the success of students in school and at work and play. People who are in hospitals, are in rest homes, or are shut-ins are also remembered. The churches are destined to survive because there is always a need somewhere.

22

The Spirit World

There are many beliefs about life after death in the world. Since Christianity is the predominant religion in America, it is the religion used for comparison in this introduction. The Christian perception of the afterlife is very similar to the Ponca concept. However, in the Christian community, there is little reference made to the spirit of man on earth. Also, there are marked differences of what one expects in the hereafter. According to Bible scholars, the idea of heaven was conceived early by the Hebrew people. And most Christians embrace and espouse this biblical thought. The apostle John, who was banished to the Isle of Patmos in the Aegean Sea, tells in his vision how he saw heaven as a city. The walls were bejeweled with the most precious stones known to mankind. Further, it had four gates containing pearls. Granted that this description may well be something other than what he described. John writes of God sitting upon a throne and many people praising Him, as well as other heavenly creatures. The creatures were described like nothing found on earth. Isaiah, the prophet of the Hebrew Testament, saw God "high and lifted up" in a temple. The apocryphal materials in the Bible further predict a long series of events that must occur before the end comes. Accordingly, the Euro-American version of the afterlife perceives (1) God on a throne, (2) creatures that fly to and fro praising God all the day long, (3) heaven with gold and other precious jewels that may be describing something else, (3) people attaining heaven after this life to praise God for all eternity, and (4) there will be no more sickness, death, hardships, and disappointments. This and more are described in a mysterious manner. The language used suggests something more perceptibly believable for adherents of the Christian faith.

During my lifetime, I have met few Native atheists or agnostics. Perhaps in modern times, because of exposure to higher education and movement into the dominant society, there may be Native unbelievers.

However, it seems that most Native peoples have never studied or heard of the likes of Nietzsche and his atheistic concepts, nor can we say that many would have any interest in these kinds of thoughts concerning the existence of God. This is because a Native believes he is part of the natural processes that he perceives in his world. In his world are inexplicable occurrences that baffle even the philosophical and scientific mind. I understand that science can explain these occurrences as the figments of imagination or with logic. But in defense of the believer, imagination is only a part of the reality of man's total person, as is the intrinsic value of morality. So through generations of experiences, the acceptance of man's spiritual concepts became part of his existence. Believing in God then, never posed a problem for most Native peoples.

The Ponca Spirit World

With the exception of the Native American Church and some ritual dancing, no particular attention is paid to the Native American religious perception of the afterlife. The simple beliefs of the people are hardly known. Like some Christians, the Ponca believe heaven is bejeweled with precious stones and gold. (God sitting on a throne does not feature in the Ponca description of heaven, and this Christian concept seems to be borrowed from the idea of European kings and queens.) Life after death is a belief that mankind will go to a place set aside for him by the Creator. Howard (1995, 98–101) discussed the Ponca religion, to some degree, on bundles and ethics. Peter LeClair, during his discourse with Howard (1995, 99), pointed out, "After we die, we go to heaven. This is *Máxeáta* in Ponca, and a man may say just before he dies, I am going underground but I will be above you. This means he believes that he will go to heaven." This story is indicative of concepts learned by our northern brothers from the non-Indian world. Ponca beliefs are told by word of mouth to each generation. The inculcation of beliefs begins at birth. The child learns through the total social interaction with his peers and mentors. During the course of his trial, Chief Standing Bear (Tibbles 1972, 62) told his former beliefs about afterlife:

> I once thought differently. I believed there were happy hunting grounds, where there was plenty of game, and plenty to eat, no sickness, no

death, and no pain. The best Indians would go to these happy hunting grounds. I thought that those who were bad would never live any more; that when they died that was the end of them.

Christian missionary endeavors by the Methodist Episcopal Church occurred in the nineteenth century near the Niobrara and Missouri Rivers in northern Nebraska. Chief Standing Bear, among other tribesmen, was converted to Christianity. This was also a time when the Ponca faced extreme hardships. It was a time when transition and the acculturation processes were just beginning. The Ponca people, unaware of their future, were desperately trying to find help. So many Ponca became Christians. The old teachings of the tribe were set aside for a while, and the new ways became more and more predominant for them.

From a time that no one can remember, the Ponca people were conscious of a God (KH, NC, AMC, JP, AL). They used to say, "*Pácà àmà, Wak'ádà íkipahàì*" (The Ponca know their God). At the most elementary point of view, according to KH, the following is taught:

> "*Wanáxeàtà ái*" . . . (place of the spirit) . . . that's what they call it. The Ponca people have a teaching . . . a place where all people will go after they die. It's a peaceful place . . . no bad thing is there . . . lots of game there . . . they don't have war . . . no argument. They got lots of things to do . . . those people enjoy it there. They're ready to accept other people from the tribe to come there when they pass on.

Unlike the Christian concept of heaven, there is an absence of a deity. No reference is made to praising and worshipping a God sitting on a throne, as mentioned in the Judeo-Christian religion. The spirit world of the Ponca people (other than Christian) has no concept of a heavenly city with streets paved with gold. *Wanáxeàtà*, or "the spirit world," suggested peace and harmony. All natural substances that are known to mankind may be present, but emphasis is placed on the reuniting of families or people and other natural interaction with nature in its perfected state (KH, NC, JP, AL). It is highly suggestive through some visions and dreams that people will have bodies but will be in their perfected state. The Ponca spirit world may be viewed from various perspectives because there are no documented written materials. The religious perception of the afterlife was evidently developed over a long span of time. The elders suggested that over millennia of years the sayings and stories concerning man's destiny after this life and his interaction with the Creator gave clues to this belief.

The term for spirit is Náxè. The spirit, they said, is that which is inside of man.[1] It is that part of man that laughs, weeps, or feels emotions. The body is only a vehicle that gives expression to those feelings. It is also that part of man that reaches out to spiritual things (KH, NC, JP, AL). They said that there were various outcomes of the spirit following death. These conclusions are general knowledge that was drawn from discussions with individuals or groups of people who related visions and visitation experiences by the deceased person's spirit. From ages past as well as in recent years, some tribal members believe this because they have personally experienced visions or dreams of the afterlife.

The topics that follow are some concepts of Ponca beliefs about the afterlife. With little or only some detail, the discussion centers around the following: The spirit of man is "tied to the earth"; the spirit cannot leave because he cannot find the way out; the spirit of man leaves immediately after the four days are ended; the spirit of man visits the spirit world in dreams before death; the spirit of man may leave the body before the person dies; the spirit of man, through the Ghost Dance, may visit the spirit world; the living may be visited by spirits from the spirit world; and other information comes from the Creator's instructions concerning the use of the Sacred Pipe of the Ponca.

The Spirit of Man Is "Tied to the Earth"

When the spirit leaves the body, it may remain in the locality of the home or other familiar places and may be seen or heard weeping. The spirit is said to be "tied to the earth" by some source of earthly influence that prevents it from leaving. This includes all family members— the parents, a husband, a wife, or children—who may not be living a proper ethical or moral life. The person himself too may have also committed some crime or unethical act that was never resolved in his lifetime. When the problem has been corrected by the living relatives, the spirit will then leave. The destination of the spirit, of course, is the spirit world. There was no mention of Hades, the underground abode of the dead in Greek mythology; Sheol, the Hebrew abode of the dead; or hell as the dwelling place of demons and Satan. Only in modern religion among the Ponca has the idea of Satan become apparent.

The Spirit of Man Cannot Leave Because He Cannot Find the Way Out

Closely related to the above, this spirit may also be seen and heard in familiar places. The Ponca say this person may have been a type while he was alive who cared for no one but himself. He may have been a selfish and unloving person. His spirit will be referred to by the people as the person he was when he lived. I heard some elderly people say about such a spirit, "I suppose it's so and so, he was so mean when he lived." The Ponca, because of respect for the dead, do not mention the name of the deceased person, but in this case it is allowed.[2] Because the person was mean and selfish, and for other similar reasons, it is said he could not find his way out to the spirit world. Sometimes this kind of spirit may remain in an area for many years. Customarily, the Ponca people might even throw out some food to him if he stands too close to their home and weeps. They usually say, "Here, take this food and get out of here!" Usually the spirit is said to leave that locality only to return at another time. In recent years, many of these spirits who were seen or heard weeping have left. Some say they left because they found the way out to the spirit world, while others say the white people scared them away.

The Spirit of Man Leaves Immediately after the Four Days Are Ended

The number four is held sacred (as mentioned elsewhere) among the Ponca and is said to be the completion of any event in life. When a person has been ill for a period and death is inevitable, it is said that within the last four days of his life the spirit may visit relatives and friends before death occurs. The elders gave several accounts of this type of spirit visitation. They related a number of different stories of how they had seen someone at a certain place only to hear later that that person was sick in bed at home or the hospital at that very moment. Sick people may also, when awakened from their sleep or a state of comatose, give a story of having "gone to see" certain people. Take, for example, the story of a dying young woman who had "gone to see" a young couple who had just adopted a baby. She described the entire scenario although she had never left her room. At the end of the four days, she died. In this case, there was an inference made that she was an upright person and, therefore, went directly to the spirit world.

The Spirit of Man Visiting the Spirit World in Dreams before Death

The elders related many stories of visiting the spirit world through dreams. Dreams of this type usually occur when a person is young. It was believed that if a young person dreamed such a dream, their life would be long. KH said when he was young he had such a dream. He said the spirit world, *Wanáxeàtà*, was described by an elder during his young days. I translated the following from his testimony:

> I was walking down a pathway and came to a place where the path divided. I followed the path that went to the right. I had walked for some time, and everything was peaceful. I notice that there was a slight breeze blowing and the grass was very green in the prairie. There were flowers everywhere. They were the kinds that grow wild. There were big puffy clouds, and the sky was clear blue. As I walked on, I came to the end of the path, and there ahead of me were a village of Indian people. There were tipis everywhere. People were carrying on in the old traditional way. There was a woman sitting on the ground preparing a meal, and there were others doing the same. Some were bringing in firewood. As I walked on, I came upon a group of men talking to each other. They were smiling and looked contented and at peace. I asked them where I was, but they didn't pay any attention to me. I tried again to talk to them because they were speaking the Ponca language and I thought they didn't hear me. But they continued to ignore me as if they didn't see me at all. Suddenly, it came to me that I shouldn't be there and I became afraid. I began to walk back hurriedly in the direction I had come. I didn't look at those people again.

After he had told his dream to the elders of the tribe, they said, "*Wanáxeàtà šì*" (You have gone to the spirit world). They told him that if he had been welcomed by the group of men, he would have had a short life. Some elders have stated that when they had such dreams, they saw their relatives and friends.

The Spirit of Man May Leave the Body before He Dies

This refers to the aged. When a person has lived a long life, his spirit may leave for the spirit world months before physical death. The elders told of an elderly woman who reached the age of ninety-five. At times she became disoriented and could not feed herself. She would communicate to others only those things that were necessary for her existence. This included the need for eating, drinking water, and personal hygiene. The psychological implications are many for this type of person, but the elders taught that this person's spirit had already left for the spirit world. Although these elderly people still live and breathe, it is said that they remain only for some time until the immediate family has accepted the fact that death is inevitable. Perhaps the family accepts the physical death much easier knowing that the spirit of the aged person is with their parents and grandparents in the spirit world.

The Spirit of Man, through the Ghost Dance, May Visit the Spirit World

The practice of necromancy among the Ponca is uncertain. But the elders said that they visited the spirits in the spirit world through the Ghost Dance. In Ponca it is called *Wanáxe wačígaxè*. The person in charge of this ritual dance is said to be *Wanáxe ídaedè*, or "has an understanding of the spirit." The dancers, with the aid of the leader, were able to travel to the spirit world to communicate with their deceased relatives. The elders said the dance was a special dance and that only certain people were involved with it. They took for granted that the spirit world truly existed and that the Ghost Dance could transport them there. The last Ghost Dance site is considered to be a sacred site on the Southern Ponca reservation. Chief White Deer of the *Níkapášnà* clan was in charge. He was also the last Ghost Dance leader among the Southern Ponca (KH, NC, JP, AMC). The dance, no longer practiced by the Ponca, is only remembered through the songs of the Ghost Dance, which they still sing in private circles.

The Spirit of Man May Be Visited by Spirits from the Spirit World

When a person is lying on his death bed, he sometimes has spirits come to him from the spirit world. There are numerous accounts of this experience. Recently, when my cousin lay at home dying, several living relatives had come to see her and pray for her. She would tell them, "Oh, I didn't know you were here, I was just talking to my mother and wasn't paying any attention to you." Her mother had been dead for many years. Sometimes a person who is dying tells those with them that somebody who died long before came to visit them. Quite often such a person says, "So and so came after me," as if to suggest that they were getting ready to leave. The elders related how a dying person may say that there were spirits present who came after another person. Those who have this particular experience will not relate the story on to other people if those people are still living and are in apparent good health. The person who has received such a message doesn't know for whom the spirits came. According to the elders, people who had these types of experiences were usually ill, bedfast, or special people who have this gift (if it can be called a gift). When such a vision was experienced, a person in the tribe would die through a sudden accident or illness. Such an experience was told to me by Mrs. Irene Warrior (now deceased):

> My husband was an invalid and blind. He was to die in the months to come. One day he told me that some spirit had come to him and told him that they had come after two men. He didn't know who the two men were, but said that they were needed. I told him that perhaps he was just imagining things. But he said it was as he said it was. He was a strong believer in the Native American Church ways, and practiced those ways. It was only a few days afterward those two Ponca men passed away. One had been killed and the other died of a heart attack.

Her husband, an invalid, spent most of his time in a wheelchair. He said the person that came to their house was the Virgin Mary or somebody like her. This is unusual because very few Ponca are Roman Catholic, and he was a member of the Native American Church. The elders, however, could relate to a story like this. They had a variety of stories that could fill many pages.

Instructions from the Creator Concerning the Use of the Sacred Pipe

As mentioned earlier, these beliefs are based on what the elders have said. Foremost in this belief is the teaching that the knowledge of the spirit world was given to the Ponca people when they received the Sacred Pipe from the Creator. This was in the beginning. In this account, the words relating to the Sacred Pipe are limited because of taboos placed on it. The elders stated that their belief about the Ponca interaction with the Creator is not speculation nor was it based on probabilities. They said there were specific instructions for the keeper of the pipe to share with the people (KH, AL, AMC). In part, this was done once a year. Through prayers to the Creator, the keeper of the Sacred Pipes requested continued sustenance for the Ponca's existence. The people were reminded that the passing from this world was only a step up to better things. Families of the tribe reiterated unwritten statutes, commandments, ordinances, and so forth, which reinforced their belief in the spirit world. For the Ponca people, their beliefs have existed for countless generations of people. They learned a lesson from nature, the symmetry and design of their world, the animals, the fowls of the air, the seeds of plants that die to become new plants, the changing of the seasons, and many other clues that point to a new era beyond this life. For the people to survive, they needed assurance from the Creator to provide this belief for them. Through the use of the Sacred Pipes they learned that if life on this earth was all that there was to our existence, and when they came to the end of it there was nothing, life then would be meaningless and senseless. This, in itself, was a sufficient reason to keep their belief and way of life to sustain them. Whatever variations of beliefs that remain among the Ponca people, it is remembered that they still have the belief of the spirit world with them to this day.

23
The Funeral Rites

There are many ritualistic practices, but only a few are cited here. The elders did not know how long some of these practices were part of the funeral experience. But they said that the tribe had always followed these procedures. The Ponca standards for the burial experience include sorrow and respect, the sacrifice of giving, the dress ethic, the giving of moral support to the bereaved, personal bereavement, never leaving the body alone, the food offering, the burial feast, dressing and combing the hair of the bereaved, and walking over the grave.

Sorrow and Respect

Suppressed by many people today, the emotion of sadness at one time was expressed openly by the people. It was not unusual for the Ponca people to weep openly for the deceased with the living relatives. In the new generation, many Indian people now suppress their inner feelings. The Euro-American ethic does not allow weeping for men--only women cry. Or perhaps the mores or social demands do not permit it. Not long ago I met an elderly non-Indian woman who asked me questions about why Indians put a black cloth over the face of the deceased lying in state. She asked a variety of questions concerning Indian practices at funerals. Finally, she told me that her husband had died and she had just finished speaking with her sister in another state about it. She spoke of how she tried to make new friends, read books, and join some clubs to get over her grief. That was the reason for her questioning about how Indians dealt with grief. I asked when her husband had died. She had spoken of it as though it happened just recently. She answered that he had passed away over ten years ago.

It may be that in mainstream America people are told to read a book or join a club to help them overcome their grief. It seems that suppression of emotions is common in many parts of America. Some believe that they can rise above the emotion of sadness. In America, for some, it has become macho to stand by stoically in moments of sadness, and as a result, behavior toward peers who weep can border on derision. So no one weeps. Television too has its influence. If a character weeps, he or she does so only in an appropriate scenario of sadness in the movie that also causes the audience to weep. So how does a person manage their lives following the death of a close relative or friend? What follows next is not a prescription of how to deal with grief; it is rather a note on the historic processes of the Ponca in times of death.

From the earliest historic practice of grieving to the mid-twentieth century, the normal expression of weeping aloud was common among the Ponca people. It was considered respectful to go to the family of the deceased and weep with them. Also, it was appropriate to take a gift to the family. In the early 1900s, friends and relatives used to bring food for the family. Sometimes they brought gifts of blankets, quilts, and dress goods that would be used in a giveaway at the appropriate time. But weeping at this time was done in a way that the family received the benefit of knowing that other people cared. The weeping not only served as an outlet for possible pent-up emotions but was also the beginning of the healing process in grieving. KH, NC, AMC, JP, and AL all agreed that the Ponca way of mourning included weeping for both men and women. They said it was better to weep because *"Đaxágeáži tedì sabáži wadíkegatè, ̨áki, gúáhidatà ̨idádą téxì ádakipatè"* (If weeping is kept back, later on, you may get sick, and you may meet up with some difficulty). In some situations, family members might hold back their emotions. These people were spoken to during their time of loss. The Ponca believed the suppressed feeling might lead to an undesirable behavior.

Contrarily, some people became overly emotional following the death experience. They wept continuously for long periods. The elders would say to the people, *"Đaxágaì kí, ̨idigdą̀ xagáigà. Edíhi, ̨ádidigè t'amašè. Égą škágaži tè, sabáži wadíkegat'è"* (When you weep, weep gently. It is then, that you will begin to feel better. If you do not do that, you may become ill). These are age-old words of advice to the bereaved. In an earlier period, the Ponca people had traditions that provided a means of expression in the weeping process.

The elders spoke of some of the ways that a person should weep.

KH, KCH, NC, JP, AMC, and NM said that among the older generation, who came to Oklahoma from Nebraska, there were those who wept and made prayers for the family or made statements about the person who had died. This was done intermittently during their emotional state of weeping. For instance, an elder might weep intermingling his words that connoted a prayer for the living, especially little children. Typical were the words *Étąbè dįgè*, or "They have no one to look to [for help]." This was a prayer for the little children who now would have to go through life without a mother or father. When a person died in a tragic accident, the person weeping might say, "*Đéxčidą·*," as if to say, "Oh, this dear one." The term is a derivative of *Đéxtidą·*. The literally meaning is *Đé* (this or that one), *xti* (very or more), and *dą·* (comes to this condition or state of being). Something similar is said to children who fall when they are learning to walk. My aunt (now deceased), at the age of eighty-five, wept at the passing of her granddaughter. Her words in the Ponca language were "My little granddaughter, dear one." The words flowed with emotion and tears as she spoke to the deceased. Since few speak the language today, practicing this custom would be next to impossible. One or two elderly women who might attend a funeral can sometimes be heard weeping and speaking to the deceased. Those who wept in years past always related their thoughts for the individual. This part of the Ponca culture is all but gone. Sometimes, quiet sobs can be heard at funerals in modern times. Only a few elders may weep aloud. Currently, we seldom see a man weeping out loud at funerals. Tears are shed, but expressions of sadness are more conservative. To have lost this practice of weeping aloud at the funeral is unfortunate. The span between us and our former cultural standards continues to widen.

The Sacrifice of Giving Away

The custom of giving away personal belongings by the immediate family in ancient times included practically everything the family owned. In the Ponca legend *The Handsome Boy and The Homely Boy*, it is suggested that everything was given away. The elders said that when the Ponca people first came to Oklahoma, they continued this custom of giving away all household items. The custom of burning the deceased person's personal belongings is still practiced. Changes in this custom in recent years include giving away some of the deceased person's unused personal belongings. For example, if an individual owned a Pendleton blanket, the family might give it to a close friend of the deceased. They have also given personal belongings to their own close friends. The types of items given away include pictures, jewelry, hunting equipment, household items, new clothing, and so forth. The capitalistic society we live in apparently has influenced our people to value material things to the extent that they would not burn them up because somebody could use them. Additionally, they may give away these items because they might serve as a token of remembrance of the deceased. Other belongings are burned.[1] This is done privately; it is not a public act.

Because funeral expenses are very costly, they are viewed as extreme by the general public. But funeral costs are seen as only one of the necessary expenses for an Indian funeral. Families also spend money on food for four days, including breakfast for people who stay up through the night with the body, lunch for family members who come to the place of the funeral throughout the day, and dinner in the evenings for family members and close friends. Lunch is also served after the wake service each night. Most families do not have enough money to take care of all this, but contributions are made by friends and relatives. Gifts of money, food, and other material goods are brought to the family. This is a common practice among the people. However, in many cases, the family is left holding the indebtedness. The fact that the cost is a great sacrifice to give does not hinder the family from spending money on the funeral. It satisfies the family that they can show their love and respect for the deceased. One family member said following a funeral experience: "There is no amount of money that we could have spent that would cause us to regret it. The life of this loved one truly gave us much to be grateful for, and we are happy that we could honor him by doing this."

The Dress Ethic

The Ponca women, when in mourning, used to take down their hair. This was a sign of death in the family and that they were grieving. Their clothing for this time of bereavement were the same clothes they were wearing at the time of the death. The menfolk and children also wore the same clothing for the four days of the funeral experience. The dress code was an act showing their love and respect for the deceased person and their deep state of mourning. The four days after death is the period the spirit remains on earth. When the spirit of the deceased departed on the fourth day, the family cleaned up their home, bathed and put on clean clothes, and went to visit friends and relatives. Additionally, an elder of the family or other tribal elder came to burn cedar to cleanse the dwelling and to fan smoke from the cedar on the family members. Cleansing means bringing a sense of peace to the mind of family members, keeping anything evil from entering into the scene, and receiving a clear mind during that time of grief. Since the old traditions have been fading away, there is probably no one living today who adheres to this age-old custom. In modern times, when a family member passes away, some women dress in black dresses, and some men wear suits; however, in more recent years we are seeing more people dressed casually.

The Giving of Moral Support for the Bereaved

A source of support is provided by relatives and friends of the deceased. Moral support for the bereaved family is somewhat hidden during a funeral and is not often seen openly. It is generally realized by the people that the loss of a family member causes the immediate family great emotional stress. Therefore, the friends and relatives are present to encourage and aide the family in any way possible. This means they may have to sit through the night with them. Sometimes nothing is said unless family members wish to speak. Friends are there to listen and give encouragement. This type of support is given because of the love these friends and relatives have for the family (KH, AMC, NC).

Personal Bereavement

Up to the early 1900s, during deep distress in their bereavement following the death of a family member, the elders said certain members of the family would cut themselves. Some women made a single cut above their knees or upper arms. It is believed that this practice is not associated with self-injury to cope with emotional pain, which characterizes a deeper psychological disorder. It is rather believed that the intensity of the women's sorrow was such that this onetime act was done to experience physical pain and suffering because of the love they had for their loved one. This practice was not carried out in every funeral rite. The woman and the deceased may have been a couple who were deeply in love and shared much of their time with their children. At this time some women also cut their hair with no careful clipping. It was said that a person deeply grieved would take a knife and cut her hair in gobs without considering her appearance following the haircut (KCH).

Some family members fasted for the four days of the initial mourning. However, it should be understood that the mourning period could go on for months to come. KH, NC, AMC, JP, and AL said the period of mourning could be as short as four to six months. However, it could go as long as a year. At the end of that period, they said, the family should have been able to accumulate some material goods and to reestablish their home situation. At this time they sponsor a feast in memorial of the deceased. The Ponca call it *Wađísì*, the act of "cleansing." Even though the feast formally ends the family's mourning period, some people might mourn for months to come, but this practice was highly discouraged. The elders said that, in the past, if a person carried his or her mourning too long, another member of their family might die.

In dealing with bereavement, according to the elders, a husband could spend up to ten nights at the burial site. The love he had for his wife might compel him to do this. When he was ready to leave the site, it is said, he was satisfied that she had gone on to the spirit world. In regard to sitting up at night at the burial site, KH told the following story of a man who had great love for his wife. This was when the historic Ponca lived along the Missouri River in the North Country.

There was a man who loved his wife. *Waú đįké đáđe áçàite* ... He love that woman very much. Everybody in the camp knows about it. Wherever he goes, she's there. Or wherever she goes, he's there. They thought of each other like that ... they said that about them. I guess they didn't have any kids ... *šįgažįgà đįgáitè*. The day came when she got real sick. People went to see them ... pray ... give encouragement ... say good things to them. But she died. In those days they used to dress them up because they going to go over there ... *Wanáxeàtà* [spirit world]. They set those poles up and fix it so they can put her body up there [scaffold burial]. Before they do that, they always put that body in a buffalo robe and sew it up. That man stayed there after everybody went back to camp . . . *Édì gḍíite* . . . He sat there. At first, he cry [wept] . . . make everybody feel bad. But each night he stayed there he start to feel better . . . even though he's sad. One evening when the sun went down . . . a wolf came out of the timber. He howled . . . went back. That wolf . . . he did that four times and never came back. That man, he don't know what it's about . . . he just sit there. *Ábà ánąžą edí gḍíite* . . . he sit there several days. Then one night . . . *Mąčú wí ahíitè* . . . grizzly bear come there. This man . . . he knows this one is dangerous. He got back there somewhere and watch. That bear . . . he come to that place where that woman is. Stand up . . . reach for that body and bring it down. That man . . . he don't have anything . . . knife, bow and arrow . . . like that. He just have to stand back and watch. That bear . . . it pick that body up and throw it up in the air. He kept doing that for some time. Each time he throw that body . . . those sewing come loose on that robe. After a while he lay that body down and walked off into the timber. That man . . . he went over there to see what that bear did. When he got there that woman was sitting up. She was alive. That man was happy . . . they talk and then went back to the camp. She live a long life . . . good life . . . that man, too. Maybe that's why some men want to sit at the graveyard when their wife die.

Whether this legend is the reason that men sit at the burial site has never been verified. As stated above, there were those men who indeed sat at the burial site, but their purposes were not the same. It was said in modern times that one Osage Indian sat at the burial site for seven days and nights to show his bravery. Those acts of individuals, however, were processes for dealing with bereavement.

A general code of behavior at funerals for all tribal members is one that is solemn and respectful. Visitors to the funeral may weep openly with the family; otherwise, they maintain a quiet atmosphere during the funeral. Children in past times were not allowed to make any unnecessary noise. Although the cooks for the funeral are busy preparing meals, noise was at a minimum.

Children are also allowed to view the body. Through this act, the children are taught that death is real and is not to be feared. They are told that there is a place where the spirit goes when it leaves the person. Children do not always understand the idea of death, but it gives them an introduction to the death and funeral experience.

Never Leaving the Body Alone during the Funeral Process, the Food Offering, and the Burial Feast

Originally, the Ponca buried their people immediately after death. KH said that people were buried the same day they died "in the old days before the sun went down." One of the last people to be buried the same day they died was a relative of KCH in 1933. His death occurred approximately at midnight. The body was kept at the home throughout the night. The next morning a funeral director from Ponca City was summoned. Following the embalming of the body, the menfolk dressed the body for the burial. The burial took place the same day. According to custom, the family mourned his death for four days. The bereaved family did not go anywhere during this period. Other friends and relatives came to call on the family during this time. They brought food and material goods and wept with the family. When the family sat down to eat a meal during this time, they also took food to the gravesite of the deceased. This ritual was done before anyone ate any food. After the four days of mourning were completed, the family left the home to visit other people. This was to show that the initial mourning was over.

The ethic of staying up with the body for four days seems to have been adopted from other tribes. This custom was evidently initiated in Oklahoma well into the twentieth century. The elders said this started during the late 1930s, when they began to keep the body for four days. They never left the deceased alone during those four days. "Staying up with the body" became a custom overnight (KH, NC, JP, AL).

A member of the immediate family, a close friend, or a relative may now take food to the deceased at the funeral location. In modern times the cooks for the funeral sometimes assume that responsibility. The amount of food taken to the deceased is usually composed of a spoonful of soup, a small piece of meat, and four or five grains of cooked corn. A pinch of bread may also be included. A small amount of water in a small glass is placed with the food. They call this *Wat'ę wadatè*, or "food for the dead." It is considered sacred, or *Waxúbè*, and must be taken back to the fireplace where it was prepared following the meal. There, it is placed into the fire to burn where the meal was prepared (KH).

The funeral feast is held on the last day of the four days of funeral. Large crowds of friends and relatives come and share in the final meal with the deceased and family. Immediately following the feast, a give-away is usually held. The family members shares their material goods and wealth with as many people as possible. Usually a speech is given about the deceased and family before the giveaway. Names are then called and those present come forward to receive the gift. The gifts, according to Ponca custom, go to non–family members. The gifts often go to friends, visitors, people who assisted in "staying up" with the body, the cooks, and other organizations who came to help or who were just simply present.[2]

Dressing and Combing the Hair of the Bereaved

This custom was initiated by a close relative or friend. The ritual dressing and combing was a private affair that was usually done at the home. When a grieving individual was observed to be going beyond the normal period of grief in the initial phase of mourning, a close relative came to his or her home with another relative or friend to visit. If this was a woman whose husband just died, it was important to be aware of her emotional state. It was at the initial time of the death of her husband that the wife unraveled her braided hair, signifying the death of her husband. The visiting relative (a woman) would tell the woman in mourning that she desired to see her resume her life in society. She then would offer to dress and comb her hair. During the ritual of combing, the visiting relative would speak gently to the grief-stricken woman assuring her that these conditions would pass. Her words were not limited to, but included "The day is coming when you will be able to remember this time in your life and not be sad. You'll remember good things you shared with him and be happy. Now you must clean up and go and visit people." There were no flattering words but encouraging words that gave heart to her that lack courage and spirit. The ritual was for any member of the family that needed help, including the children and menfolk. The elders who experienced this ancient ritual said it was done at a very timely occasion, bringing them back into the reality of living (KCH).

Walking over the Grave

According the archeological digs cited in Wood (1965), two types of graves were found in the area where the Ponca once lived. In addition to Wood's findings, the elders said there was the conventional straight east-to-west grave type, a circular burial grave shaped like a bowl, a shallow grave covered by a gable and dirt, and the scaffold burial.

Historically, when a young Ponca father passed away, his immediate family had the eldest son to walk over the grave. The child walked from the foot to the head of the grave. KH told the story of how the ritual of walking over the grave began. He related the following story:

> The old people told this story. They said one time there's a young man who been married for only a few years. He and his woman . . . they got one little boy. They think of good things for him . . . *Áxt'idaìte.* You might say they hold him up high that some day he's going to be somebody. That's the way they live. Then one day a call came out to all menfolks that there were some enemies coming. They said, "Go out to meet them." That meant get your weapon and go to fight . . . defend this place where we live. Like those other men, he went to fight. When that war was over . . . some old man come to his dwelling . . . *Ahí'ite.* He said to the father of that young man. "They said that your son . . . *Ðižíge áka* . . . he fell over there." I guess that old man got up and went to see. It was so. When they buried his son, they say, he said to those people: "You people know my son . . . and his wife. They got a little boy . . . my grandson. My son wants to see him grow up . . . now that will not be done. I want my grandson to walk over his grave. Maybe he can pick up where my son stopped . . . carry on what he had in mind." So they did that. That's where we get this practice.

According to the elders, during the time when the Ponca used the burial scaffold, they used to wrap the body in a buffalo robe, which was completely sewn together. Before the body was placed upon the scaffold, the child walked over the body. This was done at other burial types as well. The ritual was intended to encourage the oldest son to carry out the life that his father might have lived. They had hopes that the child would live a good and long life. Through this rite, the child would grow older remembering that he was fulfilling a responsibility and a promise. An elderly Ponca man told me several years ago that he walked over his father's grave as a child. He stated that, in his lifetime, there were those moments when he thought of his father. Especially when he had to make decisions, he said, "I tried to be fair to people because I thought, maybe, that's what my father would do. I look back, and I think it was an honor for me to walk over my father. I'm proud that I can think of myself as a person carrying out my father's good intentions."

The current custom of walking over the grave has changed to walking on the casket before lowering it into the grave. This custom began in the mid-1900s. The elders said that other changes also occurred because some families were unable to cope with the many deaths during that time. It seemed to have begun when an elderly man had died. The family thinking that they would perpetuate the family's stability permitted several grandchildren to walk over the body. More changes in the ritual came about as the Ponca people moved further into the twentieth century. Some of these changes included walking over the body because they felt it would enhance their chances of being like the deceased, who was a good person; they would receive blessings and be a good person; they had hopes they would avoid sickness and heartache; the deceased would not haunt them; and other reasons. The rite has evolved to meet some emotional or personal need among living relatives of the deceased. However, in recent times, the elder members of the family try to explain this ritual to the younger generation. They are bringing back the original ritual of the idea of fulfilling the dreams, hopes, and aspirations that once belonged to the deceased.

24

Ancient Ponca Burials and Practices

This section investigates the Ponca burial system as it was formerly used. Oral history tells us that Ponca villages were usually set apart from such compounds as the Ponca Fort site in Nebraska. Forts were used only in times of warfare, and individuals of high rank in the tribe in past times occupied the dwellings within the compound. The Ponca term for compound is *Ną́zà* (in modern times, the term has been attributed to the word *fence*). Reminiscent of the ancient compounds in the East and Southeast cultures, the construction and use of the Ponca Fort site by the Ponca people is probably not far removed from their previous cultural affiliation. Near the fort site, the Ponca buried their dead.

From time immemorial, according to oral history and tradition, the Ponca people occupied a territory that ranged from southeastern Nebraska to the Black Hills of South Dakota. The geographic features of the land, that is, major waterways, their tributaries, a variety of other small streams, and landmarks, were known by the Ponca. As mentioned previously, approximately twenty-eight different campsites were occupied by the Ponca. Each camp was given a name by an unusual feature of the land, the location, or an event that occurred at the time of their occupancy. The exact locations of some of these villages are not known by present-day Ponca. This is due to the lapse of time since the Ponca lived there. However, the general location of the area is known.

A Traditional Historic Journey

In 1914, following the death of his first wife, KH stayed with his uncle Jack Peniska (*P'é'niškà*) near Niobrara, Nebraska. Grandpa Jack Peniska took and showed KH many former village sites. In addition to Niobrara and the Santee Reservation, they traveled to Shannon County to the *Pahé šúšúdè* (Badlands) and to the *Pahé sábè* (Black Hills). They also visited old tribal village sites in Tripp, Todd, Charles Mix, Bon Homme, and other counties in South Dakota as well as to Chouteau Creek, where the Ponca formally lived, and to the old Fort Randall. KH also observed some village sites and significant landmarks in Nebraska, from Dakota County up the Niobrara and Missouri Rivers, and as far west to Cherry County in Nebraska. He recalled going to a place near Genoa, Nebraska, where the "old-time Poncas" had lived. He said that place was called *Wat'é*. The Elkhorn River is also called by that name. The act of "showing" locations of former Ponca lands to the younger mind interested in history is an age-old Ponca tradition that has been carried on for generations. At these locations Grandpa Jack Peniska pointed out some burial grounds to KH.

Some years ago, a University of Nebraska–Lincoln official told me that Peter LeClair had said *Mąázì* was a burial ground on the current Niobrara State Park near Niobrara, Nebraska. (I met and knew Peter LeClair when I was a young man and had much respect for his knowledge of history. He and my father had taken me to several historic places in South Dakota.) I mentioned to the official then that *Mąázì* was on the north side of the Missouri River, where there are some yellow cliffs, but that it was not a burial site. It seems that a map called the "Evans Map" marked out those cliffs, which can be clearly seen today. Ponca *Hedúškà* songs also mention the location of *Mąázì* as a well-known battleground. The burial ground on current Niobrara State Park has no name. The physical location of the burial site is on high ground above the Missouri River. This location is near a more recent village site known as *Kúhewadè*, or "Place that causes one to be scared." Implied here is that the geographic orientation from the Ponca perspective is that the burial site fits perfectly into the traditional Ponca custom of burying their people on high grounds near their villages.

Tribal Taboos

The Ponca in past times never disturbed the burials of their relatives. They knew their location by some topographical system. But they never told any outsider where and who these people were. Some years ago, it was suggested that Joe Birdhead gave away information about these burials. Birdhead was known personally by KH, AMC, NC, JP, and other Southern Ponca who spent time among the Northern Ponca for several years in the earlier part of the 1900s. It was said that Joe

Birdhead was a man who understood the Ponca traditional ways and that he had possessed "medicine" of a sort. Because communicating information about burial sites to outsiders was forbidden, it is questionable that Birdhead actually did this. Additionally, the violation of respected tribal material culture (burials) would have been particularly disturbing to one who possessed tribal medicine.

Cross-Cultural Similarities

Dr. James H. Howard, a personal friend and tutor while teaching at Oklahoma State University, told me that his unbiased opinion was that the Ponca among other tribes came from a like-cultural group from the East and Southeast following the dispersion of those cultures. The schemes of study he related were the language pattern and other cultural patterns. It seems that most of the tribes emerging from the Southeast count by fives instead of using the decimal system. The Ponca count by fives. This is only one example of the similarities. The tribes from the East and Southeast had some common characteristics in their languages and culture, although the languages could be quite different. In the state of Nebraska, there are many burial sites. In some cases, the burials of different tribes appear to be the same.

These burials to date have been attributed to other tribes by some archeologists and anthropologists, but these conclusions remain questionable.

Changes in Folklore and Customs

When I spoke with the elders, the subject of burials came up. I asked if the Ponca used the scaffold-type burial. They said yes, but the Ponca had used other methods of burial in earlier periods. Gradual changes occurred in the culture, namely, ceremonies and rites, over a span of time. Visionary and external tribal influences from various groups made an impact on the people when they entered the plains.[1] The Ponca who established permanent villages with Mǫít'i, or "earthen lodges," ultimately adopted the plains tipi. These onetime farmers adapted to the plains, where tribes were more mobile. The scaffold burial was practical and useful. For convenience's sake, cache pits were also used. The ancient burial custom in which the individual was sat up and covered with poles and dirt also disappeared. The abandonment of this practice brought about religious rituals and ceremonies never before used. Methods for addressing the tribe's needs were apparently based on respect for the earth and the actual or real needs of the people, that is, physical and spiritual needs. Former practices then evidently changed. The elders said the scaffold burial had its purpose and was an adaptation to plains influence.

Ceremonies have also changed during the last century. In the 1940s a Ponca relative, Albert Makes Cry Jr., chose to live in the white community following World War II and did not return to the Southern Ponca Reservation until 1995. As a Ponca child, he had learned tribal songs, ceremonies, and dance. Returning to the reservation in 1995, he attended the Annual Ponca Powwow. He said, "I understood and knew the songs they were singing, but I didn't know what they were doing out in the arena. They appeared to be a different tribe. I didn't see any of the old Ponca ritual procedures." This was after only a period of fifty years. Admittedly, pan-Indianism took much from each tribe in the twentieth century, but it is clearly evident that cultures do change.

Songs Tell Stories as Do Remains

In the mid-twentieth century, two outstanding singers and oral historians recorded the songs of the Ponca people. Some songs are for the women's Ponca Warrior Dance, which is commonly called the Scalp Dance. These songs confirm the assertion that the Ponca did not scalp their enemies. They took the whole head. The Indian sign language gesture describes the Ponca by drawing your right hand, face up, across your neck. This is symbolic of cutting the head off. The Ponca are also known as *P'á másè* (head cutter). One song speaks of *Žįgá P'ežì*, or "Bad Boy," who was afraid of the head of a slain enemy. That man, evidently, was killed in a battle with the Ponca. *Heɖúškà* songs too have stories relating to the taking of heads of the enemy. In 1993 I read over the field notes of Perry Newell, supplied to me by the University of Nebraska–Lincoln. In the notes, I found a discussion about the Ponca practice of taking the whole head of the enemy.

Newell also pointed out that some of the pit burials had trade goods as well as other fragments of material culture. The Ponca, at that time, were burying their people in "jug-shaped" pits. As I understood his writing, the pits were the same as those of the earlier period.

Through observed and oral tradition, we have learned that the Ponca used a buffalo (bison) skull at their annual Sun Dance. During an earlier period, they had used a human skull of an enemy warrior that was painted red. This was pointed out to me in the 1960s by Sylvester Warrior, when I was gathering information on Ponca songs. This practice was discontinued before the Ponca's arrival in Indian Territory. It should be mentioned that the Ponca had a Sun Dance leader. He was in charge of the dance and all the paraphernalia used in the dance—including the skulls. Some were said to be very old.

At the old Ponca Fort site, according to the archeological studies, the ossuaries contained "headless bodies," and in one case the body "had been mutilated" and "jammed" into the rib cage. Joseph LeRoy, Northern Ponca, once told a story of how the Ponca had defended their territory by slaying some enemy warriors. After the Ponca had mutilated the body of one enemy warrior, they took the remains and dragged them about the camp. He said,

> Later one old woman gathered up the pieces where they had been thrown in the dirt and buried them, so the children wouldn't see them lying around. She told the people who were watching her: "They deserved this for attacking us when we wanted no war, but they are humans after all." (Howard 1995, 140)

If that were the case, in our ancient history it would be reasonable to suspect that those remains could have been placed there by a Ponca person. In contrast, if the area had been inhabited by others, the burials would have been very peculiar. Those people would have had to deflesh the bodies of their relatives and stuff them into the rib cage.

We respect and appreciate the schools of archeology and anthropology and their efforts to trace the Ponca people's history or to extend it further back. To dispel conjecture and myth and put credibility into the origins of the Ponca, oral history of the Ponca's legendary migration story and the several archeological factors surrounding that story indicate that many tribes, including the Ponca, emerged from a similar or common cultural group. Additionally, Ponca burial patterns from ages past could be similar to those of another tribe. Artifactual evidence would not be a factor since the Ponca could have lived in the place previously, known the burial grounds, and come back later to use them again. Copper, which was mined by the Chippewa, or *Wax-táwį*, as the Ponca call them, was found in the graves. The Ponca, in their oral history, tell of living along the Red River near what is now Winnipeg, Manitoba, Canada. They very well may have acquired the copper jewelry from the Canadian Indians or mined it themselves.

The foregoing concerns on the Ponca Fort site and the many other sites are Ponca, as we understand our history and traditions. As oral historians and traditionalists, we believe that the human remains were Ponca and buried by Ponca. Scientific studies are sometimes determined by a minimum of proof and need not be conclusive. Some of the ossuaries in question might have or might not have been the remains of other people. But if they were other than Ponca, probably (and there are no ends to probabilities) out of some ancient religious practice and respect—even for the enemy—the Ponca buried them.

The evolution of the burial styles among the people shows a number of successful transitions from one cultural period to another. The changes probably came about because of the socioeconomic pattern they were accustomed to in the East and Southeast, in addition to the change of the environment.

In historic times, other changes came about because of the Indian Removal Act. But cultures do not change so easily because the people tend to resist change. Through the socialization processes, they retained many of their customs in regard to the funerary rites. All burials today are the same as the conventional underground burials used throughout the United States. Former customs disappeared with the historical and cultural changes mentioned. The Ponca, who have retained many of their customs, have adjusted their beliefs to Judeo-Christian practices. Although the Christian influence is explicitly seen, some underlying Ponca customs are still practiced at funerals.

25

Ponca Medicine

Learning about medicines was a personal endeavor. Usually a person left the village to find out about medicines. This was called *Nážižą*. The closest English interpretation is "praying and fasting." However, sometimes the impetus to learn was staged by an elder who was knowledgeable of herbs and their medicinal qualities. Young men and women observing the bleeding technique for headaches, for example, might find it interesting and want to learn more. If the young person showed interest and talent, the elder gradually taught him or her more of those elements of medicine he was willing to part with. KH said some "Indian doctors would not give information" simply because one asked. "I was interested in some medicine that my uncle *Wažídadį* [Robert Washington] had. I kind of hinted around about it . . . but he didn't say anything. I guess he wanted to take it with him when he died. But Logan Cerre had some medicine that somebody gave to him. He used it to help people out when they was sick." KH said that among the Ponca, a young man at puberty went out from camp and fasted four days, and if any revelation was given to him, he then would become a doctor. The elders said a person kept his revelation to himself until it was proper to share it with the tribe. This was because that revelation was given to him and would be used by him only. Apparently, there were common medicines known by most people during those times, but the Indian doctor made the prognosis of a person's illness. He was the person who knew the relationship between a medicine and a man's illness or problem. The Native people viewed sickness both physical and spiritual. The elders said the basic human physiology was understood as a means to keep people well and alive. Some practitioners of bone setting among the ancient Ponca still remain a puzzle to modern-day experts.

KH told a story of how his grandfather, *T'áíkawahò*, who was also known as *T'ą́de Ámądį* (Walks on the Ground), received medicine from some natural and unusual phenomena. The story comes in two parts. The second part includes the elements of fasting and praying:

THE FIRST PART OF THE STORY

It was many years ago. *Niášiga ámà* ... the people ... used to do things in their own way. *Witígą áka* ... my grandfather he ... sometimes he go hunting by himself. This time he's long ways from camp. *Táxt'ì wí t'ędaìtè* ... he kill a big deer. Where he kill that deer ... there was big rocks sticking out of the ground ... close to a river. He lay that deer on one flat rock ... ledge. Its kind of a deep wash there ... trees ... ditch. He lay his belongings down next to where he's butchering that deer ... *táxt'ì dįkè p'ádaìte* ... While he's working ... something ... somebody's standing behind him. He tried to see him without turning all the way round, but that person or something ... moves when he look. When he try to look from his left side ... it moves so he can't see. When he look from his right side ... he can't see. While this is going on ... he keeps butchering the deer. After a while ... he see a little hand reaching for his arrows. He lay those arrows down next to where he's working. He knows what this is now ... *Mąnádìwadè akámà* ... it was a *Mąnádìwadè*. This is the little man that leads people off. But this one ... he's different. He's trying to steal grandpa *T'áíkawahò*'s arrows. Those people who knows about these things say that maybe that little man was trying to learn about something too. They say there are things that go on in the land ... *Mąžą́* ... that nobody knows about. So, my grandpa *T'áíkawahò* ... he heard from some old people that if you can catch one of those little men ... he's going to give you something ... gift ... power to do something. People who are good people ... maybe will find a good thing in it. *Niášigà, įdádą údą udíxidèàmà, įdádą̀ idái kì ... ídaedáì, énąì* [A person who seeks something that is good when he finds it, they say, has power over it and may use that power to help others]. After he figured out how to catch him ... he turn all at once when that little man didn't expect that. He caught him ... hold him close against his chest. He try to see his face ... he won't show it. He keeps hiding it. But grandpa ... he sees his clothes. He is dressed like himself ... buckskin clothes ... moccasins ... bow and arrows. Even though he can't see his full face ... he notice he has red paint on his cheeks. They say these little men are strong ... all muscle. While he's trying to get away . . . he talks to grandpa . . . he said in Ponca, *Žídé ádištàga* . . . [Elder brother, release me]. He ask my grandfather to let him go over and over. After a while . . . toward the end . . . he said, *Áništagàtedì, ábatàštì úwii't'amikè* [If you release me, some day I will give you a gift]. When he let him go . . . that little man left . . . just like disappear. So grandpa keep these things in his mind. He finish butchering that deer. *T'á štì gaxáitè* . . . dried some of that meat to take home.

SECOND PART OF THE STORY

When *T'áíkawahò* . . . my grandfather . . . was a young man . . . he liked to be around those men who know about medicine. This was after he catch that little man . . . *Manádiwadè*. One time they told him he ought to go out . . . away from the camp . . . *Nážizà* . . . pray . . . don't eat for four days. When you finish praying . . . they told him . . . something is going to be shown to you. So he did that. Those old Indians . . . back in those days . . . pray to *Wak'áda* all the time. They do that in the morning . . . when they do something during the daytime and when they get ready to sleep.

During one foggy morning . . . he was long ways from camp . . . he woke up and got ready to travel some more. When he came to a little hill . . . he saw someone coming in the distance. So he lay down and waited. He thinks that maybe . . . it's either an enemy or ghost. He don't know. But he's ready to do whatever he has to do. When that person got closer . . . he noticed that he was not a full-grown person, but a little man. The little man spoke first . . . and said, "*Kagè, détà dišà ší ái. Áwikìpà atí*" (Friend, they said that you were coming this way. I have to come meet you). "*Ádáwahagà. Ìdádą udánetè, wípahàtamikè*" (Follow me. What it is that you are looking for, I am going to show it to you). So my grandfather followed him . . . through all kinds of places. He said that little man led him across country he never seen before. He crossed creeks . . . rivers . . . and hills. Finally, they come to a river where there was a sand bar. At one place . . . *Nidágaxà* . . . where the driftwood was piled up . . . they stopped. The little man spoke again, "*Kagè, agátií hà*" (Friend, we are here). He said he had to squeeze between some logs . . . in that driftwood. Then he had to crawl . . . some kind of tunnel in the ground. That driftwood . . . right next to a high cliff . . . is where he went. He said that he went inside that cliff. Inside . . . there was lots of room in there . . . like a big cave . . . he could stand up. In that cave . . . there were many of those little men. They all welcomed him there . . . make him feel welcome. He said that the man who brought him there . . . gave him a seat . . . told him not to move around. He was real hungry because they traveled long ways. They brought him food . . . all kinds of food . . . meat, different kinds of fruit and nuts. For four days he stayed with them . . . ate with them and watched them. They showed him lots of different kinds of tricks. One of them even picked up the fire from that fireplace and threw it to another. They did things like that and showed him . . . how to doctor . . . help a sick person. After those four days were up . . . that little man brought him out. He brought him back through a different way . . . back to that place where he first met him. The little man told him to go home . . . get ready . . . then go east . . . *Mí' édǫbe t'adišǫ* . . . toward the sunrise. When he gets to a place where there is a tree with a big limb that sticks out toward the east . . . he told him to sit there for four days. He can't eat . . . has to sit still. What he wants . . . it's going to come to him.

So he went on home and did what that little man told him to do. He said he found that tree . . . he sat there for four days. On that fourth day, he said all kinds of animals came up to him. Even birds come to him . . . land on his hand . . . shoulders. Deer, elk, and other big animals like buffalo . . . and all small animals too . . . rabbits, squirrels, raccoons . . . all come close to him. He got up and walked around them . . . touched them. After that he went home. *T'áíkawahò*, my grandfather, was a great doctor. Some people said he was what the Ponca call *Manǫ́diwadè ídaedè*. That means he understand those little people that they gave him the gift for healing people. We don't know what kind of medicine he had. Those old Indians . . . back then . . . they don't tell. Some Poncas said he was also *Ịgdǫ́ ídaedè*. That means he knows about the weather. When he got old enough . . . he married. He had six children. He named them after what happens in the weather. He called my father *Gakúwịxè*. That means "Clouds moving in different directions that come before a storm." His other children were *Tidétigdè* . . . Makes Noise, means thunder in the distance; *Nudǫ́ Mǫdị* . . . means clouds rolling on the ground coming before the storm; *Ganǫ́žị ubíxǫ* . . . Sudden Strong Rain Then Sprinkle; *Ịgdǫ́ sábè* . . . Black

Cloud; and *Niágiwaḍè* ... Let Us Get Water, his daughter. What he knows about medicine ... he didn't pass it on.

The summation of these two experiences suggests that a Ponca doctor must be an upright person with compassion for his fellow tribesmen, and a person who wants a gift from nature must desire it and have patience to acquire it. Penicillin, for example, was discovered many generations ago by Canadian Indians. How it was acquired probably will never be told. Contrarily, in modern times, the one who found the use of penicillin in his laboratory and subsequently released it to the medical field was acclaimed as the benefactor in making the discovery.

In this instance, the story of *T'áíkawahò* teaches us that the learning process comes from nature. Accordingly, nature, in its ways, presents the gift. It is apparent that *T'áíkawahò* had knowledge of certain medicines as well as curing techniques because of much discussion centered on him. In connection with this, the teaching method under the old system included other uses of the mental processes. KH said if a young man desired to accomplish something in his life he had to discipline himself early in life. Part of the procedure to attain the status of knowing, he said,

> You first have to put away fear ... *Wanápapatè itéḍagà*. Then notice things all around you ... wherever you are. Even the smallest things ... they're there for a purpose. Sometimes ... you see menfolks standing around talking. They don't look at each other ... it's part of the way. *Pącà amà* ... the Ponca, they want to know ... *Gíwáḍišnà áì* ... things clear to self, they say ... they want to see without turning their head. To do that, you have to discipline yourself. They say if somebody does this ... a person can become a big warrior ... know something.

Again, training was given only to those persons who were actively seeking to find an answer to problems of the tribe. A person with knowledge of medicine was held in high esteem among the Ponca and sometimes feared by others. The Ponca, according to KH, always say that "they used their medicine for the good of the tribe." Even though the Ponca doctors had expertise in areas of modern-day medicine, they were not considered equal to the modern-day physician. In fact, white doctors often minimized the Indian contribution of medicines and viewed Indian men of medicine as superstitious and inferior to modern medicines. However, Virgil Vogel (1990, 6) wrote, "Dr. Erwin Ackerknecht has declared that there are no good modern monographs on Indian medicine. What is especially lacking is a study of the extent to which American Indian remedies and therapeutic practices have been adopted by white society." He also cited instances in which American and South American Indians contributed hundreds of plants possessing medicinal properties. These medicines are commonly used in modern times. Since we have all this anthropological data, Indians probably contributed much more to medicine than some would like to believe. The use of fauna, flora, and the concoction of various leafs, roots, plant stems, seeds, and so forth over several millennia would ultimately produce curative medicines. Interlocked with their medicines were their religious practices and interaction in the natural world. This system allowed Indian doctors to provide for the medical and spiritual needs of their people.

A story exists of a Ponca man who had been shot in the eye by a flintlock rifle in the 1800s. The ball had entered the eye and was lodged near his brain. An Army surgeon who looked at it considered the man a casualty. But the family of the man called for the Ponca doctor, who not only removed the ball but also saved the man's eyesight. The secret of how it was done was never disclosed.

At this writing there are no Ponca "medicine men" or doctors. KH, KCH, NM, AMC, NC, and AL could only recall events they personally experienced and testify to the lost art of healing among the Ponca. Although most of the ritualism is gone, they recalled the experiences vividly. In some ways, they were proud that they had some memory of it. NC could also recall the days when the Ponca had their own medicine. He said,

> Sure, the Poncas had medicine. And it was good too. When we were young and got hurt and had pains, we always had someone to go to for help. People come around now . . . and ask about what I know. I know some things, but what I have is mine. I don't go around telling about it. When a person is getting ready to die . . . I know it ahead of time. What that means . . . I don't know. I asked an old man about it one time, what it meant . . . but he wouldn't tell me. That's why I wear

dark glasses all the time. I don't want to see people . . . in a crowd. But I help some people . . . if I can.

Although NC wouldn't tell about his own medicine, he said the Ponca used herbs, bark, charcoal, bleeding, pressing, splints, sweathouses, and artificial resuscitation. He said for example, his use of herbs as medicines included the wild gourd. He called this plant *Niášigà mąk'ą́*, or "human being medicine," because the root resembled either the male or female form.

KH said before the root was dug out of the ground, special prayers were uttered. He stated that the root must not be cut haphazardly but with extreme care. He said if a person had pains in the shoulder (bursitis?), the part of the root resembling the shoulder was shaved off and boiled in water. The patient then drank the "tea." The root has a very bitter taste, as I remember personally, but it got some good results.

NC and KH said the beaver root was also boiled and used for intestinal pains. According to the elders, the plant was taken from standing water in ponds and lakes. It is commonly called a water lily. The Ponca called it *T'édawì*. Other uses included the common cold and respiratory problems. Other plants they mentioned were the prairie ground cherry, which was used for dressing wounds and stomach troubles, and choke cherry bark, which was used for diarrhea. Either the elders were limited in their knowledge of plants used for medicines or they did not want to share information. This was a strong indication that this period in the history of Ponca medicines was at its final stages.

M. R. Gilmore (1977) listed numerous plants and herbs used by the Ponca. About the use of cedar, for instance, he said, "Red cedar was widely used fumigant among plains tribes. The Dakotas, Omahas, Poncas, and Pawnees burned twigs and inhaled the smoke for head colds, while both patient and fumigant were enclosed in a blanket" (Gilmore, 1977, 63–64, 131).

The Ponca used cedar for various purposes. According to the elders, cedar was gathered at a particular time in the year to get the maximum aroma, but it could be picked anytime. The use of cedar is simple. The "needles" of the cedar are removed from the branches and are kept in a bag until they are needed. Certain people who were considered men of medicine and prayer used cedar as a preliminary step in the healing process. Usually live coals were made available to the doctor who burned the cedar. Smoke and aroma filled the dwelling, setting the stage for both client and doctor. It is said this ritual burning of cedar "cleansed the dwelling." Other medicines were provided for the client at this time, and appropriate prayers were offered (KH, NC, AMC, AL).

Cedar was also used to bring good feelings and thoughts to clients, families, and collective gatherings of the people. Some in modern times have considered this process "getting a blessing." This is similar to a practice of the Hebrew people, who believed that blessing meant prosperity and gain on one hand and peace and contentment on the other. For instance, on New Year's Eve, the Ponca in modern times usually sponsor a dance. At midnight an elder is selected to burn cedar. The collective masses of people gather, form a line, put their hands in the smoke, and "rub" the smoke on their heads, arms, chest, and legs. Some want the elder to "fan" them with his eagle feathers, blowing the smoke on their hands and body. This is commonly done in Ponca homes and in the Native American Church. Recently young married couples who have Christian church marriage ceremonies also wish to be both "smoked and fanned." This practice is a beautiful Native American gesture showing hope that the couple will both prosper and find peace and contentment. For funeral purposes, families who give their quiet allegiance to tribal custom usually ask an elder to burn cedar at their homes after the funeral experience. Each member of the family is fanned with the eagle feathers and cedar smoke. This is called *Wegáni*, or "to fan them." The elder usually gives the families encouragement to carry on their lives with hopes that their mourning will not be too long. He then offers a prayer to *Wak'ąda* for their guidance and comfort. The family usually reciprocates by giving the elder a gift of a Pendleton blanket or money. Cedar is also used by the elder of the family when a child is going to school or is in the process of moving away from home (the reservation). The elder of the family burns the cedar and fans the son, daughter, or grandchildren so that they will succeed in their effort in school or employment. According to KH, parents used to do this in the old days when a child went off to hunt or to pursue his medicine by prayers and fasting. On a personal note, when I first went out of state (and thereafter) to attend school, my father burned cedar and fanned me. It was assuring to know that he believed in this practice and had confidence that I would achieve my goals.

The procedure for being fanned is to stand before the elder or other designated person who is doing the fanning. Standing eastward with open hands in front of you, the elder takes his eagle wing fan (Xįdá mą́šą), touches the rising smoke, and begins fanning. His first gesture is to fan your upturned hands, although it is more like hitting your hands with the eagle feathers. The charcoals are usually to his right so he continues to touch the smoke and fan your arms and all parts of your outer body. At this point, he does not touch you with the fan but causes the smoke to blow upon you. In the end, he will touch your forehead at the hairline with the tip of his eagle fan. This is the final gesture. In a collective gathering of the people, sometimes a person with a physical disability might be present. If this person is sitting away from the place where people are being "fanned off," the elder will bring the smoke to him or her with his fan. Assuming he has the skill, he will sprinkle cedar on the coals and fan the live coals until smoke begins to rise. He will take his fan and gather up some of the smoke as if it were a solid substance, causing the smoke to proceed in the front of the fan. He'll take the smoke to the person with a disability and allow him or her to use the smoke accordingly (KH, NC, AMC, JP, AL).

Charcoal, as a healing medium, was used by the Ponca to effect certain cures. The significance of its use is unclear. Stories of modern Ponca attempting to use it end in calamity. Live coals are hot, and the old-time medicine men used to put the charcoal in their mouths before administering it to the patient. A modern-day Ponca man tried to use the live coal in a similar manner, burned his mouth, and was said to have had to drink soup for the next several weeks.

KH and KCH said that a person who might be suffering from headaches, pains, and sluggishness might call the Ponca doctor to take blood from that area where the trouble was centered. Bleeding techniques were also said to be good for high blood pressure and early symptoms of tuberculosis. When I spoke to tribesmen (as well as other tribal affiliates) about this, they stated that they had blood taken from their temples, upper backs, and so forth for purposes of relieving certain illnesses. The term in Ponca is Ágaxù. Modern Ponca sometimes referred to the technique as being "hacked." Originally, a flint knife was used to "hack," but it has been replaced with modern-day knives. The procedure, I was told, is as follows (my translation): "After prayers to the Maker are made, the doctor may explain to the client the purpose of taking blood. Then the large end of a bison horn is placed over the problem area and suction from the small end of the horn is initiated to draw blood to the surface of the skin. Then small incisions are made with the knife by hacking to cause bleeding." KCH, AL, and NC were knowledgeable of the bleeding procedures. Only AL knew and practiced vein cutting. Vein cutting, or *K'ą másè*, ended with the passing of AL. This procedure is a delicate one and was done by only those who were trained in the technique. Usually blood is taken from the wrists and ankles to relieve pressure.

Stomach problems were relieved by a technique called pressing. This was used for persons who suffered from a Ponca sickness called *músisì*. It was not made clear what this bothersome internal movement was, but it was relieved by the stomach pressing procedure. Other problems like indigestion and constipation may have been dealt with by pressing. A person suffering from appendicitis was never pressed.

Splints were used by the Ponca for broken bones. According to AL, after setting the bone, the doctor usually cut a piece of flat wood to fit the area and wrapped buckskin around the arm or leg. Wraps around the chest for broken ribs were also used. This helped the individual to move about and relieved some pain. In 1994, at the University of Nebraska, one of the faculty, Dr. Karl Rinehard, showed to me the remains of a Ponca Indian held at the university. Rinehard, being a forensic pathologist, said the individual had multiple fractures in the foot that had been restored to their normal position by someone. He surmised that the Ponca, before white contact, had exceptional knowledge of bone setting. He said, even in modern times, it is difficult to set broken bones of the feet and toes.

The *Í'ųpè* (sweat lodge) is used by many plains and southwestern tribes. *Í'ųpè* may be a derivative from the word *T'í'ųpè*, which means "to enter the house or dwelling." But the sweat lodge is used for many purposes. The Ponca used it for both religious and healing purposes. The following example is given by KH as used by the Ponca:

When I was a young man . . . someone don't like me. It's this person . . .
who had medicine, bad medicine . . . who did something to me. I can't
[couldn't] sleep . . . didn't know that person *gáǫxe* me . . . caused me to
be sick. My father noticed that I don't sleep well. He asked me about
it. I told him . . . I don't know. Later on . . . sent for medicine man . . .
Indian doctor . . . to come to help me. His name was *Akíšita Žįgà*, also
known as *Wanáše Žįgà* . . . Little Soldier. My father . . . he made the
arrangements for him to come. He fixed a place where Little Soldier's
going to sit . . . and where I'm going to sit. He tied a good horse outside . . . black horse . . . one with white ankles. Little Soldier's going to
take it. When he got there . . . he come to that horse and began to sing.
My father said, it's a song for healing. When he finished singing . . . he
come in . . . went straight to where he supposed to sit. Those old people . . . they know and understand those things. After he sit down . . .
he reach into his bag and got out his pipe. When he fill it up . . . he lit it
and began to talk and pray. His words were spoken to *Níkawasà* . . . we
don't use that word anymore. It's the spirit of *Wak'ą́da,* the Maker. He
said that *Níkawasà* said he would be there when he was needed . . . that
he would heal . . . when and where it's needed. *Edí danážįtatè ešédą.* He
asked *Níkawasà* to be there. After he said his prayer . . . he put a black
cloth on me. I didn't have anything on from the waist up. He started
probing my chest . . . at the same time he made sounds like animals.

After a while . . . he sat back . . . he said, *Núžįgà akà íxtà akà.* (The
boy has been *gáǫxè*). He talked to my father . . . he said he would make
everything all right. The next day they made . . . *Í'ųpè* . . . sweat house . . .
put hot stones in there. *Išágè nąbá ahí* . . . *Hágaškadè k'i T'áxtì Ská* . . .
Old Man Playing Chief and Old Man White Deer came there. Those
stones were real hot. The only clothes old man Little Soldier wore was
a breechcloth. Rest of us . . . bare . . . from the waist up. He took out
some cedar . . . dipped it in some water. He sprinkled it on the stones . . .
a big puff of steam went to the ceiling and come down. It was hot. He
did that about four times.

Then . . . from where he's sitting . . . he blew toward me. I felt that
heat hit me . . . I bend over. Again he made animal sounds. He blew
toward me four times . . . each time . . . tell me that every thing is going
to be all right. Then he told the other two men to blow on me. They
blew four times . . . then we went out. With that medicine he gave

me . . . and coming out . . . I feel cold. But that's the way it's supposed to be. Before he doctored me, I couldn't hold any food . . . never feel hungry. My mother cooked a big meal . . . he told me to eat. I tasted the food and started to eat. Everything is normal now. I never had that problem again . . . and sleep alright.

The sweat lodge was used for cleansing purposes as well. The Ponca used it for purification rites for some ceremonies. Some used it for taking sweat baths. There is a resurgence of the use of the sweat lodge in modern times. Its meaning in modern times, of course, has been modeled like the northern tribes. The sweat lodge or hut is easily constructed. It is a smaller version of the *T'iúdip'ù* (described elsewhere), and the roof is lower. In former times bison skins were used to cover the structure, but now it is not uncommon to use tarp.

The Ponca Doctor

The Ponca had held those people who knew about medicines in high regard because of their knowledge of the mind and medicine. They are called *Wazéde*, "one who cures." Their problem solving for sickness in treatment, medicine and spiritual care, cure, and peace of mind to their people was viewed as being a special interaction with nature and their Maker (KH). The concern for healing and helping their fellow tribesmen didn't bring them any wealth. But it did bring them into social prominence in the community. They were consulted in tribal matters as well as during times of sickness. In practically every facet of tribal life, that is, illness, game scarcity, the planting season, or anything affecting the people, the Ponca doctor was consulted. Significant to him was his medicine bundle. The peculiar object sometimes was made of the whole skin of the otter. Some who received medicine from animals and birds used their skins as a container for their medicines. Howard (1995, 101) mentioned that Otto Knudsen, a Northern Ponca, had said,

Once I asked old man Whiteshirt to come over and sing for me. I gave him something to eat and after we had finished, he went to work. He had one of those big gourds and he shook it while he sang. After he sang a while, he took up his pelican and began to hit me with the beak in different places on the body. It hurt! I hadn't figured on this. I just wanted to hear him sing.

The "sacred bundle" was the pelican skin and head. He evidently used it to heal people in his personal healing procedures. The peculiarity of the bundle bemuses those uninformed of other cultures and social forms.

In 1966 I visited some Indian Methodist pastors regarding Indian medicines. One of the ministers said the following:

> My wife had a severe pain in her left shoulder which left her arm useless. She had been under the care of several medical doctors. They couldn't help her, or even relieve her of her pains. One of the members of the congregation mentioned an Indian doctor who might be able to help her. Since she was hurting so much, I encouraged her to see the man. After discussing and praying about the matter with her, she consented to go. I watched him open his bundle and take out a black handkerchief that he placed over my wife's shoulder. Whatever type of medicine he used is something I didn't see. But he grasped something with that black handkerchief on her shoulder and placed it in an empty can. He said, "She'll be okay now." She hasn't had that problem since then.

At an earlier time, one "Old Lady" Gives Water was said to have spoken to newborn babies who may have fallen ill. The following story was related to me at one time or other by several elders (KCH, MC, AL, NC) who were acquainted with her and knew her special talents:

> There was a baby who wouldn't stop crying. The parents and grandparents didn't know what to do. Somebody came to visit them and said they should tell grandma [Old Lady Gives Water] about it because she knew how to "doctor" babies. Sometime during the day they sent someone to get her. When she came, she told them to leave her alone with the baby. After she had examined the baby, she called the parents in and told them that the child's feet were hurting. After removing the baby's shoes, the baby quit crying. I'd guess that the shoes she was wearing were too tight. (KCH)

Deducing that the child was wearing wrong-sized clothing seems simple. However, given the time and period of our people's introduction to Western culture, determining size and texture of material used for modern, store-bought clothing might have been a problem.

As a young man, Albert Makes Cry Jr. heard the following story of the same woman who was a tribal doctor. Albert was in his mideighties when he related the following account of her skills. He said his parents and other relatives used to call Old Lady Gives Water *Waú Xubè*. The Ponca word means "Spiritual Woman."

> We had a baby sister by the name of Josephine. When she became very ill, they took her to the hospital to see the doctor [modern medical doctor]. He and other health professionals could not find or determine the cause of her illness. She cried constantly. A member of the family said that they should call "Old Lady" Gives Water. When she arrived, she asked to take our baby sister outside the house. After she had been gone for a period, she came in and said that our sister told her that her head hurt and she was in deep pain across her shoulders. She gave her medicines to relieve her pain, but the sickness had advanced so far she was unable to provide a cure. Our sister passed away.

Albert added that Old Lade Gives Water and the other medical doctors did not have the medical knowledge we do in modern times, so his sister's death was caused by sources unknown to them.

A variety of home remedies were used well into the twentieth century. Some of these natural medicines, such as the root of certain cedar trees, were used for stomach and bowel troubles. KH said that he used this medicine after he had had difficulties with "stomach problems." (A doctor had previously told him he had "quick consumption." Defined by Webster's dictionary, in modern times consumption apparently was and is related to pulmonary tuberculosis.) After all was said and done, KH said the Indian medicines he used were the answer.

Gilmore (1977, 63–64) said, "Cedar fruits and leaves were boiled together and used internally to coughs. For a cold in the head, twigs were burned and the smoked inhaled." I, unfortunately, had the following experience with Indian medicines: Uncle Oliver Howe Sr. was a man who used many old Indian medicines. He told me when I was a young boy that he could "fix me up" with his medicine. I had a bad chest cold. He gave my father (KH) some skunk oil to rub all over my chest and neck. He did, and I smelled like a skunk for several days. I don't remember if I got well or if my parents just simply could not stand the smell. Regardless, they sent me to school every day. Every once in a while one of the other students would say, "I smell a skunk somewhere." No one came around me for a week or two.

When anyone had an earache, an elder would blow tobacco smoke into his or her ear. This was one of the common remedies used by many families in the tribe. Sometimes some sort of liquid solution was also put into the ear. AL, KH, AMC, and others said that in the old days a small amount of a child's pee was put into their ears and then smoke from tobacco and kinikinick was blown into their ears. This was supposed to bring healing.

Ailments

Known ailments common to all mankind were described by the location of the discomfort. This is probably oversimplified given that discomfort in some parts of the body can be symptomatic of a more complicated condition. The generic term for sickness is *Wakéga*. The elders gave the following names for various ailments, types of sickness, and conditions affecting the body:

B'áxet'à	diarrhea
Díxe	mange (refers to animals)
Díxe	smallpox
Hí' níe'	toothache
Hižú nié'	gum disease
Húxp'è	common cold
Íha uxágà	chapped lips
Įšt'ásnì	sore eyes
Mą́ge niè	tuberculosis
Múdadà	throbbing
Músisì	internal pulsation
Ną́de wađaskabè	digestive problems
Ną́de wakèga	heart ailment
Nąškí nié'	headache
Nąxíde nié'	earache
Níxa nié'	stomach ache
Núde nié'	sore throat

P'á' šudáđè	nose bleed
Únièt'ą p'èžì	sexually transmitted disease (modern term)
Wahí niè	arthritis
Wamíuskíđè	diabetes
Wéđažì	blindness
Žuđį́š'į̀	Parkinson's disease or something like it
Žužíde	measles

Other words related to various maladies are listed below:

B'axđį́	mucus or snotty nose
Đa'í'í'đà	itchy
Điú'	scratching
Íbà	swollen
Ík'ip'ahązì	comatose
Įšt'abđì	tears, associated with eye infection
Įšt'áxđį̀	mucus, associated with eye infection
K'igđázù	recovering
Múdadà	throbbing
Músisì	pulsation
Náxeskàži	dizzy
Nié'	hurt/ache/pain
Niú điá'	can't breathe
Sná'	scarred
Wač'éga	tender
Wahíđagè	crippled
Wamíút'è	bruised
Xđí'	puss
Zunákadè	fever

The means whereby a person is cured is usually the focus of our attention. The ritual or ceremonialism of administering a medical procedure sometimes has hidden the real source of cure. Those who are affected by the pomp and circumstance of a religious ceremony in the high Christian church can very well miss the real purpose. So it is with those who observe Native American rites and ceremonies. In our anxiousness to prescribe a dictum of how it was done, we no doubt miss the main ingredient and will probably never know. But what is significant is the multiplicity of narratives from many sources telling of a cure's historic pronouncement and veracity. Living and coping with life's many problems, be they physical, mental, or spiritual, gave way to learning for the Ponca.

Some Problems That Caused the Loss of Indian Medicines

The main problem is obvious. White medical personnel arrived on the scene in the mid-1800s, and the longtime tribal practices were replaced with a new perspective on what medical processes entailed. The then-modern medicines seemed to overshadow the Indian medicines. Additionally, documented reports from 1869 and 1871—at the time the Ponca still lived in Nebraska—show that U.S. Army surgeons excavated the remains of Ponca Indians somewhere along the Niobrara River or Ponca Creek in Nebraska. The report states that they took the remains from the "old agency." The actions of the white doctors were detestable to the Ponca Indian doctors and their people. These remains ultimately ended up at the Smithsonian Institution in Washington DC. Their original intent apparently was to use the remains for studies in the medical field. (Modern-day studies include what the Native American Graves Protection and Repatriation Act termed invasive analysis. This process is used to determine what kind of diet the Indian people had, what kind of work they did, how healthy a particular individual was or what kind diseases existed, and so forth.)

The tribal doctors witnessed some of these white doctors taking bodies and bones. They were unable to object because the army kept their people under heavy guard. Although the Ponca doctors did not abandon their customary practices immediately, they were probably repulsed by the white doctors. Additionally, when the tribe was removed from its lands in Nebraska and South Dakota, it had difficulties in practicing medicine. One problem lead to another. KH mentioned in one story from the earlier part of the century (1900) that a "medicine man" kept on causing his wives to become ill. At that time, the Ponca still practiced polygyny. An Indian doctor was apparently called from the Comanche Tribe. During a Native American Church service, he used his medicine to cure the young woman. But in the process, during the night, he also described a man standing outside. He said, "A man is standing outside behind me. He is wearing a large hat, overcoat, and a long brown scarf around his neck. He has red yarn woven in his braids." Those present knew whom he had described. Although he had never seen the man before, he had described the woman's husband. The Comanche doctor further stated that the husband was putting "bad medicine" upon him, but he said he would finish "what he was doing" (KH). After he had returned to Comanche country, the family of the young woman received a letter from him saying that she had died from the Ponca man's medicine. Another incident occurred between two Ponca doctors. At a tribal gathering and dance, the two men stood together. One of them jokingly made a statement to the other who took it as an insult. Perhaps they had differences before this encounter. One man said, "*Eyáxtì íyè ądáià. T'enąhà, ḍat'ętanikè*" (How is it that you have the gall to say something to me like that? Look here! You are going to die!). People standing nearby became fearful, but they heard the other man retort, "*Áhą. At'ętamikè, ḍążą, ḍí ḍat'ę k'ì wagḍíškà ḍíḍat'ę t'amà*" (Yes. I am going to die, but you, when you die insects will kill you).

Both men did die soon afterward. Relatives remember the conditions in which they died. Indeed, insects emerged from the body of one of them. A horror story? This is an account of what some practices or medicines could do. It is no wonder that the next generation refused to accept any medicines from the elders. One man who practiced medicine said he had a small animal that lived within him. Before he died, those present saw a small snake come from him. He stated, "Well, it has gone back to where it belongs." Were these incidents of Indian medicine during this period, or were they experiences of witchcraft learned from some of the hill people who came and lived among the Indian people? One thing is certain: these practices are no longer among the Ponca people.

Other medicines used by the Ponca were described as "very good." The use of Ponca medicines has faded into the past. Only memories vaguely describe certain incidents of people being healed remain. Various plants, roots, and seeds are no longer used among the Ponca, and the rattles and ritual drums are now silent.

26

Journey to the School House

A multiplicity of social problems and handicaps were brought on by the domination of the Euro-American culture. The direct involvement of the federal government—through the War Department, the former Indian Department, and present-day Bureau of Indian Affairs—was and is said to be responsible for the great difficulties Indian people have encountered. It has been said that when attempts at genocide failed, the government began to initiate the processes of acculturation and socialization. The processes perpetrated losses for the people, namely, their land, their way of life, and their self-determination. This chapter will reassert and reinterpret some of these problems that affected the learning experience, review some aspects of the Ponca teaching and learning processes, and note some successes in the education experience.

When their economic system began to change, the Indian people were unprepared to enter a socioeconomic world unfamiliar to them. The agricultural Ponca knew how to grow things and hunt. This was their way of life. They knew nothing about competitive economic enterprise, much less having social and business marketing skills to negotiate trade of livestock and grain. Trade agreements for fur were the only business transactions they made that exposed them to European trade goods. They failed to enter mainstream America because they could not adjust culturally, socially, and economically.

This was the beginning of social disorganization, social maladjustment, and the distortion of their world order. World order, used in this sense, is how things such as customary modes of behavior, varied types of relationships, mores, ethics, religious rites, and ceremonies are arranged in the world. Included also is the sociopolitical and economic status of the tribe that provides freedom of movement and protection from the enemy. Adherence to tribal laws and ethics, as well as foreign restrictive laws and mores, affected personal adjustment.

Dual standards in one's world are ineffectual when understanding and knowledge of one standard is disrupted and the other is presented in a disorganized way. When it came to the laws of the white world, there was much misunderstanding. Yet these new and foreign laws were making the Ponca's own laws obsolete.

Some Ponca Indian said in the late 1800s, "The white man can do anything if there was no law against it. But the Indian can do only what the law permits him to do." Highlighting the confusion, Chief Standing Bear was said to have observed: "Are there two laws? Is there one for the white man and one for the Indian?" Early on, the Ponca people were required to pay back hundreds of dollars to early white farmers for destroying their farm buildings and house on formerly shared hunting grounds. For the white farmer, it was acceptable to take and use formerly Indian lands because their law said it was acceptable. Indian people frequently violated the federal laws, and charges were filed against them. The laws and rules of the non-Indians pertaining to people were not clear to Indians nor was there any clarification of the penalties imposed upon them. Unfortunately, penalties were imposed upon them to alter their behavior. The list of laws of the dominant society probably seemed as innumerable as the stars. Herein lies the dichotomy that affected the Ponca's success in entering mainstream America. Consequently, these conditions impeded the acceptance and practice of many laws regulating the dominant society. In addition to the laws, other cultural components to be learned in the new world included a foreign language, a multiplicity of social mores, and various religious philosophies.

To implement the standard Euro-American mores among the Indian population required acceptance, interpretation, and finally, practice. The Ponca understood and practiced their tribal ethics governing personal behavior. Because Ponca ethics and mores conflicted with American ethics and mores, the Ponca became a people in a quandary. Deviating from the Euro-American norm, these perplexed, suspicious, and doubtful people became resistant to the socialization process imposed by the government. On the reservation, many people showed evidence of social and psychological disorders. In modern times, sociologists have interpreted those problems as resulting from the Ponca's "warrior image." Some of our people made incorrect decisions because of misinformation or miscalculated interpretations. And that is a far cry from the genuine "warrior image." To adopt another culture by abandoning one's own is unreasonable even from the most elementary point of view. However, the hard hand of the government did cause change. Inculcating another way of life through forced acculturation and socialization was the beginning of the destruction of the Ponca way of life.

The Ponca people's culture had been ingrained into the generations over many centuries. It was hardly reasonable to think that the people would forsake their own ways and take on a new way completely. During the period when they were losing their identity, there was an undercurrent of rebellion. Not the kind that speaks of revolution or war, but of a quiet, solemn, and unuttered statement of dissent. Big Snake, for example, cognizant of his brother's case in Nebraska in 1879, left the reservation periodically without permission. Even though this man lost his life, he received praise from his tribesmen. According to the elders, he was a man who challenged many unjust decisions handed down by the government. Had he become complacent about the new way, he may have been criticized. In this case, he did one of the most common things in life. He traveled at will—without the permission of the federal authorities (KH, NC).

During the transition period, many problems centered on unfamiliar laws and ideologies. For example, for five hundred years, the white people had experimented with laws that founded the American education philosophy. Historically, the American education system was formulated to meet their specific needs.[1] The determined Europeans had strong desires for freedom from tyranny and for capitalistic gain. The educational philosophy in America went through many changes, but eventually found a practical avenue for making money called "supply and demand." The criteria for instituting the American educational system drew on centuries of exploration in philosophy, religion, government, and economics. However, during this time, individual politicians working in some capacity for the government were always present with no plan or system on how to educate other cultures. But the Indian people were a source of revenue for the government. Reservations brought many politicians, private entrepreneurs, and other white workers good profits. For example, a report in the *Arkansas City Traveler* (Arkansas City, Kansas) indicated that lots of lumber and other building materials were bought from private companies with federal dollars in 1879 and the 1880s to build a school and homes for employees for the Ponca Indian Boarding School. Building an education system for personal gain is a selfish economic venture and is just one example of American capitalism.

Inasmuch as the Indian school was an economic venture, the well-paid personnel evidently did teach. The teaching method was not an immediate success. For years it didn't work, and the causes of the failure were conclusively identified by the experts and were stated in one sentence: "Indians don't think like we do." Subsequently, one-lined statements were also made to correct the problem. Some of these statements were as follows:

"Give an Indian a chance and he'll do as well as anybody."

"If Indians had the same opportunity, they'd do as well as anybody."

"Indian people are capable when they have the right incentive."

"Substantially increase their educational opportunities and they'll do well."

"Get him off of the reservation and show him how the white man lives and he'll do exceptionally well."

These among many other statements were somewhat reasonable and challenging but did not suggest specifically how to fix the problem. No significant plans were put into effect. However, the Ponca did, through extreme discipline, learn to read. In retrospect it is obvious that the teaching method did not work because the Ponca did not understand the dominant culture and its demands.

In modern times, most college students have adjusted and have done exceptionally well (see chapter 27). According to tribal records of students entering college, many were married men and women.[2] Some of the women were single parents. The records show that more of these students completed their degree programs than did the younger students. These older students were more settled and had a better understanding of the economic demands of the modern world, and they had to decide what to do with their lives.

Although the time, culture, and conditions are not the same, valid processes of learning in former times included a period of deciding one's life's calling. This resulted in a stable adult life. Thus, beginning at an early age, the mastery of the language and simultaneous learning of the social mores provided specific interpretations of life (KH, NC, JP, AL). People who were said to be settled successfully coexisted with their fellow tribesmen. In this respect, the integrated ideology of language, tribal philosophy, and religious order suggests to us the basic premises of the tribal orientation to world order.

The Ponca teaching processes entailed specific items to be taught. In each instance, the information given was precise to each individual. Under this type of tutelage, the Ponca learned the appropriate behavior and their place in the world order (KH, NC). Because the Ponca learning system was part of their lives, the modern method of teaching and learning was hindered. The following sections reiterate some aspects of the Ponca learning processes and culture under the tribal order as well as in the modern setting.

The Ways of Learning

When the Ponca people still lived in the North Country, their children were taught in the true Ponca tradition. They were breastfed and spoken to by their mothers. According to KH, KCH, NC, and AMC, the early stages of learning were structured around the children's immediate surroundings and were overseen by their mothers. A mother taught her children to keep away from the fireplace, to behave at mealtime, to respect items in the dwelling and other members of the household. She taught them the importance of sitting still, being quiet, and not wandering off. The patriarch, grandfather, or father set rules in the household as well as for expected behavior in public. These rules were enforced by both mother and father. Grandparents also had a role in the training of the children.

Certain crafts were taught to each succeeding generation. Girls learned from other female relatives and friends of the family. The art of (porcupine) quillwork, for instance, was done by women. Natural dyes were identified and named by female relatives and shown to young girls, who later would be sent out to gather them. Identifying plants in their natural state as well as at their mature stage was taught to both young men and women (KH, NC). Tribal or clan designs were taught to children at an early age. Designs of their own choosing came later, as they developed their ability to create some variation of their clan affiliation. Women also made everyday and ceremonial clothing and cooked for the family. Girls participated in these activities, learning these skills early in life. There was a method for processing meat for which men and boys were responsible, although women were involved. But both men and women cooperated in dehydrating foodstuffs. Young people learned these techniques by helping their parents.

As boys grew older, they were taught by their fathers and other male members of the family. Older brothers played an important role for younger brothers because, whatever they did, the younger brothers did the same. Men also made various crafts that were taught to younger men. Some of these crafts included the techniques for making bows and arrows, shields, and various dwellings; tanning hides (both men and women did this); transplanting trees and certain other plants; and gardening (KH). Howard once told me that in his personal research on ancient village sites, there was strong evidence of the transplanting of various plants.

Children also learned about tribal mores and ethics, and much of the learning seemed to be centered on respect for the natural things of earth. It is said that through interaction with nature and other persons, young people summed up a right or wrong behavior. Hearing stories about people who through some unique human situation solved problems also contributed to children's learning experiences. Some of these types of stories were very effective in the learning processes. These kinds of stories were told by parents, grandparents, or visiting relatives or friends. Many of these stories were bedtime stories called *Hígà*. Some stories were about the *Íštinikè*, a mischievous creature who was always committing misdeeds. There was also the *Maščíge*, a certain rabbit who did good deeds. But there is also a story of a rabbit that had bad manners and did bad deeds. There were stories of real or legendary people who also did good deeds. They are characterized as people who accomplished heroic deeds of bravery. These are stories of men who hunted alone and made an unusual kill or defeated the enemy single-handedly. In connection with some of the stories, the Ponca devised a means of retaining knowledge of actual or real incidents by singing about it, as mentioned earlier. The songs were designated to those young men who had interest in history and possessed the ability to sing (KH, AL).

Language, a Key to Learning

A good teaching method is derived from the use of terminology that has understandable meanings and is oriented toward one's world order.[3] With this in mind, this section will concentrate on several examples of language uses and experiences wherein every tribal member understood his place in society. In former times, the learning and use of the Ponca language encompassed that which the Ponca understood and lived.

Through their language, the Ponca interpreted their world. The elders pointed out some common words that entailed more than that which meets the eye. For example, the terms for a tribal hunt is *Páca áma ábaye gaxą adái*. The words relate to an organized bison hunt, but in general use, the term means "The Ponca hunt as a group."

For obvious reasons, preparation and organization for the hunt was motivated by experiences of the past. The foreknowledge of possible mass hunger in the future required the tribe to organize their economy by setting times for the hunt. The communication of individual to individual summed up the need (KH). When the clan leaders were certain that game was present, they designated the proper time to proceed. The call to hunt, "*Wanąsedè ugípì!*" means "The place of the hunt is full." This did not simply mean that there indeed was game out there, but to a greater degree, it informed the people that it was time to prepare for the hunt. The preparation for a hunt entailed necessary and careful procedures. Appropriate prayers were offered to the Creator from the start. This was done to assure the hunters that *Wak'ąda* would give them guidance and success. The plans for the hunt would determine what method would be used to make a kill or mass kill. Those who knew how to approach the bison would be called on to give direction. According to the elders, there were several ways to kill bison—individually or collectively. Some of these methods were making a kill from a horse; approaching the bison as another animal (some wore the skin of the coyote or wolf) to get a close shot; and guiding the bison to a known kill site where the animals were herded into a ravine or over a bluff. The plans would also determine how many cows, calves, and bulls would be taken. The Ponca believed that the bison cow had tender meat as did the calves and that their skins were soft. The bow and arrows (and related equipment), hunting horses, housing, the hunters, and their families were all part of the hunting trip. When the actual hunt was taking place, there was no time for repairing equipment; therefore, all preparation was done before the hunt. The call to hunt then "*Wanąsedè ugípì!*," a vital part of the learning process, secured and stabilized the group for the hunt (KH, NC, JP, AL).

The matters of language are relative to one's environment. Communication is never altered. But because his surroundings were constantly changing, a person in the Ponca world had to understand the demands his environment was making on him. So from the beginning phases of his life, he was taught the various levels for his existence and the language it required. Some of these statements and terms were related to a level of understanding that would take him to the next level. Take, for example, a young man wanting to learn the things of a warrior and of medicine. According to the elders, there were several steps. The first was *Wanąpažìgá*, or "do not be fearful." The second was *Wažį̀ tè ská gikídagà*, or "develop a clear mind." The third was *Mąžą́ kè ígipahągà*, or "know your country." The fourth was *Ųkíte ámà wágazù wébahągà*, or "know your enemies." Being fearless, or *Wanąp'aži*, does not mean a person can be foolish and do something foolhardy. Close scrutiny of one's environment and enemy and the anticipation of what can happen at any given time entailed a careful analysis of the world the Ponca lived in.

Human error too was reduced. Anytime we ventured into the wilderness, KH used to tell us as young boys, "watch where you step, but look around you and see where you are." Broken legs and ankles were not part of growing up. Still, some would dare to test the limits of their physical stamina. It was tempting to jump from a high bank into a sandy dry riverbed. Doing that could easily result in a sprained ankle or broken leg, but simply sliding down the embankment made more sense. Doing something foolish by testing one's strength is not fearlessness. However, to face the enemy unflinchingly was a mark of fearlessness. KH, AMC, NC, and JP said certain members of the Ponca *Heđúškà* society called *T'ę́ nápažì* (Not afraid to die) exemplified fearlessness by their willingness to fight to the death in a war experience.

When elderly men visited and spoke with one another, they had a significant mannerism of not making eye contact. Always looking off into the distance, they spoke, laughed, and sometimes became solemn. Through the development of their peripheral vision and mind (*Waží tè ská gikidagà*), these Ponca men were able to see the actions and reactions of other individuals. Through the use of hearing, they could sense movement from any direction. Being dependent on their senses for their survival, the acuity of their hearing became highly developed (KH, NC, JP, AMC). According to the elders, what Indian hunters were able to perceive through the stimulation of their nasal olfactory nerves also would be considered phenomenal today. I personally went deer hunting with a man from Arizona a few years ago. We sat to rest after we had traveled for some miles to a place where there were deer. We sat for a moment, it seemed, when he said, "Okay, let's keep going." Then suddenly he said, "Wait! Hold on a minute! There's a deer up ahead!" I looked but couldn't see anything but scrub cedars and sand. "He's up ahead toward that big clump of bushes over there," he whispered. At least, I knew the wind was in the right direction. After we walked about another twenty-five yards, he said to stop again. Standing very still, he pointed up ahead slightly to the right. Among the cedars stood the deer. Without waiting, he drew a bead on him and knocked him down. I asked him, "How'd you know he was there in first place?" He said, "You can smell him, they smell bad." A clear mind and undefiled physical senses probably is the answer. He lived in Arizona on an Indian reservation all his life.

The environment (*Mąžą́ kè ígipahągà*) the Ponca understood ranged from their knowledge of rivers to forestlands, plains, and mountains. Common to the people, of course, was their immediate territory. Children brought up in Ponca territory found no difficulty coexisting in their natural surroundings, the land and streams. They learned to respect the things of nature: the earth, plants, and animal life. Unlike the modern family, to a greater extent, they understood plant growth and the birthing habits of wildlife. KCH told us, as children, that we should not kill rabbits and squirrels during the spring and summertime. She also taught us that there were only two weeks in the spring when we might find edible fungi called morel. The Ponca term is *Mikáe xdí*. Learning about the environment included knowing the names of plants, animals, and landmarks and their locations. In modern times, wild blackberries still grow on the Ponca reservation in Kay County, Oklahoma. There are many places in the North Country where a great number of chokecherry trees are located. Today there have been chokecherry trees transplanted at rest areas along major highways in the northern states. The traditional learning process was one that enabled individuals to know where to find food in the days of our ancestors.

Knowing your enemies, or *Uk̇íte ámà wágazù wébahągà*, was of importance to those who traveled.[4] On one occasion, my great-grandfather Cries for War was recorded by Dorsey (Ðási) as saying that they were highly outnumbered when the Pawnee attacked them. This attack on a small number of Ponca took place after Cries for War and another boy had taken some vegetables from a Pawnee village. Of the group, only he and three others survived. Knowing your enemy was not restricted to knowing the powers at hand; it was also being aware of their lifestyle and daily practices. This story shows that as a young boy, Cries for War failed to understand the enemy. As he matured, however, he practiced more caution when he traveled. In the story of *Mąčú Žįgà* (Little Bear), we see a mature warrior, his strategy in surveying the enemy camp, and the multiple successes of his achievements. He knew his environment as well as his enemy. His success depended on this foreknowledge.

This discussion of terms and statements that imply a responsible reaction to any given situation leads to another process of communication. Body movements are a part of every civilization. The next discussion shows how the Ponca people used this medium.

Body Movement (Sign Language)

Probably the most obvious of body signals as an influencing factor in learning is the Ponca sign language. The elders said gestures were predominantly used by the plains tribes. Since hand gestures are interpretable, they play an important role in the teaching process. Additionally, there are specific body movements that lead to an understanding of the acts of another person. They are part of the learning process. During my early college years, I had an assignment on "body movement" as I understood it. The following was part of my paper:

Humans of all shapes, sizes, creeds and races send signals to other persons with certain types of body movements. The signals or movements tell us to prepare, dodge, relax, stop, go, come, etc., or they tell us something about another person, group or thing. We read signals all the time because they are part of our human development and socialization. Without them we would be helpless to determine a proper reaction to a situation. When a person waves to me, for instance, I usually wave back. This means that we are friends. More complex signals are sent from our bodies and are read by the receiver or we may read signals sent by others. If a person approaches me with a smile, I know our encounter will be a friendly one, but if the approach includes a clenched fist I should prepare for another type of encounter. Eye movement too may signal friendship or enemy, anger, hate, etc. Facial expressions tell us if a person is happy, unhappy, distressed or perplexed. The stance of a person also signals information without speech. A person, for instance, slouched in a chair may tell us he is tired or asleep. A person sitting on the edge of a chair tells us they are in a hurry, uneasy, nervous, or has a sore bottom. A person with hands on hips may be signaling readiness or may even be arguing with someone to prove a point. A standing person who is speaking to a crowd, rising upon his toes occasionally, tell us he is telling some truth as he fully understands it and is a high point in his talk. A gesture of the hands speaks a various language that describes, mimics, imitates, and shows peace. A nudge of the elbow followed by a nod of the head in the direction of a situation tells another to take notice. Handshakes too tell us friendship, sympathy and love, as well as nervousness, uncertainty and apathy. So on it goes, language without words, shaping our lives and lifestyle.

American Indians too had certain kinds of body signals that the Ponca used. Some factors that influence and aid in determining types of body signals include the environment, philosophy, and religion, as well as the family unit, clan, tribal, and intertribal groups. Perhaps the most significant of Indian body language is the use of hand gestures. Those of us who were raised by the elders know some of the hand gestures, but we have largely lost the usage of these gestures for everyday living. The use of hand gestures in former times was essential and determined outcomes of intertribal encounters (KH, NC, AMC,

JP, AL). The following examples and descriptions were given in the Ponca language by KH:

The show of a lifted bare right hand signifies peace upon an encounter with another people or person. If a person you haven't seen for a long time meets you, he may rub his open hands together. This is a sign that shows he is glad and happy to see you again. A clenched fist with the forearm extended forward along side of the body and brought down with a short but soft jerk signals for one to be seated. If a person places his curved hand at his right temple and draws it downward to his chest, he is referring to a male person. If he moves his right curved hand from his right front shoulder over and curling back over the right shoulder, he is referring to a female person. Both gestures are based upon the hairstyle of men and women. Ponca men wore their braids in the front, and Ponca women wore theirs in the back. If a person makes a circular motion with his right palm facing his stomach area, he is telling you that he is hungry. When you tell some kind of information or ask a question requiring a yes answer, the other person may answer in the affirmative by using the following gesture: His right hand with three outer fingers curled in and his pointing finger extended out with a slight curl, and the forearm elevated at a left 45 degree angle in front of the body with the pointing finger in the direction of the speaker the hand is drawn toward his chest in a short jerking motion and the pointing finger is curled in simultaneously with the movement.

These are but examples of many types of unspoken words through the use of hand gestures. Hand gestures of the Ponca describe experiences, conditions, attitudes, things in nature, things in the home, and people and, generally, include the total realm of the human situation. It can be said that Ponca hand gestures do not extend the full length of the arm in any gesture, that is, hand gestures are made in the near front of the chest area to the top of the head and shoulder areas. This means that the elbow is bent at the person's side and hands are directly in front of the individual (KH, NC, AMC, JP). Hand gestures are common among most plains Indian tribes, but there remains the question of whether there were other body movements that could be characterized as body signals.

To the Ponca, the way a person walks, stand, sits, or moves cannot always tell significant behavioral patterns. A person's body movement in former times was quite reserved and seemingly unattached to any situation (KH). It seems some people still think "Indians are stoic." Much of the time the emotion of an individual Indian is not expressed as openly as that of a non-Indian (except at ballgames). Perhaps the layman of Indian studies too needs interpretation of stoicism. This philosophy is not applicable to the Ponca or likely other tribes either because Indians like to laugh, smile, and cry and at times may become remorseful or suffer depression. Feelings were not hidden nor suppressed; neither were the Ponca unfeeling. Of course, in modern times, the Indian people rely on our modern American concepts of body movement to determine a person's behavior. As mentioned already, at the beginning of this section, we are all subjected to signals every day of our lives. So then what about Ponca body signals? What conditions or situations warrant silent speech? What kinds of motor movements can be observed as to be body signals? The answer to these questions rests, likewise, in the actions of the individual. Facial expression and sound also may be part of the body signals aside from hand gestures. The relationship of body movement as an influencing factor in the socialization process is a consignment of mannerisms in which the individual's perception factors are instilled. The salient features of behavioral patterns, unlike in the dominant society in the modern world, were quite significant to the people. Children were taught how to act and react to any given situation early in life as a part of the maturation process. For instance, if a medicine man came to a dwelling because of sickness, the children would go out to play as if nothing were happening. The children, although aware of the sickness in the home, were cued to play. The psychological deterrent to play instead of worrying and crying placed the children in a positive mental attitude. This allotted behavior was not self-induced or sought out by the individual child but was rather taught at an earlier period. The closest form of psychological adjustment is probably compensation, in which the otherwise weary and worrisome experience is counterbalanced by achieving another behavior. This does not mean that the children were "freed" from anxieties over the sickness in the home. For the Indian family members, it is better for the children to occupy their time with other activities while the condition of sickness exists in the household. This alleviates the children from worry and provides them with a positive emotional outlet. How does a person tell when there is sickness in the home? Through body signals as per mannerisms? Seeing that all children are at play, would it not be reasonable to assume that all children are happy? Yes and no. One would expect the children from the household where sickness exists to appear downcast and somber. The mature eye of an adult takes into account the behavior of the child and can determine that something is awry within the household. Certain variant behavior can be seen, and further inquiry will lead an adult to the story (KH, NC, AMC, JP, AL).

Another known, and practiced, behavior is the manner in which a man folds his arms. Among the Ponca, if a person sits with his arms folded with his right hand covering his chin, we know that everything about him is normal, that is, his life and his household. But if he sits with arms folded with the left hand covering the chin, we know that there is an apparent problem. Further inquiry will lead an individual to the truth. KH said if a man in former times was sitting in such a position, he could be holding a weapon with his right hand under his left arm. Other learned behavior patterns that are significant body language include signals that are made while working, walking, and sitting. These types of signals that go out from a person are also apparent at ceremonies, burials, play, and so forth. Yet the underlying signals we look for are not obvious, as we understand them in the modern world. To the Ponca people, in former times, having knowledge of body signals was just as important as learning to speak (KH, NC, AMC, JP).

Fear Used as a Teaching Tool

In the past some Ponca families, when disciplining and teaching children, used fear as a medium to teach children. Fear was used as an instrument for teaching or training children primarily to eliminate unwanted behavior. But some of the elders said this was not practiced extensively when the Ponca lived in the north. However, in recent years some felt fear was used because of the oncoming new culture and the cultural transition experience. For example, some Ponca families said that if a child cried for something incessantly, the parent would sometimes say, "The bogeyman is going to get you if you keep crying" or "If you keep crying, I'm going to let that white man get you." This would cause the child to be quiet. This was indeed done among the Ponca but cannot be verified as a Ponca custom (KH, AMC, NC, JP, AL). It was not unusual for parents to "use" other persons of the tribe as the focus of fear. Toddlers usually perceive strangers as a part of their immediate surroundings. Perhaps persons who resemble their "world" are considered acceptable. However, on occasions, a person may not fit the proper description and the child will fear that person. Once this is realized the parents, at certain times, will use that person as a focus of fear for the child. When that person happens to visit the family and the child misbehaves, for example, he'll say, "If you don't behave, I'm going to cut your ears off." The child, from then on, will fear that person. But, it is said, during the "fear" period, he will learn the proper behavior expected of him.

Wordless Expressions That Teach

Interjections are used in most languages. Expressions in America today include many sounds that are understood by all hearers. For example, Webster's Collegiate Dictionary says the interjection *wow* "is used to express a strong feeling of pleasure or surprise." Expressions seem to be more of a representation of the actual word or description of a condition that an individual might otherwise use. Both Ponca men and women had their own expressions that connoted an emotional response to joy or surprise or otherwise bewailed a situation of pain or surprise. Some of the male expressions learned at an early age are listed below:

Wuh!	Male expression showing surprise at the appearance of an unexpected person or sound or at the revelation of a thing, idea, or statement.
Hái!	Male expression that means the same as "oops" in English.
A'haú	A conjunctive male expression meaning "okay" or "all right." Usually used as a pause between statements

Aó or *haó*	Male expression of approval following a speech.
Hı̨daké or *Hı̨dá*	"All right" or "okay," usually used following another person's statement or request to do something.
T'ená or *T'enahà*	"Listen!," precedes a statement of seriousness.
Xénàha'	Male expression for "Oh! I was mistaken" or "Oh, I made a mistake."

It has been said that pain is a fundamental teacher. Expressions that connote pain are used by both men and women. A man and woman who inadvertently hurt themselves will say "*Ą́nąną̀.*" When a child hurts himself, the parent says, "*Ádudù,*" expressing that what happened hurt. The child too, later on, will use the expression. At the moment he scratched or cut himself, he will say, "*Ádudù!*" If his parent did not hear him cry out when he hurt himself, at a later time he'll show the scratch or cut to the parent and call it a "*Dudú.*" Another example is if a toddler approaches the fireplace, his mother usually utters an expression of warning. Of course, the mother's first reaction is to bring the child away from the fire. However, as curiosity grows and not knowing the danger, the child will attempt to come closer. As the child reaches for the fire, the mother pulls the child away and says, "*Jijí!*" Unless the child actually touches the fire and learns from experience that the fire hurts, the expression "*Jijí*" will consistently be used until the child learns to keep away from the fire. The expression is also used by the father.

The following are expressions use by women that declare joy, a mistake, unbelief, and so forth:

Hı̨jé·	Female expression of joy in receiving a gift or finding a collectible item.
Hı̨ or *Hı̨ɖa*	Female expression that connotes "oops" but also suggests the forgetting of something.
Eną́	Expression of disapproval of another's behavior or speaking.

Xu	Velar flat voiceless fricative sound made with rounded lips suggesting distaste or unbelief of a statement or a condition that could be considered comical.
Ídidì or *Dí·*	Female expression connoting an element of disgust in regard to someone's speech, words, or actions. Also overdoing something that goes beyond the excess of normality.
Xé· or *Xénà*	Female expression for "Oh! I was mistaken" or "Oh, I made a mistake."

The timing and conditions of a situation must be as such for expressions to be the most effective. In the 1960s, when Indian men began to grow their hair long on the reservation, one of the tribal leaders attempted to join the neo-Indian fad. When his hair grew passed his shoulders he tried to braid his hair. This amounted to two little funny-looking braids that stuck outward. He came to the Indian agency at the White Eagle Community to do some business, and there was a group of women sitting in the waiting room. When he passed by them, they said nothing. But as he walked out, one of the women said, "*Xu·.*" He heard the laughter as he left the building. Most Ponca speakers today seldom use the expressions; interestingly, many of the younger people who do not speak the language use *É'čainà* (pronounced "Ay-China").[5]

Hígà or Stories That Teach

Another method of teaching children was through storytelling. The time for storytelling was at night or bedtime during the winter months. As was the custom for sleeping arrangements, the storyteller usually slept near the children. When visiting relatives came or a person of a different family visited, they were usually asked to tell the stories. Some elders were very skillful storytellers and held the attention of the children until they were sound asleep. According to KH, the person telling the stories usually included a variety of subjects:

> They always teach children about different things . . . always tell story about something . . . maybe about how to treat animals . . . horses, dogs, and friends. They tell about different menfolk being brave . . .

strong men, who do something for the tribe. Sometimes about cheating, lying, and stealing from one another . . . take something not yours. *Hígà ámà* . . . those stories tell lots of different things.

The coyote, for some tribes, is the villain in children's stories. The Ponca have only one coyote story that the elders could think of at the time of this research. The story was a means of teaching fair play. The coyote was not the villain. It was one of many stories told to children. Dorsey (1890) records several stories told by the Ponca. In Dorsey's book are several stories of the *Éštínikè*, *Mąčú*, *Maščíge*, and others. Many stories recalled by the elders include those recorded by Dorsey. There are stories of the *Wasábe* (black bear), *Šą́t'ągà* (wolf), *Čígaďišížè* (name for a young man), *Haxégà* (name for a young man), *Wésa* (the snake), and many others. Some stories have Indian titles as the English have titles for their stories. To get the storyteller to start, as children we asked for certain stories to be told first. These included the following: "The *Mą́ščà* and the *Miká*" (The Crawdads and the Raccoons), "The *Maščíge* and the *Zizíkà*" (The Rabbit and the Turkeys), "The *Gé*" (The Turtle), "The *T'é Núgà Dáďį̀*" (The Deranged Bison), "The *Míkasì* and the *Éštínikè*" (The Coyote and a Pesky Animal), "The *Wasábè* and the *Éštínikè*" (The Black Bear and a Pesky Animal), and others. In modern times, any primate, that is, monkeys, apes, gorillas, and so forth, is called *Éštínikè*. Some have thought that because of its antics and sometimes comical behavior, the term may have been a slang name used for the otter (*Nušną́*). There is also a story of the Ponca traveling southward along the Rocky Mountains into Mexico and into South America in ancient times. The story includes a segment that says they saw a little man with a tail. And they called him *Éštínikè*.

Some stories that were told on a regular basis had historic overtones that included names of actual individuals of the tribe. The names were included in the storytelling process. The problem with some stories according to the elders is that they were tales from European folklore, probably told by their French parentage. These kinds of stories are easily detected because they have a nice logical ending with a moral teaching. Some Ponca stories seem to be totally illogical and have no neat conclusion. Other stories with unusual endings, in addition to stories that are inconclusive or have no logic, are left to the listener to interpret. The genuine Ponca teachings are left for the children and even to teenagers to figure out. The following stories include some of these characters.

The Éˀštínikè and the Turtle

One time an *Éˀštínikè* was walking along the way when he came upon a turtle who was also walking in the same direction. He thought to himself in a certain way, "Now, here could be something to my advantage." So he retreated a little ways and came running and hollering, "Hey! All you there! There's a big flood coming! All the little animals are heading for the hills!" The turtle paid little attention to the *Éˀštínikè* and kept walking. The turtle thought, "Why should I head for the hills? Water is my kind of territory." But the *Éˀštínikè* persisted and ran toward the turtle. Passing up the turtle, he kept hollering, "There's a big flood coming! All the little animals are heading for the hills!" The turtle thought it over and hollered to the *Éˀštínikè*, "Elder brother! Wait for me!" So the *Éˀštínikè* and the turtle went walking along together. While they're walking along, the *Éˀštínikè* never again mentioned the flood. But he said to the turtle, "When people walk, they always walk with their necks sticking way out." Without taking precautions, the turtle listened and stuck his neck way out. As he walked along with his head bobbing up and down, the *Éˀštínikè* looked for a club. He finally saw the old bone of a larger animal and carried it with him. When he thought it was just right, he hit the turtle on the head and killed it. He said, "*Ába wì šti gáwakią ḍįhè*" (That's just the way it goes for me some days). He carried the turtle down beside the creek, where he built a fire to cook it. After the fire was built and the turtle was cooking, the *Éˀštínikè* became sleepy. He said, "I'm going to take a nap. When you're done, say, s-s-s-s-, and I'll wake up and eat you." So he went to sleep. Meanwhile a coyote was sitting nearby in the deep grass watching everything. When he was certain that the *Éˀštínikè* was fast asleep, he crept down to the cooking turtle and ate it up. When he finished eating it, he carefully put the bones back into the turtle shell and crept back up to his sitting place. When he was ready, he said, "s-s-s-s." The *Éˀštínikè* woke up, stretched his arms, and reached for his turtle he was going to eat. When he grabbed a leg from the turtle, it all fell apart. He said, "*Wuh!* Oh yes, I ate my turtle before I went to sleep. Nooo . . .

I said I would sleep first and then eat my turtle. No, it couldn't be. I ate my turtle and then went to sleep." So while the *É'štinikè* was arguing with himself, the coyote hollered down at him, "So how is the ole man!" The *É'štinikè* looked up and said, "So you're the one!" He got up and began to chase after the coyote. The coyote ran and ran. He ran through holes in the ground, and the *É'štinikè* was right behind him. Finally, the coyote ran through a hole in the ground, and the *É'štinikè* got caught in it. Only his rear end was sticking out. The coyote came back around where the *É'štinikè* was stuck and mated him. The coyote went his way afterward, and the *É'štinikè* finally got out. Later the *É'štinikè* was walking along the way when he suddenly got a stomachache. So he sat down to relieve himself, and as he did so a little coyote rolled out and ran. He got up and continued on only to be stopped again by another stomachache. And again, a little coyote rolled out and ran. After this happened one or two more times, the *É'štinikè* was very angry. He said, "You're not going to do that again." He wrapped himself very tightly with his blanket thinking he would catch the next one that might roll out. When he had walked a short distance, his stomach again began to hurt. So he tightened himself up and got ready to catch the little coyote. Only this time, it wasn't a coyote. He *že'd* all over himself and his blanket. Much later, he was going up a pathway toward the community, and he came across some little skunks that were saying, "What are people saying about the *É'štinikè*? They're saying, He *že'd* all over his blanket." And they sang a song telling about it. *Šetą́* (The End)

The É'štinikè *and the Black Bear*

One time an *É'štinikè* was walking down the road, and by chance he met a black bear. They went along, strolling side by side. The *É'štinikè* said to the black bear, "Unh . . . unh . . . unh, my lips are so chapped, and they hurt so much. If only I had a small piece of fat, I could wipe it on my lips, unh . . . unh . . . unh." The black bear did not pay any attention to him. The *É'štinikè*, however, continued to complain, "If only I had some fat to put on my lips, it would relieve my pain. Friend . . . you have a lot of fat on you. Would you give me just a little piece from your side." The black bear didn't listen to him, but the *É'štinikè* kept complaining. Finally, the black bear agreed to let him have a small piece. So the *É'stinikè* told him to lie down. He took his knife out and placed it on the black bears side and suddenly pushed the knife into the bear's side killing him. Then he said, "*Ą́ba wì šti gáwakią̀ dįhè*" (That's just the way it goes for me some days). So he dragged the black bear down by the creek and butchered it up. As was the custom, he cooked up the heart and kidneys and sat down to eat. Just as he was opening his mouth to eat the first piece, some limbs on a nearby tree squeaked. He put the food down and looked up at the tree. Again, he started to open his mouth to eat when the tree squeaked a second time. When it happened the third time, the *É'stinikè* said, "Why are you squeaking at me? If you do that again, I'm coming up there!" So, he began to eat, and the tree squeaked, and the *É'stinikè*, angry and bent on breaking a limb, climbed the tree to the limbs. He said, "Where are you, you that squeaked at me?" shaking the limbs. Suddenly a gust of wind came up, and the *É'stinikè* had his arms caught between two limbs. For some time, he pulled and pulled but couldn't get loose. At length he became repentant and said, "I was just playing. Let me go friend. I was just playing." But the tree would not let him go. A little while later, as he sat perched on top of the tree with his arms caught, he saw a pack of wolves passing by in the distance. The wolves had no idea that the *É'stinikè* was caught in the tree and that there was an abundance of meat cooking. But ole *É'stinikè* hollered at them, "Hey! You! Over there! Go way around that way because I have some meat over here! You might smell it if you come closer!" The leader of the pack raised his head and sniffed around and said, "The ole man said he was cooking?" They all came as a group and ate up all the meat and left only the bones on which they urinated. When they had left, the tree let the *É'stinikè* go. He climbed down and looked at the remains of his kill. He tried to lick the bones for anything that was left. *Šetą́* (The End)

In addition to such stories, there are antithetical stories that deal with heroism and good deeds, as opposed to complicity and sham behavior. These stories center on a heroic rabbit that lives with his grandmother and a conniving, lying rabbit that also lives with his grandmother. Grandmothers usually told these stories. Could it be they were telling us something?

The Rabbit and His Grandmother

One time a rabbit was living with his grandmother. He told her that there were some turkeys down by the creek, and he was going to get some. In preparation he took with him his bow and arrows, a knife, a rope, a sack, and a drum. He lured the turkeys by announcing that there was a handgame and dance going on, and he started beating on his drum and called out, "*Įutį tągà k'í wačígaxè adį t'amà. Bdúgaxtì díkuì*" (They're having a big handgame and dance. All of you are invited). But the lead turkey, feeding on seeds downstream, said, "Oh, we've been to dances before. We don't need to go." The rabbit didn't give up. He kept calling to them. The turkeys finally gave in and one said, "We'll just dance a few rounds and leave."

The rabbit had chosen a place by the creek where there was a cave. He had built a big fire in it so it would look inviting to the turkeys. As they entered the cave, he kept beating on his drum. Close by him he had his bag ready. The turkeys went inside as he sang songs. The turkeys began to dance around him and his drumming. He sang, "*Įbe dą diąje . . . Įbe dą diąje*" (Shake your tail feathers . . . shake your tail feathers). Then he called out, "*Tągá mašè, ágahadè wačígaxaìgà*" (You bigger ones . . . dance closer in). So he sang some more, saying, "*Įbe dą diąje . . . Įbe dą diąje.*" Then he called to them to close their eyes as they danced. And the turkeys did as he said. As they danced with their eyes closed, he started putting the bigger ones in his sack. Finally, one of the little turkeys opened his eyes and saw what he was doing and yelled out, "Hey! He's about to clean us all out!" And all the turkeys flew away. But the rabbit caught some and killed them. He took them home and told his grandmother to cook them. He told her that he had invited the Pawnees over to feast with him. His grandmother was so proud of him that she said, "Oh, some people think so much of my grandson." So when she had finished cooking the turkeys, the rabbit said to her, "Now go out into the deep weeds and sit low as the Pawnees will soon be here." So she went out and did as he told her. He waited for a while, and then he pretended to have people come in. He would make noise and speak Pawnee saying, "*Hé wadąbe sidémąka.*" He continued to make noises and speak Pawnee loud so his grandmother would think that there really were Pawnees present. When he had eaten all the turkeys, he again pretended that the Pawnees were leaving and said, "*Hé wadǫbe sidémǫka.*" Later, he called to his grandmother, "You can come out now, the Pawnees have all left and have gone home."

The Rabbit and His Grandmother (#2)

One time there was a rabbit that lived with his grandmother. One day he said, "I think I'll go hunting." His grandmother cautioned him saying, "You be careful. They say there is a hill swallower (*P'ahé wadáhunì*) around somewhere. He can swallow you up if you're not careful." So the rabbit left, carrying his bow and arrows and knife. His grandmother hollered after him saying, "*Uhé ágahadì íhaà!*" (Walk on the higher plains!)

So the rabbit set out on his hunting trip. When he was far from his home, seeking his prey, he hollered out, "*P'ahé wadáhunì águdì niá?*" (Hill-swallower, where are you?) As he crept along, he had his bow and arrow ready to shoot. While he was hollering out, suddenly everything became dark. The hill swallower had already swallowed him, and he didn't know it. When he realized he was no longer where he thought he was, he used his fire maker to make a little fire. Then he saw people sitting around. Some were very skinny and about dead, as they had been swallowed long ago. There were others too who appeared to be skinny, but not like some of the others. There were those like himself who had just been swallowed. He didn't know he had been swallowed and asked where he was and what was going on. Someone spoke up and said, "Don't you know that you have been swallowed by the hill swallower?" As he looked around, he saw all the meat everywhere. He also saw the heart of the hill swallower and said, "Why aren't you people eating all this meat in here? These are good to eat." He looked at the heart, liver, and those things that are inside an animal. So right off, he started cutting the meat, including the heart. When he did this, the hill swallower fell apart. All the people were happy and began to take pieces of the meat. They had a big feast and prepared the rest of the meat and went home. The rabbit took his portion home to his grandmother. When he got home, he called to her saying, "I have come home and have killed the hill swallower." His grandmother was very happy and said, "*Hijé·*, my grandson has killed the hill swallower and has brought back some meat to eat." And she cooked the meat for them to eat together.

Inquiries began early in life, and Indian teachings were often learned through communication with the elder members of the family, namely, the grandparents. They told stories containing certain types of behavior, and reinforced this behavior by seeing to it that the children practiced it. A good use of the language was essential in the learning process of good Ponca ethics.

Certain tribal rituals and ceremonies were practiced by leaders and men of medicine that were not told to children until they became older. But as mentioned earlier, if a child showed exceptional interest, he was encouraged to seek this knowledge. According to tribal custom, the time allotted for him to find this knowledge was never closed. And those who consistently pursued their objectives were eventually rewarded. According to KH, the want of knowledge too had its drawbacks, but the inquiring mind of youth, if given the opportunity, would stop at no point.[6] But the youth also had to make time to understand the custom of inquiry. As in any civilization, in the Ponca Tribe the knowledge of good and evil is always present. The elders say that there is a knowledge that anyone can possess, but in other cases, that knowledge is left to those to whom it belongs and to whom it will be given at a proper time. In addition to that, certain knowledge belonged to a select few and was respected by the tribal members. If the person possessed certain knowledge of a thing, he would not impart it at the asking. This is because it belonged to him. The elders stated that if it were intended for another to have it, then it would have been given to them. But if the person who originally received the gift desired to do so, he could pass it on to another person. For example, if knowledge of medicine was desired by a young person, he would eventually be taught. This was done only when there was a strong indication that he had definite interest, some talent, and some knowledge by the standards of the tribe. In some instances, when certain family members had a leading role in their knowledge of tribal religion, philosophy, psychology, and arts, this knowledge could be passed on to the eldest son. If the same knowledge was desired by the younger siblings, more often than not, they were ignored. When the time was proper for the eldest son to receive the gift, the knowledge and technique was usually given by the father or grandfather.

The following story is given to show a teaching method based on a student's desire and resourcefulness in acquiring knowledge. The story told by KH is translated from the Ponca language.

ČÍGAÐIŠÍŽÈ

This is a story of a man and his son. The teaching of the way is puzzling but can be understood if one wants to know. *Čígaðišížè* was the son. One day his father lay on his back behind his dwelling and was looking into the sky. There were big puffy clouds slowly moving across his view when suddenly the father saw the plume of an eagle lying below one of the clouds. Observing the plume for a moment, he said with startling discovery: "*Xa·, Įdádąpáxetè ądą́bextì gðí ną́bì*" (What is this! Anything I do, he always watches me). Then he arose above the cloud and was a center tail feather of an eagle. Realizing he had been discovered, *Čígaðišížè* came down as a swift hawk ... *Gðedą́*. His father followed him as an eagle ... *Xiðá*, chasing him. When *Čígaðišížè* came close to the forest, he became a deer and ran. Likewise his father too became a deer and chased him. When *Čígaðišížè* came to a stream of water, he became an otter and swam and ducked under water and hid behind reeds and driftwood. But his father too followed as an otter, still pursuing him. After he changed his form into many different animals, he finally came into the tipi and hid. His father knew he was in the tipi and came in as a flea and crawled into the crack of a tipi pole. Sitting there, he looked to find *Čígaðišížè*, but could not find him for a long period. Suddenly he noticed a sunbeam shining through the skins covering the tipi and knew it was his son. Realizing he was discovered, *Čígaðišížè* went out, proceeding to the right as he circled the tipi.

After a little while, his father too went out proceeding to the right around the tipi.

Behind the tipi he saw a mangy dog lying. He walked up to it and kicked it so that the dog ran and cried. At the end of the fourth day *Čígaðišížè* died.

Čígaðišížè's death was attributed to his father, but why did he kill him? And why such description of changes in form? What was the primary reason for telling the story in the first place? The story is a challenge to interpret for those who want to know. As a child, I asked what the story meant, and I was ignored. I became conscious of the saying, "To some it is given, and to others it was not intended for them to know." Persevering, however, I eventually knew the meaning of the story. At this announcement, my father began to impart to me all that I inquired of and much more.

Major keys for survival are understood through oral history. The story of the "Crazed Bison," mentioned earlier by KH, indicates how to survive in a crisis situation during a hunt. This story essentially marked the level for bravery and survival. If one can perceive himself outside the modern world and able to travel back into time to that period when survival was dependent on scrupulous decisiveness, he would see that socialization was developed through many human situations. If, for example, his life's sustenance was dependent on wild animals, it follows that he must know and understand the behavior of animals.

The ingenuity of man is observed in this episode of survival by overcoming a bison single-handedly. Although no system governed this type of activity, this does not suggest that the hunters were undisciplined. Tribal hunters, especially young men, learned that in every given situation on the hunting grounds, alternative methods were open to them. It is unknown how old the story is, but it is interesting that the Ponca used the restrictive forces of water to break horses in modern times. Knowing the environment, climate, topography, and limits of their physical stamina, they acquired the means for survival. Exceptional abilities and knowledge obviously marked those who were outstanding members of the tribe. Although they did not set out with the intention to receive personal recognition for deeds of bravery, these men invariably would be honored. Little Bear accomplished many deeds of bravery that are remembered to this day. Acts of gallantry and achievement; methods developed for hunting, fishing, and planting; the sharing and acquiescence in the use of methodology all contributed to that special condition in life whereby one found his place in society. The socioeconomic system, an integral part of the culture that was taught, learned, and developed over centuries, evolved into a congruent and workable system that affected all Ponca.

Discipline Results in Societal Recognition

Some rites and ceremonials were created because a good deed was performed by one or more individuals. In other situations, a rite was made to cause a person or people to perform a service to the people. Over time, these rites and ceremonies also gave birth to proverbs, aphorisms, morals, and ethics (KH, NC, AMC). That being the case, over a long span of time, behavioral expectations for all tribal members were based on the reasonableness of thought as it affected their social world.

In the socialization processes concerning children and their expected behavior, the adult member was the essential motivating factor in establishing acceptable standards. As mentioned, appropriate behavior was taught by both the parent and grandparents. Because children thrive on attention, parents took advantage of this feature in maturation and led them through a series of steps as they matured (KCH). A mature and knowledgeable parent would, for instance, always praise the child for his exhibited accomplishments. The mother did special things with and for the child. And there were those daily chores in which each family member participated. Other activities included friends who shared in the same activity. VBSH said she and a group of other girls her age went to a place where wild potatoes grew.

> We walked in pathways that led between the foggy hills to a creek where these potatoes grow.[7] There were only five or six of us. As we were busily digging for the potatoes, we were cautious because the Sioux were attacking the Ponca at that time. But we felt reasonably safe. As we were digging, suddenly we heard someone say, "There's some over there." We thought it was the Sioux and became frightened. We ran and left everything where we were working. Later on, we learned that there were no Sioux around and that some of our own tribesmen were watching us. An elder told us what we heard must have been a meadowlark speaking to us.

The communal farming and gathering system was ingrained in these young girls at an early age. Although there is no recognition for gathering potatoes or other foods, it is possible that these young girls would one day receive a just reward for their faithfulness in participating in family and communal efforts.

But see what the underlying meanings of ceremonies and rites tell us. For one, they connote that all persons at one time or other will receive recognition. The socialization of the child, under these conditions, would ultimately teach him or her that the ceremonies and rites were the most appropriate method of receiving recognition. There was no place in the socialization process that permitted people to bring attention to themselves. The ceremonies and rites for the young were significant, and recognition for deeds of bravery in later years would fulfill the need for personal recognition. When a child misbehaved in public places, especially when rites were being performed, what did the parent do to correct the behavior? Something like a time-out was used. He might be denied activities that he liked. Much of the time, according the KCH, the parent helped the child to focus on the ritual at hand. She prompted him, saying that the day is coming when he too would be receiving some reward or recognition. In a moment of misbehavior and subsequent reprimand, in addition to the promise of recognition, the parent could cause the child to refrain from the unwanted behavior.

Socialization and Discipline

Desirable and undesirable behavior displayed by a child is part of growing up. The stimuli, good and bad, that cause individual children to feel contented or dissatisfied are common to all people. If a child did something outside the context of acceptable behavior, what did the parent do to correct the unwanted behavior? It has been stated previously that the child, from the time he was able to comprehend what behavior was expected of him, followed the cue from the parent through reprimand in its most appropriate form. But there were other means through socialization that aided in the child's upbringing.

Howard once told me about attending a modern Indian church birthday prayer meeting in the North Country. It was in the middle of winter and during the time when Indians burned wood for heating. It was held at a private home where friends and relatives came to celebrate with a five-year-old boy. Howard said when you entered the home, you could feel the atmosphere of prayers and birthday cheer. After the child was given his gifts, one man, who came in late, was sitting by the door. He had brought no gift, but as he prepared to leave, he took off his worn jacket and presented it to the child. The parents arose and thanked him as they shook his hands.

First thoughts about such an act might lead one to conclude that the jacket was old, too big, and inappropriate; it was winter, and the man would have to walk out into the cold without it; and this was an unreasonable act. However, according to KH, when the principle of social interaction is understood, it is truly not the gift but the act. He said the man could not have participated in the occasion without being a part of it and could have shown no greater love but to give all that he had. That child will be told what happened on his fifth birthday, and he will remember that his time will come when he too may have to make a sacrifice. The probability that the man's act would elevate his status was not the issue. Rather the issue is that his act of sharing be perpetuated.

Other Cultural Perspectives

The current cultural status of the tribe is a derivative of the former lifestyle of our ancestors and the merging with the American culture. Gathering information about the Ponca culture seems to be a simple matter. But to understand it, one must cross the cultural barrier. And to cross the barrier and draw intelligible conclusions about the lifestyle, one must separate himself from Western thought and Western civilization. To know some truths that can be explored or interpreted essentially means that one must be or become an Indian. It is thought that the Ponca culture and religion should be shared without discretion like other world philosophies and religions. However, the ethical values of the tribe suggest that to do so would violate some sacred principles. Some segments of the culture and religious practices have been subjected to criticism and stereotyping. This has somewhat been eliminated, but the stereotypes probably will continue for another generation or so. In the process of acquiring information from the elders, their interest was more in saying "This is all we know and we will not lie to you" with no apologies. The nexus that follows is open to criticism.

There was a coexistent relationship of the Ponca and nature. This was because the Ponca religion was derived via interaction with the environment. The understanding did not provide logical explanations of behavior for private or public use of rites and ceremonies. The acceptance of man's life as it is and the use of those rites was all that was necessary for reaching the accessible benefit. The rudimentary basis for continuing and sustaining life rested in this acceptance (KH, NC, AMC, AL, JP). For some tribes, the phrase "harmony in nature" is the key in understanding American Indian religion. That may be so, but the elders felt that social patterns established over a thousand years entered every facet of life and had a purpose. If one was born into a world of noncompetitive spirit, with a philosophy of sharing and a cooperative lifestyle, the European concepts of self-aggrandizement, achievement, and the like could hardly be understood. To the culturally oriented Indian, competition breeds competition. For the non-Indian, competitive creativity and discovery may be enriching and rewarding, but to the culturally oriented Indian, it may be repugnant to his way of life.

For the Ponca, discovery was restricted to observing of the natural things of life, and nature was left untouched and unblemished, that is, the natural things of earth, such as rocks, wood, and trees, were left as they were. To remove a rock that was in the path would have violated the natural processes. It was better to go around it. It had its place in the whole scheme of things. However, there were exceptions to the rule. When a person gathered wood for fire, for example, he or she spoke to the wood for its use. This was done because all natural things were alive and had life. The elders said, "Įdádą bdúgà nítà uží" (Everything has life in it). In Ponca mythology, a tree "holds on" to a creature, a hill can "swallow" people, and religiously, water is "life." They said in every facet of life, a person requested permission from the Creator to move the natural things. In success and defeat, appropriate prayers were made for hunting and warfare. The pattern had been set so that their actions and prayers were part of the natural processes. In some instances, failure to carry out the required practices was said to result in heartache, sickness, famine, or eventual death to an individual or a member of his family (KH, AMC, NC, JP, AL). The elders of the tribe remind the younger generations to observe the rules that Wak'ą́da (God) is present in all that is done by mankind. Some of those words of wisdom are listed below:

IN REGARD TO TRAGEDY

Íyè wadánąą̀žì tedì, dégą šit'amašè.

"When you do not listen to your elders, this is the way your life will end."

Šégą̀ danít'à mąnítedì, ábataą̀štì daxáge daną́žį̀ t'amašè.

"When one lives in this manner, you who live will stand weeping."

Éde dít'a wí gatái ki, dí, kí t'íúži dit'à, kí dihą́ kí diádì, ną́dè waxpádì wadé t'amà.

"When one in your family dies tragically, it will cause your family, your mother and father, to have deep heartache." (This statement was made in regard to a family member who did not adhere to proper ethical codes for living.)

IN REGARD TO PARENTS

Diádì kí dihą́mà į̀dádą̀ údą̀ udídaìkì, wádanąą̀xtì dagdí tè.

"When your father and your mother tell you something good for your welfare, you should sit quietly and listen."

Išágeàmà égidąì, údą̀ mąnítedì kášì danít'à mąnítanikè.

"The elders say if you live ethically good, your life will be long."

Diádì íyè ádanąą̀žìtedì, ą́ba guáhidąt'à, udúgdaxtì ną́de waxpádì damą́nit'atè.

"When you do not listen to your father speak, some time in the future, you will live a life of regret, sorrow and heartbreak."

IN REGARD TO CHILDREN

Šígažį̀gà dít'amà wédagihusàigà kí į̀dádą̀ údą̀ wégązàigà.

"Admonish your children and teach them good things."

Šígažį̀gà dít'àmà úšką údąì kì, dip'íxt'ì uhíwadadetè wét'ąì.

"When your children are ethically good, it is noticeably clear that you have brought them up well."

Šígažį̀gà wásp'eáži madíáma, "wegą́ze digé" énąì.

"When children misbehave, it is said that they have not been taught."

Wásp'eáži kí nąxíde digé mąnítedí, t'iúži dít'a kí dihą́, diádi ną́dè waxp'ádì mądít'amà.

"If you do not walk scrupulously, you and your family—your mother, father—will have deep heartache."

IN REGARD TO WOMEN

Atą́štì waúamà úšką̀ et'áitè úkinąđì ną́i, xádè wiáxc̀ì kedì íkìnąxđè ukíhi.

"Sometimes a woman's ways can be so deceiving that she can hide behind a blade of grass."

Waúamà, nú waą́đamà, šą́gè íđaži ékìgą̀, uc̀íže kí xđabé kedí égihà ną́ge mą̀đí ną̀ì.

"When a woman leaves her husband, she runs like a blinded horse that runs through brush and trees."

Waú úđamà wíke mą̀địitedì, wac̀ígaxáikì t'ą̀gádihà wadíʃdexti ną̀ží ną́i.

"A woman who lives ethically well and dances at giveaways will give abundantly."

IN REGARD TO LIFE

Đanít'a mą̀ní kedì, mą́hi gap'ái ègą ái, úną̀k'à wađái.

"It is said that life is like a sharpened knife; it is very easy to hurt yourself."

Pahą́gadì įđádą p'iáž̀ì škáxète, ą́bàtą̀št'ì, guáhiđąt'à áđakigđahiđè t'anikè.

"The wrong you have done in the past, somewhere in the future, it will blow back upon you."

Wađác̀igaxè tedì, úđixixidagà. Sabáži wí įđádą ađiáži địkè edí gđí k'í, eí wa'đíʃđè ú'ìgà.

"When you dance, look about yourself. You may see one who is in need sitting there; give to that one."

Pą́ca úškątè đagíąđà tedì, ą́batą̀štì guáhiđatà, éđè điđít'àxtì áđakipàkì wéđagišpahą̀žìt'amašè.

"When you have abandoned your Ponca ways, in the future, you may meet a relative and will not know each other."

The examples given above are classic sayings, but it has been said "there are as many sayings as there are Sayers." Some of the sayings have been interpreted by others. There are no curse words in the Ponca language; otherwise they might have been included in the above sayings. These cultural teachings began when children were beginning to experiment. Perhaps this is why Peter LeClair in his *Ponca History* condensed some of these statements. When the end product was written, they appeared to be very similar to the Hebrew Commandments.

The development of the culture in morality, for instance, has no sayings relating to adultery and fornication, although these concepts may be inferred by certain terms. The elders said that this does not mean that the possibility of extramarital relations never took place. The claim here is that to commit such offenses was no simple behavior that could be done without notice. Furthermore, in the old days, the apparent punishment meant public embarrassment or even death to clandestine couples.[8] Although the morals and ethics of the tribe could be questioned by others, we are reminded that to survive in those days, there was a need for complete cooperation from all tribesmen. There was warfare with neighboring tribes. Sometimes game was difficult to find. Drought on the plains is still common today. To preserve the high values of loyalty and social cohesiveness, the Ponca demonstrated examples of high ethical and moral standards for tribesmen.

The teachings of ethics and morals were a high priority with the people. These teachings were incorporated in a real-life experience of the people. The following story was also told by KH when we were young boys (my translation):

UGLY BOY AND PRETTY BOY

One time there was a beautiful Ponca girl who was liked by two young men. They were both different from one another. One of the boys was very handsome and flamboyant. The other boy was not too good looking but was a young man who carried himself in dignity and self-control. The first boy is called "Pretty Boy." He always comes around the girl even though he was not invited. She was always cordial and friendly toward him but thought that he was too forward and aggressive. There were times when some activity was happening in the camp, such as a dance, he would make sure he was across from her so she would see him. He sometimes would do some foolish act he thought was funny or comical trying to impress her that he was somebody to be around.

The other young man is called "Ugly Boy." He too liked the girl but was more reserved to express himself as openly as Pretty Boy. He too went to the dances, but always sat with the other men who displayed their status as warriors of the tribe. He danced like the other men and showed his prowess as a warrior as he danced. In his manner of courtship to the girl, he, at night, would go to the hillside away from her and her parents' dwelling and sit to play a love call with his flute. Everyone in the village knew it was he that played so she knew who was playing the flute.

Pretty Boy also knew what was happening and became jealous. He had thought he was the only one showing interest in the young girl. So his way of courting her became more intense and bolder. But the girl remained unimpressed with his audacious acts. Even though she knew how he was, she wanted to find out more about both young men. One evening at sundown she walked quietly through the village toward Pretty Boy's dwelling. It so happened that he was cooking himself a leg bone of the bison called the *Wažíbe*. The cooked bone was usually eaten by old people who ate the marrow. When he saw her coming in the distance, he took the bone and rolled it out to the back of the tipi. She had seen what he did. When she got there, she picked up the bone and took it around to the front where he was sitting and gave it to him saying, "Here is your *Wažíbe*. Somehow it rolled out of your tipi!"

Later, she went on to see Ugly Boy's living conditions. Interestingly, unlike the other boy, whose parents were not present, Ugly Boy was home with his parents and sisters. They did not see her, but she peered into the tipi to see that his mother was cooking a meal for him and his sisters were combing his hair as he sat in the most prominent place in the tipi. In our language, his living conditions being commendable is called *Wadį*. It means "possesses much." It meant to her that he was loved by his family and that meant he was a good man.

Then one day a call was made to all warriors to get their weapons of knife, war club, bow and arrows to go meet the enemy who were coming to battle the Ponca. Now, in those days, the wives of the men going to battle would follow their men and watch from afar. The young girl joined them. In this story, as the battle raged on, many of the Ponca men were killed or wounded, but Pretty Boy and Ugly Boy continued to fight. Then without warning Pretty Boy cut Ugly Boy's bowstring causing him to be captured as he [Pretty Boy] sneaked away. The young girl saw what happened. She saw the enemy take Ugly Boy captive and saw Pretty Boy run away.

After she returned to her parents, she told them that Ugly Boy was taken captive, and she was going to go where they had taken him and would try to get him released by whatever means it took. Meantime, Pretty Boy told everyone that Ugly Boy was captured and would be executed. This was certain to happen, so according to custom his parents gave away everything they owned to mourn the death of their son. They moved into a small hut outside the village circle for their period of mourning.

For days the young girl followed the trail of the enemy to their village. When she finally arrived there, she saw that Ugly Boy was tied to a post in the middle of a great circle of tipis. That afternoon, she meditated upon how she would get him away. For whatever reason it was, she fashioned a makeshift baby cradle from the bark of a certain type of tree. It was a large crude piece of bark wrapped with small pieces of bark. It was about the size of a baby. After sundown, she heard somebody singing. [At this point in the story, a song is sung in the remembrance of the Ponca chiefs.]

The village was quiet, but you could hear people talking among family members. It was then the young girl walked circling the village. Carrying the cradle as she walked she began to hum a lullaby as though she was causing her baby to sleep. As she did this, she caused the entire village to sleep. When she was certain that the village indeed was asleep, she went to release Ugly Boy from his bonds, and they returned home on horses she had taken.

Arriving late at night, Ugly Boy was told that his family thinking him dead had given away all they had and moved into a hut outside the village circle. There he was reunited with his family, who were overjoyed to have him return. They hugged and embraced him now that he was alive and well. The next day the town crier (Iyé bahà) went through the village hollering and announcing that Ugly Boy was not dead, but alive and was home safe.

The Ponca people have an unwritten law concerning what is now called capital punishment. In this story, the law of banishment was to be applied to the violator.

While the village was delighted that Ugly Boy was safe, those who knew what had happened at the battle site concerning Ugly Boy's captivity were about to enforce the law of banishment on Pretty Boy. But the parents of Pretty Boy knowing what was going to happen had hurriedly prepared food and necessary items for survival for him. Unseen, he left the village and was never heard of again.

The survival of the people was dependent on these principles. In this story we see the human element at work in their daily lives. In the unethical act of one man, we see clearly that extreme action sometimes had to be taken to maintain order and stability among tribesmen.

The best possible way to describe the purpose of cooperative living is found in the idea of sharing one's wealth. In modern times we seem to be more family oriented when giving is concerned. The personal acquisition of material goods in modern times prevents us from acquiring to give things away.

The ancient custom of sharing too could lead one to believe that another could eventually become dependent on the receiving end of the sharing. But that didn't happen. I am reasonably certain that the old practice of sharing is no longer existent. It is a common saying today among Indian people that there are certain persons who will be presented gifts at giveaway dances. And those same persons will be giving back to those same "givers" at the next giveaway dance. This practice today has been altered to mean something other that the original meaning (AL, NC, NM). But the custom is still practiced. When a fellow tribesman becomes afflicted with some illness, other tribesmen usually go to him with gifts of food, money, and prayers. This is common among Indian people today. At a recent gathering of the tribe, it was announced that a tribesperson had died. Many Ponca went to the deceased person's spouse and presented to him many gifts, which included foodstuffs, Pendleton blankets, shawls, and money. In this sense, certain aspects of sharing are still intact.

The Ponca people never viewed nature as something they could control; rather, they saw themselves as a part of nature. They didn't impose their will on another, except when the enemy violated their peaceful existence in their own territory. The basis of unfair competition in modern times would have violated the accepted social patterns. In this regard, there is an obvious difference in the rational between the Indian people and the non-Indian world. To the Indian people, close association with nature provided techniques for survival. In nature he saw the social pattern that best fit him into the scheme of his existence. The changing of the seasons, the coming of the new moon, the continuing life cycle of plants and animals all contributed to his knowledge of rules for his existence. Within this chain of occurrences, he saw himself as part of that life cycle. According to KH, if a person were to find his life's calling or move into the world of daily living, he would have to leave the village and go to find his calling. He said persons who became especially knowledgeable in medicines had probably spent a lot of time fasting and praying. Through this experience, they may have, for example, encountered something that revealed answers to some problems that otherwise could not be solved. The revelation, under these circumstances, was said to be given to them by nature. KH said the natural processes of man in nature lead to these kinds of special gifts. Those special gifts from nature were referred to as *Waxúbè*. The word implies something sacred to be revered and respected. Ultimately, this lead to the understanding of some aspect of religious practices and medicine.

In Dorsey's research on the Ponca, it was suggested through his interpretation that *Wak'ǫ́da* was a power or Great Mystery.[9] He quoted a woman as supposedly saying, "*Nú wiwítàmà Wak'ǫ́da wádixèštiwǫ̀, agíkǫbdà.*" The interpretation is "Even if my husband is pursuing those things of mystery, I want him back." A person's aspirations or hopes in life were pursued (probably more at "finding") with intent; that is, a person wanted to be endowed with the special talent for spiritual or medicinal powers.

A good example of finding aid for the tribe was given by AL in 1962. By telling the story of the eagle and cedar his intent was to tell us that life could continue normally if we used these ancient customs. This was told to my brother and me in private when our other brother died tragically. The following is an approximate translation from Ponca:

One time, many years ago . . . in the old days before the white man came, the Ponca were facing hard times. We don't know what it was, but it must have been bad enough for menfolks to look for an answer to what was happening to them. They say a man traveled many days from where the Ponca lived trying to find the answer. Maybe he could find a medicine or anything that the Creator might show him to correct that thing that was bothering them. The story goes that one day as he approached a small knoll, he noticed dust rising in the air. The weather happened to be dry . . . maybe like a drought. No wind was blowing, so the dust he saw was going straight up. He crawled to the top of the knoll, and lying flat on his stomach, he could see what looked like a whirlwind. But as he lay there, he could make out something on the ground that appeared to be spinning. He thought, maybe it was two animals fighting. At that distance it was hard for him to see clearly, so he moved closer trying to keep hidden as there were a few trees in the area. He finally came close enough to see that the animal was a wounded eagle. One of its wings appeared to be broken . . . and as it flapped its good wing, it caused itself to spin in a circle. As it did this the dust rose up. He watched for a while and then decided that that eagle will probably die from starvation or be killed by some other ani- mal. He left the area to continue his search for the problem facing the Ponca people. Traveling two or three days later, he began to wonder if, maybe, the Creator had shown him something in that wounded eagle and he overlooked it. So, they say, he returned to that place where he seen that eagle. When he got there, that eagle was still there trying to flap its wings. Even though the eagle was tired and wounded, he noticed that it was trying to use its broken wing. As it lifted its good wing, it would also lift its broken wing. He had observed when he first passed by the eagle was dragging the wing. But now he saw that the eagle was lifting the wing almost as good as the other wing. As he watched from a distance, he noticed that the eagle would rest a while and then continue its flapping.

They say on the fourth day of his watch, he saw clouds forming in the distance. A slight breeze had also come up. The eagle was now hopping and flapping its wings. Then suddenly it hopped toward a tree and jumped to the lowest branch and began to climb the tree by jumping and using its beak to pull itself to each higher branch until it reached the top. The eagle sat with its wings spread for some time swaying in the breeze on that tree with something in its beak. Trying to get a better look, he came closer and saw that it was a small twig with the leaf attached to it. The tree he sat upon was a large cedar. Then, all at once, as a strong wind came, the eagle made a big jump into the wind and began to rise upward. He watched as the eagle began to rise circling . . . riding on the air, until it went beyond the cloud . . . *Umą́di etáike akíitè* . . . where eagles live. The man went to the tree where that eagle flew. There he found a tail feather of the eagle lying upon small branches of cedar. This, he picked up and carried back to the village. They say he told the tribe that the Creator had given it to him. They say he made a central fire and burned the cedar and asked those who would come to use the fire and smoke from the cedar, and fanned them with the eagle feather as he called upon the Creator to heal their spirits and hardship. He ended up by saying if the eagle had sat there still, its wing would have grown wrong and would not have been able to fly again. By flapping its wings, it healed itself. So the people were encouraged to try to overcome their hardships.

The use of cedar (*Mázì*) and eagle feathers (*Xidá mą́šą*), which are known by most plains tribes, has its deepest meaning in the act of healing. The legend of how the eagle feathers and cedar came to the Ponca by a certain man who had found a solution to some problem has a deep meaning to the people. According to the legend, the Ponca man received the gift from the Creator. The gift was that a person with illness, under special circumstances, should be more active. He had learned that immobilization could cause sickness to remain fixed or motionless. In sickness, many, if not all, would rather lie still. Laterally, a secondary problem related to complacency was not doing anything about problems with which people were confronted. There were solutions to many problems in the world, but they had not sought them out. In this scenario, the man of medicine, in every human situation, used the eagle fan and cedar to impart strength and courage to the tribe or individual.[10] The burning of cedar and a simple fanning motion with the feather did not constitute an act of healing, but its psychological impact with the use of other medicinal herbs and prayers brought healing to the sick. Additionally, a proper approach to individuals with personal problems and a community with mounting problems found relief. To restore a harmonious relationship between man and nature, then, the fan and cedar were used. Some uses of the fan included fanning and praying for individuals in mourning, memorials of individuals, birthday celebrations, the honoring of warriors, formal thanksgiving to other individuals, and all everyday human situations in which fanning would be appropriate. The fanning of the deceased person also had its own meaning (KH, NC, AL, AMC, JP).

Some historic stories of the tribe are passed on from generation to generation. The story of how the Ponca acquired the hand game in the wilderness was told to me by KH. The following is my translation from the Ponca language:

HOW THE HAND GAME CAME TO THE PONCA

One time a man went on a search for some hunters who had not returned for many months. They say he traveled a long distance from the village. He used to hunt for small animals when he needed to eat something. In those days they also carried parched corn. One evening he came to a place where there was a timber. He noticed that a small creek ran through the timber, and out in the middle of that creek was an island. On one side, where he stood, he noticed that there was no water running in that part of the creek. Water was running on the other side.

He put up his camp on the west side of the timber a small hill. From there he could see the sunset, and to the east he could see the timber and timberline. At sundown, when he prepared for a night's rest, he heard the howl of a wolf. This was not unusual as wolves were everywhere in the North Country. He sat besides his campfire meditating before he would go into his temporary lodge. Suddenly he heard that wolf howl again. But this time it was directly toward the timber's edge. After some time had elapsed, the wolf came closer and howled again. This happened four times. After that wolf howled the fourth time, it began to sing. [At this point in the story, the storyteller sings the "Wolf Song."] When the wolf left, all was quiet. Then, suddenly, he heard people singing and laughing as though they were celebrating some event. He looked toward the timber and saw a big fire burning on that island he had seen earlier. Curious of what was happening, he went toward the fire. It was then that he saw people playing some sort of game. Two people would hide something in their hands and a person would guess what hand they were hiding something. At one end of the circle, men beat a drum in a fast study rhythm with their singing. When the guess was made correctly, one side of the circle would shout and laugh. On and on it went as he watched. Intermittently, they would stop playing and some would get up and dance to a different tune and drumbeat.

As he came closer to the fire, where people were talking and laughing, he saw that the fire began to grow smaller and the people were quieter. When he finally got to the place where the people were, there was no noise or talking, and there was only embers glowing in the darkness. He could barely see that there were people lying on the ground or leaning against a tree. As he looked around, he noticed some of them appeared to be skeletons. Others seemed to be near death. Looking closer, he heard a man speak weakly beckoning him to come closer.

The man asked him who he was. He told him he was Ponca and searching for some of his people who left the village long ago who did not return. The man told him that it was them who left. He said they hunted for a long time until they ran out of food. He said they became lost, and this is where they came. He told him as they were starving and becoming weaker a wolf came to them and told them about this game. The wolf said if you are able to guess the place where they hid the small stone in their hands, they would be strengthened and find their way home. It gave them hope to do this.

The man told him he was going to die like the rest of the people with him, but he wanted him to take this game and songs home with him. He said it would help the people when they need to be encouraged and that they would find joy and happiness in their lives.

There are many cultural aspects that might have been included in this discourse; however, this section has chosen only those elements of the culture that seem appropriate in their development and use.

Language and Socialization

The development of language and socialization was probably based on the welfare of the tribe. In some cases certain words became complex and were relegated to meanings significant to those people who understood them. There are many words regarding the natural things of earth that include a variety of techniques in usage. In the learning process, they are interlinked with rites, ceremonies, and other human situations. There was a proper usage and identity of words. Everyone was taught the correct behavior so that the attitude toward the situation was universal. They had a reverence that encompasses the whole of the ceremony, rite, or other experiences. Each individual knew his part, and others too followed the practice accordingly (KH). The Ponca language can classify objects, events, ideas, experiences, and so forth. The words can also describe a set of the same. The language, which contained meanings from their environment (the land, dwellings, people, experiences, etc.), was quite different from the world in which we now live. The word meanings contained concepts of that world, especially of religion and normal daily functions, that somehow seem inapplicable in the modern setting. Terminology for normal communication is the same. Words, however, still exist in the language that once concerned their interlude with things in nature.

The elders indicated that there were no words of profanity in the Ponca language, like those used in the English language. They said it would be ridiculous, for instance, to call a person the son of a dog. The breeding habits of animals were observed as a natural process in the animal world. In the human world, a word to connote such behavior could not be culturally, socially, or philosophically applicable. Dorsey, in his handwritten manuscript, recorded that the Ponca men learned some English profanity. In his discourse he commented on "civilizing the Indian." He wrote that should the Indian be civilized, all he would be is like the whites on the "borders." He projected that if the Indian were civilized and Christianized, he would be respected like all "good citizens." In regard to profanity, he made the following statement:

It is remarkable that when a Ponka wishes to curse or swear, he must do so in the language of his White neighbors; and even then it frequently happens that he uses the words without being aware of their true meaning, but simply because the White men use them when they get angry.

KH said there was an argument between two elderly women that a number of Ponca tribal people heard. The year was about 1910. The major language of the people at that time was the Ponca language. Coming from a period when the Ponca language was the only language spoken, they used two terms that the onlookers surmised to be "cuss" words. However, no one present had an idea what the words meant. All present were born in the late 1800s. In the heat of the argument, one of the women stated, "Dągínanihè!" The other retorted, "Xaa! đí mą́žą pagđe ní." According to the elders, everyone that heard began to laugh because they didn't know what was said.

In former times, the socialization of the child was based on learning as many aspects of the language that would affect his existence. His perceptions and beliefs may have been quite different if he had learned a different language. The Ponca related or perceived their world through words and meanings that shaped their development as individuals in their time and environment. In this sense, the language aided the family in socializing the child. And because he was socialized with the use of his native language, he understood and interpreted the things of nature through his language (KH, KCH, NC, AMC, JP, AL).

Motives and attitudes relating to perception, which was a part of his total person, gave rise to certain behavioral and cultural practices. Anyone who pursued the "things of mystery" had to be patient and follow the processes in nature as well as the social patterns of life. He may not have known what it was that he was seeking, but it was usually revealed to him. Some factors involving the "pursuit" of his calling included water, fire, wind, animal, and plant life. The objective of finding was connected to these natural elements and the seeker. In the process of finding the revelation, he was also aware of his surroundings (KH, KCH, NC, AMC, JP, AL). In the following, the elements are discussed only as they are commonly understood. The Ponca interpretation of how they might affect their lives is intertwined with some mystery of outcomes in their daily lives.

Water

The word *water* is perceived as a physiological drive. The Ponca word for water is *Ní'*. A child learns this word very early in life, and it is about as important as "mama." To a child, the word "mama" may associate with hunger and thirst, that is, if the child says "mama," she will determine his need. When he is old enough and is thirsty, he will get his own drink. As he matures, his thinking and perception expands, and he finds ways to satisfy the thirst he experiences. When drought occurs, he especially realizes the importance of water. As a part of his total existence, he knows that water is a necessary element. He may further conclude that without it, nothing can survive. Some people perceiving the in-depth meaning of water may even philosophize about it. The elders, for instance, said that there is life in it and its source of being may only be attributed to the Creator (KH, NC, AMC, AL). Water, or *Ní'*, then, through his perception of it, becomes sacred. KH said that water is sacred and should not be played with and that we should drink a little before we eat, thanking the Creator for our lives. He said that water is alive and is like man: it can kill or let you live. So in giving thanks to the Creator for his existence, the mature man concludes that water is sacred, or *Ní' akà waxúbaì*; and therefore, he will drink little of it before each meal or at any ceremonial gathering as directed by the ceremony leader. In past times, members of the family drank from the same dipper that was passed around before the meal. This practice has been absent from the people since they came to Oklahoma. Most Ponca families up to the late 1950s always set water at the table. At tribal feasts the custom of drinking water is still practiced by the Ponca. Usually, a very small amount of water (about one tablespoon) is poured from a dipper into a cup for each individual attending the feast. The water is drunk immediately. Following the water are a variety of foods that are served in generous portions to each person. If the feast is in connection with a funeral, a small glass of water is usually taken, along with food, to the deceased. It is placed by the deceased for the remainder of the feast (KH).

The Native American Church as one part of its rituals has a water carrier, or *Niádi*. KH said that following the singing of songs pertaining to the "water bird" in the morning of the peyote meeting, the *Niádi* brings water into the tipi. Once inside the tipi, she sets the water before the fireplace near the entrance. Here she kneels and offers thanks to the Creator for the water, other life-sustaining foods, and good health. She may pray for many things, but she always gives thanks for the water. After a night of praying, the participants in the meeting partake of the water first and then other foods that are brought into the tipi. Each food, of course, is considered sacred and is partaken of in the spirit of honor and respect (KH, NC).

The Ponca *Hedúškà* usually recruits a "water boy" whose primary job is to provide water for dancers and singers. The intent is to quench the thirst at these gatherings, but the water is still taken in the spirit of honor and respect. The water boy carries a pail with a dipper to each dancer and singer. In past times, each dancer and singer drank from the same dipper without wiping it clean. Today, one will see styrofoam cups, or you may see someone wipe the dipper or drink from the opposite side of the cup.

Water was also said to be held as a sacred medicine by the *Hísadà* clan of the tribe. When clan members died in the old days, it is said, it would surely rain. Having the responsibility of officiating funerals over the years, I have witnessed rain occurring at the time of an individual *Hísadà* clan member's death. Coincidence? Members of this clan were also known as rainmakers. Virginia Buffalohead once told me that her mother, who was a member of that clan, said if a member of their clan threw water on a person, it would rain. Others claim if they hung out feathers to dry, it would rain.

Fire

From earliest times fire was considered important to the Ponca people. It had many uses and was considered sacred in some religious practices, but it was never worshipped. Its use was of a practical nature and included cooking to keeping warm, hardening spear points to heating stones for applying to aching bones, making pottery to bending shinny clubs, and so on. Its place in the ceremonial circle usually was considered sacred and was treated as such because of the nature of some rituals. For example, the *Xdexdé* ritual required the heating of an instrument used to tattoo a person. The heat purified the instrument, and then the instrument was allowed to cool so as not to burn the skin. The elders said that during that time, the man or woman performing the ritual made statements regarding the fire as being given by the Creator.

The Native American Church also uses a center fireplace called *Unéde*, which is kept burning throughout the night. KH said at appropriate times cedar is added to the fire to make smoke. It was said to be like the prayers rising up to the Creator. Participants desiring to pray roll their tobacco in corn shucks. With assistance from the fire keeper, the tobacco is lit with the lighting stick from the fireplace.[11] The significance, again, is the smoke that rises as prayers are uttered to the Creator. The fire's main function is to provide the means whereby prayer rituals can be completed. In this, the fire is considered sacred to the Ponca people.

Other rituals using fire include the sweat lodge, Íʼụpè, in connection with healing. Large perforated rocks, about ten to twelve inches in diameter, are heated and brought into the sweat lodge. Following the medicines administered by the Ponca doctor, the sick person is taken into the sweat lodge. Here other rituals are performed.

In August 1994 a reunion of the Southern and Northern Ponca took place at the first annual powwow of the Northern Ponca at Niobrara, Nebraska. A speech was given by Thomas Roughface Sr. He addressed a crowd of approximately a thousand people in attendance at the gathering. Two fires were built outside the arena or dancing area. The fire on the south side represented the Ponca from Oklahoma. The fire on the north side represented the Ponca of Nebraska. At the east center of the arena, wood was placed. AlJo Picotte (now deceased), great-grandson of Chief Standing Bear, represented the Ponca Tribe of Nebraska and George White Eagle (also deceased), great-grandson of Chief White Eagle, represented the Ponca Tribe of Oklahoma. In the lighting of the center fire, each carried a torch from the fire representing their tribal villages. Together they lit the center fire symbolizing the union of both tribes. The singing of a one-slow-beat song was dedicated to the ancestral fathers for the land of northern Nebraska and southern South Dakota, our original homelands. Ponca from both tribes participated in the dance. I offered a prayer in the Ponca language. Edwin Little Cook Sr. (now deceased), a member of the Native American Church and a traditionalist, put cedar on the ashes of the fire. A very moving experience took place as all Ponca people present, individually fanned themselves with the smoke from the fireplace.

The place of fire in Ponca history shows its many uses. At funerals, for example, food taken from the fireplace to the deceased in former times was returned to the fire to be burned (KH). It was believed that the destroyed foodstuff, through the fire, would accompany the deceased to the other world. When bison roam in giant herds on the northern plain, Ponca bison hunters set fire to the dried prairie grass to cause new grass growth in the early spring. It was believed that the bison would smell the new grass and come.[12]

Wind

The Ponca consider the four winds as sacred. They focus on the seasons in that the north wind brought the bitter cold as the south wind brought heat. The west-northwest and west-southwest brought all storms—rain, thunder, and snow. East winds were said to be gentle and blew back as the storms left. There was a saying that if the east wind blew hard, there would be a tremendous storm. (Lightning also told the tribe which way the storm was headed. The angle of a single bolt of lightning suggested a direction to the left or to the right of you. If the lightning was straight up and down, it was coming toward you.)

The respect for the wind (*Tadé*) begins with the breath of life. They call breath *Níú'*. It is certain that without this life ceases. The elders, when they were present at the death of their close relatives, noted the cessation of breathing. When this occurred, one would say, "*Núítè bišt'ái, náxe akà agdáì.*" This means, "He has stopped breathing, and his spirit is going back." The sacredness of this moment is associated with the breathing. The departure of the spirit becomes independent of the body and returns to its Maker.

The teachings of the wind too are perceived on the plains and in the forest. A gentle breeze could mean that conditions for the people are good. According to Fletcher and La Flesche, Chief White Eagle told how the wind could also be detrimental to bison hunters:

> The father cut all the edges of the man's robe, so that nothing about him could flutter should the wind blow. The spirit of a murdered person will haunt the people, and when the tribe is on the hunt, will cause the wind to blow in such a direction as to betray the hunters to the game and cause the herd to scatter, making it impossible for the people to get food. [The Omaha have the same belief about ghosts scattering the herds by raising the wind.] After the man's robe was cut it was sewed together in front, but space was left for his arm to have free-

dom . . . Then his hair was cut short for fear it might blow and cause the winds to become restless.[13]

This story was told about a man who had caused the death of another tribesman and about the subsequent effects of his actions. The wind in this regard might have been considered unfavorable because of the man's actions.

The winds in the forest also tell their own story. Some men found secrets to life in the directing sounds of the wind in the leaves or grass. One tribal elder said regarding the wind in the woods:

> I was looking for a certain plant that grows on the floor of the timber. After about one half of day, I heard the wind rustling the leaves above me. At first I thought it's just windy, but it got louder and louder in one place. I walked away from there, but I kept hearing that wind so I went in the direction it was blowing. When the wind stopped blowing, I stopped walking. I began to look around, and sure enough there was that plant at my feet.

The respect given to wind is noted in the name-giving process. It was said by the elders that some children were named according to the wind conditions. For example, if it was a pleasant but windy day, an infant girl might be named *Tadéwį* (Wind).

Animals and Plants

The meanings of words that described mammals have been lost to the past. Some root meanings are known but have only a broad association with varied species. The prefixes for the following are examples of such words:

> The prefix *T'á-* has no significant meaning to us but seemed to suggest to those early Ponca that animals might have the same lineal descent:[14]

T'áxtì	deer
T'atą́gà	large deer (elk?)
T'ačúge	antelope
T'atą́gà	bison (?)

Šą́- appears to categorize those animals in the same family:

Šą́gè	horse
Šą́gèt'aną̀hà	wild horse, mustang
Šą́tągà	wolf
Šą́nudà	dog
Šą́žįgà	pup or small dog

Mą́- refers to dirt or the ground in the Ponca language. These types of animals perhaps burrowed into the ground for nesting or hibernating:

Mą̀čú	grizzly bear
Mąščį́gè	rabbit
Mąd̦į́kàšižè	fox
Mąščį́skà	jackrabbit
Mąžą́hà	red fox
Mą́šcà	crawdad
Mą́gà	skunk
Mąd̦į́xudè	prairie dog
Mąd̦į́gà	mole

An exception for the rule for Mą́- is the burrowing owl, Wapúhagadà, and the grey fox, which is T'ík'axudè.

Mí'- means "moon" in these animal names. These animals were considered nocturnal by the Ponca.

Mí'k'asì	coyote
Mik'á	raccoon

Į́- is a prefix designating certain rodents:

Įštíp'a	opossum
Įčą́t'ągà	rat
Įčą́ga	mouse
Įčágaskà	weasel

Some of the meanings of the cited prefixes are lost. However, the classification of the animals clearly suggests that the early Ponca had an understanding of the animal world in which they lived. These classifications, in turn, became a way for the Ponca to determine species that benefited them for their physical needs. Not all animals were considered foodstuff. It was believed that some animals had medicinal properties and were sometimes consumed for that purpose only. Otherwise, their diet consisted mainly of vegetables and other wild plants. They supplemented their plant food with venison and other small animals. Fish too was used for foodstuff. According to experts, the Ponca people became bison hunters once they were established in the plains. Our interest here, however, deals primarily with how the Ponca understood their world. As noted above, they evidently classified most animals and plants as to their importance.

A common shorthaired dog called *Įštá dubà*, or "four eyes," and was used for various purposes. It received its name because of the round marks above each eye. This animal was used primarily as a pack animal. Sometimes a small travois was attached to the dog. It was believed that the animal was a gift from the Creator from the beginning. KH told the following story of how the dog came to the Ponca:

One time a Ponca man was coming home from great distance away . . . *Agíitè* . . . he's coming back. *Wąískigè adíitè* . . . He's carrying a heavy bundle on his back. *P'ázè ahiíkì, ázegidè nąštaìtè* . . . When evening had come, he stopped to rest. But he doesn't want to stay there. There's something there he don't like. He cook something and keep coming. While he's walking, there's somebody or something following him. When he stops, that thing back there stops too. *Hádąitè* . . . It must have been at night. It's dark. But he knows that something is following him, so he gets his club ready. This thing is coming real close to him now. So when it's right behind him . . . he turns around and lift his club. He's ready to hit that thing . . . but when he's going to hit . . . that thing talk to him. It said, *Ąwátiážigà. Ikágèwigidè k'ábdà* . . . "Don't hit me. I want to be your friend." *Egidè šánudà akámà* . . . It was a dog. It talk again and said, "If you let me come with you and feed me when I'm hungry, I'll protect you. I'll bark when somebody comes to your home. I won't sit right in front of your home . . . but I'll sit away from your home so I won't get in the way. But if someone tries to come there . . . I'll let you know. If you go on a journey, I'll help you by carrying some of your things. And if any member of your family gets sick, you can kill me when I'm young and eat me . . . my flesh will make them well. When you go hunting . . . *Ábaì né'tedì, udúwihè mąbdítamikè. Ųwíwikątamikè* . . . I will follow you. I will help you [hunt]. If there is no food to eat, you can kill me and eat my flesh, and you will live." I guess he talk like that to this man. So he brought that dog to the Ponca people . . . he's been there ever since. They believe that the Creator gave it to them.

In the Ponca tradition, the dog had many uses. It followed hunters and warriors and assisted them in every way. It became a companion and friend and protected them. Some wolf-like dogs were spoken of by the elders but said they were wild and could serve only as attack dogs. They didn't know what breed of dog they were. AL said that some of these dogs were honored for their participation in warfare by placing a feather on them.

The following story was told to me by Albert Makes Cry Jr. in 1989. It is a story of a heroic dog named Old Man Bear (*Mąčú Išáge*).

There's song that was made for a dog. *Šánudà wí wáą wí' gí'gaxaì tè.* They said that this dog was a close friend to his owner. He used to go with him wherever he went. Everybody in the camp knew this dog. When they went hunting, he would go with him. His name was *Mąčú Išáge* . . . Old Man Bear. They say he even went on the buffalo hunt with the menfolk. *Gaxą adá kí' wiúhe adé nąite.*

One day an alarm was made by the tribal lookouts . . . *Úwadąbè.* They said there is a group of men coming this way. In those days the lookouts could tell how far away a person or a group was from the village. That was their job you might say. Those men who were always ready for such a thing were from the *Đíxidą̀* and *Níkapášną̀* clans. They were the first to meet the enemy. This was part of the Ponca strategy to go into warfare. As they began to leave the village, *Mąčú Išáge* started to follow them because his owner was a member of the group. But his owner talked to him and told him he could not go. He said, "We may fight over there and you might get kicked and get hurt. You have to stay." But *Mąčú Išáge* wouldn't stay back. His owner pretended to hit him with a little stick, and *Mąčú Išáge* ran back toward the village.

As the men approached the enemy, they suddenly noticed that the enemy was in a turmoil. When they came close, they saw *Mąčú Išáge* jumping at the enemy's legs and biting them. Their horses were buck-ing and turning round and round. The Ponca battled the enemy, and when it was over, they looked for *Mąčú Išáge*. But they could not find him. So they returned to the village victorious but without *Mąčú Išáge*.

About four days later, a man came to the owner's dwelling and said, "There is a dog lying in the bushes. It looks like your dog." He immedi-ately went to see with other men. Sure enough, it was *Mąčú Išáge*. He was hurt but he was alive. The man who doctors people and animals came. Also present was a song maker . . . *Waą́ gáxe*.

> *Áwatè t'éxiadą̀ ną́'ą̀wap'a ąkídedą̀*
>
> Second, *Áwatè t'éxiadą̀ ną́'ą̀wap'a ąkídedą̀*
>
> Chorus, *Áwatè t'éxiadą̀ Šaą́ žįgà ną́'ą̀wap'a ąkídedą̀*
>
> *Áwatè t'éxiadą̀ šéwábdi bde yo heye theye thǫ*
>
> *Mą́ču Išágeà, Áwatè t'éxiadą̀ Šaą́ žįgà ną́'ą̀wap'a ąkídedą̀*
>
> *Áwatè t'éxiadą̀ šéwábdi bde yo heye theye tho.*

This is the song he made for *Mąčú Išáge*, a heroic and brave dog.

In this section, the embodiment of Ponca ways are seen in the lan-guage. These words described the world in which they lived, and that perception subsequently interpreted all stimuli in their environment.

27

Into the School House

The term *Western civilization* connotes a philosophy stemming from Greco-Roman traditions and culture. This, in fact, seems to be the root of modern civilization as we know it. The influx of the European people into North America brought with them that overshadowing system, not just by word, deed, and thought but also by sheer numbers of people espousing the same philosophy. The power in numbers brought the inevitable change that the Ponca somewhat reluctantly accepted. Requiring their cooperation in every way to accustom themselves to the new culture, the first missionaries and federal agents worked with those Ponca who showed special interest. There is some evidence that many Ponca were accepting and learned to read and write beginning in the mid-nineteenth century. Unfortunately, many rejected the system in the beginning, which resulted in far-reaching problems. Apparently, the signing of treaty agreements with representatives of the federal government gave those first Ponca insight into what the future held for their people.

The first two treaties of 1817 and 1825 made no commitment to the Ponca concerning their education and compensation for lands ceded. The language in the treaty agreements spoke primarily of friendship and admission that they, the Ponca people, resided within the territorial limits of the United States; that they, the Ponca people, would not retaliate against the Americans; and that they, the Ponca people, would agree to trade with them. The initial compensatory benefit for the Ponca people appeared in the treaty of 1858, which was signed in Washington DC. Part of the treaty stipulated a provision for one saw mill and a grinding mill to provide employment for tribal members. A training program (school?) was started but amounted to the building of a commissary. This project lasted for three years.

It wasn't until the Ponca had come to Indian Territory that acculturation issues entered the scene. Those problems were primarily due to the methodology used in the inculcation processes. The methods enforced, by the government, were inconclusive. In retrospect, it is certain that procedures used in teaching the need for employment and household management could have been more effective. The forced acculturation proved to be a deterrent toward acceptance of the new way.

The Ponca Indian Boarding School

Part of the 1858 treaty agreement was apparently the first attempt to train young Ponca men as apprentices and assistants and subsequently to make the Ponca tribesmen self-sufficient in accordance with European standards. Following the removal to Indian Territory, a boarding school was established on the Ponca Reservation. According to KH, KCH, AMC, NC, and others, the building itself was three stories high and included a dormitory, a kitchen, a dining room, classrooms, and offices. They indicated that other buildings surrounded the school, which included houses for government employees; a mess hall for teachers; a barn; a corral for livestock; sheds for farm implements; a corn crib; a chicken house; a laundry; a shoe shop; a machine shop; cellars; and other outhouses. The school owned a variety of livestock, including horses, cows, hogs, and chickens. It had its own orchard and vegetable gardens. As a self-supporting operation of the federal government, the school had no reason to purchase any perishable foodstuff from the city unless it may have been for a special occasion for government dignitaries. The cultural pattern of the Ponca, very noticeable and different from the European-American way of life, was to be changed.

The school program focused on teaching reading, writing, and arithmetic. The teachers of the school neither spoke Ponca, nor did they use interpreters. All elders reiterated how frustrating the experience was during those early years. KH said,

> We were pitiful . . . we didn't know one word of English. We were not allowed to talk in Ponca. If we did . . . we were punished. Sometimes . . . whipped . . . make us chop wood or maybe dig ditches. That was all part of learning how to talk English.

The main method for teaching the English language was with the use of a large cardboard on which letters from the alphabet were placed beside a picture of an object or objects to show the name and sound of each letter. The teaching methodology was called the sound-symbol technique. (This was conveyed to me in 1980 by Robert Ford, assistant superintendent, Ponca City Schools.) The children then learned the sounds of the alphabet as the teacher pointed to each letter and voiced the sound of the letter. The letters and sounds were then placed together to make a word. The method enabled Ponca children, who only spoke the Ponca language, to learn a foreign language.

KH and KCH said the school had no competitive sports but did provide intramural sport activities for all students. They learned and played baseball, football, and basketball (which was considered a girls' game at the time). There was no track. The girls played ball among themselves using a flat piece of board for a bat and a homemade ball. The girls, more often, enjoyed playing the Ponca women's game *Wabášnadè*. The game was played much like the men's shinny game. Boys too played shinny during the springtime. Another game the boys played was kicking a basketball toward goals. This was a game created by the boys to play with the big ball because the girls played basketball with it. Soccer originated in England beginning in the mid-nineteenth century and was hardly known in America.

Detailed work at the school included helping in the kitchen and bakery. Here students had a work experience as well as an opportunity to earn their keep. In the farm department of the school, students had their own livestock and were responsible for them. Each student also had their own plot for planting vegetables. Clothing worn by students was government-issued uniforms for classroom, work, and Sundays. According to KH, AL, and NC, the uniforms for the boys during school time and Sundays were a three-piece outfit consisting of a shirt, pants, and a cap. The girls, according to KCH, wore ankle-length dresses with a white apron, fluffed at the shoulders, and large ribbon in their hair. Boys' hair was clipped short like the crew cut. The girls were allowed to wear their hair long, probably based on the Christian biblical standard. All students wore the same kind of shoes, a high-topped work boot. The school according to the elders had its own laundry as well. Originally, they used the washboard and tub, but eventually they acquired a steam-operated engine for laundry. Boys were detailed to cut wood and keep the fire going to produce steam.

Domestic chores, such as house cleaning, cooking, canning, and planting gardens, were part of the learning process (KH).

Disciplinary measures taken on students who violated rules by, for example, chewing gum, being tardy, or speaking the Ponca language varied according to the offense. Students who broke these rules were sometimes whipped and made to sit on a bench for long periods. Food was also kept from them as a means of punishment. (A practice contrary to the Ponca culture, in which children were neither spanked nor whipped and were never deprived of food.) Extra detail for violators was most common. Educating Ponca children could have been effectually done without that type of discipline.

The idea of work among Native Americans was always connected to survival. The same idea was somewhat indoctrinated as students were taught the essential idea of the work world of the white populace. The white concept of work somewhat contradicted the Ponca concept of work, which entailed a communal effort. They, however, gave their fullest possible cooperation in the work-study program of the school. KH, who spent six years at the Ponca School, said the work detail was carried out easily by Ponca students:

> Every student had a small plot for gardening. He planted his own seeds and cared for his plot. Some students ... boys ... had their own livestock ... cows ... they had to take care of them every day. We like to do that. Everybody at school did some kind of work. Some worked in the kitchen, laundry, and halls, sweeping ... mopping up. They cut weeds too. When they got that steam engine ... it's for the laundry ... we used to cut wood to keep the fire going. That work ... it wasn't hard to do.

The concept of work in the education environment in other government schools was the same. The federal government did not conceive of a "free" education for Native Americans. The workload they carried from day to day probably exceeded the current work-study programs in most colleges. For instance, the Chilocco Indian Agricultural School also had their own farm implement to raise their own crops. They had a large herd of varied livestock and operated their own dairy, producing their own milk products. NM said she worked "year round" at Chilocco as well as at the Ponca Indian School:

I went to Ponca School first, and after that I went to Chilocco. While we were at Ponca School, we all dressed the same. I worked all the way through school. I worked with Agnes Headman, Katherine No Ear, and Cordelia Hairy Back. We used to bake about five hundred loaves of bread a day. I stayed there for five years straight and never went home . . . I was raised there, but my parents came to see me every once in a while. I was paid eight dollars a month during the summer.

The initial funding for the establishment of the government schools in Kay County, Oklahoma, came from the federal government. Entrepreneurs in Arkansas City, Kansas, profited greatly from building these schools for the federal government. But the schools were self-supporting in food production. Teacher's salaries, however, were paid by the government and were very good.

Other Government Schools

When the Ponca Indian Boarding School could not provide further training for the students, they were sent to one of several government schools in the country. Some of the schools that Ponca Indians attended were the Chilocco Indian Agricultural School, Chilocco, Oklahoma; Haskell Institute, Lawrence, Kansas; Carlisle Institute, Pennsylvania; Phoenix Indian School, Phoenix, Arizona; Cantonment Indian School, Canton, Oklahoma; and Genoa, at Genoa, Nebraska.

Chilocco Indian School, in the early years following the turn of the twentieth century, provided a practical training program that many Ponca received. The training included welding, electricity, plumbing, printing, painting, heavy equipment operating, auto mechanics, dry cleaning, journalism, the culinary arts, baking, cosmetology, and agriculture. Practically no one wanted to be a farmer because of the stigma placed on the profession by the students themselves. The training, originally, was designed to help the school retain its self-supporting status. In the end, the training at Chilocco became the precursor for a quality trade school.

Even though the students, especially boys, didn't want to be farmers, they were required to work on the farm and enjoyed it. This experience was probably one of the better features of the school. Most foods were produced on the school property. Well into the twentieth century, the school operated a complete dairy system, chicken farm, hog and sheep lot, beef and dairy cattle, horses and horse barn, apple orchard, and so forth. Some activities included dehorning cattle, neutering hogs and sheep, vaccinating chickens, operating the milk machine, making ice cream and cheese, butchering, and plowing and planting. The students did many other chores such as transporting milk cartons to and from the kitchen, gathering eggs, cutting grass, and general clean up on the campus grounds, buildings, and dormitories.

Under expert supervision from the power plant, students received training by assisting those who repaired electrical breakdowns, keeping all electrical appliances in working order, maintaining all power plant functions, and providing a steam heat system for the campus in working order. The bakery and kitchen prepared a variety of menus three times a day. The bakery was responsible for making enough bakery products to feed over nine hundred students by the 1950s. The school's laundry provided cleaning services for bedding for six dormitories in addition to clothing, if requested by students who paid a fee. Otherwise, students did their own laundry by hand. The print shop provided training by publishing a school newspaper, bulletins, special cards, announcements, and so forth. The paint shop was responsible for painting all campus buildings and homes.

The school maintained an orderly system, and all students participated in the work-learn trade program. In the academic department, students learned American history, English, mathematics, general science, geography, social studies, and so forth. Some courses in algebra, business, and journalism were also provided. The school participated in competitive sports such as boxing, football, basketball, baseball, wrestling, and track. Excelling in boxing, Chilocco boxers won practically every match with other schools and boxing teams. Famed footballers and track men too, like Louis "Rabbit" Weller, Caddo Indian, set records unmatched by high school players today. The trade school concept gave impetus to the acculturation processes. Although disadvantaged by many problems, it was a positive step forward into the dominant society. Ponca students who had attended the government boarding schools since their inception have now favorably found gainful employment in many cities throughout the country. In May 1980 Chilocco Indian School closed as did some other government schools.

The Indian Education Acts

To counterbalance the school closings, the Office of Indian Education, a division of the Education Office of the Department of Health and Education, in 1972 provided grant assistance to local education agencies throughout the United States. The assistance was given to Native Americans, Alaskan Natives, and Native Hawaiians. The educational programs were essentially established to supplement funds to meet the special educational and culturally related school needs of students enrolled in public schools. The eligibility requirements for assistance included having specific educational needs; being economically disadvantaged; having special educational and material needs; and determining how this project would be carried out. The eligibility of Native Americans was based on a needs assessment survey. This survey would determine whether an Indian community was really in need. That disadvantaged condition then would make the community eligible for the federal assistance. This eligibility was to demonstrate that there existed an actual physical or material need in the educational environment. It had to be demonstrated with specific instances of proof that the Native American children lacked in certain educational achievements, accomplishments, and other evidences of inactivity in school functions. This was self-evident. In Ponca City, practically all non-Indian graduating students received special scholarships to go on to college. There is no known Native American who has received such scholarships.

Assuming a school was eligible, the monies received then would provide opportunities for the children. Ponca children did not participate in school activities, and the money was intended to encourage them to become more involved. An Indian counselor was hired to help curb problems that students were facing. Some of these problems included excessive absenteeism, tardiness, drug abuse, fighting, arguing with teachers, and dropping out of school. Since there was a lack of communication with Indian parents, the counselor provided liaison between the school and Indian community. Six teacher's aides had been previously hired to assist in six of the elementary schools. Their job was essentially to assist teachers and the attendance office. As the federal Indian education programs began to make their impact

in the schools, their purposes were termed instructional, supportive services, and experiences. This meant the project provided guidance, counseling, and cultural enrichment. Other assistance covered
school supplies and other educational costs that might be defined as
a specific need existent among Native American children that could
increase their educational opportunities. Dr. Allen Robson, superintendent in the 1970s, provided excellent guidance and leadership to
Native American parents. To substantiate the local program to the
Washington office for funding, consultation was made with tribal
authorities and parents of the children. Subsequent to the funding
of the project, a repository was kept in the local education agency for
interpretation of the project, which included documentation of meetings, minutes, committee member selection procedures, and members
themselves. Since accountability is the basis for success and interpretation for future programming, a strict administration of the funds
was essential with the Native American populace being knowledgeable of the administration of the funds.

The Inception of the Ponca Johnson-O'Malley
Program and Title IV-A Projects

Mrs. Hazel Headman, Mrs. Genevieve Pollak (deceased), Mrs. Helen
Overland (deceased), and Mrs. Bonita Fite (deceased) cooperated in
establishing the first Indian education program in 1969 in the Ponca
City Public Schools. Although it was difficult to promote, the program was secured. First, an official of the State Board of Education,
Indian Office, suggested that the Ponca City Public Schools were inel-
igible because Ponca City was an "affluent town." Second, he said the
Ponca and other tribes residing within the school district did not
meet the necessary "Indian" enrollment percentage to qualify for
a project. To qualify, he said, an Indian group was required to have
"10 percent Indian enrollment" of the total school enrollment. The
enrollment of Native American students in the district was always
approximately two hundred for the ten years before the Indian education programs. Criteria for eligibility had disqualified the Ponca
because the total enrollment was always approximately sixty-five hundred or there about. At this rate, the Indian enrollment had to be 650.
Whether the state employee was honest in quoting the requirements

for the program is unknown. Additionally, it was uncertain whether he was within his legal rights to make an arbitrary decision for the federal and state governments. These funds were known as entitlement funds and should have been distributed to schools where Native Americans attended classes from kindergarten through the twelfth grade. After much discussion of the economic problems, and especially the high dropout rate of the Ponca students, the official stated that perhaps the school fees could be paid for. This was the beginning of the Johnson-O'Malley (JOM) program. The JOM Committee was composed of five parents of children in the school district. At regularly scheduled meetings with a representative of the school district, they ultimately were able to procure funding for a bus and six teacher's aids. The same parent committee, as it was called, also initiated Title IV-A project, which had a separate committee because of communication with the funding agency. The committee was also composed of five parents of students, three student representatives, and one teacher. Ex officio members were one Ponca Tribal Council member and the Indian counselor who also became the coordinator of the project. The function of the committee was to approve new students applying for services through the project, in addition to determining the current needs of students. Some results of the project in the years 1974–79 were monitored and showed that student involvement in athletics increased from one or two to twenty-four students. Better communication between Indian parents and teachers was established, especially through the Indian counselor. Identity was made with the educational environment through the teacher's aides (all Ponca). A positive attitude toward school was evident by the retention of 87 percent of all Indian students for the 1978–79 school year.

Higher Education

Those Ponca students graduating from high school or completing the General Equivalency Diploma (GED) program usually continue their education.

After the Second World War, some servicemen entered vocational schools, while very few entered college. The greater majority of those entering colleges or trade schools began in the second half of the twentieth century. In 1975 a survey conducted by the tribe showed that over five hundred people had completed training in various trades. Toward the end of the 1990s, approximately eighty graduated from accredited colleges and universities with anything from an associate's to a doctorate degree. The bulk of these people graduated from college in the last quarter of the twentieth century.

In the beginning of the twenty-first century, tribal records indicate a larger number of adult students entering or going back to school. Their reasoning for reentering school is usually the want of higher earning potential to fulfill a desire to become a business manager, teacher, or specialist in some profession. These older students were shown to have a preconceived notion of what they wanted when they entered college.

Areas of study in college show that more women entered practical nursing, with advanced studies in registered nursing. More men and women achieved undergraduate and graduate degrees in elementary and secondary education. More men entered business administration, industrial and computer technology, and civil engineering. In specialized fields, both men and women were successful in the field of fine arts, psychology, religion, law, and political science. Records for 2016 show at the doctorate level four received advanced degrees in law, three in education, one in psychology, and one in medicine.

This section has cited some data on the educational achievements of the Ponca Tribe of Oklahoma. Some of these graduates joining the workforce have remained close to the reservation area and are employed by the Ponca Tribe of Oklahoma. Others have successfully established their residence and employment in other cities in the state as well as other locations around the country.

28

Warriors of the Ponca

While traveling in Canada some years ago, I met an itinerant Sioux Indian evangelist who reiterated stories of conflicts his band of Sioux had with the Ponca in the "old days." His people were from the Devils Lake Indian Reservation in North Dakota. He apologized to the congregation that evening by saying, "but in modern times, we are now brothers." Ancient stories of the Ponca also relate the conflicts they had with other tribes of Indians. It is evident that there was an ongoing conflict with the surrounding tribes during those times. According to some historians, the Ponca were not liked by their neighbors. Why that happened is a mystery; however, it does suggest that the Ponca had enemies.

According to most historical records, the Ponca never waged war against the United States. According to KH, NC, and AL, certain pioneers crossing their land, squatting, or establishing farms were targeted by Ponca warriors to be burned out. In their own way, these men of war attacked and destroyed many white farms. The attempt, in retrospect, must have appeared futile and foolish to government representatives.

The government penalized the tribe by demanding they repay those families for their losses. For instance, the sixth part of the 1858 treaty agreement provided that the Ponca set aside a sum of $20,000 to repay private citizens who claimed that Ponca tribesmen committed "depredations" upon them. Additionally it stated that these "citizens of the United States" were to receive "full consideration" from the tribe. One Jesse Williams was to be paid in full in the amount of $1,000 for his claim. Thus began an experience that taught the Ponca they were aliens in their own land.

But after going through a maze of fifty-six years of forced acculturation and socialization, the Ponca were now ready to go to war for the United States.

As a part of the American social, cultural, and economic processes at work in their lives, the Ponca developed a deep sense of patriotism and obligation. The ingrained ideology of military training during the early years at government schools and their own tribal regimentation resulted in high support of the United States when it entered the First World War of 1914–18. Tribesmen volunteered for the U.S. armed forces in the First and Second World Wars, the Korean conflict, the Vietnam War, and the War in the Persian Gulf out of this sense of obligation and responsibility to the country and family. The enemy, to the Ponca, had been anyone who had trespassed on their land or who might have violated other tribal laws. This constituted reason for retaliation. Now, if these new conflicts never reached American soil, how then did they justify their action to join? First, reservation life had little to offer economically. Second, there was that sense of patriotism developed through socialization. Their perception of the American way of life was equally theirs as well as other non-Indian people's. When the war began, the U.S. government called on the tribe to help. So friends and relatives joined up and went willingly. Those able-bodied Ponca who went from the reservation to serve in the First World War were as follows:

Buffalo, Alfred

Callshim, George, Sr.

Cerre, Ben

Collins, William, Sr.

Cry, Norman "Willie"

DeLodge, Baptiste

Gayton, Dick

Headman, Kenneth

Hinman, Richard "Dick"

Hinman, Roy

Howe, Oliver, Sr.

Kemble, McKay

Kemble, Willie

King, Browning

Knight, Tony (Non-Ponca)

LeClair, Charles Richard

LeClair, Mike

Makes Cry, Albert, Sr.

New Moon, George

Others, Robert

Ribs, Harry

Walking Sky, Woolsie

Waters, Albert

Yellow Bull, Frank

According to the elders, some of the men were drafted. The draft system was established about this time, but in legal terms it was a questionable act of the government (see chapter 29). For the most part, the Ponca men volunteered for service. According to tribal enrollment records, the Ponca men above represented every eligible tribesman. As soldiers, they served well and received tribal praise and commendation for their services performed. Songs were made for some of the men as song making goes. Some men kept their own family songs, by which they were honored.

Practically every eligible Ponca man volunteered for the draft during the Second World War. They served in all branches of the armed forces, and the tribe was represented by at least one member in all major invasions by the United States. In the European theater, some were involved in fighting in Sicily, Italy, France, Belgium, and Germany. In the North African campaign, the Asiatic theater, the South Pacific theater, and other operations Ponca men fought alongside other American soldiers. Many Ponca will tell where they fought but do not go into detail. They were in places called Anzio, Omaha Beach, Utah Beach, Burma, Siam, and even in China. Some said, "We were somewhere in Europe." The predominant fighting period with the Japanese was in the Pacific Islands. Here, they spoke of Okinawa, the Philippines, Luzon, Guadalcanal, Laiti, and other islands. Like other soldiers, some Ponca were wounded or killed.

A general description of the Ponca involvement in the war was solicited from some veterans. Sgt. Wiley Howe (deceased) told KH (his uncle) the following about how the invasion at Utah Beach took place:

He said his group was about second or third group to make a landing. His superior officer told them that they were to dig in on the hillside as another group went farther into the interior. The plan was to cause the enemy to chase the Americans back toward the beach. The plan worked, and Sergeant Howe and his group opened fire upon them from that lateral position. He said there were many casualties. But this allowed great numbers of American soldiers to go in defeating the enemy and gaining ground.

There was a part of this episode that Sergeant Howe remembered that was unlike anything he ever seen or heard of. The American soldiers were issued alcoholic drinks to give them calmness in the thick of the battle. He said he heard one soldier cry for his mother as he was dying. Some were intoxicated and should have lived, he said. But because of their carelessness, they lost their lives.

The following is a World War I episode that transpired into the making of Ponca *Heⁿdúška* songs for an enemy war leader. The story was told to me by Joe Rush, a World War II veteran (my translation).

In the major war campaigns, it seems there was always a Ponca Indian present. In the First World War, at least one of the three Ponca men who fought with American troops in Europe told the story of how one of the enemy's main military officials ran for his life. It was told he left his soldiers behind to fend for themselves. It was so noted by all the Ponca soldiers that they considered that act as an act of cowardice. The story was conveyed to tribal members back home in Oklahoma. Those who made songs for such men immediately composed four *Heⁿdúška* songs for that enemy leader. [Songs such as these are call *Wéxaxà waą̀*, "make fun of" or "mockery songs."] Three of the songs were Soldier Dance songs that tell of the man's cowardice and running to save his life. One of the songs was a Straight Dance song of the *Heⁿdúška*.

Leaving out the gory details of war, Gilbert Cole Jr. (now deceased) related his duties as a Marine antiaircraft weapons specialist:

I joined the Marines in February 1943 and took my training in boot camp at San Diego for two months. I volunteered with Olin Kemble, Amos Primeaux, Neal Blueback, and C. J. Fisher, a white guy that lived among us Poncas. We all didn't join the Marines. We were just looking for adventure when we volunteered. I was trained and put in an antiaircraft outfit . . . 20 and 40mm special weapons. Following boot camp, I went to Camp Pendleton for special weapons for six months training. Just before Ponca powwow time, we were told that we were going to ship out, and I got a ten-day leave to come home. I went back to Pendleton and then went out on the high seas for about sixty days in a convoy. We stopped in Hawaii for refueling and went on to the Marshall Islands into combat. These islands were well fortified by the Japanese, but these were knocked out by the Navy Fleet and then the "salt troops" moved in and took over half of the islands. We moved in at night, and the Japanese opened fire on our landing crafts, and we had to back out and went to another area, but we secured the island in two days. I spent two weeks there, and we set up our antiaircraft guns on the airstrips. Japanese bombers came in and bombed us, and many got killed. I was on guard duty that night and heard the first bomb fall and got knocked down. When I came to, I looked around and the whole island was a mess. I started running for cover. The bombing had ended, and we cleaned up the mess. After that, we were sent back to Hawaii . . . at the transit center and more training. We then went to Okinawa. While we were going there, we heard that Germany surrendered but the Japanese were still fighting. Our troop ship was bombed by a Japanese kamikaze plane, but we were lucky and didn't get hit by anything. About one-third of the island was still occupied by the Japanese. The Navy Fleet shelled it, and then we moved in to set up our antiaircraft guns again on the airstrip. We were bombed two times by the Japanese, but I came out okay. I was there for four months, and it was during this time that the A-bomb was dropped on Japan. After the Japanese surrendered, everybody got excited and started shooting their weapons into the air, and some guys got killed by their own shells. After that we were shipped home.

Isaac Headman, who served in the U.S. Navy in the Second World War, said, while in the South Pacific, his ship went through many hazardous waters delivering fuel in a tanker. His ship was attacked by Japanese kamikaze planes. He said they had shot the Japanese down before they crashed into the ship.

Like the veterans of the First World War, these men also were recognized by the tribe for their valor. Tribal honors of the past again surfaced, and appropriate songs and commendations were given to them. Getting more information from these new Ponca warriors was next to impossible. During these interviews, most of the veterans usually said, "Yeah, we were there." However, their courage and fortitude is attested by their wounds, medals, and commendations. During the Korean and Vietnam Wars in the 1960s and 1970s, again eligible tribesmen volunteered to serve in the armed forces. They served as foot soldiers, paratroopers, sailors, guardsmen, and so forth. Some boys of sixteen years of age also volunteered and completed a tour of duty. During the Korean War, quite a large number of Ponca men served in the famed Forty-Fifth Thunderbird Division of the Oklahoma National Guard.

According Sgt. George White Eagle, USAF Ret., a platoon was composed primarily of Ponca men. He said World War II veterans Sgts. Elmer Primeaux, Paschel LeClair, and Russell Primeaux, who had combat experience, provided leadership. This group of men was involved in some fighting in the Cherwon Valley. They suffered no losses, but Neal White Tail and Mike Roy (both now deceased) were wounded. Mike told his experience in Korea:

I joined the Forty-Fifth Division in the summer of 1950 and took my basic training at Camp Polk, Louisiana. Then we were called to go to Japan in March 1951 . . . we spent about seven to eight months at Hokkaido. We were called to go to Korea to relieve the First Calvary. We arrived there in the winter of '52 . . . in January. They put us on the line there . . . there wasn't much activity there, but we would go out on patrols . . . and make contact. At that time I was wounded . . . it was in March. I forget the date, but it was early in the morning. We were sent out to investigate a movement. We had to find out about it . . . which we did. We were on our way back when we were ambushed. It happened so fast that . . . I remember I was hit by hand grenade fragments, plus a concussion grenade. It didn't hurt me. We were surrounded at the time. They called back in, and the artillery sent a barrage on that hill. They got us off the hill. There were fifteen guys in the squad. There were three of us Poncas . . . Herbert Eagle, Lancelot Primeaux Jr., and myself. Herbert was leading, in the front, when we were ambushed.

I don't know how he made it. He must have gone down the hill . . . I don't know how he survived it when they shelled that area . . . he was in the middle of it. The guy behind me got it [killed]. When I was hit, I fell and rolled. I didn't know I was hit at the time. I guess I was lucky because there was a ditch nearby and I laid in it. Later, I was sent to the field hospital. They removed the fragments and sent me on to the hospital at Pusan. After thirty days there, I was sent back to my outfit.

Men served in other branches of the armed forces as well. When Gen. Douglas MacArthur commanded the forces in Korea, Joe Thicknail and Nathaniel Page (both now deceased) were among the troops in the Twenty-Seventh Calvary of the regular army. The story of the Twenty-Seventh Calvary is known by most history buffs. Thicknail earned two bronze stars while in pursuit of the North Koreans to the Manchurian border. In the following, Sgt. Joe Thicknail, also a nephew of KH, shared his experience of how he was awarded one of the two bronze stars (my translation).

In a convoy headed for the Yalu River in North Korea, the troops were impeded by a single enemy machine gunner at one curve on the hillside.

The commanding officer asked for volunteers to proceed forward to "knock out" the machine gunner. Several attempts were made with no success. Not because of glory but because it had to be done, Private Thicknail volunteered. He related that he climbed behind the high hillside and came in from the back of the gunner. Unaware of Thicknail's presence, the enemy was terminated. The troops were now able to proceed.

Page too received commendation for his acts of bravery. Ponca men who served in the Marine Corps are exemplified by Sgt. Bruce Howe (now deceased), who served in the First Marine Division, D Company, the Second Battalion of the Fifth Regiment. Of his involvement in the Frozen Reservoir operation, he said, "I started out as rifleman, and then was machine gunner. As squad leader, I spent 109 days at the front. I don't remember all those little towns' names. That was long time ago." Howe went to Korea in January 1951. He said they encountered many North Koreans and "did in a whole bunch." His brother Keith (USMC Ret., also deceased) was also in the Marine Corps during this time and experienced frontline action. When I spoke with Sgt. Oliver Howe Jr. (USMC Ret., now deceased), he said his outfit "hit" Inchon in 1950. He said, "We were about the fifth wave that went in following the ground troops." He was with a Marine aviation group. Tyrus Headman (deceased), a member of the famed 187th Regimental Combat Team, was also involved in heavy and intense fighting. Robert Roy, U.S. Army, was counted as the only Ponca casualty during the Korean conflict. For his services performed beyond the call of duty, he was honored by the tribe. As a fitting memorial to him and his service to his country, the tribe placed a plaque at the Ponca Indian Cemetery in Kay County. The plaque is located in the veteran's section of the cemetery.

During the Vietnam War, some Ponca men volunteered. The questionable status of the war affected many of these veterans. Some of them had great difficulty in killing people who looked like themselves. Yet they did what they had to do. Kennis Headman, U.S. paratrooper, spent weeks encountering and fighting the Vietnamese. He was decorated with the bronze star twice for saving the lives of his comrades.

Printed stories of feats accomplished could fill many pages and volumes on the Ponca who participated in U.S. wars. Those men who gave their lives in service on the front lines for the United States and the world are listed below:

WORLD WAR II CASUALTIES

Claremore Smith

James Fire Shaker

Cornelius Hardman Jr.

Floyd Little Cook

Kenneth McClellan

Floyd Primeaux

KOREAN WAR CASUALTY

Robert Roy

VIETNAM WAR CASUALTY

Prentice Dale LeClair

Raymond Fire Shaker

Gale New Moon

MILITARY CAREER MEN

Sgt. Keith Howe, deceased, USMC/U.S. Army Ret.

Sgt. Oliver Howe Jr., deceased, USMC Ret.

Sgt. Wallace Iron, deceased, U.S. Army Ret.

Sgt. Fred Primeaux, deceased, USN/USAF Ret.

CPO Carleton Rhodd, deceased, USN Ret.

Sgt. Gordon Roy, deceased, USAF Ret.

Sgt. Vincent Warrior, USMC/USAF Ret.

Sgt. George White Eagle, deceased, USAF Ret.

While Ponca men dedicated their lives and time to military service during World War II, their families at home too participated. They gathered scrap iron around their homes and brought it to a central area on the reservation. At the old White Eagle School, District No. 90, a mountain of old iron was brought by students and parents and then picked up and carted away by trucks. The recycled iron became guns and military weapons. The school participated in government-sponsored savings bond and stamp drives, in which some Ponca participated. The American Red Cross support programs were initiated at White Eagle School, and flags and banners hung at every home. The support of America and its soldiers was essential to every tribal member. Like all of America, the Ponca people also received ration stamps to buy food, clothing, and fuel.

Ponca Women in the U.S. Armed Forces

According to the elders, in ancient times, wives accompanied their husbands when they went to war. Women who were hearty, had stamina, and knew medicines followed to aid the men should the need arise. These women too bore arms of knives and clubs and were prepared to do battle if necessary.

In modern times women with various technical skills joined the armed forces to support. During World War II, those women joining in the military were Delphine Cerre Rhodd, Cena Rhodd Zaitcek, May Hinman, Melvina Primeaux Kemble, Jacqueline Collins, Angeline DeLodge Laravie, Yolanda Knight, and Maxine Biggoose. Women who served during the Korean conflict and peacetime included Nellie Roughface Obregon and Sarah Roughface Paul (these women both entered at the rank of second lieutenant), Naomi Eagle, Francine Eagle Biggoose, Suzie Hinman Hara, and Martha Ann Hinman. Following the Vietnam War, Adele Steeprock joined in the U.S. Navy. The peacetime volunteer following the Desert Storm episode was Christen Hinman.

American Legion

Although there were other men who served during World War I, there were only three Ponca men who served on the front lines. They were Alfred Buffalo, George Callshim, and Richard "Dick" Hinman. Subsequent to the First World War, an American Legion Post was established. The post was organized by Albert Makes Cry Sr., Mike LeClair, and Tony Knight and was called Buffalo Post #38, named for Alfred Buffalo. Historically, the Ponca Indian Post was the first all-Indian American Legion Post in the state of Oklahoma and possibly the United States. Post #38 in 1980 operated according to the *American Legion Manual and Guide*. They listed some of the functions and activities of the organization:

Assisted American Legion Home in Ponca City
Assisted veterans going to the Veterans Administration (VA) Hospital
Assisted veterans who are eligible for various veteran benefits
Sponsored eligible high school students at Boys State in Oklahoma
Assisted veterans' widows seeking pensions
Provided financial assistance to veterans' widows
Provided food drive for the needy at Christmastime
Provided financial assistance to elderly for gas or propane bills
Provided honor guard and military funerals
Observed all national holidays, such as Memorial Day and Veterans Day

At special traditional Ponca dance ceremonials, they give special recognition to veterans who served in all wars. Their fund-raising projects through the tribal dances support the above-listed activities. They paid annual dues and sponsored a bingo game as a fund-raiser. Their membership in 1980 was thirty-two but has varied up to more than fifty. Annual reports are submitted by the post every year to the state commander of the American Legion. Some of the officers of the post are commander, vice commander, secretary-treasurer, post adjutant, service officer, post chaplain, sergeant-at-arms, historian, judge advocate, and others, plus various committees as they become necessary. The post also has an organized women's American Legion Auxiliary that has been reorganized since 1955 and is still functioning with similar activities as the post. In the early 1970s, a Veterans of Foreign Wars (VFW) group was organized by the late Louis Dole.

29

Political Governance

The special relationship that Indian tribes have with the U.S. government was established at the initial entry of the Europeans into this country. The first treaties ever made were not only made with the British, but also with the Dutch, French, and Spanish governments. The reasons for the treaties varied from tribe to tribe but essentially ranged from keeping peace, preventing war, and gaining tribes as allies. These treaties considered Indian tribes as nations within themselves. When the United States became the controlling government of the country, the Indian tribes remade numerous treaties with them (RDH).

Since the earliest periods of exploration and colonization of this country then, the U.S. government created this unique relationship with Indian tribes that has lasted to the present. Some of the policies of the government were "regulating commerce . . . with Indian tribes," observing "good faith . . . toward Indians," and providing "peace and friendship among them." These early agreement policies were eventually replaced by other legislation because of the westward expansion of the whites. During this time the whites thought of Indians as people without souls (RDH). However, Indians believed that they had rights as other people or private citizens did. Also, Indians were considered uncivilized because they did not understand legal transactions according to European standards. The inherent sovereignty of each tribe, although conceivably understood by each individual tribe, as they perceived themselves, is self-evident. Chief Justice John Marshall in the 1800s stated that Indian tribes were not only sovereign entities but also were "domestic dependent nations." According to RDH, tribal legal assistant (now deceased), this meant that tribes were governing their own members and territory before the entry of the Caucasian races into this country. Additionally, Indian tribes had retained this inherent right and were recognized by the federal government. Further still, he said, the Supreme Court ruled in 1832 that Indian nations were "distinct political communities" and that a state could neither intervene nor legislate matters pertaining to tribal authority.

Federal policy regarding Indian tribes includes a concept called "federal trust relationship." It is based on ownership of land and the assumption that Indians are incapable of handling their own financial affairs. This, in effect, places the Indians as "wards" of the government. These policies have changed periodically because expectations were not met by the Indian tribes. Noticeable policies that were difficult to interpret concerned farming, lumbering, water rights, and public domain. Land usage, for example, by Indian tribes under legal terms remains a problem. To acquire a fee patent to sell their lands to private citizens is illegal. From the years following the passing of the Dawes Act of 1887, government agents, who apparently had a share in the dealings, had authorized land sales. When higher echelons of the government caught wind of what was happening, they dismissed the agents from their jobs. But the replacements were no better.

Although hundreds of treaties and government policies were enacted, only a few are listed below to show the extent of government and Indian relations from the nineteenth century to the present:

1794–1868	The period of treaties
1819	Congress appropriated funds to provide aide to prevent extinction of Indian tribes.
1850s	Indian reservations began to be established.
1871	Congress said it would no longer enter treaties with Indian tribes.
1887	The Dawes Act provided a division of land parcels for individual Indians to become farmers.
1870	Congress made its first funding for schools for Indian tribes.
1884	Day schools were initiated through federal money.
1921	The Snyder Act provided that the secretary of the interior administer services to Indians "throughout the United States" to support and educate Indian tribes.
1924	The Indian Citizenship Act conferred citizenship to all American Indian tribes.

1928	The Meriam Survey report included the inadequacies of federal Indian boarding schools.
1934	Johnson-O'Malley Act authorized the U.S. Interior Department to contract with states to provide education, medical, and agricultural assistance to Indian tribes.
1950s	Sen. A. Watkins of Utah attempted to terminate government relations with Indian tribes. Relations with some tribes were terminated, but it created extreme hardship for them.

The enactment of public laws by the federal government has affected and benefited most Indian tribes. But these public laws and benefits were unknown to tribes until recent years. Ponca tribal councilman Dana Knight provided the groundwork for oncoming programs and projects for the tribe. The most important have been those pertaining to education. From 1950 to 1978, many projects and programs were made available to Indian tribes. For example, the Indian Self-Determination Act of 1975 had provisions enabling tribes to contract for federally funded programs. This meant that an Indian tribe could apply for federal assistance as a prime sponsor for a given project within the limits of the tribal jurisdiction, that is, the reservation boundaries. Programs for education, labor, housing, and health are made available to all citizens of America. Indian programs too are recognized as special projects because of the federal trust relationship that federally recognized Indian tribes have with the U.S. government.

The federally funded programs are from tax dollars paid by all citizens. Ultimately, the federal dollars derived from taxation on lands, personal property, income, and so forth are all paid directly or indirectly back to the taxpayer. These federal dollars are allocated for military purposes, various scientific studies, educational institutions, and a multiplicity of government subsidies to assist enterprises deemed advantageous to the public. The singular tax that Indian tribes do not pay and are exempted from is the tax on lands. The federal trust and restricted land laws prohibit the taxing of reservation lands. Indians pay other taxes like all American citizens. The government-sponsored programs on Indian reservations and in other Indian-populated areas contribute to the entire economy of cities, counties, and states. This means that the Indian populace does not alone benefit from these programs but that the community at large receives all the advantages from Indian business transactions.

Since the term *trust relations* is a broad concept, and its implications may extend to mean a number of things. For one, the Indians, in concurrence with Congress, interpret the concept as meaning that the U.S. government has agreed to provide for Indian education, health, and so forth. The extended meanings may go further in that the government may obligate itself to a total or overall status of protecting Indian tribes because of their (the tribes') incompetence. The term *incompetent* in governmental interpretation normally relates to the disposition of lands owned by Indian tribes. The transferal of lands by deed to another, for instance, requires federal approval. For example, if an Indian wanted to build, farm, or get a lease on their lands, they must have permission from the Bureau of Indian Affairs. Just how far-reaching the policies on Indian trust lands are can only be known if one is an Indian. Under this legal interpretation then, Indians are incompetent (RDH). Be that as it may, the impact of land ownership on tribal and federal government remains tied to the "incompetence" idea. The treaties, old and from the past, are still in effect. As early as 1882, Congressman William S. Holman appealed to the conscience of America. He said these treaty obligations, if they were to be fulfilled, had to provide all guarantees promised.

The student of Indian history recognizes that the U.S. government, to provide lands for white settlers, had to establish a means whereby it could acquire land from Indian tribes and justify it. The problematic concepts include Manifest Destiny and other similar reasoning that the land was not really being used. These concepts were the God-directed basis for taking the land. A statistic shows that in fewer than four hundred treaties with Indian tribes, the government acquired nearly one billion acres of land. The rest was simply taken. (The contiguous United States encompasses 3,787,425 square miles, which equals to approximately 2,423,952,000 acres of land). The taking of lands resulted in the tribes' loss of culture and way of life. The internal governing systems too were upset or destroyed (RDH). The encroachment of white settlers near Indian reservations disrupted a feasible system provided by the government for Indian tribes. In addition to the loss of lands, there was a loss of self-esteem. The Indian people suffered a cataclysmic trauma that affected self-determination as well as a will toward socialization and acculturation in the white-dominated society.

The reservation idea too was a created mechanism that the government used to move Indian tribes to certain geographic areas. This system allowed the government to account for the location of Indian tribes and keep them under control (RDH). RDH said that five types of Indian reservations have affected all tribes in the territorial limits of the United States. These were instituted, he said, according to the actual conditions that the U.S. government dealt with. They are (1) reservations created by acts of Congress, (2) executive order reservations, (3) treaty reservations, (4) acquisition of title by purchase, and (5) title derived from other sovereigns. The Ponca were affected by two. First, when they ceded lands to the government in 1825, 1858, and 1865, they were left with a treaty reservation in the amount of approximately 125,000 acres of land. The second (the present Ponca Reservation) was an executive order reservation in Indian Territory created by government appropriation of some $30,000 and a subsequent order from the president to remove the Ponca from Nebraska.

The federal government disassembled the tribal political system and did not recognize the Ponca chiefs' role as the authority of the tribe. The government issued a federal mandate saying it would only deal with an elected "business committee" of the tribe (RDH). The current Ponca Tribal Business Committee then is an offspring of that mandate issued at the turn of the twentieth century. Had the chiefs been capable of expressing their tribal sovereignty, inherent sovereignty, and inherent powers, RDH said, they could well have retained the hereditary governing body to this day. The main governing body of the tribe then began to cease in operation from that time on. Only a few continued to encourage the people to accept their human situation in life and attempt to coexist with the oncoming new way. Those who had previously attended school could now speak the English language and assume a leadership role for the tribe.

No formal council or committee was ever selected or elected until the former mandate (to select a business committee) was reemphasized by the Indian Reorganization Act (IRA) of 1934. The Citizens Act of 1924 too bestowed a dual citizenship on the tribe; that is, the tribe members were citizens not only of their own reservation but also of the United States. The IRA came short of its mark for tribes to organize under its provisions for a business committee. The Oklahoma Indian Welfare Act of 1936 provided a similar mandate to get Indian tribes to organize. This act provided that if the Indian tribes failed to organize, the Interior Department would write a constitution for them. The Ponca did not write a constitution until 1950—fourteen years later. What the government failed to understand was that most tribes had neither the writing skills nor the technical knowledge in reading the legal language of the mentioned acts. The Constitution and Corporate Charter of the Ponca Tribe of Indians of Oklahoma was written with the help of the Bureau of Indian Affairs. The idea was to organize the tribe to operate under its own constitution, while the tribal business committee would operate under its corporate charter to conduct all its business transactions. In essence, the BIA was primarily responsible for the writing of the document. The provisions in it gave the tribe operational powers under the auspices of the Department of the Interior. Additionally, partial external controls are given to the secretary of the interior. Since 1950 the two instruments have been used by the tribe.

The onslaught of young Native American leaders throughout the country examining the legal definitions and government policies regarding their people has resulted in volumes of findings. These researchers and attorneys have revealed legal material that is relevant to the times in which we now live. Federal government officials too have cooperated to provide a better understanding of the special relationship that exists within and between the tribal and federal governments. Old documents, which are eminent in tribal and federal relations, are brought to light and, when translated in the layman's language, become significant and aid the tribal members toward self-determination and political solidarity. A careful analysis of the Ponca constitution and charter was done in connection with other federal government policies. In 1981 RDH provided an analysis of the powers of the Ponca Tribe as provided by the tribal constitution.

The universally accepted inherent powers of tribal government have been authoritatively set forth in 55 Interior Decisions 14,[1] *Powers of*

Indian Tribes, October, 1934 by the Department of the Interior, Solicitor Margold. This treatment of tribal powers is quoted below. The inherent powers of self-government unless terminated by law or waived by treaty are:

1. The Power of an Indian Tribe to define its form of Government. This is self-explanatory; it gives the tribe the right to choose what type of government to abide by.
2. The Power of an Indian Tribe to Determine its Membership.
3. The Power of an Indian Tribe to Regulate Domestic Regulations. This is important. To regulate the domestic relations of its members by instituting rules and regulations concerning marriage, divorce, legitimacy, adoption, the care of dependents, the punishment of offenses against marriage relationships, to appoint guardians for minor and mental incompetents, and to issue marriage licenses and decrees of divorce. And, to adopt such state laws that seem advisable and/or to establish separate tribal laws.
4. The Power of an Indian Tribe to Govern the Descent and Distribution of Property.
5. The Taxing Power of an Indian Tribe.
6. The Power of an Indian Tribe to Exclude Non-members from its Jurisdiction.
7. The Powers of an Indian Tribe over Property.
8. The Power of an Indian Tribe in the Administration of Justice. To administer justice with respect to all disputes and offense of or among members of the tribe other than the ten major crimes reserved to the federal courts.
9. The Power of an Indian Tribe to Supervise Government Employees.
10. Power of Eminent Domain.

The above stated powers of an Indian Tribe are inherent in tribal self-government. These powers have been concealed from us by the lack of understanding Indian law and the federal trust relationship with the United States Government. In a U.S. Supreme Court ruling it was stated that the inherent sovereignty of tribal government was in existence before the United States was a country. And the tribes' governmental power of inherent sovereignty came from its tribal members and not from the U.S. Government.

The powers of the tribe are recognized by the federal government and as such have enhanced the Ponca toward self-sufficiency. It is a fundamental proposition that the Ponca use their enlightenment for the advancement of their fellow tribesmen. Being dependent on their ideas, with assistance from the federal government, they must perceive their future with exactness and promote the highest ideals for the tribe. In this perspective they will be able to serve not only the Ponca but also all those with whom they come into contact. The democratic system of the United States, our only advocate and source of reliance, serves its people as the people serve its intentions and objectives. The primary objectives then are that—contingent upon government or congressional action—the Ponca may one day emerge from their present socioeconomic status and function as other Americans throughout the United States.

The Ponca Tribe of Indians in Oklahoma operational procedures begins with the tribe's Business Committee. Stacy Buffalohead (now deceased), elected chairman of the committee in 1980, gave an overview of the status of the Ponca government and services provided to the Ponca people.

> In 1950, the Ponca tribe and members of the governing body became acutely aware of the need to formalize their tribal government. To initiate a formal type of organization, a tribal constitution was adopted which would provide a general foundation on which the governing body could implement their government. Tribal operations and services were minimal and any services that were available came directly from the Bureau of Indian Affairs.
>
> From 1960 to the present (1981) the Ponca tribe has developed some programs. The tribe acquired a grant from the Department of Housing and Urban Development to construct twenty frame houses for tribal members. In 1970, ten low-rent units were acquired; and three years later, one hundred and forty houses were constructed.
>
> The North Central Inter-Tribal Council, Inc., comprised of the Kaw, Pawnee, Ponca, Otoe-Missouria, and Tonkawa tribes acquired a planning grant from the Department of Health, Education and Welfare. The purpose of the grant was to strengthen tribal governments in their development and to research, plan, and implement programs for the tribes. Each tribe received mutual benefits from the programs.

In 1974, the tribe acquired a grant from the Economic Development Administration to renovate the old White Eagle School into office space for tribal operation. Since then, numerous programs have been acquired through various federal agencies allowing and providing services for the tribal constituency.

The Ponca Tribe also acquired the Comprehensive Employment Training Act (CETA) program which enabled them to employ and provide training for tribal members.[2] The tribe also initiated a loan to construct a clinic that would provide services for its constituency, as well as for neighboring tribes and other eligible persons. Also, of major importance was the enactment and passage of Public Law 93-638, the Indian Self-Determination and Education Assistance Act which set a new direction for Federal Indian policy. The Act specifically recognizes the right to contract directly with state and federal agencies. Pursuant to P.L. 93-638, the Ponca tribe initiated a number of contracts with state and federal agencies to provide direct services.

In 1971, the tribe acquired the Indian Action Team program that served as an employment agency and provided tribal services for community projects. The same year the tribe acquired a grant from the Economic Development Administration to construct a Cultural Center for recreational opportunities. In 1979, a grant from the Department of Housing and Urban Development was acquired to provide housing rehabilitation, economic development and street repair.

Prior to the 1980s the programmatic operations of the tribe were weak in financial and managerial aspects, and each program functioned separately. This autonomy caused problems in the areas of communication, which led to confusion and disruption in general operations. However, with the change in administration, a high mobile period of transformation was initiated in all areas of programmatic functions. The need to centralize all systems was cited as a priority for program operations. Accounting and management systems were modified to provide effectiveness and efficiency. Personnel were placed in positions that would allow for maximum utilization of their expertise.

Special emphasis was placed on the development of the mid-management section of program operations, mainly to stabilize and assure efficiency. Program people were mandated to evaluate program functions and personnel. A review of program finances was initiated for cost effectiveness thus providing a greater degree of control and accountability. As a result of the implementation of the new systems, greater efficiency has been programmed into tribal operations which will allow for expansion and development of additional programs. As a progressive tribe, only good can evolve.

These administration program directors were college educated. Following Buffalohead's tenure, Sherman Warrior became chairman of the Business Committee. Chairman Warrior had a master's degree at that time and now possesses his doctorate degree. Two other committee members were college graduates with business degrees. The combination of Business Committee and staff professionalism provided the Ponca people a classic administration for tribal operations. Following that administration, a new tribal Business Committee was elected, and the hoped-for progress began to waver. As in most Indian communities, large families carry many votes. The people always determine who they want on the Business Committee. Plans for additional tribal enterprise were not implemented until the 1990s, when a vigorous effort was made to upgrade administrative functions and a move toward self-sufficiency was again initiated. Chairman A. Lionel LeClair, the Business Committee, and a very capable staff with various backgrounds have brought in and maintained many new projects for the tribe.

In concluding this section, the foregoing interpretations are the realities of the political governance and working instruments of the tribe. Each administration has always hired well-trained employees, and the working relationship with the federal government has improved.

Afterword

History tells us the influx of many white Europeans seeking shelter and refuge from tyranny in their countries crowded into the American East Coast. It further tells us the Indian Removal Act of 1830 caused the Native peoples to be relocated west of the Mississippi River. This was done many times by force, and many people died en route to Indian Territory. Oral history tells us the Ðégihà people had moved before this period from their former lands--the Smoky Mountains to the Atlantic Coast.

After traveling to many places into the north central plains, the Ponca established their territory in what is now Nebraska and South Dakota. Eventually being forcefully moved to Indian Territory in 1876–77, the elders stated they were "captives" of the United States. Although Chief Standing Bear won a landmark civil rights case (1879) in Nebraska, it did not immediately affect other Native peoples including the Southern Ponca. In 1924 the Ponca officially became citizens and had the right to vote in national elections.

It is not clear where the Ponca people were when various federal acts were passed. Such acts as the Dawes Act of 1887 and the Indian Reorganization Act had a direct effect on the tribe. It seemed like a good plan for individual tribal members to have their own plot of land; however, the plan was short-lived once the government allowed white farmers to purchase "Indian lands." (RDH said purchase of Indian lands was allowed primarily owing to the "ward of the government" idea.) This caused the loss of thousands of acres of land for the tribe.

As the tribe moved into mainstream American, the elders said, President Franklin Roosevelt's New Deal in the 1930s brought some employment for the Ponca. The Civilian Conservation Corps (ccc) paid one dollar a day wage to workers from 1933 to 1942. The program employed young men to perform work (then called "common labor") on the reservation lands and highways passing through the reserva-

471

tion. KH stated the crew he worked with built ponds on Indian lands. But he said some workers did some projects that seemed meaningless. The elders said they camped out where the projects were being done.

In 1933 the Tennessee Valley Authority, a federally owned corporation, under the supervision of the U.S. Army initiated a separate program for Native Americans. It provided some employment for tribal members. Tribal member Louis McDonald assisted in record keeping for that Ponca program. In 1935 the Works Progress Administration (WPA), a national labor program, created construction work. The current Ponca powwow ground's bleachers were built under this program. (However, in the beginning, the bleachers were built as seating for baseball games.) Although the Department of Labor had programs during the Great Depression, they lasted only a short time on reservations. It is surprising that as the nation was undergoing economic depression, the Ponca economy went up because for the first time employment was available to the people.

The ill-fated relationship of the Ponca with the dominant society is an undeniable reality. Before and during the years of Native American protests, the condition of our socioeconomic status became apparent to all of America. The Ponca people were one of several, if not all, Native peoples who suffered economic depression for decades. Following years of struggle to get a better education, the Ponca became noticeably strong with the younger generations that there was more to living as we had in the old traditional ways. Interestingly, we never knew we were economically deprived.

Following the passing of Public Law 93-638, the Indian Self-Determination and Education Assistance Act of 1975, federal funding became available. The enactment brought many challenges to the tribe. Under the leadership of Dana Knight, Leonard Biggoose, Ed Pensoneau, Thurman Rhodd, and others, new programs were begun to benefit the tribe. The first and foremost of the tribal programs is difficult to name. Every program or project available was important. Many of the men and women in and around the Ponca Reservation had no formal skills for employment. However, programs that provided employment seemed to be the main objective for the tribe. Under the Department of Labor, the Ponca acquired the Comprehensive Employment and Training Act (CETA) program, which provided work for low-income families and summer jobs for students. The jobs lasted for a period of twelve to twenty-four months on the reservation and in some places in the general public. The program was supposed to help individuals to move into the mainstream workforce. The program was part of the Works Progress Administration program from the 1930s. A project under the BIA was the Indian Action Team, which also provided work on the reservation. A project called the Jobs Bill, under the auspices of the BIA employment/training program, was a disaster for the Ponca.

Before the passing of the Self-Determination Act, some established federal programs were implemented in other cities and communities. As tribal leaders became of aware of such projects and programs, they began to make applications for federal assistance. Under the federal Housing and Urban Development program, Delphine Cerre Rhodd initiated the Ponca housing project. Genevieve Pollak and Bill Stabler did a survey for an elderly meals program, which provides meals for the elderly. Maynard Hinman wrote the proposal for the food distribution program, which in its first years also served the Osage Nation. The tribe contracted the BIA higher education program in late 1970s, and I wrote the proposal for the tribe. The Native American Graves Protection and Repatriation Act provided means to repatriate human remains and tribal artifacts. That project was funded under the National Park Service. The Indian Child Welfare program too serves the people. Each of these programs and projects still serve their purposes.

In the early 1980s tribal chairman Dr. Sherman Warrior initiated a high-stakes gambling operation. With the help of RDH, who was well-versed in federal and Indian law, the tribal council began a bingo operation that ultimately developed into a casino. It is believed to be the first Indian casino in the nation, except for the casino of the Seminole Tribe of Florida. Casino-type gambling brought all sorts of problems for the federal and state governments. They scrambled to establish a stance to take on high-stakes gambling on Indian reservations in Oklahoma. Somehow the state wedged itself between the tribes and the federal government and got its share of economic gain.

Cultural Changes

During a period of cultural change, the Ponca's economic status shifted toward a more stable condition for the people. It may be that many

Ponca recognized the federal programs were the right thing for the government to do in terms of the economic needs of the people. The concern here, however, is that the Native cultural standards began to change. The term *neo-Indianism* is applicable to today's nativistic practices. The ongoing perpetuation of Native culture is fraught with vast changes.

Native Ponca culture, like other cultures, has a system that integrates knowledge, beliefs, and practices into the human experience of life. There are simple but genuine religious patterns in the Ponca's social and material world. These values, attitudes, and conventional practices characterize the Ponca world. This concept of culture was typical for the first and second generations of Ponca in Indian Territory. But as the people entered the white-dominated world, drastic changes began to appear on the reservation as well as in cities where they lived. Even though some have made progress in the modern world, the ever-changing cultural condition on the reservation leaves one thinking that the stability of the old standard Ponca cultural ways has been lost to the past.

One of the things that is obvious in cultural changes is the adoption of "the white man's ways." This begins with the loss of our language. Our language embodies and embraces all cultural practices––rituals and ceremonies. This means when our language was still use, we were able to address our human situation according to our cultural standards. Take, for example, the *Wá'waǫ* ceremony. Question: Why did the previous generations use the plume of the eagle in this ceremony? As described earlier, the *Hįxpé'* is the down feather or plume placed on the *Wá'waǫ* celebrant. Why not use a tail or wing feather of a crow or a meadowlark? The answer is, first, they chose the most magnificent bird of prey that builds its nest in a place unreachable by other predators. The following description was given by the elders: At a high precipice, large limbs are built around the base of the nest followed by smaller branches. With the small branches, thorny limbs and rocks were also included. This was covered with coarse weeds and grass. Then the downy feathers of the mother were laid atop the nest. There the mother eagle laid her two eggs. The down or plume is warm and light so as to hide the mother eagle's eggs when she is away. The elders said, *"Wét'a ugǫ̀e ke edì hįxp'éte itéde nǫi. Xiǫá mà, giǫ adé*

nądì wét'atè ánąxdè egą̀ gáxe ną́i" (The eggs are placed upon the plum-
age in the nest. It looks like the eagle hides the eggs [in the plumage]
when it flies off). It also trapped warm air to help protect the eaglets.
It also served as a camouflage for the eggs and chicks once hatched.
When the eaglets matured, the mother began to remove the down
feathers and rocks from the nest, allowing the thorns to emerge. This
caused the eaglets to move away from the comfort of the nest forc-
ing them to learn to fly.

So the elders of an earlier period selected the plume of the eagle.
This ornament was representative of the characteristic trait of the
eagle caring for its young. The recipient of this honor was to live a
life of being helpful, aiding the needy, healing the sick, ministering
to the downhearted, or whatever the need may have been in the village. Consequently, the individual who wore the *Wá'waą̀* eagle plume
represented that kind of protection from the elements of hardship
and sickness. It gave a signal to others that there was help available
from those who wore the ornament. It told others that the one who
wore the plume would provide aid when there was a need. This means
that the individual had been trained and dedicated to perform those
duties as one who was set aside for that purpose.

The Change

When I spoke to a number of the younger generation, they indicated
that the eagle plume was an ornament placed on a young woman so
that she could enter the powwow arena to dance. The practice is called
being "plumed." In our fast-changing white world, we have been taken
far from the original meaning of wearing the eagle plume. The practice
is oversimplified. What is evident is that the people in today's world
know only in a very small part what the plume means. Whether we
know altogether or in part, the dominant culture *is* dominant. The
old culture has gradually faded away.

Respect for the elders, leaders, men of medicine, and others who
were significant in the community is another aspect of cultural change.
In my lifetime, I was taught, witnessed, and saw the correct behavior expected of people when a person of respect came around. In the
1960s I was present at the Oklahoma Indian Missionary Conference of
the United Methodist Church in Antlers, Oklahoma. One of the con-

ference grounds is located centrally on the Choctaw Reservation in southeastern Oklahoma. Present were pastors and church representatives from various tribal churches throughout the state. There was mutual respect for each other with lots of laughing, sharing, and eating. On the afternoon when the bishop arrived, there was a strange hush on the grounds. When Bishop Angie Smith stepped out of his vehicle, it seemed that the entire conference grounds became quiet. You could hear only the birds in the trees singing their songs. A deep respect and honor was given to this man of God. I believe this practice of respect was significant to all tribes in those days.

I remember my first lesson of showing respect for the elders when I was present at the noon meal served at a Native American Church meeting. As a boy of six or seven years of age, I was admonished by my father for walking in front of a man of medicine as the men sat down to eat. I was told that I could not walk in front of him but had to go as far around him as was possible in that enclosure. This rule was also applicable to the elders of the tribe. We were taught never to walk in front of them.

Respect for female relatives was another rule that was impressed on young men by that second generation of Ponca born in Indian Territory. Brothers and sisters were allowed to play together until they were about eleven or twelve years of age. Brothers assumed a protective role over their sisters. Sisters honored their brothers by bringing him food at meal times and observing other conventional tribal pleasantries in the realm of social relationships. This respectful relationship extended to other women and young girls. I learned this rule when I was about twelve years of age, when Grandmother Headman told others to tell me I could no longer play with my first cousin. Alice and I used to ride bicycles and horses, swim together, climb trees, play tag, and a sundry of other things. I didn't understand it at first, but one day I saw her wearing clothes like the big girls and then it struck me. My playmate was no longer the little girl who laughed, ran, and played the same games. The social roles in our relationship changed.

The Powwow World

The Ponca *Hedúškà* was the only male organization where men of a high caliber came together to plan and provide aid, such as food, clothing, and shelter, for orphaned children and widows. They also looked after the social concerns of the tribe. In their meetings, they danced (as previously discussed). The songs of the fraternal organization were songs made for men who accomplished honorable deeds, whether in war or in the community. The songs usually tell in a few words the involvement of an individual in some worthwhile deed, a war, or a benevolent act. In modern times, most songs relate to a veteran who went to war or was simply a veteran. This condensed view of the *Hedúška* and its purpose was the precursor to the modern powwow.

In 1965 Howard researched some aspects of Ponca history and culture. He concluded that at one point all the Native peoples were merging their culture, a phenomenon he termed *Indian nationalism*; however, he stated that it was an all-Indian movement, which he called pan-Indianism. This meant that the people were sharing, borrowing, and copying dance styles, songs, and procedures in the dance circle. In another work, Petrullo (2018, 26) wrote,

> The reservation system has caused the old tribal animosities to disappear, and there has arisen a sympathetic attitude of the various tribal units toward each other, with the result that intercourse between them has become common, and each other's rites are observed and studied with the avowed purpose of comparison. This constant interchanging of ideas is giving rise to a novel feeling for Indian nationality. As welcome as this may be to one interested in the progress and development of the Indian, it must not be underestimated as being of prime importance in the disintegration of tribal culture patterns.

So the powwow world today is a conglomeration of various Native American tribes converging at some location to sing, dance, camp out, mingle, laugh, and eat. There's nothing wrong with that. But where are those attributes of tribal identity that once dominated the Ponca ethos? In the late 1960s, a Native person of insight said at a Native American Church meeting, "We're not Ponca, Osage, Caddo, or Pawnee anymore . . . we're 'Pan-Indians.'" Although the line is humorous, for the speaker it was a way to say we are now the same as one another. Those fundamental traits of the tribe seem to have merged into what is now call by some "the powwow mentality." It is common knowledge that you often hear one claiming modern customs as "our ways," or "this is the—way."

I want to venture out to recognize some features of the modern-day powwow dances as intertribalism. The elders said in modern times the War Dance has a "head dancer." They stated his place was to signal others to dance as he arises to dance. But they indicated that the concept of the head dancer is new. There are head dancers for every group that participates in the activity. All dances have a man, woman, boy, girl, little boy, and little girl head dancer as well as head dancers for the Gourd, War, and other dances. In defense of these practices, it is said that standard rules for the modern-day dances are formed out of necessity. The dancer, for instance, must be knowledgeable of the dance steps required for certain dances. Among the Ponca, there is a different step for the *Sésasà wačĭgaxè* (Trot Dance) as compared to the *Nąstáp'i wačĭgaxè* (Tiptoe Dance). These dance styles are part of the *Heđúškà* organization. The elders said the head dancer should know these differences.

According to the elders, in the old days there was no head dancer. There was no need for one as a respected warrior or elder stood to dance. This *Heđúškà* dancer simply stood on the first drumbeat and began to dance as the song began. Once he began to dance, other dancers followed him. It also must be understood that each Ponca *Heđúškà* organization sponsored their separate activity, and before the removal to Oklahoma, there were as many as six different *Heđúškà* organizations.

There are also head singers for such events. In former times, the elders said the lead singer also called on others to lead. He evidently was respected for his ability to sing and have knowledge of various ceremonies and rituals. Again in modern times, the head singer is selected out of necessity because of the vast number of singers in various tribes. And the head singer must be knowledgeable of songs. For many years, the Osage have called on the Ponca singers. Albert Makes Cry Jr. said,

> The Osages often sent a letter to Grandpa Oscar to bring singers to Gray Horse. He and the other singers took their families by wagon. It took two days to get to Gray Horse. We would camp out along the way as though this was part of the joy and celebration of going there to sing.

The Osages were very rich and paid Grandpa well. They provided fresh cuts of meat and other foodstuffs for the duration of the celebration.

That special relationship with the Osage has lasted for generations now. Some of the Ponca singers whose names are remembered for the first half of the twentieth century include Oscar Makes Cry, Charlie Waters, Robert Little Dance, Josiah Thicknail, Leonard Smith, Tim Little Voice, Adam LeClair, Albert Waters, Sylvester Warrior, Lamont Brown, Joe Rush, Louis Yellow Horse, and Harry Buffalohead. The head singer for the Osage *Elǫ́ška* can be its own tribesman today, but occasionally, Ponca singers are called to lead.

Origin of *Heǡúškà* Songs

Some suggest that these songs originated somewhere other than among the Ponca people. It must be understood that these songs are not "War Dance" songs. The elders said that younger people should not confuse the songs with the organization. They said the songs came from a different source. The *Heǡúškà* fraternal organization has always been part of the Ponca Tribe's cultural practice (as mentioned elsewhere).

Dr. Karl Rhinehard, University of Nebraska–Lincoln professor of forensic pathology and anthropology, said that the human remains of the Ponca that were taken from various burial sites showed injuries resulting from being in a battle. Comparatively, remains of one of the other tribes in Nebraska showed little or no evidence of being in war. This he stated was the result of that tribe being peaceful and tolerant of other people. This then is one verification of how we came to confirm that the songs of the Ponca (and there are hundreds of songs) are indeed of Ponca origin. Two or more songs tell the same story but with different words, a different tune, and a different drumbeat. This then is how the tribe retains Ponca oral history. Not all songs pertained to war or battles but also included good deeds done by various tribal members. In this, the common man or woman in the tribe might be honored for his or her acts of benevolence or accomplishments.

The Town Crier

The term *town crier* is used often in and around Ponca *Heǡúškà* dances. The term *Iyébahà* means "tell with words." In modern times, the younger generation heard the term *Wajép'a*, which has its origin among the Osage. Because the Ponca discontinued their usage of their own term, the Osage version is used among the younger people. But that is understandable as two generations before their time, the Ponca had abandoned the use of the Ponca term because of the loss of the *Heđúskà* organization (KH, NC, JP). When the *Heđúškà* was reinstituted by Sylvester Warrior and others in the 1960s, the term *town crier* was used. As a result, our Ponca word was ignored or simply forgotten.

The *Iyébahà*, in the early twentieth century, used to ride a horse throughout the camp, hollering intermittently to advise the people to keep their camping area clear of debris and to admonish children to respect other campers and visitors. The elders stated that during the time the Ponca lived in the North Country, the people themselves told the *Iyébahà* of matters pertaining to their village. He rode his horse throughout the village advising and admonishing the people about the concerns at hand. The *Iyébahà* was a necessary spokesperson for the tribal council, which managed the affairs of the people. He was not necessarily a council member.

As for the *Heđúškà*, the elders said the *Iyébahà* was the person who announced an event in the dance procedures. He hollered and then announced what would follow. Hollering necessarily was done to get the attention of the attendees. The hollering was vocables that sound like "Hey!-yeh-yeh-yeh-yeh-hah! Hey!-yeh-yeh-yeh-yeh." This was repeated twice, and then in the same tempo, the *Iyébahà* began to speak. For example, he hollered before the dance began, announcing the intention of the organization; when a dancer or a group of dancers entered the arena or dancing circle; when there was a pause in the day or evening dance; when the meal was ready, so that the singers could complete the series of songs they were singing; when it was time to sing the cook's song; and so on. This procedure is partially still intact with the Osage. A town crier is used in the absence of a Native-language speaker explaining each phase of the dance.

The Gourd Dance

This dance is credited to the Kiowa, Cheyenne, and Arapaho Tribes in Oklahoma. Its history and purpose have significant accounts by these tribes. The Ponca began to participate in the Gourd Dance in the late 1960s. The purpose of the dance is unclear, but some sources relate the following: Among the Cheyenne, it is a dance solely for war chiefs, warriors, and priests of the tribe. The Kiowa say the dance honors veterans of war and the songs are personal songs, but names have been lost to the past. It was once a part of the Kiowa Sun Dance. The Ponca, in modern times, were "given" the Gourd Dance by a Kiowa man by the name of Nelson Big Bow. The Gourd Dance has no significant meaning for the Ponca, but they enjoy singing the songs and dancing. Some aspects of Kiowa and Cheyenne customs are carried out as in the gift-giving practice of honoring somebody. Most tribes having powwows usually do the gourd dance before the main event of powwow.

The Ancient Ponca Gourd Dance

The Ponca also use the gourd to dance. The gourd is part of the hand game and is used at intervals during the game. The songs are called *Šǫ́t'ǫgà waǫ̀* (wolf songs) and *Míkasì waǫ̀* (coyote songs). Mentioned elsewhere, a legendary story tells us that a wolf gave the game and songs to the Ponca. It is a woman's dance. In today's dance, although still awe-inspiring, frivolity takes the place of the serious mood of the ancient dance and song. That "serious mood," according to the elders, combined encouragement, hope, and inspiration joined together with laughter and having a good time. Interestingly, some of the songs tell the same stories we hear in the warrior *Heɖúškà* songs.

According the elders, the *T'ę́' nǫ́p'ažì*, or "not afraid to die," society composed of seasoned warriors of the ancient past used to shake a rattle or gourd in time with the drumbeat as they danced in one place. It was said that when they danced, they carried arrows in their free hand signifying their status as ready to go to war. This dance too was part of the men's *Heɖúškà* fraternal organization. This is no longer practiced among Ponca *Heɖúškà*.

Hobbyist

In the twentieth century there was a revival of the Ponca *Heɖúškà* organization in which Sylvester Warrior had a strong input. Others involved with the newly organized *Heɖúškà* were Johnny Steel, Owen Walking Sky, Abe Conklin, Perry LeClair, and others. This group along with singers Lamont Brown, Joe Rush, Harry Buffalohead, and others formed the fraternal organization of good men. The dancers were primarily Ponca dancers with an occasional invitation to Osage *Elóškà* dancers. Like any organization that becomes successful, the Ponca *Heɖúškà* became known through various individuals interested in Native American lore and culture.

During this period of resurgence of Native cultural practices among several tribes, hobbyists too took special interest. The California Hobbyist Association requested the Ponca *Heɖúškà* group to share with them the basic structure and principles of the organization. Because of their special interest and want of further involvement in the practices of this ancient organization, a special song was composed by Harry Buffalohead. The lyrics and vocables are as follows:

Gáhiɖè ámà wadą́babè yo he ye de ye *wadą́babè*
Gáhiɖè ámà wadą́babè yo he ye de ye *wadą́babè*
Gáhiɖè ámà wadą́babè yo he ye de ye *wadą́babè*
Gáhiɖè ámà wadą́babè yo he ye de ye do

Chorus:
Nudą́ hą̀gà ną̀žį́ga yo he ye de ye *wadą́babè*
Waɖáeɖè nį̀ ną̀žį́ga he ye de ye *wadą́babè*
Gáhiɖè ámà wadą́babè yo he ye de ye *wadą́babè*
Gáhiɖè ámà wadą́babè yo he ye de ye do

Interpretations:
Gáhiɖè ámà wadą́babè
"Behold these people far from here."
Nudą́ hą̀gà ną̀žį́ga
"War leader, arise!"
Waɖáeɖè nį̀ ną̀žį́ga
"You who show compassion or show generosity arise!"

Note: Some singers have suggested the word *Waɖáeɖè nį̀* is rather *Waɖį́áɖįhè*, which means "You who show generosity."

Other hobbyists in Midland, Texas, Baltimore, Maryland, Detroit, Michigan, and others have joined in with the Ponca style of dancing and singing. These groups have ongoing meetings and dances with the Ponca tribal *Hedúškà*. Biannual dances are held during the fall and springtime in the Ponca community. They still subscribe to the ancient practice of gift giving to the elderly and widows.

The Statue

In early 1990s a statue was erected by Ponca City commemorating the first white person coming into the Cherokee Outlet to stake a land claim. That land was originally known as part of the Cheyenne Indian Reservation, which later became part of the Cherokee Reservation. It is commonly called the Cherokee Outlet. Somehow the federal government allowed that portion of land to be opened to anyone who was not an Indian to stake a claim. It must have been an exciting venture for many non-Indians. So the statue represented to the community the first non-Indian to stake a claim. The statue was named *This Land Is Mine*. Land was valuable to the non-Indian. To the Indian, land was culturally part of their existence on this earth. Ownership of parcels of land by individuals was not a part of their concept of private property. Some lands were shared by the people in certain territories for hunting purposes. Other lands unmarked by boundaries were known to be inhabited and were respected by neighboring tribes. During the land run, one old Ponca man by the name of Charley Collins, while watching the white settlers, said, "I didn't know a person could kill for a small piece of land. But I saw it with my own eyes." The statue and the name of the statue were immediately offensive to many young Native Americans who had just held protests on a variety of social issues concerning their status in America. Tribes of Native Americans from across the country came and made a peaceful protest as they marched around the civic center in Ponca City.

After a cooperative effort to negotiate a new name for the statue, it was renamed *The First Settler*. One of the city's fathers, Mr. Carl Renfro, who stood out among many, initiated an equally good gesture to erect a statue of a historic Native American. Many names were suggested at that time as to whom the tribal committee of elders would like to see representing all Native Americans. The then elders of the Ponca tribe, being modest, suggested men like Sitting Bull, a medicine man of the Lakota; Geronimo, a war leader of the Apache; Sequoyah, a half-breed Cherokee who developed a syllabary to write the Cherokee language; and others. I, being the youngest on the committee, spoke to Ms. Genevieve Pollak about Chief Standing Bear. At first she, like the others, didn't want to "put ourselves up" as though we were bragging. But she relented and agreed that the chief did indeed represent all Native Americans for what he had done.

After viewing several artistic depictions of the chief, the committee selected Orland C. Joe, a Navaho / Southern Ute Indian, to sculpt the twenty-some-feet-tall statue. Today the statue stands on the south side of the city on land donated by the Continental Oil Company. A museum and a powwow arena are part of the Standing Bear Park. Visitors across the nation and foreign countries now visit the museum and hear the story of one of the first civil rights leaders, Chief Standing Bear, who won constitutional rights for all Native Americans. The profundity of the statement made by Judge Elmer S. Dundee in 1879 still resonates: "An Indian is a person" within the meaning of the law and is entitled to all benefits under the constitution of the United States of America.

Native American Graves Protection and Repatriation Act, 1990

The Native American Graves Protection and Repatriation Act (NAG-PRA, 1990) was passed because the Native peoples in the United States were dissatisfied that Native human remains were displayed and studied in public places, such as museums, colleges, and universities. The act addresses the rights of Native lineal descendants, Native American tribes, Hawaiian organizations, and cultural items, including human remains, funerary and sacred objects, and objects of cultural patrimony. For the Native peoples, the primary use of this public law was to recover human remains and associated funerary objects and artifacts and subsequently to rebury the remains and maintain such objects and artifacts in a safe place.

The Ponca received their first notification of human remains uncovered by the U.S. Army Corps of Engineers at the Steed-Kisker archeological site north of Kansas City, Missouri. At the time this information was passed on to me, I knew nothing of the NAGPRA ruling. A committee was formed at the Ponca tribal headquarters at the White Eagle Community to study the federal regulation and participate in recovery of remains and objects pertaining to the Ponca people.

The Ponca elders in 1993 were reluctant to participate in the program. Those who were invited to help rejected the invitation. The next generation was more open to do something about it. The Ponca had their committee. At the University of Oklahoma and the University of Nebraska, we studied and learned the federal regulation. In the next four or five years, we participated in recovering over six hundred human remains and burial artifacts that were appropriately repatriated.

Following correspondence from various museums summarizing Ponca artifacts, we visited the museums to read all accession records and view the artifacts to determine the course of action according to the NAGPRA ruling. Eight museums in eight major U.S. cities, including the Smithsonian Institute in Washington DC, were visited. Twenty-eight artifacts were recovered from the Smithsonian. The Ponca Tribe of Nebraska chose to display them in its museum with agreement that after ten years they would be shipped to the Southern Ponca. To date (2016), no other artifacts have been recovered.

After the School House

An elder of the tribe once made a statement that still rings true in some ways: *"Úškǫ ǫgút'aitè, ḍigét'atè ádǫ, žigánǫmašè wagáze neꜗté·. Xįháskà úškǫtè wánipꜗi tedì údǫ mǫnít'amaše"* (Our old ways are going to be gone, so you younger people should go to school and learn the white man's ways. Then you will be better off). These words were spoken over a hundred years ago.

Characteristic of those who have merged into the dominant society are those who have found gainful employment away from the reservation. At home near the reservation, some tribal members have entered the business world, such as Jesse Fisher, who sells furniture and other household products and has opened stores in five locations. Carl "Lacy" Pollak runs a successful body shop in Ponca City. A few worked at Conoco in Ponca City. Some were satisfied with status quo positions until retirement. There's nothing wrong with that. Ben Waters, Johnny Williams, Isaac Headman, Buddy Brown, and others all retired from Conoco. Dr. Phillip Knight still practices medicine in Ponca City. Many Ponca live elsewhere and are doing well in their employment or community affiliations. Roswell "Jimmy" Primeaux, now deceased, civil engineer, retired from Tinker Air Force Base, in

Midwest City, Oklahoma. Practicing law are Vincent Knight, JD, and Yvonne Knight, JD. The Rev. Dr. Thomas Roughface Sr. was general superintendent of the Oklahoma Indian Missionary Conference of the United Methodist Church until his demise.

The Ponca, like other Native Americans, have found gainful employment in many cities across the nation. The Higher Education Office indicated that college or vocationally trained Ponca men and women are in the workforce in the dominant society across the country. This includes positions in the medical, education, industrial, and public services fields of employment.

The Future

When reviewing all that I heard and wrote from the elders, my contemporaries, and youth of my tribe, I thought I could be remiss or casual in my perspective of tribal history. Whether they approved or disapproved of the questions I asked left me with the thought that their responses and statements were absolutely trustworthy and reliable. In every case, their viewpoints were seldom negative or vague. They inevitably concluded a story or historic episode with "See, that's what happened. But look what happened afterward." Stories always ended with an optimistic outlook.

Whether ultimate reality is formed by the Creator or whether we make it, the history of the Ponca people indicates a positive direction. Mother Teresa once said, "The biggest disease today is not leprosy or tuberculosis, but rather the feeling of being unwanted." The first Americans felt that despair and hopelessness. The creatures of the Creator are of intrinsic value. Looking back, the maze was broken through in many places to reach the goal of success, and this attests to the determination that the future can and will be as good as mankind desires.

Appendix

U.S. Treaty Obligations to Indian Tribes

The U.S. government set forth treaties with American Indians. The Ponca Tribe of Indians had four treaty agreements with the United States. These treaties were mostly signed in part to establish certain kinds of rights, benefits, and conditions for both the Indian tribe and the United States. They also included the giving up or the ceding of Ponca homelands to the United States. Furthermore, under the treaties, the Ponca would be under the protection of the United States. The U.S. Constitution authorized the executive and judicial branches of government to communicate and engage in contractual relationships with Indian tribes. Through these varied treaties of the U.S. government with Indian tribes, it became apparent that the government charged itself with the highest level of moral obligation of responsibility and trust to Indian tribes. This in effect is a legally enforceable fiduciary obligation on the part of the United States to protect those assets, resources, lands, and treaty rights made with federally recognized American Indian tribes.

TREATY OF 1817

Between the Ponca Indians and the United States of America

A treaty of peace and friendship made and concluded between William Clark and Auguste Chouteau, commissioners on the part and behalf of the United States of America, of the one part, and the undersigned chiefs and warriors of the Poncarar tribe of Indians, on the [their] part and of their said tribe of the other part.

THE partes being desirous of re-established peace and friendship between the United States and their said tribe, and of being placed, in all things and every respect, upon the same footing upon which they stood before the late war between the United States and Great Britain, have agreed to the following articles:

ARTICLE 1.

Every injury or act of hostility by one or either of the contracting parties against the other, shall be mutually forgiven and forgot.

ARTICLE 2.

There shall be perpetual peace and friendship between all the citizens of the United States of America and all the individuals composing the said Poncarar tribe; and all the friendly relations that existed between them before the war shall be, and the same are hereby, renewed.

ARTICLE 3.

The undersigned chiefs and warriors, for themselves and their said tribe, do hereby acknowledge themselves to be under the protection of the United States of America, and of no other nation, power, sovereign, whatever.

In witness whereof, the said William Clark and Auguste Chouteau, commissioners as aforesaid, have hereunto subscribed their names and affixed their seals, this twenty-fifth day of June, in the year of our Lord one thousand eight hundred and seventeen, and of the independence of the United States the forty-first.

William Clark, [L. S.]
Auguste Chouteau, [L. S.]
Aquelaba, the Fighter, his x mark, [L. S.]
Gradonga, Fork-tailed Hawk, his x mark, [L. S.]
Shondagaha, Smoker, his x mark, [L. S.]
Kihegashinga, Little Chief, his x mark, [L. S.]
Necawcompe, the Handsome Man, his x mark, [L. S.]
Ahahpah, the Rough Buffalo Horn, his x mark, [L. S.]
Showeno, the Comer, his x mark, [L. S.]
Bardegara, he who stands fire, his x mark, [L. S.]
Witnesses present:
Lewis Bissel, acting secretary to the commissioners,
Manual Liea, United States Indian agent,
Benja O'Fallon, United States Indian agent,
R, Graham, Indian agent for Illinois,

Dr. Wm, J. Clarke,

B. Vasques,

Saml. Solomon, interpreter,

Stephen Julien, United States Indian interpreter,

Joseph Lafleche, interpreter.

TREATY OF 1825

Between the Ponca Indians and the United States of America

FOR the purposes of perpetuating the friendship which has heretofore existed, as also to remove all future cause of discussion or dissension, as it respects trade and friendship between the United States and their citizens, and the Poncar tribe of Indians, the President of the United States of America, by Brigadier General Henry Atkinson, of the United States' Army, and Major Benjamin O'Fallon, Indian Agent, with full powers and authority, specially appointed and commissioned for that purpose of the one part, and the undersigned Chiefs, Headmen, and Warriors, of the Poncar tribe of Indians, on behalf of said tribe, of the other part, have made and entered into the following articles and conditions, which, when ratified by the President of the United States, by and with the advice and consent of the Senate, shall be binding on both parties—to wit:

ARTICLE 1.

It is admitted by the Poncar tribe of Indians, that they reside within the territorial limits of the United States, acknowledge their supremacy, and claim their protection. The said tribe also admit the right of the United States to regulate all trade and intercourse with them.

ARTICLE 2.

The United States agree to receive the Poncar tribe of Indians into their friendship, and under their protection, and to extend to them, from time to time, such benefits and acts of kindness as may be convenient, and seem just and proper to the President of the United States.

ARTICLE 3.

All trade and intercourse with the Poncar tribe shall be transacted at such place or places as may be designated and pointed out by the President of the United States, through his agents; and none but American citizens, duly authorized by the United States, shall be admitted to trade or hold intercourse with said tribe of Indians.

ARTICLE 4.

That the Poncar tribe may be accommodated with such articles of merchandise, &c. as their necessities may demand, the United States agree to admit and license traders to hold intercourse with said tribe, under mild and equitable regulations: in consideration of which, the Poncar tribe bind themselves to extend protection to the persons and the property of the traders, and the persons legally employed under them, whilst they remain within the limits of the Poncar district of country. And the said Poncar tribe further agree, that if any foreigner, or other person not legally authorized by the United States, shall come into their district of country, for the purposes of trade or other views, they will apprehend such person or persons, and deliver him or them to some United States' superintendent, or agent of Indian Affairs, or to the Commandant of the nearest military post, to be dealt with according to law. And they further agree to give safe conduct to all persons who may be legally authorized by the United States to pass through their country; and to protect, in their persons and property, all agents or other persons sent by the United States to reside temporarily among them.

ARTICLE 5.

That the friendship which is now established between the United States and the Poncar tribe should not be interrupted by the misconduct of individuals, it is hereby agreed, that for injuries done by individuals, no private revenge or retaliation shall take place, but instead thereof, complaints shall be made, by the party injured, to the superintendent or agent of Indian affairs, or other person appointed by the President; and it shall be the duty of the said Chiefs, upon complaint being made as aforesaid, to deliver up the person or persons against whom the complaint is made, to the end that he or they may be punished agreeably to the laws of the United States. And, in like manner, if any robbery, violence, or murder, shall be committed on any Indian or Indians belonging to said tribe, the person or persons so offending shall be tried, and if found guilty shall be punished in like manner as if the injury had been done to a white man. And it is agreed, that the Chiefs of said Poncar tribe shall, to the utmost of their power, exert themselves to recover horses or other property, which may be stolen or taken from any citizen or citizens of the United States, by any individual or individuals of said tribe; and the property so recovered shall be forthwith delivered to the agents or other person authorized to receive it, that it may be restored to the proper owner. And the United States hereby guaranty to any Indian or Indians of said tribe, a full indemnification for any horses or other property which may be stolen from them by any of their citizens: Provided, That the property so stolen cannot be recovered, and that sufficient proof is produced that it was actually stolen by a citizen of the United States. And the said Poncar tribe engage, on the requisition or demand of the President of the United States, or of the agents, to deliver up any white man resident among them.

ARTICLE 6.

And the Chiefs and Warriors, as aforesaid, promise and engage, that their tribe will never, by sale, exchange, or as presents, supply any nation or tribe of Indians, not in amity with the United States, with guns, ammunition, or other implements of War.

Done at the Poncar Village, at the mouth of White Paint creek, the first below the Qui Carre river, this 9th day of June, A. D. 1825, and of the independence of the United States the forty-ninth.

In testimony whereof, the said commissioners, Henry Atkinson and Benjamin O'Fallon, and the chiefs, head men, and warriors, of the Poncar tribe, have hereunto set their hands and affixed their seals.

H. Atkinson, brigadier-general, U.S. Army, [L. S.]

Benj. O'Fallon, United States agent Indian Affairs, [L. S.]

Shu-de-gah-he, or He who makes Smoke, his x mark, [L. S.]

Ish-ca-da-bee, or Child Chief, his x mark, [L. S.]

Wah-ha-nee-che, or He who hides something, his x mark, [L. S.]

Wah, or The Hoe, his x mark, [L. S.]

O-nam-ba-haa, or Lightning, his x mark, [L. S.]

Ti-e-kee-ree, or Big Head with tangled hair, his x mark, [L. S.]

Wa-we-shu-shee, or The Brave, his x mark, [L. S.]

Ou-de-cowee, or the one that has been wounded, his x mark, [L. S.]

Ne-ou-gree, or Prairie apple, his x mark, [L. S.]

Woh-ge-a-mussee, or The flying iron, his x mark, [L. S.]

Pee-la-ga, or Buffalo, his x mark, [L. S.]

Wah-buc-kee, or The bull that leads, his x mark, [L. S.]

Wah-ha-nega, or He that has no knife, his x mark, [L. S.]

Mah-shar-harree, or He that walks on land, his x mark, [L. S.]

Mach-souch-kee-na-pabee, or He that fears no bears, his x mark, [L. S.]

Ca-hee-tha-bee, or Black raven, his x mark, [L. S.]

Gah-he-ga, or The relative of the Chiefs, his mark, [L. S.]

Na-hee-tapee, or He that stamps, his x mark, [L. S.]

Na-ne-pa-shee, or One that knows, his x mark, [L. S.]

Witnesses:

H. Leavenworth, colonel, U.S. Army.

S. W. Kearny, brevet major First Infantry.

D. Ketchum, major, U.S. Army.

G. H. Kennerley, U.S.S. Indian agent.

John Gale, surgeon, U.S. Army.

J. Gantt, captain, Sixth Infantry.

Wm. Armstrong, captain, Sixth Regiment Infantry.

S. MacRee, lieutenant, First Infantry.

J. Rogers, lieutenant, Sixth Infantry.

Thomas Noel, lieutenant, Sixth Infantry.

S. Wragg, adjutant, First Regiment Infantry.

R. Holmes, lieutenant, Sixth Infantry.

Thos. P. Gwynn, lieutenant, First Infantry.

Levi Nute, lieutenant, Sixth Infantry.

Jas. W. Kingsbury, lieutenant, First Regiment Infantry.

M. W. Batman, lieutenant, Sixth Infantry.

Wm. L. Harris, First Infantry.

R. M. Coleman, assistant surgeon, U.S. Army.

Wm. Gordon,

A. Langman,

P. X. Promo,

A. L. Langham, Secretary to the Commission.

TREATY OF 1858

Between the Ponca Indians and the United States of America

Articles of agreement and convention made and concluded at the city of Washington, on the twelfth day of March, one thousand eight hundred and fifty-eight, by Charles E. Mix, commissioner on the part of the United States, and Wa-gah-sah-pi, or Whip; Gish-tah-wah-gu, or Strong Walker; Mitchell P. Cera, or Wash-kom-moni; A-shno-ni-kah-gah-hi, or Lone Chief; Shu-kah-bi, or Heavy Clouds; Tah-tungah-nushi, or Standing Buffalo, on the part of the Ponca tribe of Indians; they being thereto duly authorized and empowered by said tribe.

ARTICLE 1.

The Ponca tribe of Indians hereby cede and relinquish to the United States all the lands now owned or claimed by them, wherever situate, except the tract bounded as follows, viz: Beginning at a point on the Neobrara River and running due north, so as to intersect the Ponca River twenty-five miles from its mouth; thence from said point of intersection, up and along the Ponca River, twenty—miles; thence due south to the Neobrara River; and thence down and along said river to the place of beginning; which tract is hereby reserved for the future homes of said Indians; and to which they agree and bind themselves to remove within one year from the date of the ratification of this agreement by this Senate and President of the United States.

ARTICLE 2.

In consideration of the foregoing cession and relinquishment, the United States agree and stipulate as follows, viz: First. To protect the Poncas in the possession of the tract of land reserved for their future homes, and their persons and property thereon, during good behavior on their part. Second. To pay to them, or expend for their benefit, the sum of twelve thousand dollars ($12,000) per annum for five years; commencing with the year in which they shall remove to and settle upon the tract reserved for their future homes; ten thousand dollars ($10,000) per annum for ten years, from and after the expiration of the said five years; and thereafter eight thousand dollars ($8,000) per annum, for fifteen years; of which sums the President of the United States shall, from time to time, determine what proportion shall be paid to the Poncas in cash, and what proportion shall be expended for their benefit; and also in what manner or for what objects such expenditure shall be made. He shall likewise exercise the power to make such provision out of the same, as he may deem to be necessary and proper for the support and comfort of the aged and infirm members of the tribe. In case of any material decrease of the Poncas in number, the said amounts shall be reduced and diminished in proportion thereto, or they may, at the discretion of the President, be discontinued altogether should said Indians fail to make satisfactory efforts to advance and improve their condition; in which case such other provision shall be made for them as the President and Congress may judge to be suitable and proper. Third. To expend the sum of twenty thousand dollars ($20,000) in maintaining and subsisting the Poncas during the first year after their removal to their new homes, purchasing stock and agricultural implements, breaking up and fencing land, building houses, and in making such other improvements as may be necessary for their comfort and welfare. Fourth. To establish, and to maintain for ten years, at an annual expense not to exceed five thousand dollars, ($5,000,) one or more manual-labor schools for the education and training of the Ponca youth in letters, agriculture, the mechanic arts, and housewifery; which school or schools shall be managed and conducted in such manner as the President of the United States shall direct; the Poncas hereby stipulating to constantly keep threat, during at least nine months in every year, all their children between the ages of seven and eighteen years; and that, if this be not done, there shall be deducted from the shares of the annuities due to the parents, guardians, or other persons having control of the children, such amounts as may be proportioned to the deficiency in their time of attendance, compared with the said nine months, and the cost of maintaining and educating the children during that period. It is further agreed that such other measures may be adopted, to compel the attendance of the children at the school or schools as the President may think proper and direct; and whenever he shall be satisfied of a failure to fulfil the aforesaid stipulation on the part of the Poncas, he may, at his discretion, diminish or wholly discontinue the allowance and expenditure of the sum herein set apart for the support and maintenance of said school or schools. Fifth. To provide the Poncas with a mill suitable for grinding grain and sawing timber, one or more mechanic shops, with the necessary tools for the same, and dwelling-houses for an interpreter, miller, engineer for the mill, if one be necessary farmer, and the mechanics that may be employed for their benefit, the whole not to exceed in cost the sum of ten thousand five hundred dollars, ($10,500;) and also to expend annually, for ten years, or during the pleasure of the President, an amount not exceeding seven thousand five hundred dollars, ($7,500,) for the purpose of furnishing said Indians with such aid and assistance in agricultural and mechanical pursuits, including the working of said mill, as the Secretary of the Interior may consider advantageous and necessary for them; the Poncas hereby stipulating to furnish from their tribe the number of young men that may be required as apprentices and as assistants in the mill and mechanic shops, and at least three persons to work constantly with each laborer employed for them in agricultural pursuits, it being understood that such laborers are to be employed more for the instruction of the Indians than merely to work for their benefit. The persons so to be furnished by the tribe shall be allowed a fair and just compensation for their services, to be fixed by the Secretary of the Interior. The Poncas further stipulate and bind themselves to prevent any of the members of their tribe from destroying or injuring the said houses, shops, mill, machinery, stock, farming utensils, or any other thing furnished them by the Government; and in case of any such destruction or injury, or of any of the things so furnished being carried off by any member or members of their tribe, the value of the same shall be deducted from the tribal annuities. And whenever the President shall be satisfied that the Poncas have become sufficiently confirmed in habits of industry, and advanced in acquiring a practical knowledge of agriculture and the mechanic arts, he may, at his discretion, cause to be turned over to the tribe all of the said houses and other property furnished them by the United States, and dispense with the services of any or all of the persons hereinbefore stipulated to be employed for their benefit and assistance. Sixth. To provide and set apart the sum of twenty thousand dollars ($20,000) to enable the Poncas to adjust and settle their existing obligations and engagements, including depredations committed by them on property of citizens of the United States prior to the date of the ratification of this agreement, so far as the same may be found and decided by their agent to be valid and just, subject to the approval of the Secretary of the Interior; and in consideration of the long-continued friendship and kindness of Joseph Hollman and William G. Crawford toward the Poncas, of their furnishing them, when in distress, with large quantities of goods and provisions, and of their good counsel and advice, in consequence of which peace has often been preserved between the Poncas and other Indians and the whites, it is agreed that out of the above-mentioned amount they shall be paid the sum of three thousand five hundred dollars, ($3,500,) and the sum of one thousand dollars ($1,000) shall in like manner be paid to Jesse Williams. of Iowa, in full for his claim, as such has been admitted by the Poncas for depredations committed by them on his property.

ARTICLE 3.

The Poncas being desirous of making provision for their half-breed relatives, it is agreed that those who prefer and elect to reside among them shall be permitted to do so, and be entitled to and enjoy all the rights and privileges of members of the tribe; but to those who have chosen and left the tribe to reside among the whites and follow the pursuits of civilized life, viz: Charles Leclaire, Fort Piere, N. T.; Cillaste Leclaire Pottowattomie, K. T.: Ciprian Leclaire. St. Louis, Missouri; Julia Harvey, Omaha, N. T.: Jenny Ruleau. Sioux City, Iowa; David Leclaire, Amelia Deloge, and Laura Deloge. at the Omaha mission, there shall be issued scrip for one hundred and sixty acres of land each, which shall be receivable at the United States land-offices in the same manner, and be subject to the same rules and regulations as military bounty-land warrants. And in consideration of the faithful services rendered to the Poncas by Francis Roy, their interpreter, it is agreed that scrip shall, in the like manner and amount, be issued to his wife and to each of his six children now living, without their being required to leave the nation. Provided, That application for the said scrip shall be made to the Commissioner of Indian Affairs within five years from and after the date of the ratification of this agreement.

ARTICLE 4.

The United States shall have the right to establish and maintain such military posts, roads, and Indian agencies as may be deemed necessary within the tract of country hereby reserved for the Poncas, but no greater quantity of land or timber shall be used for said purposes than shall be actually requisite; and if, in the establishment or maintenance of such posts, roads, and agencies, the property of any Ponca shall be taken, injured, or destroyed, just and adequate compensation shall be made therefor by the United States. And all roads or highways authorized by competent authority, other than the United States, the lines of which shall lie through said tract, shall have the right of way through the same; the fair and just value of such right being paid to the Poncas therefor by the party or parties authorizing the same or interested therein: to be assessed and determined in such manner as the President of the United States shall direct.

ARTICLE 5.

No white person, unless in the employment of the United States, or duly licensed to trade with the Poncas, or members of the family of such persons, shall be permitted to reside, or to make any settlement, upon any part of the tract herein reserved for said Indians, nor shall the latter alienate, sell, or in manner dispose of any portion thereof, except to the United States; but, whenever they may think proper, they may divide said tract among themselves, giving to each head of a family or single person a farm, with such rights of possession, transfer to any other member of the tribe, or of descent to their heirs and representatives, as may be in accordance with the laws, customs, and regulations of the tribe.

ARTICLE 6.

Such persons as are now lawfully residing on the lands herein ceded by the Poncas shall each have the privilege of entering one hundred and sixty acres thereof, to include any improvements they may have, at one dollar and twenty-five cents per acre.

ARTICLE 7.

The Poncas acknowledge their dependence upon the Government of the United States, and do hereby pledge and bind themselves to preserve friendly relations with the citizens thereof, and to commit no injuries or depredations on their persons or property, nor on those of members of any other tribe; but, in case of any such injury or depredation, full compensation shall, as far as practicable, be made therefor out of their tribal annuities; the amount in all cases to be determined by the Secretary of the Interior. They further pledge themselves not to engage in hostilities with any other tribe, unless in self-defence, but to submit, through their agent, all matters of dispute and difficulty between themselves and other Indians for the decision of the President of the United States, and to acquiesce in and abide thereby. They also agree, whenever called upon by the proper officer, to deliver up all offenders against the treaties, laws, or regulations of the United States, who may be within the limits of their reservation, and to assist in discovering pursuing, and capturing all such offenders, whenever required to do so by such officer.

ARTICLE 8.

To aid in preventing the evils of intemperance, it is hereby stipulated that if any of the Poncas shall drink, or procure for others, intoxicating liquor, their proportion of the tribal annuities shall be withheld from them for at least one year; and for a violation of any of the stipulations of this agreement on the part of the Poncas, they shall be liable to have their annuities withheld, in whole or in part, and for such length of time as the President of the United States shall direct.

ARTICLE 9.

No part of the annuities of the Poncas shall be taken to pay any claims or demands against them, except such as may arise under this agreement, or under the trade and intercourse laws of the United States; and the said Indians do hereby fully relinquish and release the United States from all demands against them on the part of the tribe or any individuals thereof, except such as are herein stipulated and provided for.

ARTICLE 10.

The expenses connected with the negotiation of this agreement shall be paid by the United States.

In testimony whereof, the said Charles E. Mix, commissioner, as aforesaid, and the undersigned delegates and representatives of the Ponca tribes of Indians, have hereunto set their names and seals, at the place and on the day hereinbefore written.

Charles E. Mix, Commissioner. [L. S.]

Wah-gah-sah-pi, or Whip, his x mark. [L. S.]

Gish-tah-wah-gu, or Strong Walker, his x mark. [L. S.]

Mitchell P. Cera, or Wash-kom-mo-ni, his x mark. [L. S.]

A-shno-ni-kah-gah-hi, or Lone Chief, his x mark. [L. S.]

Shu-kah-bi, or Heavy Clouds, his x mark. [L. S.]

Tah-tungah-nushi, or Standing Buffalo, his x mark. [L. S.]

Executed in the presence of—

Edward Hanrick,

E. B. Grayson,

James R. Roche,

Moses Kelly,

Joseph Hollman,

Jno. Wm. Wells,

J. B. Robertson, United States Indian agent,

Henry Fontenelle, United States interpreter,

Francis Roy, his x mark.

TREATY OF 1865

Between the Ponca Indians and the United States of America

Supplementary treaty between the United States of America and the Ponca tribe of Indians, made at the city of Washington on the tenth day of March, A. D. 1865, between William P. Dole, commissioner on the part of the United States, and Wah-gah-sap-pi, or Iron Whip; Gist-tah-wah-gu, or Strong Walker; Wash-com-mo-ni, or Mitchell P. Cerre; Ash-nan-e-kah-gah-he, or Lone Chief; Tah-ton-ga-nuz-zhe, or Standing Buffalo; on the part of the Ponca tribe of Indians, they being duly authorized and empowered by the said tribe, as follows, viz:

ARTICLE 1.

The Ponca tribe of Indians hereby cede and relinquish to the United States all that portion of their present reservation as described in the first article of the treaty of March 12th, 1858, lying west of the range line between townships numbers (32) thirty-two and (33) thirty-three north, ranges (10) ten and (11) eleven west of the (6) sixth principal meridian, according to the Kansas and Nebraska survey; estimated to contain thirty thousand acres, be the same more or less.

ARTICLE 2.

In consideration of the cession or release of that portion of the reservation above described by the Ponca tribe of Indians to the Government of the United States, the Government of the United States, by way of rewarding them for their constant fidelity to the Government and citizens thereof, and with a view of returning to the said tribe of Ponca Indians their old burying-grounds and corn-fields, hereby cede and relinquish to the tribe of Ponca Indians the following-described fractional townships, to wit: township (31) thirty-one north, range (7) seven west; also, fractional township (32) thirty-two north, ranges (6,) six, (7,) seven, (8,) eight, (9,) nine, and (10) ten west; also, fractional township (33) thirty-three north, ranges (7) seven and (8) eight west; and also all that portion of township (33) thirty-three north, ranges (9) nine and (10) ten west, lying south of Ponca Creek; and also all the islands in the Niobrara or Running Water River, lying in front of lands or townships above ceded by the United States to the Ponca tribe of Indians. But it is expressly understood and agreed that the United States shall not be called upon to satisfy or pay the claims of any settlers for improvements upon the lands above ceded by the United States to the Poncas, but that the Ponca tribe of Indians shall, out of their own funds, and at their own expense, satisfy said claimants, should any be found upon said lands above ceded by the United States to the Ponca tribe of Indians.

ARTICLE 3.

The Government of the United States, in compliance with the first paragraph of the second article of the treaty of March 12th, 1858, hereby stipulate and agree to pay to the Ponca tribe of Indians for indemnity for spoliation committed upon them, satisfactory evidence of which has been lodged in the office of the Commissioner of Indian Affairs, and payment recommended by that officer, and also by the Secretary of the Interior, the sum of fifteen thousand and eighty dollars.

ARTICLE 4.

The expenses attending the negotiation of this treaty or agreement shall be paid by the United States. In testimony whereof, the said Wm.

P. Dole, Commissioner as aforesaid, and the undersigned, chiefs of the Ponca tribe of Indians, have hereunto set their hands and seals at the place and on the day herein-before written.

Wm. P. Dole.

Wah-gah-sap-pi, or Iron Whip, his x mark. [SEAL.]

Gist-tah-wah-gu, or Strong Walker, his x mark. [SEAL.]

Wash-com-mo-ni, or Mitchell P. Cerre, his x mark. [SEAL.]

Ash-nan-e-kah-gah-he, or Lone Chief, his x mark. [SEAL.]

Tah-ton-ga-nuz-zhe, or Standing Buffalo, his x mark. [SEAL.]

Executed in the presence of—

Chas. Sims.

Stephen A. Dole.

Newton Edmunds.

J. Shaw Gregory.

George N. Propper.

Notes

1. Beginnings

1. The cognate groups of people emerging from the cultures of the aforementioned southeastern parts of the United States include many tribes. It would be presumptuous to assume that these entities could have fallen under the umbrella of one main tribe. (The concept of one king or queen over all the people has its roots in Europe and Africa.) The attempt to syncretize these cultural patterns with world cultures would be most inappropriate.

4. Chief Standing Bear

1. An act passed on March 3, 1871, provided that Indian tribes would not be recognized as a separate nation or government. A policy was also enacted that Indian policies and tribal government would be phased out and would not be recognized as a true government (RDH).

9. The Ponca Giveaway

1. It should be understood that "redistribution" of gifts did not always mean the same gifts were received and passed on to another. The term here is used to indicate that a person who has much or who has been given to over a period has the opportunity to give back to others.

13. Ponca *Heđúškà* Songs

1. The name Headman is derived from the Ponca word *Nudá̧ há̧gà*, which means "war leader." The chief was born about ten years after the Great Meteor Shower of 1833. The Ponca referred to this phenomenon as *Miká'e Uxp'áde teđą̀dì* (When the stars fell).

2. The word *Haská* (flag) in these songs symbolizes the principles of freedom, liberty, or in general, the democratic way of life. This is one of two songs composed by Sylvester Warrior for Vietnam veterans. He said this first song should be sung only at Ponca *Heđúškà* dances. He indicated that the second song, which follows, has been sang at various powwows, but it was his desire that the song should be sung only at the *Heđúškà* dance. There were numerous young Ponca men who were in the Vietnam war. Prentice Dale LeClair was listed as the only casualty; however, many returned home wounded and emotionally drained from that infamous international conflict.

3. "Went" connotes more than to go. It is more like charging the enemy.

15. Marriage and Property

1. Some non-Indian historians have suggested that a man could "buy a girl with ponies." Historians who made this assessment were unqualified to write about the customs of the people. To substantiate assessments like this one, they often quoted others who also knew nothing of Native American customs. This quote is from the

nineteenth to early twentieth centuries, and we are behooved to set the Ponca story straight.

16. Clans of the Ponca

1. *Néšta* is the eighth clan of the Ponca, which became extinct shortly after 1900. According to KH and NC, two elderly women who bore the name Kemble were the last two members of this clan.

2. *Wáxe* is a misnomer. The proper term the Caucasian race is *Xįhá ská*.

17. Ponca Names

1. The purity of names has been lost in the twentieth century. Crossover use of names has been commonplace with the modern Ponca.

2. The names listed in this section are names that are common in the Ponca Tribe of Indians. In this segment of names, the clan affiliation has been omitted to allow the reader to note the type of name given as well as the structure of terms that determine how a name might be composed.

3. The term *Mí* is normally used for the sun. For most female names, *Mí* means moon. *Mí Ðágđì* was also Grandmother VBSH's name.

4. The census documents referenced in this chapter are housed in the Commission of Indian Affairs, Washington DC.

5. All documents were handwritten and could not be readily read.

20. The Ponca Native American Church

1. The term *meeting* is used universally by all tribes for the Native American Church ceremony.

2. "Use" means to touch the object. In this and other rituals, the Ponca usually touch the object and then touch themselves on their hair, forehead, or chest. Sometimes they will touch an area of their body where they may be suffering pain from sickness, such as the shoulders, arms, knees, and so forth. It is believed that God, in His generosity, will heal them through these items. It is like a prayer through which they communicate with *Wak'ą́dà*.

According to Napoleon "Bird" Buffalohead, they discontinued singing eight songs, believing it was too long. Also the chief peyote of the Comanche ritual was sometimes passed around to allow the participants to *use* it. The NAC, as a religious organization among the Ponca, has seen significant changes in the ritual procedure (KH, NC, AMC, JP).

21. The Church in the Community

1. Mr. Howe's aunts, Viola and Loretta, kept a diary, old letters, newspaper clippings, and pictures of their father's work in Nebraska. These items came to Mr. Howe after their demise.

2. This doesn't suggest that differences between tribal members do not exist. On the contrary, people are people in all walks of life in every culture, and differences will occur among people.

22. The Spirit World

1. KH said the term for the Northern Lights is *Níkà nąxè*. Interpreted literally, it means "the spirit of man." There is no known Ponca religious belief or ritual in con-

nection with this phenomenon. The Peguis Cree Indians of Manitoba, Canada, have a belief that the Northern Lights are their ancestors coming close to visit. If a person whistles to them, they are said to come closer to them. The term *Wanȟxè* refers to the spirit of a person that wanders on earth.

2. The term *Ðigé ákà*, or "the one that is gone," refers to the one who is deceased. If there is need to be specific, they may name the individual and add *"Ðigé"* as in "John *ɖigé.*"

23. The Funeral Rites

1. According to the elders, the tradition of burning material belongings allowed the deceased to take those things with them, especially those clothing items that he or she wore often or liked.

2. The food prepared for the family and guests of the family is now prepared at the funeral location with the exception of the funeral chapel. These meals are held at one of the local churches: the Ponca Indian Nazarene Church, Ponca Indian United Methodist Church, Ponca Indian Baptist Church, and Ponca Indian Full Gospel Church. The body is sometimes taken to the Ponca Tribal Cultural Center.

24. Ponca Burials and Practices

1. Dr. Karl Rinehard, professor at the University of Nebraska–Lincoln who did extensive studies on Ponca remains, told me the former Ponca horticulturists coming into the plains attained a modified economic base. The Ponca became bison hunters.

26. Journey to the School House

1. The American education system was founded on centuries of social and economic history beginning in Europe. The following is an excerpt of American education history:

1. In the fifteenth century, the white people entered this continent.

2. They received assistance for survival from the Native peoples.

3. They instituted schools: The Latin school propagated that one learns about the past. It provided no practical purpose. It espoused a philosophy that if they learned of a better past, it would contribute to the present. Everything was written in Latin. In the late fifteenth century, the schools began to break away from the Latin school tradition, and as a result, there was a birth or rebirth of a purposeful education system for the Caucasian community. Up to this time, education was available for only a select few, say 3–5 percent of the people. The King James Version of the Bible was available to all people, and it was written in the English language. The Reformation too expanded the Renaissance in that it provided education through schools. Then in 1635 the Latin Grammar School came to America. From the 1600s through the 1800s, there were massive discoveries in education; it was essentially an era of explorative progress.

4. The discovery of the New World brought people from all parts of the world for various purposes. The Spanish came to South America to hunt for gold and destroyed the Aztec civilization—for gold. The Incas were also destroyed for their gold. The French came to Canada for lumber. Their purposes were apparently designed to supply their country with lumber to build ships to con-

trol the world. They also capitalized on beaver pelts. The English came to Central America—from about where Maine is today to the north of Florida. Their attempts too were to improve their naval supplies. By the early 1600s, they felt they had received the poorest deal. Occupying and claiming a 250-mile strip of land from Maine to northern Florida, England decided to purge itself of all its evil people, and this became a kind of a prison camp. Australia was also their prison camp. By the standards of the King of England, they sent shiploads of people to the New World. The first were the Puritans. These were considered radicals and fanatics and were hated by the aristocrats of England. They taught the belief that God did not direct their king. They came to what are now Massachusetts and the Boston area. These people were not delightful, clean people. They were said to have a Spartan spirit. But they were afraid and wanted to go back to England. Most of them stayed because the boat captain wouldn't let them get back on the boat. The Puritans were dedicated to one idea: that they were correct, and if anyone deviated from them, they were wrong. Since they believed that God was on their side, they aimed to build a new Zion—a perfect society. Old England was corrupt. The perfect life would have (a) absolute laws and (b) leaders and followers. Women were followers. The leaders would have social power from heaven, and theirs would be the government of the people. The followers' end would be hell because they had nothing.

5. Purpose of the school: To assist in weighing the people—to find out who would be leaders and followers. A second purpose was to educate the people as to their place in society. The leaders were then taught to be leaders. This was about 5 percent of the elite group. During a five-year period, they decided what their schools should teach and what they would be like. This resulted in the aforementioned Latin Grammar School. The curriculum included Latin and Greek, and only male children at the age of fifteen were admitted. Learning Latin took the first through the eighth year, and learning Greek took the first through the second year. Those students entering the ministry were required to take Greek. Students were expected to be proficient in Latin, which took a great deal of memory work. The teachers had the students repeat each day what was memorized the day before. They were tested often. No errors indicated a child to be successful. If errors occurred, the child was lost. The Latin school produced scholars from 1635 to 1699. It failed. Why did it fail? Because Latin couldn't help anyone to survive. The Latin school was then expelled from society. They could not create their own model for education. Education then was theoretical for men at that time. Women had practical education at home.

6. Chesapeake Bay Area. They developed farming techniques, and their major crop was tobacco. Grown in the New World, tobacco was a favorite of the English and other Europeans. It became a good crop for cash. The British built large farms called plantations, which demanded many laborers. They tried to get the American Indians to do it, but they would not. So they went to Africa to get slaves. The English plantation was owned by the English elite, and the English farmer owned only small parcels of land. They were called yeoman and were very poor people.

The laborers were the black people, and the host was the American Indian. The plantation owners wanted education as did the yeoman. Education was illegal for the blacks, and the hosts wanted no part of it but were considered "hopefully to be educated and Christianized."

7. Yorktown. Only the plantation owner could afford schools or get an education. All others were excluded. Common people were to work. Only leaders could go to school because of the imposed fees. The fee prevented others from entering. Their education was by tutor, and the tutor came from England. They were uncertified, but they taught Latin and Greek from 1620 to 1692. When children completed the course, they were entitled to go to Oxford or Cambridge in England. By 1692 high education was too expensive, so they formed their own university called William and Mary College in 1692–93. It was named for the King and Queen of England, who gave permission for founding the university.

8. System of education for excellence. This would be quality education. William and Mary was a quality education school. Boston had mass education as opposed to quality education. Harvard accepted any student but was no more than a glorified high school. William and Mary, on the other hand, had students from the tutored group, and they were good students. They had to be good.

9. Middle Colonies (New York, New Jersey, Pennsylvania). This area was occupied by the Dutch originally and was vacated by 1664 and opened to the English. The British monarch divided the land into division. The Pennsylvania Dutch built communities around churches, as did the French and German communities that had their own denominations, namely, Lutheran and Roman Catholic. This was basically the European style of life. The British made decisions about the communities and decided to leave them as they were.

10. Quakers (English). They were pushed out of England and settled in Pennsylvania. They made significant contributions to education. In fact, it is said they made breakthroughs in education in the 1600s. Led by William Penn, they approached the education processes from a practical point of view. They knew that the people needed certain things to survive. Their educational system was built more on the principles of the modern vocational training schools. They were taught to build farm implements, guns, and boat parts. This was the beginning of the development of school as we know it today.

2. The tribal records referred to are the Ponca (BIA) Higher Education Files, 1980 to 1994.

3. A BIA statistic some years ago showed the American Indian to have very low English proficiency. This is not surprising because most families were speaking the Ponca language for the first half of the twentieth century. (As of this writing, the Ponca have a very low Ponca-language proficiency.) When English began to replace Ponca, it was apparent that the Ponca's limited use of the English language resulted in a limited vocabulary. Those students who had a greater use the English language had the advantage and were more successful in the learning processes. Given that the English language was necessary to attain a reasonable explanation for the under-

standing and appreciation of the new world order, it was one segment of a series in the socialization and acculturation processes.

4. The term *to travel*, or *Ugášą̀*, meant to investigate the land or to go hunting.

5. The term is a corruption of the word *Ét'abè edégą̀*, meaning "You think that is what I would have said." The original term went through a variety changes primarily due to the younger generation. From the original, the second change was *É'čabedégą*, which is a corruption of the original term. It was then followed by *É't'aina*, which is another Ponca word meaning "They might say." Then came "*É'čainà*" or "Ay-China." The meaning has also changed. Today the term connotes doubt or unbelief of what has been said by another person.

6. The youth who searches for his people's way of life, that is, their culture, seems next to impossible in modern times. First, to integrate school and learning of the white world with the Indian culture would create a problem. Second, education under Western thought eliminates Native American thought and philosophy. The youth may find information about who he is and where he came from, but what he is doing here and where he is going would present a situation in which there are no answers. Even to seek information from his father would seem fair enough to most people, but he may receive some sarcastic answer or may be ignored altogether. This is because the father may have no knowledge of his tribal customs.

7. The fog that hangs low between the hills was referred to as *Xékì* in the Ponca language.

8. The elders said that the penalty for committing adultery, first, permitted the husband to cut off the penis of the perpetrator and tie it to his wife's hair, where she would be required to wear it out in the public. In a teasing fashion, they told boys, "If you do that, so-and-so will be wearing your penis in her hair." The rule also applied to unmarried young men and women.

9. KH, AMC, NC, JP, and others said *Wak'ą́da* has always meant "God" in their lifetime.

10. Any gift coming from *Wak'ą́da* is considered *Waxúbe* (sacred) to this day and should be treated as such.

11. A carved and decorated wood piece about twenty inches long and three inches in diameter.

12. Perhaps the bison returned to their ancestral breeding grounds in the north at this time.

13. The quote is from "The Omaha Tribe, Vol. 1," an edition reproduced from the Twenty-Seventh Annual Report of the Bureau of American Ethnology to the Secretary of the Smithsonian Institution, 1905–6, and housed in the National Anthropological Archives.

14. Also means dehydrated meat or jerky. *T'anúkà* is edible animal flesh.

29. Political Governance

1. 55 10 Sec 14 so Selector's Opinion.

2. The Department of Labor since then has new titles for the same program. It has been titled Jobs Training Program Act (JTPA) and now Workforce Investment Act (WIA).

Bibliography

Archives and Manuscript Materials
Commission of Indian Affairs, Washington DC.
Department of the Interior, Washington DC.
National Anthropological Archives, National Museum of Natural History, Smithsonian Institution, Suitland MD.
National Archives, Washington DC.
Nebraska Historical Society, Lincoln NE.
Tract Books Indian Schedules, Vol. 22 (December 7, 1894).

Published Works

Dorsey, James Owen. 1884. *Omaha Sociology*. Washington DC: Smithsonian, Bureau of American Ethnology.

———. 1890. *The Ðegiha Language*. Washington DC: Smithsonian, Bureau of American Ethnology.

———. 1891. *Omaha and Ponka Letters*. Washington DC: Smithsonian, Bureau of American Ethnology.

Fletcher, Alice Cummings, and Frances La Flesche. 1992. *The Omaha Tribe*, with an introduction by Robin Ridington. Lincoln: University of Nebraska Press. (Original work published in 1911.)

Gilmore, M. R. 1977. *Uses of Plants by Indians of the Missouri River Region*. Lincoln: University of Nebraska Press. (Original work published in 1919.)

Howard, James H. 1970. "Known Village Sites of the Ponca." *Plains Anthropologist* 15(48):109–34.

———. 1995. *The Ponca Tribe*. Lincoln: University of Nebraska Press. (Original work published in 1965.)

Jablow, Joseph. 1974. *Ethnohistory of the Ponca with Reference to Their Claim of Certain Lands*. A Report for the Department of Justice, Lands Division, Indian Claims Section. New York: Garland.

Lake, James A., Sr. 1981. "Standing Bear, Who?" *Nebraska Law Review* (60):451–503.

Nasatir, A. P., ed. 2002. *Before Lewis and Clark: Document Illustrating the History of the Missouri, 1785–1804*, with an Introduction by James P. Ronda. Norman: University of Oklahoma Press. (Original work published in 1952.)

Petrullo, Vincenzo. 2018. *The Diabolical Root: A Study of Peyotism, the New Indian Religion, among the Delewares*. Philadelphia: University of Pennsylvania Press. (Original work published in 1934.)

Skinner, Alanson. 1920. *Medicine Ceremony of the Menomini, Iowa, and Wahpeton Dakota, with Notes on the Ceremony among the Ponca, Bungi Ojibwa, and Potawatomi Indians.* Indian Notes and Monographs, Heye Foundation, Vol. 4. New York: Museum of the American Indian.

Tibbles, Thomas Henry. 1972. *Standing Bear and The Ponca Chiefs,* edited with an introduction by Kay Graber. Lincoln: University of Nebraska Press.

Vogel, Virgil J. 1990. *American Indian Medicine.* Norman: University of Oklahoma Press. (Original work published in 1970.)

Whitman, William. 1939. "Xúbe, A Ponca Autobiography." *Journal American Folklore.* (52):180–93.

Wilson, James G., and John Fiske, eds. 1887. *Appleton's Cyclopedia of American Biography,* Vol. 2. New York: D. Appleton.

Wood, W. Raymond. 1965. "Redbird Focus, the Problem of Ponca Prehistory." *Plains Anthropologist* 10(28):80–145.

Index

Louis V. Headman (Ponca elder) (Oklahoma) is the project coordinator of the Ponca Language Grant and pastor of the Church of the Nazarene in Ponca City. He is the author of *Dictionary of the Ponca People* (Nebraska, 2019).

Sean O'Neill is an associate professor of anthropology at the University of Oklahoma. He is the author of *Cultural Contact and Linguistic Relativity among the Indians of Northwestern California* and the coeditor of *Northwest California Linguistics*, volume 14 of *The Collected Works of Edward Sapir*.

www.ingramcontent.com/pod-product-compliance
Lightning Source LLC
Chambersburg PA
CBHW021841290326
41932CB00064B/333